Environmental Side Effects of Rising Industrial Output

Environmental Side Effects of Rising Industrial Output

Edited by

Alfred J. Van Tassel
Hofstra University

Heath Lexington Books
D. C. Heath and Company
Lexington, Massachusetts

Table of Contents

List of Figures

List of Tables

Preface

Ecology is a fashionable word these days. It is usually defined as the "scientific study of plants and animals in relation to their natural environment." The evidence is increasing that man himself is one of the most powerful forces shaping the world in which he lives. For a long time it appeared that man had made only superficial scratches on the earth's surface, but it is now clear that far-reaching changes have been set in motion and that the geological time scale has been severely compressed by acts of man.

Although geographers, planners and other social scientists have been issuing warnings for years, it is only recently that the American people in general have awakened to the fact that they have been fouling their own nest and perhaps those of others. This new awareness can be considered in part a by-product of our space program. Only last year, in full view for all to see, a space capsule was on its way to the moon — a striking example of a life system in a closed environment. For the astronauts to have polluted heedlessly the inner environment of their space capsule would have been quickly to convert a living space into a mausoleum. The more perceptive of those who watched and reflected were soon aware that the earth is nothing more than a space capsule — another closed system moving through the solar system.

Our smoke-filled skies, polluted waterways and littered landscapes have made us aware of our transgressions in more down-to-earth terms. Why is the impact suddenly so severe? America has always spent its resources profligately. But only twenty years ago the central concern of the Paley report was whether our natural resources would last. Today, we wonder if we will be buried under the wastes we generate.

Many see the problem as one of a too-rapidly expanding population. In the United States the problem is as much a matter of affluence as numbers. In the underdeveloped countries of Asia, hundreds of millions manage to exist free of the awful specter of being buried in their own waste. Where dung serves as fuel, fertilizer, or building material, cycles are completed and raw materials disappear into the earth. Not so in the more sophisticated economies where product transformations may yield irreversible reactions and indestructible refuse, and where output is so enormous that the rapid accumulation of debris in the atmosphere and waters and on the earth is inevitable unless appropriate measures are taken.

This complex of problems was the subject of a research seminar in the School of Business at Hofstra University. As Dean of the School, I am proud that our work has produced this timely and important volume and pleased that Heath Lexington Books is publishing it. We feel that it says something about the Hofstra approach to education when subjects of such vital current interest to business and the community serve as the subjects of our research. This book may be looked upon as a companion to an earlier study edited by Dr. John E. Ullmann entitled *Waste Disposal Problems in Selected Industries.*

The authors of *Environmental Side Effects of Rising Industrial Output* brought to the seminar varied backgrounds and training in such fields as business, accounting and engineering. The seminar built, of course, on the work of others, especially that of Resources for the Future, Inc., whose monumental survey was the source of the projections used in this volume. The study would not have been possible, either, without reference to the many recent inquiries by governmental agencies whose results were efficiently collected and catalogued by the Documents Library at Hofstra. The director of the seminar and editor of the volume, Dr. Alfred J. Van Tassel, has long had an interest in natural resource questions. This volume continues his contributions to the examination of the economic implications of technological change.

Harold L. Wattel
Dean, School of Business
Hofstra University

August 29, 1970
Hempstead, New York

Environmental Side Effects of Rising Industrial Output

1

The Environment and Rising Output: Methodology for a Study

Alfred J. Van Tassel

It was a clear summer night and a brilliant half moon hung over New York City's Central Park. There, on an area known as Sheep Meadow, 135,000 people were jammed, waiting for a free concert by Barbra Streisand sponsored by a local beer company. The huge turnout was a striking tribute to the popularity of America's "Funny Girl," but the next morning park officials found little to laugh about. The Sheep Meadow was strewn with what was described by the *New York Times* as "thousands of pounds of garbage and litter" including half-eaten sandwiches, empty cans and bottles, newspapers and blankets. The cleanup task took three days and cost the beer company $3,000.

Such episodes, though normally on a smaller scale, have become increasingly characteristic of our disposable society. The plight of harried municipal officials is eased but not eliminated when people are disciplined enough to dispose of their trash through the proper collection channels. The fact is that many large cities are running out of space in which to throw away the mounting column of debris arising from our industrial civilization. Incineration might appear a suitable outlet for trash disposal except that in many cities this may exacerbate air pollution already at critical levels from other sources. Similarly, garbage grinders which macerate trash for down-the-drain disposal may overload the assimilative capacity of waterways already burdened with incompletely treated sewage.

A wide variety of pollution problems are rendered more acute by the prosperity that has persisted since World War II. Dilution can be an important factor ameliorating the harmful effects of many forms of air and water pollution. During the 1930s, when the population was one-third less than it is today and industrial activity was at a much lower level, stream and air flows often diluted pollutants below critical levels, even in the absence of sound treatment and control measures. But the almost uninterrupted growth of population and national product since the 1930s has made evident the need for improved antipollution measures to avoid a serious deterioration in the quality of the environment. There is, of course, no certainty that the economy will continue to grow at the rate that has prevailed for the last three decades, but there is at present no clear evidence that it will not.

A shortage of the natural resources needed to sustain uninterrupted growth of the economy was a possibility that received a good deal of attention during the postwar period. In 1963, Resources for the Future, Inc. (RFF), an institution supported by the Ford Foundation, published the results of an investigation designed to determine insofar as possible the adequacy of the resource base to support various levels of economic growth from 1960 to the year 2000 [1]. Based on all available United States data through 1960, this landmark study by RFF developed an internally consistent set of projections of the output of virtually every commodity used in the nation whose production involved a significant natural resource input. The authors were careful to note that such projections were not to be regarded as forecasts of the future. Rather, they explained a projection "in economic parlance . . . generally refers to the process of determining what a given set of starting assumptions means for the future course of some economic or social statistical measure" [1:55].

The starting assumption was that human needs and wants in the United States during the remainder of the century would continue to increase and to be more nearly satisfied with each passing decade. This assumption − consistent with the American experience in the first half of the century − implies a steady increase in the per capita national product. Given this series showing per capita national product in each succeeding year, a projection of figures for population in the same period yields a series on estimated gross national product (GNP) by a simple process of multiplication.

To convert the overall GNP projections to series for individual commodities, it is necessary to know the constituents that make up the total output and then to make assumptions concerning future changes in this national market basket. Once these changing values were estimated and plugged into the GNP series, individual end-use commodity projections were generated and the implications of these for demand for intermediates and raw materials were explored. Finally, individual commodity and raw material output series were checked against one another extensively to make sure that they were internally consistent, and where they were not, the entire estimating procedure was retraced. Thus, by a process of iteration, the RFF approached closer to a comprehensive projection of future national output. While such comprehensiveness was time-consuming, it had the virtue of forcing internal consistency and of illuminating many problem areas that might otherwise have gone unnoticed.

It may be noted that the RFF procedure relied heavily on population projections which are notoriously hazardous and subject to rapid obsolescence. The United States Bureau of the Census which developed in 1960 the specific series employed by RFF has since issued a revision which projects a lower rate of population increase for the United States. This revision has little effect on RFF projections to 1970, but would reduce appreciably the RFF projections for later years. However, with respect to per capita consumption trends, the evidence suggests that RFF projections tend in most instances to understate the increases and an adjustment for this might largely offset the effect of lowered population estimates.

It goes without saying that any undertaking as heroic as this involved hundreds of individual assumptions concerning factors affecting demand for specific commodities and that many of these will be proven wrong by developments. Because such errors are unlikely to be consistently additive, this need not impair the general usefulness of the study.

However, there are two fundamental, underlying assumptions of the RFF study which must be met if the projections are to have any value. These are "that there will be, during the period under study, no general war and no major depression. If either comes to pass, all of the projections must be considered invalid" [1:500].

The production and consumption projections of RFF were only a means to an end, namely, "to uncover any serious situations of (resource) scarcity or surplus that seem likely to occur if present trends continue . . ." [1:4]. At the conclusion of its study, RFF found that there was unlikely to be "any general running out of resources in this country during the remainder of the century," but that there was "great likelihood of severe problems of shortage . . . from time to time in particular regions or segments of the economy, for particular raw materials" [1:4 and 5].

It has become evident that the vast expansion of output in recent years has had profound repercussions on the quality of American environment, and it is reasonable to suppose the enormous increase in the GNP projected by RFF could have proportional impacts. These environmental side effects were given no more than passing mention by RFF in its study. In part, this was because they were not germane to the central thrust of the investigation. More important, perhaps, was the practical necessity of limiting as much as possible the attempted coverage of a study already monumental in scope.

That there would be extensive environmental side effects from any such increase in GNP as that envisioned by RFF seemed evident. The present study seeks to supplement the RFF study by exploring the implications for the quality of the enviornment of the RFF projections. If consumption of gasoline in motor vehicles follows RFF projections and more than doubles from 1960 to 1980, what would be the consequences for air pollution, already a major problem in several American cities? Power production is projected to increase five and one-half times by the year 2000 and much of the addition is expected to be generated from atomic fuels. Would safe disposal of the resulting radioactive wastes impede the realization of such an end?

The means for conducting such an investigation of environmental side effects of increasing industrial output were at hand in the research seminars conducted as part of the Master of Business Administration program of the Hofstra University School of Business. Under this program developed by Dean Harold L. Wattel, each candidate for the MBA degree does a defined portion of a general research project carried out by a seminar under the direction of a member of the faculty. The collection of individual theses prepared by members of the research seminar, under the editorship of the faculty leader, is then published by the University in a series which includes nineteen volumes to date [2].

The present study is the product of such a research seminar under the direction of the editor on the subject of the *Environmental Side Effects of Rising Industrial Output,* divided into fourteen distinct topics as indicated by the headings of Chapters 2 through 15. The editor contributed an introductory Chapter and a Summary of Findings.

Each of the subject matter chapters explores the side effects likely to follow if the REF projections relevant to his subject are realized or approached in the future. Every effort was made to project such side effects in quantitative terms, but where this proved infeasible a qualitative or relative judgment was made. For example, if paper production were to expand in accordance with RFF projections, what would be the extent of the resultant pollution of the nation's waterways? This called for more than a mechanical projection of pollution effects. Advances in manufacturing practices have made it possible to reduce to a fraction of former levels the amount of water pollution associated with a given volume of paper production. The effect of such improvements in technology were to be taken into account.

The phenomena designated here as side effects have been studied and pondered for years by economists. The great English economist Alfred Marshall used the smoke that once filled the air over Pittsburgh as an example of an external effect of iron and steel production. Thus, Marshall recognized that there was a social cost of iron and steel production expressed in air pollution that was not paid by the producers. Such externalities, or diseconomies, as they have been designated by others, are the central subjects of the present inquiry. It is worth noting that Marshall used the smoky skies of Pittsburgh as his example because improvements in iron and steel production technology and rigorous municipal requirements for smoke control have largely cleared the air of the steel city even though output has increased since Marshall wrote. Thus, air pollution can be corrected by technological advances and strict controls.

It is interesting, also, that Los Angeles smog has replaced Pittsburgh smoke as the symbol of air pollution, with the private automobile rather than industry as the principal source. Thus, consumption, as well as production, may result in diseconomies.

Each seminar member developed to the degree possible a projection of the side effects of increased production of the commodities coming under his chapter, allowing for the likely extent of adoption of known technologies capable of offsetting such side effects. However, it was not permitted to treat technological progress as a *deus ex machina* blandly assumed to be capable of overcoming all difficulties. To bar such evasions, seminar members were enjoined from introducing exotic technologies as a solution to the increase in the volume of pollution otherwise to be expected as output rose. Accordingly, the possible reduction in air pollution that might be achieved by the widespread adoption of electric or steam powered automobiles was not considered. On the other hand, projections were made assuming various degrees of adoption in automobile engines of the emission control devices now in existence, with allowance for further improvement in this auxiliary equipment along present lines of development.

The projections of diseconomies in this volume are based, for the most part, on the commodity and service output projections of RFF. Accordingly, they share with that volume the underlying assumptions of a rising GNP uninterrupted by major depression or general war. Involved, as well, are assumptions concerning individual commodities and substitutions between alternative raw and semifinished constituents. The basic projection mechanism begins with an assumption of a sizeable increase in population amounting to a compound annual rate of growth of 1.55 percent net increase per year, a little below the rate that prevailed from 1940 to 1960, substantially above the rate from 1920 to 1940 but lower than the rate for any twenty-year period before 1920. Principally because of changes in the age composition of the population, the labor force is expected to increase at a faster rate than the population as a whole and to roughly double in size between 1960 and 2000. The productivity per member of this growing labor force is expected to increase at an annual rate of roughly 2 percent in terms of GNP. The logical consequence of these interrelated assumptions is a projection envisioning "slightly more than a doubling of GNP between 1960 and 1980 and approximately the same again between 1980 and 2000" [1:19]. When this quadrupling of GNP is translated into outputs of individual commodities dramatic projected increases are inevitable in most instances and are still more striking in the case of those sectors expected to gain faster than the economy as a whole. Generation of electricity, for example, is expected to increase by more than five and one-half times between 1960 and 2000.

It is neither necessary nor feasible to set forth here the detailed assumptions included in projections for individual commodities or services. It may be noted that these generally appear to be consistent with broad trends prevalent in the economy, namely, (a) the increase in extent and intensity of processing per unit of primary raw material consumed; (b) decrease in the importance of the output of farms, forests, and mines relative to that of industry; and (c) the ascendancy of synthetics in preference to natural raw materials; and (d) the shift of a larger portion of the consumer dollar to services as against commodities as affluence increases.

The RFF projections were made using data available through 1960. Data for a more recent year (usually 1966, 1967, or 1968, depending on the commodity or service in question) are now available and it is therefore possible to check on the accuracy of the RFF projections thus far. This can be done by comparing actual results for the most recent year with an interpolation of the RFF projection for the same year. These comparisons are shown in Appendix A.

RFF underestimated the extent of the increase in prosperity in the 1960s as evidenced by the fact that the high projection of personal consumption expenditures (PCE) more nearly corresponded to the actual figure than the medium projection for the same year. Expenditures on most consumer durable goods were underestimated to about the same extend as PCE as a whole, but actual purchases of private automobiles exceeded even the high projection by RFF.

RFF was also overconservative on its estimate of the increase in electric power production during the 1960s. Coal output benefited from the increase in electric power generation; more importantly, coal made major gains in the competition with other fuels. The result was that the increase in coal output slightly exceeded the high projection.

Output of most other industrial commodities and services during the 1960s most closely approximated RFF's medium projections. These projections represent enormous increases over the entire period to 2000 and it seems unlikely that they will be exceeded on balance for many commodities or services in the long pull. This does not exclude substantial share-of-the-market shifts which could — as in the case of coal — result in high figures for individual series.

The central purpose of the RFF study was to reveal any situations of serious shortage of natural resources that might develop if output expanded as projected. Of course, such a condition of shortage might affect the projections themselves if increased costs forced up market prices and reduced demand.

Of particular interest in this respect is the supply of fossil fuels. Coal reserves were judged adequate for the indefinite future, and the same conclusion applied to natural gas. The outlook for oil was not as clear cut, but in the light of the demonstrated ability of the industry to locate new sources and the existence of enormous secondary supplies such as shale oil, it was concluded that no shortage was likely. No serious general shortages were foreseen in respect to raw materials for manufacture of consumer durables, paper, chemicals, steel, construction materials, or fertilizers, though this did not bar localized shortages of specific raw materials such as wood for pulping. Water supplies were unevenly distributed throughout the country and shortages in many western localities seemed certain. However, none of these shortages situations were expected to interfere substantially with the realization of RFF projections.

2

The Social Costs of Expanding Paper Production

Robert Gordon

No more important single problem faces this country than the problem of 'good' water. Water is our greatest single natural resource. The issue of pure water must be settled now for the benefit not only of this generation but for untold generations to come. The need for good quality water for all our Nation's uses — public and private — is a paramount one [39:viii].

One of the industrial projections made by RFF concerned the production of paper products. The projected increases will have an effect upon the level of effluent discharged into our waterways; the severity of this problem is the topic of this chapter.

Figures from the 1959 Census of Manufacturing show the pulp and paper industry in third place among all industry groups in the United States in total intake of water of 1,937 billion gallons for the year. When reuse of water is included, the paper industry leads all industry groups at 5,989 billion gallons or 24 percent of all industrial water use. The discharge to surface waters is shown to be 1,765 billion gallons. By the nature of the paper industry, much of this discharged water carries dissolved and suspended wastes. Therein lies one of the major problems confronting the industry [5:51].

Paper products are both items of end consumption and intermediate items which facilitate the production of many other endproducts; RFF discussed this product grouping in Chapter 8 of their volume. The gross annual consumption of paper and paperboard is about 40 million tons a year; in 1950 it was about 30 million tons, and 1929 not even 15 million [17:170].

The major components of the paper production series are newsprint, printing paper, fine paper, sanitary and tissue paper, coarse and industrial paper, boxboards, and other special paperboards. Each of these will be considered individually. Historical data on the production of paper by type is presented in Table 2-1; Table 2-2 reflects the RFF projections.

Newsprint, as the name implies, is used for newspapers. It is mainly made from groundwood pulp. Because the paper has a high lignin content (the substance that binds the fibers together in the tree), it turns yellow and brittle in a relatively short time. Newsprint requirements were related by RFF to population with the assumption that per capita consumption will continue to increase but at a decreasing rate; this per capita growth is attributed to increasing daily circulation and average number of pages per newspaper.

Uncoated groundwood, book, and coated papers are often grouped together as printing papers. Uncoated groundwood grades are similar to newsprint and its uses include drawing, tablet, album paper, and wall paper. Coated papers are used largely in magazines; paper coated on only one side is used for can labels.

Table 2.1

Historical Data on Production of Paper
(Million tons)

Year	News-print	Printing Paper	Fine Paper	Sanitary & Tissue	Industrial Paper	Boxboards & Special	Container-Board	Other	Total
1947	.83	3.05	1.11	1.08	3.27	1.62	4.89	5.26	21.11
1948	.88	3.19	1.10	1.18	3.43	1.76	5.02	5.34	21.90
1949	.92	2.97	.97	1.19	3.06	1.86	4.63	4.72	20.32
1950	1.01	3.31	1.16	1.36	3.72	2.16	5.77	5.89	24.38
1951	1.11	3.51	1.32	1.47	4.09	2.20	6.19	6.16	26.05
1952	1.11	3.36	1.26	1.35	3.66	1.68	5.69	6.31	24.42
1953	1.07	3.59	1.27	1.51	3.92	2.29	6.54	6.34	26.53
1954	1.20	3.58	1.25	1.61	3.91	2.28	6.34	6.55	26.72
1955	1.46	3.91	1.42	1.76	4.23	2.60	7.35	7.41	30.14
1956	1.62	4.31	1.54	1.78	4.58	2.47	7.62	7.42	31.34
1957	1.81	4.04	1.48	1.91	4.31	2.56	7.39	7.20	30.70
1958	1.73	4.02	1.54	1.95	4.26	2.57	7.41	7.34	30.82
1959	1.92	4.19	1.72	2.13	4.75	2.83	8.09	8.42	34.05
1960	2.01	4.71	1.74	2.22	4.75	2.80	8.16	8.07	34.46

Source: *Resources In America's Future*, Table A 8–1. Hereafter referred to by title and page in tables.

Table 2.2

Projected Production of Paper (Million tons)[a]

	1970			1980		
	L	M	H	L	M	H
Newsprint	3.1	3.1	3.4	4.5	4.8	5.5
Printing Paper	5.8	6.0	6.5	7.4	8.2	9.6
Fine Paper	2.2	2.4	2.6	3.0	3.3	4.0
Sanitary & Tissue	3.2	3.5	4.1	4.5	5.4	7.0
Industrial Paper	6.0	6.6	7.2	7.6	9.2	11.2
Boxboards & Special	3.5	3.7	4.1	4.3	5.0	6.0
Containerboard	11.6	12.7	14.0	15.9	19.2	23.4
Other	9.5	11.0	13.2	11.5	14.5	19.7
Total	44.9	49.0	55.1	58.7	69.7	86.4

	1990			2000		
	L	M	H	L	M	H
Newsprint	5.8	6.6	8.1	7.1	8.7	11.4
Printing Paper	9.4	11.0	14.1	11.6	14.6	20.4
Fine Paper	4.1	4.8	6.1	5.3	6.7	9.4
Sanitary & Tissue	5.7	7.7	11.2	6.6	9.8	17.1
Industrial Paper	9.7	13.1	17.5	12.5	18.5	27.2
Boxboards & Special	5.3	6.6	8.8	6.2	8.7	12.6
Containerboard	21.3	28.4	38.1	28.0	41.3	60.8
Other	13.4	19.0	29.1	15.6	25.2	44.8
Total	74.7	97.2	133.0	92.9	133.5	203.7

Source: *Resources in America's Future*, Table A 8–2.

[a]L = low; M = medium; H = high.

Book papers go into books, magazines, and pamphlets, and are used in commercial printing as well as in business stationery and envelopes.

Fine papers are among the highest grades of paper made; most are made from chemical wood pulp. The projections for printing and fine papers were related to disposable personal income.

Industrial papers vary according to the specific need. Folding boxboard is used to carton common household products: cereals, toothpaste, soap powders, and so on. The outer surface is designed to take a fine printing, while the inner part gives the bulk, rigidity, and protection necessary for a carton. The production of both types is linked with levels of output; the former is related to output of all goods, the latter to that of consumer nondurables.

Sanitary and tissue papers are self-explanatory; population growth is the basis for the projection.

Containerboard is the largest single grade of paper made. There are two major kinds: linerboard and corrugated material. Projections for containerboard were based on total goods output, assuming a slightly faster rate of increase in the former. Although paper is being displaced from part of the flexible packaging market by plastic films and aluminum foils, it is at the same time enlarging its share of the rigid container market by invading many of the markets formerly supplied by wood. With further substitutions for metal and wood possible, paperboard use is likely to grow at a faster rate than the container and packaging market as a whole, ans slightly ahead of the output of all goods in the economy.

Included in the "other" category are special foodboard, and building paper and boards. Special foodboard is used to package moist and oily foods; the projection is related to the growth of nondurables output which has been growing at a fairly stable rate. Building paper and board projections are related to total construction including maintenance and repair.

Pollution from the Manufacturing Process

The 1963 Encyclopedia Americana states that "stream pollution is any degradation of stream waters by runoff from inhabited areas, eroding soil, sanitary sewage, industrial wastes, and in fact, by any liquid or material not naturally present in the stream. The word stream is used to represent any natural water. Abatement of pollution requires large amounts of money and will take years to accomplish." To understand the relation of paper production to water pollution, the manufacturing process should be explained.

The four basic elements required for making paper are wood, water, power, and labor. Wood reaches a pulp mill in several forms, the commonest probably being four foot logs. The initial steps in converting the wood to paper are washing and removing the bark from the logs. The washing is done by water showers or immersion to remove dirt and other foreign material which the logs pick up as they are dragged from the forests. The barking operation removes the

Table 2.3

The Various Pulping Processes

Pulp Classification	Name of Process	Annual U. S. Production, 1960 (tons)	Number of Pulp Mills in U. S. 1960
Chemical	Sulfite	2,578,000	62
	Kraft	14,590,000	85
	Soda	420,000	11
Semichemical	Neutral Sulfite	1,841,000	40
	Bisulfite		
	Acid Sulfite		
	Kraft		
Chemimechanical	Chemigroundwood	100,000	1
	Mason	1,205,000	48
	Asplund		
	Cold Soda	150,000	9
	Hot Sulfite	1,500	2
Mechanical	Groundwood	3,292,000	93

Source: U. S. Department of Commerce, Area Redevelopment Administration, *Technical and Economic Feasibility of* *Establishing a Hardwood Pulp and Paper Mill in an Eight-County Area of Western Kentucky*, August 1964.

bark which does not produce good paper and can cause black specks in the finished sheet. The more common methods of removing the bark are by tumbling the logs in rotating cyclinders 12 to 15 feet in diameter or by using high pressure water sprays which lift the bark off the log.

After the logs are cleaned and peeled, they are made ready for pulping; there are two basic approaches for making a pulp of the logs — chemically and mechanically; Table 2-3 compares the prevalence of each.

Pulp prepared by the kraft, soda, or sulfite processes accounts for about 73 percent of total United States pulp tonnage (see Table 2-3). These processes are all subdivisions of the chemical pulping classification. In the various chemical processes, pulp is prepared by dissolving out of wood the natural binding material, lignin, which holds the fibers together in the log but causes paper to turn yellow. The dissolution of the lignin is accomplished in closed vessels at elevated temperatures and pressures in the presence of a dissolving liquor. The entire process is called cooking, the vessels are called digesters, and the operators are often referred to as cooks. To facilitate the penetration of the cooking liquor into the wood, the logs are reduced to three-quarter inch chips by feeding them through a chipper. It has rotating discs which are equipped with knives set into the face of these discs. Before cooking, the chips are screened to remove sawdust generated during the chipping operation. Following this the chips are fed into the digester where they are covered with the cooking liquor and heated by steam for a specified period to over 300 degrees Fahrenheit and about 125 pounds per square inch pressure.

After the cooking, which takes anywhere from 2 to 12 hours, depending upon the type of cooking liquor used and the pulp being made, the digesters are discharged or blown into vessels which hold the pulp until it can be fed to the next processing operation. By now the chips have been transformed into pulp by the cooking operation, but the result is a brown sodden mass which must be treated further before it can be fed to the paper machines.

The next step is to wash the pulp with water which removes the cooking or black liquor with the decomposed lignin and resins from the fibrous pulp. After the pulp has been washed it has the light brown color of wrapping paper. The black liquor is concentrated and burned in large furnaces to generate steam and recover the residual cooking chemicals. Following the washing, the pulp is screened to remove lumps caused by knots or incompletely cooked pieces of wood. If white paper is being made, the pulp is bleached to rid it of the brown color and washed and screened again. If blue, yellow, or other colors are being made, a dye is added to the pulp after bleaching.

The final step before the pulp is transformed into paper on the paper machine is a beating or refining operation. There are several methods for accomplishing this step, but basically the surface of the wood or cellulose fibers are roughened so that they will lock together to form a strong paper.

Now the pulp is ready to be made into paper on the paper machines. These machines are huge, often measuring over 100 yards and capable of performing a most remarkable transformation.

The machine receives a mixture consisting of 99½ percent water and ½ percent pulp and converts it to dry, finished rolls of paper at speeds of up to 30 miles per hour. To do this, the pulp and water solution is poured onto an endless wire screen (the Fourdrinier) which permits the water to drain and form a very wet sheet. The sheet is dried by running it between rollers similar to a washing machine wringer and then over steam-heated cyclinders until the residual moisture is about 5 percent or less.

A variety of techniques are used to give the paper a smooth glossy finish: passing it over a series of hardened steel calender rolls, coating it with a thin film of clay, and various combinations of these.

Varying, but basically similar processes are employed in the further treatment of the remaining 27 percent of pulp tonnage produced by one of the other semichemical, chemimechanical, or mechanical methods (see Table 2-3).

The Pollutants

This chapter examines the relation of production of paper products to water pollution. In this connection, a discussion of the pollutant nature of the production of effluent is appropriate.

The following statements allude to the severity of the pollution problem associated with the pulp and paper industry.

No industry has made more trouble and more violent public relations because of river pollution than the pulp and paper companies [6:149].

A few industries — paper and allied products, ... , which are typically composed of a relatively few, relatively large plants, use most of the nation's industrial water and produce most of the nation's wastes [33:62].

Perhaps one-fifth of the total pollution load in the effluent discharge by industry into American streams originates in groundwood and chemical pulping mills [1:175].

The major steps necessary to minimize stream pollution problems in the pulp and paper industry are: (a) suspended solids removal; (b) to reduce biochemical oxygen demand (BOD); (c) and color removal.

Suspended Solids

Suspended solids consist of finely divided particles of clay, broken fibers, and bark fines that escape the filtering systems. These suspended solids may settle on the stream bottom to form sludge banks which are unsightly and occupy space that might be utilized by aquatic life or may float in masses on the water surface. They slowly decompose and in so doing reduce the oxygen level of the water. The removal of suspended solids from pulp and paper mill effluents has received more attention in this industry than any other phase of stream pollution.

Biochemical Oxygen Demand

The oxygen-consuming properties of pulp and paper mill effluents arise from the fact that wood, the basic raw material, is organic. The residues from the pulping processes and wastes from the paper machines are subject to decomposition by microorganisms. The oxygen required by bacteria for the breakdown of organic matter is referred to as the biochemical oxygen demand (BOD). "When organic matter is present in water, there is competition between the microorganisms and aquatic life for the dissolved oxygen; the microorganisms are usually the victors in the struggle for existence" [18:362].

The BOD test measures the amount of oxygen required for the biological decomposition of organic solids to occur under aerobic conditions at a standardized time (normally five days) and temperature (normally 20 degrees Centigrade). The BOD is the major test made to determine the polluting power of a waste, because it measures the total amount and rate of oxygen which will be needed to prevent odor nuisance and oxygen depletion of streams.

Thus, it is the single most important test on which the engineer bases the design of the waste treatment facilities [39:19].

The process of oxygen consumption proceeds in two distinct stages. When an untreated waste is put into a stream, a major draft upon dissolved oxygen occurs as the wastes are degraded by bacterial action. Thereafter, the dissolved oxygen level tends to recover. About five days later, a second stage occurs as the nitrogen embodied in organic sewage is converted to nitrite and to nitrate by aerobic bacteria. This second stage does not tend to reduce the level of dissolved oxygen as much as the first stage. Both effects can be carried on in a treatment plant rather than in the receiving water. However, orthodox treatment measures do not fully complete either process and so the water's self-purification capacity is always called upon to a degree [15:7].

In pulp mill effluents, the major contribution to the oxygen demand is spent sulfite liquor. This is spent cooking liquor containing the nonfibrous material removed from the wood chips during the cooking process. It has no direct effect on health of human beings since it is sterile and nontoxic. Harmless water organisms in the water break down the spent liquor readily, but in doing so, they use up oxygen from the water at a rate which may adversely affect fish and other aquatic life if the stream is overloaded. Moreover, the capacity of the stream to combat biological pollution from other sources, notably from sewage wastes, is correspondingly reduced. Thus, streams which receive large quantities of pulp and paper mill wastes may be especially susceptible to biological pollution.

Wastes containing wood sugars are excellent food for the small water organisms which form the basis of the food complex. This complex progressively leads to larger organisms and eventually to fish. Small amounts of this food, therefore, are actually beneficial. When too much is added, however, these water organisms multiply at terrific rates of speed, to do this they require oxygen and obtain it from the water. This can deplete the oxygen to the point where the fish suffocate. The problem is to make certain that streams are not overloaded and that sufficient oxygen is maintained.

In pure water, only about 8 parts of oxygen may be dissolved in one million parts of water at summer temperatures. If this low initial concentration is reduced by much more than about 50 percent the aquatic environment may be affected; at levels lower than 3 parts per million fish mortality may occur, and the foul odors of anerobic decomposition develop [29:6-1].

Color

Although treatment of mill effluent for suspended solids removal and reduction of oxygen demanding chemicals is quite common today, the color characteristics of the effluent usually remain unchanged. The brown color of pulping effluents is due to the presence of lignin and tannins dissolved from the wood during digestion and bleaching. Color standards for water in some industrial uses are higher than for drinking water. "The U.S. Public Health Service drinking water standards set a maximum of 20 color units for potable water. Allowable maximum for process water for textiles, fine paper, pharmaceuticals, and soft drinks range from 0 to 5 units" [28:6-3]. (For an example of recent developments in color treatment, see comments about Interstate Paper Corporation mill in a later section of this chapter.

From where do difficult waste problems emanate? The pulping process is a consistent source of problems in connection with pollution control. In sulfate pulping, the unrecovered black liquor (from cooking) is a major factor in wastewater treatment; it has a high concentration of BOD, oxygen demanding chemicals, a very high color content, and a high foaming potential that readily offers visual evidence of pollution. "Reduction of problems associated with the black liquor from kraft pulping is best achieved by a liquor recovery system in which chemicals are reclaimed, while oxygen demanding organic materials and color-causing lignin are burned" [34:19].

The difficulties encountered in sulfite pulping also emanate from its spent cooking liquor. Many calcium based sulfite mills continue to discharge their spent liquor directly into wastewater streams without any chemical recovery or secondary waste treatment. The spent sulfite liquor contains very high concentrations of oxygen demanding chemicals, solids, color, and acidity. Semichemical pulping problems are similar to those of sulfite spent liquor.

Wastewaters from bleaching operations containing high amounts of oxygen-demanding chemicals and dissolved organic and inorganic materials are relatively difficult to treat. The waters are generally colored by lignins and tannins removed from the pulp. Cellulose material in the wood fiber, the lignins, and tannins are not easily attacked biologically. Foaming is also a problem associated with the filtrates from the washing cycles; preventing spills and overflows is important in foam control and will simultaneously increase the efficiency of the washing cycle. Paper machine wastewaters contain high concentrations of fine suspended solids.

The technical problems in pollution abatement in the pulp and paper industry are very complex, but are all characterized by one common central fact: the amount of water that the industry uses is so large and the pollutional material in it is so small. Although wastes per gallon may be reduced, the volume of water required is certain to be great.

Table 2-4 presents water requirements; Table 2-5 compares waste discharges. Although the ratio is frequently several thousand to one, the consequences may be grave.

The Consequences

The nature of the resulting problem is suggested by the following quotation from a recent work:

Table 2.4

**Water Requirements for Selected
Pulping Processes**

Process	Gallons fresh water per ton of pulp[a]	
	Maximum	Minimum
Kraft and soda (unbleached)	88,500	33,000
Kraft and soda (bleached)	144,500	39,500
Sulfite (unbleached)	79,000	8,300
Sulfite (bleached)	126,300	8,300
Groundwood (unbleached)	69,000	1,000
Groundwood (bleached)	92,400	1,000
Semichemical (unbleached)	12,400	6,980
Semichemical (bleached)	30,000	12,960

[a]These figures are for mills integrated with paper manufacture.

Source: U. S. Department of Commerce, *Technical and Economic Feasibility of Establishing a Hardwood Pulp and Paper Mill in an Eight-County Area of Western Kentucky*, August 1964, p. 5–7.

One giant mill on the Coosa River, which runs through Georgia and Alabama, pours into the stream wastes equivalent in oxygen demand to untreated sewage from a city of 200,000 persons. It must be repeatedly underscored that such wastes, although not toxic or dangerous in the sense that sewage and certain by-products of the chemical industry are, has essentially the same end effect since it robs the water of oxygen needed to assimilate the more perilous junk. Papermill waste liquors break the 'chain of food' in a river at several links, since all assimilation processes in fresh water, except putrefaction, require oxygen [6:150].

K. W. Kapp in his *Social Costs of Business Enterprise* put the matter this way:

The costs of controlling water pollution either by prior treatment of the materials discharged or by otherwise disposing of them is likely to be much lower than the social costs arising from the neglect of these measures. . . .The main social costs of water pollution are not those sustained by individuals in the form of injuries to health or property or recreational values, but rather those which arise from the depletion of a major economic resource.

Table 2.5

Comparative Waste Discharges

Industry	Unit of Input or Output	Waste Water (gals. per unit)	B.O.D. (ppm)[a]	Suspended Solids (ppm)
Groundwood pulp	1 ton dry pulp	12,000	645	n.d.[b]
Soda pulp	1 ton dry pulp	58,000	110	1,720
Sulfate (kraft) pulp	1 ton dry pulp	64,000	123	n.d.
Sulfite pulp	1 ton dry pulp	48,000	443	n.d.
Paper mill	1 ton paper	40,000	19	452
Paperboard	1 ton paperboard	14,000	121	660

[a] Ppm = Parts per million

[b] n.d.–no data

Source: E. A. Ackerman and G. O. G. Lof, *Technology In American Water Development* Baltimore: Johns Hopkins Press, 1959), p. 130.

The pollution of this resource, like the pollution of the atmosphere, is a social cost which needs to be fully assessed. Only systematic research conducted under impartial scientific auspices can provide the basis for estimating the social costs of water pollution with a reasonable degree of accuracy [cited in 11:84].

Just how serious is the water pollutant resulting from paper production?

In the year 1964, according to the Public Health Department, 18.4 million fish were killed by water pollution. Industrial pollution of lakes and streams was the cause of 12.7 million fish deaths [6:165].

The Pacific Coast has erupted with protests against industrial destruction of fish. Justice William O. Douglas experimented near the mouth of the Williamette River at Portland, Oregon. He put healthy rainbow trout in a cage and lowered them into the water; they died of suffocation immediately. Although this was mostly due to local sewage contamination, much pollution was provided by paper mills.

In the Northwest the feud between commercial fishermen and industrial river pollution is as savage as the ancient enmity between cattlemen and farmers on the Great Plains. The fishermen on the lower Columbia have set forth a manifesto in behalf of their own bodies as well as fish.

They wanted, for example, a coliform standard for the river of 250, which is very low, it is swimming pool quality, unheard of in a modern river. Their words were most passionate: This is our working environment. We are in this water; our hands are in this water, we have it on our faces and arms; we eat and live on this water all day. Why should we not have the same protection from bacteria that someone going to play for a half hour in a swimming pool has? [6:171].

This manifesto was presented to the states of Oregon and Washington and to the United States Public Health Service. The coliform standard of 250 was adopted.

The coliform count is a useful index to disease potential of polluted water. Bacteria of the coliform group reproduce in human intestines and are excreted in enormous numbers. The usual measurement is the number of coliform organisms per 100 milliliters of water (about half a glassful). If a sample has less than 100, the water is considered safe to drink. At 2,000 it is still considered safe to swim in [24:56].

It remains to be seen if the rigid coliform standard of 250 will be enforced.

Salmon in Puget Sound have to pass through the Bellingham Harbor area. The extreme toxicity of this water was proved by the suffocation of fish lowered into the water. Sulfite waste liguor less than those which rob the water of oxygen cause deformations of embryo oysters. For the Port Angeles-Everett area oyster larvae abnormalities reach as high as 50 percent [6:171].

The battle against water pollution is not only being waged on the Pacific Coast. Senator Muskie of Maine still claims, apparently with some degree of inverted pride, that the Androscoggin River of his native state is the worst polluted in the country. Years ago a dam was built which trapped behind it effluent from numerous pulp and paper mills. Even if there were no further pollution, he maintains that this trapped pollutant would make fish life impossible for many years, perhaps forever.

Below is a list of rivers which the Federal Government is trying to clean up because they are so badly polluted; only those whose pollution is attributed in whole or in part to pulp or paper production have been listed.

Rivers	Location	Industries Using
Androscoggin	N. H., Me.	Pulp & paper
Columbia (Lower, Upper) and Puget Sound	Wash., Ore.	Pulp & paper
Conneticut	Mass., Conn.	Paper, chemicals, textiles, metals
Coosa	Ala., Ga.	Paper
Escambia	Ala., Fla.	Paper

Menominee	Mich., Wis.	Paper, packaging
Pearl	La., Miss.	Paper, chemicals
Merrimack-Nashua	N.H., Mass.	Textiles, paper
Savannah	Ga., S. C.	Paper, food processing
Snake	Idaho, Wash.	Paper

The following are considered to be dangerously polluted, but no action has started yet.

River	Location	Industries Using
Batten Kill	Vt., N.Y.	Pulp & paper
Chowan	Va., N.C.	Pulp & paper
Delaware	N.Y., Pa., N.J., Del.	Pulp & paper among others
Deerfield	Vt., Mass.	Pulp & paper
French Broad	N.C., Tenn.	Tanning, textiles, pulp & paper
Hocking	Ohio, Pa.	Paper, gravel processing
Housatonic	Mass, Conn.	Textiles, paper
Kalmath	Ore., Calif.	Lumber, pulp & paper
Little Tennessee	Ga., N.C.	Pulp & paper textiles
Mill	Mass., R.I.	Textiles, paper, metal plating
Muskingum	Ohio, W. Va.	Paper, among others
Pigeon	N.C., Tenn.	Pulp & paper
Quinebung	Mass., Conn.	Paper, textiles
Rock	Wisc., Ill.	Paper

Saco	N.H., Me.	Paper, among others
St. Joseph	Ind., Mich.	Pulp & paper, meat packing
St. Louis	Wis., Minn.	Pulp & paper among others
St. Marys	Ga., Fla.	Pulp & paper
Tennessee	Ga., Tenn., Ala.	Paper among others
Wabash	Ill., Ind.	Paper, among others
Walloomsac	Vt., N.Y.	Paper
Withlacoochee	Ga., Fla.	Paper

Of a total listing of 114 rivers, 32 were associated with paper or paper industries [6:141].

Why are our waterways so heavily polluted? An argument which is often cited claims:

Abuse of water and air resources comes about largely because air and water are undervalued. Air and water are regarded as free goods. Because water and air resources are underpriced, private costs are less than social costs [11:13].

Allen V. Kneese, an economist for RFF, feels that factors of profit and loss do not enter sufficiently into the waste disposal problem. He suggests the charging of fees for the use of streams and bodies of water for dumping grounds or as sources of process water for industry.

A New York Times editorial said "Water pollution would not have become a federal responsibility if so many state and local governments had not been negligent in protecting their rivers" [12:22]. The reasons for this neglect were deemed to be (a) that polluters were communities and cities and that it would be politically embarrassing to move against them; and (b) that in many instances big polluters are big employers and there is keen competition among states for industrial establishments.

The extent of the waste disposal problem of the chemical pulping industry is indicated by the large volume of the material that must be eliminated; Table 2-6 presents comparative volumes of waste discharges in 1964. There are first the chemical residues of the various washes, bleaching agents, and spent digesting liquors. In addition, large quantities of lignin, wood sugar, and other materials from the wood enter the cooking liquors in the digesting process. Since almost one-third of the untreated wood consists of lignin, the potential volume of these wastes can readily be appreciated. "It was estimated a few years ago that the

Table 2.6

**Estimated Volume of Industrial Wastes
Before Treatment, 1964**

Industry	Wastewater Volume (Billion Gallons)	Process Water Intake (Billion Gallons)	BOD (Million Pounds)	Suspended Solids (Million Pounds)
Food & Kindred Products	690	260	4,300	6,600
Textile Mill Products	140	110	890	N.D.
Paper & Allied Products	1,900	1,300	5,900	3,000
Chemical & Allied Products	3,700	560	9,700	1,900
Petroleum & Coal	1,300	88	500	460
Rubber & Plastics	160	19	40	50
Primary Metals	4,300	1,000	480	4,700
Machinery	150	23	60	50
Electrical Machinery	91	28	70	20
Transportation Equipment	240	58	120	N.D.
All Other Manufacturing	450	190	390	930
All Manufacturing	13,100	3,700	22,000	18,000
For comparison: Sewered Population of U. S.	5,300[a]		7,300[b]	8,800[c]

Note: Columns may not add due to rounding. N.D. - no data.

[a] 120,000,000 persons x 120 gallons x 365 days.

[b] 120,000,000 persons x 1/6 pounds x 365 days.

[c] 120,000,000 persons x 0.2 pounds x 365 days.

Source: Federal Water Pollution Control Administration, *Cost of Clean Water*, v. 2, *Detailed Analyses*, January 1968, p. 63.

sulfite pulping industry in North America annually discharged 7 million tons of lignin into surface streams as wastes" [10:177].

Only recently has an awareness of the problem of air and water pollution developed. Prior to this, the discharge of industrial effluents were not considered important to control. The current state of pollution, for the most part, developed in this earlier period; it is this careless accumulation that has created a most serious problem.

Factors Influencing the Discharge of Effluents

The paper industry, perhaps more than any other industry, is dependent upon large quantities of water for the production of its many products. Because of this, the industry has been acutely aware of the need for water quality and is today grappling more forcefully than ever with one of the greatest problems it has encountered in its long history: that of eliminating — or, at least, controlling — the wastes from the effluents produced in the manufacture of pulp, paper, and paperboard [23:22].

Technological Change

The paper industry uses about four billion gallons of water each day; compare this with all of New York City which uses one billion gallons each day. This means that great care must be taken in locating the mills in areas where these large quantities of water are available. The enormous requirements of the paper industry cannot be met by public utilities so that water treatment and waste disposal plants are an integral part of each mill. "The technical know-how of pollution abatement, the state of the art, and the practicality of operation have advanced more in the last decade than in the entire century preceding it" [4:5]. Major advances have been made in the manufacturing subprocesses and the treatment of wastewaters.

The greatest factor in pollution abatement in the paper industry has been the shift from the sulfite to sulfate pulping:

... the production of a ton of wood pulp by the older sulfite process results in 20 to 40 times the waste strength of a similar amount of pulp produced by the now dominant sulfate process. Since about 1940, most of the expansion that has occurred in the pulp and paper industry has taken the form of growth of sulfate production. As a result, pulp output has increased roughly two and a half times as fast as have wastes of pulp manufacture. To put the matter in another perspective, if all pulp now produced by the sulfate process were being produced with sulfite pulping, BOD of the pulp and paper industry at current production levels would exceed 20 trillion pounds per year — or just about as much as is now produced by all manufacturing [33:73].

One of the great advantages of the kraft and soda processes for wood pulping, as compared with sulfite pulping, is the practicality of recovering the chemicals employed in the cooking liquor, of using the separated lignin as a fuel, and in some cases, of producing by-products from the effluent.

Today the major pollution problem of the pulping industry centers upon the disposal of the calcium — bisulfite waste liquors involved in sulfite pulping. . . . . . there is no simple way to recover the pulping chemicals or to evaporate the liquor to the point where this organic matter can be burned. . . . Nearly all of the total BOD of the sulfite pulping effluent originates in the spent cooking liquor [1:180].

In the sulfate (kraft) pulping process, the system of waste treatment inherent in the method of handling spent cooking liquors makes possible recovery of more than 95 percent of the chemicals and the wood substances present in them [9:195].

The demands placed upon water for the disposal of these very objectionable wastes are accordingly reduced. However, the plant effluent may contain relatively high concentrations of waste material derived from the other pulping operations and from the recovery process; comparative data have already been presented in Table 2-6.

Three Production Process Streams

Since the extent of pollution per unit of input of finished product varies with the level of technology, the Federal Water Pollution Control Administration has found it useful to distinguish three production process streams: (a) a subprocess series representative of an older processing technology; (b) a typical series of subprocess which are most prevalent today; and (c) a series representative of a still newer processing technology [34].

Since many of the existing plants limit technological improvement to specific areas of their fundamental process or subprocesses, it is not uncommon for a mill to have older technology in one process and newer technology in another. Except in the design of a new plant, clear cut designation of a plant into one of the three technology levels is often difficult. Based on overall performance, the percentage of mills with process streams that fall into one of these three categories has been estimated for the years 1963, 1972, and 1977; estimated percentages are shown in Table 2-7.

The mill sizes associated with these three technology levels are also indicated in Table 2-7. It can be seen that the trend is towards the establishment of larger mills. To categorize size relative to pulping process, sulfate kraft mills are relatively large; sulfite, semichemical and groundwood mills are relatively small. In many cases, groundwood, deinking, and semichemical pulping processes are integrated in the sulfate or sulfite mills.

On the average mills producing less than 250 tons per day are "small," 250 to 700 tons per day are "medium," and more than 700 tons per day are "large."

It is no longer possible to build an economically sound mill in the United States with a production capacity of less than 300 tons a day. New pulp mills are producing from 600 to 800 tons per day [5:169].

Table 2.7

**Percentage of Plants According to Tech-
nology Level and Production Capacity**

Technology Levels	Estimated Percent of Plants in Year			Range of Plant Sizes tons/day
	1963	1972	1977	
Older	24	11	6	20 – 500
Today's typical	68	58	48	100 – 1,000
Newer	8	31	46	200 – 1,500

Source: FWPCA, *Paper Mill Profile*, p. 21.

Some examples of size are provided by new mills listed in a trade directory. The West Virginia Pulp and Paper Company plant in Wickliffe, Kentucky, and the Weyerhauser Company plant at New Bern, North Carolina, have listed capacities of 600 tons per day [28:371].

Average wasteloads and wastewater quantities associated with the fundamental processes and subprocesses are presented in Table 2-8. Each mill has a wide variety of fundamental processes, subprocesses, and combinations from which to choose under the older, present, and newer technology; except for mills being built, it is impossible to estimate the exact operating sequence of any individual mill, much less estimate the number of mills that would select the same sequence. It is, therefore, impossible to determine precisely wasteloads and quantities for the three mill sizes as related to the different technological levels; variations in wasteloads and quantities according to mill size are also not readily obtainable.

The data for average wasteloads are not intended to be additive because of the complexity of the operations involved in the different pulping processes, various degrees of water reuse from one process to another, and product related problems. Instead, total waste quantities and wastewater volume, based on available data covering bleached sulfate (kraft), unbleached sulfate (kraft), and bleached sulfite processes, and for each of the three technology levels are presented; these three type mills constitute the major portion of paper industry production. Groundwood, semichemical, deinking and other types of mills are in the minority.

Even considering the many process improvements made, the typical biochemical oxygen demand of sulfate pulping effluent is undesirably high when

Table 2.8

Average Wasteloads and Wastewater Quantities (Wasteload in lbs./ton of product)

Processes	Older Technology			Today's Technology			Newer Technology		
	Solids	BOD	Wastewater[a]	Solids	BOD	Wastewater[a]	Solids	BOD	Wastewater[a]
Wood Preparation	- -	44	12,000	13	3	3,400	4	.2	1,700
Pulping									
Groundwood	340	16	7,000	- -	- -	- -	50	10	2,000
Sulfate (kraft)	162	52	20,300	164	23	5,600	81	21	4,600
Sulfite	2,440	362	14,600	411	235	10,900	305	70	6,300
Semichemical	155	43	12,000	200	30	7,000			
Pulp Screening									
Groundwood									
Sulfate	80	18	9,600	62	14	3,600		Generally	
Sulfite	35	5	9,100	27	8	6,000		No	
Semichemical	150	30	7,800	- -	- -	- -		Waste	
Pulp Washing									
Groundwood									
Sulfate	107	35	10,000						
Sulfite	165	19	11,000						
Semichemical	400	85	6,000						

(continued)

Table 2-8 (continued)

Processes	Older Technology			Today's Technology			Newer Technology		
	Solids	BOD	Wastewater[a]	Solids	BOD	Wastewater[a]	Solids	BOD	Wastewater[a]
Pulp Thickening									
Groundwood	107	47	10,000	75[b]	33	7,500	27[b]	10	1,900
Sulfate	71	7	15,000	142	25	7,000	50	8	2,000
Sulfite	108	19	17,000	131	18	7,500	68	11	4,100
Semichemical	40	5	14,000	93	24	5,400			
Bleaching									
Sulfate	400	--	45,000						11,500
Sulfite	335	40	43,000					7	6,000
Semichemical	--	--	45,000						
Papermaking	160	20	32,000				70	10	7,500
Total Mill Effluent (integrated pulp and paper mills)									
Bleached sulfate and paper	1,100	200	110,000				390	90	25,000
Unbleached sulfate and paper	650	--	90,000				260	80	16,000
Bleached sulfite and paper	1,320	500	95,000				450	100	30,000

[a] gallons/ton

[b] These figures for washing and thickening

[c] Remainder of figures not included

Source: Federal Water Pollution Control Administration, *Cost of Clean Water*, v. 3, *Industrial, Waste Profiles, Paper Mills*, November 1967, Tables A-3, A-4. A-5.

discharged in such great volume. The presence of suspended or floating solids and toxic materials as well as substances causing objectionable odors indicates the desirability and often the necessity of waste treatment. Three types of treatment practice are important: controlled discharge of the mill effluent, submerged dispersal, and reduction of its biochemical oxygen demand (BOD) by mechanical or biological means. In the first method, the effluent is impounded in large storage lagoons or retention basins from which it can be discharged into receiving waters as conditions warrant. The mill effluent often varies considerably in strength in the course of a day's operation, and one of the advantages derived from the use of storage lagoons is that the fluctuating pollutional load of the wastes can be equalized. More important is the fact that the wastes can be retained during seasonal periods of low flows in receiving waters. In some cases, sufficient storage capacity is provided to hold the entire waste for a portion of a year. Discharge can then be scheduled only when stream flows are at their peak so that serious pollution can be avoided by adequate dilution.

Other methods of treating sulfate mill effluent are directed toward BOD reduction. In almost all cases, an attempt is made to reduce the biochemical oxygen demand of the liquid wastes mechanically by removing suspended and floating solids by filtration. These filters frequently are augmented with settling basins and clarifiers. Before discharging mill wastes to nearby waterways, their BOD may be lowered further by various biological oxidation techniques, the most important being retention in oxidation ponds, natural purification, and accelerated aeration. Chemical and physical techniques such as ion exchange, dialysis, and electrical methods to reduce BOD have been tried and found economically unfeasible or mechanically unworkable.

Where the process of natural purification is relied upon in biological treatment, the waste effluent is passed down a stream or canal in which a culture of appropriate biological organisms hastening oxidation has been developed. Under favorable conditions, significant BOD reductions can be effected.

The accelerated aeration method of effluent oxidation is carried out in an aeration tank by a biological sludge. A large sulfate mill has begun to treat its effluent, in excess of 16 million gallons a day, by the activated sludge process. Because of the very high BOD reductions, this constitutes one of the most significant recent developments in handling of pulping wastes [1:175-183].

The activated sludge process is a system in which biologically active growths are continuously circulated and contacted with organic waste in the presence of oxygen. The biological life assimilates the food contained in the waste. Oxygen is fed into the aeration tank in compressed air injected in the form of fine bubbles under turbulent conditions. This is a second stage treatment. This process involves many variations and utilizes many different types of aeration tanks and aeration equipment [8:400].

A large activated sludge plant constructed for the treatment of pulp and paper mill wastes is in service at Westernport, Maryland. Its function is to clean up pollution in the North Branch of the Potomac River, in compliance with long standing urgings of Maryland officials. It is designed to handle not only wastes from the vast Luke, Maryland, plant of West Virginia Pulp and Paper Company, but also sewage from three nearby municipalities, Luke and Westernport, Maryland, and Piedmont, West Virginia. The major participant in the joint program is the company. For this overall industrial installation, the total investment in waste treatment approached $4.5 million [36].

Because of the difficulties and expense of evaporating sulfite pulping liquor, considerable effort has been expended in developing methods for recovering high-value by-products from the residues. Limited success has been achieved. One process treats spent digester wastes with lime to produce a solid lignin compound which may be used either as a boiler fuel or as a lignin raw material; another uses a multiple effect evaporator to obtain an effluent syrup which can be burned in liquid form [1:180].

Although a substantial share of the market for vanilla flavoring is being taken by synthetic vanillin made from sulfite waste liquor, this high-value by-product is of relatively minor importance in waste disposal. "United States sulfite pulp mills produce enough waste liquor in two days' operation to meet the nation's demand for vanilla for a full year" [10:177].

"Millions of gallons of unevaporated sulfite spent liquor have been used in Wisconsin and other places as a road binder, by applying to dirt, sand, or gravel roads at a solids content of about 10%" [7:205]. The successful development of methods for concentrating sulfite spent liquor by evaporation has opened up markets for this material over and above its use as a fuel. Partially evaporated sulfite spent liquor has been suggested for use as an adhesive, in the preparation of tanning agents, dye bases, fertilizers, soil conditioners, and insecticides. It can also be employed as an additive in resinous plastics and special purpose concrete.

In addition to these efforts to secure a high-value use for lignin constituents of sulfite wastes, a number of other effort concern the use of material in the mill effluent. In some countries alcohol is produced from recovered wood sugars; in the United States the sulfite wastes of one mill in Washington are being used for this purpose.

The alcohol produced must compete with that made from the fermentation of blackstrap molasses or grain and that made by synthesis from petroleum, which in general are cheaper processes. Consequently, the production of alcohol from sulfite spent liquor is not extremely attractive... [7:211].

Spent cooking liquors of sulfite mills are being used as a culture medium in the production of yeast and substantial reductions in the BOD of the effluent discharge are obtained. As early as 1943, the Sulfite Pulp Manufacturer's Research League started growing yeasts on waste sulfite liquor; today nearly every sulfite plant has a yeast plant next to it. These are not enough, however, to make much of a dent in the total flow of pollutants.

Because use of the sulfite wastes as fuel has generally not been economical, and because development of large markets for by-products is low, much effort has been directed toward the development of cheap, practical methods of treating the final mill effluent. Lagooning has long been practiced and various soil filtration techniques have gained considerable importance in recent years. Numerous other methods, such as the use of trickling filters and foam phase aerators, have been intensively explored, but they appear to be prohibitive in cost despite the impressive reductions in BOD which they make possible. Artificial stream aeration; the addition of a dissolved oxygen to a stream by compressed air diffusion, has shown considerable promise during experiments and may have applicability under certain conditions. Because of the high concentration of wastes in sulfite pulping effluent, however, the treatment problem is difficult and it is not likely that an effective technique will be developed which is not expensive. Also, the recovery and purification of soap has established a firm market for this product and it has proved to be a substantial source of revenue to the sulfate pulp mill [5:168].

Another method of handling sulfite waste ensures their rapid dilution by the receiving waters. Instead of discharge at one single point, the effluent is distributed into the receiving stream through a long submerged perforated pipe or some other device that facilitates its dispersal and dilution. Ample stream flow is a complementary requirement for use of this disposal system.

Satisfactory waste disposal thus has not been as successfully achieved for sulfite pulping as for the sulfate process. The simplicity and comparative economy of the recovery practices employed in sulfate pulping have undoubtedly promoted the industry's increasing reliance on this process. Not only is an important saving effected in the use of chemicals, but the recovered lignosulfonate is an excellent fuel. About half a ton of coal or its equivalent is needed in the manufacture of a ton of chemical pulp; by burning the lignin, a substantial part of this need is met.

A major factor in the growth of sulfate pulp manufacture also has been the improvement in both quality and usefulness of the product. The introduction of bleached kraft has been especially important, making a finer product capable of replacing sulfite pulp for a number of purposes. Improved quality, along with the lesser waste disposal problem, account for the dominance which this method of pulping has achieved. In 1920, the kraft process accounted for only three percent of the wood pulp output, while today more than half is made in this way. In the last three decades, almost the entire growth of the industry has been in sulfate pulping. The output of sulfite pulp, although not decreasing, is today less than one-third as important as it was. The rapid expansion of sulfate pulping is suggested by the fact that the capacity of such mills have increased fivefold between 1936 and 1953.

A significant development is altering the waste disposal situation and will unquestionably affect this general trend. For more than twenty-five years, interest has been directed toward the possibility of replacing calcium in sulfite cooking liquor with more soluble bases which could be recovered practicably. Ammonia and magnesia base processes have been adopted. These modifications in the pulping process are important for waste disposal because they result in considerable reduction in stream pollution and provide substantial heat economies. "Weyerhauser engineers developed an entirely new sulfite pulping process, the MGD process, which reclaims more than 85 percent of the wastes previously discharged into receiving waters" [38].

On January 16, 1968, the Great Northern Paper Company announced in a press release distributed by the company that it would invest approximately $10 million in pollution control and abatement facilities at one of its plants in Maine. The changes include conversion to the manufacture of sulfite pulp by the magnesium oxide process and the construction of a new recovery boiler to burn waste products and recover the chemicals used in the wood cooking process. In addition to fulfilling the need for water improvement, the company expects to obtain a significant monetary return since the recovery process will enable the reclamation of between 70 and 80 percent of its pulping chemicals and will generate increased power from the burning of waste liquor as fuel.

The magnefite process developed at Howard Paper Mills, Ltd., Cornwall, Ontario uses a magnesium base. It allows for (a) manufacture of pulp from a wide variety of wood species; (b) manufacture of pulp of high yield and great strength; (c) elimination of stream and air pollution; and (d) highly efficient recovery of chemicals. "Current (1962) production of magnesium base sulfite pulp in the United States is estimated to be 790,000 tons out of a total sulfite capacity of 3,400,000 tons" [5:161]. This is an indication of the changing trend.

The disposal of mill wastes so as to prevent serious pollution in the receiving waters continues to constitute a major problem for the pulping industry, but much progress has been achieved. "Although production has increased fourfold in 25 years, total pollution has actually decreased" [13:104].

Despite this accomplishment, severe waste disposal problems still exist; this is particularly true where there are numerous plants on the same stream. Costs are an added expense in manufacture. In a speech in October, 1968, a Kimberly-Clark executive, Mr. R. M. Billings, suggested that two to four percent of capital expenditures for new projects in the paper industry will go for abatement facilities; also, the cost of removing BOD is about four cents per pound. The economic feasibility of recovery practices has been supported by the growing recovery rates and the use of by-products which has materially increased.

In building a plant at a new location, a firm has a tremendous advantage. It usually knows the pollution standards; it has freedom in design and layout, and it knows what is technically available and economically practical and can analyze costs.

The quantity and quality of water available to meet present and future demands is a very important consideration in the selection of a mill site, being just as important as transportation facilities for the raw materials and available markets. When the site is being selected, the method of used-water disposal must also be studied because at least 90 percent of the water entering the plant leaves it either as a by-product source of enzymes and chemicals, as vapor, or as waste effluent down the sewer and back into the stream. The waste-carrying used water usually forms the greatest volume and must be disposed of in conformity with regional or local stream — pollution-abatement regulations [18:144].

Mills that were built in the past have seen the pollution climate change rapidly over a space of a relatively few years. Many of these mills were built during a period when stream conditions were not regarded as subject to control and do not have waste treatment facilities. It is impossible to bring many of them to the efficiency of a modern installation. A decision may be required as to whether an old plant can be technically improved enough to make it satisfactory or whether it cannot be improved enough and must be junked.

Since a number of promising disposal methods have been developed, it is likely that further progress may be achieved merely by wider application of successful techniques. It seems certain that there will be no single waste disposal practice meeting the needs of the entire industry, but the problem will continue to require a variety of solutions. As success is achieved, the water requirements for waste disposal correspondingly will be reduced.

The potential effectiveness of technological advances in meeting the problem of stream pollution by allowing older plants to meet today's standards can be exemplified by the success at the Weyerhauser Company Springfield, Oregon, kraft pulp and containerboard plant. Latest controls were installed when the plant was built in 1949. It is situated on the McKenzie River, nationally known for its trout and salmon fishing; the flow of the river lessens during the summer months. Complaints began to be registered from fishermen who objected to odors coming downstream from the plant. There was also foam on the river's surface and slime growth on the river bottom. Technicians were set to work seeking a solution to the problems. In 1961, the new techniques and refinements of old control methods earned the commendation of the Oregon State Sanitary Authority, and the plant was awarded the Industrial Air and Water Protection Award by the Pacific Northwest Pollution Control Association. The BOD load of effluent per ton of product was lowered from 58 pounds in 1956 to 18 pounds in 1963 [37].

Legislation and Standards

Some twenty years ago, in response to the realization that rivers and streams were being overloaded with wastes, an aroused public clamored for strict controls and Congress passed legislation to correct the situation. In 1948, a Federal Water Pollution Control Act was passed, providing financial and technical assistance for the construction of water facilities for municipalities and making research grants available.

The Federal Water Pollution Control Act of 1965 expressly states: 'It is hereby declared to be the policy of Congress to recognize, preserve, and protect the primary responsibilities and rights of the States in preventing and controlling water pollution.' The act allows states to recommend standards applicable to interstate waters and to adopt plans for enforcement. If this is not done, the Secretary of the Interior will set forth the standards [39:62].

Much had been done by the states prior to the issuance of this edict; this is evidenced by the numerous revisions and reorganizations that have taken place since 1950. "By 1965 sixteen states had created statutory agencies within the health department, twenty one had created independent pollution control agencies, and one had placed authority in its Fish and Game Commission" [39:55]. Interstate agencies have been created in a number of regions to deal with water pollution problems that overlap state boundaries.

The Council of State Governments endorsed a Suggested Water Pollution Control Act in 1950; about 40 states have used this as a model [39:60]. Formulating statewide standards is a complex and difficult task; many states have developed standards as specific cases required. "In two states, New Hampshire and Maine, the legislature established four classes of receiving waters and standards for them, and then classified every major body of surface water. Vermont used a similar plan, but left the classification to the control board. New York's act provides that there are variable factors; the Water Pollution Control Board adopts standards and classifications of quality and purity" [39:61].

A number of different standards of stream quality have been developed. Usages which are available as measures of permissible pollution include: 1) preservation of natural-state (so-called wild) river, 2) use as a source of potable water supply, 3) preservation of fish and wildlife, 4) safety for agricultural use such as stock watering or irrigation, 5) safety for recreational use such as swimming and water skiing, 6) use for industrial purposes such as cooling and process water, 7) freedom from nuisance, 8) commercial use such as navigation, 9) use for water carriage of wastes [39:14].

Industry has also moved to study the nature of its industrial wastes and worked closely with local and state authorities on the processing and control of waste materials, with much being accomplished over the years. In 1943, the pulp and paper industry created the National Council for Stream Improvement, a nationwide organization. With headquarters in New York and five regional groups located throughout the country, the Council carries out basic research seeking solutions to the industry's waste problems and makes these findings available to members for introduction in their mills. Before that, in 1939, the Sulfite Pulp Manufacturers' Research League was formed and charged with the responsibility of improving stream conditions.

Today, the industry must adhere to existing local, state, and federal regulations. There is no state where standards for comparable areas vary significantly for new mills. The problem of setting requirements for old mills which can only be modified to a certain extent still remains; there is a limit to what can be done to improve an old installation.

In Vermont, secondary treatment of all waste discharges is required. Essentially, this requires 85 to 90 percent reduction of biochemical oxygen demand and removal of objectionable wastes such as foam, scum, and floating material. The industries throughout the state are, in general, in some stage of engineering planning for the required facilities. Waters are classified into four categories, A, B, C, or D, according to use. Enforcement by the state attorney general can be used to enjoin offenders from polluting waters.

The most serious industrial waste pollution problem in the state is on Lake Champlain opposite Ticonderoga, New York. The International Paper Company at Ticonderoga has discharged wastes for many years which have built up a considerable sludge deposit in the lake. These deposits and the continuing effluent discharge affect water quality throughout a wide area of the adjacent lake waters; the water depth has decreased from over 18 feet to less than 2 feet in some locations.

In 1965, the Vermont Department of Water Resources conducted a water quality study in the area. The following year the study was furthered with the cooperation of the New York State Health Department and the Federal Water Pollution Control Administration. The total lake area known to be seriously affected by the wastes and its sludge deposits is approximately 1450 acres.

The water is dark gray to black and often contains floating sludge mats; an odor like rotten eggs emanates from the escaping hydrogen sulfide. Biochemical oxygen demand values as high as 205 milligrams per liter have been measured; normal BOD values to be expected in a lake of this nature would be less than one milligram per liter.

In response to this problem, the International Paper Company is presently planning to move their operation from the present location to a new site on Lake Champlain. It is expected that the new plant will incorporate adequate water pollution control facilities. Although further pollution will be controlled, it is expected that these waters will remain in their present condition for many years due to the massive sludge deposits in the bay unless remedial action, such as dredging, is undertaken [35].

In a letter dated April 4, 1969, Mr. Thomas L. Kamppinen, Regional Water Quality Supervisor for Michigan, states that "abatement of pollution in the interstate waters of Michigan is to be accomplished by June 1, 1972." The Menominee River has previously been cited as being seriously polluted due to paper mill waste discharges; the paper companies are "now in compliance with the interstate standards adopted by the State of Michigan and approved by the Federal Water Pollution Control Administration." Upgrading of treatment facilities in the St. Joseph River basin, also cited earlier, is in progress. On the Kalamazoo River, paper companies "have reduced the BOD loading to that river by approximately 50 percent in the last two years." Primary treatment is provided at the plants of the majority of the companies and contracts provide for secondary treatment at municipal plants. Like many other states, use designation for the interstate waters were adopted in March, 1969; these are not yet available. In addition to setting water quality standards, a bonding program of 335 million dollars for pollution control facilities was overwhelmingly endorsed in November, 1968.

Severe industrial pollution of important streams may lead to the impression that the problem is more nearly insurmountable than it really is. For example, Senator Muskie of Maine has frequently called attention to the serious pollution of the Androscoggin River in Maine. The Androscoggin is also polluted in New Hampshire below Berlin where the Brown Company has a large plant which manufactures pulp and paper, as is the Ashuelot River in southwestern New Hampshire on which five paper mills are located. However, the upper reaches of both rivers and the vast majority of New Hampshire streams are relatively unpolluted.

The New Hampshire Water Pollution Commission reports that

Since the passage of the Water Pollution Control Law in 1947, studies made and legislation enacted have resulted in the classification of over 11,000 miles of streams. This is about 76 percent of the estimated 14,500 miles of streams in the state [22:7].

Four major classifications are used.

Almost 97 percent of these streams have been assigned an A or a B-1 classification. Only 336 miles or 3.1 percent of the classified stream mileage have been designated for those uses not requiring bathing quality water [22:10].

From East to West, state and local governments are initiating water control programs. Mr. Jerry L. Harper, Senior Engineer for the Washington Water Pollution Control Commission, responded to an inquiry in a letter dated March 12, 1969. He noted that

There has been considerable improvement to the quality of the Snake and Columbia Rivers within the past twelve months due to completion of construction of solids-removing equipment at the five major pulp and paper mills located on these rivers. These projects provided primary treatment of effluent from these mills at an approximate cost of seven million dollars. One of these mills has recently closed its pulping operation entirely, thereby eliminating a major source of pollution.

Two of the remaining mills have additional major projects to complete within the next two years which will eliminate another major segment of strong pulp mill wastes. These projects will cost about twenty million dollars. As you can see, we are making very good progress in our pollution abatement programs for these rivers, as well as other state waters.

The state of Washington also uses four major classifications and requires permits to discharge waste effluents.

To be optimumly effective, legislation should fit the problem: Standards should not be the same, but should vary according to the characteristics and uses of the waterway. Certain rivers can be set aside for the express purpose of preserving them in a natural condition, but not all waterways. (The cost of such a proposal could cripple many industries.) "The cost of waste abatement for the nation as a whole has been estimated by the Federal Water Pollution Control Administration to be $100 billion between 1968 and the year 2000" [14].

A Look Ahead at Pollution Due to
Paper Production

The technological advances and legislative controls described in the preceding section have had an effect in reducing pollution largely because of growing

Table 2.9

**Regional Incidence of Paper Industry
Waste Discharge, 1964**

Region	Percent of Wastewater Discharge
Northeast	23.5
Southeast	26.4
Great Lakes	12.4
Ohio	2.6
Tennessee	3.4
Upper Mississippi	5.6
Lower Mississippi	1.6
Missouri	.1
Arkansas	3.4
Western Gulf	1.4
Pacific Northwest	16.7
California	1.2
Total Regionally Assignable Discharge	98.3

Source: FWPCA, *Detailed Analyses*, p. 65.

public awareness of the problem. Increasing output may add to the obstacles to be overcome. This section examines the implications of the future projected level of paper production on pollution problems in terms of the regions in which expanded output is expected to occur.

Due to the heavy reliance upon proximity to woodlands and adequate water supplies, future plant location is limited to certain areas. Table 2-9 presents the regional location of waste discharge of the paper industry in 1964, Table 2-10 shows the change in plant locations over a ten-year period, and generally corroborates the discharge allocation. The North American pulp and paper

Table 2.10

Location of Pulp and Paper Mills

Location	1969 Edition	1963 Edition	1958 Edition
Alabama	17	11	12
Alaska	2	2	1
Arizona	2	2	1
Arkansas	11	9	9
California	37	29	30
Colorado	1	1	2
Connecticut	23	23	22
Delaware	6	6	6
District of Columbia	0	0	0
Florida	16	16	15
Georgia	20	17	15
Hawaii	0	1	1
Idaho	2	1	1
Illinois	28	31	36
Indiana	15	16	17
Iowa	3	3	3
Kansas	2	2	2
Kentucky	2	0	0
Louisiana	18	15	12
Maine	26	27	30
Maryland	6	9	8
Massachusetts	58	66	76
Michigan	37	48	46
Minnesota	12	13	12

Table 2.10 (*continued*)

Location	1969 Edition	1963 Edition	1958 Edition
Mississippi	11	7	7
Missouri	9	10	7
Montana	1	1	0
New Hampshire	22	26	26
New Jersey	35	39	45
New Mexico	1	1	1
New York	86	122	129
North Carolina	15	12	11
Ohio	47	52	55
Oklahoma	5	2	2
Oregon	29	27	24
Pennsylvania	57	56	57
Puerto Rico	2	2	1
Rhode Island	1	1	1
South Carolina	8	5	4
Tennessee	12	12	12
Texas	16	17	15
Vermont	11	10	9
Virginia	14	14	15
Washington	27	30	28
West Virginia	3	3	4
Wisconsin	48	54	54
Total	804	851	864

Source: Robert Sanford (ed.), *Lockwood's
Directory of the Paper and Allied Trades*
(New York: Lockwood Publishing, 1968,
1962, and 1957), 1968 p. 147; 1962 p. 139;
1957 p. 131.

Table 2.11

New Mills Planned in the United States:
1968 to Early 1970

Alabama	2	Mississippi	1
Arkansas	3	New York	1
Alaska	1	North Carolina	2
Colorado	1	Oklahoma	1
Connecticut	1	Oregon	2
Florida	1	Pennsylvania	3
Georgia	1	South Carolina	1
Hawaii	1	Tennessee	1
Illinois	1	Texas	4
Kentucky	2	Washington	1
Louisiana	3	West Virginia	1
Maryland	1	Wisconsin	1
Minnesota	1	Wyoming	1
		Total	39

Source: *Pulp and Paper*, December 16, 1968, p. 71.

industry plans to spend $4.5 billion in capital improvements from 1968 to the early 1970s. There are 65 new mills planned, 39 in the United States and 26 in Canada. The distribution of the new plants in the United States is presented in Table 2-11 [25:71].

These three tables indicate the current trend in plant location in the paper industry. The total number of plants is decreasing; this is the result of large new plants replacing smaller plants built under the older technology. Regionally, the South and West have been the principal areas of expansion for the paper

Table 2.12

Total Wasteloads and Wastewater Quantities by Technology Levels in 1963

Manufacturing Technology Levels	Solids (lbs/ton)	BOD (lbs/ton)	Wastewater (gal/ton)	Estimated Percent of Industry
Older	1000	200	84,000	24
Today's	670	135	40,000	68
Newer	350	80	25,000	8

Source: FWPCA, *Paper Mill Profile*, p. 25.

industry; this has been true over the past ten years (Table 2-10) and planned expansion will continue this trend (Table 2-11). Conversely, the Northeast and Great Lakes have experienced marked declines in the number of paper plants and planned expansion will not alter this trend.

In order to project into the future, a point of origin must be established; Tables 2-7 and 2-8 have presented summaries of the three technology levels. The status of wasteloads and technology levels in 1963 is presented in Table 2-12.

The estimated shift in technology levels is seen in Table 2-8. The concomitant decrease in waste discharge is unknown; however, the past can provide evidence of substantial reductions through technological change. A shift in the sulfite base, as already noted, could greatly reduce the polluting effects of effluents. To proceed, certain assumptions regarding future developments must be established

(1) The mid values of the RFF production projections will be used. For 1970, 1980, and 1990, and 2000 these were, respectively, 49.0, 69.7 97.2, and 133.5 tons.

(2) The percentage shift in technology levels will be approximately as reflected in Table 2-13.

(3) Improved technology should reduce waste discharge levels. These reductions will probably focus on the new and today's technology levels; estimated BOD of discharge per ton of product are shown in Table 2-14.

Relating the above estimations of waste discharge levels and technology shifts to the data in Tables 2-10 and 2-11 provides an implicit picture of future developments in the pollution problem associated with the paper industry. New improved plants will probably be located in the South and in the West; the plants in the Northeast and Great Lakes can possibly be partially improved, but more probably will be abandoned.

Table 2.13

Estimated Shift in Technology Levels

Technology Levels	Percentage of Plants				
	1963[a]	1970[a]	1980[a]	1990	2000
Older	24	11	6	3	–
Today's	68	58	48	38	28
Newer	8	31	46	59	72
Total	100 percent	100 percent	100 percent	100 percent	100 percent

Source: Table 2.7.

Table 2.14

Estimated Waste Discharge Levels

Technology Levels	Estimated BOD of Discharge (lbs. per ton of product)				
	1963[a]	1970	1980	1990	2000
Today's	135	120	105	90	75
Newer	80	70	60	50	40

Source: Table 2.12.

Magnitude and Impact of Waste Discharge

The quantitative measure of BOD discharge resulting from the above assumptions is expressed in Table 2-15. Of prime importance is the relation of discharge to production; although production increases by two and a half times, the absolute level of the BOD of the discharge is not expected to change significantly. Technological change is responsible for the declining ratio. This is an extension of the historical trend which has seen production far outstrip the discharge of wastes.

If these projections are realistic, the problem of effluent discharge associated with the paper industry should be controllable. The fact that this discharge is readily localized provides added optimism. City, county, and state offices are in a good position to decide how to approach the specific improvement required.

Table 2.15

Projected BOD of the Discharge

	1970	1980	1990	2000
Tons of Product[a]	50.0	70.0	100.0	130.0
Tons at Older[b]	5.5	4.2	3.0	–
Today's	29.0	33.6	38.0	36.4
Newer	15.5	32.2	59.0	93.6
BOD (millions of lbs.)[c]				
From Older	1100	840	600	–
Today's	3480	3528	3420	2730
Newer	1085	1932	2950	3744
Total	5665	6300	6970	6474

[a]RFF mid values.

[b]Calculated using percentages in Table 2.13.

[c]Calculated using discharge rates in Table 2.14.

An example of success at a specific plant is exemplified by the treatment of the suspended solid discharge at Kimberly-Clark's deinking mill at West Carrollton, Ohio.

The Miami Conservancy District needed 70,000 cubic yards of fill to complete the flood control levee for the West Carollton side of the river. This 70,000 cubic yards came from our (Kimberly-Clark's) 28 acre disposal tract. The hole left will be filled with sludge from the treatment plant. To properly thicken the sludge, substantial amounts of lime are required. This lime is obtained in slurry form from the nearby plant of Air Reduction Company, Inc. where it occurs as a waste by-product in the manufacture of acetylene. This solves a disposal problem there. Disposal of cinders from the Kimberly-Clark power plant in turn further stabilize the sludge itself. Local knowledge of local problems produced a local solution [3].

It has been noted earlier that the Northeast and Great Lakes will probably be the scene of partial improvement in current plants and little future expansion; in fact, a diminishing importance in the regional location of the paper industry. Will the improvement in current plants enable these areas to contain effluents?

An indication of the potential effectiveness of improvements in current plants is noted in Wisconsin when Wisconsin's Department of Resource Development was charged with formulating, no later than July 1, 1968, a long-range, comprehensive state water resources plan for prevention and abatement of water pollution and for maintenance and improvement of water quality. There, the need for organized control of water pollution first became evident in 1925:

A tremendous fish kill occurred on the Flambeau River due to the discharge of wastes from a sulfite pulp mill. Tons of fish floated to the surface; not poisoned by the spent liquor as some believed, but asphyxiated because the slug of decaying organic material had robbed the water of its dissolved oxygen [40:2].

The Wisconsin and Fox Rivers have the largest number of pulp and paper mills. Water quality standards have been adopted for the state's interstate waters utilizing four classifications.

There is clear-cut evidence that the amount of pollution per ton of pulp and paper production has gone down. However, operations have increased and the overall amount of pollutional material reaching the Wisconsin River is about as much as ever.

With increasing production, further reductions in pollutional discharges are needed to prevent further stream degradation and substantial abatement is necessary to bring about improvements [41:11].

As in the aggregate projections in Table 2-15, the data for the Wisconsin River, as presented in Table 2-16, show production advancing at a greater pace than pollutional load.

Since the majority of new plants will be located in the South and West, these areas can guard against a water pollution problem if effective legislation is enacted and enforced. As noted earlier, the Kimberly-Clark plant in Shasta County, California, is an example of the industry's ability to conform to rigidly enforced standards. Another example can be cited in Georgia where a plant opened in May, 1968, was the first to apply primary, secondary, and color-removal treatment to mill effluent. The $27 million plant designed to produce 400 tons per day had to meet state effluent standards. "The Georgia Water Control Board limits color content to 30 parts per million, suspended solids to 10 and biological oxygen demand to 800 pounds per day" [25]. The mill's waste treatment system is unique in the industry; the waste treatment system was built at the cost of $2.5 million. The chemical coagulation color-removal process is the factor which makes this plant unique; this color-removal process is a demonstration project of the Federal Water Pollution Control Administration for which the company has received a demonstration grant.

These examples hold the promise for an expansion of large clean plants in the South and West. Other areas will not be assisted by the construction of modern plants; current plants may be improved and old plants may be closed. These factors, if they prevail according to current indications, should enable the paper industry to control the water pollution problem associated with increasing production.

Table 2.16

Wisconsin River Pulp and Paper Statistics

Year	BOD (t.p.d.)	Pulp and Paper Production (tons)
1950	297	3175
1955	260	3777
1959	315	4641
1960	386	4629
1961	349	4878
1962	424	5122
1963	460	5326

Source: State of Wisconsin, "Report on an Investigation of the Pollution in the Upper Wisconsin River Drainage Basin Made During 1963 and Early 1964," June 30, 1964, Tables 3 and 4.

[a]Data is for total of 15 plants.

Another indication of the potential success of pollution abatement programs in the paper industry is the increasing number of joint treatment plants built to treat industrial and municipal wastes. Grant money is available to municipalities and sewerage authorities that is not available to industry alone. It reduces the necessity for a high capital investment, although cost to industry is still substantial. Certain federal and state incentive may be made available to defray part of this expense; these could include cash grants, low-cost loans, accelerated depreciation, increased allowance for investment credit, and reductions in property taxation. Some of these have already been effected to encourage companies to make expenditures necessary for significant improvements in stream conditions.

Also, there remains the fact that the water resource will replenish itself perpetually if allowed to do so; this is the reason that streams can be and are being improved. As a waterway flows, natural counteragents help to restore water quality. Sedimentation in stillwaters filters out suspended matter; waterfalls provide aeration to restore oxygen content; sunlight bleaches color; and biological agents cleanse the water. These counteragents contribute to the self-purification of streams; time, temperature, and the character of the pollutants are important factors influencing a stream's progress toward purity. Future technological improvements should allow this progress to continue, despite the increase in paper industry production as forecasted by RFF.

3

Water Pollution and Expanding Production in the Steel, Chemical, and Petroleum Industries

Thomas E. Christman

This chapter discusses the problem of industrial water pollution. The steel, chemical, and petroleum industries have been chosen as representative examples of the many industries that discharge large volumes of harmful wastes into waterways.

In recent years, it has come to the attention of all levels of government that the industrial water pollution problem poses serious threats to the health and welfare of our nation. In response to these threats, Federal, state, and local governments have created comprehensive water pollution abatement laws and water conservation programs. Several of these laws and programs are examined in terms of their content and effectiveness. Industries' efforts to control effluent discharges have been prompted by pressures of public opinion, fear of water pollution law enforcement penalties, and perhaps personal conscience. Influenced by the above mentioned sources of motivation, the steel, chemical, and petroleum industries have devised numerous effective waste treatment techniques which are also examined.

The Steel Industry

The steel industry in comparison to most other industries is plagued with an especially large waste and water pollution problem. A tremendous quantity of waterborne wastes are the undesirable by-products of the numerous processes involved in the production of steel. In this industry, waste streams flow at 10,000 to 25,000 gallons per minute [28:8].

In recent years, the steel industry has been making greater use of alternative methods of executing fundamental manufacturing processes. Often a steel mill uses two or more processes within each of the fundamental areas of production, depending upon the type of raw materials available and the product desired. These processes are significant examples of the industry's technological advances; they produce a lighter unit weight product at a high-speed, high-volume output rate [28:7-8]. However, these alternate methods are often responsible for an increase in the volume of wastes produced.

Wastes are generated in proportion to the surface area of the steel exposed during rolling and finishing operations and in proportion to the relative gas-liquid interfacial areas in ironmaking and steel-making operations: the newer technologies, which tend to maximize these areas, generate greater waste loads [28:10].

The waterborne wastes of the steel industry can be categorized into several groups which include suspended solids, oils, heated water, waste acids, plating solutions and dissolved organic solutions, soluble metals, emulsions, and coke plant chemicals. These substances appear as wastes in various combinations and are characteristic by-products of each particular phase of production [28:6-12].

In the ironmaking process, which takes place in the blast furnace, iron ore is converted into pig iron. This process creates large waterborne waste loads which include suspended solids, phenols, and ammonia. In accordance with air pollution abatement regulations, blast furnace flue gas must be washed with water before it is expelled. The water used to scrub the exit gases becomes polluted with the above mentioned wastes [28:17]. Suspended solids also appear in the water which is used to wash the gas produced by the steelmaking furnace. Steelmaking gas-washer water volumes can range between 600 to 2000 gallons per minute [28:18]. The steel casting process which transforms molten steel into molds called ingots produces a wastewater flow of 2,000 to 7,000 gallons per minute. The ingots are converted into slabs or billets, and then into plates, strips, and other shapes in hot rolling mills. Steel casting and hot rolling mills produce wastewaters containing oil, dirt, and scale which are washed from the surface of the steel during these operations [28:18-19]. Steel cleaning operations prepare the surface of steel for plating. There are several subprocesses of steel cleaning operations. In the pickling subprocess, oxides and scale are removed from the surface of steel by acid solutions. In another subprocess, alkaline cleaners are especially effective in the removal of mineral fats and oil from steel. Caustic soda, phosphates, soda ash, and silicates are efficient alkaline cleaners. Although the steel cleaning operation produces acidic and alkaline waste solutions, spent pickling solutions and acid rinsewaters constitute the largest volumes of wastes produced by this process. The volume of pickling wastes produced and expelled by large pickling tanks can exceed 104 gallons per minute [28:19]. Cold rolling is a steel finishing operation that gives steel a smooth, shiny finish. Depending upon the size of a cold mill's operations, between 1,000 and 1,500 gallons of cold mill effluents, such as scale and emulsions, are produced each minute per mill [28:19, 32].

Figure 3-1 illustrates the many plant operations involved in the production of steel and indicates the process areas in which water is utilized and also the various wastes produced therein.

The Petroleum Industry

Most of the production processes operating within a petroleum refinery complex create several kinds of undesirable by-products. The most obvious effluents produced by the petroleum industry are oils and oil coated solids which can be traced to almost all phases of production. Strict regulations have been imposed upon the petroleum industry by government in order to prevent waste oils and coated solids from leaving the plant site. However, these undesirable by-products often do reach waterways.

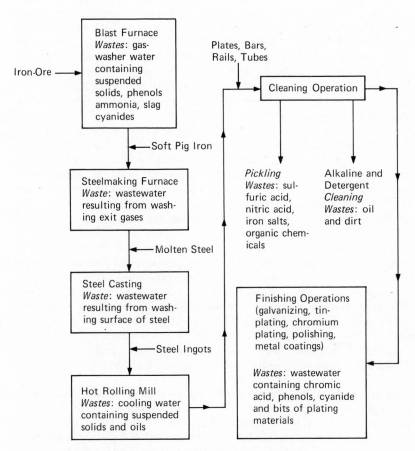

Figure 3-1   Flow Diagram for Steel Mills.

Crude oil and storage tanks are used in petroleum refineries to insure an adequate, free flowing supply of oil to the various process units. These tanks are also used as storage containers for finished oil products. Because these tanks are filled and handled so often, the occurrence of leaks and other accidental losses of crude oil or oil products is rather frequent. Crude oil and product storage drainoffs create a high rate of biochemical oxygen demand (BOD) within receiving waterways [29:S-1, 20]. "BOD is a quantity (quantitative measure for concentration of metabolic subtrates) of oxygen disappearing from a solution by the activity of micro-organisms" [12:287-288]. The severity of an organic waste pollution problem can be measured in terms of BOD; the rate of BOD indicates the degree to which the water's oxygen supply is being taxed by the decomposition of organic wastes.

The electrical method of crude desalting removes inorganic salts and suspended solids from crude oil before the oil is passed on to the fractionation process. In the crude desalting process, crude oil is mixed with water to form an emulsion. The desalted crude oil is then separated from the water, which contains the dissolved crude oil impurities. Crude desalting wastewaters contain sulfides, suspended solids, phenols, and ammonia. Crude desalting wastewaters create thermal water pollution problems because the temperature of desalted wastewater can exceed $200°F$ [29:F-3].

The complex process of crude oil fractionation results in the breakdown of crude oil into various substances such as gases, gasoline, and kerosene. A larger quantity of water is used in the crude oil fractionation process than any other phase of crude oil refining. Crude oil fractionation wastes have three main sources: (a) wastewater drawn off from overhead gasoline product accumulators contains a substantial amount of sulfides, chlorides, and phenols; (b) oil which escapes from sampling lines also contributes to the wastewater problem; and (c) barometric condensers, used to create the pressure needed in vacuum distillation units, sometimes create oil emulsions which are very difficult to treat [29:F-5].

In the process of thermal cracking, heat and pressure are used to break heavy oils down into several lighter oils such as domestic heating oil. Thermal cracking is rapidly being replaced by catalytic cracking which utilizes lower temperatures and pressures, and catalysts to produce greater amounts of high-octane gasolines, furnace oils, and other products [29:S-2]. Catalytic cracking is a main source of refinery wastewaters which contain highly undesirable sulfur compounds. Other catalytic cracking wastes are phenols, oils, and ammonia which form a highly alkaline waste stream and generate a high rate of BOD in receiving waterways [29:F-8-9].

Hydrotreating is a catalytic process that removes sulfur, nitrogen, and oxygen compounds from cracked petroleum. The resulting oil products are improved in terms of odor, color, and storage stability. Many alternate methods or subprocesses are included in the general category of hydrotreating. Although different catalysts are employed, the various subprocesses are otherwise basically the same [29:F-21].

Sulfur compounds, carbon dioxide, and other impurities are removed from liquid petroleum products (including gasoline, kerosene, jet fuel, and domestic heating oils) by the drying and sweetening processes. Large volumes of waste-waters are discharged by the drying and sweetening processes. These waste-waters are caustic in nature because they contain a substantial amount of phenols and sulfides. Spent caustic wastewaters generate a high rate of BOD in receiving waters [29:F-26].

The lube oil finishing process also creates significant amounts of waterbound wastes. The wastes produced by this process include acid rinsewaters, sludge, dissolved and suspended solids, sulfates, and stable oil emulsions [29:F-28-30].

A quantitative analysis of the various waterbound wastes produced by petroleum refineries is not readily available. However, Figure 3-2 identifies the refinery processes that do create significant amounts of harmful wastes.

The Chemical Industry

The chemical industry projects a vast sphere of influence over industry, agriculture, and medicine. Many manufacturers depend on the chemical industry for a supply of synthesized raw materials. Agricultural prosperity depends greatly upon chemical products such as fertilizers and insecticides. The chemical industry also aids man in his search for a longer and more comfortable life by producing drugs, health products, and grooming aids. Unfortunately, the chemical industry, like many other vital industries, produces undesirable waste products that compound the water pollution problem.

The chemical industry can be divided into three general categories. The first branch manufactures basic chemicals, including inorganic chemicals, inorganic acids, alkalies, and salts. Basic chemicals are used by other industries to manufacture materials such as nylon, antifreeze, and paint. They are also used by other branches of the chemical industry. A second branch manufactures intermediate chemicals which are converted or further developed basic chemicals. Plastics, synthetic fibers, fats, and oils are intermediate chemicals; these products are sold to other manufacturers. The third branch manufactures finished chemicals such as drugs, cosmetics, soaps, and explosives.

Within the abovementioned branches of the chemical industry, there are numerous production subdivisions which are implemented at individual plant sites. Thus, it is evident that the chemical industry is too vast to be discussed in its entirety in terms of the technological causes of industrial water pollution. This paper will focus attention on the water pollution problems of one subdivision of intermediate chemical manufacturing: plastics and resins.

There are more than nine different products, each with its own manufacturing process, included in the category of plastics and resins. This paper places particular emphasis on the manufacturing of cellulosics, vinyl resins, and polystyrenes.

Cellulosic plants produce regenerated cellulose, which is more widely known

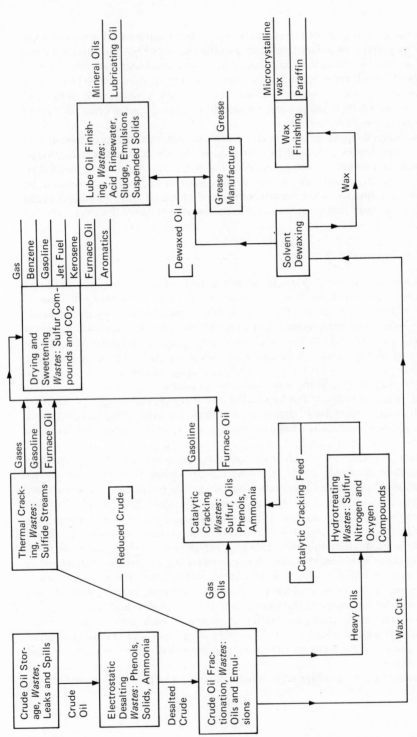

Figure 3-2 Flow Diagram for the Production of Petroleum Products.

as cellophane. Regenerated cellulose is primarily used to manufacture cellophane film. In 1963, 480 million pounds of regenerated cellulose were produced and 75 percent of that amount was used to make cellophane film [30:9]. The xanthate process is the most widely used means of regenerating cellulose in the United States. In the xanthate process, cellulose (extracted from wood pulp and cotton linters) is treated in a solution containing water, caustic soda, and carbon disulfide. The resulting solution, cellulose xanthate, is then converted into a continuous film by an acidification process. The regeneration of cellulose creates several types of wastes, including biodegradable cellulosic wastes, sulfates, and scrap cellophane. Regenerated cellulose wastes create a significant rate of BOD in receiving waterways [30:9-11].

Cellulosic plants also manufacture cellulose esters: cellulose acetate, cellulose propionate, and cellulose butyrate. Acetate, propionate, and butyrate are manufactured in suspension processes that are similar to one another. Figures 3-3 and 3-4 indicate the production areas that produce significant amounts of wastes in the regenerated cellulose and cellulose ester processes.

The production of vinyl resins has been increasing as the demand for this highly functional material has also increased. Although the volume of vinyl resins being produced is increasing rapidly, production methods have not changed nor are they expected to change in the near future. Consequently, the type of wastes produced will remain the same. However, wastewater volumes are likely to increase somewhat as production volumes increase [30:21].

Vinyl resins can be manufactured by suspension polymerization, emulsion, or bulk polymerization. Suspension polymerization is the most widely used production method. Between 85 and 90 percent of all vinyl resins are produced by suspension polymerization. In this process, tiny drops of vinyl chloride are dropped into a solution of water and a suspension-inducing agent such as polyvinyl alcohol, gelatin, or esters. The resulting solution is heated in a reactor containing a catalyst such as benzol and the polymerization process is initiated.

The polymerization process unites simple chemical elements or chemical compounds to create a complex chemical compound. The newly created polymerized compound, still in solution, is circulated through a stripping tank where any vinyl chloride which has escaped polymerization is recovered and returned to the mixing tank for another polymerization treatment. The stripped polymerized suspension solution is then combined with other batches of the same solution. This mixture of batches is then pumped into the centrifuge where it is washed and dewatered. The resulting synthetic is dried by rotary dryers [30].

The centrifugal step in polymerization creates the most significant volumes of waterbound waste loads. The effluent stream discharged as a result of centrifugation includes suspended solids, catalysts, suspending agents, a small amount of vinyl chloride, and fine particles of the polymerized product. Chlorinated organic solvents (such as carbon tetrachloride and chloroform) appear in the wastewater of the polymerization process. The above mentioned wastes generate a high rate of BOD in receiving waters.

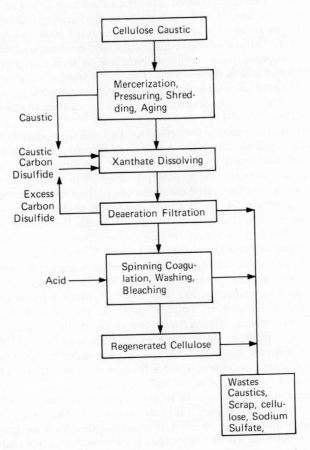

Figure 3-3 Flow Diagram for the Production of Regenerated Cellulose.

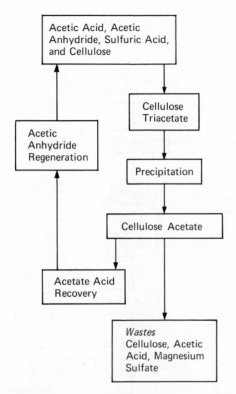

Figure 3-4   Flow Diagram for the Production of Cellulose Acetate.

Figure 3-5 indicates the process areas in the polymerization process that create significant amounts of wastes.

The production of polystyrene resins has also been increasing rapidly. Polystyrene is a clear colored plastic which has many practical applications. This substance can be used to make phonograph records, film, insulation, lightweight molded items, and protective package padding for appliances and other fragile items.

The manufacturing process for polystyrene resins are bulk polymerization and suspension polymerization. Styrene, which is the raw material utilized in the production of polystyrenes, is purified by either distillation or caustic washing in order to remove elements that would inhibit polymerization. The purified raw materials are polymerized in the presence of a catalyst. Polymerization takes place in a temperature of about 90°c. Reaction water and wash water are the two main components of the significant amount of wastewater expelled by a polystyrene manufacturing process [30:29]. Figure 3-6, flow chart for the production of polystyrenes, is located on page 55 of this paper. Although a

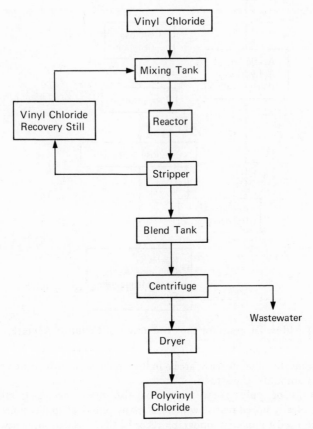

Figure 3-5   Flow Diagram for the Production of Polyvinyl Chloride.

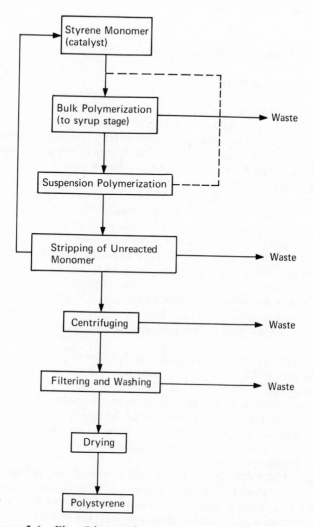

Figure 3-6   Flow Diagram for the Production of Polystyrene.

major portion of the wastes produced in conjunction with the manufacturing of polystyrene resins is discharged into municipal sewage systems, the balance of these wastes escapes to waterways.

Factors Having an Offsetting Influence
Upon the Growth of the
Industrial Water Pollution Problem

In recent years, government (on a federal, state, and local level) has exhibited great concern over the ever increasing industrial water pollution problem in the United States. In an effort to combat industrial water pollution, government has taken legislative action on several occasions. Industrial water pollution legislation has had two basic aims. First, stricter water pollution control standards have been imposed upon industries in order to force them to develop a water pollution conscience and to take steps to check the tremendous volumes of pollutants indiscriminately expelled into waterways. Secondly, legislation has been enacted in an attempt to inspire and finance research to discover effective means of dealing with the industrial water pollution problem.

One of the first antipollution laws of major importance was Public Law 845, known as the Water Pollution Control Act, passed by Congress in 1948. This law assigned to the federal government the ultimate responsibility for curbing the pollution of streams by industrial wastes. Public Law 845 also gave the federal government the authority to disperse funds to state governments for the purpose of enforcing the act as well as the authority to compel states to enforce it [1:325].

Greatly needed action was taken again by the federal government in 1965 when Congress passed the Water Quality Act. One of the main accomplishments of the Act was the establishment of the Federal Water Pollution Control Administration, a bureau within the Department of Health, Education, and Welfare; in 1966, the F.W.P.C.A. became part of the Department of the Interior. The main purpose of this organization has been to establish and maintain minimum interstate water quality standards and to help organize the states attempts to curb water pollution.

Recently, the F.W.P.C.A. has been assisted by various other federal agencies. The Department of Health, Education and Welfare has become cooperatively active in F.W.P.C.A. water pollution abatement programs. The U. S. Geographical Survey has contributed valuable information to the F.W.P.C.A. which has been used to regulate water quality standards. The Department of Agriculture also has been called upon to aid the F.W.P.C.A. [37:4].

The Water Quality Act also authorized the expenditure of $20,000,000 a year for three years to state governments for the purpose of initiating research and improving existing facilities used in dealing with the sanitary and storm sewage problem [31:21-22]. Moreover, the Water Quality Act urged individual states to begin drafting their own water quality standards. Thus far, all fifty states have submitted water quality standards to the Secretary of the Interior for Federal approval [13:4].

The Water Quality Act of 1965 was followed by the Clean Water Restoration Act of 1966 which liberalized the dollar amounts to be spent by the federal government for water pollution abatement. While funds were still to be allocated to the states for the specific purposes determined by the Water Quality Act of 1965, the Clean Water Restoration Act of 1966 also included many other important provisions, one being the allocation of $20,000,000 a year to state governments for water purification projects and industrial waste treatment. This Act also gave the Secretary of the Interior the authority to enforce the Oil Pollution Act which demands that anyone responsible for the dumping of oil into waterways must either remove it or bear the cost of removal by federal authorities [31:23-24].

The Water Quality Improvement Act of 1968 (H.R. 15907), which was introduced in the House of Representatives, is an extension of the Water Quality Act of 1965. H.R. 15907 was designed to encourage state and local governments to enforce federally approved water quality standards and to provide state and local governments with greatly needed financial assistance for the construction of efficient pollution reduction treatment facilities [38:4-6]. The federal government has also concerned itself with the need to revive waterways which already have been devastated by industrial water pollution. However, it has been suggested by federal water pollution abatement officials that the failure of industries to measure accurately and reveal the nature of and quantity of wastes discharged is a major detriment to the quick and effective cleanup of polluted waterways [2].

In the years between the Water Pollution Control Act of 1948 and the Clean Water Restoration Act of 1966, state and local governments generally were rather lax in dealing with their water pollution problems. However, several worthy state and regional organizations were formed at various times to solve specific pollution problems. One such group, the Committee of Water Pollution Control Council, Pacific Northwest Area, developed standards by which industrial water pollution can be measured and abated. These standards, which have also been adopted by the Washington State Pollution Control Administration, clearly indicate the minimum water pollution control requirements to be adhered to by industry. For example, wastes produced by the steel industry must be treated so that the pH values of the wastes register in a range between 6.0 and 9.0. Also, concentrations of toxic metals should be reduced in order to spare aquatic life from harm. A determination of a safe level of concentration for each of the various wastes produced by the steel industry was also made by the Committee [1:336-344]. At various times, the F.W.P.C.A. has sponsored interstate water pollution abatement conferences in an attempt to encourage state and local governments and industrial concerns to join together in a cooperative effort to solve a regional water pollution problem. One such conference was held in 1965, during which Illinois and Indiana, the city of Chicago, and several industrial representatives discussed ways of diminishing the Lake Michigan water pollution problem. As a result of the conference, the abovementioned participants in the meeting are presently working together toward a solution of the water pollution problem in Lake Michigan [32:10].

It appears that the Clean Water Restoration Act of 1966, the Water Quality Improvement Act of 1968, other current legislative programs, and public opinion are having a motivating influence upon several state governments. In recent months, Maine has become increasingly more aware of its industrial water pollution problem. Maine has undertaken a one million dollar program to preserve its waterways; municipal and industrial wastes will be drawn away from major cities via pipes, thereby eliminating the indiscriminate dumping of large volumes of wastes into waterways. Governor Kenneth M. Curtis has said, "The plan is the first concrete evidence of Maine's determination to have industrial development through conservation" [19].

In January 1967, Governor John H. Chafee of Rhode Island created the Rhode Island Water Pollution Advisory Board which has been appointed the task of examining the state's water pollution program. The Advisory Board has devoted much effort to making a critical analysis of The Division of Water Pollution Control of the Rhode Island Department of Health. With the Advisory Board's guidance, The Division of Water Pollution Control has revised Rhode Island's water pollution laws and has clarified its water quality standards and antipollution enforcement laws. Additionally, the Advisory Board has carefully studied the water pollution abatement programs of various industries located within the state and has established time schedules of compliance with the state's water pollution regulations for these industries [45:1-4].

For many years New York State has been faced with a very serious water pollution problem which, from a financial viewpoint, has been beyond the control of local governments. However, since the enactment of The Pure Waters Program of 1965, all levels of government within the state have taken positive steps to restore polluted waterways and to control the volumes of waterbound pollutants to be dispersed in the future. In accordance with the provisions of The Pure Waters Program of 1965, the New York State Legislature has taken action to provide funds to local governments for the purpose of dealing with water pollution control problems. Secondly, the Legislature has prefinanced Federal assistance in order to quickly initiate the construction of adequate water pollution abatement treatment facilities. There is considerable evidence of substantial progress in cleaning up the Hudson River under the Pure Waters Program in the stretch from Troy to New York City. At a conference in September, 1967 it was stated that 99.5 percent of the polluters on this portion of the river had agreed to a treatment facility construction timetable which should result in the termination of all pollution of the Hudson by 1972 [35:11-24 and 43-45].

Two qualifications concerning this optimistic forecast must be noted: (a) Unfortunately, New York State has had some difficulty in enforcing treatment facility construction timetables; (b) Little was said at the conference concerning control of the tributary Mohawk River which is especially subject to pollution from industrial sources. Thus, the success of The Pure Waters Program and other antipollution legislative programs depends greatly upon how well the provisions of such programs are enforced. Critics of governments' handling of the industrial water pollution problem believe that the monetary costs and aesthetic losses incurred as a result of industrial water pollution do not fall upon the waste discharger; because the waste discharger is not directly affected by these undesirable costs, the harmful effects of pollution will not be considered in industrial management's decision-making. Accordingly, manufacturers will not be induced to design manufacturing processes to limit the output of wastes nor will they restrict certain waste contributing inputs. However, if industries were made to bear the costs associated with the removal of wastes from waterways, the recycling of waste materials and other effective techniques would receive immediate attention in process design [39:632-633].

New Jersey claims to have a very conscientious water pollution abatement program, directed by the New Jersey State Department of Health. New Jersey's antipollution laws, dating back as far as The Potable Water Act of 1899, pertain to the disposal of both industrial and municipal wastes. New Jersey law requires that a permit be obtained from the State Department of Health before a manufacturer establishes a plant site on any potable watershed within the state. Furthermore, all permits for the construction and operation of sewage and industrial waste treatment plants include a condition that licensed operators be in charge of the treatment plants. Also, owners of industrial waste treatment plants are required by law to make monthly reports on plant operations to the State Department of Health; the State Department of Health examines these plant sites annually, or more frequently if necessary. New Jersey has recognized its responsibilities as a neighbor and is presently cooperating with New York and Connecticut in an attempt to restore the polluted Hudson River [9:1-2].

Pollution can be checked by the implementation of various standards of control. Input standards regulate the quantity or quality of the pollution producing agent used by the industrial processors. Regulation of industrial expansion in a highly polluted area would serve as a useful means of controlling pollution levels [11:1]. Discharge standards may also be utilized to control pollution by setting maximum limits on the quantity of pollution discharged. Pollution resulting from industrial processing can be controlled by establishing waste treatment requirements, by reusing discharged water, and by filtering bulk waste and sludge before discharging water. Establishing discharge standards would probably be the most effective method of controlling industrial water pollution; industrial wastes create various pollution problems, with each industry making its unique contribution to the problem. Discharged soluble organics result in a depletion of dissolved oxygen, restricting the capacity of the receiving waters for assimilation. Heavy metals, cyanide, and toxic organics discharge can be extremely harmful to aquatic life. Oil and floating materials destroy the aesthetic beauty of the water. Undesirable algae growth occurs as a result of nitrogen and phosphorous discharged into lakes and ponds.

Ambient standards are intermittent controls, exercised only during critical pollution periods and withdrawn upon termination of the emergency condition. In the area of water pollution resulting from industrial wastes, it appears that ambient standards would include regulating waste discharges during drought periods and during periods when the pollution concentration reached a dangerous level.

The Steel Industry

The steel industry has taken various steps to modify the volumes of waterborne wastes that are created by the various production processes. Blast furnaces produce gaswasher wastewaters containing suspended solids. Sedimentation, a waste treatment process, has a 93.8 percent removal efficiency of suspended solids. The removal efficiency could be increased to 98.8 percent if gaswasher waters are recirculated through the blast furnace. The use of coagulation sedimentation in the treatment of rolling mill effluents can result in a 95.4 percent reduction in suspended solids and an 80 percent reduction in oils [28:72]. In cold finishing mills, waste treatment practices include the recirculation of soluble oil solutions which permits a 75 percent reduction in the volume of cold mill oil effluents. Cold mill wastes in the form of suspended solids can be reduced in volume by the recirculation of emulsions and by the use of magnetic separators. In coke plants, there can be an 81 percent decrease in phenol effluents, a 98 percent decrease in cyanides, and a 99 percent decrease in ammonia when coke is quenched with benzol plant wastes and if the cooling water is recirculated. Wastes produced by the various plating processes are disposed of by subjecting these wastes to an ion exchange treatment process, with a 95 percent rate of effectiveness. Deep well disposal of plating wastes is 100 percent effective. Pickling solutions can also be disposed of in deep wells [28:73-74]. The deep well waste treatment method is also employed by the chemical industry; a description of this treatment process is included in a discussion of the chemical industry's waste treatment practices.

While the steel industry has devised some very effective waste treatment methods, certain factors have worked against the industry in its attempt to control water pollution. For instance, as the technological level of a plant increases, so also does the volume of waterborne wasteloads increase, resulting in additional waste treatment costs. Table 3-1 illustrates the relationship between the newer modes of technology and the wastewater problem in the steel industry.

As newer, more technologically advanced plants are put into operation, the steel industry will have to devise technologically advanced treatment programs that will be capable of dealing with the growing waste production problem. In the past, industrial management has attempted to cope with its water pollution abatement responsibilities by placing the burden upon individual plant sites. This approach to the water pollution problem often has been quite costly and not always very effective. Perhaps it would be feasible, when geographical location permits, for various production plants to share the cost and use of waste treatment facilities, to recycle common scrap, and to benefit from savings on fuel and combustion residuals [39:634]. At the present time, existing plants will have to operate their waste treatment facilities at maximum efficiency levels.

Table 3.1

**Relationship Between Newer Modes of
Technology in the Steel Industry and
the Waste Water Problem**

Level of Technology	Wastewater[a]
Old	9,860
Typical	10,000
Advanced	13,750

Source: U. S., Department of the Interior, *Industrial Waste Profile No. 1: Blast Furnaces and Steel Mills*, p. 10.

[a]Gallons of waste water produced per ingot ton per day.

The Petroleum Industry

Petroleum refining is one of the largest and most important industries in the United States. Much has been done within the petroleum industry to curb water pollution. The 1966 estimated replacement value of United States refineries' waste treatment equipment, totaling $255,000,000, substantiates this claim. Unlike the steel industry, the petroleum industry can boast of a continuing decrease in the amount of effluents and wastewaters produced as the technological levels of its refineries become more advanced. The decrease in amounts of petroleum refinery effluents being produced has been attributed to the development of more effective waste treatment techniques and to the utilization of alternate production processes that create lesser amounts of undesirable by-products [29:S-1, S-14]. Table 3-2 illustrates the relationship between technological levels and waste production in the petroleum industry.

In the petroleum industry, approximately 90 percent of the total water input is used for cooling purposes. Water for cooling purposes is especially necessary in the processes of thermal cracking and catalytic cracking. (In these processes, heat and pressure are used to break down heavy oil fractions.) Between 1954 and 1964, the total amount of water used by the petroleum industry increased 48.5 percent. However, due to water reusage techniques, only 13.2 percent of the total increase required additional water input [29:S-6].

There have been several advances in cooling water technology which will be responsible for an even greater degree of water reuse by the petroleum industry in the future. For instance, air-cooled finned tube exchangers will replace existing cooling towers, thereby eliminating evaporation losses [29:S-7].

Table 3.2

**Relationship Between Technological
Levels and Waste Production**

Level of Technology[a]	Flow mgd	BOD lb/day	Phenol lb/day	Sulfide lb/day
Older	23.1	12,500	3,500	2,200
Typical	9.9	5,400	1,650	625
Newer	4.5	4,200	850	680

Source: United States Department of the Interior, *Industrial Waste Profile No. 5: Petroleum Refining,* p. Summary-13.

[a]A hypothetical 100,000 bpsd (barrels per stream [operating] day) refinery was selected as a base for quantitative waste evaluation for the three technological levels.

Also, it has been realized that if there could be a continuous flow of refinery products through the various production phases rather than the intermediate storage of refinery products between processes, the products would not have to be cooled and reheated as often. Thus, the amount of cooling waters needed would be greatly reduced.

Although there is a shortage of quantitative data pertaining to wastewater flow and to the effectiveness of waste treatment methods upon each of the petroleum industry's production wastes, there is a substantial amount of information available concerning the treatment procedures devised by the industry to curb water pollution. There are five general methods of treatment used by the petroleum industry: (a) physical; (b) chemical; (c) biological; (d) tertiary treatment; and (e) in-plant treatment methods [29:S-14, 15]. The most widely used technique in the category of physical methods of waste treatment is gravity separation. In this process, earthen basins or API (American Petroleum Institute) separators skim 50-90 percent of floatable oils from production effluents. At the same time, solids are settled and disposed of as land fill or by means of incineration. The chemical methods of waste treatment include coagulation, sedimentation, and chemical air floatation. These processes are especially effective in the treatment of emulsified oils. The most effective biological method of treatment is activated sludging. Details of the activated sludging treatment method are given later in this chapter. It is the job of tertiary treatment methods to remove taste and odor elements from biologically treated wastewaters. In-plant treatment methods include sour water stripping, ballast water treatment, slop oil recovery, and temperature control. At Mobil Oil refineries, methods of waste treatment control are designed to meet the specific needs of individual plants and the communities in which they are located. The extent of waste treatment administered at each plant depends upon (a) the property adjacent to the refinery; (b) prevailing meterological conditions of the location; (c) the degree of toxicity or unpleasantness of the waste materials; and (d) statutory regulations [16:1-2].

It is estimated that during the ten-year period between 1967 and 1977, the petroleum industry will make greater use of API separators, activated sludging, and many other modern biological and chemical waste treatment methods [29:S-15]. The Humble Oil & Refining Company is experimenting with a new waste treatment technique called ponding. Humble operates this pilot project at the Baytown refinery, located on the Houston Ship Channel. Wastewater which has already been treated by the refinery's regular treatment facilities is pumped into the first section of a pond at a rate of 6,000 gallons per minute. As the volume of wastewater increases in the first section (176 acres in size), it is gradually released into a second section of the pond which is 84 acres in size, and then on to a third section of 120 acres. After a period of approximately 45 days in the pond, the water is released into the Houston Ship Channel. During its confinement in the pond, the wastewater is purified by the natural processes of aeration and assimilation. Ponding has proven to be a highly successful means of purifying refinery wastewater. However, the large acreage required for ponding bars this treatment method for many refineries [15:4-5].

Natural assimilation and aeration, which take place quite effectively in ponding, are highly desirable means of controlling water quality. Aeration and assimilation are processes that oxidize waste materials (organic carbons) and convert same into carbon dioxide. The algae in the waterway absorb the carbon dioxide, and through the process of photosynthesis transform the carbon dioxide back into oxygen. This new supply of oxygen is released into the water where it is used again by the bacteria to oxidize more organic carbon. Aeration and assimilation occur in all waterways. However, when the volume of wastes expelled into a waterway exceeds its assimilative capacity, the physical indications of pollution become evident. In the future, spatial arrangement could be a very effective means of controlling the quantities of waste discharged into a waterway and would allow natural aeration and assimilation to occur. Spatial arrangement would provide a geographical location with a carefully planned ratio of industrial, residential, and recreational activities, and would minimize the strain upon the assimilative capacity of the area, including its waterways. Furthermore, water based recreational areas would not be located in areas of industrial concentration nor would production plants be located near waterways that are valuable to the community, either recreationally or commercially [3:18-19].

The Chemical Industry

During the last few years, chemical companies have begun to spend large sums of money in order to restore polluted waterways and to finance abatement research. The DuPont Corporation, which has always been eager to test the newest pollution abatement techniques, has been a water pollution abatement leader within the chemical industry. In 1958, DuPont encouraged nine other chemical companies to participate in a research program sponsored by the West Virginia Water Resources Division and the U.S. Geographical Survey. This research program resulted in the formation of feasible waste reduction goals designed to serve as guidelines for the establishment of effective water pollution abatement programs at individual plant sites [4:153-156].

On several occasions, the Allied Chemical Corporation has demonstrated a desire to cooperate with state and local authorities and to assume its fair share of responsibility for the cleanup of various industrially polluted waterways. Allied Chemical is presently working in cooperation with Onondaga County, New York, to dredge the Nine Mile Creek and to beautify its shores, making the entire area highly suitable for recreational purposes. It is estimated that Allied Chemical will contribute $250,000 to this project. In the last 25 years, Allied Chemical has spent approximately 11.2 million dollars on water pollution abatement programs. Most recently, Allied Chemical has joined forces with Syracuse University in order to study the social, economic, and political influences of water pollution upon a community. Ten thousand dollars will be contributed to this study by Allied Chemical [5:12-14].

Depending upon the products produced, chemical plant wastes may require only neutralization or removal of color or other ingredients; on the other hand, other more complex chemical wastes require extensive treatment. The waste treatment process for removing phenols and phenolic compounds from chemical plant wastes is most complex. The Dow Chemical Company deemed it necessary to install two treatment plants, one for the treatment of general waste, exclusive of phenolic wastes, and the other for the treatment of phenolic wastes. The treatment of general chemical wastes is usually accomplished by the implementation of an activated sludge system, a continuous system in which flocculated biological growths are mixed with wastewater and aerated. Biological growths are subsequently separated from the treated waste by settling. Although there are numerous modifications of this process, there are only two basic process variations. The conventional process accomplishes the absorption, flocculation, and synthesis process in a single step. The contact-stabilization process accomplishes the same task; however, oxidation and synthesis of expelled organics takes place in a separate tank. Wastes, in a suspended or colloidal form, which would generate a high rate of BOD in receiving waterways are generally treated by the contact-stabilization process [11:153-155]. Flocculation, which is part of the activated sludging treatment method, can also be employed as an independent treatment method which purifies wastewaters by removing suspended materials. Chemicals, referred to as flocculants, are added to wastewater. The flocculants cause particles of waste material to cluster into large masses which are more easily removed than smaller untreated particles. In the past, aluminum, calcium, and iron salts have been used as flocculants. However, the Dow Chemical Company has created a synthesized organic polymer,

PURIFLOC, which is a very effective flocculant [6:2]. PURIFLOC flocculants are being used by many industries. This flocculation process can be incorporated into almost any industry's waste treatment program, as this process only requires the installation of a small pump and storage tank. One of the most important uses of PURIFLOC flocculants is the clarification of potable waters.

The plant for phenolic wastes employs trickling filters before processing the wastes through the activated sludge system. The trickling filter is a bed of irregularly shaped pieces of stone, brick, or concrete. Controlled volumes of wastes are discharged into the trickling filter. The wastes trickle down between the pieces of stone which become covered with slime in a short period of time. The slime is composed of aerobic bacteria which feed on the organic matter in the wastes. As the organic wastes (which generate a high rate of BOD in receiving waters if discharged untreated) are deteriorated by the aerobic bacteria, the ability of these wastes to generate a high rate of BOD is also reduced [1:136].

The Dow Chemical Company has developed a trickling filter bed, SURFPAC, which is superior to beds made of stone chips. SURFPAC filters are basically made of large plastic sheets that look much like honeycombs. The SURFPAC filter can handle a greater capacity of wastes in a more compact treatment area than the stone filters can.

It is interesting to note that activated sludging and trickling filtration are mechanical techniques which are imitations of natural waste treatment processes that occur in waterways. However, natural waste treatment processes quickly become overtaxed when large volumes of industrial and municipal wastes are continually dumped into a waterway [14:41-42]. Because large quantities of oxygen and aerobic bacteria are vital to the treatment of organic wastes, hundreds of miles of a waterway would be needed to accomplish the same amount of treatment that an activated sludging or trickling filtration process could achieve [8:6].

Deep well disposal — the injection of liquid wastes into a well which can be between a few hundred to over 12,000 feet deep — is another treatment method employed by the chemical industry [22:2]. This method of waste treatment is particularly useful in the disposal of wastes that are not easily precipitated, decomposed, or neutralized [6:1]. At Shell Chemical's Houston, Texas plant (the largest of all the company's plants, producing approximately 1-1/4 billion pounds of products annually) water pollution abatement techniques include deep well disposal and deep sea disposal of various types of wastes. The Houston plant's deep sea disposal sites are located 100 miles from land and are at a depth of four hundred fathoms. This waste disposal technique is utilized when other means of disposing of highly concentrated wastes are not suitable [20:1-5].

By-Product Utilization

The primary objective of the treatment of industrial wastes is the abatement of water pollution. However, industry (and government) has been conducting research in order to devise efficient treatment methods by which potentially harmful and undesirable wastes could be recovered and reused for a financial profit. The financial success of a by-product recovery endeavor depends greatly upon how easy or difficult it is to separate a desired substance from other wastes and wastewaters. If complex, expensive recovery equipment must be installed in a plant that is costly to operate, substantial profits might not be attainable. Also, the factor of product demand must be taken into consideration; recovery may be profitable only if the by-products are marketable.

To date, little success has been achieved in the area of by-product recovery. One of the few industries which has financially profited from waste recovery and reuse is the petroleum industry. The main pollutant expelled by refineries into streams and lakes is waste oil. However, when American Petroleum Institute (API) basins are used at refineries, several thousand barrels of waste oil can be recovered daily and sent through the manufacturing processes. The reprocessing of waste oils amounts to a large dollar savings for the petroleum industry [1:304, 314-316]. Another major by-product of the petroleum industry is sulfur which is recovered from sour waters and the hydrotreating process. It has been estimated that recovered sulfur was worth $40,000,000 in 1966. The value of by-product sulfur is expected to increase rapidly as stricter air pollution abatement measures increase the demand for low-sulfur fuels [29:47].

On the other hand, a great many industries are not able to realize any profit from waste recovery and reuse. In the case of chemical manufacturing, certain wastes and waste acids are recoverable. However, recovery has proven to be unprofitable from an economic point of view. The Allied Chemical Corporation produces thousands of tons of valueless wastes each year. The disposal of such wastes is a serious problem. Speaking at a meeting of the Syracuse Citizens Foundation in 1967, John T. Connor, president of the Allied Chemical Corporation, said:

The frustrating truth is: we have hundreds of tons a day of waste — for which there is as yet no known use. We have spent a fortune searching for ways — either to use it or to dispose of it. But — I fear — in vain. So far. We can't burn it; we can't bury it. . . . So we do the best we can within our capabilities. We put it in neat, orderly piles; we give it time to settle; we cover it with soil; we landscape it, we screen it with trees; we help fill in some of Central New York's swamps with it . . . . we have turned over a large area of these sedimentation beds to New York State, which may have plans to incorporate them into a sizable park and recreational area [5:12-13].

The recovery of by-products is a basic part of waste treatment procedure in the steel industry; but wastes are principally recovered for the purpose of reutilization and/or waste load reduction rather than for the purpose of marketing. Suspended solids, found in the blast furnace gaswasher waters, are recovered and returned to the blast furnace for reprocessing. Another recovered waste element is acid which is returned from spent pickling solutions. The acid is returned to the pickling tanks and is reused in the steel industry's cleaning operations. Recovery and reuse of by-products is also practiced in coke plants;

about 40 percent of the gases produced during the coking process are recovered and reused as fuel for the coking process [28:13, 33].

The Social Costs of Industrial Water Pollution

Each year, thousands of pounds of industrial wastes are dumped into this nation's waterways, often causing grave water pollution problems. The act of discharging wastes into a body of water does not necessarily initiate a water pollution problem; the characteristics of the wastes, the quantities in which they are discharged, and the assimilative capacity of a waterway are important factors to be considered. Various elements such as copper, iodine, manganese, and iron are not necessarily harmful to waterways unless they are discharged in high concentrations [18:6]. On the other hand, certain kinds of wastes such as oils, phenols, and waste acids are responsible for much damage caused to waterways and aquatic life. These elements, even when discharged in relatively small quantities, can alter the quality of the water and create a water pollution problem. Thus, whether or not a waste is a pollutant depends upon the influence that the waste has upon the quality of the receiving waters [33:214].

There are several kinds of wastes that create water pollution problems: (a) wastes that contain elements that are harmful to animal and vegetable life along the shorelines of a waterway; (b) wastes that destroy bridges, piers, and warehouses; (c) wastes that clog riverbeds and docks, occasionally causing flooding; (d) wastes that give off obnoxious odors as they decompose; (e) wastes that make waterways unsafe for drinking purposes; and (f) wastes that make the waterway undesirable or unsafe for recreational or navigational purposes.

One of the most obvious and serious damages caused by the dispersal of harmful wastes into waterways is the destruction of aquatic life. Industrial wastes interfere with and destroy aquatic life in several ways. Wastes can impair the vital processes of reproduction and maturation. Fish deposit eggs at the bottom of a stream where the eggs are hatched and the young fish grow to maturity. Large accumulations of sediment from ineffective petroleum refinery waste treatment operations or from ironmaking plants prohibit these processes from occurring successfully; the eggs often become mixed with sediment and die. Such has been the case in the polluted waters of Lake Erie. The Lake's blue pike has become extinct because the eggs of the blue pike have been repeatedly smothered by sediment. Waste oils which sometimes escape from petroleum refineries coat fish gills and prevent fish from obtaining an adequate oxygen supply. Pollution can also influence the supply of food available to fish. An insect known as the mayfly has become extinct in the Lake Erie region and its disappearance has been attributed to pollution. The mayfly had been an excellent source of nourishment to growing fish. Now, fish living in Lake Erie must feed on sludge worms and are consequently growing at a noticeably slower rate. Some fish take so long to grow that they die of old age before they are fully mature [33:104]. Solid wastes are also harmful to aquatic life and when disposed into waterways causes turbidity. Sunlight cannot penetrate highly turbid waters. A lack of sunlight within a body of water can cause the oxygen-producing photosynthesis process to cease. Also, when water lacks sunlight, fish find it very difficult to locate food.

Aquatic life must also endure another hardship caused by industrial water pollution. When organic wastes are deposited into a waterway they cause harm to aquatic life by depleting the water's oxygen supply. As organic wastes are broken down by aerobic bacteria that cause decay, large volumes of oxygen are used up. In a given volume of water, only a certain amount of oxygen can be dissolved at a given time. If there is too much organic waste material in the water at one time and the level of oxygen is being depleted there will be a high rate of BOD. When the BOD of a stream is at a high level, young fish that live in the deepest portions of the waterway are robbed of oxygen which is already scarce at that level. Many of these fish die and are later found rotting along the shoreline. The wastewaters of the petroleum industry exert a tremendous oxygen demand upon the receiving waters. Crude and product storage, product finishing operations, solvent refining, and cracking are processes that generate a high BOD.

The severity of the fish kill problem is reflected in a sample of Lake Erie fish kill statistics. Since 1900, several valuable species of fish such as sturgeon, cisco, whitefish, and pike have disappeared and have been replaced by heartier fish such as catfish and smelt. Thus while the volume of fish caught in Lake Erie annually is about the same (1,000,000 lbs.), the volume of quality fish has diminished. Between 1885 and 1925, 25,000 lbs. of cisco were caught from Lake Erie annually. Today, only 1,000 lbs. are caught annually [24:127-128, 131]. The scarcity of valuable fish in Lake Erie has had some economic repercussions. Tourists and sport enthusiasts no longer care to visit Lake Erie on fishing expeditions. Commercial fishing has also been curtailed.

The problem of thermal pollution will be discussed in detail in Chapter 5. However, it is sufficient to note at this time that thermal pollution will contribute to the overall industrial pollution problem.

Large volumes of industrial wastes containing solids and sediment are discharged into waterways and subsequently create serious water pollution problems. Dredging is an effective but temporary means of dealing with this type of water pollution problem.

As sediment accumulates in a riverbed, the level of the water rises. If the riverbed is not periodically dredged and if restrictions are not placed upon industries contributing to the problem, the waterway will eventually overflow. Along the Grand Calumet River near Gary, Indiana, flooding was reported in 1967. A United States Steel complex in Gary was dispersing large volumes of sediment into the Grand Calumet, causing serious flood damages to the local sewage treatment plant and to the city. The company took immediate but temporary action and dredged that area of the waterway to lower the water level by six inches [32:60]. The presence of solid industrial wastes, such as bits of iron which are discharged in the wastewaters of the various steel manufacturing processes, discourages boating enthusiasts and swimmers from using a waterway for recreational purposes. Often the decay of solids is accompanied by obnoxious odors. This can create a serious problem from an economic point of view in a community that depends on tourism. The Presque Isle State Park in Pennsylvania's section of Lake Erie is the most frequented of all of the Lake's beaches. Local authorities are determined to keep this section of Lake Erie free from unsightly pollutants that would discourage a present yearly attendance of more than three million visitors and decrease their current annual income of $45,000,000.

Certain wastes contain high concentrations of acids or alkalies that attack structures along the waterway. Acid wastes will attack iron and steel structures in the water as well as boat bottoms. The acidity of a waste water is usually caused by the presence of carbon dioxide, sulfuric acid, and salts of strong acids and weak bases. Acids are found in the pickling liquors that occasionally escape from steel mills. Alkalinity is caused by the presence of carbonates, bicarbonates, phosphates, and organic substances in a waterway. High concentrations of alkalies in wastewaters, such as ammonia, can cause corrosion.

The color of water may be attributed to natural, mineral, or vegetable origins. However, waters may also be colored by organic or inorganic wastes from many industries including the petroleum refining industry and the chemical industry.

Navigational problems are multiplied in waterways that have high pollution levels. The presence of phosphates and nitrogen compounds, mainly attributable to nonindustrial waste treatment processes, encourages the growth of rooted vegetation which interferes with navigation. Floating materials also inhibit movement on a waterway. Oil clings to boats and mars their outward appearance. Sediment clogs up docks and decreases the depth of a waterway. In order to keep the navigational channels of the Buffalo River open, over 100,000 tons of sediment must be dredged annually. A good deal of this sediment comes from many oil, steel, and chemical plants along the Buffalo River. For example, the Socony Oil Refinery Company has been cited as a polluter, discharging phenols, cyanides, and suspended solids. The Donner-Hanna Coke Co. also contributes phenols, ammonia, and solids. Republic Steel also adds its share of solids and phenols to the Buffalo River. The General Chemical Company distributes large volumes of inorganic wastes into this waterway [33:259]. As we can see, evidence discloses that a number of the larger American corporations are the major contributors to the industrial water pollution problem.

Industrial wastes contain many harmful elements. If these wastes remain untreated and are dumped into receiving waters, they not only create water pollution problems but also limit the uses of the waterway.

Wastes with a high acid content will generally restrict the usage of waters by downstream municipalities. Industrial water pollution can also limit the use of a waterway for recreational purposes. Although discolored water is not harmful, most individuals avoid it. Bathing in water containing acids would be discouraged for acids and other chemical elements will cause irritation to the eyes and skin. Some sections of Lake Erie can no longer be used for recreational purposes; many beaches along this waterway have been temporarily or permanently closed. Downstream industries are sometimes affected by industries above that discharge chemicals or other elements which affect the product or processes of the downstream users.

Industrial wastes can also limit the use of water for drinking purposes. Phenols, acidic compounds found in petroleum and steel industry wastewaters, cause taste and odor problems, especially when the water is chlorinated. In the case of Lake Erie, 835,000 residents of New York State and 2,442,000 people in other states draw drinking water from Lake Erie. If the pollution level of the Lake continues to rise, another source of drinking water will have to be tapped [33:19].

Trends in Pollution Levels

Trends in industrial pollution levels are closely linked with related industrial production output trends. As industrial production increases, pollution levels rise. RFF historical data relative to chemical, steel, and petroleum production are presented in Table 3-3. Table 3-4 reflects projected production data.

The actual 1966 Federal Reserve Board indexes of industrial production for the three industries with which this chapter is concerned were compared with values for the same industries for 1966 derived from RFF projections. These values were obtained by interpolation between the "actual" 1960 value in each case and the corresponding projected value for 1970. For iron and steel, and chemicals and products, it appears that the high value approximates the actual production trends. The medium value most closely resembles the actual trends of production of petroleum products.

Consequences of Shifts in Technology

Meaningful projections of future waste loads can be accomplished by relating production trends with trends in production technology. No emphasis has been placed on shifts in technology in the chemical industry since modern technology has been employed by those chemical processes selected for analysis and no shifts to a newer process is presently anticipated [30:13, 24, 31].

Table 3-5 reflects 1963 actual technological levels and projected shifts in technology in the petroleum and iron and steel manufacturing processes.

Waste Load Projections

Tables 3-6, 3-7, and 3-8 reflect projected waste loads of selected pollution contributors assuming no shift in technology. Chemical and petroleum waste loads were measured in terms of BOD; however, steel waste loads were measured

Table 3.3

Historical Industrial Production Indexes (1957 = 100)

Year	Iron & Steel	Industry Chemicals & Products	Petroleum Products
1947	81.7	45.4	63.8
1948	85.5	49.1	69.1
1949	73.0	48.4	66.9
1950	89.9	60.5	73.8
1951	100.5	68.6	82.5
1952	88.5	71.7	84.4
1953	102.0	77.5	89.5
1954	80.0	76.8	88.8
1955	105.7	89.2	95.4
1956	103.2	95.5	100.1
1957	100.0	100.0	100.0
1958	75.4	99.7	98.8
1959	85.9	114.3	105.4
1960	87.9	121.2	108.1

Source: *Resources in America's Future*, Table A1-30, pp. 564–578.

in terms of pounds of net waste discharged. Suspended solids account for a substantial portion of the overall pollution input related to the steel industry [28:6].

In comparing projections of future pollution levels in the steel and petroleum industries, it is apparent that newer technology significantly reduces waste

Table 3.4

Projected Industrial Production Indexes
(1957 = 100)

	Iron & Steel	Chemicals & Products	Petroleum Products
1970:			
Low	92	158	125
Medium	122	195	141
High	156	258	159
1980:			
Low	95	209	153
Medium	151	294	185
High	220	475	237
1990:			
Low	105	273	186
Medium	190	435	248
High	317	855	357
2000:			
Low	112	348	230
Medium	247	642	342
High	474	1516	553

Source: *Resources in America's Future*,
Table A1–30, pp. 564–578.

Table 3.5

Shifts in Production Technology Relative to Waste Load Quantities

Type of Technology	Contribution to Waste Load in 1963	1963	Projection–Percent of Plants Employing Level of Technology[a]			
			1970	1980	1990	2000
Petroleum Refining						
Old	40/55	36.0	28.8	23.0	18.4	14.7
Today's typical	10/55	56.9	51.2	46.1	41.5	37.3
Newer	5/55	7.1	20.0	30.9	40.1	48.0
Iron & Steel						
Old	9.9/12	33.3	28.5	24.0	20.2	17.0
Today's typical	1.0/12	55.4	42.0	29.0	19.4	13.0
Newer	1.1/12	11.3	29.5	47.0	60.4	70.0

Source: *The Cost of Clean Water–Industrial Waste Profile No. 5: Petroleum Refining,* Appendix A, Table 2 and 6; *Industrial Waste Profile No. 1: Blast Furnaces and Steel Mills,* pp. 56, 57, 61, 67.

[a]For iron and steel, used 1977 projected figures from above source as 1980 data. Computed 1990 and 2000 data based on above projected trends. Computed petroleum refining shifts in technology by assuming a 20 percent decrease per decade in old technology and a 10 percent decrease per decade in typical technology.

Table 3.6

**Projected Steel Waste Loads Assuming
No Shift in Technology (10^6 pounds of
net waste discharged per year)**

Waste Component	1963 Actual	1970	Projected[a] 1980	1990	2000
Suspended Solids	957.00	1416.36	2009.70	2890.14	4316.07
Lube Oils	211.90	313.61	444.99	639.94	955.70
Acids	1010.20	1495.10	2121.42	3050.80	4556.00
Soluble Metals	5.57	8.24	11.70	16.82	25.12
Emulsions	19.20	28.42	40.32	57.98	86.59
Coke Plant Chemicals	6.68	9.89	14.03	20.17	30.13
Flourides	3.54	5.24	7.43	10.69	15.97

Source: The Cost of Clean Water--*Industrial Waste Profile No. 1: Blast Furnaces and Steel Mills*, p. 79.

[a]Assigned index value of 105.3 to 1963 data based on interpolation between 1960 index and RFF projected high value for 1970. 1970–2000 trend based on high value data in Table 3.4.

discharge levels. A comparison of the steel projections, (assuming no shift in technology, Table 3-6, and assuming shift in technology, Table 3-9) indicates that the anticipated shifts in technology will offset projected pollution levels for the year 2000 by approximately 33 percent. The petroleum projections (Table 3-8 and Table 3-10) indicate that the anticipated shift in technology will offset projected pollution levels for the year 2000 by approximately 44 percent. Considering the favorable effects of shifts in technology, the anticipated pollution levels for the year 2000 are staggering. However, industry has not been forced to control pollution levels; thus it can be assumed that antipollution technology has not reached an optimum point. It appears that a speedup in technology could substantially alter present pollution trends.

Pollution trends will vary from state to state and will vary from location to location within a state's boundaries. Of course, those areas containing numerous industrial plants will be affected the most. Several states have been selected and

75

Table 3.7

Projected Selected Chemical Waste Loads Assuming No Shift in Technology (10^6 pounds per year of BOD waste loads)

Waste Component	1963 Acutal	1970	Projected[a] 1980	1990	2000
Regenerated Cellulose	6.4	10.9	19.6	35.3	62.7
Cellulose Esters	3.2	5.3	9.8	17.6	31.4
Vinyl Polymers	16.0	26.6	49.0	88.2	151.7
Polystyrene Resins and Copolymers	15.0	25.0	45.9	82.7	147.0

Source: The Cost of Clean Water--*Industrial Waste Profile No. 10: Plastics and Resins*, Vol. III, pp. 15, 22, 32.

[a]Assigned index value of 154.6 to 1963 data

based on interpolation between 1960 index and RFF projected high value for 1970. 1970–2000 trend based on high value data in Table 3.4.

Table 3.8

Projected Petroleum Waste Loads Assuming No Shift in Technology (10^6 pounds per day of BOD waste loads)

Type of Waste	1963 Actual	1970	Projected[a] 1980	1990	2000
Total Petroleum Refinery	1.04	1.26	1.64	2.20	2.95

Source: *The Cost of Clean Water--Industrial Waste Profile No. 5: Petroleum Refining*, Vol. III, Appendix A–Table 8.

[a]Assigned index value of 117.2 to 1963 data

based on interpolation between 1960 index and RFF projected medium value for 1970. 1970–2000 trend based on medium value data in Table 3.4.

Table 3.9

Projected Steel Waste Loads Assuming Shift in Technology (10^6 pounds of net waste discharged per year)

Waste Component	1970	Projected[a] 1980	1990	2000
Suspended Solids	1274.72	1607.76	2086.68	2805.45
Lube Oils	282.25	355.99	462.04	621.21
Acids	1345.59	1697.14	2202.68	2961.40
Soluble Metals	7.41	9.36	12.14	16.33
Emulsions	25.58	32.26	41.86	56.28
Coke Plant Chemicals	8.90	11.22	14.56	19.58
Fluorides	4.72	5.94	7.72	10.38

[a]computed by applying weighted average of projected technology shift (as reflected in Table 3.5) to waste load statistics in Table 3.6.

Table 3.10

Projected Petroleum Waste Loads Assuming Shift in Technology (10^6 pounds per day of BOD waste loads)

Waste Component	1970	Projected[a] 1980	1990	2000
Total Petroleum Refining	1.09	1.23	1.45	1.65

[a]computed by applying weighted average of projected technology shift (as reflected in Table 3.5) to waste load statistics in Table 3.8.

an analysis has been made of the unique industrial water pollution problems affecting these geographical areas.

The Social Costs of
Industrial Water Pollution
in Localized Areas

The harmful effects associated with the disposition of industrial wastes into waterways are discussed in qualitative and quantitative terms. The assistance of many industrialized states has been solicited in an attempt to pinpoint the specific industrial water pollution problems of localized areas within the nation. Unfortunately, not all of these states responded by forwarding information pertinent to the study of water pollution problems generated by the steel, chemical, or petroleum industries.

The Lake Ontario and St. Lawrence River Basins study conducted by the Federal Water Pollution Control Administration illustrates the problems [34:3-10, 15-23, 38-45]. In New York State, the Lake Ontario and Saint Lawrence river basins have been greatly affected by the industrial complexes that inhabit the area. Since the early 1960s, there has been a definite trend toward a greater degree of industrialization in the Lake Ontario region. Industrial employment is mainly concentrated in five counties within the basin: Erie, Niagara, Monroe, Onondaga, and Oneida. Rochester and Syracuse (in Monroe and Onondaga counties respectively) employ approximately 40 percent of the entire basin's working population.

The chemical and steel industries are integral parts of the economy in the Lake Ontario basin. Chemical plants are located mainly in the Syracuse, Lockport, and Rochester areas. Allied Chemical operates the largest soda ash-caustic soda plant in the world on the banks of Onondaga Lake. Rochester is the home of the Eastman Kodak Company which manufactures organic chemicals, pharmaceuticals, and photographic chemicals. The shores of the Niagara River are the site of many large chemical plants including Hooker Chemical, Olin-Mathieson, DuPont, and Stauffer Chemical and Carborundum. In the vicinity of Massena, near the St. Lawrence River, Reynolds metal aluminum plants and General Motors aluminum plants, and several other manufacturing operations make substantial contributions to the water pollution problems of the Lake Ontario-Saint Lawrence river basins.

The rotting Cladophora which covers the shores of Lake Ontario each summer is indicative of the seriousness of the Lake's water polution problem. Cladophora is a green algae that thrives on elements contained in many industrial waste discharges. These nutritional elements include nitrogen, phosporous, potassium, calcium, iron, and sundry organic substances. As Lake Ontario is oversupplied with these nutrients (by Lake Erie, Lake Onondaga, the Niagara River, and their tributaries), the algae can multiply at a fantastic rate during the summer months, sometimes covering a large portion of the Lake and growing to depths of about 30 feet. Often the Caldophora is washed on to the shores of the Lake where it rots and emits a terrible stench. Consequently, beaches along the shores of Lake Ontario must often be closed during the summer months when tourists and residents of the region could enjoy them.

Much of the industrial waste materials that mar the water quality of Lake Ontario are supplied by the Niagara River, its banks being highly industrialized. This waterway, which is infested with Cladophora, also contains large quantities of phenols and oils discharged from the Mobil Oil Refinery, the Donner-Hanna Coke Plant, and the Buffalo Dye Plants. The Ashland Oil and Refining Company discharges oil wastes which cling to the eastern shores of the Niagara River, consequently harming wildlife inhabiting the River's shores. Ashland also discharges approximately 36 mgd of wastes containing phenols into the Niagara. At another point along the Niagara, Ashland and Allied Chemical discharge a combined, high phenol content, waste load amounting to 33 mgd. Although the Hooker Chemical Company dispels a comparatively small volume of wastes, this company's waste loads are highly concentrated and detrimental to water quality. Thus, the Niagara's waters are highly turbid, foaming, unsightly in color, and unsafe for municipal purposes unless treated for bacterial, taste, and odor problems.

Lake Onondaga also has a serious water pollution problem. More than sixty large industries, located in or near the city of Syracuse, discharge pollution causing effluents into Lake Onondaga. Below the level of twenty-five feet, the Lake is almost completely devoid of oxygen. The bottom of the Lake is covered with piles of sludge, and sodium and calcium carbonate deposits. A heavy algae growth covers portions of the Lake which has a light penetration depth of about three feet. Lake Onondaga also contains large amounts of chlorides, and suspended solids. Among the major industrial polluters of Lake Onondaga are Crucible Steel and the Allied Chemical Corporation. Crucible Steel discharges 300 lb/day of iron 150 lb/day of chromium, and 8,200 lb/day of suspended solids. Allied Chemical contributes an estimated 3,100 tons/day of chlorides; 3,600 tons/day of dissolved solids; and 300 tons/day of suspended solids.

Among the more than two hundred industrial plants located in the Lake Ontario basin, only a few industries have adequate waste treatment facilities. The inadequacy of industrial waste treatment facilities is exemplified in the pollution abatement practices of industries situated on the Niagara; the General Motors Chevrolet Division is the only one of more than twenty industries located on the shores of the Niagara that has adequate waste treatment facilities in operation. Unless industries take responsible measures to curb water pollution, the Lake Ontario and Saint Lawrence River basins will continue to suffer serious water quality damages.

In the southeastern section of New York, the Hudson River is the center of much concern as municipalities and industries regularly dispose of large quantities of inadequately treated wastes into this waterway. While most of the pollution of the Hudson is directly attributable to municipal sewage discharges, several industries have contributed substantial amounts of harmful wastes to the Hudson River and its tributaries. These industries include the Texaco Oil Company, which discharges oil into the Fishkill River; the Sterling Drug Company, which discharges wastes from the manufacture of pharmaceuticals into the Hudson; and the Allegheny Ludlum Steel Company, which discharges metal finishing wastes into one of the smaller tributaries of the Hudson at Colonie, New York [35:204-211].

New Jersey

New Jersey's vast industrial development is equaled in size by its industrial water pollution problem. Much of the state's industry is located in the vicinity of Raritan Bay, the Arthur Kill Strait, and the Raritan River which is Raritan Bay's main tributary. These waterways have been utilized for various purposes. Industries draw upon these water supplies; however, industrial use of these waterways entails the application of waste treatment processes in order to raise the water's quality level to acceptable standards for cooling and condensing purposes. Commercially, Raritan Bay is of great value to New York as well as to New Jersey. It is a part of the Port of New York and approximately 25 percent of all New York harbor oceanic traffic either departs or arrives there. The Bay also has many recreational uses including swimming, boating, waterfowl hunting, and sport and shell fishing. New Jersey wants to maintain a high level of water quality in Raritan Bay to provide citizens with attractive recreational facilities. The major portion of wastes discharged directly into Raritan Bay are municipal in origin. Most industrial water pollutants enter Raritan Bay via the Arthur Kill and the Raritan River. Evidences of industrial water pollution in Raritan Bay include shellfish that are saturated with phenols, oil, and grease slicks, and in certain sections of the Bay, a diminished oxygen supply.

The Arthur Kill Strait is heavily supplied with industrial wastes. Twenty-one industries, including four petroleum, nine chemical, and four metal producing companies discharge 320 mgd of wastes per day into the Arthur Kill. These wastes include high concentrations of phenols, oils, and minerals, and generate a high rate of BOD in receiving waters. Oil slicks which cover the surface of the water prevent residents and tourists from using the Arthur Kill for recreational purposes. As a result of large accumulations of sediment and a seriously depleted oxygen supply, the Arthur Kill is devoid of normal aquatic life. Several companies such as Reichhold Chemicals and U.S. Metals Refining discharge harmful wastes into the Arthur Kill without any treatment. Humble Oil and Refining Company, the Chevron Oil Company, American Smelting and Refining Company, and various other chemical, steel, and petroleum manufacturers can be credited with only partial treatment of effluent discharges.

The Raritan River receives the effluent discharges of ten industrial plant sites, all of which treat wastes to varying degrees. Industrial pollutors include the Union Carbide Corporation, Tenneco Chemicals, and several other chemical companies. In parts of the Raritan River, the dissolved oxygen supply is nonexistent. At one time, the Raritan River was used for boating, fishing, and swimming. These recreational activities have been discontinued as foam, gases, and obnoxious odors have rendered the waterway unsafe and undesirable for many types of activity [36:47-62, 225-29, 362].

Indiana — Illinois

Northern Indiana and the Chicago area of Illinois comprise one of the largest industrial regions in the United States. Highly populated and industrialized cities in this area include East Chicago, Gary, Whiting, and Hammond, in Indiana; and Calumet City, Chicago Heights, and part of the south side of Chicago, in Illinois.

The state of Indiana is the homesite of ten major steel manufacturing plants, five petroleum companies, and several chemical companies. A large number of steel, petroleum, and chemical plants are also located in Illinois. The above mentioned industries, mainly clustered along the Calumet River, the Indiana Harbor Canal, and the Grand Calumet River, have created serious water pollution problems in the neighboring states of Indiana and Illinois. The Calumet River has suffered serious damages resulting from the inadequately treated effluent discharges of the iron and steel, and chemical industries; approximately 396,000,000 gallons of industrial wastes are poured daily into the Calumet River. The level of industrial water pollution of the Grand Calumet and the Indiana Harbor Canal has been increasing rapidly in recent years. Since 1965, the concentration of iron, phenols, and cyanides in these waterways has increased 100 percent, 50 percent, and 50 percent, respectively.

The Calumet River, the Indiana Harbor Canal, the Grand Calumet, and their tributaries display the physical evidences of severe water quality degradation. These waterways contain large amounts of chlorides, ammonia, iron, phenols, cyanides, spent pickle liquor, sulphate, sludge, foam, dissolved solids, and floating debris. The abovementioned wastes, especially phenols and cyanides, create taste and odor problems in drinking water supplies. Sludge, floating debris, and sedimentation have caused flooding problems on the Grand Calumet [32:39-40, 45-64, 160-161, 229, 428-438].

In Illinois, two other main waterways have suffered the effects of industrial water pollution. The Carus Chemical Company, Baird Chemical Company, and the American Nickeloid Company are among the largest contributors of harmful pollutants to the Illinois River. The Lower Des Plaines River displays much evidence of water quality damages which have been attributed to the inadequately treated wastes of the Texaco Company and the Amoco Chemical Company [42:13-14].

The Ohio River, which originates in the Pittsburgh area at the junction of the Allegheny River and the Monongahela River, flows south on the borderline between the states of Indiana and Kentucky and then continues flowing in a southwestern direction along the sourthern border of Illinois. As far back as

World War II, the Ohio River was considered to be a disaster in terms of water quality level. Beginning in 1948, the Ohio River Valley Water Sanitation Commission has been trying to improve water quality of the Ohio. However, many industries continue to display a total disregard for the importance of the restoration of the Ohio. Among the main pollution contributing industries to the Ohio are the Wheeling-Pittsburgh Steel Corporation, the Allied Chemical Corporation, the U. S. Steel Company, the Crucible Steel, and the Jones & Laughlin Steel Corporation. Harmful waste discharges from the abovementioned manufacturers include oil and colored chemicals (which color the Ohio black, blue, red, green and muddy-brown), phenols, caustics, poisonous chemicals, sludge, suspended solids and floating debris. The negligent disposal of such wastes has resulted in curtailment of the usage of the Ohio River for recreational, municipal, and certain industrial purposes [10:1].

California

In the next fifty years, the population of California is expected to expand at a very rapid rate. In 1967, California's population was 19,500,000. By the year 2020, this state's population is likely to exceed 54,000,000. The pleasant climate, the geographic beauty of the region, the expansion of industrialization, and the availability of attractive job opportunities will continue to bring new residents to the state in years to come. As the population, and the technological and industrial level of the state rise, so also will the demands made upon the state's waterways be increased. Thus, while California is presently experiencing some industrial water pollution problems, the water pollution abatement problems of tomorrow are of greater concern to state and local governing officials, and to informed citizens.

The California State Water Pollution Control Board and nine statewide regional water pollution control boards are striving to obtain the complete cooperation of municipalities and industries in the matter of water pollution abatement. These government agencies hope to curb the current trend toward greater pollution levels in several of the state's waterways, particularly the San Francisco Bay [40:1-11]. The Bay has shown evidence of a detrimental increase in the volume of chlorides, dissolved solids, and toxic substances in its waters. An unfavorable lowering of the Bay's dissolved oxygen level has also been noted. Thick patches of green algae cover portions of the Bay and dead aquatic life which is not hardy enough to survive in polluted waters rots along sections of the Bay's shoreline.

In California, the chemical industry is expected to increase to more than eight times its present size by the year 2020. A particularly large expansion of this industry is likely to occur in the San Francisco Bay area. The Bay area will also be the homesite of a significantly increased number of steel-producing complexes. The Bay area presently produces approximately 600,000 tons of steel. Steel production estimates for the Bay area in the year 2020 indicate that production will be increased to 12 million tons per year. Petroleum refineries, which are located on the shores of the San Pablo Bay and the San Suisun Bay, are expected to multiply in size and number in the next fifty years. It has been estimated that the volume of refined petroleum produced in California each year will rise from 165 million barrels per year to 1,200 million barrels per year [41:Chap. 3, pp. 11-13; Chap. 4, pp. 6-9].

It is apparent that if California intends to preserve its water resources for municipal, industrial, and recreational purposes, existing pollution must be curbed and the anticipated water pollution problems of the future must be avoided.

Rhode Island

Recognizing the consequences of industrial water pollution, the Rhode Island Department of Health, Division of Water Pollution Control, has been soliciting the cooperation of the state's industries in a drive to curb pollution and preserve waterways. Additionally, Rhode Island has updated its water pollution control laws in recent years; newest amendments require that industries apply for permits before building any new plant site within the state and also before discharging wastes into any of the state's waterways. For instance, in July 1967, the Kaiser Aluminum and Chemical Corporation applied for a permit to locate a new plant in Portsmouth. As there is no local sewer system at this location, Kaiser had planned to discharge wastes into Narraganset Bay. However, the permit was denied as water pollution officials decided that such a discharge would result in the closing of valuable shellfish areas in the Bay. After a period of research, it was decided that Kaiser's treated wastes could be safely discharged below the ground and the Kaiser Aluminum and Chemical Corporation was granted a building permit [43:24].

Among the industries responsible for the pollution of the Pawtuxet River is the Geigy Chemical Corporation which discharges significant amounts of damaging wastes into this waterway. Research is being conducted in order to find the means whereby the strength of these wastes can be reduced and discharged through the city of Cranston's sewer system. The Hoechst Chemical Company has also marred the Pawtuxet River by discharging wastes and dyes into this waterway. The Pawtuxet River is also polluted by the American Tube and Controls Company. Highly acidic metal wastes which contain large concentrations of chromium enter the Pawtuxet through the town of West Warwick's storm drain [43:2-3, 22-24].

Conclusion

Regardless of the claims made by the public relations departments of various industries, little or no responsible action is being taken voluntarily by industries to curb substantially the quantities and qualities of wastes discharged daily into waterways. This chapter reviews the various contributions made by industries in order to curb rising trends in industrial water pollution. Unfortunately, the low quality level of many major waterways indicates that whatever has been done clearly is not sufficient.

In measuring future pollution levels, it was assumed that with the exception of an anticipated shift in technology all relative forces would maintain a proportionally static influence over the environmental conditions. Although no major shifts in technology are anticipated in the chemical industry, the steel and petroleum industries are expected to offset pollution levels projected for the year 2000 (assuming no additional shift in technology) by approximately 33 percent and 44 percent respectively. Obviously, this is a significant factor which must be pondered when considering the overall ramifications of industrial pollution. However, one must not become overly influenced by the material reduction in pollution levels attributable to modern technology and lose sight of the fact that absolute quantities of industrial pollution will continue to rise. The paramount question is whether or not (assuming favorable shift in technology) the waterways will be capable of assimilating the pollution levels projected for the year 2000.

Although the quantity of pollution anticipated for the year 2000 is staggering, especially in the chemical industry, it should be pointed out that favorable shifts in technology have demonstrated significant influences over pollution trends, even though moderate trends in technological shifts were assumed. Considering that in the past industry has not been hard-pressed to control pollution emissions, it can be assumed that research and development in the area of antipollution production techniques has not been exhausted. Through tax incentives, direct government pressure, or social conscience, industry must be persuaded to respond to environmental pollution problems by speeding up research and development in the area of environmental pollution. Some have suggested that such research and development be sponsored by the federal government and be made available to industry for implementation. Regardless of the source of research and development, it is important to recognize that a speedup in technology could substantially alter present pollution trends.

It is extremely difficult to determine, based upon projections for the year 2000 and assuming no speedup in technology, whether or not the waterways will be capable of assimilating estimated pollution levels; however, it appears sufficient to say that the overall quality of the waters will deteriorate approximately in proportion to the increase in output unless there is a marked acceleration in antipollution progress. At a minimum, additional restrictions will be placed on the waterways. Waters presently considered safe for bathing will perhaps only be useful for navigational purposes.

It is apparent that numerous pollutants contribute to the industrial water pollution problem. However, it must be emphasized that individual pollutants do not cause the same degree of degradation in all waterways. The degree of pollution is determined by the strength and volume of the pollutant and the assimilative capacity of the receiving waterway. In turn, the degree of pollution determines the type of usage restrictions placed upon a waterway. Low levels of pollution may restrict the use of water for drinking purposes while higher levels of pollution may limit bathing and recreational uses or possibly interfere with the use of water by downstream industries. Navigational restrictions upon a waterway would indicate that the water had become virtually unusable.

The industrial water pollution problem is both complex and serious. It will not be easy to either conceive of or execute highly effective industrial pollution abatement programs. However, drastic measures must be taken in the near future if the many polluted waterways throughout this nation are to be saved from total degradation. It is obvious that government will have to create and enforce stricter penalties for the expulsion of inadequately treated wastes into waterways.

Factors external to industry could also play an important role in the industrial water pollution problem. Effective desalinization programs could very well alleviate fresh water withdrawals for drinking or bathing purposes and reduce the severity of the entire problem. Hard-hitting state and federal antipollution legislation would materially offset the trends of pollution levels. Other unmeasurable variables also play an important role in pollution trends. For instance, examples have been cited whereby the implementation of air pollution abatement controls have actually created increased levels of water pollution.

It appears that significant accomplishments will be made in the area of industrial water pollution abatement; however, the rate of progress will probably not far exceed the level of progress required to avoid a critical situation.

4

Population Growth and Nonindustrial Water Pollution

Charles H. Weidner

Introduction

The topic of population growth and nonindustrial water pollution would normally entail the study of a large number of pollutants and the problems they cause. Some topics which could be put forward for consideration are (a) pollution from such sources as cesspools, privies, and septic tanks and other individual means of disposal; (b) ground water pollution of various types; and (c) marine pollution from such sources as boat privies.

Although the above listed types of pollution are all of some importance, it is quite reasonable to expect that during the period which is under consideration, 1970 to 2000, these means of pollution will be very small in relation to the problem of mass sanitary sewage disposal. What is meant by mass sanitary sewage disposal is that sewage effluent which is transported to a central location, usually by means of a sewer system.

Sanitary sewage may be defined as "that which originates in the sanitary conveniences of a dwelling, business building, factory or institution" [26:332]. In 1950, approximately 77 million persons in the continental United States were served by sewer systems. This number represented 51 percent of the total population. By 1962, the population served increased to about 118 million which represented 64 percent of the then larger population. The nonsewered population was thus reduced from 74 to 68 million. These figures indicate the increasing importance of the disposal of collected sewage as against individual disposal. This trend is expected to continue [29:192]. Thus, what will be considered is the manner by which this sewage effluent is disposed of from the central points to which it has been transported.

Furthermore, a large part of the population that is not served by sewers lives in low population density areas where the sanitary sewage effluent may be easily disposed of with little worry of pollution providing certain health standards are followed. The manner of such disposal and further reasons for not considering other sources of pollution will be discussed later in this chapter along with the associated technological problems.

Because of the rather obvious fact that the amount of human wastes excreted is directly proportional to the population, of central importance in this study are the population projections for the period 1970 to 2000. These will directly relate to the amount of potential pollutants to be produced and thus available to pollute this country's streams, rivers, and other bodies of water.

There are two basic RFF projections which have significant bearing on the problem of nonindustrial water pollution: (1) population growth; and (2) urban population growth.

Sanitary sewage effluent is principally a product of human wastes and, therefore, a direct function of population. For instance, although sewage flows also depend upon water consumption, the flows in most areas of the country range between 80 and 90 gallons per day (excluding infiltration by rain water and ground water into the collection system) [13:50]. Thus, population gives a good indication of the amount of sewage which is produced.

Since sewers are only economically feasible in areas of relatively high population densities, it is important to know the expected part of the total population which lives in metropolitan areas, i.e., the cities and suburbs. This projection will supply needed information on the total quantities of centrally collected sanitary sewage which is under consideration.

The importance of the waste dilution flow projections is to indicate the extent of pollution anticipated and thus, the level of treatment required to prevent the pollution from becoming detrimental to various water uses such as drinking, recreation, swimming, fishing, and so on.

The two projections by RFF are detailed in tables 4.1 and 4.2.

The projections give a general indication of the expansion of the problem of nonindustrial water pollution on the national level. Unfortunately, the problem is not one which can be generalized, since the population of this country is by no means spread out to the degree that would be required to obtain truly meaningful results from a national, or even regional, study of population growth. Because population has collected in urban pockets with no forethought to the problem of sewage disposal, the only true in depth study that can be made is one which at the very least breaks the problem down to individual river basins. This will be attempted to at least a small degree later in this chapter.

Population projections for the nation as a whole do, however, provide an indicator, regardless of how general, of the degree of the problem which this nation faces. They are therefore, of some significance.

Water Pollution Terminology

Biological oxygen demand (BOD) of sewage or other specific pollutants "indicates the rate at which dissolved oxygen is drawn upon in a waste receiving water [17:273]. The BOD of sewage is very important because it indicates, by a formula to be detailed later in this chapter, the amount of dissolved oxygen which will be required for the biological oxidation of the sewage. Since this oxidation process requires large amounts of dissolved oxygen, the level of dissolved oxygen in the waterway may be greatly reduced. If the dissolved oxygen content is seriously lowered, the capacity of the waterway to oxidize sewage, without deleterious effects in the form of readily observable pollution, is greatly reduced or eliminated [26:465]. Water, on the average, may be assumed polluted and, therefore, not capable of supporting fish life when the dissolved

Table 4.1

Population Projections for United States,
1960 – 2000 (population in millions)

| | *Actual* | Projected | | | |
	1960	*1970*	*1980*	*1990*	*2000*
low projection		202	226	249	268
medium projection	179.9	208	245	287	331
high projection		223	279	349	433

Source: *Resources in America's Future*,
p. 517.

Table 4.2

Urban Population Projections for United
States, 1960 – 2000 (population in
millions)

| | *Actual* | Projected | |
	1960	*1980*	*2000*
low projection		171	213
medium projection	125	193	279
high projection		225	378

Source: *Resources in America's Future*,
p. 371.

oxygen content of the water is below four parts oxygen per one million parts of water; or more commonly referred to as four parts per million (ppm) [17:273]. To prevent pollution it is thus necessary to maintain a fairly high dissolved oxygen content in the sewage receiving water. This may be done by reducing the biological oxygen demand of the sanitary sewage effluent. Treatment efficiency may therefore be defined in one form as the percentage of oxygen demanding organic materials removed from sanitary sewage effluent [29:126]. This percentage removal will then be the approximate percent, by which the oxygen demand of the sewage effluent, on the body of water into which it is discharged, is reduced.

Once the above definitions are understood, understanding of the term *treatment by dilution* becomes quite simple. Stream water freely flowing and relatively free of pollutant demanding oxygen would carry close to its capacity of dissolved oxygen. For a water at $5°C$ that saturation would be about 12.8 ppm of dissolved oxygen [4:239]. This water would thus have over three times the amount of dissolved oxygen necessary to preserve fish life. It could give up, therefore, over two-thirds of its dissolved oxygen to aid in the bacteriological decomposition of sewage effluent without becoming polluted. This generalization neglects the beneficial effect of the continual addition to the waterway of dissolved oxygen through natural reaeration [26:465]. This matter will be considered in the study of individual rivers later in this chapter.

The dissolved oxygen content should not, however, be considered the sole measurement of pollution. The dissolved oxygen may be relatively high in content, while for instance, bacteria deleterious to man's health may be the dangerous pollutant. This might be caused by the pollutant entering in relatively small quantity close to the location of the waters removal. The bacteria which entered the water with the sewage would still be alive; the stream had not had proper time to purify itself.

The fact that streams, rivers, estuaries, and in fact, all bodies of water can purify themselves by biooxidizing the vast majority of pollutants which would be associated with sanitary sewage means that, providing proper controls are used, pollutants in reasonable quantities may be added to the body of water continually. One factor affecting this addition is the natural reaeration of the body of water because in order to bio-oxidize, additional oxygen must be continually available at a rate no smaller than that used in the process. Also obviously important is the efficiency of any prior treatment to which the pollutant may have been subject. Generally speaking, if the efficiency of such treatment was about 90 percent, ten times as much sewage might be so disposed of with the same pollutant effect on the body of water as if no treatment had been performed. This comparison is not precisely true — it is only a good indication since there are other significant factors which will be considered more completely later.

Adequacy of Water Resources
for Waste Dilution

Just as indicated earlier in connection with sewage produced per capita, when considering adequacy of water resources for waste dilution, national figures have little bearing. RFF has, in fact, made no national estimates for water resource needs because high transportation costs in relation to value eliminate the possibility for a nationwide market for water [17:379]. Therefore, RFF has broken its study of water resource needs into three regional sections; the East, the West and the Pacific Northwest. RFF further acknowledges that "there would be advantages in having an even larger number of regions because the regions selected are still too large to represent a meaningfully localized demand" [17:380].

The reason why localized or at least water-basin-for-dilution demand is the most important part of the pollution problem should be obvious. If a stream does not have enough water volume of a sufficient dissolved oxygen content to sufficiently dilute a sanitary sewage pollutant, how much additional water is available in another river in the same region is of little importance; the stream will still be polluted.

The East has a very large quantity of water available for dilution, but its large population creates pollution problems. Providing treatment efficiencies are significantly improved there are adequate water resources, in general, for the east.

The west has large arid and semiarid areas and in general has far less available water resources than the East. Although as yet the population of the West is only about one-third that of the East, the available water resources are only about one-fifth those of the East. To complicate matters further, the population of the West is growing at a much faster rate and by the year 2000, the West should be about one-half the size of the East in population [17:824]. The West's problem is, therefore, far more critical than that of the East. In certain areas and/or at certain times of the year, available water resources are by no means adequate for other uses aside from waste dilution as indicated by the Arizona ground water overdrafts. This means that ultimately, direct waste water reuse may be the only economical salvation possible for areas of the West.

The Pacific Northwest does not as yet have sufficient population to create regional waste dilution problems. Localized problems must still be met and dealt with.

External Effects Associated with
Sanitary Sewage Pollution

Water pollution may have deleterious effects on (a) recreation, including swimming, boating, sport fishing, and miscellaneous water sports such as water skiing; (b) agricultural reuse; (c) industrial reuse; (d) use of water for public water supply; (e) general public health and aesthetics; and (f) the fishing industry.

Recreational needs of nonpolluted water are both direct and indirect. Direct needs include the four specific needs listed above. In the 1963 Senate Hearings on Water Pollution Abatement, James M. Quigley, Assistant Secretary of the Federal Department of Health, Education, and Welfare, stated that recreation requires a water quality close to that for drinking supplies [29:9]. This stand is by no means held by all those dealing with water pollution. After extensive studies by means of water quality testing and health questionnaires, Flynn and Thistlethwayte concluded that there is no evidence to justify that any current coliform standard is warranted in determining the public classification of water for bathing. For the average case, they believe that bathing would become aesthetically unpleasant before any serious public health hazard is created [11:11]. The topic is an interesting one for obvious points can be made for both sides. One might say that since swimming does not entail the large scale consumption of water, it does not require standards quite as high. Another might well say that since the water would normally be treated before consumption, providing the treatment was adequate, the water could perhaps be even slightly lower in quality than that used for swimming.

Maintaining pollution standards for the sake of agricultural and industrial reuse is often necessary to the economy of an area. Many industrial water uses require water of a relatively high quality; therefore, the maintenance of cheap available water supplies is often essential to the economy of an area. If the water is not available in sufficient quality and quantity, new industry may not move in and existing industry may be forced to relocate [29:8].

Water of sufficient quality, free of bacterial pollutants, may be required for agricultural uses [4:526].

The use of polluted water for public water supply is perfectly reasonable from a technical point of view. The additional treatment required may well be economically prohibitive in comparison to treating the pollutant at its source. The economy of this type of program would have to be considered for each location together with other use requirements.

The city of Windhoek, in Southwest Africa, which lies in an arid region similar to parts of the western region of the United States, has successfully experimented with the reclamation of sewage effluent. A prototype plant in operation is capable of treating effluent to the degree that it may be processed by a normal water purification plant. The cost of this treatment is about forty-five cents per thousand gallons which, in their case, is cheaper than alternate means of supply available [33].

The danger of pollution to the fishing industry is twofold. First, as previously discussed, if the pollutants biosynthesis reduces the dissolved oxygen content of the water below four parts per million, fish life normally cannot be sustained. This makes pollution a real danger to fresh water fishing. Secondly, the lower pollutant contents normally found in a relatively larger quantity of water in estuaries usually mean that the dissolved oxygen is high enough to sustain fish life. The bacterial pollutants found in sanitary sewage effluent, however, often are in high enough concentration to create the danger of the fish becoming carriers. This is especially true of shellfish, which may carry salmonellae and enteric viruses. [25:34-35]. Because of this danger, pollution may greatly hurt our large shellfish industry since many shellfish are obtained from estuaries.

The problem of aesthetics in water pollution may not seem to be as important as the other diseconomies created, but it is nevertheless important. For proper enjoyment of recreation facilities, it is necessary that adjoining water not be polluted. Pollution might greatly reduce the property values of adjoining homes both because of the aesthetics and the smell which usually accompanies pollution. Pollution is the enemy of conservationists both because of its direct effects on the fish and water creatures and its indirect effect on animals in the vicinity of the pollution.

Table 4-3 shows the New York system for classifying water for its best and safest use. The system uses both qualitative and quantitative means to classify and serves as a good example of one state's opinion on this matter. These standards were set up by New York State under the direction of the Federal Water Quality Act of 1965 which directed the states to determine the uses that are to be made of a particular body or stretch of interstate waters, set criteria required or allowed for such uses, and develop a specific and enforceable plan to meet the criteria [6:1]. The New York standards are generally quite similar to those of most other state's.

The deleterious effects of nonindustrial water pollution indicate the reason for the need to prevent water pollution except possibly where it is under perfect control, or in other words, causes no deleterious effects. A thorough study of the technical literature available shows that it is well within our capabilities to purify sanitary sewage effluent until it is fit for consumption in the form of industrial or agricultural reuse, or even drinking water as indicated by the Windhoek Case. The economic and social costs, which would be attached to this form of treatment, could well be enormous. This cost problem and its effects will be further discussed in the concluding section of this chapter.

The degree of treatment of effluent in sewage treatment plants in this country varies considerably even for the same type of plant, just as the efficiencies of individual motors vary. Present plants in operation are constructed for the removal of three principal components of the effluent: solids, suspended matter, and bacteria. Reduction in BOD as defined previously measures the amount of biodegradable material removed from the effluent. Table 4-4 indicates cost per capita in terms of treatment process and efficiency.

In actuality, there are many varieties of each of the methods of treatment listed in Table 4-4. Each method has its own efficiencies and costs, which would also vary depending on the size of the plant and the effectiveness of the plant management. Weather of the locality, or more specifically, average temperature, is also a factor since higher temperatures benefit digestive processes. The efficiencies and costs shown are fairly average except for primary treatment where the efficiencies and cost of chemical precipitation, the best method now in use, are shown.

Primary treatment of sewage is the phase in which "the grosser solids are removed from the sewage by utilizing screening and sedimentation" [13:318]. Secondary treatment is the second phase of the sewage treatment. It "involves biological oxidation of the organic matter to stable forms" [13:318]. Typically, primary treatment first removes the larger solids and then secondary treatment further improves the quality of the water. In practice, however, many cities because of the expense involved only perform primary treatment, which is often far more ineffective in relation to secondary treatment, than indicated by Table 4-4.

Secondary treatment is performed by means of such methods as trickling filters, oxidation ponds, chlorination, wet combustion, or activated sludge

Table 4.3

New York State Classes and Standards for Fresh Surface Waters

Class and Best Use	Dissolved Oxygen in milligrams per liter	Coliform Bacteria Median, Per 100 Milliliters	pH	Standards of Quality	
				Toxic Wastes, Deleterious Substances, Colored Wastes, Heated Liquids and Taste and Odor Producing Substances	Floating Solids, Settleable Solids, Oil, and Sludge Deposits
AA–Source of unfiltered Public Water Supply and any other usage	5.0 minimum (trout) 4.0 minimum (nontrout)	Not to exceed 50	6.5 to 8.5	None in sufficient amounts or at such temperatures as to be injurious to fish life or make the waters unsafe or unsuitable	None attributable to sewage, industrial wastes or other wastes
A–Source of filtered Public Water Supply and any other usage	5.0 minimum (trout) 4.0 minimum (nontrout)	Not to exceed 5,000	6.5 to 8.5	None in sufficient amounts or at such temperatures as to be injurious to fish life or make the waters unsafe or unsuitable	None which are readily visible and attributable to sewage, industrial wastes or other wastes
B–Bathing and any other usages except as a source of Public Water Supply	5.0 minimum (trout) 4.0 minimum (nontrout)	Not to exceed 2,400	6.5 to 8.5	None in sufficient amounts or at such temperatures as to be injurious to fish life or make the waters unsafe or unsuitable	None which are readily visible and attributable to sewage, industrial wastes or other wastes

Table 4.3 (*continued*)

				Standards of Quality	
C—Fishing and any other usage except Public Water Supply and Bathing	5.0 minimum (trout) 4.0 minimum (nontrout)	Not applicable	6.5 to 8.5	None in sufficient amounts or at such temperatures as to be injurious to fish life or impair the waters for any other best usage	None which are readily visible and attributable to sewage, industrial wastes or other wastes
D—Natural drainage, Agriculture and Industrial Water Supply	3.0 minimum	Not applicable	6.0 to 9.5	None in sufficient amounts or at such temperatures as to prevent fish survival or impair the waters for agricultural purposes or any other best usage	None which are readily visible and attributable to sewage, industrial wastes or other wastes

Source: Irving Grossman, "Experiences with Surface Water Quality Standards," *Journal of the Sanitary Engineering Division,* American Society of Civil Engineers, Vol. 94 (February, 1968), p. 15.

Table 4.4

Plant Efficiency vs. Cost

Type of Treatment	BOD Reduction	Bacteria Reduction	Suspended Matter Reduction	Const. Cost per Capita	Annual Operational Cost per Capita
Primary	60%	70%	75%	$ 3.00	$0.40
Primary + Trickling Filters	82%	90%	85%	10.50	0.80
Primary + High Rate Filters	80%	82%	80%	6.00	0.65
Primary + Activated Sludge	88%	95%	88%	7.00	1.50

Source: Information taken from Ernest W.
Steel, *Water Supply and Sewage* (4th ed.;
New York: McGraw Hill Book Company,
1960), pp. 462, 623.

[14:399-400]. Although sometimes only one of these processes is used, it is not abnormal for more than one to be used in the plant sequentially.

Primary and secondary processes are highly effective in removing about 80 to 95 percent of the BOD and suspended solids. These treatments do not, however, produce a purity of water suitable for such applications as recreational, industrial, and domestic use. Depending upon the assimilative capacity of the stream receiving the effluent, it may not even be suitable for discharge [27:1122-1123].

There are numerous third phase (tertiary) treatments under study presently. The goal of tertiary treatments is to make the effluent treated by secondary methods adequate for reuse. Tertiary treatment does not consist of just one additional all-purpose treatment, but a series of individual treatments, each designed to bring the effluent to reusable standards in its particular field.

Table 4-5 shows the methods recommended in a recent study of waste treatment to make the effluent fit for reuse. Indicated are the methods, their estimated cost, including possible economies of scale, and the total cost necessary to make the effluent fit for normal reuse.

It should be noted that some of the figures given in Table 4-5 for some of

Table 4.5

Estimated Unit Costs for Waste Treatment Processes

Process (1)	Cost, in cents per 1,000 gallons Plant size, in million gallons per day		
	1 (2)	10 (3)	100 (4)
Conventional Processes			
Primary treatment	12	6.3	3.5
Activated sludge (includes primary treatment)	18	11	6.6
Filtration	1.8	1.5	1.2
Microscreening Sand or graded media	7.7	3.5	1.6
Phosphate Removal			
Coagulation, sedimentation	4.0	3.7	3.4
Coagulation, sedimentation, filtration	12	7.2	5.0
Ammonia Stripping	3.3	1.6	1.4
Granular Carbon Adsorption (High Removal)	16	8.0	4.0
Electrodialysis	21	14	8.7
Total Cost for Reuse Treatment	78	45.3	27.3

Source: Robert L. Steinburg, John J. Convery, and Charles L. Swanson, "New Approaches to Wastewater Treatment," *Journal of the Sanitary Division*, American Society of Civil Engineers, Vol. 94 (December, 1968), p. 1135.

the tertiary treatments are purely estimates since prototype installations, especially in the case of the larger size plants, have not been constructed.

In particular, the phosphate removal is required, especially where reuse is possible more than one time. The presence of excessive amounts of nitrates and phosphates "stimulate excessive growth of phytoplankton" [15:159]. This growth especially causes discoloration of the water. Very high concentrates of phosphates and nitrates, especially a problem if continued reuse as water supply is anticipated, can be deleterious to fish and other marine life.

Ammonia stripping may be necessary because high concentrations of ammonia can be extremely deadly to fish [15:158].

The carbon adsorption is used "for removal of non biodegradable organics, color and residual BOD"[27:1132].

Demineralization by electrodialysis "will not ordinarily be required for pollution control purposes, but will be necessary for reuse applications involving domestic supplies, some industrial uses, and underground injection where dissolved salts in the ground water are already at maximum allowable concentration levels"[27:1133].

It should be noted that the costs listed in Table 4-5 are for plant operation and maintenance only. These costs clearly indicate that, providing the prototype plants can be as inexpensive as believed, tertiary treatment for water reuse is not uneconomical. Depending on the size of the plant, Table 4-5 indicates that the total cost of all tertiary treatment (including the sometimes not needed electrodialysis) varies between 19.1 and 52.3 cents per thousand gallons of effluent treated. These prices become more reasonable when it is remembered that the water reclaimed by this process is made saleable for reuse in various applications. The cost is smaller than that for the previously discussed Windhoek plant except in the million gallon per day range. Windhoek was designed to operate at the rate of two million gallons per day. The quality of the Windhoek effluent is, however, as good as that quality envisaged for the use of all processes in Table 4-5.

The very low cost per thousand gallons shown in Table 4-5 for the hundred million gallon per day plant is somewhat deceptive because it does not take account of the sewage transportation system, which would be required to collect sufficient waste to operate on this scale. It is likely that only very densely populated areas would be able to economically construct a plant of that size. For less densely populated areas, the cost of the collection system would become prohibitive. Since the sanitary sewage flow generated by an average person per day is about eighty to ninety gallons, to which must be added the additional amount of flow due to ground water intrusion into the collection system and other sources, it would take a population of over three-quarters of a million people in a relatively small area to make this type of plant economical [13:50-51]. There are less than 25 metropolitan areas in this country that could thus require a plant of that scale [28:19].

In addition to the technological factors already mentioned, there is an enormous amount of research continually being performed to aid man in his continuing fight against the deleterious effects of water pollution. This research is centered not only upon the reduction in cost and increase in efficiency of present treatment methods but also along the lines of entirely new concepts in reducing our pollution problem; many of which only indirectly involve sewage treatment.

An example of this beneficial research is the work of Dr. Bohnke of Germany who has constructed a technical formulation for the determination of the capacity of waterways to accept sewage while the pollution content remains within acceptable limits. Included in Bohnke's research is a method of calculating the rate of reaeration for specific bodies of water under specific conditions [3:157-158]. The first section of the research is obviously helpful in determining a stream's capacity for assimilating waste. Reaeration is, however, a process which can be accomplished naturally as Bohnke has determined formulas for, but this method is fairly slow in relation to mechanical reaeration.

The faster that the stream water can be reaerated, the greater the BOD the stream can accommodate. Mechanical reaeration and other methods of instream treatment have been proven feasible under certain conditions in prototype installations in Germany [16:88-89].

The technology, as presently available, is quite capable of purifying sanitary sewage effluent to the desired degree; however, further research which could reduce the enormous cost of this purification is needed.

Santee, California, is another instance in which man has done a great deal to adapt the requirements of purification to his environment. In Santee, a research project has successfully used waste effluent to provide varied water type recreational facilities for the local inhabitants. This was accomplished in an area of southern California where water is difficult and expensive to obtain. Thus, the recreational facilities provided could not have been made available without the reuse of the effluent except at enormous cost. The facilities included a series of four lakes for swimming, boating, and fishing. Also, as part of this project was a reeducational program for the local inhabitants to eliminate any distaste for making use of adequately purified sanitary sewage effluent. Although this project has encountered problems with maintaining such standards as the nutrient level of the lakes (which has resulted in fish kills), it has been an overall success [19:3-5].

The Per Capita Problem of
Increased Sewage Production and
Offsetting Effects

It is possible to construct what will be called a per capita pollution ratio relating the increase in the BOD of sewage that could be expected to the potential increase in population. This ratio would be somewhat synthetic since a third variable, available flow for waste dilution, must also be considered. Perhaps the cost per thousand gallons of effluent treated by various means given in Table 4-5 would have more practical use in some ways, but the per capita pollution ratio will give a better indication of potential pollution.

It has been calculated by Hardenbergh and Rodie that average amounts of organic matter produced per person per day in domestic sewage is equivalent to about 0.17 lb. of 5-day BOD [13:318]. If the ratio is then computed on a per thousand person basis, it will be necessary to neutralize 170 lbs. per day to prevent any polluting effects through the using up of dissolved oxygen.

A next step in creating a usable per capita pollution ratio would be to determine the amount of flow per day necessary to dilute this pollutant. It is here necessary to set a minimum acceptable standard for dissolved oxygen content before the ratio calculation may be furthered. Four parts per million (ppm) was discussed as the minimum acceptable for maintaining fish life and this seems reasonable for use here.

For a stream with an average dissolved oxygen content of 8.2 ppm, the available dissolved oxygen in one million gallons of water for maintaining the 4 ppm level would be 35 lbs. in 5-day BOD equivalent [13:321]. Thus, an average daily flow of 4.86 million gallons would be necessary for each one thousand people producing sewage effluent. There are principally two very significant factors which can alter this ratio.

The foremost factor which can influence the per capita pollution ratio is the degree of treatment of the effluent which is accomplished. The 4.86 million gallons would be that amount of flow necessary to neutralize one thousand persons' output of raw sewage. If the sewage were treated with 95 percent efficiency for BOD, only 243 thousand gallons of dilution flow per day would be required. 99 percent efficiency would reduce the flow required still further — to less than 50 thousand gallons.

The other very significant factor to be considered is the dissolved oxygen content of the stream. This content is appreciably lowered by an increase in temperature of the water since the capacity of water for holding dissolved oxygen is inversely proportional to the temperature [26:469]. Another factor seriously affecting the dissolved oxygen content of the water is the amount of pollutant previously disposed of in the waterway. The BOD of that pollutant may have already lowered the dissolved oxygen content by a considerable amount, perhaps below the acceptable 4 ppm level.

Examples of how the dissolved oxygen content of the waterway may affect the required dilution flow are as follows. If the dissolved oxygen content was raised to 10.3 ppm, the required dilution flow would be reduced to 3.23 million gallons per day; while if the dissolved oxygen was decreased to 6.1 mg./1., the required flow would have to be raised to 9.72 million gallons per day.

A system of reaeration of the waterway could perhaps be worked out inexpensively for use if the dissolved oxygen level of the waterway or the volume of water available should slip below the prescribed level for short periods of time [16:88].

The flow itself is affected by the conditions such as drought, flood, and other related factors in the tributary basin. Because of this, it is necessary to determine what flow will be considered as the design flow.

As a design flow, the Federal Water Pollution Control Administration recommends the use of a 10-day, 25-year flow criterion. [23:507]. This means that the flow used is that minimum average flow for a ten-day period, which by standard hydrological practices would be expected to occur only once every twenty-five years. Virginia, on the other hand, uses a 7-day, 10-year flow criteria for determining a stream's capacity for waste assimilation [23: 507-508].

In connection with the Virginia Code, hydrological data has been studied in depth, and it has been found that 99 percent of the daily flows exceed or equal that suggested design level [23:508]. This then appears to be a very reasonable, if not conservative, criteria. These design flows, however, tend to be considerably smaller than the average daily flow on a yearly basis; therefore, it may be feasible to augment these small design flows which are often as little as 10 percent of the average flows.

Probably the simplest method to augment these design flows would be to impound quantities of the water in storage reservoirs during periods of high flow and then release it in controlled quantities during periods of low flow, just as is already done in some parts of the country. When the storage water is available for other uses such as recreation, power supply, and water supply, pumped storage may be economically and technologically feasible where the construction of normal reservoirs is not [30:170].

The relation of the per capita pollution ratio to cost, both social and economic, has already been described in Table 4-4 and in other sections. It is important, however, to note that if certain ambient standards are to be maintained at specific levels and the goal is not to be the maximum purity of water possible, then variable efficiency treatment may well be the most efficient. By this, it is meant that degree of treatment of the effluent could vary with the ambient conditions of the waterway.

When stream flow is relatively high, only primary treatment might need to be performed. During normal periods of flow, both primary and secondary treatment of the effluent could be performed, while tertiary treatment would be used only during extremely low flow conditions. Oxidation ponds could also be used to store sewage during periods of low flow. Variable treatment methods such as these might significantly lower the average operational costs of the treatment processes.

Offsetting effects associated with the expanding output of sewage effluent are basically of three types: (1) legislative action caused principally by the continually worsening pollution problem; (2) technological innovations spurred on by the increasingly difficult problems associated with pollution which are developing; and (3) beneficial external effects such as use of processed effluent for fertilizer and fluid reuse possibly helped by economies resulting from the expanding volumes available.

Probably the most important piece of legislation to date in the battle against pollution has been the Federal Water Quality Act of 1965. Inquiries were sent to ten states (Arizona, California, Illinois, Kansas, Maryland, Minnesota, Missouri, New York, Pennsylvania, and Virginia) and all provided copies of their recently enacted Water Quality Regulations prompted by the Federal Act. The individual acts were all somewhat similar to the New York requirements detailed in Table 4-3.

It is impossible in a study of this size to detail the water pollution control laws of our fifty states or even in the sample of ten listed above. In the breakdown of projections in the next section, certain pertinent laws of the above listed states will be further discussed.

Aside from the passing of laws concerning water pollution which are often difficult to enforce, probably the major instrument state legislatures have in their hands to fight pollution is the ability to form agencies — either interstate, if other state legislatures agree there is a joint need, or intrastate, if the problem is a local one. An example of an interstate commission which has been set up is the Ohio River Valley Water Sanitation Commission (Orsanco).

Orsanco was set up in 1948 by joint action of the legislatures of eight states bordering on the Ohio or its tributaries [5:3]. The purpose of the interstate compact was principally to study the existing laws in the member states and make recommendations for their improvement and/or uniformity. It was generally believed that the work of Orsanco should be distinguished by its ability to impel rather than compel. As a result the staff emphasized development of community action programs, radio and television projects, and the production of documentary films and brochures [5:89].

In 1948, when the compact was signed, 38 percent of the urban population was served with treatment plants; in 1965, 94 percent of an increased urban population were served by sewage treatment plants. 90 percent of the industrial plants have installed industrial waste treatment facilities [5:216-217].

In general, it has been found that stream quality within the Orsanco program area has improved within the last ten years; however, there are still many streams having stretches which would not qualify as clean enough to satisfy reasonable use requirements [5:221]. Thus, the compact has probably been beneficial to the region.

A similar program on an intrastate basis was started in 1960 for the San Francisco Bay-Delta in California. This water quality program instituted the use of a computer to determine the exact effect which a pollutant added to any stream which ultimately enters an estuary will have on the water quality at any point in the estuary [24:914-916]. The study and research required to write that type of program is very great, but so are the benefits. Enormous economies may be observed since the worst sources of pollutant may be readily indicated. Often, the economic outlay for obtaining a desired water quality may be greatly reduced by this method.

Of the laws and potential legislative enactments studied, one in particular seems especially promising in its potential effects on water quality. In 1966, the Governor of Maryland appointed a commission to determine a program for water pollution control to be used in that state. That commission published a set of recommendations in early 1968 which are somewhat revolutionary in the field of waste water management.

The key finding of the commission was that a "Waste Acceptance Service" should be set up which would be in essence, "a statewide sanitary district obliged to serve all communities and industries in the state" [14:289]. This service would be required to provide treatment for municipal and industrial waste before the waste could be discharged into any stream or river in the state. Industrial and individual treatment service would be maintained on a paid retail basis. The service would sell its services to municipalities on a wholesale basis, allowing the municipality to determine retail charges. By this and other similar means, local autonomy would be maintained [14:289-290].

This concept of a statewide sewage disposal corporation is an interesting one because, for the first time, local bickering over who is creating the problem would be removed within each state. A uniform, carefully controlled approach within each state would result in economies of scale as well as increased uniformity and consistency.

If Maryland does follow the recommendations of the commission and set up this waste acceptance service, it will be very interesting to study its functioning feasibility in order to determine its possible applications to our national problems.

One of the forces complicating the legislators' role in the solving of our water pollution problems is the continually changing technological concepts which affect the waste disposal. Because of these new developments which continually necessitate change for the sake of economy, it is proper that legislative enactments be limited to generalizations, giving the power for enactment to highly skilled individuals thoroughly familiar with the changing developments in their field. Some examples of new concepts in pollution control and water quality management are described in the following paragraphs.

During the late 1950s and early 1960s, the public became increasingly aroused by foam or "head" which developed in many of our streams and water supplies. The foam was created by the nonbiodegradable detergents used principally for washing. Since it was not biodegradable, normal means of treatment could not remove the detergent from the water, and through added use and reuse the concentrations and thus the heads created became greater and greater.

The detergent which caused this problem was alkylbenzenesulfonate (ABS). In the early 1960s, local ordinances began to appear prohibiting the production and sale of ABS. Legislation was soon pending in several states and Congress (34). In response to this problem, the detergent industry spent $100 million on research, development, and new equipment to produce a new, more biodegradable detergent. All this was done simply to remove a pollutant whose only major deleterious effect was to aesthetics. No other serious result of this type of pollution, in reasonably expected concentrations, has been found [34].

When several new, and not yet fully proven, research studies are compared, providing they are all as sound as their authors believe, it is found the ABS problem might have been dealt with as an indirect benefit of a possible revolutionary new process.

Dr. James E. Etzel, a professor of sanitary engineering at Purdue University, has developed a process which uses irradiation to kill germs and coagulate the solids in sewage [22:61]. The sewage is thus concentrated by coagulation to reduce its volume. Once concentrated, it can be economically pumped to areas where it can be cheaply disposed of. According to Dr. Etzel, it could be pumped economically and efficiently as far as 200 miles. This means of disposal, providing a cheap method of final disposal could be found, could reduce the cost of sewage treatment for Chicago from $56 a ton to as little as $16 a ton [22:61].

A separate research project by H. R. Spragg has found that irradiation of sewage degrades ABS detergents, and so, eliminates foaming troubles. Spragg's study indicated that the cost of treating sewage with radiation for the sole purpose of degrading ABS was not economical [15:161]. When Spragg's and Etzel's studies are combined, however, the impressive possibility of economies of scale become very evident. This comparison is meant only to serve as an example of the vast possibilities available in today's research.

Another possible future aid in the field of waste treatment is pumped storage. Although pumped storage has never been tried for this purpose, it probably could be done quite economically, provided the storage served other purposes as well; such as peak power delivery, recreational needs, and preventing salt water surface intrusion in water supply inlets [30:167-168].

An example of this surface salt water intrusion was the problem Philadelphia encountered due to the low flow of the Delaware during the 5-year drought in the Northeast during the early 1960s.

Increasing the minimum flow will reduce the amount of treatment required to meet prescribed water quality standards.

The beneficial external effects from the treatment of sewage are at present quite limited, as will be detailed later; however future research may well discover further uses, especially as our natural resources of such elements as nitrogen and phosphate are depleted.

Sewage sludges have moderate value as fertilizers but are inferior to manure due to lack of potassium for crops needing potash. High transportation costs make it necessary to obtain sludges with a low moisture content (less than 50 percent) if the sludge is to be economically used for fertilizer [15:185]. Professor Etzel's radiation treatment is, of course, made more impressive by this requirement, especially since it disinfects the sludge which is required by the laws of several states if it is to be used for the fertilization of eatable crops [4:6].

Properly conducted composting of sewage sludge will produce a germ-free inert material with good economic value when the quantity produced is not excessive [15:189-190]. The humus produced, thus, provides an excellent means of economical (and possibly profitable) disposal of sludge.

Economical reuse of the liquid effluent is also quite possible. Indirect reuse has been an accomplished fact for some time. After effluent has been discharged into a waterway, the water from that source is often used for drinking, industrial, recreation, agricultural, and other uses, even in polluted form. If polluted, before the water is fit for some of these uses such as drinking, more treatment than would normally be required must be performed.

Direct reuse is not as often accomplished. The amount of treatment required to make effluent available directly for the above listed indirect uses is often economically prohibitive. It is, however, quite possible to treat effluent to the stage that it may be used for drinking water [4:526-534].

The use of effluent for ground water recharge is often an excellent and economical means of disposal. Sewage effluent is normally adequately purified by this means for reuse providing care is taken in the placement of the recharge basins away from such hazards to proper purification as underground streams. Recharge with effluent offers the following advantages: (a) supplementation of natural recharge, (b) reduction of aquifer overdrafts; (c) control of saline intrusion, and (d) control or aid in combating land subsidence problems [1:167].

Recharge is, thus, an economical means of effluent disposal with several beneficial results.

The basic problem with providing beneficial effects from effluent and sludge disposal is often one of matching location of source with the location of the need. If transportation were costless, disposal would not only be economical, but possibly profitable [4:534].

Projections of the Future Magnitude of
the Nonindustrial Pollution Problem

Using the urban population projections described earlier, with the five percent downward adjustment, the expected sewage contributing population for the entire nation for the year 1980 will be about 175.8 million people. As merely an example of the computation method described previously, for 95 percent treatment efficiency 42.7 trillion gallons of water per day would be required for dilution purposes based on a reasonable assumed dissolved oxygen content for the waterways of 8.2 parts per million. This is about 427 times the flow which RFF computed would be available 95 percent of the time, based on 1954 storage facilities. There are some obvious fallacies in this computation [17:380]. First, a large percent of the urban population considered would live adjacent to an estuary of an ocean or the ocean itself; thus, the effluent could be directly disposed of without polluting the rivers and streams with which RFF was concerned. Also, the characteristics of the streams, which allow them to purify themselves, mean that pollutant may be diluted into the same flow several times before it ultimately reaches the ocean or estuary.

On the other hand, there is probably little chance that the degree of treatment in practice will actually reach 95 percent efficiency by 1980, especially when the number of combined sewers currently in use are considered. These intangible factors, very difficult to quantify, make the problem very difficult to discuss above the local level.

On a regional basis, there can be little doubt that the most critical area is in the West. It is projected that the urban population in the West will reach 79.2 million by the year 2000, excluding the five percent reduction [17:824]. This compares with urban population for the East of about 189.9 million. As previously shown, however, the West's available dependable runoff is only about 18 percent of the East's [17:824]. This, combined with the inequitable distribution of the water resources in the region, make the West the most critical region by far [17:383].

The largest unit with which the water pollution problem can be effectively and efficiently dealt with is the river basin. In 1967 the Federal Water Pollution Control Administration (FWPCA) divided the nation into twenty major river basins for planning purposes. Each basin would be studied individually for the best methods to improve the water quality in the particular river basin. The purpose of the plan was to facilitate the control of pollution within the river basin on both a short and permanent, long-term basis [6:2-3].

With the setting up of the FWPCA under the Water Quality Act of 1965, "140 stream monitoring stations on interstate streams throughout the United States" were established [6:2]. These stations monitor quality of the bodies of water they are on and, thus, the water quality. Inquiries to the ten states mentioned previously indicated that before 1965 few states had sampling systems and, therefore, little information is readily available about instream water quality in most river basins before 1965.

A reasonable method to project future water pollution problems to be expected in river basins would be as follows (1) projection of sewered populations could be determined for the river basin under consideration; (2) the present sewage treatment efficiencies could be graphed with past efficiencies and future efficiencies could be projected; and (3) these two sets of projections could be correlated with present pollution readings at various points in the river basin to give a semiquantitative result.

This projection method has several flaws but it should provide a generalized qualitative result for each river basin when several other considerations are included. Some of these considerations are (1) the trend of legislation and government spending should be studied to determine whether the spending will be adequate to provide for the projected treatment efficiency — or in fact provide for a greater or lesser efficiency; (2) other sources of water pollution must have their effects taken into consideration in their effect on past and future pollution readings; and (3) consideration must also be given to the effect which new technology, droughts, new water requirements, or any other unforeseen circumstances might cause.

Although a truly precise projection for thirty years in the future would be nearly impossible, a reasonably sound, semiquantitative, almost qualitative result through this method seems reasonable. The water pollution problem, unfortunately, has not been vigorously attacked in many areas until recently, as indicated by the lack of stream monitoring stations and interstate organizations. Since the vast majority of information available, especially for major river basins, does not predate the FWPCA, accurate past data on average sewage treatment efficiencies and stream quality are not available. Furthermore, the river basin study groups set up by the FWPCA have not yet had sufficient time to assimilate data and develop comprehensive programs. It is, therefore, difficult to arrive at positive results in a study of many river basins. The majority of the states and regional offices of the FWPCA written to, indicate that much of the data are simply not readily available as of this time.

Adequate information was obtained to provide a reasonable insight into the potential pollution problem in several important river basins.

Population projections prepared by the Missouri Basin Region of the FWPCA show that the urban population of the basin is expected to increase from 4.5 million in 1960 to 10.5 million by the year 2000 [31]. This increase of 133 percent is approximately in line with the national increase projected earlier. Charles H. Hajinian, Acting Director of that FWPCA office of water quality management, stated in recent correspondence that "Present sewage treatment methods are capable of disposing of the waste generated" within the river basin [31]. Mr. Hajinian further observed that to meet future projected requirements, additional funds will be needed for the construction of sewage treatment plants. Mr. Hajinian's view of the Missouri as a reasonably unpolluted river is corroborated, at least within Missouri, by data from Missouri's Water Pollution Board. Sampling stations in Missouri indicate that only at Kansas City does the dissolved oxygen content of the river normally fall below 4 parts per million. Even in the Kansas City region of the river, this only occurs during periods of extreme low flow when dilution is minimized. Other pollution indicators such as pH and BOD are reasonably good [20:1-2].

Unfortunately, adequate data have not allowed a specific projection for the water quality to be expected in the Missouri basin by the year 2000. It does appear, however, that the problem in that basin will be somewhat typical of that to be expected for the largest part of the nation, and especially the East. The water quality from sanitary sewage dilution is not too bad now, but a great deal of funds will have to be expended simply to maintain the status quo. This matter will be further discussed in the concluding section.

The next river basin to be considered is that of the Salt River, draining much of central Arizona including the metropolitan area of Phoenix. The water shortage being experienced in Arizona and much of the southwest has increased to the extent that "outflow from the central Arizona area is negligible [2:11, 7]. Because of the water shortage, Arizona requires a minimum of secondary treatment complete with chlorination for all domestic wastes [2:43]. Effluent from the Phoenix area is discharged into the usually dry Salt River bed. Although some of the effluent is used for irrigation or reaches the ground water table, most of it evaporates. Plans are currently being prepared to reclaim the water more fully [2:1].

It can thus be seen that Arizona has no problem of waste dilution because the value of water is so high due to its scarcity that maximum treatment is nearly a necessity.

The next basin to be considered will be the Mohawk River basin in New York State. The Mohawk River section of the Hudson basin is polluted primarily by sanitary sewage effluent, discharged for the most part in raw condition by the cities and towns between Rome and Schenectady. By the 1960 census, about 350,000 people contribute sewage to this 100-mile stretch of the Mohawk. As of 1967, approximately one-third of the sewage produced was treated and that third was treated only by primary treatment [32].

Figure 4-1, prepared by the New York State Department of Health, shows a

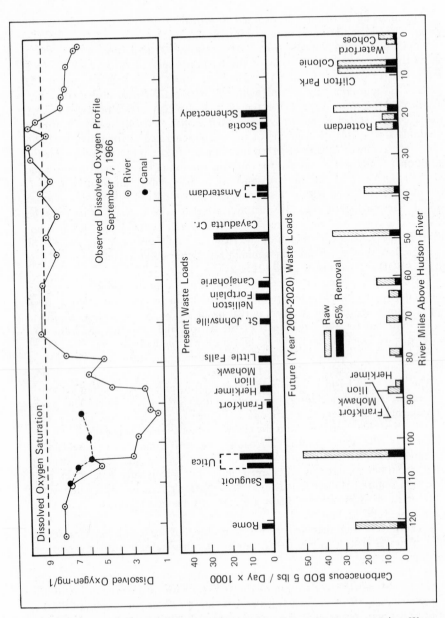

Figure 4-1 Dissolved Oxygen Profile and Present and Future Major Waste Inputs, Mohawk River. Source: Letter dated April 14, 1969, from George K. Hansen, Sanitary Engineer, Basin Development Section, New York State Department of Health.

plot of dissolved oxygen content of the Mohawk during a period of low flow. Therefore, the dissolved oxygen shown is a lower level than would be the yearly average. The graph indicates that the only area in which a severe problem is being felt is that 20-mile section of river between Utica and Mohawk.

Below the plot of dissolved oxygen readings are two bar graphs which show the present output of 5-day BOD and that output projected for the period between 2000 and 2020. The darkened areas show the equivalent loading in 5-day BOD while the cross-hatched sections of the "Future Waste Load" chart show what the loading would be without the forecast 85 percent removal through treatment.

The graphs indicate that, despite the greater loads to be expected from population growth, the quality of the river should substantially improve.

Actually, much of this improvement should take place well before the year 2000, for New York has enacted "Pure Waters Program" through which the state and federal government combine to contribute up to 85 percent of the cost of constructing sanitary sewage treatment plants. The state will further contribute 30 percent per year to the cost of operating and maintaining the plant if its effluent meets water quality standards [21:3-4]. Much of the financial burden is removed from the municipalities and construction expedited. Because of this liberal reimbursement plan, the number of projects underway considerably oversubscribes New York State's share of funds under the Federal Clean Water Act of 1966 [21:63]. The Mohawk basin thus does not appear of prime concern for the future; although there are water quality problems now, the outlook for the future is improving.

As can be seen from the three river basins considered, the effects of the population growth expected between 1970 and 2000 vary in their effect on water pollution. These basins considered, represent a fair cross-section of the problem of nonindustrial water pollution as it is being felt in various river basins within the United States. For more precise results, each basin must be considered separately in the manner previously indicated.

For the total effect on any river basin, it will of course be necessary to include studies of other sources of pollution as pertinent, such as industrial pollution and thermal pollution.

Social and Economic Costs of
Improved Sewage Treatment

As has been indicated, it is quite possible technologically to treat sewage to a point where the effluent is fit for direct human consumption. It is, therefore, necessary to make some sort of a cost versus benefit appraisal in comparing the value of fighting water pollution with the social uses of the funds available. For instance, what determines how a dollar of government funds available should be divided between such worthy alternates as hospitals, education, transportation, welfare, pollution control, and many other alternates? It is beyond the scope of this book to make an in-depth study of this difficult question; however, it is important that this difficult problem of proper allocation of resources be recognized.

If a formula for the proper allocation of funds could be worked out, it would almost definitely vary, depending on the region, state, county, city, and perhaps even village which was being considered. This would be because of existing conditions, the public needs for the various social services which a unit of government can give would vary. The reasons for this variance would be on account of such things as past service history, geographic problems such as weather, economic problems of the area, and many other variables. For this reason, two cities on the same river close together but perhaps in different states might have a considerably different relative amount of funds available to fight pollution. Therefore, the efficiency of treatment might vary considerably to the extent that one city dumps raw sewage into the river while the other treats its sewage by secondary processes to 95 percent efficiency.

Thus, as shown in the above example, regardless of the amount of funds the one city spends, its river may still be badly polluted. Because of the social costs involved and possible economic problems within the state, the second city may not be able to make available adequate funds for the treatment of sewage. To do so might be to take funds from other critical needs. It is problems such as these which complicate the task of minimizing water pollution.

From the absolute cost standpoint, the Federal Water Pollution Control Administration (FWPCA) estimates eight billion dollars will be required between 1969 and 1973 to meet adequate water quality standards [7:2-3]. The standards referred to are those of the Federal Water Pollution Control Act for the nation's clean water needs. That Act required that a study be made of the economic impact on affected units of government of the cost of providing clean water. This study found that the total cost, in addition to the eight billion listed above, units of local government would have to spend an additional seven billion dollars on sanitary collection sewers before 1973 [7:2-3]. This total potential expenditure of fifteen billion dollars appears very large when compared to approximate total outlay of $5.3 billion in the 1961-1966 period [7]. Even when adjusted for construction cost increases, the estimated expense in the 1969-1973 period is almost three times as great [8:56-57].

This increase in cost will thus have serious economic and social costs. Of this amount, the Federal Government has authorized $3.5 billion in the form of Federal Aid [7:3]. This will help allay some of the economic impact upon the affected units of Government. Any delay in this program will increase its cost by slightly more than three percent per year.

The major means by which states and local governments finance capital outlays such as these is by debt offerings in the form of bonds. The Federal Government gives these bonds the advantage of their interest being income tax free to the debt holders. This allows these governmental units to market the securities at a lower interest rate than would otherwise be required. During 1966, the total state and local capital outlays financed by this means amounted to $22.3 billion [7:48]. The FWPCA study indicates that the governmental units may expect to float their bonds at an average interest rate of 4.5 percent. Current events and changes in the interest rate which have occurred since the study was made indicate that this estimate is lower than might now be expected; but even at this perhaps understated rate, the yearly cost to meet this debt service will be about $500 million a year.

The cost to these governmental units for the operation and maintenance of these new facilities must also be considered. Assuming that the program reaches the estimated completion by 1974, the additional expense of $225 million annually will be required for operation and maintenance [7:76].

The FWPCA study emphasizes that the economic and social effect on units of local government will be enormous unless the federal government finances a larger share of this program than the $3.5 billion previously mentioned.

The level of government at which the cost is met is not the most important consideration. Whether the funds required for this work come from the national budget or that of other governmental units is not the key. The effect will be approximately the same on the country as a whole since what would probably be accomplished in most cases is a redistribution of funds among federal programs. The net cost to the nation's gross national product would not substantially change. The seriousness of this financial problem should thus in no way be underestimated.

The FWPCA study does not make any projections past the year 1975 but it generally indicates that depending upon changes in the technical and quality requirements of the program, future requirements should be in line with those listed.

The problem of priorities is obviously a difficult one; but our future problem with water pollution in the period under consideration is clearly dependent upon the economic priority the nation attaches to the solving of that problem.

Conclusion

In conclusion, reasonable projections for urban population as obtained from Table 4-2 with the five percent correction discussed earlier, indicate the following percent increases in population: The 1980 urban population will be 47 percent greater than the 1960 urban population and the 2000 urban population will be 114 percent greater than that of 1960. Since the amount of human waste created is directly proportional to the urban population, the amount of potential water pollution should increase by approximately these same percentages.

Sanitary sewage is, however, being treated to a constantly increasing efficiency to the point that its polluting effects upon the waters it is discharged into is being reduced. The principal question of this study has been: Will the efficiency of treatment improve more than that amount required simply to offset the growth in pollutant, and if so, to what degree?

Unfortunately, adequate data do not now appear to be available to provide an adequate quantitative answer to these questions. Technology is now more than adequate to treat the effluent to whatever degree required; however, the economic and social costs of such treatment are very high. Because of these high costs, the problem is relegated from one of technological feasibility to one of prognosticating the amount of concern which the nation will have for the problem of pollution. It is probable that only if concern is high will adequate funds be made available to significantly improve our waterways, for these funds must be taken from other needy recipients such as welfare, transportation, and education.

At present, public concern does appear to be high. This concern has fostered the Federal Water Pollution Act of 1965 and subsequent federal, state, and local water pollution acts. If this trend continues, there appears little doubt that in general our waterways should be superior to their present condition in the future, regardless of projected increases in population. The degree of improvement will probably vary for each river basin in relation to the ambient needs within each basin.

The water pollution present in a waterway is, of course, dependent on more than just the sanitary sewage pollution, but also the other sources of pollution such as industry. Government, however, usually directly controls sanitary sewage treatment and therefore has little excuse not to improve it. This control should make the sanitary sewage pollution problem easier to solve than those of other sources of pollution.

There is the possibility of some further technological breakthrough which will decrease significantly the cost of treatment and therefore reduce the non-industrial pollution problem. The source of this breakthrough might be greater need for by-products of the treatment process such as water for reuse or sewage for fertilizer. In areas of great water need, such as central Arizona and Santee, California, this is already being attempted. Any new process which could significantly reduce treatment costs could perhaps make the treatment of effluent profitable, at least in paying for operation and maintenance.

As mentioned, all things considered, it appears likely that the water quality in the nation's waterways will improve, at least as far as sanitary sewage pollution is concerned. This prediction must, however, be hedged. During the 1960s, this nation has had the greatest period of prosperity in its history. The nation's attack on the problem of water pollution may well be a product of the affluence created by this long period of prosperity. Should we return to a period of recessions, much of the nation's zeal for the problem of water pollution may wane. In such a period, expenditures for sewage treatment might well be cut by required constrictions in state and local budgets. If this is the case, obviously the projections of this chapter for the improvement of water quality may be in error.

Regardless of this problem, it does appear that the water quality of our waterways will improve, at least to some extent, during the period under consideration.

5 Thermal Pollution

J. R. Crespo

As soon as I had gotten out of the heavy air of Rome, and from the stink of the smokey chimneys, thereof, which being stirred, pour forth whatever pestilent vapor and soot they held enclosed in them, I felt an alteration of my disposition [37].

This was said in the year 61 A.D. by the Roman writer Seneca in referring to the then capital of the western world. Thus it can be seen that man has worried about the cause and effects of pollution for many centuries, but perhaps of more significance is the fact that man has continued to pollute the air and the water for as long as he has worried about it. Over these many centuries there have been numerous misconceptions regarding the real effect of different types of pollution. The inability of man to measure accurately the long-range effects of pollution has added to the uncertainty in dealing with the problem.

Although some forms of pollution are rather ancient, as man's technology becomes more complex, new pollutants are coming into existence. One of the most recent forms of pollution which has come to man's attention is thermal pollution.

Projected Output of Electric Power Production

Thermal pollution, or the process by which heat is added to water as a result of the end of an industrial cooling cycle, is a common occurrence in power production and some other industries. Industrial cooling waters are considered to be the major contributors to thermal pollution. In particular, cooling waters from thermal power plants are at present the prime source of this new pollutant. However, it should be pointed out that thermal pollution can take place in a variety of ways. The presence of a dam, the depletion of streams, and discharges from industrial processes and municipal effluents with modified temperature characteristics are also sources of thermal pollution [29:119].

This chapter concentrates on thermal pollution as a result of power production. *Resources in America's Future* summarizes and projects the expected use of electricity in the years to come [36:837, A 15-1]. Since the production of electricity is the main cause of thermal pollution, it is of interest to establish future requirements. In this way some judgment concerning the future magnitude of the problem is possible. The projections in *Resources in America's Future* show total power generation required increasing from 845 billion kilowatt-hours in 1960 to 4711 billion kilowatt-hours in the year 2000, see Table 5-1.

Table 5.1

Projected Consumption of Electricity
(billion KWH)[a]

		1960	1970	1980	1990	2000
	L		287	428	541	677
Residential	193 M		353	594	843	1188
	H		492	857	1300	1961
	L		170	254	340	467
Commercial	113 M		190	308	416	554
	H		243	387	501	624
Industrial	L		86	103	125	162
(Iron, Steel,	76 M		111	160	224	324
Non–ferrous metals)	H		153	261	398	654
	L		45	64	82	105
Non–Industrial	32 M		49	75	99	128
	H		60	92	121	155
	L		339	500	720	1001
Manufacturing	221 M		388	635	1011	1599
	H		442	842	1551	2771
	L		20	26	32	39
Mining	16 M		24	33	46	61
	H		28	44	68	108

Table 5.1 (*continued*)

		1960	1970	1980	1990	2000
Atomic Energy		L	60	60	60	60
Commission		60 M	60	60	60	60
Installations		H	68	75	83	90
		L	70	115	171	251
Others		42 M	82	149	243	391
		H	104	205	362	636
		L	120	156	184	212
Losses		92 M	143	215	294	406
		H	190	325	498	768
		L	1197	1706	2255	2974
Total Generation		845 M	1400	2229	3237	4711
Required		H	1780	3088	4882	7767

Source: *Resources in America's Future*, p. 837, Table A 15-1.

[a]L = low; M = Medium; H = High.

The RFF projections were made on the basis of 1960 data and it is now possible to compare the projections with actual results. This is clearly a desirable step if we are to draw valid inferences concerning the future magnitude of the thermal pollution from projections of the consumption of electricity. A comparison of data reflecting the medium RFF projections of electricity consumption with actual consumption for recent years suggests that RFF underestimated the rate of increase slightly. However, the RFF projections are certainly within the appropriate range when both the medium and high projections are considered in the comparison. Also these projections of total production appear to be realistic when compared with other projections from the Edison Electric Institute [38:10, 31-33].

Adequacy of Natural Resources Required

Different types of fuel are consumed to produce electricity. One obvious requirement in order to gauge the validity of the projections in *Resources in America's Future* is to determine whether or not there are sufficient natural resources available to produce the electric power which will be produced. The present projections by type of fuel for total power production requirements are presented in Table 5-2.

There are basically four sources of energy for power production. Projections of the availability of these sources have included assumptions regarding the level of technology for extraction. *Resources in America's Future* has established the supply of gas and coal to be adequate unless a very pessimistic outlook is taken. The adequacy of oil supply presents an interesting problem since oil is a nonrenewable resource. Nevertheless, the adequacy of future oil supplies is also a highly probable assumption if the availability of oil is considered from the United States as well as the Middle East and Venezuela.

The adequacy of supplies of nuclear fuels is directly proportional to the supply of fissionable materials. However, future development of reactor technology is a more important factor than the level of reserves.

Technological Basis for External Effects

It has been found that the discharge of large amounts of heated water may have detrimental effects on aquatic life. The harmful effects may result from either one or both of the following set of circumstances. Heated water added to a body of water may result in the raising of ambient water temperatures and thus throw off balance the critical equilibrium of animal and vegetable life. The other possibility is that added heat may induce the growth of algae and other plants. The subsequent consumption of oxygen by vegetable growth would leave less of it available for fish and other animal life of a lower species which fish use as part of their diets. There is no doubt that the aquatic environment, when subject to disturbances of continuous extraction of large amounts of cold water in the initial state of the input cycle and large additions of heated water at the end of the discharge cycle, could suffer damaging transformations. Especially, it should be kept in mind that these disturbances take place not over minutes or hours, but over many days and years.

Table 5.2

Power Production by Type of Fuel
(billion kwh)[a]

		1970	1980	1990	2000
Gas-based	L	279	313	315	304
	M	335	402	411	429
	H	445	578	691	863
Oil-based	L	59	60	66	69
	M	70	77	86	97
	H	93	111	144	196
Coal-based	L	592	830	932	1008
	M	712	1067	1217	1422
	H	944	1535	2044	2865
Nuclear	L	20	220	620	1230
	M	35	400	1200	2400
	H	50	580	1680	3480
Hydro	L	NA	NA	NA	NA
	M	248	283	323	363
	H	NA	NA	NA	NA

Source: *Resources in America's Future*, p. 844, Table A15-10.

[a]L = Low; M = Medium; H = High; NA = Not Available.

There is little doubt that the entire question of thermal pollution is one that is being watched closely. In hearings held by the Subcommittee on Air and Water Pollution in August 1967, Udall, Secretary of the Interior, said:

... the electric power needs in this country are growing so rapidly that we are going to get most of this power from thermal plants, coal plants, nuclear plants, and so on. This is going to create a tremendous problem in terms of water quality and what we call thermal pollution [25:505].

✳The main concern in thermal pollution is that water will be heated through hot water discharges to the point where the heat can have detrimental effects. Pure water reaches its maximum density at $4°C$ ($39.2°F$) and it becomes lighter as it is heated or cooled.

To appreciate the effects of thermal pollution it is necessary to understand the manner in which physical factors exert effects that are interrelated in the overall ecology of water. This has been described by scientists of the Department of the Interior [22, 11-16]. The weather seasons induce cycles of a physical and chemical nature which are conditioned by temperature. Only during a few days in the spring is the temperature of a body of water uniform from top to bottom. It is during this period that it becomes possible for the wind to mix the water completely, circulating oxygen and nutrients from all layers. As the water begins to warm up with the advance of summer, circulation from top to bottom quickly stops as the vertical density of the body of water becomes non-homogeneous. As the water gets lighter it rests on top of the heavier and colder water [22:11-12].

In natural deep bodies of water, such as lakes and ponds, the difference in vertical density eventually creates three layers of water. These layers are known as the upper layer or epilimnion, the middle layer or thermocline, and the lower layer or hypolimnion. The epilimnion is the most freely flowing layer of water and its temperature is uniform throughout its depth which could vary from 10 feet or less in shallow lakes to 40 feet or more in deep bodies of water. The middle layer, or thermocline, exhibits rapidly changing temperatures which decrease $1.8°F$ for each 3.28 feet increase in depth. The hypolimnion is the coldest region. It has uniform temperature, does not circulate with the upper waters and, therefore, receives no oxygen from the atmosphere during stratification.

When autumn begins, the water cools, the epilimnion increases in depth until the vertical density of the water becomes once again uniform. Again complete mixing begins. The occurrence of this circulation will vary from region to region, but it should occur between September and December.

Circulation stops some time during these months until the following spring and during this time either one of two things occurs: (a) the body of water freezes over, or (b) changes in density reestablish the stratification that had existed after summer set in. From the end of November until the following spring only the epilimnion has any direct contact with the air.

Thermal stratification takes many different forms depending on the climatological conditions, location, depth of the body of water, and volume of water. For example, in places where the surface winds are moderate, stratification could mean a gradient of 5°F to 10°F from top to bottom. If man-built reservoirs or underground springs feed other bodies of water, the colder water carried by the springs which comes into the reservoir at a low level could create a thermocline below the water surface. It can be seen that a rather delicate equilibrium exists in the temperature of bodies of water, and the physical factors which may affect the temperature are various and numerous. If water is taken out from the body of water, any one of the following factors could define the effect of the withdrawal: (1) volume of water withdrawn in relation to mean stream flow; (2) surface area of withdrawn water; (3) depth of water; (4) orientation with prevailing wind direction; (5) shading; (6) elevation; (7) temperature of inflow water in relation to temperature of impounded water; or (8) downstream flow rates during the critical temperature period.

The manifestations of thermal pollution in rivers and streams, although similar to that in lakes and ponds, does have its own characteristics. The main difference between these types of bodies of water is that every stream has a definite flow downstream. One simple way to analyze the effect of temperature in rivers and streams is to consider the area affected by the discharge as a triangular area whose apex is the point where the discharge enters the river. Normally, the water discharged will spread over the surface of the river because of the flow and leave the bottom rather unaffected. The length of the triangular area which will be affected by the heated waters will depend on the flow of the river as compared to the flow of heated water into the river, the mixing effects of rapids, the configuration of the river bottom and jetties, the width of the river, the velocity of the river, and, obviously, the normal temperature of the river and discharge [24:67]. It appears that generally the danger of thermal pollution in streams and rivers is lessened by the fact that water flows at a more or less rapid rate.

No one factor which results in established effects on water temperature can be singled out as more important than another. The effect would all depend on the particular set of circumstances prevailing at each location. Therefore, one conclusion which can be reached is that man has the ability to upset the thermal equilibrium of lakes, ponds, streams, and rivers by discharging or withdrawing large volumes of water, but nature is still the most complicated factor to be accounted for in determining the overall effect on the body of water. Nature's varied conditions from geographical location to geographical location will determine the thermal variations which will take place in a body of water. Because bodies of water differ from season to season the criteria for thermal pollution must vary correspondingly.

Although it is difficult to determine exactly the discharge temperature of water from power plants, a range of 55°F to 75°F appears to be reasonable. Also, it has been established that, due to the inefficiencies of the cooling or condensing process, the overall effect of using water from a steam or lake is that the temperature of the water discharged is $20°F$ warmer than the water at the intake point [29]. For example, water taken in at $50°F$ will be discharged at approximately $70°F$.

The National Technical Advisory Committee on Water Quality Criteria issued an Interim Report in June 1967, in which it issued specific thermal criteria for rivers, lakes, and coastal water for a variety of fish species. The criteria were in the form of limits of temperature rise and maximum allowable temperatures. The Committee recommended a limit on temperature rise of $5°F$ for rivers and streams and $3°F$ in the epilimnion of lakes. The increase is based on the monthly average of the maximum daily temperature. The Committee further advised that heated effluents should not be discharged into the hypolimnion of lakes nor water pumped from it. Perhaps the most significant recommendations made by the Committee referred to maximum temperatures which should not be exceeded for various species of fish. The practical importance of thermal pollution has been increased by the desire for outdoor recreation associated with the rise in the standard of living of the country.

Finally, the Committee set guidelines for marine and coastal waters. Instead of setting maximum permissible temperatures it recommends that discharge of water should not raise the monthly average of the daily maximum temperatures by more than $4°F$ during the fall, winter, and spring; and not more than $1.5°F$ during the summer. The Committee further recommended that no external cause other than natural phenomena should raise water temperature in excess of $1°F$ per hour.

In addition to the effect on fish life, there are biological problems associated with thermal additions to the aquatic environment. These effects range from directly lethal effects of temperature on individual organisms to subtle behavioral and metabolic problems [39:1047]. Heated discharges may also have an effect on the foodchain relationships. Plant life is the base food for all aquatic organisms. Plants are eaten by crustaceans, snails, and by some fish which in time become food for larger fish. Plants and algae consume oxygen from the water during hours of darkness, but since they discharge oxygen during the daylight hours, the net effect is the addition of a considerable amount of oxygen to the water in every twenty-four hour period [8:67].

The heat which is added to the water by thermal discharges accelerates tremendously the growth of vegetable life and algae. This additional growth will occur at the upper layers and eventually make it more difficult for oxygen to filter down to the lower levels of the body of water. The growth of algae and plants in the epilimnion results in the accumulation of organic matter which settles down into the hypolimnion. The decomposition of this matter has the effect of reducing the total oxygen available for animal life in the deep waters. Moreover, the addition of warm water to the epilimnion could prolong the period of stratification and thereby shorten the vital mixing period which restores oxygen to the hypolimnion [18:5]. Thus it can be seen that heated discharges can have long-term genetic effects.

Table 5.3

**Maximum Temperatures Recommend-
ed as Compatible with the Well–Being
of Various Species of Fish and Their
Associated Biota**

93 F: Growth of catfish, gar, white or yellow bass, spotted bass, buffalo, carp-sucker, threadfin shad, and gizzard shad.

90 F: Growth of largemouth bass, drum, bluegill, and crappie.

84 F: Growth of pike, perch, walleye, smallmouth bass and sauger.

80 F: Spawning and egg development of catfish, buffalo, threadfin shad, and gizzard shad.

75 F: Spawning and egg development of largemouth bass, white, yellow, and spotted bass.

68 F: Growth or migration routes of salmonids and for egg development of perch and smallmouth bass.

55 F: Spawning and egg development of salmon and trout (other than lake trout).

48 F: Spawning and egg development of lake trout, walleye, northern pike, sauger, and Atlantic salmon.

Source: U. S. Department of the Interior, National Technical Advisory Committee on Water Quality Criteria. *Interim Report.* Washington, D. C.: U. S. Government Printing Office (June, 1967).

One of the points which needs emphasis is that the discharge temperatures are not as important as the amount of heat discharged. This amount of heat is best measured in BTU per hour. The net heat rate is the amount of heat exchanged and is the main concern regarding nuclear power plants. This is because the process by which steam is condensed and heat removed is less efficient in nuclear power plants than in the more conventional fossil units. The net heat rate of nuclear plants in operation in 1965 had an average of 29 percent thermal efficiency, and the average for all fossil fueled plants was 32.6 percent. Although some of the more recently built fossil power plants have an efficiency of 39 percent. more than 6 percent above the industrial average, it is not expected that the efficiency of nuclear plants will be increased much beyond the present industry average [29:15].

The possibility of thermal pollution in the waterways has attracted attention as a result of the increased demand for power in the last decade. The present tendency is to plan and construct larger power plants which will have greater cooling water requirements. The complex economics of power plant building and the increasing demand for electricity make the construction of power plants of large capacity necessary and attractive.

A Projection of Social Costs

Despite the tremendous use of water in thermal power generation, the most interesting aspect of the phenomenon is that the water is not actually consumed. With the exception of a very small percentage of the water which evaporates in the cooling process, the rest of the water is in most cases returned to the very same environment from which it originally came. This simple phenomena is the root of the problem at hand. After the condensing process, when the water is returned to its source, it carries with it large amounts of heat. Whether or not there is a threat of thermally polluting the body of water to which the discharge is being made depends on many factors [38:31].

It is apparent that power plants will tend to be concentrated in those areas with large concentrations of population. Therefore, it is not surprising to note that over 50 percent of the existing and proposed nuclear power plants in the United States are concentrated in the Northeast and Great Lakes region. Since the biggest factor in thermal pollution in the years to come will be the construction of nuclear power plants, particular attention should be paid to those areas of the country in which the largest concentration of nuclear power plants is expected [25:202-203].

Two prime factors have been established as being of importance in considering the projected social costs resulting from the anticipated output of electrical power generation, namely, the type of body of water from and to which the heated discharges flow, and in a more broad sense, the region or part of the country where these discharges appear to be concentrated [38:31].

To develop an estimate of the effects of water requirements and the effects of its discharges of future thermal power plants, the following must be identified and analyzed:

(a) power plants in which the water is taken from and returned to a river;
(b) power plants in which the water is taken from and returned to a natural pond or lake;
(c) power plants in which water is partially taken from and returned to an artificial pond or lake; and
(d) power plants in which salt or brackish water is taken from and returned to coastal water and estuaries [38:31].

In all the situations considered above, the one item in common is that the water is discharged completely unchanged except for the increase in temperature. Although the water circulated through a power plant is directly dependent on the number of hours of operation, regardless of the source of the water, the quantity of water is a function of the thermal efficiency of the plant and the change in temperature from water inlet to output. Thermal efficiency is a design criterion which determines the amount of heat rejected to the condenser. When several power plants are located along the same river the water is from the same source and the effects are likely to be compounded.

In the case in which water is being drawn from and returned to artificial ponds, it is possible to analyze the amount of heat being dissipated and the amount of heat being returned to the environment. In the case in which water is being drawn from a natural river it is a little more difficult to determine the amount of heat being returned to the river since it would depend on the volume of the river, variations in streamflow, and the average stream temperature. The other case in which thermal plants use cooling water from coastal and estuary sources apparently does not present as serious a problem.

The Federal Power Commission has divided the country into eight geographical regions by which it makes its forecasts and keeps historical data and records.' Northeast; East Central; Southeast; North Central; South Central; West Central; Northwest; and Southwest.

In order to discuss further the possible social costs which may result, it will be necessary to investigate the forecast of power generation for each one of the regions, with focus on the Northeast and East Central regions. Tables 5-4 and 5-5 summarize the forecasted power production by region and the associated water consumption required for power production, as well as the type of body of water from which it is taken and to which it is discharged. Table 5-4 shows actual FPC forecasts and Table 5-5 represents a straight line extrapolation based on Table 5-4.

Two things are apparent from the previous tables. If the projections of the Federal Power Commission are correct, most of the cooling water for future use in 1970 and 1980 will be coming from rivers and coastal waters. Fortunately, although potentials of thermal pollution exist in the coastal waters and rivers, they are less serious and relatively easier to handle than similar threats to lakes and ponds. At present, heated discharges do not pose a very serious problem for coastal waters, and on the other hand, the flow of the rivers makes the problem of pollution a less serious one since a lot of the discharges stay at the surface and are dissipated. The problem of thermal discharges in rivers is easy to control by means of river flow management. Gates are constructed upstream and are opened or closed to increase or decrease correspondingly the flow of the river at times when it is required because of the discharges.

It can also be seen that the Northeast and East Central regions, with the greatest concentration of population and industry, have a relatively heavy demand not only for electric energy but also for cooling water, especially from sea water and rivers, respectively. Since it has been recognized from the start

Table 5.4

Projected Energy Requirements from Thermal Plants and Associated Cooling Water Requirements by Regions and Source – 1970 and 1980

Regions	Energy Reqmnts. (Billion KWH)	Rivers	Lakes	Cooling Water Circulated in Thermal Plants (billion gallons of water circulated per year)			Total
				Sea and Brackish Water	Cooling Towers	Reservoirs	
1970							
Northeast	268	4179	578	6951	370	33	12111
East Central	267	8701	3761	- -	403	- -	12865
Southeast	310	4019	312	4560	76	378	9345
North Central	152	4506	1762	- -	288	160	6816
South Central	197	2067	1620	2146	3694	1563	11090
West Central	35	242	135	- -	274	51	702
Northwest	109	28	- -	- -	211	- -	239
Southwest	142	- -	- -	2798	1319	- -	4117
Total	1481	23842	8168	16455	6635	2185	57285
1980							
Northeast	459	6659	1218	11466	604	33	19980
East Central	494	14206	7378	- -	786	- -	22370
Southeast	612	7976	1408	6756	1128	692	17960
North Central	277	8053	2696	- -	433	460	11642
South Central	440	4888	2384	4358	8586	3657	23873
West Central	72	406	176	- -	861	51	1494
Northwest	193	391	- -	- -	574	- -	965
Southwest	248	176	- -	5345	2514	- -	8125
Total	2795	42755	15260	28015	15486	4893	106409

Source: United States Senate, *Water Resources Activities in the United States*; Select Committee on National Water Resources, 86th Cong., 2nd sess., pursuant to S. Res 48, 1960, pp. 10 and 32.

Table 5.5

Projected Energy Requirements from Thermal Plants and Associated Cooling Water Requirements by Regions and Source – 1990 and 2000

| Regions | Energy Reqmnts. (Billion KWH) | Cooling Water Circulated in Thermal Plants (billion gallons of water ciruclated per year) | | | | | |
		Rivers	Lakes	Sea and Brackish Water	Cooling Towers	Reser- voirs	Total
				1990			
Northeast	640	9139	1858	15981	838	33	27849
East Central	721	19711	10995	- -	1169	- -	31875
Southeast	914	11833	2504	8952	2180	1006	26575
North Central	402	11500	3630	- -	578	760	16468
South Central	683	7709	3148	6570	13478	5751	36656
West Central	119	570	217	- -	1448	51	2286
Northwest	277	754	- -	- -	937	- -	1691
Southwest	354	176	- -	8072	3709	- -	12133
Total	4109	61668	22352	29575	24337	7601	155533
				2000			
Northeast	831	11619	2498	20496	1072	33	35718
East Central	948	25216	14612	- -	1552	- -	41380
Southeast	1216	15690	3600	11148	3232	1320	35190
North Central	527	14947	4564	- -	723	1060	21294
South Central	926	10530	3912	8782	18370	7845	49439
West Central	166	734	258	- -	2035	51	3078
Northwest	361	1117	- -	- -	1300	- -	2417
Southwest	460	176	- -	11409	4904	- -	16141
Total	5424	80581	29444	51135	33188	10309	204657

Source: The above figures represent a straight–line extrapolation based on Table 5.4. The same growth forecasted to take place between 1970 and 1980 is also assumed between 1980 and 1990 as well as between 1990 and 2000.

that the problems of thermal pollution cross state lines, it would be of interest to see how the forecasts of Tables 5-4 and 5-5, regarding the water requirements by region, would compare with a similar breakdown by natural drainage areas.

The breakdown by drainage areas gives a good idea of which bodies of water in a broad sense will carry the burden of supplying the cooling water for future power generation. Of particular interest are the discharges into the North Atlantic, Upper and Lower Hudson and Coastal Area, Delaware, Ohio, and the Great Lakes since these are the main drainage areas for the Northeastern and Great Lakes region.

One of the questions which often arises in the discussion of social costs of thermal pollution is how much heat is required to raise the temperature of a body of water $1°F$; that is, how much will the temperature of a body of water be raised for every kilowatt-hour of electricity generated. The answer to these questions are rather complex since it depends not only on the heat dissipated by the generation of electric power but also on the size of the body of water the discharge goes into, the velocity of the flow of water, ambient temperatures, and other factors. According to present estimates, 50 percent of the new power plants to be constructed will use nuclear fuel. The thermal efficiency of 29 percent of nuclear power plants represents a net heat rate for power plants in operation in 1965 of 11,680 Btu per kilowatt-hour compared to 8700 for conventional plants [29:123].

Since a kilowatt-hour of electricity is equivalent to 3413 Btu of energy, that means that 8267 (11680-3413) Btu of energy are wasted for every kilowatt-hour of electricity produced by nuclear energy compared to 5287 (8700-3413) Btu for every kilowatt-hour produced by conventional methods [29:121].

It is difficult to forecast the social costs of dealing with thermal pollution more than a few years in advance because of the uncertainty as to the type and construction of power plants. However the Federal Water Pollution Control Administration estimates that to reduce the effects of thermal pollution associated with power production from 1969 to 1973 to acceptable levels would require an investment of 1206 million in 1968 dollars. Since the largest rise in power production and especially in that portion generated by nuclear fuels is foreseen for the period after 1973, it is evident that the program to combat thermal pollution will be costly indeed.

Forces Tending to Offset Thermal Pollution

The potential for thermal pollution varies from location to location and, of course, the problem also varies in magnitude. On the other hand, the ability of nature to adapt to changing conditions should neither be underestimated nor overemphasized. If utilities are going to accept the challenge of social responsibility created by problems of pollution, a great deal of imaginative work will be required.

In the instance of a small nuclear plant built in Rowe, Massachusetts, hot water discharges flow back to a cold lake which flows into the Deerfield River.

Table 5.6

Cooling Water Requirements by Drainage Area 1970 and 1980

Drainage Area	Rivers	Lakes	Cooling Water Circulated in Thermal Plants (billion gallons of water circulated per year)			Total
			Sea and Brackish Water	Cooling Towers	Reservoirs	
			1970			
North Atlantic	440	- -	1643	43	- -	2126
Upper Hudson	488	- -	- -	- -	- -	488
Lower Hudson & Coastal Area	- -	- -	3623	- -	- -	3623
Delaware	2135	- -	461	33	13	2642
Chesapeake	895	- -	1452	164	126	2637
Southeast	3890	312	4332	76	214	8824
Tennessee– Cumberland	- -	- -	- -	141	58	199
Ohio	8898	- -	- -	408	- -	9306
Eastern Gt. Lks– St. Lawre.	224	3200	- -	- -	- -	3424
Western Great Lakes	111	2668	- -	15	- -	2794
Missouri–Hudson Bay	734	244	- -	528	42	1548
Upper Mississippi	3980	96	- -	201	160	4437
Lower Mississippi	1562	- -	308	157	148	2175
Arkansas–White– Red	454	528	- -	1227	185	2394
Western Gulf	- -	1120	1838	2112	1230	6300
Colorado	23	- -	- -	945	9	977
Great Basin	5	- -	- -	145	- -	150
Pacific Northwest	3	- -	- -	- -	- -	3
South Pacific	- -	- -	2798	440	- -	3238
Total	23842	8168	16455	6635	2185	57285

(continued)

Table 5.6 (*continued*)

| | | Cooling Water Circulated in Thermal Plants (billion gallons of water circulated per year) | | | | |
Drainage Area	Rivers	Lakes	Sea and Brackish Water	Cooling Towers	Reservoirs	Total
			1980			
North Atlantic	541	- -	2869	16	- -	3426
Upper Hudson	826	- -	- -	- -	- -	826
Lower Hudson & Coastal Area	- -	- -	5466	- -	- -	5466
Delaware	2881	- -	1148	30	13	4072
Chesapeake	1998	- -	2295	427	126	4846
Southeast	7249	1408	6444	1046	497	16644
Tennessee–Cumberland	- -	- -	- -	127	89	216
Ohio	14890	118	- -	827	- -	15835
Eastern Gt. Lks.–St. Lawre.	607	6169	- -	- -	- -	6776
Western Great Lakes	82	4753	- -	70	- -	4905
Missouri–Hudson Bay	1840	244	- -	1229	43	3356
Upper Mississippi	6623	115	- -	357	460	7555
Lower Mississippi	3751	- -	686	158	133	4728
Arkansas–White–Red	897	981	- -	2734	783	5395
Western Gulf	- -	1472	3672	5153	2740	13037
Colorado	199	- -	- -	2319	9	2527
Great Basin	5	- -	- -	508	- -	513
Pacific Northwest	366	- -	- -	- -	- -	366
South Pacific	- -	- -	5435	485	- -	5920
Total	42755	15260	28015	15486	4893	106409

Source: United States Senate, *Water Resources Activities in the United States*, p. 32.

Table 5.7

Cooling Water Requirements by Drainage Area 1990 and 2000

Drainage Area	Cooling Water Circulated in Thermal Plants (billion gallons of water circulated per year)					
	Rivers	Lakes	Sea and Brackish Water	Cooling Towers	Reservoirs	Total
			1990			
North Atlantic	642	– –	4095	27	– –	4726
Upper Hudson	1164	– –	– –	– –	– –	1164
Lower Hudson & Coastal Area	– –	– –	7309	– –	– –	7309
Delaware	3627	– –	1835	27	13	5509
Chesapeake	3101	– –	3138	690	126	7055
Southeast	10608	2494	8556	2016	780	24464
Tennessee–Cumberland	– –	– –	– –	113	120	233
Ohio	20882	336	– –	1246	– –	22364
Eastern Gt. Lks.-St. Lawre.	990	9128	– –	– –	– –	10128
Western Great Lakes	53	6838	– –	125	– –	7016
Missouri–Hudson Bay	2746	244	– –	1930	44	5164
Upper Mississippi	9266	134	– –	513	760	10673
Lower Mississippi	5940	– –	1064	159	118	7281
Arkansas–White–Red	1340	1434	– –	4241	1381	8396
Western Gulf	1824	6505	8194	– –	4250	19774
Colorado	365	– –	– –	3693	9	4077
Great Basin	5	– –	– –	871	– –	3876
Pacific Northwest	729	– –	– –	– –	– –	729
South Pacific	– –	– –	8072	530	– –	8602
Total	61668	22352	39575	25337	7601	155533

(continued)

Table 5.7 (*continued*)

| | Cooling Water Circulated in Thermal Plants (billion gallons of water circulated per year) | | | | | |
Drainage Area	Rivers	Lakes	Sea and Brackish Water	Cooling Towers	Reservoirs	Total
			2000			
North Atlantic	743	--	5321	11	--	6026
Upper Hudson	1502	--	--	--	--	1502
Lower Hudson & Coastal Area	--	--	9143	--	--	9143
Delaware	4373	--	2522	24	13	6939
Chesapeake	4204	--	3981	953	126	9264
Southeast	13967	3585	10660	2986	1063	33284
Tennessee–Cumberland	--	--	--	99	151	250
Ohio	26875	454	--	1665	--	28893
Eastern Gt. Lks–St. Lawre.	1373	12097	--	--	--	13480
Western Great Lakes	24	8923	--	180	--	9127
Missouri–Hudson Bay	3652	244	--	2639	45	6972
Upper Mississippi	11909	153	--	669	1060	13791
Lower Mississippi	8129	--	1442	160	103	9834
Arkansas–White–Red	1783	1887	--	5748	1979	11397
Western Gulf	--	2176	9340	11235	5760	26511
Colorado	541	--	--	5067	9	5627
Great Basin	5	--	--	1234	--	1239
Pacific Northwest	1092	--	--	--	--	1092
South Pacific	--	--	10709	575	--	11284
Total	80581	29444	51135	33188	10309	204657

Source: The above figures represent a straight-line extrapolation based on Table 5.6.

The dilution of the discharge is so substantial that it creates no thermal pollution problem. In other instances, although local standards are being set, problems do arise. An example is a plant located on the Columbia River in Richland, Washington. The temperature of the river has been raised slightly by the heated discharges. Some states, such as Oregon, have set guidelines of a maximum temperature of $69°$ F and $2°$ maximum increase at any time. Still, however, the greatest complications arise in those cases where interstate waters are involved. For example, there is a nuclear plant being constructed in Vernon, Vermont, on the banks of the Connecticut River, using water from that river. The Connecticut between Vermont and New Hampshire flows through Massachusetts into Connecticut, ending in the Long Island Sound. Although the standards of the states through which it flows do not differ significantly, the fact is that the plant is potentially subject to regulation by four states and the federal government.

Many states would like to see either the Atomic Energy Commission take care of the problem or be forced to consult with the states' Water Resources Council before issuing licenses. Utilities cannot build nuclear power plants without approval of the Atomic Energy Commission. However, the Atomic Energy Commission has claimed that it has no jurisdiction over heated discharges, and their effects unless such authority is given by Congress. The Federal Power Commission has been suggested by others as a possible regulatory agency in this matter, but this solution would also create difficulties [18:3].

The problem of proper enforcement of thermal pollution discharge standards is at present still an unsettled matter. In July 1966, President Lyndon Johnson signed Executive Order 11288 on Prevention, Control, and Abatement of Water Pollution by Federal Activities and in Section 4 of this order, put forth most of the present regulations on thermal pollution at the federal level. Under part B of Section 4 it says:

If discharge of cooling waters is expected to create problems by significantly increasing the temperature of the receiving waters, facilities shall be installed, or operating procedures shall be established, to maintain water temperatures within acceptable limits.

The ambiguity of the terminology clearly indicates the magnitude of the jurisdictional problems when dealing with interstate waters. The term *interstate waters* is defined to refer to all rivers, lakes, and other waters that flow across or form a part of state boundaries, including coastal waters [40:22].

Standards are varied in nature from one state to another. They are both general and flexible. In Vermont, standards are based on a sliding scale of temperatures, whereas in Pennsylvania, the Advisory Committee on Control of Stream Temperatures passed a regulation which said:

The heat content of discharges shall be limited to an amount that could not raise the temperature of the entire stream at the point of discharge above $93°$ F, assuming complete mixing [21:78].

When the Water Quality Act of 1965 was enacted, it gave the states three years in which to establish their own water quality standards. The deadline was

June 30, 1967. To date only 37 states have received federal approval, although standards from other states are presently being received. The purpose of federal standards is to accelerate control efforts which are badly needed, not so much for thermal pollution but for other types of water pollution problems. The Federal Water Pollution Control Administration (FWPCA) was created by the Department of the Interior for the purpose of coordinating water pollution control efforts with the states. Under the law, the states are given an opportunity to set their own standards. However, the effort has been a joint state-federal one from the start. One of the main objectives of the FWPCA has been to establish a review process by which standards submitted by the states can be properly evaluated using all available information. Another purpose of the FWPCA has been to avoid lengthy delays which could result if the standards of a state were turned down because they were not appropriate in every respect.

The standards approved up to this point, apart from a few basic parameters such as temperature, oxygen, and pH are primarily of a qualitative nature. This ambiguity is chiefly a result of the tremendous range of pollutants which can affect the water quality requirements. The National Technical Advisory Committee points out that the unknowns in this field far outweigh the knowns [10:1601-1603].

The FWPCA has been instrumental in bringing the problem of thermal pollution to the surface. For example, it has begun a study in the Columbia basin to gain knowledge to aid in the proper identification of heat sources and management of river flow programs. Once standards are arrived at in the remaining 13 states, it might be possible to implement federal programs which at the very least would identify the type of research required to find some of the answers which are being sought by government and industry [10:1605].

In cases where the thermal pollution problem has already become apparent and attempts are being made to deal with it, the use of cooling ponds and towers seems to be the best solution, although they in turn create problems of their own. Also, presently, the utilization of infrared detecting devices is being brought into focus.

The simplest way to deal with heated discharges is to build large artificial ponds or reservoirs in which the water is allowed to cool by transferring its heat to the air before returning to the power plant or to the body of water from which it came. It has been estimated that approximately one acre of reservoir surface 10 to 60 feet deep is required to provide adequate cooling for 1,000 kw of generating capacity. The cost of building such a reservoir is approximately $2.5 per kilowatt. The cost of building artificial reservoirs is low when compared with the cost of other methods [24:48-49]. Nevertheless, it is a slow process which requires additional land and which may not always be feasible.

The building of cooling towers is done in order to accelerate the cooling process. Cooling towers may be classified primarily into two types, namely, the wet and the dry. A wet type or open cycle cooling tower is one in which the air and water come into direct contact. The dry or closed cycle tower is one in which the cooling air comes in contact with the water indirectly through heat exchangers. Each one of these types of cooling towers can be subdivided further into natural draft and mechanical draft towers [24:51].

In the natural draft wet type water is sprayed into a lattice network and thus broken into droplets through which air circulates and transfers heat. The natural draft dry type is less efficient than the wet type. In the natural draft dry type, cooled water from the tower is introduced into a direct-contact jet condenser where the water picks up heat and then returns to the tower for cooling. The towers are very bulky and likely to be unsightly. For example, the first tower to be built in the United States was 320 feet high and 245 feet in diameter at the base and was capable of cooling 120,000 gallons per minute. The mechanical draft type towers are similar to the natural draft towers in every respect except that fans are used to induce the drafts [24:54].

Although the cooling towers help alleviate the problem of thermal pollution and are more effective in reducing discharge temperatures than artificial reservoirs, they are costly in construction and operation. The typical costs for these types of towers are $7.00 per kilowatt for induced draft wet type; $11.00 per kilowatt for natural draft wet type; $25.00 per kilowatt for natural draft dry type; and $27.00 per kilowatt for induced draft dry type [24:54].

It can be seen that cooling towers, as an immediate solution to the problem of thermal pollution, are both costly and unsightly. In addition, due to chemicals which must be used to help in the process, many indirect problems are created. Furthermore, the drift of vapor from large cooling towers could prove to be a nuisance to nearby residents [24:82].

It will aid in dealing with thermal pollution if it proves possible to detect its effects before it reaches alarming levels. Some of the possible methods available for detection or thermal pollution are noted here.

Since the impact of thermal pollution will vary from season to season, being more severe at times when water temperatures are high, there appears to be an effective way of dealing with the problem provided that adequate detection methods are available. The idea is that instead of having to cool the discharge water throughout the entire year, it can be cooled by whatever method is available whenever it is necessary. One possible method which has been attracting some attention is the method of infrared detection. The principle is a simple one, since all bodies emit infrared images provided their temperature is above absolute zero. This type of detection can best be done by airborne devices. The method has already been used to detect heated water discharges and to define their currents and patterns. Specifically, it has been used to map thermal circulation and diffusion patterns at the proposed atomic site at Cayuga Lake in New York and at an existing site along the Connecticut River [19:1].

When utilizing this type of detection it must be kept in mind that thermal sensitivity is dependent upon surface area. The larger is the surface area that is exposed, the greater will be the sensitivity. Therefore, when scanning bodies of water it is possible to detect extremely small thermal differences due to the uniform emissitivity. It has also been found that night flights produce better results than those in the daytime because during the day solar radiation creates problems with shadows and reflections from other bodies [20:2-3].

Studies have been made which show the possibility of making surveys of bodies of water and determining their temperature within $1°$ or $2°C$ rather consistently. Furthermore, it has been found that with precision techniques, accuracies can be established within $0.2°C$ [14:432]. Thus suitable methods of thermal pollution detection may well be available. Their accuracy is certainly most impressive and perhaps this type of infrared detection would be the key to the extent that they relate to the problem of thermal pollution. Detection is the proof of existence and the first step necessary in dealing with thermal pollution as well as any other pollutant.

It is often the case in problems of pollution as well as in other matters that more time and effort is spent discussing and publicizing the bad effects than the good effects. Thermal pollution is perhaps one of the few forms of pollution that may well have beneficial consequences. In moderation and under control heated discharges not only attract fish but also allow them to breed and remain at a given place over the winter months.

Despite the publicity of the damaging effect that thermal pollution could have on fish life, the fact is that historical records of fish kills from 1960 to 1965 show that out of 531 reported fish kills only two can be specifically associated with power production. These two fish kills totaled 620 fish, as compared to 11,393,439 total fish killed by all other types of pollution [30:10].

Shellfish are especially susceptible to damage due to biological pollution. Nevertheless, it has been shown that shellfish which are sensitive to extreme changes in water temperature can benefit from heated discharges, which can be used to control spawning and to lengthen the growing season. It is almost certain that improvements will be achieved by the selection of the best oysters, clams, mussels, and other shellfish and placement in optimal conditions [31:9]. At present, an experiment of this type is taking place at a power plant on Long Island, New York. The sea water is piped into discharge basins at the end of the cooling cycle. The discharge basin is being used as an oyster nursery. After a year of research it was found that the baby oysters could live in the basin during winter or summer as a result of the moderating effect of the heated discharges on the water temperature. Warm sea water is used in the development of young oysters in the hatchery to induce a new oyster generation and then promote vigorous growth during certain early states [41].

Studies at Martin Creek, Delaware, have shown that with the exception of the summer months, the best fishing may be found a short distance downstream from where the discharge canal enters the river [24:68].

This abundance of fish in the area downstream from discharge canals has been observed at many other power plant sites around the country.

It has also been observed that most fish habitate the waters they do by choice. In other words, fish do not subject themselves to an environment in which they would be under physiological stress. Fish do show temperature preferences and will withdraw from waters which are too warm. It is perhaps a bit presumptuous to assume that it is to man's advantage to have fish living in every acre of water. It would seem that a little less moralizing by those concerned with the problem would aid in placing the advantages and disadvantages of thermal pollution in the proper perspective [15:29-30].

A Projection of the Implications of
Thermal Pollution

A desirable conclusion to this discussion would be some measure of the impact that thermal pollution will have in the future. At present, it is not possible to establish clearly whether thermal pollution will have a significant impact in the future or whether it is a serious problem requiring prompt attention. The President of the National Coal Policy Conference, Joseph E. Moody, in testimony before the Senate Subcommittee on Air and Water Pollution on February 3, 1969 cautioned that issuing regulations to stop something without having knowledge of the effects could produce harm as well as good [42:45].

The National Coal Policy Conference engaged the Travelers Research Corporation (T.R.C.) of Hartford, Connecticut, to study and issue a report of its findings on the problems and future implications of thermal pollution. Some of the report's findings were summarized in the *Air/Water Pollution Report* of Feburary 10, 1969:

1) Equipping nation's electric power system with mechanical draft cooling towers, to comply with emerging regulations could range from cumulative 1970-80 total of $2.4-billion to $6.8-billion, depending upon type of controls adopted. These estimates are based upon use of evaporative mechanical draft cooling towers because cost data are available. The lower estimate is based upon the assumption that one-third of new units and one-fourth of existing units will be required to recycle water, an additional one-third of new units will meet abatement requirements at cost of nearly 50% of wet tower recycling costs, and remaining new and existing units will be exempt.

2) Complete recycling costs for fossil-fueled plant would range between 0.3-0.4 mills per kilowatt hour, for comparable size nuclear plants from 0.46-0.70 mills per kwh.

3) Cost of recycling equipment would add 10-14 percent to cost of generating nuclear power and 7-9 percent to fossil fueled plants.

4) Prospective costs of abatement would increase electricity costs to consumers at the most by 1-1/2 to 2 percent.

5) More positive approach to thermal pollution is to put energy in waste heat to work for beneficial purposes, such as shellfish production and in agricultural irrigation. Much more research is needed here [42].

The above findings from the T.R.C. report are primarily for the period 1970 to 1980 and are easily correlated to Tables 5-4 and 5-6. Between 1970 and 1980 the projection of the generation of electricity almost doubles. The actual ratio of 1980 energy requirements to 1970 is 1.9, and referring to Tables 5-5 and 5-7, the corresponding ratios for the years 1990/1980 is 1.5 and for 2000/1990 is 1.3. If the same assumptions made by the T.R.C. report are extended to the decades ending in 1990 and 2000, some conclusions can be reached regarding the cumulative costs. If the low projection is taken, a total expenditure of $6.8 billion will be required, and if the high projections are followed, the expenditures would be $16.3 billion by year 2000. In view of this enormous expense, the power industry should investigate the maximum possible use of waste heat in conjunction with cooling towers for beneficial purposes in cooling lakes and ponds.

Thermal pollution is perhaps one of the few pollutants that man has detected at an early stage. At present, there appears to be no reason for alarm, but a careful and continuing study of its effects on marine life is desirable. In addition, the presence of thermal pollution in the water could result in accelerating the effects of other types of pollutants. This development should not be overlooked. Thermal pollution by itself may cause no alarm, but its interaction with other pollutants could have a different effect. The fast growing rate of power consumption will require a constant surveillance of thermal discharges so that no serious problems are allowed to develop.

The projected concentration of new nuclear power plants in the heavily populated areas of the Eastern and North Central regions could result in thermal pollution being blamed for the effects of other pollutants. The reason for this is that these areas are also highly industrialized areas with great sources of industrial and sewage pollution.

Possible sites for future power plants should be studied to determine the existence of other forms of pollution in the water. The sites should be studied after the power plant has gone into operation to determine to what extent thermal pollution has contributed to accelerating other forms of pollution. Although simple to do, these types of studies will take time, but only through them will the real effect of heated discharges on other pollutants be established.

It appears clear at this point that it is generally agreed that not enough is known about the cause and effect of thermal pollution. On the other hand, warning signs are rather obvious and significant. It is also clear that the knowledge required to deal with the problem, when and if it becomes a problem, is available today. The alternative of having to construct cooling towers although costly is not out of reach. A recent article in *Scientific American* perhaps best summarizes the findings:

Thermal pollution of course, needs to be considered in the context of the many other works of man that threaten the life and richness of our natural waters; the discharges of sewage and chemical wastes, dredging, diking, filling of the wetlands and other interventions that are altering the nature, form and extent of the waters. The effects of any one of these factors might be tolerable, but the cumulative and synergistic action of all of them together seems likely to impoverish our environment drastically.

Fortunately, thermal pollution has not yet reached the level of producing serious general damage; moreover, unlike many other forms of pollution, any excessive heating of the waters could be stopped in short order by appropriate corrective action [43, 26].

The increase in power production and consumption projected by RFF is predicated on a rising level of GNP and personal consumption expenditures. But a rising demand for outdoor recreational facilities is also expected to accompany the ascending GNP. Outdoor recreation facilities may be seriously impaired by water pollution and such impairment is also likely to be most pronounced in the heavily populated Eastern and North Central regions of the country. Since there will be an increasing demand on the part of the public for clean water and research takes a long time, it is not too early for industry to begin taking the necessary steps.

Nuclear Power Production and Problems in the Disposal of Atomic Wastes

Jack Gordon

Introduction

Resources have been exploited and consumed throughout American history with little regard for the disposal of its waste by-products. The expanding nation seemed to have infinite capacity to absorb the trash, the effluent, the waste generated within the production/consumption cycle of industry. We are only recently acquiring an awareness that the capacity of the land to act as a sponge is quite finite, hence the need for courses of action necessary to prevent an inundation.

The harnessing of the atom for the production of energy, or nuclear power, represents one of the more recent producers of manmade waste. The development of atomic radioisotopes was preceded by the knowledge that potentially harmful emissions radiated from these materials. Thus, the need to contain and isolate radioactivity developed concurrently with the development of atomic energy. Radioactive containment is an ordinary part of the nuclear industry, in contrast to the emergency measures invoked in some areas of waste management only when crises are imminent. The learning curve of effective waste and contamination control has been rapid, though painful. Poorly controlled use of radioactive drugs and paints, for example, have resulted in tragic loss of life [42:34-42]. Problem identification, ensuing research, and legislation have all aided in materially reducing unnecessary risk.

The Problem

A rapidly growing nuclear power industry is engaged in the utilization of a family of materials classed as radioisotopes, serving as a source of thermal and radioactive energy. The consumption and production of such sources of energy gives rise to the production of waste that is deleterious to living matter. Thus, the disposition of such pollutant materials must be rendered with great discretion and foresight to insure that

(1) safety to the public domain is maintained;

(2) adequate planning is conducted to provide for the future increases of radioactive matter; and

(3) economic feasibility is sustained to prevent curtailment of a major growing industry.

The current philosophy in handling radioactive wastes has not taken the ideal approach of total isolation from man and his environment. Rather, it has proven feasible to permit very weak concentrations of radionuclides, diluted in large quantities of water to render it harmless, to be dispersed to the environ. Additionally, a smaller quantity of high strength radioactive waste, concentrated and hazardous, is stored for eternity in specially constructed tanks, remotely located and with redundant safeguards to prevent accidental contamination of the site through spillage or leakage.

Standards of Control

The inability of the environment to absorb wastes without causing widespread damage necessitates the controls that will tend to minimize such effects. Pollution by uncontrolled waste dispersion can be harmful to living matter, can reduce the ability of our resources to serve us, and can damage our economic well being. Hence, the importance of the development of uniform, objective, unbiased standards of control that

(a) are attainable;
(b) are reasonable and equitable in cost and responsibility;
(c) do not impede progressive research and development; and
(d) are measurable and enforceable.

To meet such criteria, it is necessary to establish at which points in the production/consumption cycle such standards should be injected.

Atomic Pollution and Factors of Control

The prevention of pollution by uncontrolled disperion of atomic wastes is mandated by federal legislation and implemented through the Atomic Energy Commission, whose authority extends to the licensing and revocation of users and producers of radioactive materials. The degree of control is the result of several decades of research and development to determine the characteristics and long-range effects of radiation exposure. The prevailing approach of the Atomic Energy Commission (AEC), the Federal Radiation Council, and the International Commission on Radiological Protection is one of extraordinary conservatism requiring that exposure to radioactivity in and near nuclear work sites to be less than in a dentist's office.

The emission of particles of matter, and high-frequency rays from radioactive substances can cause deterioration of life cells or genetic mutation. Further, the harm may not be immediately apparent, but it is cumulative and sometimes requires many years to manifest itself. The need for controls to maintain safety and for continuing efforts to seek further improvements is obvious. Expert monitoring teams measure control effectivity by sampling the air, earth, and water for presence of radioactivity in the neighborhood of all nuclear activities [2:14].

Radioactive wastes generated during the production and consumption of fission materials have necessitated the development of safety controls. The outstanding cooperation between AEC and the users who generate the radioactive waste has resulted in close observation of safety and continuing improvement through research. Current production of enriched fuels and its attendant waste management has been well controlled and safe, and there are no foreseeable undue restrictions. Storage sites for waste containment appear to be plentiful; shielding techniques are adequate, with programs developed for 600-year storage periods [3:18-22].

On the basis of several considerations we may hypothesize that the future appears to offer continuing stability:

(a) reservations for waste storage appear adequate beyond the year 2000;

(b) technology is reducing the per unit waste generated in nuclear fuel consumption;

(c) methods of concentrating bulk waste are improving;

(d) higher fuel burning efficiencies are anticipated, with resulting reduction in fuel reprocessing and waste generated. (Current utilization of fuel energy at 50 kilowatt-hours output per gram of uranium is only one percent of theoretical attainment.); and

(e) reactor technology is projected to increasing breeding of fuels during the fission process, resulting in longer fuel burning periods and reduced amount of fuel reprocessing [4:5].

Nuclear Power

Nuclear power plants produce electricity much as conventional fossil-fuel steam plants. The heart of the reactor is the shielded container housing a configuration of radioactive fuel elements. A controlled process of neutron bombardment results in an enormous liberation of heat, used conventionally to boil water into steam. The steam's energy spins a turbine, whose action acts as primemover for an electric generator. The process of nuclear heat liberation leaves an atomic residue that is the major source of radioactive waste.

Quantities of atomic waste are expected to increase with increasing nuclear power generation. Because the cost of nuclear powered electricity appears to be gradually decreasing to below the cost of conventional electricity, extraordinary growth of nuclear power production is projected [44:21]. RFF estimates a rise from 35 to 2400 billion kilowatt-hours from 1970 to 2000 in energy consumption, from nuclear sources in the United States [30:844]. Other sources (see figure 6-3) such as The Long Island Lighting Company anticipate higher preference for the nuclear plant, projecting 85 to 4300 billion kilowatt-hours growth in the same time frame.

Atomic Wastes

The process that converts raw ore to usable uranium fuel involves a lengthy series of physical and chemical conversions utilizing volumes of water that runs to the billions of gallons annually. Due to the low level of radioactivity emitted by the processed ore, much of this liquid effluent is harmless and may be simply diluted and returned to its source river or lake [32:9-28]. Higher levels of radioactive strength, generated in the process of fuel irradiation, may contain thousands of curies per gallon of effluent waste. (The curie is a measure of rate of radioactive disintegration, approximately equal to 370 billion nuclei disintegrations per second, or, the rate of decay of one gram of natural radium.) Highly deleterious to living cells, such wastes cannot be dispersed, but instead are concentrated to sludge to reduce bulk and are stored in shielded, isolated tanks which are buried under many feet of earth and monitored with detection devices for minute leakage. Some wastes have been discharged to deep fissures in the earth several thousand feet deep. This method is discouraged due to the possibility of external leakage to surrounding areas [39:46]. Design criteria for nuclear reactors must consider the remotest possibility of accidental contamination. Failures within the reactor vessel, fuel cladding, or the cooling system are conceivable sources of leakage of radioactivity. A combination of redundant safety controls, continuous surveillance, failsafe controls, and close quality control of component manufacture, combine to reduce the probability of an accident to nearly zero. The licensing procedure and authority vested in the AEC provides reasonable assurance that those permitted to carry on the business of handling and disposing of radioactive substances are competent and qualified [4:24-30].

Sources of Atomic Waste

The predominant source of atomic wastes — and by far the most important for two decades (1942 to 1962) — originated from the production of plutonium-239 for use by the military in the nuclear warheads of atomic bombs. The production reactors at Hanford, Oak Ridge, and Savannah River converted uranium-238 to plutonium-239 with the attendant generation of thousands of tons of waste radioisotopes. The actual quantities of the fissile and waste production are secret for reasons of national security, however, production for military consumption may have accounted for 90 to 99 percent of all nuclear fuel manufacture in the 1940s and 1950s [23:Ch.10]. According to Amphlett, nuclear power plants, to generate one billion kilowatt-hours, required approximately 25 tons of fuel. In 1945, the consumption of nine billion kilowatt-hours, burning 225 tons of fuel, generated some half-million gallons of high-strength waste requiring storage, when the fuel was processed for recoverable uranium-235. By 1965, in excess of 600 million gallons of contained wastes had been accumulated.

The great impetus toward peaceful uses of the atom, gathering momentum since the 1950s, has largely manifested itself in the use of nuclear fuels for electric power production. Electric power consumption, to satisfy the need for energy in home and industry, is currently growing by six percent annually, or doubling in little more than ten years. Although a decrease in rate of growth is forecast by 1980 by RFF due to saturation of use of electrical devices in the home, energy consumption from electricity is expected to rise from 1400 billion kilowatt-hours in 1970 to a range of 5000 to 6000 billion kilowatt-hours by year 2000. See Figure 6-3. Accompanying this growth is the more rapid growth of nuclear power plants as the prime source of electricity, projected to supply more than half the electric energy needs of the nation by 2000, growing from a modest five percent in 1970. Thus, a rise in atomic fuel usage, and therefore, in the generation of high-strength radioactive waste disposal by tank storage may be inappropriate to the future if the quantities of such wastes will change to the extent anticipated.

Intent of Report

It is intended to view and interpret the correlation that may exist between the projected rise in the generation of nuclear waste matter, and the problems attendant on the disposition of the waste. An attempt will be made to determine whether it is feasible to maintain current methodology in the disposal of atomic wastes, or if new techniques must be mandated due to impending problems and undesirable side effects. Attention will be directed at two such considerations: (1) the reduction in both quantity and cost of disposal of the waste; and (2) the consideration of conversion from waste to a valued source of thermal and/or radiological energy.

The production of waste is interrelated to the growth of population, the gross national product and the growth of consumption of electric energy. The increasing generation of atomic wastes is a direct result of the rising dependence upon electricity which, in turn, is closely related to gross national product which appears to be accelerating more rapidly than the population trend. Figure 6-1 suggests this close correlation of electric energy usage being dictated in terms of national wealth, a function of gross national product.

The nuclear reactor, the major source of atomic wastes, is becoming a significant source of electric power, soon to approach the fossil fuel power plant as a major supplier of electricity. The preference for the nuclear electric source is largely a matter of economics, with nuclear technology expected to steadily reduce the cost of generated power to perhaps half the cost of fossil fuel supplied electricity, by 1980 to 1990. In testimony before a senate committee on technology and the human environment, Dr. Seaborg predicted that compared to a current national average of six to seven mills per KWH for electric generation, major nuclear reactors will supply power at four mills per KWH by 1980, and possibly two to three mills per KWH by 1990 (15). The projected result of such advantage is that 50 to 60 percent of all electricity will be furnished from nuclear sources by the end of the century [55]. Mr. Morrison

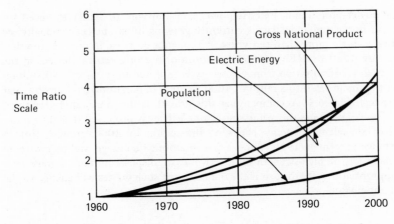

Figure 6-1 Projected Growth of Population, Gross National Product, and Consumption of Electric Energy. Source: Table 6-1.

Table 6.1

Growth and Correlation of Population, Gross National Product, and Consumption of Electric Energy

Parameter	Units	1960	1980	2000
Population	Millions	180	245	331
	Ratio to 1960	1.0	1.36	1.84
Gross National Product	$ Billions	500	1060	2100
	Ratio to 1960	1.0	2.10	4.20
Electric Energy	Quadrillions of BTU's	9	21	37
	Ratio to 1960	1.0	2.20	4.00
The ratio of *Gross National Prod.* to Electric Energy		1.0	0.95	1.05

Source: *Resources in America's Future*, pp 18, 20, 73.

forecasts a medium range projection of electric energy requirements by 2000 of 5,000 billion kilowatt-hours, with nuclear plants contributing 60 percent of the total.

The Correlation of Electricity
and Atomic Power

The relationship between nuclear power generation and the consumption of nuclear fuels provides the basis for estimating the production of atomic wastes (with appropriate factoring for reductions due to improving technology, methods, and reuses for the radioactive by-products). Several forecasts of growth of electric energy consumption (see figure 6-3) fall within the high and medium RFF projections. An average value will be utilized to compute the estimated quantities of nuclear waste accumulated by year 2000. The hypothesis that the nuclear industry can handle adequately the radioactive wastes in the coming decades is believed by the writer to be valid for the highest projection of nuclear electric generation (see figure 6-4).

The Generation of Atomic Waste

The importance of the concept of nuclear fission as a growing source of energy is clearly evidenced by the projected growth of the use of the nuclear reactor (see figure 6-4) for the production of electricity and heat. Additional utilization of radioisotopes for research and development projects, radiological and biological programs, nuclear powered transportation, and so on is also projected by authoritative sources, but is generally based on the use of activation products extracted from the waste generated within the power reactor [32:21-25]. Thus, such usage does not materially add to the production of atomic wastes but rather reallocates its handling and disposal. Quantitatively, the reuse of waste radioisotopes is quite small; according to Mawson, in 1965, it amounted to less than 0.1 percent of the total fission products stored in that year.

The Common Denominator

Atomic wastes arise from all phases of the nuclear fuel cycle. The methods of dealing with waste matter are varied, but are all predicated on two common factors, namely safety and economies.

Safety: The International Commission for Radiological Protection (ICRP) is dedicated to the establishment of safe levels of radioactivity that may exist in

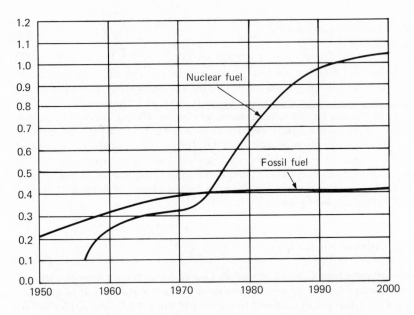

Note: Efficiency is defined, here, as the ratio of output energy over input fuel energy. Coal is the fossil fuel under consideration. Coal is estimated to improve in burning efficiency from a 1960 value of 10,000 BTU's, to 7,500 BTU's by 2000, per kilo-watt hour output. Breeder reactors will convert fertile radio isotopes to fission fuel in quantities equal to or greater than the startup fuel, hence efficiencies greater than unity.

Figure 6-2   The Efficiency Trend of Fossil Fuel Compared to Nuclear Fuel. Sources: Hans H. Landsberg, et al, *Resources in America's Future*, (Baltimore: Johns Hopkins Press, 1963), pp. 287, 288, 845; W. C. Davidson, "Need for Advanced Reactor is Moscow Meeting Refrain", *Electrical World* (October 14, 1968), pp. 34-37.

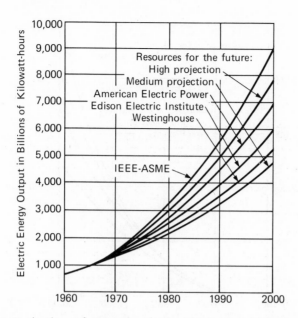

Figure 6-3 Projection of Growth of Electric Energy Consumption in the United States for the Period 1960 to 2000. Sources: Hans H. Landsberg, et al, *Resources in America's Future* (Baltimore: Johns Hopkins Press, 1963), p. 844; Edison Electric Institute, *Report on Power Projections* (New York, 1968); Phillip Sporn, *Energy Forecasts,* American Electric Power Report, 1968; W. E. Morrison, *U.S. Bureau of Mines Projections,* IEEE-ASME Joint Power Conference: San Francisco, July 26, 1968, p. 4.

the environment without causing harm to all forms of flora and fauna. The USAEC (United States Atomic Energy Commission) is an active member of the ICRP, participating on its research, developmental, experimental and advisory committees. Due to the complex nature of radioisotopes, their toxicity, rate of radiation, longevity and effect on living tissue, the ICRP recommends safe levels of radioactive discharge for each of the hundreds of radioisotopes synthesized through irradiation. For example, radium-226, when discharged to public waters, must not exceed 10^{-13} grams per liter of water [6]. The AEC periodically monitors and analyzes the levels of radioactivity in the environment contiguous to facilities associated with discharge of nuclear pollutants. Excessive discharges, when detected, are corrected by order of the Commission, whose authority can revoke a license, or bring litigation in the event of misuse of radionuclides.

Economics and Legislation Waste handling must be performed at minimum cost if the nuclear industry is to survive, due to intense competition from fossil fuel power production and developing sources of energy such as the fuel cell and

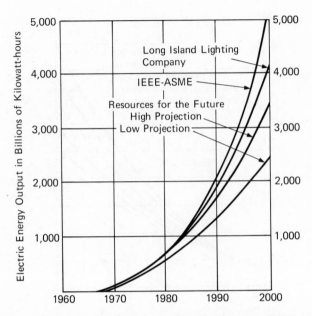

Figure 6-4 Projection of Growth of Electric Energy Consumption from Nuclear Power in the United States, 1965-2000. Sources: Hans H. Landsberg, et al, *Resources in America's Future* (Baltimore: Johns Hopkins Press, 1963), p. 844; W. E. Morrison, *U.S. Bureau of Mines Projections,* IEEE-ASME Joint Power Conference (San Francisco, July 1968), p. 3; John Martone, Manager, Nuclear Power Engineering Division, Long Island Lighting Co., *Nuclear Power Projections,* 1968 [47].

generation by magnetohydrodynamics [1:19-24]. Consequently, the degree of containment and standards of atomic waste must be held to reasonable levels. The AEC, working from international standards drawn from the ICRP dictates policy with just such economics in mind. An integral part of the AEC licensing and approval process for private enterprise includes public hearings at which the public must be assured and guaranteed freedom from harmful atomic waste pollution [4:24-30].

Sources of Atomic Waste

The generation of atomic waste is a function of the growth of nuclear power plants. Although wastes are created at all stages of nuclear radioisotope production and consumption, Mawson observes that perhaps 99.9 percent of all radioactive waste is concentrated in the waste residual of spent fuel [32:35].

Major emphasis is placed on research and development of improvements in the economies and safety techniques involved in extracting reusable nuclear materials and safely disposing of the remaining products created during the burnup of atomic fuel. The remaining sources of waste generation (one-tenth of one percent of the total) arise from the release of natural radioisotopes from uranium ores during manufacture of fuel and the minute discharges to air and water from power reactors during the fuel fission process.

One-Tenth of One Percent of The Problem

The processing of uranium ore concentrates, necessary to production of the salts of uranium for nuclear fuels, liberates atomic pollutants such as radium, radon, and radon-decay products, all hazardous and toxic [31:232]. The uranium itself is safe to handle with light gloves due to the very short range of its radiation emission. The uranium milling process with its grinding, washing, and extractions releases radon dust to the air, mixed with particles of radium, thorium, and other decay-chain radioisotopes [28:32]. The toxic dusts are removed by entrapment through ventilation and filtration to maintain a healthful working environment (not to exceed 10^{-4} microcuries per cubic foot, as required by ICRP). The major concern is for the mine or mill worker, vulnerable to carcinogenic and genetic diseases if overexposed to the radioactive dusts.

Careful inspection and frequent removal of contaminated filters and associated equipment are required to sustain a safe atmosphere. The production of ore concentrates (called "yellow cake") produces a waste liquor called tailings, that is washed into storage ponds. A separation, by ion-exchange, acidleach, liming, and so on, removes a highly radioactive sludge (as much as 1,000 curies per gallon of water) for permanent storage and a very weak, highly diluted aqueous remainder to run off or drain to local ponds or swamps. In this manner, the giant processing plant operated by the AEC at Hanford on the Columbia River may disperse 40 to 50 billion gallons of low-level aqueous waste in a single year. Radioactive wastes have been monitored in quantities of 2×10^{-12} grams per liter of discharge water, or approximately one-fifth the maximum repetitive level recommended by ICRP. Proper design and maintenance of the ponds are required to provide correct leaching rates [12:59].

Gaseous effluents emitted from the stacks of nuclear reactors contain some radioactive materials even after being cleansed and scrubbed. Trace radioisotopes of argon, xenon, krypton, and iodine have been detected in quantities of one-thousandth of the safe limits prescribed by AEC [33:204]. Additionally, activated radioactive products are found in the cooling waters discharged by reactors. Isotopes of sodium, phosphorus, iron, and so on are found in small quantities by chemical analysis often too weak to measure by detection devices. Even so, under AEC requirements, cooling waters are always monitored for presence of radionuclides. Low-level radioactive wastes may be discharged to the environment as long as their cumulative effect is harmless and safe by regulatory standards. Levels of strength of radioactive waste defined by the *Nuclear Engineering and Science Congress,* Geneva, 1958, are

a. High level:	1.0 to 100 curies per litre
b. Medium level:	0.1 to 1.0 curies per litre
c. Low level:	0 to 0.1 curies per litre

Low-level radioactive wastes may be highly toxic and hence dangerous when found in quantities exceeding the limits set forth by the Geneva Congress. Each radioisotope is unique in its radiant and particulate emissions and ability to penetrate living tissue.

The low-level waste liquids are generated in the washing and extraction processes for ore refinement and in the waste removal process for fuel recovery. The highly efficient techniques for capturing radioactive residues and solubles in the waste stream reduces the strength of the effluent to one-tenth of the dispersions permitted by ICRP. After introduction to streams, rivers, swamps, and settling ponds, low-level radioactive wastes are further diluted by a factor ranging from 10,000 to one to 250,000 to one [23:197]. The public fear of radioactive poisoning necessitates such hyperconservative practices. The factors of dilution reduce the radioactive content of the discharge waters to a level that is safe even when projected to the year 2000 [13:406-457].

Further purification of low-level waste waters is not economically feasible due to the high cost of replacement of existing capital equipment with systems capable of entrapping more particulate matter and long lived nuclides such as cesium-137 and strontium-90. Little gain would be realized in further cleansing of waters that is safe for drinking, swimming, and fishing even close to the point of entry of the effluent [23:14-30]. Trace elements of strontium and cesium, both long lived and highly toxic when in sufficient strength, must be dealt with primarily due to public fear; accordingly, some developmental research has been undertaken for their extraction for commercial value. However, economics dictates that secondary sources of energy should be sought perferably from the high-level radioactive scrap heap where very much higher energy levels are found.

The enormous dilution of low-level wastes after discharge to rivers produces a safety factor of some 200,000 to one according to ICRP standards. Thus, even if the projected increase noted in figure 6-5 were 100 rather than 7 between 1970 and 2000 the radioactive content in the waters would scarcely exceed 2×10^{-3} of the maximum set forth by the ICRP.

There does not appear to be any justification for a departure from the current practice of low-level discharge and general dispersion. In this manner, several millions of curies of activity are released without measureable harm to the environment. The safety factor is such that the quantities of low-level wastes cumulatively discharged by year 2000 can be handled using present day methods.

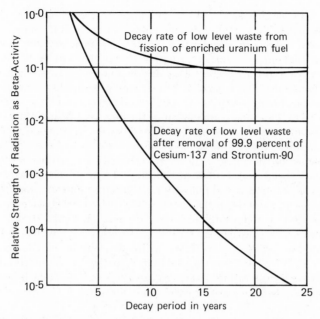

Figure 6-5 A Comparison of the Rate of Decay of Untreated Low Level Fission Product Waste and Same with Cesium-137 and Strontium-90 Removed. Source: E. Gluekauf, *Chemical and Process Engineering*, "Nuclear Waste Treatment", Volume 23 (1956), p. 54.

High-Level Radioactive Wastes

99.9 percent of The Problem

Fuel is expended within the nuclear reactor in the form of liberated heat and radiated energy. The complex fission process gradually tends to smother the fuel due to the tendency of the activation ash to cling to the fuel, stifling the neutron flux beam. The reduction of neutron irradiation causes electrical output to decline as the nuclear mass cools off. Fuel efficiency thus declines to a point that necessitates fuel replacement. The intensely hot fuel element is still rich in uranium-235 and plutonium-239, recoverable, and reusable. The complex recovery process generates more than 99.9 percent of all waste radioactivity in the nuclear industry, according to Mawson.

Fuel recovery is profitable due to the value of the recoverable fissile materials. Natural yellowcake, refined uranium ore, contains 0.7 percent of uranium-235, and sells for eight dollars a pound. Recovered fissile fuel currently commands about $81,000 for the fifteen pounds of uranium-235 and plutonium extracted from a metric ton of spent fuel [36:26-28]. Obviously, the major cost of fuel is in its enrichment. Typically, a power reactor may replace 20 tons of its fuel store, per year, with recovered fuel valued in excess of $1.6 million. Such a high priced commodity in the hands of private enterprise indicates that licensing agencies must maintain the most careful scrutiny to insure the continuing integrity in safe handling and containment of the extracted fission products [4]. Radioactive pollution is detected very easily and swiftly, insuring prompt action against improper handling and containment of radioisotopes.

The problems of handling radioactive materials are neither exotic nor mysterious. Extensive research and experimentation have provided the base lines for safety in containment and allowable dispersion. Further, detection of particulate and gamma emission has been refined to an exact science, able to distinguish between isotopes and the types of emission. Public Health Service and AEC teams periodically deposit radioisotope tracers in air, water, and soil to test their capability of detection. Heavy hydrogen (tritium) was detected in a flowing stream five miles from its point of insertion, at a concentration of 3×10^{-11} parts per million [18:107]. Radioactivity was so weak, it could not be detected separately from ambient cosmic radiation.

Detection and Radioactive Exposure

The combination of public concern and the little understood effects of low-level chronic exposure produces a considerable pressure for safety measures in the use of radioisotopes. Detection devices can measure concentrations of the order of 10^{-15} microcuries of radiation per milliliter of water. These types of detection devices are (a) pulse counters which measure passage of radiation and rate of disintegration; (b) integrating instruments which measure the total dosage of radiation over a period of time by the flashes of light emitted from radioactive salts; and (c) flux rate which measures the dose rate of radiation level by the chemical changes due to disintegration. Such instruments are sensitive to far below the maximum concentrations recommended by ICRP [29:232-288]. Another form of measurement is used to detect absorption of radiant emissions in the body. Film badges are used, worn on one's jacket when working in potentially radioactive or radiant locales. Film exposure is proportional to body energy absorption measurable in roentgens (or rems).

Handling of High-Level Radioactivity

A 600 megawatt nuclear reactor may contain a fuel charge of 100 tons of enriched uranium fuel, consisting of some 400 fuel elements each containing 500 pounds of fuel. An individual fuel element yields approximately 40 million

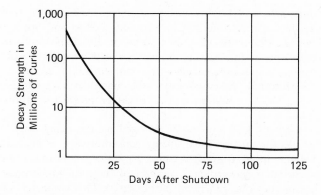

Figure 6-6 Rate of Decay of Nuclear Fuel After Shutdown of Nuclear Reactor. Source: USAEC, *Report on Nuclear Fission Production,* Report WASH- 740, (Washington, D.C.: Government Printing Office, 1957), p. 7.

kilowatt-hours of energy through a four-year time frame, until its replacement. (John H. Martone, Manager, Nuclear power division, Long Island Lighting Company, gave this figure in describing the characteristics of the company's new 800 megawatt Shoreham Number 1 plant, scheduled for 1975 turn-on.) The spent fuel, after 100 days of cooling storage, would exhibit a radiant strength in excess of 150,000 curies per fuel element from a total reactor initial fission strength of 400 million curies (see figure 6-6). The transfer of spent fuel to storage is a carefully sequenced process with adequate safeguards to prevent thermal or biological contamination. AEC approved shipment for reprocessing includes specially designed containers and transporters [7]. Fuel shipping casks are designed for thermal cooling and total shielding and to withstand accidents, fire, and water immersion. Although six accidents in transportation occured from 1940 to 1964, no container leakage was detected.

High-Level Waste

The throughput of the spent fuel element in the recovery process casts off large amounts of high-level radioactive waste. The process is initiated by dissolving the fuel element in a series of powerful solvents followed by a sequence of chemical and physical separations that utilize large volumes of water. A fuel element is simply a supply of fuel within a metallic, protective cladding. The element may be an array of 40 to 80 tubes, each 12 feet long and three-quarter inch diameter. The tubes of stainless steel or zirconium are filled with fuel slugs and sealed. Cleanliness, purity, integrity of the cladding, and a specific geometry are all essential to efficient operation. Each separation process, by filtering, scrubbing and ion-exchange, withholds increasing quantities of the fission and other wastes dissolved or suspended in water. Ideally, all of the waste materials would thus be extracted leaving the pure washing waters to be returned to its source. In practice, process limitations, according to Mawson, Collins and others, fail to extract as much as one-tenth of one percent of the radioactive residues. Industrial experts maintain that it is neither economically feasible nor biologically necessary to perform further extraction [26:497]. The high-strength residues are concentrated by evaporation and contained as a sludge whose volume ran from 1000 to 1400 gallons per ton of processed fuel, through the 1950s.

The accumulation of high-level waste is based on the rising magnitude of nuclear-supplied electric energy. Such energy consumption is estimated at 100 billion kilowatt-hours in 1970 (see figure 6-4). At 1,000 gallons of waste per ton and 10,000 (thermal) megawatt days per ton of fuel; 0.8 million gallons of high-strength waste could be generated during 1970. This compares favorably with projections derived by Mawson [32:54], who finds that such quantities are easily contained at existing waste storage sites. The current methodology of containment of waste sludges has thus far been adequate by virtue of advance construction of high quality underground facilities, whose design and safety minimizes the possibility of leakage and contamination.

At the major fuel processing sites, radioactive sludges containing 10 to 15 curies per litre are stored in below grade, steel, concrete reinforced tanks. The tanks are constructed to provide for gaseous discharge, spontaneous boiling, and high heat. Typically, the tanks are 40 feet high and 75 feet in diameter, containing from 0.7 to one million gallons each. Tank farms with one or two such tanks per acre are economically practical. Storage at up to three dollars per gallon per year constitutes less than three percent of the total value of enriched fuel. In this manner, 65 million gallons of high-level waste had been stored at the Hanford (Washington) AEC reprocessing site on the Columbia River by 1956 [10:389].

Storage tanks are constructed and put into operation according to AEC requirements. Close inspection for quality assurance, isolation from habitable areas, an extensive catch basin system for accidental spillage, and construction for 100 years life and 50 year replacement assures the safe usage of tank farms for future generation of nuclear wastes.

Fuels

The cost of fuel reprocessing is a significant factor in the cost of power generation. Hogerton estimates that by 1970 the cost of nuclear fuels will contribute about two mills ($0.002) out of a total of seven mills per kilowatt-hour for generated electricity from nuclear plants [4:25-26]. (Northeast United States fossil fuel plants are running at three mills fuel cost out of six mills per kilowatt-hour for generated electricity.) Nuclear fuel cost breakdown is noted:

Fuel element fabrication	40 percent
Net fuel burnup	30 percent
Use charge (rent)	10 percent
Fuel reprocessing	20 percent

Technological progress is effectively reducing the cost of fuel. Projections are anticipating fuel cost to drop to one mill per kilowatt-hour by 1980 [50]. Higher energy extraction, in terms of burnup per ton of fuel, contributes to the cost reduction. Burnup of fuel refers to the energy in megawatt-days per ton of fuel, and may be extracted from the fuel charge during its service in the reactor. For example, a fuel rated 10,000 megawatt-days per ton, operating at a power density of 10 megawatts, runs 1,000 days at this level. In practice, for reasons of stability and uniformity, 25 percent of a reactor's fuel elements may be replaced every twelve months if fuel life is estimated at four years. This is currently being extended to six years according to Frederic de Hoffman of Gulf Atomic General, a major company in nuclear manufacture and fuel processing. Fuel replacement is accompanied by relocating the remaining elements to new positions within the vessel, to minimize overexposure to hot spots.

Research, conducted to improve burnup levels, is expected to make possible levels of 50,000 to 100,000 megawatt-days per ton, permitting extended periods of fuel use and a corresponding reduction in processing per ton of fuel per year. Greatly increased burnup capability is theoretically attainable, but practically limited by a maximum safe enrichment, physical stability of the fuel element, potential damage to the cladding, eventual neutron absorption, and accumulation of fission products that reduces operational efficiency. Burnup time is further improved by increasing thermal transfer through optimum element arrangements and by maintaining extraordinary cleanliness. In this manner, power reactors are attaining power densities of 20 megawatts per ton and energy levels at 40,000 megawatt-days per ton with fuel use approaching periods of six years.

The breeder reactor further increases burnup by its ability to produce more fissionable material than contained in the original fuel. The principle of high-speed accelerated fission converts uranium-238 to fissile plutonium 239 [4:32-35]. Breeders are currently experimental and are expected to be operational in the 1970s and fully competitive in the 1980s. The ability to create fuel without the tedious labor involved in fuel processing gives rise to a measurable reduction in waste radioisotopes. The breeder may extend the burnup to 100,000 megawatt-days per ton of fuel, with reprocessing required due to fission contamination and weakening of the fuel cell structure [37:34-37].

Nuclear Reactors

The basic reactor contains three essentials: fuel, a moderator (to slow down the stream of neutrons for more effective radiation), and the coolant to carry the

Table 6.2

Reactor Efficiency and Fuel Burnup

	Cycle Efficiency in Percent		Average Fuel Burnup Megawatt–days per ton	
Reactor Type	*1970*	*1980*	*1970*	*1980*
1. Pressurized water	28	32	13,000	24,000
2. Boiling water	29	33	11,000	30,000
3. Superheat	-	36	-	32,000
4. Organic cooled	30	34	4,500	24,000
5. Sodium graphite	34	41	11,000	22,000
6. Fast breeder	34	40	18,000	50,000
7. Heavy water	23	26	4,000	7,000
8. Gas cooled, natural uranium	24	26	3,000	4,000
9. Gas cooled, enriched uranium	33	36	10,000	24,000

Source: USAEC Report TID–8517, *Civilian Power Reactor Program*, (Washington, D. C.: Government Printing Office, 1960), Part 2, p. 425.

heat of fission to the turbine-generator. Many workable combinations of materials are available and in use, or in development, for operation of reactors. The selection depends on a trade-off of advantages and undesirable features in materials, economies, availabilities, degree of safety, waste generation, and system efficiency. A summary of reactor materials and their characteristics are provided in table 6-2 to illustrate some of the choices offered to the reactor designer. Tables 6-3 and 6-4 provide additional information such as efficiencies, power densities, burnup rates that are currently realized and projected. The data in these tables provide the basis for anticipating long-range improvements in fission waste reduction.

Table 6.3

Some Nuclear Reactor Materials

Material	Use	Advantages	Disadvantages
1. Light water	Moderator, coolant	Inexpensive	High neutron capture
2. Heavy water	Moderator	Low neutron capture, natural U	Expensive
3. Liquid sodium	Coolant	Inexpensive plant costs	Inefficient, high operating costs
4. Gas.	Coolant	Good heat transfer	High waste accumulation
5. Lithium	Coolant	Thermally good	High neutron absorption
6. Natural U	Fuel	Inexpensive	Low efficiency, low burnup
7. Enriched U	Fuel	High output	Expensive, high waste output

Source: ASME *Nuclear Reactor Plant Data*, Parts 1 and 2, (New York: McGraw–Hill, 1959), pp. 72–77.

Projections for the Future

Trends of Increasing Atomic Waste

The economics of nuclear power generation indicates that total cost to produce electrical energy will decline with the improving technology of reactors, fuel, and fuel recovery. Even 1970 will see nuclear plants of 500 to 900 megawatt capacity delivering energy at seven mills per kilowatt-hour compared to fossil-fuel plant cost at six to seven mills [26:774-775] . Intensive, world-wide research and development is improving the efficiency of the nuclear/power cycle. Dr. Glasstone offers a detailed cost analysis of energy delivered from coal fired power plants. He concludes that 6.99 mills per kilowatt-hour is appropriate for fuel purchased at 35 cents per million BTU and 6.04 mills for fuel at 25 cents per million BTU. Nine mills per kilowatt hour was estimated for nuclear power costs from boiling water reactors with capital costs of $250 per kilowatt of plant

Table 6.4

Reactors: Their Categories and Pertinent Facts

Reactor	Comments	Thermal Density Kilowatts/Cu.Ft.	Fuel
1. Ordinary water moderated	Pressurized, boiling, and superheat	1500 800 1000	Enriched UO_2
2. Heavy Water	Moderator and coolant	500	Natural uranium
3. Organic cooled	May also serve as moderator	400	Enriched UO_2
4. Sodium–graphite	Liquid sodium as coolant; graphite as moderator	300	Highly enriched UO_2 or UC
5. Gas–cooled	Heavy water as moderator	15	Natural uranium
6. Gas–cooled	Liquid sodium as moderator	220	Enriched UO^2
7. Fast breeders	Liquid sodium as coolant	21,500	Highly enriched UO_2 or P_uO_2
8. Fluid fuel	Liquid metal fuels		

Source: Samuel Glasstone and Alexander Sesonske, *Nuclear Reactor Engineering* (Princeton: D. Van Nostrand, 1963), p. 714.

and three mills for net fuel cost. Capital costs for nuclear plants are declining to $150 per kilowatt reducing the fixed charges to 3.5 mills per kilowatt-hour [44:21-24]. Fuel costs have also declined from three to less than 2.5 mills. 1980 is projected to provide nuclear energy at less than six mills per kilowatt-hour, according to estimates presented at the Nuclear Power Industry Conference seminars held at Washington, D.C. in August of 1968. The lower costs are predicted on a number of considerations:

A. Reactor vessels are improving to permit higher burnup rate and higher capacity due to increased power densities, operating temperatures, and pressures. The resulting reactors will be more efficient, with improved fuel utilization. (At the Nuclear Power Conference H. W. Muller, West German representative, estimated efficiency of a proposed 1975 600 megawatt high temperature, gas cooled reactor at 50 percent.)

B. Reactors are increasing in size, with attendant economies of scale. From the modest 90 megawatts produced by the 1957 unit at Shippingport, current reactors are in the range of 500 megawatts, with near future units such as Brown's Ferry (TVA) designed for 1,000 megawatts. The capital costs per kilowatt for plant construction decreases with size of plant; early plants of 1960 vintage cost $250 per kilowatt; 800 megawatt plants of 1970 are projected to cost $150 per kilowatt.

C. Fuel is declining in price per kilowatt-hour of output. A. M. Weinburg, Oak Ridge National Laboratory, estimates that large molten-salt converter reactors of the next decade will have a fuel cost of under one mill per kilowatt-hour. Fuel technology is increasing efficiency and burnup time, while reducing waste production per ton of reprocessed fuel. Gluekauf and Collins separately show evidence of reduction of waste bulk from 2,000 gallons per ton to 1,000 gallons per ton of reprocessed fuel in the period between 1950 and 1962. The General Electric Nuclear Fuel Recovery Operation at Santa Clara, California shows significant reduction in bulk fission product separation by a unique solvent extraction technique that contains 99.9 percent of the waste product in approximately 100 gallons for each ton of fuel processed [46]. Further concentration and calcination results in about 2.5 cubic feet of high-level waste mix per metric ton of fuel processed.

The forces of progress appear to be reducing the per unit generation of atomic wastes. An examination of the net effect on increasing electric production should yield some meaningful conclusions as to the consequences of assuming increased usage of nuclear fuels. We may accept without further examination, the statement that atomic waste matter is toxic to some degree to all forms of life. The current methodology of containment of radioactive wastes has retained a degree of safety and relative economy that has permitted the growth of the nuclear power industry. Waste containment requires extensive facilities to provide absolute assurance against the possibility of accidental spillage and area contamination. The hypothesis is conceivable and must be tested that the production of atomic waste will outrun available safe storage facilities in view of the enormity of the projected increase in nuclear power production.

A survey of several electric load forecasts indicates that nuclear power will provide 50 to 60 percent of all electric generation in the United States by year 2000. An average growth pattern extracted from figure 6-4 is provided for quick evaluation. The rise in nuclear power output is expected to increase by 16 between 1970 and 2000. Assuming no change in the current level of fuel burnup at 20,000 megawatt-days (thermal) per ton of fuel, at an efficiency conversion of 0.3, combined with fuel processing methodology that discharges 600 gallons of high-level radioactive waste per ton, it may be shown that annual waste generation could rise from 0.8 million gallons in 1970 to 40 million gallons annually by 2000. The cumulative effect for the period would thus approach 450 million gallons, or 1.1 billion gallons for the period 1940 to 2000. In 1965, there was approximately 650 million gallons of high-level waste accumulation in the United States, primarily generated during the decades of research and development of nuclear weapons with an inefficient extraction technique that delivered some 2000 gallons of liquid waste per ton of reprocessed fission material [32:62].

The land areas available to long-term storage at the existing AEC sites (Hanford, the Idaho test facility, Savannah, Oak Ridge) and those of private firms such as Nuclear Fuel Services and Atlantic-Richfield indicate that over a billion gallons of fissile waste liquids could be contained in large tank modules (up to one million gallons each) buried in the earth. The Nuclear Fuel Service Corporation, for example, has established a tank farm on 4,000 acres at West Valley, New York, specifically for the containment of nuclear waste storage. Approximately 1,000 acres are available for tank installations; at one tank per acre and one million gallons per tank, one billion gallons of nuclear sludge could be stored at this site.

The above calculation omits from consideration the technological improvements taking place currently and expected in the future. As summarized by table 6-5, and figure 6-7, continuing reductions in per unit generation of high-level wastes cause the estimated 1.1 billion gallons total accumulation to reduce to 0.86 billion gallons accumulated by year 2000. This assumes no significant reductions in wastes currently contained.

Continuing progress is anticipated in the reduction of waste per ton of processed fuels, and is expected to reduce the accumulations noted above. Further reductions in land area requirements are attainable by construction of deep, vertical tanks requiring only one-fourth the land surface taken by conventional tanks. Some of the factors relevant to such reductions are:

1. The increasing trend in fuel exposure will extend the time betweeen fuel removal and processing [46]. Although fuels processed after ten years of consumption have considerably different isotopic makeup and energy content than fuels with less burnup, producing a more dense waste mix, the per unit volume of the waste will not change materially. (Carson states that active waste products may vary from 20 to 50 kilograms for fuels ranging in burnup capability from 20,000 to 45,000 megawatt-days per ton. For either case, 99.9 percent of the waste high-level products can be contained in 100 gallons of liquid.)

Table 6.5

Factors for the Determination of Projected Rise of High-Level Radioactive Aqueous Waste Volume in the United States

Parameter	Units		1970	1980	1990	2000
Energy	Billions of kilowatt-hours from nuclear power		100	800	2100	4300
Power	Thousands of megawatts from nuclear power		40	150	330	675
Fuel burnup	Kilowatt-hours per ton x billions	therm.	0.5	0.75	1.00	1.25
		elec.	0.14	0.23	0.36	0.43
Fuel processed	Tons x 1,000		1.4	7.0	12.0	20.0
High-level waste	Aqueous effluent in gallons per ton of fuel		600	500	400	300
High-level waste	Thousands of gallons per year		840	3500	4800	6000
High-level waste	Total accumulation in thousands of gallons, since 1970		840	22,000	64,000	118,000
High-level waste	Accumulation in billions of gallons since 1940		0.65	0.68	0.74	0.86

Note: Fuel burnup is tabulated for thermal and electric values, with efficiency rising between 1970 and 2000, from 0.28 to 0.35.

Sources: A. B. Carson, General Electric Nuclear Energy Division, *Fuel Recovery Operation,* personal correspondence dated March 14, 1969; Dr. Gerald F. Tape, Former Commissioner, AEC, "Nuclear Power and Social and Technological Change," *Seminar on Technology and Social Change* held at Men's Faculty Club of Columbia University, May 9, 1969; William E. Morrison, Bureau of Mines, *IEEE-ASME Joint Power Conference,* San Francisco, July 26, 1968.

2. The operation of breeder reactor plants will further extend fuel burnup periods beyond even ten years due to their inherent ability to create fissionable matter during operation. Thus, burnup is estimated to increase from four years in 1970 to six years in 1980 to eight years in 1990 and ten years by 2000. High-gain breeders with fuel burnup of 50,000 megawatt-days per ton are under design for completion in the late 1970's and sustained operation projected for 1980. At a power density level of 20 megawatts per ton, a period of eight years between fuel replacement may be attained. Nuclear experts are researching exotic materials and techniques capable of reaching 100,000 megawatt-days per ton [51]. At a conference in 1968 Professor Benedict of MIT advised of the planning of large 1,000 megawatt/100,000 megawatt-day breeder reactors utilizing uranium carbide fuel and liquid metal coolant; Westinghouse, at the same time, announced plans for 1980 completion of a 100,000 megawatt-day per ton breeder with conversion ratio of 1.4

3. A reduction in quantity of stored wastes appears feasible by evaporative concentration of the tanked liquids to an almost solid consistency. Immersion heaters have been used to boil away nonactive liquors, leaving a solid sludge of 25 percent of the original bulk. Recently developed and under field test, this could theoretically reduce the storage at Hanford from 94 million to 25 million gallons in 1968. The technique is usable, but expensive, and is not expected to become fully operational until the cost of purchase and operation of the four megawatt, nine ton heaters is less than the storage capacity it makes available [38:6]. A bonus appears in the form of reduced hazard from leakage due to the solidity of the remaining sludge. It is assumed that increasing costs of land and tankage will eventually make this technique widely used. It is estimated that waste volumes generated by 1980 will thus be reduced by a factor of two with further reduction by a factor of three by 1990.

4. The economic utilization of land can be enhanced further by the sinking of deep shafts, sealed and shielded to prevent leakage. A pilot shaft near Carlsbad, New Mexico, ten feet in diameter and 1250 feet deep was completed July, 1961 at a cost of $600,000. Designed to contain the high-energy release of nuclear explosions, it can readily be modified for long-term waste storage of 800,000 gallon capacity, using surface area of only one quarter acre [15:1-48]. The cost, even when escalated to $1.2 million for 1970 costs, with modifications, is competitive at $1.50 per gallon. In this manner, land surface is more conservatively utilized than conventional sludge tanks occupying one acre per tank.

The above factors lead to a reduction of atomic waste generated per ton per acre of surface. These data are only relevant in terms of projected capabilities for the indefinite storage of concentrated wastes. The reduction in waste output per ton of processed fuel could attain a level of less than 200 gallons through increased burnup and improved methods of concentration; however, even a more conservative value of 300 gallons by year 2000 would reduce the projected 1.1 billion gallons total accumulation to approximately 0.86 billion gallons of high-level waste stored in the United States by year 2000. This amount is only

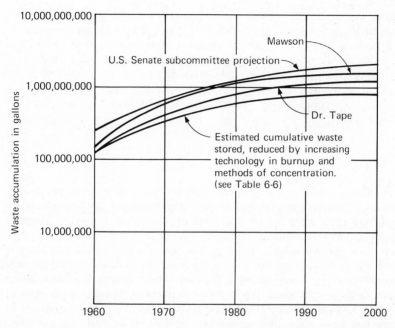

Figure 6-7 Projected Rise of Accumulation of High-Level Nuclear Waste. Sources: United States Senate, Subcommittee on Air Pollution, *Hearings on Industrial Radioactive Waste Disposal,* (Washington, D.C.: Supt. of Documents, 1959) Vol. 3, pp. 2346-50; Collin Ashley Mawson, *Management of Radioactive Wastes,* (Princeton: D. Van Nostrand, 1965) Ch. 3, p. 62. Dr. Mawson's projections are based on the generation of approximately 1,000 gallons of aqueous effluent per ton of reprocessed fuel; Dr. Gerald F. Tape, *Seminar at Columbia University,* "Nuclear Power and Social and Technological Change", May 9, 1969. Dr. Tape's projection assumes a constant of 600 gallons of concentrate per ton of fuel.

one-third more than the current stored waste and facilities to accommodate it are readily available at existing facilities. This assumes no reduction in existing volume of stored wastes.

The 1967 Nuclear Industry Report for the Atomic Industrial Forum Conference at Chicago, November 6, 1967, summarized that "It can be concluded, based on AEC experience, that: (1) radioactive waste management practices have not resulted in any harmful effects on the public, its environment, or its resources; and (2) the general problem of radioactive wastes need not retard the future development of the nuclear energy industry." The same report notes that continuing research and development in the field of waste management of nuclear fuels is showing significant promise in several areas relating to per unit waste reduction and additional storage facilities [20:164-165].

Waste Product or Productive Waste

A potentially beneficial characteristic of radioactive waste lies in its high-energy content, both thermal and biological. The hot irradiated fissile mass, when removed from the reactor, contains millions of curies of decay energy, liberated principally as heat. Considerable research has and is being devoted to finding economic uses for this source of energy. The use of atomic waste as a thermal source of energy has not generally been exploited due to its relatively high cost. The special handling, recontainment, heat exchanger system, and diminishing heat level could not economically compete with conventional sources of heat, where fossil fuels are plentiful and inexpensive. Special situations may justify waste nuclear heat when fuel replacement is difficult or fuel is inaccessible. Some applications under current consideration include the powering of spacecraft, underwater propulsion systems, and waste water reprocessing. The most notable of such uses of radioisotopes are the AEC development of Systems for Nuclear Auxiliary Power, (SNAP) supplies for remote areas and underwater research. For example, the SNAP-7D is a power supply used for weather station buoys at sea. Using Strontium-90 derived from atomic wastes, this well-shielded supply will provide 60 watts of power for ten years. The unit weighs 4600 pounds and produced electricity at ten to twenty times the cost of residential power in the United States [34:180-183].

Waste products contain an abundance of fission, activation, and corrosion products in the form of radioisotopes. Extraction and purification is justified for numerous isotopes that are useful and of value. Strontium-90 and cesium-137 are useful as high-level sources of radiation for work in research and industrial studies. Both are long lived with half life of order of twenty-five years and contribute heavily to the toxicity and heat generation in waste material. Waste products, with 99.9 percent of the strontium and cesium-137 removed, would permit ground disposal after some twenty years storage [35:475]. This consideration is largely academic as the industrial needs for these materials is less one percent of the total content in spent fuels. Additionally, the cost of removal far exceeds the current bulk storage cost of high-level waste products.

Radioisotopes are highly valued for their many uses. Further, the very existence of the nuclear industry has promulgated associated activities with the net result of industrial growth and expansion. Some considerations are:

Commerce and Industry. A vast spectrum of commercial goods are required for all aspects of handling and manufacture related to the nuclear industry. Many goods, adequate for the prenuclear era, were not suitable to radioactive handling due to leakage, deterioration, failure, poor reliability, or poor design for the new technology. Consequently, extensive improvements, innovations, new materials, and techniques have been developed in such commodities as pumps, valves, seals, piping, instruments, gauges, lubricants, bearings, containers, concrete, and so on. The net result has been to stimulate many industries with new ideas, money, manpower and general expansion. The need for remote surveillance and control has also created a need for innovations and higher quality in optics, mechanical handling systems, and sensitive, quick response closed loop logic systems.

Radiation Chemistry. Radioisotopes are used extensively for tracers, gauges, pest control, growth stimulation, sterilization, disease control, food preservation, chemical processing, radiography, medical therapy, analysis of materials and numerous other uses. Some specific applications are noted:

Medical and biological research
    a. Sodium-24   Tracers for body and bloodstream
    b. Iron-59   Metabolism studies
    c. Iodine-131   Anti-cancer research
Medical diagnosis and therapy
    a. Deuterium, tritium, bromine-82   Blood, heart and body diagnosis
    b. Strontium-90, thulium-170   gamma-ray treatment
Agriculture
    a. Calcium-25, phosphorus-32, carbon-14   soil studies
    b. Zinc-65   plant tracers
    c. Sulphur-35, calcium-45   Plant disease studies
Animal research
    a. Cesium-137, cobalt-60, molybdenum-99   Metabolism studies

Power Systems. Small, long-lived sources of electric power have been devised, utilizing waste radioisotopes for the thermal conversion of radioactive heat to electricity. Many SNAP generators have been built for situations where high reliability, long life, and inaccessibility are prime requisites [34:184].

Sewage Treatment. Sterilization of raw sewage by irradiation renders it free of odor and germs. Professor James Etzel of Purdue University would use Cobalt-60 gamma radiation on sewage sludge and pump it to remote farms as rich humus. It is estimated that this process could reduce the total cost of sewage handling in the United States by one billion dollars if fully implemented [40:384].

The factor common to all uses of radioisotopes extracted from spent fuels is that their quantities are small when compared to the total amount generated by nuclear fission for power production. Thus, the impact on waste quantities would not affect the future projections for stored wastes. Further, reused wastes are themselves subject to incomplete decay and the residue must again be relegated to nuclear waste repositories.

Conclusion

The generation of wastes in recent decades has been viewed by many with alarm as the rising quantities are creating a blight to man and the environment. A lack of planning, public apathy, inadequate legislative controls, the cost of disposal, and less than adequate waste management have all contributed to the problem. The results have been widespread pollution and the production of waste outstripping the means to cope with it. Finally, as the problem approaches irretrievable proportions, forces are gathering to clean up the man-made filth and contamination at enormous cost.

An outstanding exception to the general mismanagement of waste handling has been in the disposition of radioactive wastes. Cognizance of the hazards of radiological emissions dating back to the research of the 1930s firmly established a respect and fear of the toxic effects of radiation. Setbacks have occurred through ignorance of the potency of radioisotopes that are capable of poisoning the body after prolonged contact. Although the need for caution and proper shielding has been known since the nineteenth century, a technology has evolved of the methods to be maintained in handling and disposing of radioactive materials and in its detection. Before 1940, quantities of radionuclides used in research, medicine, industry and luminous watch face manufacture were extremely small and generally solid in consistency. Wastes were simply stored in drums which were sealed and buried. World War II and the impetus of the atomic bomb saw the development of large radioisotope production plants with the subsequent generation of tens of millions of gallons of aqueous wastes of all intensities. The technology, the competence, and the isolated storage sites were all available to cope with the potential pollutant. The Atomic Energy Commission was organized with devoted, eminent scientists and administrators who established a watch dog vigilance over the infant nuclear processing industry. The surveillance of the safety aspects of radioactivity and the efforts of all concerned have been rewarded by the benefits derived:

1. Waste management has been effective in its ability to plan, control, and maintain safety. Storage facilities for high-level radioactive wastes appears to be adequate even at year 2000. Containment is so effective that radioactivity near storage sites cannot be distinguished from and does not add appreciably to cosmic radiation.

2. Waste control and economy of disposal has been constantly improving so that it occupies a minimum portion of the total pricing spectrum of fuel

manufacture and reprocessing. This permits nuclear fuels to hold a competitive position with other sources of energy, and thus has allowed the continuing growth of the nuclear power industry.

3. Research and development is a continuous process that reviews and improves the methodology of waste disposal, dispersion, and storage with regard to safety, feasibility, cost, and future reuse.

4. Waste materials are under constant evaluation as to their value as sources of thermal and biological energy. To date, many isotopes are extracted from the waste, whose radiant energy is useful to industry, medicine, agriculture, and space exploration.

The accumulation of wastes is not a constraint upon the growth of the nuclear power industry, which until recently was unique in that its commodities are priced to include its waste containment. The increasing burning efficiencies, reduction in plant, fuel and reprocessing costs, and elimination of pollutants associated with the burning of fossil fuels all favor nuclear power plants over conventional fossil fuel types. In consequence, fifty percent of power plants placed on order in the United States between 1966 and 1969 are atomic units, representing $10 billion in capital investments, and $35 billion in fuel commitments over a thirty-year period [48]. This projects to a $2 billion annual fuel bill by 1980. With approximately three percent of the cost in waste extraction and disposal, .06 mills would represent the waste handling portion of the 1980 anticipated two mills per kilowatt-hour for total fuel cost. The favorable economics of nuclear fuels makes it a stabilizing element in electric costs that is independent of geography, permitting industrial growth where high-energy costs may have been a deterrent to expansion.

Two major factors that might limit the growth of nuclear power are the potential depletion in world reserves of nuclear fuel and high heat emission with attendant thermal pollution, both under scrutiny for corrective developments. The breeder reactor will make usable the fertile uranium-238, by conversion to fissionable plutonium, replacing the uranium-235 whose estimated reserves in the United States would be depleted long before 2000, according to Landsberg. In the second matter, technology is closing the efficiency gap between nuclear plants (currently at 0.32) and fossil fuel plants (0.40) so that heat emission from both types of plants may soon be approximately the same.

Waste bulk per ton of processed fuel is diminishing with improving technology. Only limited by its concentrated heat generation, waste residues in aqueous form have significantly reduced in bulk over the past decades from 2000 gallons per ton or processed fuel in 1940 to 1400 gallons in 1950 to 1,000 gallons in 1960 to 300 gallons, currently estimated by Tape [48]. Finally, General Electric's Nuclear Fuel Recovery Plant, through a solvent and evaporative process, will, in the near future, extract 99.9 percent of waste fission products concentrated within 100 gallons of effluent. The aqueous concentrate may be solidified via calcination, to some 2.5 cubic feet of solid material for each ton of reprocessed fuel.

Waste containment by the current method of storage in buried tanks with continuous surveillance for detection of radioactive leakage, container failure, overheat, or earth disturbances has exhibited a record of almost total reliability. The present array of government and private waste tank farms is adequately prepared to add 200 million gallons of aqueous high-level waste (expected total accumulation to year 2000) to the existing 600 million gallons stored from accumulations since 1939 (primarily from military plutonium production plants). Further reductions in stored bulk are attainable and could be implemented if economically justified or required through legislation, by evaporative concentration of the stored solutions (additional cooling by extended heat exchangers would be required due to the increased density of heat emission of the concentrated waste sludges). Additionally, Gluekauf has shown that 99.9 percent removal of cesium-137 and strontium-90 would leave a residue whose radioactivity would diminish sufficiently in twenty years to permit dilution and dispersion to ground waters and fissures. The cesium and strontium, thus removed, would require special handling due to their high thermal and radiant energy content but could be contained within a 0.3 to 0.5 cubic foot volume per ton of processed fuel [46].

There is concern that waste storage sites are vulnerable to enemy attack, earthquakes and other destructive forces. The AEC has given such possibilities careful evaluation, concluding that the waste itself cannot be made explosive, and would cause, in the event of total tank destruction, only local ground and water contamination, controllable due to the remoteness of such installations from peopled areas [4]. In fact, the detonating force of a missile or atomic bomb would render any waste contamination negligible.

The industries associated with nuclear production are harvesting the fruits of a waste management science that was well conceived, is well implemented, and assures a bright future of growth, expansion, and safety.

7

Air Pollution and the Projected Consumption of Fossil Fuels for Purposes Other than Internal Combustion Engines

Norman Wesler

As the postwar United States economy has driven to ever higher output levels, the rising demand for energy has set the pace. From 1940 to 1960 the demand for energy in all forms more than doubled and the 1960 figure is expected to be increased by a further 75 percent by 1980 and to be almost tripled by 2000. This chapter and the one that follows will attempt to assess the effect of this enormous increase in terms of air pollution.

Table 7-1 gives a more detailed picture of the sources of the increased energy output. The two bottom lines indicate that the portion coming from sources that make no significant contribution to air pollution – hydro and nuclear power – is projected to increase from 3.6 percent of the total in 1960 to 8.1 percent and to 16.1 percent in 2000, principally because of a sixfold expansion of nuclear sources in the last twenty years of the period. A large and growing portion of the total is expected to be derived from the use of petroleum products in internal combustion engines, over one quarter in 1960 and about a third in 2000. As a percentage of the energy derived from fossil fuels, the internal combustion share is even more striking, projected to increase from 27 percent of the total in 1960 to about 31 percent in 1980 and to 39 percent in 2000 as may be seen from Table 7-1. The internal combustion engine, principally in private automobiles, is far and away the main source of such air pollutants as oxides of nitrogen, carbon monoxide, and unburned hydrocarbons. Air pollution from internal combustion engines will be the subject of Chapter 8.

The center of interest in the present chapter is in those fossil fuels used for external combustion – notably, coal, natural gas, and fuel oil. Coal which is the main fuel burned in thermal power stations is projected to lose part of this market to nuclear fuels, especially in the last twenty years of the century. Thus, the share of coal in supplying energy for power plants is projected to decline from 24.5 percent in 1960 to only 13.3 percent in 2000, as shown in Table 7-1. The same source shows, however, that the absolute amount of coal which is expected to be consumed increases sharply during the same period, rising by 44 percent from 1960 to 1980 and by another 14 percent in the next twenty years. Electricity generation provides a small but steady market for fuel oil, but residential space heating is the principal outlet for this fuel. Natural gas provides stiff competition for fuel oil in space heating, is extensively used in power generation (especially nonutility), and is projected to find a rising market in various manufacturing and commercial applications. Natural gas liquids are used mainly for residential space and other heating purposes principally in rural areas where their combustion makes no significant contribution to air pollution [2:192]. Natural gas liquids are not considered further in this study.

Table 7.1

Demand for Energy by Source, 1960,
and Medium Projections for 1980 and
2000

Source	1960	1980 Physical Quantities	2000
Petroleum (billion barrels)[a]			
Used in internal combustion	2.14	4.06	8.16
Used in external combustion	1.05	1.28	1.87
Total petroleum	3.19	5.34	10.03
Natural gas (trillion cubic feet)	12.87	23.47	32.78
Natural gas liquids (billion barrels)	.34	.75	1.56
Coal (million tons)	436	630	718
Hydro power (billion kilowatt hours)	149	283	363
Nuclear power (billion kilowatt hours)	- - -	400	2,400

[a]Total petroleum demand from RFF Table 15-3. Portion used in external combustion from Table VII-6; portion used in internal combustion by subtraction. The figure designated "used in internal combustion" includes petroleum in asphalt and road oil and other miscellaneous non-combustion uses such as lubrication; this portion represented 12.1 percent of figure for "internal combustion" in 1960, declining to 11.6 percent in 1980 and 11.1 percent in 2000.

Source	1960	1980	2000
		Percentage Distribution	
Petroleum[b]			
Used in internal combustion	26.2	28.3	33.0
Used in external combustion	12.9	8.9	7.5
Total petroleum	39.1	37.2	40.5
Natural gas	29.2	30.5	25.0
Natural gas liquids	3.6	4.3	5.1
Coal	24.5	19.9	13.3
Hydro power	3.6	3.4	2.1
Nuclear power	- - -	4.7	14.0
Total:	100	100	100

[b]In RFF Table 15-3, the physical quantities shown above were converted to energy equivalents which are not reproduced here. However, this percentage distribution by source is of energy equivalents and is based upon identical figures in RFF Table 15-3.

Source: *Resources in America's Future*, Table 15-3, p. 290.

Table 7.2

Consumption of Coal for 1960 and
Medium Projections for 1970, 1980,
1990, and 2000, by Use (million short
tons)

Use	1960	1970	1980	1990	2000
Electricity generation	208	296	407	426	457
Manufacturing[a]	152	162	169	187	220
Commercial	22	11	9	8	8
Residential	20	12	11	3	–
Total:[b]	402	481	596	624	685

[a]From lines for "iron and steel industry" and "other manufacturing in RFF Table A15–16, p. 854. Also included is "railroads", 3 million tons in 1960 (less than 1 percent) and 1 million tons in 1970 (about two–tenths of one percent), with zero entries for other years.

[b]Bureau of Mines reported total 1960 domestic consumption at a level approximately 1 percent below the total by identified uses shown here. Projected totals may be subject to a corresponding percentage adjustment downward.

Source: *Resources in America's Future*, p. 854.

The procedure which will be followed is to determine for each of the principal fossil fuels the projected volume consumed in external combustion and then to explore the implications of these projections for air pollution, assuming no improvement in current control standards. Next, the opportunities and prospects for control of air pollution from external combustion will be examined and conclusions drawn.

Coal Consumption by Uses

Table 7-2 shows coal consumption by uses for 1960 and RFF medium projections at ten year intervals to 2000. By far the most important of these uses is for electric power generation which accounted for 52 percent of total coal use in 1960 and was projected to increase in relative importance to 67 percent of the

Table 7.3

Emission Factors for Coal Combustion
(pounds per ton of coal burned)

Pollutant	Power Plant Unit	Industrial Unit	Domestic and Commercial Unit
Carbon monoxide	0.5	3	50
Hydrocarbons	0.2	1	10
Nitrogen oxides	20	20	8
Sulfur oxides	$38S^a$	$38S^a$	$38S^a$

[a]S refers to percent of sulfur in the coal which should be multiplied by 38 to give pounds of pollutant per ton of coal burned. Example: If the sulfur content of a coal is 2 percent, the emission of sulfur base pollutants would be 2 times 38 or 76 pounds of sulfur dioxide per ton of coal burned.

Source: U. S., Public Health Service, *Compilation of Air Pollutant Emission Factors* (Washington, D. C.: Government Printing Office, 1968), p. 5.

total in 2000. Next most important use for coal is in manufacturing, notably iron and steel production, which accounted for slightly more than half of all coal used in manufacturing in each year shown in Table 7-2. Coal has lost out in competition with petroleum products in many applications. Railroads, once an important consumer, have ceased using coal almost entirely, and the market for coal in residential and commercial space heating has likewise suffered erosion, first from the competition of fuel oil and more recently of natural gas. Combustion of coal for residential and commercial heating accounted for about 10 percent of total consumption in 1960 and this percentage is projected to decline to about 3 in 1980 and to only 1 in 2000.

For a variety of reasons which will be examined in more detail later, it is likely to be economically feasible to achieve high levels of air pollution control where usage is highly concentrated. Accordingly, the fact that coal consumption is expected to be increasingly concentrated in electric power stations and large manufacturing plants should favor an improvement in air pollution control. For the present, however, it will be useful to project the volume of pollutants to be emitted from the combustion of coal, assuming no improvement in pollution control, in order to assay the magnitude of the task to be performed.

The U.S. Public Health Service which has federal responsibility for study of air pollution has issued estimates of the volume of air pollutants formed per ton of coal burned. These are presented in Table 7-3. The contribution of coal

Table 7.4

**Estimates of Certain Gaseous Pollutants
Produced from Combustion of Coal in
1960 and Projections for 1980 and 2000,
Assuming No Improvement in Pollution
Control** (millions of pounds)

| | Estimate | | Projections | | | |
| | *1960* | | *1980* | | *2000* | |
Use	*Nitrogen Oxides*	*Sulfur Oxides*	*Nitrogen Oxides*	*Sulfur Oxides*	*Nitrogen Oxides*	*Sulfur Oxides*
Electricity generation	4,160	15,808	8,140	30,932	9,140	34,732
Manufacturing	3,040	5,776	3,380	6,422	4,400	8,360
Commerical	176	1,672	72	684	64	608
Residential	160	1,520	88	836	--	--
Total	7,536	24,776	11,680	38,874	13,604	43,700

Source: Computed from data in Table 7.1
for selected years and appropriate emission
factors as shown in Table 7.2. Sulfur content for "Manufacturing" coal assumed as
1 percent; 2 percent for all other.

combustion to gaseous pollutants such as carbon monoxide and unburned
hydrocarbons is negligible compared to the amount emitted by the automobile
(see Chapter 8). This is because unit emission factors relating to carbon
monoxide and hydrocarbons are low for power plants and industrial units as
shown by Table 7-3. While these unit factors are high for domestic and
commercial heating, these uses account for a small and declining fraction of the
total. Accordingly, attention is focused here on the volume of oxides of nitrogen
and sulfur formed, to which coal makes a substantial contribution.

Table 7-4 gives estimates of the weight of nitrogen and sulfur oxides formed
from the combustion of coal in 1960 and projections of these estimates at 20
year intervals to 2000, assuming no improvement in pollution controls. The
oxides of nitrogen react with other constituents to form the brown haze known
as smog which has so plagued Los Angeles. The sulfur oxides are regarded as
especially hazardous because if oxidation proceeds as far as sulfur trioxide,
sulfuric acid will be formed upon solution in the moisture of the atmosphere.

Smoke formed by discharge of particulates is a visible nuisance, more evident than the sometimes dangerous oxides just discussed. Table 7-5 gives estimates for 1960 and projections for 1980 and 2000 of the volume of particulates emitted in the combustion of coal, again assuming no improvement in pollution control after 1960. The estimated weight of particulates released to the air in 1960 from the burning of coal amounted to more than 10 billion pounds or 5 million tons, mostly in populated areas. Again electric power stations were responsible for the bulk of the problem in 1960.

Pollutants Formed by Combustion of Fuel Oil

The consumption pattern for fuel oil in 1960 was in sharp contrast to that for coal. Electric power generation was the least important use for fuel oil and residential consumption the most important, precisely the opposite of the situation in coal. However, residential sales of fuel oil were projected to decline steadily after 1960, reaching a point nearly a third below the 1960 level in 2000. In contrast, manufacturing use of fuel oil was expected to nearly triple from 1960 to 2000 and commercial use to increase in about the same proportion. Data on fuel oil uses are presented in Table 7-6, and emission factors for fuel oil consumption in Table 7-7.

Based on the data of these two tables, Table 7-8 presents estimates for 1960 of the weight of oxides of nitrogen and sulfur emitted in the combustion of fuel oil and projections for 1980 and 2000. It is striking that fuel oil burned in residential heating was by far the most important fuel oil source of sulfur oxide pollution in 1960. It is also evident that relative to coal, fuel oil is an unimportant point of origin for oxides of nitrogen. Since residential fuel oil consumption is projected to decline in 1980 and 2000, the main source of fuel oil air pollutants will shift to manufacturing where effective control measures may be more feasible economically because of the larger scale of operations.

Table 7-9 gives estimates of particulate emission from combustion of fuel oil in 1960 and projections for 1980 and 2000, again assuming no improvement in pollution control. It will be noted that the estimated 624 million pounds of particulate matter emitted in 1960 during combustion of fuel oil is about 6 percent of the comparable figure for coal in the same year.

Table 7-10 gives data on natural gas consumption in 1960 and medium projections by ten year intervals to 2000. Table 7-11 presents emission factors for natural gas consumption prepared by the U.S. Public Health Service. The emission factors for natural gas combustion are quite low except for nitrogen oxide and for particulate matter output.

Based on the data in Tables 7-10 and 7-11, Table 7-12 shows estimates of oxides of nitrogen and sulfur emitted during combustion of natural gas in 1960 and projections for 1980 and 2000, assuming no improvement in pollution control. The addition to sulfur oxide pollution from natural gas combustion is negligible in all uses, but the contribution to output of oxides of nitrogen of

172

Table 7.5

Estimates of Particulate Emissions from Combustion of Coal in 1960 and Projections for 1980 and 2000, Assuming No Improvement in Pollution Control (millions of pounds)

| | Estimate | Projections | |
Use	1960	1980	2000
Electricity generation	5,200	10,175	11,425
Manufacturing	3,800	4,225	5,500
Commercial	550	225	200
Residential	500	275	--
Total:	10,050	14,900	17,125

Source: Computed from data in Table 7.2 and emission factor of 25 pounds particulate per ton of coal burned in accordance with "average" degree of control, as given in U. S. Public Health Service, *Atmospheric Emiss-* *ions from Coal Combustion* (Washington, D. C.: Government Printing Office, 1968), Public Health Service Publication No. 999-AP-24, Table 2-3. p. 5. No improvement assumed in later years.

natural gas consumed in 1960 in electricity generation and manufacturing was substantial. Assuming no improvement in pollution control and expanded consumption as projected, the contribution of natural gas to output of the smog producing oxides of nitrogen would be 36 percent of that of coal in 1980 and nearly 43 percent in 2000.

Table 7-13 gives estimates of weight of particulate matter emitted during combustion of natural gas in 1960 and projections for 1980 and 2000, assuming no improvement in pollution controls. It is clear that considered in terms of the particulates that make up smoke, natural gas is the cleanest of the three fuels considered here. In 1960, particulate matter released to the air in burning natural gas was less than 2 percent of that resulting from coal and only about 29 percent of that formed in burning fuel oil. This is more striking when it is noted by reference to Table 7-1 that the heating value of the natural gas consumed in 1960 was 19 percent greater than that of the coal and well over twice as great as that of the fuel oil burned in the same year.

Summary: Coal, Oil, Natural Gas

Table 7-14 summarizes for all three fuels considered here the estimates of volume of oxides of nitrogen and sulfur emitted in external combustion in 1960

Table 7.6

Petroleum Consumed in External Combustion in 1960 and Medium Projections for 1970, 1980, 1990, and 2000, by Use
(millions of barrels)

Type of Consumption	1960	1970	1980	1990	2000
Electricity generation	101	123	126	129	136
Manufacturing[a]	353	441	560	747	1018
Commercial	138	187	232	300	403
Residential[b]	462	406	366	342	314
Total:	1054	1157	1284	1518	1871

Source: *Resources in America's Future*, Table A15–13. p. 848.

[a]Total of following lines in RFF Table A15–13: General manufacturing; Iron and steel industry; Nonferrous metals; Petroleum refinery fuel.

[b]Total of following lines in RFF TAble A15–13: Residential – space heating; Residential – all other.

and projections of these estimates for 1980 and 2000, assuming no improvement in pollution controls. Table 7-15 presents a similar summary with respect to particulate emissions. Finally, Table 7-16 gives a percentage breakdown of Tables 7-14 and 7-15 by type of consumption.

Most of this chapter leans so heavily on projections that it may be well to point out that the 1960 estimates of pollutant emission depend upon nothing more than the best figure available concerning pollutant emitted per unit consumed and overall output statistics. Thus, if the unit emission factors arrived at by the U.S. Public Health Service are accepted and the generally agreed upon statistics of fuel consumption are used as multipliers, the following gross quantities of pollutants entering the atmosphere in 1960 through external combustion of fossil fuels are arrived at (in millions of pounds): oxides of sulfur – 38,859; oxides of nitrogen – 11,893; particulates – 10,852. Expressed in tons, these figures rounded off are still in the millions, namely, oxides of sulfur – 19, oxides of nitrogen – 6, particulates – 5. Five million tons of particulates is a very large amount of dust.

Moreover, such pollutants were generated for the most part in the most densely populated areas of the country where air pollution due to automobiles was the most severe. Considered in per capita terms, the total volume of pollutants emitted by external combustion in 1960 added up to a not so tidy package of 342 pounds per person.

Table 7.7

Emission Factors for Fuel Oil Combustion (pounds per 1,000 gallons of oil burned)

| | | Type of Unit | | |
| | Power | Industrial and Commercial | | |
Pollutant	Plant	Residual	Distillate	Domestic
Aldehydes	0.6	2	2	2
Carbon monoxide	0.04	2	2	2
Hydrocarbons	3.2	2	2	3
Nitrogen oxides	104	72	72	12
Sulfur dioxide	$157S^a$	$157S^a$	$157S^a$	$157S^a$
Sulfur trioxide	$2.4S^a$	$2S^a$	$2S^a$	$2S^a$
Particulate matter	10	23	15	8

Source: *Compilation of Air Pollutant Emission Factors*, p. 7.

[a] S equals percent of sulfur in the oil which should be multiplied by the number appearing next to S to give pounds of pollutant per 1,000 gallons of fuel oil burned.

Even more sobering is the consideration of what the volume of pollutants from external combustion will be if there is no progress in pollution control and if output expands as projected. The horrendous totals of Tables 7-14 and 7-15 suggest the total weight of pollutants emitted by external combustion would be in excess of 91 billion pounds or 45 million tons in 1980 and 112 billion pounds or 56 million tons in 2000.

It is entirely unlikely that the volume of pollutants reaching the air will increase in accordance with the projections of Tables 7-14 and 7-15. The calculation of the tremendous volume of air pollutants that would be forthcoming if there were no improvement in controls may find its principal usefulness in pointing up the urgency of the situation. Others may feel that this is forcing an open door since industry has given sufficient evidence of its intentions to make a decisive reduction in the air pollution problem.

The most decisive reason for believing that the projection of pollutants in Tables 7-14 and 7-15 is much too high lies in the data of Table 7-16. This latter table shows that the electric power industry accounts for over half of the oxide pollutants and more than 60 percent of the particulates for 1980 and 2000. The

Table 7.8

Estimates of Oxides of Nitrogen and Sulfur Emitted During Combustion of Fuel Oil in 1960 and Projections for 1980 and 2000 Assuming No Improvement in Pollution Control (millions of pounds)

	Estimate		Projections			
	1960		*1980*		*2000*	
Use	*Nitrogen Oxides*	*Sulfur Oxides*	*Nitrogen Oxides*	*Sulfur Oxides*	*Nitrogen Oxides*	*Sulfur Oxides*
Electricity generation	441	1,352	550	1,687	594	1,821
Manufacturing	1,067	4,715	1,693	7,479	3,078	13,596
Commercial	417	1,843	702	3,099	1,219	5,382
Residential	233	6,170	184	4,888	158	4,194
Total:	2,158	14,080	3,129	17,153	5,049	24,993

Source: Computed from data in Table 7.6 for selected years and appropriate emission factors as shown in Table 7.7. Sulfur content of fuel oil in all uses assumed to be 2 percent. Sulfur oxides is sum of sulfur dioxide and sulfur trioxide. The barrel used in petroleum statistics contains 42 gallons. Accordingly, the figures in Table 7.6 were multiplied by 42 and the final results were divided by 1,000 to adjust to the 1,000 gallon units in which Table 7.7 is stated.

only reason the calculated increase in the volume of pollutants associated with electricity generation in 2000 is not more marked is that by 2000 nuclear power is projected to take over a substantial share of the energy supply from coal. As it is, Tables 7-14 and 7-15 show that electricity generation in 2000 is projected to account by itself for 97 percent of the total volume of pollutants generated by all external combustion sources in 1960.

If it is unlikely that the volume of air pollutants in general would expand as projected in Tables 7-14 and 7-15, it is more unlikely still that the electric power industry would permit air pollution from its plants to increase as projected there. The public utilities are subject to continuous and searching popular scrutiny and it is to be expected that they will have abundant incentives to reduce their contribution to air pollution and that they will respond affirmatively to pressures to correct the situation. There is good reason to believe that the electric power industry — far from standing still in pollution suppression —

Table 7.9

Estimates of Particulate Emission From Combustion of Fuel Oil in 1960 and Projections for 1980 and 2000 Assuming No Improvement in Pollution Control

Type of Consumption	Estimate 1960	Projections	
		1980	2000
Electricity generation	42	53	57
Manufacturing[a]	317	503	915
Commercial[b]	110	185	322
Residential	155	123	106
Total:	624	864	1,400

Source: Computed from data in Table 7.6 and appropriate emission factors as shown in Table 7.7. Data adjusted to reflect 42 gallon barrels as explained in note on Table 7.8.

[a]Oil consumption assumed to be 80 percent residual and 20 percent distillate so resultant particulate emission factor is 21.4 pounds per 1,000 gallons burned.

[b]Oil consumption assumed to be 50 percent residual and 50 percent distillate so resultant particulate emission factor is 19 pounds per 1,000 gallons burned.

will, instead, be the scene of major advances in that area. It is reasonable to suppose that improved measures for air pollution control will find their first application in the electric power industry and that the utilities will show the way for other industries to follow. Accordingly, advances in air pollution controls will be discussed first with relation to electricity generation.

Measures to Reduce Industrial Air Pollution

The passage of the Air Quality Act of 1967 enormously stimulated interest in devices to control air pollution. This attention was heightened by the publication in the Federal Register of February 11, 1969 of the national criteria and control techniques recommended by the Department of Health, Education and Welfare to implement the Air Quality Act. Under the Act, the states were given 180 days to adopt suitable standards, following the Department's action,

Table 7.10

Natural Gas Consumption in 1960 and Medium Projections for 1970, 1980, 1990, and 2000, by Use (trillion cubic feet)

Type of Consumption	1960	1970	1980	1990	2000
Electricity generation[a]	2.50	4.16	4.77	4.68	4.65
Manufacturing[b]	3.57	5.20	7.33	10.36	14.62
Commercial	.89	1.21	1.53	1.60	1.61
Residential	3.08	4.30	5.47	5.74	5.78
Total:	10.04	14.87	19.10	22.38	26.66

Source: *Resources in America's Future*, Table A15–14, p. 850.

[a]Includes values on line designated "Public" in RFF Table A15–14 which was judged to be used mainly in electricity generation according to footnote 9 of RFF Table A10–24.

[b]Includes consumption in general manufacturing, iron and steel industry, nonferrous metals, petroleum refining, carbon black manufacture. In all of these industries except the last, natural gas is assumed to be used principally as a fuel in external combustion. Carbon black manufacture accounted for 5.5 percent of all manufacturing consumption in 1960, but this proportion was projected to decline to less than 2 percent in 1980 and less than 1 percent in 2000.

and an additional 180 days to begin to implement and enforce the standards. This was expected to result in a noticeable stiffening of existing state statues [11,12].

Those concerns which had pioneered in the development of methods for capturing pollutants after combustion were expected to benefit most in increased business [16]. (The concerns were Research-Cottrell, Inc.; Monsanto Company; Joy Manufacturing; Koppers Company; Buell Engineering Company; M. W. Kellogg Company; Babcock and Wilcox Company; and SCM Corporation.) Among the more common methods used in abating air pollution are electrostatic precipitation, catalytic oxidation, mechanical collection, gas scrubbing, and bag filters. The first two of these methods are discussed in more detail later. Mechanical collection techniques are employed generally where the particles suspended in the flue gas are relatively large and where the high efficiency

Table 7.11

**Emission Factors for Natural Gas Com-
bustion** (pounds per million cubic feet
of natural gas burned)

	Type of Unit		
Pollutant	Power Plant	Industrial Process Boilers	Domestic and Commercial Heating Units
Aldehydes	1	2	Negligible
Carbon monoxide	Negligible	0.4	0.4
Hydrocarbons	Negligible	Negligible	Negligible
Nitrogen oxides	390	214	116
Sulfur oxides	0.4	0.4	0.4
Other organics	3	5	Negligible
Particulates	15	18	19

Source: *Compilation of Air Pollutant
Emission Factors*, p. 6.

electrostatic precipitator is not required. The gas scrubbing technique operates
by the injection of water into the stream of flue gas, followed by an atomization
process. The atomized droplets of water then collide with the particulate matter.
Dust particles are thereby trapped by the droplets, stripped from the burning
gas, and carried away.

When dealing with a dry, low temperature flue gas, bag filters are generally
used to remove particulate matter from the gas discharge. The bag filter works
on the principle of the vacuum cleaner. The bag filter is then periodically
emptied into hampers for ultimate disposal.

The electrical precipitation process is a method of removing suspended
particulate matter from flue gases. An electric field is set up across two
electrodes between which the gas to be cleaned passes. As the dc voltage
difference between the electrodes is increased, a corona discharge is produced
and suspended matter is attracted to the collecting electrode.

Precipitators can be either of the dry type or wet type. In dry precipitation,
the dust particles adhere to the collecting electrode and are removed by a
mechanical rapping process. In the wet type of precipitation, weirs are
positioned over the collecting electrodes. A liquid is then used to wash the
particles down as they collect.

Table 7.12

Estimates of Nitrogen Oxides and
Sulfur Oxides Emitted During Combus-
tion of Natural Gas in 1960 and
Projections for 1980 and 2000 Assum-
ing No Improvement in Pollution
Control (millions of pounds)

| | Estimate | | Projections | | | |
| | 1960 | | 1980 | | 2000 | |
Type of Consumption	Nitrogen Oxides	Sulfur Oxides	Nitrogen Oxides	Sulfur Oxides	Nitrogren Oxides	Sulfur Oxides
Electricity generation	975	1	1,860	2	1,814	2
Manufacturing	764	1	1,569	3	3,129	6
Commercial	103	-	177	1	187	1
Residential	357	1	635	2	670	2
Total:	2,199	3	4,241	8	5,800	11

Source: Computed from data in Table 7.10
for selected years and appropriate emission
factors as shown in Table 7.11.

The electrostatic precipitator is frequently used in series with mechanical collection equipment. The latter removes the larger particles at lower operating cost per unit, and the electrostatic precipitator then cleans up the finer particles remaining in the flue gas. The high fly ash collection efficiency found in the combination of the electrostatic precipitator and high efficiency cyclone equipment makes them a popular team in electric power generating stations and high capacity space heating installations.

While electrostatic precipitation finds use primarily in removal of particulate matter from flue gases, catalytic oxidation is employed in eliminating gaseous pollutants, among which the sulfur oxides, especially sulfur dioxide, rank among the most hazardous associated with coal. Catalytic oxidation of the sulfur dioxide in flue gases is a key step in a process developed by the Monsanto Company. By oxidizing the sulfur dioxide to sulfur trioxide and absorbing the latter in water to form sulfuric acid, Monsanto hopes to secure a by-product the sale of which will substantially offset the cost of pollution abatement.

The process provides for the removal of particulate matter in the first step by use of a hot electrostatic precipitator which will remove 99.5 percent of the dust suspended in the flue gas. All remaining dust will be removed in subsequent steps where the gas passes through scrubbing towers.

Table 7.13

Estimates of Particulate Matter Emitted During Combustion of Natural Gas in 1960 and Projections for 1980 and 2000 Assuming No Improvement in Pollution Control (millions of pounds)

Type of Consumption	Estimate 1960	Projections 1980	Projections 2000
Electricity generation	38	72	70
Manufacturing	64	132	263
Commercial	17	29	31
Residential	59	104	110
Total:	178	337	474

Source: Computed from data in 7.10 for selected years and appropriate emission factors as shown in Table 7.11.

The precipitator exhaust gas is passed into a converter where its sulfur dioxide is oxidized in the presence of a catalyst to the trioxide form. Monsanto expects to maintain a conversion efficiency of 90 percent in this stage. The flue gas, rich in sulfur trioxide, then enters a packed-bed type absorbing tower where the trioxide is absorbed as sulfuric acid in a counterflow of liquid. The acid is cooled to room temperature and then pumped to storage tanks which are usually located adjacent to a railroad siding where the acid may be transferred to tank cars for transport to market. Heat exchangers absorb waste energy at each stage for transfer elsewhere in the power plant to be used in such functions as preheating boiler waters.

In addition to producing a by-product whose sale can substantially offset air pollution abatement costs, Monsanto feels the process offers other advantages: (1) removes virtually all fly ash from the flue gas; (2) keeps sulfur dioxide emissions well below anticipated legislative requirements, even when lower-cost, high-sulfur fuels are burned; and (3) makes unnecessary high smokestacks which are costly to build and maintain.

The U.S. Bureau of Mines considered and rejected a process for the catalytic oxidation of sulfur dioxide in favor of its opposite — a reduction process. In pilot plant experiments, sulfur dioxide and trioxide are removed from the flue

Table 7.14

Estimates of Nitrogen Oxides and Sulfur Oxides Emitted from Combustion
of Coal, Fuel Oil and Natural Gas in
1960 and Projections for 1980 and
2000 Assuming No Improvement in
Pollution Control (millions of pounds)

Type of Consumption	Estimate 1960		Projections			
	1960		1980		2000	
	Nitrogen Oxides	Sulfur Oxides	Nitrogen Oxides	Sulfur Oxides	Nitrogen Oxides	Sulfur Oxides
Electricity generation	5,576	17,161	10,550	32,621	11,548	36,555
Manufacturing	4,871	10,492	6,642	13,904	10,607	21,962
Commercial	696	3,515	951	3,784	1,470	5,991
Residential	750	7,691	907	5,726	828	4,196
Total:	11,893	38,859	19,050	56,035	24,453	68,704

Source: Table 7.4, 7.8, and 7.12.

gases by absorption in solid alkalized alumina. The absorbent is then regenerated by heating with hydrogen or a steam formed natural gas, in the course of which the sulfur oxides are reduced to elemental sulfur.

The Bureau of Mines feels that the sulfur recovered by the reduction process is much easier to store and therefore will be a more convenient and profitable by-product for disposal [3:353-358;6,781-786;7].

The coal industry has been able to effect some reduction in coal's pyritic sulfur content through separation employing the electrostatic, magnetic, pneumatic, and hydraulic methods. Other sulfur separation methods still in the development stages are solvent extraction/filtration and hydrogenation [8].

Major coal users, such as the electric utilities, use all their engineering knowhow in the effort to achieve maximum combustion efficiency which is associated happily with low emission of pollutants. In general, completeness of combustion and hence efficiency increases as the air input rises, but overall efficiency is eventually reduced by the cooling effect of added air [13:25].

Among the improvements suggested by the Public Health Service as worthy of research is the substitution or addition of pure oxygen in place of air. This would increase combustion completeness, might "essentially eliminate emissions

Table 7.15

**Estimates of Particulates Emitted from
Combustion of Coal, Fuel Oil, and
Natural Gas in 1960 and Projections
for 1980 and 2000 Assuming No
Improvement in Pollution Control**
(millions of pounds)

| Type of | Estimate | Projections | |
Consumption	1960	1980	2000
Electricity generation	5,280	10,300	11,552
Manufacturing	4,181	4,860	6,678
Commercial	677	439	553
Residential	714	502	216
Total:	10,852	16,101	18,999

Source: Tables 7.5, 7.9, and 7.13.

of nitrogen oxides" and might serve as "a means of reducing the volume of stack gases to make treatment of such gases (for removal of sulfur oxides) more economical [13:95].

Dilution as an Air Pollution Modifier

The discussion thus far has dealt with the chemical and mechanical methods of capturing air pollutants before they leave the smokestacks of power stations. Those pollutants which do escape have importance mainly insofar as they contribute to dangerous concentrations of noxious gases in metropolitan areas. The air basins over such metropolitan areas receive pollution from many other sources in addition to electric power stations, notably from automobiles and fuel oil combustion for space heating. Whether the pollutants discharged into the air by power stations add significantly to the level of pollution depends in large measure on how much they are diluted. The sulfur oxides and particulate matter discharged by a power plant located in a rural area some distance from the nearest metropolitan area are likely to be so diluted with clean country air as to be of no consequence. However, power losses in transmission increase roughly in proportion to the distance between the generating station and the point of

Table 7.16

Percentage Distribution by Type of Consumption of Pollutants Emitted in the Combustion of Coal, Fuel Oil, and Natural Gas, 1960, Estimated, 1980 and 2000 Projected Assuming No Improvement in Pollution Control

	Estimate 1960			Percent Distribution 1980			Projections 2000		
Type of Consumption	Nitrogen Oxides	Sulfur Oxides	Particulates	Nitrogen Oxides	Sulfur Oxides	Particulates	Nitrogen Oxides	Sulfur Oxides	Particulates
Electricity generation	47	43	49	55	58	64	47	53	61
Manufacturing	41	27	39	35	25	30	43	32	35
Commercial	6	9	6	5	7	3	6	9	3
Residential	6	20	7	5	10	3	3	6	1
Total[a]	100	99	101	100	100	100	99	100	100

Source: Computed from data in Tables 7.14 and 7.15.

[a]Totals may not add to 100 due to rounding.

Table 7.17

Comparison of "Medium" and "High"
Projections of Coal Consumption in
Electric Power Generation (millions
of short tons)

Year	Medium	High
1970	287	380
1980	395	568
1990	414	695
2000	444	895

Source: *Resources in America's Future*,
Table A15–10, p. 844.

consumption. This limits the economic feasibility of locating power stations at sufficient distances from metropolitan areas — always major points of consumption — to accomplish significant abatement of air pollution.

A very high smokestack may accomplish somewhat the same effect of massive dilution by directing the discharge into the faster-moving airstreams well above ground level. With a high enough smokestack the power station may be located in the metropolitan area without contributing critically to air pollution. There are, of course, substantial costs attached to either the rural generation of power or high smokestack solutions of air pollution problems.

**Electric Power's Use of Coal is
Increasing Faster than RFF Projected**

So far as the electric power industry is concerned, accelerated control efforts are especially necessary because there is substantial evidence that the *potential* volume of pollutants it produces may increase even faster than is suggested by Tables 7-14 and 7-15 which are based on the assumption that coal consumption in electricity generation will increase in accordance with the medium projections of RFF. Actually, coal consumption in electricity generation has increased during the 1960's at a rate more nearly corresponding to the high than to the medium projection of RFF. The two projections are compared in Table 7-17. This is true of the demand for electric power in general.

Moreover, as has been noted, coal is "dirtier" than other fuels, that is, produces more air pollutants per heat unit generated than other fuels. Thus, if

Table 7.18

**Projections of Emissions of Particulate
Matter from the Combustion of Coal
in Electric Power Generation Assuming
High Increase in Consumption and
Substantial Progress in Pollution Control**

Year	Projected Coal Consumption in Electric Power Generation[a] (million short tons)	Particulate Matter Emission (pounds per ton coal burned)	Projected Particulate Matter Discharge (million pounds)
1980	568	10^b	5,680
2000	895	2^c	1,790

[a]From Table 7.17, corresponding to RFF High Projection.

[b]Assuming universal adoption by electric power industry of current Good standards of particulate matter control by electric power industry. See Table 7.19.

[c]Assuming universal adoption by electric power industry of particulate matter control equipment of 99 percent collection efficiency used with coal of 10 percent ash content.

electric power output is increasing faster than Tables 7-14 and 7-15 allow for and if an increasing portion is generated from coal, there are two reasons for assuming that Table 7-14 and 7-15 understate the electric power industry's potential for the emission of pollutants. On the other hand, it has been noted that Tables 7-14 and 7-15 grossly overstate the volume of air pollutants likely to be released in electricity generation because they make no allowance for improved pollution control whereas dramatic improvement in this respect is possible and even probable. An experiment with a better balanced approach allowing for a more rapid rate of increase in coal consumption for electricity generation *and* improved pollution control may be worthwhile.

The results of such an experiment are shown in Table 7-18 which represents the consequences of assuming the RFF high projection of coal consumption in electricity generation and a rate of increase in control of particulates by the industry which is substantial, but believed to be well within reach. Specifically, the universal adoption of the degree of particulate control designated as good in Table 7-19 is assumed in calculating the particulate emission estimates of Table 7-18. A comparison of the projections set forth in Table 7-15 is of interest. It will be noted that the projection for 1980 of Table 7-18, regarded as the more realistic of the two, allows for an emission of the still considerable amount of 5,680 million pounds of particulates by the industry. This is 2,100 million pounds, or 7.5 percent, greater than estimated particulate emission by the

Table 7-19

**Estimate of Controlled Particulate
Emissions from Coal Combustion**

| | Particulate Per Ton of Coal Burned, Pounds | | |
Degree of Control	Electric Generating Plants	Industrial Plants	Domestic and Commercial Plants
Average	25	25	25
Good	10	15	20

Source: U. S. Public Health Service, *Atmospheric Emissions from Coal Combustion* (Washington, D. C.: Government Printing Office, 1968), Public Health Service Publication No. 999-AP-24, Table 2-3, p. 5.

electric power industry in 1960 from combustion of all types of fuels, reflecting the effect of increased volume of coal projected for consumption in 1980. On the other hand, the 1980 figure of Table 7-18 is only 55 percent as large as the equivalent figure of Table 7-15, reflecting the more realistic assumption concerning progress in pollution control. The difference is even more striking for the year 2000 because continued progress is assumed in pollution control. Thus, the figure for 2000 in Table 7-18 is only about 15 percent of the equivalent figure in Table 7-15, and is even 66 percent below the estimated particulate emissions from electricity generation in 1960.

It is reasonable to suppose that reductions in emission of nitrogen and sulfur oxides from electricity generation will be comparable to those in Table 7-18. In general, there are several persuasive reasons for anticipating marked improvements in pollution control by the electric power industry: (1) the utilities are very much in the public spotlight and conscious of the public relations value of reducing their contribution to pollution; (2) rate regulating agencies are likely to look kindly on investments and additions to cost necessary to bring utilities into compliance with federal and state antipollution legislation; and (3) some pollution control measures such as certain of those used to suppress sulfur oxide emissions rely on sale of by-products to help defray their cost. This is most likely to be economically feasible for large scale fuel users such as the electric utilities.

The second-largest coal-using industry — iron and steel — is likewise in a good position to apply those pollution control techniques that depend for economic feasibility on scale of operations. Moreover, for other reasons the industry is rapidly extending its use of methods involving oxygen-enriched combustion which should favor pollution control. Other industrial fuel uses involve situations so varied as to defy generalization for the most part. It can be said that effective legislative control of pollution is likely to be easier to accomplish for large than for small users for reasons already noted in connection with electric utilities, namely, (1) large users are likely to be more aware of the public relations value of early compliance with pollution control measures; and (2) the economic feasibility of some pollution control measures such as those used in suppression of sulfur increases with a rise in the scale of operations.

Commercial and residential fuel consumers may be considered as analagous with respect to air pollution to small industrial users. All but a handful of the largest commercial and residential users are small in comparison to most industrial consumers of fuel.

In general, it is to be expected that air pollution control measures by all classes of users will benefit from the technical progress that is likely to be stimulated in the first place by the problems and needs of large fuel consumers. Thus the plants of the electric power industry and other major industrial users will probably be the site of the first applications, if they are not, in fact, the birthplace of a new generation of more advanced and efficient air pollution control devices.

Some aspects of residential and commercial uses of fuel oil present problems that are worthy of special comment.

Commercial and Residential Uses of Fuel

The type of fuel consumed is the most important factor affecting the volume of air pollutants associated with the commercial and residential consumption of fuel. The shift in the type of fuel consumed is most pronounced with respect to residences where all the expansion in fuel use is projected to be in natural gas.

Thus, residential consumption of natural gas is projected to increase by 78 percent from 1960 to 1980 and by an additional 10 percent at the 1960 figure during the following 20 years (see Table 7-10). In contrast, residential consumption of coal is projected to decline to 55 percent of the 1960 figure in 1980 and to be virtually nil in 2000 (see Table 7-2). Fuel oil is expected to retain a larger share of the residential market than coal, but also to decline steadily in both absolute and relative importance in residential use. Thus, projected 1980 residential consumption of fuel oil is 79 percent of the 1960 figure and that of 2000 only 68 percent (see Table 7-6). As a consequence of this projected shift in type of fuel consumed to the cleaner natural gas, it is expected that the contribution of residential fuel consumption to air pollution will be decisively lowered even under the assumption of no improvement in pollution control. Thus, the emission of sulfur oxides in residential fuel consumption, assuming no improvement in pollution control, is projected to decline to 74 percent of the 1960 figure in 1980 and to 55 percent of the same in 2000 (see Table 7-14). The projected decline in particulate emission under the same assumptions is even more pronounced, dropping to 70 percent of the 1960 figure in 1980 and to 30 percent of the same in 2000 (see Table 7-15). Only with respect to emission of nitrogen oxides from residential consumption is there an indication of a small increase from 1960 levels shown in Table 7-14.

As in residential use, commercial consumption of natural gas is projected to increase rapidly, rising by 72 percent from 1960 to 1980 and by an additional 9 percent of the 1960 level in 2000 (see Table 7-10). Also as in residential use, Commercial coal consumption is expected to decline to 39 percent of the 1960 level in 1980 and further to 36 percent of the same in 2000 (see Table 7-2). However, in contrast to the residential scene, the commercial market for fuel oil is expected to be an expanding one, increasing by 68 percent from 1960 to 1980 and further to 292 percent of the 1960 figure in 2000 (see Table 7-6).

Since the shift to the cleaner natural gas is projected to be much less pronounced in commercial uses than in residential, there is less pronounced improvement in the projected outlook for air pollution. Again, making the assumption of no improvement in pollution control, the volume of sulfur oxides emitted in commercial combustion of all fuels is projected to increase slightly by 8 percent from 1960 to 1980 and sharply to 170 percent of the 1960 figure in 2000 (see Table 7-14). The projected increase from 1980 to 2000 is attributable to the fact that all the expected expansion of demand for fuel is projected to be met by fuel oil, from which sulfur oxide emissions are relatively high. The projected increase in nitrogen oxides from commercial fuel consumption under the same assumption of no improvement in pollution control boosted the 1980 figure to 137 percent of the 1960 level, and further to 211 percent of the same in 2000 (see Table 7-14). With respect to particulates from commercial combustion, however, the situation is markedly improved and both the 1980 and 2000 figures under the usual assumptions are well below that for 1960 (see Table 7-15).

Actually, the situation with respect to pollutants actually reaching the atmosphere from both residential and commercial fuel combustion is likely to be much better than the projections discussed in this section would suggest. It is safe to assume that virtually all of the surviving residential and commercial uses of coal will be in very large installations, probably in 1980 and almost certainly by 2000. There is no reason why such large-scale residential and commercial coal users should not achieve high levels of pollution control comparable to those suggested earlier as likely in electric power. Accordingly, the assumption used in constructing Tables 7-14 and 7-15 of no improvement in pollution control would not be tenable. This same qualification would be likely to hold for a very large percentage of the commercial fuel oil applications.

High Sulfur Fuel Oils

It has been noted that the decline in use of fuel oil projected for residential space heating is not expected to be matched by a similar drop in commercial usage where consumption is projected to expand steadily from 1960 to 2000.

Much of this growing commercial demand as well as that of other major users such as manufacturers and the electric power industry has been met by low cost, high sulfur residual oils, especially in the populous northeastern and central states. In these highly urbanized areas, the sulfur oxides emitted in combustion of high sulfur residual oils have been joined by similar pollutants from automobile exhaust and the smokestacks of power stations burning coal with a substantial sulfur content. In 1964, the New York metropolitan area consumed 113 million gallons of residual oil and 87 percent of this total was imported from western hemisphere sources and had an average sulfur content of nearly 2.6 percent [5:154]. Low sulfur fuel oils are available from Libyan and Nigerian sources which can be blended with the sulfur laden South American oils to reduce sulfur content to acceptable levels. New York City has enacted legislation requiring that sulfur content of oil be limited to an average of 2 percent by May 1969 and calling for a further reduction to 1 percent by October 1969 [19]. A major technical difficulty in the enforcement of the 1 percent limit is that the sweet, low sulfur oils do not flow through equipment as easily at ordinary temperatures as had the sour or heavily sulfurized oils. This does not affect the small homeowner who has used the diesel type of lighter residual oil for years. Nor does it affect such major consumers as the utilities who had installed expensive equipment needed to keep the oil at free flowing temperatures. But many factories, large apartment houses, office buildings, and institutions were not similarly equipped. Such users will have to adjust to the legislation or enforcement will break down. That the oil industry expected air pollution control officials to hold the line is evidenced by the fact that the article which detailed these difficulties also reported that "the petroleum industry is spending hundreds of millions of dollars to rush the desulphurization plants to completion [17].

Conclusion

Air pollution from fossil fuels is unquestionably a function of energy source. The six major forms of energy sources in the United States are petroleum, natural gas, natural gas liquids, coal, hydro power and nuclear power. Of the six major energy sources, hydro and nuclear power are essentially free of air pollutant emission. Natural gas and natural gas liquids produce almost untraceable amounts of sulfur oxides and, therefore, have a negligible impact on the sulfur oxide pollution problem. Sulfur oxide pollutants have long been the main concern of the pollution control agencies because of their detrimental effects to human and plant life and for their corrosive and discoloration effects on materials.

Because the sulfur content of a fuel is of such vital importance, a study was made to determine the natural state practical sulfur content of the energy sources under consideration. For coal, a one percent sulfur content is about the best that can be expected in the near future. The state-of-the-art content of the low sulfur-bearing petroleum fuels can be expected to be not much lower than two percent. It is possible to remove sulfur from the fuel either prior or subsequent to the combustion process. Most of the modern processes remove the sulfur oxides subsequent to the combustion process.

Air pollution is a disease of urban America. If fuels were uniformly consumed throughout the United States, the quantity of pollutants released to the atmosphere would not tend to create many local or regional air pollution problems. The great majority of fuel consumed in the United States is in populated areas near saltwater ports, with the Atlantic Coast megalopolis being the greatest offender.

If we are not to choke to death, if our plant life is to continue to survive, if our cities and towns are to remain free of pollutant products, we must continue to support air pollution abatement legislation. The amount of air available to our inhabitants is most certainly fixed in volume. With no known method for increasing this air volume it becomes prudent to control the air pollution sources.

8

Air Pollution and the Expanding Consumption of Fuels in Internal Combustion Engines

Alan Thierman

One of the greatest problems in our society is air pollution. Motor vehicles, especially the automobile, have contributed more to creating air pollution problems than any other source. The side effects associated with the use of the automobile are relatively recent, due to the tremendous growth in automobile usage after World War II. In 1945, there were 26 million passenger cars registered in the United States, whereas in 1960 the number of registered vehicles had increased to 59 million [65:660]. The growth in automobile usage continued at a rapid rate through the 1960s. By 1966, there were 78 million passenger cars on the nation's streets and highways — a threefold increase over 1945 [72:31]. America's population, however, increased only 39 percent for the same period. The American economy was not prepared for the tremendous growth in automotive fuel consumption or for meeting the resulting air pollution problems.

During the postwar period, little research had been conducted on the effects and quantities of emissions from the internal combustion engine. Medical research, however, did link air pollution with several diseases and chronic conditions. As automobile travel increased, the problems of urban America with regard to air pollution grew worse. Since passenger cars are mainly concentrated in the major metropolitan areas, it is these areas which suffer the greatest air pollution problems. As air pollution conditions worsened, and with projections for the increased usage of automotive fuels, legislation was enacted in the late 1950s and throughout the 1960s to abate some of the harmful emissions from the internal combustion engine and automobile exhaust [22:12-15].

Despite federal legislation, the overall automotive air pollution problem may be growing worse. One of the main weaknesses with existing laws is that older vehicles are not covered by emission control legislation. Standards have not yet been developed at the federal level for controlling the emission of nitrogen oxides and lead resulting from the burning of fuels. Legislation of the 1960s, however, has established federal responsibility for coordinating the effort to control pollution of the air. Emission control devices are installed on 1968 model cars, but their degree of effectiveness is yet to be determined. Federal legislation has also resulted in the development of ambient air quality standards by all states and has provided a stimulus for research and development activities by automobile and oil companies. It will be several years before the effectiveness of the air pollution legislation can be evaluated. Many technological advances have been made in recent years by industry and government; however, more research is needed in order that the quality of the air in our environment can be maintained or improved [28:1-3].

The principal function of this paper is to investigate the extent of future air pollution caused by the internal combustion engine, based on anticipated increases in fuel usage to the year 2000. As a source of information on the projected consumption of fuels, data contained in the study *Resources in America's Future* are being used [65:640-668].

In setting the framework for this study, two constraints will be imposed. Firstly, the projections in *Resources in America's Future* (RFF) will be accepted as being valid indications of the future. These projections are the result of several years of research and study, with great care taken in formulating data on the supply and demand for natural resources. Secondly, it has been assumed that present technology will not change with regard to use of the internal combustion engine and that there will be no radical shifts in future supply and demand. Currently under study are the electric and steam-powered automobiles which are possible alternatives to automobiles powered by the internal combustion engine. For purposes of this chapter, no effort will be made to evaluate the results of adopting such vehicles to meet future pollution problems in the atmosphere.

Automotive Air Pollution Relates
to the American City

Since the side effects associated with the projected increase in fuel usage relate mainly to the automobile, this study will deal mainly with automotive pollution problems. Much attention will be directed toward developing the causes and adverse conditions of air pollution, examining pertinent legislation and technological advances in the field, and evaluating the magnitude of the automobile air pollution problem. Air pollution is mainly a problem for urban Americans since automobiles are concentrated in metropolitan areas. As such, the problems of specific urbanized areas will be examined. Air pollution projections will be developed for these areas to the year 2000, based on statistical projections for passenger cars.

Projections of Automotive
Fuel Consumption to the Year 2000

It has been projected by RFF that the total stock of passenger cars will double by 1980 from 1960 levels [65:641]. The study further predicts that by the year 2000, four times as many passenger cars will be on the nation's roads than in 1960. This data, as noted on Table 8-1, is based on RFF medium projections. By the year 2000, 244 million passenger vehicles may be in use, according to Table 8-1. Since the U.S. Bureau of the Census estimate of population at January 1, 1967 was 197 million, passenger cars in 2000 are expected to exceed current population by 47 million [71:13]. When considering the high projections by RFF in Table 8-1, the passenger car stock is expected to increase six times by the year 2000 from 1960.

Table 8.1

Projected Stocks of User-Operated
Passenger Vehicles from 1970 - 2000

	1950	1955	1960		1970	1980	1990	2000
				L	81.0	113.7	151.7	199.4
Total stock of vehicles (millions)	36.5	48.5	59.3	M	83.3	120.2	168.6	243.5
				H	91.0	143.6	229.3	372.2

Source: *Resources in America's Future*, p. 641. Projected data refers to all types of user-operated vehicles, including airborne. Historical data, however, are confined to automobiles.

Data for the projected fuel requirements to the year 2000 are summarized on Table 8-2. Automotive fuel consumption is expected to double by 1980 and increase fourfold by 2000 from 1960 fuel consumed (Table 8-2, medium projections). Truck fuel consumption will increase at a faster rate than for the passenger car, mainly due to the expected increase in the average size of trucks [65:147]. Table 8-2 indicates that fuel consumption for trucks will increase five times by 2000 from 1960 levels. On the other hand, bus fuel consumption is not expected to increase more than 50 percent by the year 2000 from 1960. Total fuel consumption for passenger cars, trucks, and buses is anticipated to increase four times from 1960, according to the RFF.

In analyzing the fuel requirements for various means of transportation using the internal combustion engine, the automobile clearly uses the greatest volume of fuels (71 percent in 1960) and is projected to consume 67 percent by the year 2000. Trucks consume approximately 27 percent of fuels, but relatively fewer pollutants are emitted by the diesel-operated truck than from the automobile. Fuel consumption of both the bus and airplane are considered negligible when compared to fuel usage by the automobile. When considering the problem of air pollution caused by the internal combustion engine, the projected consumption of fuels from the automobile must be the problem of major concern to the American people.

*Relation of Fuel Consumption Projections
to Air Pollution*

The expected expansion of fuel usage, as shown in Table 8-2, will most certainly create or increase existing problems in controlling vehicular pollution. As more

Table 8-2

Projected Vehicle Mileage and Fuel Requirements for Motor Vehicles — 1970-2000

	1940	1945	1950	1955	1960
Passenger cars:					
Total stock (millions)	26.2	25.6	36.5	48.5	59.3
Miles per vehicle (thousands)	9.5	7.8	10.0	10.1	9.9
Passenger-car-miles (billions)	250	200	364	488	588
Miles per gallon	15.3	15.0	n.a.	14.5	14.3
Fuel consumption:					
Gallons (billions)	16.3	13.3	n.a.	33.5	41.2
Barrels (millions)	388	317	n.a.	798	981
Trucks:					
Total stock (millions)	4.7	4.8	8.0	9.8	11.6
Truck-miles (billions)	50	46	91	111	126
Miles per gallon	9.7	9.1	n.a.	8.3	7.9
Fuel consumption:					
Gallons (billions)	5.16	5.06	n.a.	13.3	15.9

	1970	*1980*	*1990*	*2000*
L	81.0	113.7	151.7	199.4
M	83.3	120.2	168.6	243.5
H	91.0	143.6	229.3	372.2
	9.8	9.8	9.8	9.8
L	794	1,114	1,487	1,954
M	816	1,178	1,652	2,386
H	892	1,407	2,247	3,648
	14.5	14.5	14.5	14.5
L	54.8	76.8	102.6	134.8
M	56.3	81.2	113.9	164.6
H	61.5	97.0	155.0	251.6
L	1,305	1,829	2,443	3,210
M	1,340	1,933	2,712	3,919
H	1,464	2,310	3,691	5,991
L	14.2	17.9	22.6	28.8
M	16.4	23.0	32.2	45.7
H	19.0	30.1	47.4	76.2
L	155	195	246	314
M	179	251	351	498
H	207	328	517	831
	7.3	6.9	6.5	6.5
L	21.2	28.3	37.8	48.3
M	24.5	36.4	54.0	76.6
H	28.4	47.5	79.5	127.8

(continued)

Table 8-2 (*continued*)

	1940	1945	1950	1955	1960
Barrels (millions)	123	120	n.a.	317	379
Buses:					
Index of growth (1960 = 100)	–	–	–	–	100
Interurban buses	–	–	–	–	100
Local commercial buses	–	–	–	–	100
School buses	–	–	–	–	100
Buses-miles (billions)	2.7	3.8	4.1	4.5	4.4
Fuel consumption: Gallons (billions)	.44	.70	n.a.	.77	.83
Barrels (millions)	10.5	16.7	n.a.	18.3	19.8
Total fuel consumption: (bil. bbl.)	.52	.45	n.a.	1.13	1.38

	1970	1980	1990	2000
L	505	674	900	1,150
M	583	867	1,286	1,824
H	676	1,131	1,893	3,043
L	91.0	87.6	86.7	85.6
M	108.1	120.5	137.3	146.9
H	127.4	162.2	210.6	272.2
L	77.5	66.7	56.4	52.5
M	93.6	95.1	94.1	89.2
H	109.3	123.0	145.6	180.4
L	75.8	70.5	63.2	58.9
M	100.0	109.5	117.9	123.2
H	125.3	158.9	202.1	268.4
L	134.7	143.3	165.3	173.3
M	140.0	170.7	224.0	258.7
H	152.7	215.2	304.0	389.3
L	4.0	3.9	3.8	3.8
M	4.8	5.3	6.0	6.5
H	5.6	7.1	9.3	12.0
L	.76	.73	.72	.71
M	.90	1.00	1.14	1.22
H	1.06	1.35	1.75	2.26
L	18.1	17.4	17.1	16.9
M	21.4	23.8	27.1	29.0
H	25.2	32.1	41.7	53.8
L	1.83	2.52	3.36	4.38
M	1.94	2.82	4.02	5.77
H	2.16	3.47	5.63	9.09

Source: H. H. Lansberg, L. L. Fischman, and J. L. Fisher, *Resources in America's Future* (Baltimore, Md.: The Johns Hopkins Press, 1963), Table A5-15, p. 661. Readers wishing more detail concerning the sources and assumptions involved in deriving this table are referred to the extensive footnotes in the above RFF volume.

emissions from fuels are projected into the nation's constant air mass, more air pollution will be the inevitable result. Increased fuel consumption indicates that more people will be affected by air pollution in the future unless action is taken at the present.

Since the RFF projections were made on the basis on 1960 data and since data for more recent years are now available, it is possible to check on the accuracy of the trends implied by the RFF projections. Such a comparison suggests that fuel consumption in motor vehicles is increasing significantly more rapidly than RFF projected. Substantially, this arises because of a considerable underestimation by RFF of the rate of increase in the stock of automobiles in use, rather than an error in such factors as miles per gallon of fuel. With respect to the stock of passenger cars, however, an interpolation for 1966 between 1960 actual and RFF 1970 projected gives 69.9 million for the medium value and 73.0 million for the high (see Appendix A). In 1966, however, the Bureau of Public Roads reported the number of passenger cars registered as 78.4 million, or 12 percent above the RFF medium projection and 7 percent above even the high RFF value [72:49].

In Chapter 1 the possibility that resource depletion might interfere with the realization of RFF projections was considered and rejected as unlikely for the most part. There seems no reason to change this view with respect to the resource base for automobile fuels, certainly not for the period before 1980. However, the possibility of increased fuel prices due to resource scarcity by the end of the century cannot be excluded, though such forecasts have been proven wrong frequently in the past.

The Side Effects Associated with the Expanding Output of Automotive Fuels

RFF projections indicate that the usage of motor fuels will grow at a faster rate than the total population. The projections in Table 8-2 indicate that the passenger car stock by the year 2000 will exceed current population by 47 million, according to U. S. Census Bureau data [71:13]. Relatively more people will thus be affected by unclean air in the future.

Emissions from all motor vehicles are directly related to the amount of fuels consumed. As motor vehicles consume more fuels, more air pollution is the result. This relationship is shown on Table 8-5. In 1966, a survey was conducted by the Public Health Service of total air pollution in the United States. The results of this survey indicate that motor vehicles contribute more to the creation of air pollution than any other source (Table 8-3). Table 8-3 indicates that motor vehicles emitted 66 million tons of carbon monoxide in 1966 of total emissions of 72 million tons. Vehicle emissions also contribute most of the hydrocarbons to the air we breath as well as 46 percent of the nitrogen oxides. Other emissions by the motor vehicle are not considered material.

Table 8.3

Total U. S. Air Pollution by Source–1966
(millions of tons per year)

Source	Carbon Monoxide	Sulphur Dioxide	Nitrogen Oxides	Hydro-carbons	Partic-ulates
Space Heating	2	3	1	1	1
Refuse Disposal	1	1	1	1	1
Motor Vehicles	66	1	6	12	1[a]
Elect. Gen. Plants	1	12	3	1	3
Industry	2	9	2	4	6
Total	72	26	13	19	12

Source: U. S. Department of Health, Education, and Welfare, Public Health Service, *The Sources of Air Pollution and Their Control* (Washington: Government Printing Office, 1967), pp. 3–13.

[a]Total does not include lead emissions of 190,000 tons per year.

Based upon the Public Health Service air pollution data presented in Table 8-3 and data compiled by the Bureau of Public Roads on 1966 fuel consumption (Table 8-4), it is possible to derive an air pollution index for various emissions from the motor vehicle (Table 8-4). This index of pollution indicates the average amount of air pollution caused by one gallon of gasoline in 1966 for various emissions. The data indicates that carbon monoxide is the main emission from the internal combustion engine. Table 8-4 shows that one gallon of fuel consumed results in carbon monoxide emissions of 1.76 pounds. Hydrocarbon emissions average about one-third of a pound, and emissions of nitrogen oxides and particulates average approximately one-sixth of a pound per gallon of fuel consumption.

Projections of Total U.S. Air Pollution – 1970-2000

Utilizing the air pollution indexes developed in Table 8-4, it is now possible to project total future air pollution caused by motor vehicles for 1970 to 2000 (Table 8-5), based on fuel consumption projections in Table 8-2. These

Table 8.4

**Air Pollution Per Gallon of Gasoline
Consumed for Motor Vehicles
Operated in 1966**

Fuel consumption for all motor vehicles:[a]

(billions of gallons)	75

Motor veh. emissions[b]   (millions of tons)

carbon monoxide	66
oxides of nitrogen	6
sulphur dioxide	1
hydrocarbons	12
particulates	1
lead	.19

Air pollution per gallon of gasoline (tons)

carbon monoxide	.0008800
oxides of nitrogen	.0000800
sulphur dioxide	.0000133
hydrocarbons	.0001733
particulates	.0000800
lead	.0000025

Air pollution per gallon of gasoline (pounds)

carbon monoxide	1.7600
oxides of nitrogen	.1600
sulphur dioxide	.0266
hydrocarbons	.3466
particulates	.1600
lead	.0050

Source: [a]U. S. Department of Transportation, Bureau of Public Roads, *Highway Statistics–1966* (Washington, D. C.: Government Printing Office, 1967), p. 49. Motor vehicles include passenger cars, buses, and cargo vehicles.

[b]Data from Table 8.3.

projections are based on the assumption that future emissions will be left uncontrolled as in 1966. Although motor vehicle emissions are not likely to remain unchanged in the future, the nature and extent of the change in vehicle emissions is not easily predicted. Air pollution control legislation and technological advances may influence the amount of future emissions. It is extremely difficult to evaluate the effectiveness of present legislation or anticipate future technological advances.

Projections in Table 8-5 are based on the assumption that air pollution will increase proportionately to motor vehicle fuel consumption. On this basis, air pollution will double by 1980 from 1960 levels and increase fourfold by the year 2000. According to the 1966 Public Health Service survey in Table 8-3, 86 million tons of pollutants were emitted by motor vehicles. The projections on Table 8-5 indicate that air pollution in the year 2000 will be 298 million tons for vehicles operated using the internal combustion engine if there is no improvement in automotive pollution controls above 1966 levels.

The air pollution projections in Table 8-5 give a general indication of the magnitude of the problem facing the American people. The projections, however, have assumed that future motor vehicles will be controlled by 1966 standards. Another weakness in these projections is that no consideration is given to the future air pollution of individual localities. Air pollution is a problem confined mainly to urban areas and specifically to large cities. The problems of air pollution in individual cities will be considered in a later section of this paper, and projections will be made for the air pollution of specific metropolitan areas. The total air pollution problem caused by motor vehicles is basically a problem of the cities; therefore, the overall projections of air pollution (Table 8-5) are not too revealing.

Air Pollution a Problem of Urban America

In a Public Health Service survey, it was determined that all major cities with populations over one million, according to the 1960 census, have major air pollution problems [27:9]. The data presented on Table 8-6 are the result of surveys taken of state and local air pollution officials. Although opinions of these experts in the field will vary with regard to the degree of severity of the problem, the data do present a good cross-section of views on the urban air pollution problem. The data in Table 8-6 indicates that 308 major urban places with populations over 2,500 have major air pollution problems, an increase of 84 over a similar survey conducted ten years earlier. Approximately 70 percent of the urban places with populations between 500,000 and one million have a major air pollution problem, according to Table 8-6. For cities with populations between 250,000 and 500,000, 45 percent have great problems in controlling pollution of the air, and 45 percent are experiencing moderate air pollution problems. According to Table 8-6 about one-third of the American people live in urban areas with major air pollution problems. An additional 22 percent of the

Table 8.5

Projected Future Air Pollution From Motor Vehicles If Emissions Are Left Uncontrolled As In 1966

		1970	1980	1990	2000
Projected fuel consumption[a] (billions of gallons)		81.7	118.6	169.0	242.4
Air pollution per gallon of gasoline consumed[b] (tons)					
carbon monoxide	.0008800				
oxides of nitro.	.0000800				
sulphur dioxide	.0000133				
hydrocarbons	.0001733				
particulates	.0000800				
lead	.0000025				
Projected future air pollution (millions of tons)					
carbon monoxide		71.9	104.3	148.7	213.3
oxides of nitrogen		6.5	9.5	13.5	19.4
sulphur dioxide		1.1	1.6	2.2	3.2
hydrocarbons		14.2	20.5	29.2	42.0
particulates		6.5	9.5	13.5	19.4
lead		.2	.3	.4	.6
Total		100.4	145.7	207.5	297.9

[a]Data obtained from Table 8.2. Middle projections of fuel consumption were used for passenger cars, buses, and trucks.

[b]Data obtained from Table 8.4. These rates have been assumed to remain constant to the year 2000 for purposes of this analysis.

population reside in urban areas with moderate problems in controlling the quality of the air. Table 8-6 also indicates that about 7,300 urban places over 2,500 in population, housing 60 percent of the nation's population, have an air pollution problem. The problem of air pollution thus appears to be confined mainly to urban areas. Most of the American people live under conditions of polluted air.

It has been established that air pollution is mainly a problem of areas with large concentrations of population. The Public Health Service survey presented in Table 8-6 was made in the early 1960s. Since the survey was conducted, both urban population and motor vehicle fuel consumption have increased, according to the U. S. Bureau of the Census [71] and the American Petroleum Institute [66:178], respectively. According to Table 8-2, fuel consumption is expected to double by 1980 from 1960 levels. Since the motor vehicle creates most of the air pollution in the United States, air pollution problems have probably worsened through the 1960s based on increases in motor fuel consumption at a faster rate than total population. According to U. S. Census Bureau data "the metropolitan population overall increased about twice as rapidly as the nonmetropolitan between 1960 and 1965, and the proportion of the population living in metropolitan areas, now more than 3 out of 5, continued its upward trend [70:10].

Table 8-7 presents data on the anticipated urban population to the year 2000. In 1960, 48.3 percent of the United States population lived in cities with populations of over 50,000. In 1980, it is projected that 59.4 percent of the people will be residing in the larger cities. By the year 2000, more than two-thirds of the population will live in major metropolitan areas. It has been projected, according to Table 8-7, that 85 percent of all Americans will live in urban areas with populations over 2,500 by the year 2000. The trend toward urbanization of America is thus apparent.

The continuing movement of an ever larger percentage of the population into urban areas has concentrated the discharge of wastes from combustion into a very small proportion of the atmosphere, hereby intensifying the problem of air pollution. This results in the exposure of more and more people to more and more pollution without any corresponding increase in the available air supply [27:6].

Since air pollution is a problem of the cities and trends indicate that relatively more people will reside in cities in the future, a greater percentage of the population will be exposed to conditions of pollution of the air. The number of urban places with air pollution problems in Table 8-6 will increase in the future, assuming technological advances and governmental controls do not change radically.

None of the larger cities are without a major problem of air pollution, and the indications are that the problem will continue due to the trend toward urbanization and the creation of the megalopis [29:1,32-33].

Table 8-6

Estimated[a] Number of Places in U.S.
with Air Pollution Problems and
Population Exposed to Air Pollution[b]
(1960 population in thousands)[c]

| | All urban places | | Major problem | | |
| | | | Places | | |
Population class	Number in class	Approx- imate popula- tion	Per- cent	Num- ber	Approx- imate popula- tion
Urban places:					
1,000,000 or more	5	17,500	100	5	17,500
500,000 to 1,000,000	16	11,100	70	11	7,800
250,000 to 500,000	30	10,700	45	13	4,800
100,000 to 250,000	81	11,600	25	20	2,900
50,000 to 100,000	201	13,800	20	40	2,800
25,000 to 50,000	432	14,900	10	43	1,500
10,000 to 25,000	1,134	17,600	8	91	1,400
5,000 to 10,000	1,394	9,800	3	42	290
2,500 to 5,000	2,152	7,600	2	43	150
Unincorporated parts of urbanized areas		9,900			3,800
Subtotal	5,445	124,500	5	308	42,940
Urban & rural places under 2,500	14,345	11,100			
Grand Total	19,790	135,600	5	308	42,940
Percent of total U. S. population[e]		76			24

Source: U. S. Congress, Senate, "A Study of
Pollution-Air," *A Staff Report to the
Committee on Public Works*, 88th Congr.,
2nd sess., 1963, p. 9.

[a]Accuracy of estimates not to be inferred
from number of significant digits reported.

[b]Urban places as defined by U. S. Department
of Commerce, Bureau of the Census.

[c]The data in this table were gathered through
surveys by the U. S. Public Health Service
concerning opinions of state and local air
pollution officials. The data indicate major
air pollution problems in 308 urban places,
an increase of 84 in ten years. The table
also shows that about 7,300 places (housing
60 percent of the nation's population) have
an air pollution problem.

Moderate problem			Minor problem			All problems		
Places		Approximate population	Places		Approximate population	Places		Approximate population
Per-cent	Num-ber		Per-cent	Num-ber		Per-cent	Num-ber	
0	0	0	0	0	0	100	5	17,500
30	5	3,300	0	0	0	100	16	11,100
45	14	4,800	10	3	1,100	100	30	10,700
50	40	5,800	25	21	2,900	100	81	11,600
35	70	4,800	45	91	6,200	100	201	13,800
25	108	3,700	45	194	6,700	80	345	11,900
20	227	3,500	37	420	6,500	65	738	11,400
12	168	1,200	35	487	3,400	50	697	4,890
10	215	760	28	602	2,100	40	860	3,010
		2,300			2,300			8,400
15	847	30,160	33	1,818	31,200	53	2,973	104,300
					—d	30	4,300	3,300
15	847	30,160	33	1,818	31,200	37	7,273	107,600
		17			17			60

d Problems are mostly minor.

e Total U. S. population in 1960 was 179,323,000.

Table 8.7

Anticipated Urban Population Distribution

| | Major Metropolitan Areas (over 50,000) | | All Urban Areas (over 2500) |
	Number	% of Population	% of Population
1960	78	48.3	67
1980	117	59.4	75
2000	145	65.9	85

Source: U. S. Bureau of Census, *The Automobile and Air Pollution: A Program for Progress*, Part 1 (Washington D. C.: Government Printing Office, 1967), p. 33.

Table 8.8

Summary of Emission Factors for Automobile Exhaust[a]

| Type of Emission | Emissions | | |
	Pounds per 1000 vehicle-miles	Pounds per 1000 gallons of gas	Pounds per vehicle-day
Aldehydes	0.3	4	0.007
Carbon monoxide	165.0	2300	4.160
Hydrocarbons	12.5	200	0.363
Oxides of nitrogen	8.5	113	0.202
Oxides of sulphur	0.6	9	0.016
Organic acids (acetics)	0.3	4	0.007
Particulates	0.8	12	0.022

Source: U. S. Department of Health, Education, and Welfare, *Compilation of Air Pollutant Emission Factors* (Washington, D. C.: U. S. Government Printing Office, 1968), p. 50.

[a]This table presents emission factors for uncontrolled automobile exhaust. The emission factors are based on an average route speed of 25 miles per hour in urban areas. The factors are also based on average automobile mileage of fourteen miles per gallon and daily driving of an average vehicle of 3.25 trips of eight miles in length.

Table 8.9

Summary of Emission Factors for Diesel Engines (pounds per 1,000 gallons of diesel fuel)[a]

Type of Emission	Emission Factor
Aldehydes	10
Carbon monoxide	60
Hydrocarbons	136
Oxides of nitrogen	222
Oxides of sulphur	40
Organic acids (acetic)	31
Particulate	110

Source: U. S. Department of Health, Education, and Welfare, Public Health Service, *Compilation of Air Pollutant Emission Factors* (Washington, D. C.: Government Printing Office, 1968), p. 52.

[a]Diesel engines are currently uncontrolled by federal authorities. Emission factors for diesel engines are considerably lower than those for autombiles in the emission of hydrocarbons and carbon monoxide. The emission factors for oxides of nitrogen and sulphur, aldehydes, organic acids, and particulates are higher than for the automobile.

The Automobile is the Greatest Contributor to Air Pollution of All Motor Vehicles

"Automobile exhaust gases are the major source of hydrocarbons, oxides of nitrogen, and carbon monoxide emissions to the atmosphere in our metropolitan areas [33:50]. As was indicated by the RFF projections summarized in Table 8-2, passenger cars contribute 71 percent to fuel consumption, based on 1960 data. Table 8-8 indicates various emission factors for the automobile exhaust which is basically uncontrolled. Table 8-9 summarizes emission factors for diesel engines, which are used mainly by trucks and buses. When comparing the emission factors on the two tables which are expressed in pounds per 1,000 gallons of fuel consumed, it should be noted that emission factors for diesel engines are considerably lower than those for automobiles in the emission of hydrocarbons and carbon monoxide. The average uncontrolled automobile, according to Table 8-8, emits 2,300 pounds of carbon monoxide per 1,000 gallons of gasoline. The uncontrolled diesel vehicle emits only 60 pounds of this pollutant for every 1,000 gallons of diesel fuel. Hydrocarbon emissions from the

Table 8-10

Summary of Emission Factors for Aircraft Below 3,500 Feet (Pounds per flight[a])

Type of Emission	Jet Aircraft, four-engine Conventional	Jet Aircraft, four-engine Fan-Jet	Turboprop Aircraft, four-engine	Piston-engine Aircraft, four-engine
Aldehydes	4.0	2.2	1.1	0.5
Carbon monoxide	35.0	20.6	9.0	326.0
Hydrocarbons	10.0	19.0	1.2	60.0
Oxides of nitrogen	23.0	9.2	5.0	15.4
Particulates	34.0	7.4	2.5	1.4

Source: U. S. Department of Health, Education, and Welfare, Public Health Service, *Compilation of Air Pollutant Emission Factors* (Durham, N. C.: National Center for Air Pollution Control, 1968), p. 49

[a]The term flight has been defined as both a landing and a take-off.

automobile are 50 percent greater than from diesel vehicles. On the other hand, diesel-operated trucks and buses emit twice as many oxides of nitrogen as the automobile. Particulate emissions are also higher for the diesel engine per pound of fuel consumed, as are emissions of sulphur oxides.

Table 8-10 lists emission factors per flight for various aircraft. The table indicates how many pounds of specific emissions are generated into the atmosphere below 3,500 feet during an average landing and take-off. According to RFF, civilian aircraft account for 3 percent of total transportation fuel consumption and military aircraft contribute about four times the consumption of civilian aircraft [65:147]. As shown on Table 8-10, it appears that aircraft do not contribute materially to the air pollution problem, in view of the relatively minor contribution of the airplane to total fuel consumption. The data in Table 8-10 do indicate that there are large variations for the emission factors for jet, turboprop, and piston-engine aircraft. The average conventional jet aircraft emits 111 pounds of pollutants into the atmosphere per flight whereas the turboprop aircraft emits only 19 pounds of pollutants for every landing and take-off. Piston-engine aircraft cause the most air pollution; however, this type of aircraft is not used as much as jet and turboprop airplanes. It should be noted that most emissions from aircraft are confined to airports and surrounding areas.

It can be concluded, therefore, that the automobile is the major contributor to air pollution of all motor vehicles. The passenger car consumes the most fuels and emits the most pollutants into the atmosphere as a result of the combustion process. Henceforth, the automobile pollution problem will be the topic of main concern in this study. The following statement will summarize the diesel pollution problem.

As a source of pollution the diesel engine is notorious for smoke and odor of its exhaust. Because these characteristics involve primarily esthetic values, there have been few attempts in applying objective measurement to them. In addition to smoke and odor, diesel exhausts carry significant concentrations of unburned hydrocarbons, nitric oxides, oxygenated compounds, and carbon monoxide. The concentration levels of pollutants as emitted from the diesel engine are deceptively low if compared with similar data from auto exhausts. This is because diesel engines are operated with an unthrottled air intake and induct large quantities of excess air that dilute the combustion products. Comparable dilution does not occur with spark-ignited engines (automobile engines) [13:82-83].

Table 8-8 lists a summary of exhaust emission factors for the automobile. In addition, air pollution is generated from other sections of the passenger car, including the crankcase, fuel tank, and carburetor. Table 8-11 indicates the relative contribution of each of these sources to air pollution. It should be noted that the automobile exhaust system emits almost all of the carbon monoxide, nitrogen oxides, and lead; therefore, the emission factors presented in Table 8-8 represent total emissions for the average automobile. According to the data in Table 8-8, the average car emits 165 pounds of carbon monoxide for every thousand miles traveled and generates over four pounds of this pollutant into the atmosphere in a day. Nitrogen oxide emission factors for the average passenger car, according to Table 8-8, are 8.5 pounds per 1,000 vehicle miles and one-fifth of a pound per vehicle in one day. These emission factors are based on samples taken from uncontrolled passenger cars.

According to the data presented on Table 8-11, 55 percent of hydrocarbons are emitted from the auto exhaust, 25 percent are generated from the crankcase, and 20 percent of emissions result from carburetor and fuel tank evaporation [30:30-31]. By applying these rates to hydrocarbon exhaust emissions of 200 pounds per 1,000 gallons of gasoline (Table 8-8), it can be determined that approximately 180 pounds of hydrocarbons for every 1,000 gallons of gasoline are generated into the atmosphere from other sections of the automobile.

On 1968 model cars, controls have been imposed on the automobile exhaust and crankcase. Emission control levels have not yet been set for the carburetor and fuel tank in controlling evaporation losses of hydrocarbons [28:21-25]. A discussion of government controls and legislation is reserved for a later section of this study.

The engine of the automobile has been remarkably efficient in meeting our transportation requirements, but has been ineffective in the burning of fuels. Incomplete and inefficient combustion of fuels have led to the emission of several pollutants from the engine and exhaust of the automobile. The major

Table 8.11

Automobile Emissions by Source for
Passenger Cars Operated in 1966

Source	Percent
Crankcase:	
hydrocarbons	25
Carburetor – Fuel Tank	
Hydrocarbons	20
Exhaust:	
Hydrocarbons	55
Carbon monoxide	99
Oxides of nitrogen	99
Lead	100

Source: U. S. Department of Commerce, *The Automobile and Air Pollution: A Program for Progress*, Part 2 (Washington, D. C.: Government Printing Office, 1967), p. 1.

types of emissions have been summarized on Table 8-8. Each has been proven to adversely affect the quality of our environment. Hydrocarbon emissions result from the inadequate combustion of gasoline in the automobile [2:89-90]. Hydrocarbons are gaseous in form and may react with other gases in the air to form ozone. Ozone is poisonous and is a major cause of rust and corrosion [30:4-5]. "The primary concern with hydrocarbon emissions is their indirect effect through participation in the photochemical reactions which lead to the formation of smog" [29:14]. Certain hydrocarbons, such as benzpyrene, have been found to cause cancer in animals [39:6].

Oxides of nitrogen are gaseous in form and also contribute to the phenomenon of photochemical smog. Nitrogen dioxide is mainly responsible for the poor visibility in the city of Los Angeles, which is plagued by smog [30:3]. "Plant damage, eye and respiratory tract irritation, and reduced visibility are all associated with the formation and prevalence of photochemical smog" [29:14]. Nitrogen oxide emissions from the automobile react with oxygen to form nitrogen dioxide, which has been found harmful to humans. Nitrogen dioxides react with ozone and other oxidants in the air to form smog. "The benefits from a reduction of the nitrogen oxides are dependent on the effectiveness of hydrocarbon controls. Unlike emissions of carbon monoxide and hydrocarbons, which increase under conditions of poor combustion, the nitrogen oxides characteristic of the combustion process increases as combustion efficiency improves" [37:51]. It is this problem which has prevented effective control over nitrogen oxide emissions.

Carbon monoxide is a gaseous emission which is extremely toxic when the concentrations are high. Carbon monoxide poisoning has resulted in death and severe brain damage to humans.

Carbon monoxide is dangerous because it has a strong affinity for hemoglobin, which carries oxygen to body tissues. The effect of carbon monoxide is to deprive the tissues of necessary oxygen" [2:73].

Carbon monoxide emissions are caused by the insufficient burning of fuels in the automobile engine. The incomplete combustion results from a lack of oxygen being generated through the engine at the time of the burning process. The absence of sufficient oxygen produces carbon monoxide rather than the harmless carbon dioxide. An efficient automobile engine should produce only carbon dioxide as a waste product of combustion. Carbon monoxide is the largest emission from the automobile (Table 8-3).

As shown in Table 8-8, emissions of lead, sulfur oxides, and particulates are minor in comparison to carbon monoxide, hydrocarbons, and nitrogen oxides. Lead and lead compounds are solid particles emitted from the exhaust system of the passenger car. Lead has been proven harmful to the human body; however, lead concentrations caused by the automobile are not sufficient to be a cause for great concern at the present time. Lead deposits on exhaust emission control devices have been found to adversely effect the performance of these devices [2:124-131].

Sulfur oxide compounds are, also, emitted by the automobile, but the amount of these emissions do not greatly influence the quality of the atmosphere. The problem of sulphur dioxide, a poisonous gas, is mainly a cause for concern for those who use fuels for heating and power generation. As shown on Table 8-8, particulate emissions are not significant from the auto. Particulates are solid particles emitted from the auto exhaust system.

Doctors have yet to determine the precise effects of automotive emissions on the human body over long periods of time. It is yet to be proven how much of this gaseous matter can be absorbed without bodily damage. It is known, however, that auto emissions are harmful and adversely affect the environmental quality. Doctors have linked several diseases to the polluted air; however, evidence is not conclusive. Among these diseases are heart disease, chronic bronchitis, emphysema, eye irritations, asthma, pneumonia, tuberculosis, the common cold, and cancer. For further discussion of the effects of air pollution, refer to the annual reports of the Public Health Service and to

The Physician's Guide to Air Pollution, and the *Interstate Air Pollution Study on the Effects of Air Pollution* [10:1-20:35, 1-62]. Wastes in the air, also, cause damage to vegetation and soil; however, this is mainly a problem for rural Americans. Emissions from the automobile thus adversely influence our environment.

The emission of wastes by the internal combustion engine has created certain economic and social costs for society. Economic costs which have been attributed to air pollution are cleaning costs, earnings loss due to sickness, fuel losses, and loss in property value. Comprehensive studies have been made of these economic costs of air pollution by Professor Ronald G. Ridker [11]. Social costs which are related to air pollution are difficult to measure monetarily. A social cost of pollution might include the poor visibility which adversely influences the esthetic beauty of the environment. Social costs may also take the form of reduced sunlight in our cities as a result of air pollution. The temperament of man is influenced in part by the air. Although economic and social costs have been incurred by society as a result of air pollution, little has been spent in offsetting these side effects of the dirty air. The projected increase in air pollution to the year 2000 (Table 8-5) will most certainly increase the economic and social costs to our society. In order to offset these costs, huge expenditures must be incurred by government, industry, and the public.

When the automobile emits pollutants into the atmosphere, certain economic and social costs are being transferred from the producer and user of the car to society as a whole. The costs of driving an automobile are not confined only to gasoline, tolls, and maintenance. The costs of polluting the air are also costs incurred by the automobile producer and user. Unfortunately for society, the costs of pollution control have not been paid by those responsible for auto pollution. The result has been a deterioration of air quality in our environment. Economists say that a person who does not drive a car is incurring external diseconomies. The costs of air pollution have thus been transferred to the nondriver unfairly [11].

The Great Cost of Clean Air

It has been estimated that the cost of automobile control devices (afterburners) in the next fifteen years may amount to $2.5 billion [23:605]. One and a half billion dollars is expected to be spent for installation of such devices and $1 billions is estimated to be spent on operating maintenance [23:605]. The costs incurred in controlling air pollution must be weighed against the benefits to be derived from clean air. It has been mentioned that many of the costs of air pollution are difficult to measure quantitatively in terms of money. Automobile users do not consider the great economic cost to them of unburned gasoline which may be the greatest cost of pollution [16:136]. It is not the purpose of this study to evaluate the various costs of air pollution to society or to weigh these costs against the benefits of satisfactory air quality. It should be noted that the costs of polluting the air are great; however, society has not yet paid for these costs. One conservative estimate of the cost of air pollution is that per capita cost in the United States each year is about $50 [2:216].

Weather and Geographical Conditions
Influence Air Pollution in Cities

Weather and geographical conditions are important contributing factors to air pollution in cities. The degree of air pollution may be influenced by wind speed and direction, relative humidity, temperature inversions, rainfall, air density, topography, cloud cover, temperature, and seasonality [4:1-160]. The city of Los Angeles, which has numerous temperature inversions in its atmosphere, is continuously plagued by photochemical smog. Due to its high percent frequency of inversion, the components in the atmosphere which produce smog in Los Angeles are not allowed to disperse. Cities with large rainfalls may have a cleaner atmosphere than cities where there is little rain. A large rainfall brings many of the air pollutants to the land surface, thereby dispersing these pollutants. Wind speed is also a contributing factor to air pollution. A city with a strong westerly wind, such as San Francisco, is less likely to have an air pollution problem than Los Angeles, which does not have strong ocean breezes. Topography of a city is, also, an important factor in air pollution. A city located in a valley is more likely to have an air pollution problem than one in mountainous regions. Mountains surrounding a city situated in a valley may trap air pollutants in the lower atmosphere so they cannot disperse [4:1-160].

The causes of an inversion are unknown at the present time. This phenomenon is created when upper levels of the atmosphere become warmer than at the ground level. This results in cooler air on the ground level becoming stagnant. Pollutants which ordinarily rise with the cooler air are forced to remain in the lower atmosphere.

The intensity and duration of inversion depends upon how rapidly the earth cools at night and warms in the morning. These rates are affected by clouds, topography, and the season. Fall months generally have more total hours of inversion conditions, but a single inversion condition is likely to last longer during the winter [27:11].

Inversion generally develops during the peak evening 'rush hours' and lasts usually until 3 or 4 hours after sunrise. The inversion thus influences the emission of pollutants when auto traffic is highest; during morning and evening rush hours. These pollutants from passenger cars are not allowed to disperse due to the inversion.

In the fall of 1966, the eastern United States was affected by a severe temperature inversion which lasted several days. Pollutants were not allowed to disperse due to the low wind velocity, and thus, accumulated at the ground level during the inversion period. The increase in death rates in New York City during

Table 8.12

**Annual Percent of Hours of Inversion
Based At or Below 500 Feet**

Regions	Percent
Atlantic Coast	10–35
Appalachian Mountains	30–45
Great Lakes	20–30
Gulf Coast	10–35
Central Plains	25–40
Rocky Mountains	35–50
Northwest Pacific Coast	25–30
West Coast	35–40

Source: U. S. Senate, "A Study of Pollution: Air," *A Staff Report to the Committee on Public Works,* 88th Cong. 2nd sess., 1963, p. 11.

this period may have been attributable to the high concentrations of pollutants trapped in the lower atmosphere. Conditions of severe air pollution appear to occur mainly because of adverse weather conditions (such as the temperature inversion during a period of low wind) rather than a sudden increase in the amount of pollutants emitted into the atmosphere. Air pollution episodes in 1966 caused large segments of the nation's most populous region to be exposed to potentially dangerous conditions due to the inversion [31:1-2, 35].

Inversion conditions vary for the different regions in the United States. Table 8-12 indicates the relative frequencies of inversion for these regions. It should be noted that the western states have inversion occurrences more frequently than other regions. The Rocky Mountain states have especially high annual percent hours of inversion. Inversions occur from 35 to 50 percent of the time. These states, however, have low levels of automobile fuel consumption [72:2]. In the populous West Coast, inversions occur 35 to 40 percent of the time. The large cities of Los Angeles and San Francisco are thus affected by this high inversion frequency. The Atlantic states are fortunate because inversions are only present 10 to 35 percent of the time. States within the Atlantic region consume the greatest amount of gasoline [72:2]. The populated Great Lakes states have inversion frequencies of 25 to 30 percent. Inversions affect large

Table 8-13

Motor Fuel Consumption by Month—
1966 (millions of gallons)

Month	Motor Fuel Consumption
January	5.9
February	5.6
March	6.4
April	6.5
May	6.8
June	7.1
July	7.1
August	7.4
September	6.8
October	6.7
November	6.6
December	6.7
Total	79.6

Source: U. S. Department of Transportation, Bureau of Public Roads, *Highway Statistics: 1966* (Washington, D. C.: Government Printing Office, 1967), p. 4.

cities where there is a large concentration of pollutants in the atmosphere. It should be noted that man at the present time has no control over inversions and other weather conditions which lead to air pollution problems.

Motor fuel consumption varies with the seasons and months of the year. Table 8-13 indicates that more fuels used for transportation are consumed during the summer months. These months coincide with the main vacation period of Americans. Inversion conditions occur mainly during the fall months which represent the second highest period for auto fuel consumption and emissions into the atmosphere (Table 8-13). The least amount of fuels are

Table 8.14

Average Horsepower of Automobiles
Manufactured from 1958 to 1966

Year	Average Horsepower
1958	227.3
1959	214.2
1960	188.2
1961	175.1
1962	176.4
1963	195.7
1964	219.6
1965	220.3
1966	232.9

Source: *Petroleum Facts and Figures–1967*
(New York: The American Petroleum Institute, 1967), p. 179.

consumed during winter when inversions are expected to last longest [27:11].
According to Table 8-13, more air pollution is generated from motor vehicles
during the summer months. Emissions from the motor vehicle are least during
the winter. Therefore, there appears to be no relationship between motor fuel
consumption by month and inversion frequency.

Table 8-14 indicates that during the 1960s there has been a trend toward an
increase in the average horsepower of the automobile. In 1961, when a compact
car was popular with the American motorist, the average horsepower of the auto
was 175. By 1966, as a trend developed toward larger and more powerful cars,
the average horsepower increased to about 233. *Resources in America's Future*
has projected that the average consumer will experience an increase in the
standard of living of almost 50 percent from 1960 to 1980 [65:83-84]. This
expected increase in the standard of living and resulting consumption expenditures may indicate that Americans will continue to buy larger and more powerful
cars in the future.

In general, as the average horsepower of the automobile increases, the amount of fuel consumption and resulting emission of pollutants increase. In 1965 and 1966, fuel consumption of the average passenger car amounted to 667 and 679 gallons, respectively [72:49]. Average horsepower, also, increased for these years. In 1965, the horsepower of the average car was 220, whereas in 1966, horsepower had increased to 233, according to Table 8-14.

An increase of housepower in the engine of the passenger car increases the total amount of explosions per second. More energy must be expended by the automobile in fulfilling the requirements of a more powerful engine. The increase in the energy requirement resulting from an addition to horsepower means that the automobile must use more fuel [29:25-32]. The trend toward an increase in average horsepower may compound the air pollution problem.

Oil companies have increased the octane ratings of gasoline through the use of lead. As was mentioned earlier, lead is poisonous and is generated into the atmosphere through the automobile exhaust. The increase in the use of the automobile has been accompanied by a rise in the use of lead additives in gasoline. This trend is expected to continue into the future [29:21, 23-24]. "The major fears from rising lead levels in the environment stem from a belief that many of the adverse health effects may be chronic or cumulative and not early, or easily, detectable" [29:23].

Some aspects of automotive pollution may be reduced by the imposition of different types of standards by government. For example, the emissions of lead and sulphur may be reduced by specification through legislative means of an upper limit for their content in gasoline. This is the imposition of an input standard. The quantity of unburned hydrocarbons and carbon monoxide emitted from the auto may be controlled by requiring that certain devices be added to the engine and exhaust to affect more complete combustion. This constitutes a discharge standard. The danger attributed to automotive pollutants may vary with weather conditions requiring the imposition of specific and rigorous ambient standards at certain times. Standards are generally imposed by federal, state, and local governments by law [3:1-107].

A definite relationship has been established between automobile speed and the amount of pollutants. The Public Health Service study summarized on Table 8-15 indicates that cars travelling in the congested business districts of cities at an average speed of ten miles per hour emitted the most pollutants. Carbon monoxide emissions were found to be .35 pounds per vehicle-mile and emissions of hydrocarbons were .023 pounds. When travelling at 45 miles per hour on highways, emissions were reduced to .10 and .009 pounds per vehicle-mile for carbon monoxide and hydrocarbons, respectively. Data on Table 8-15 thus indicate that as the driving speed of the average car increases, less pollution is generated into the atmosphere.

In another study conducted by the National Air Sampling Network in several major cities, it was found that commuters, in the central city where driving speed is lowest, experience the greatest exposure to carbon monoxide. Tests conducted at locations adjacent to expressways indicated that carbon monoxide concentrations were not as high as in the central city business district

Table 8-15

Emission Factors for Automobile Exhaust by Type of Route Travelled
(pounds per vehicle-mile)[a]

Type of Route Travelled	Average Route Speed (miles per hour)	Hydrocarbons (pounds)	Carbon monoxide (pounds)
Business	10	0.023	0.35
Residential	18	0.015	0.21
Arterial	24	0.013	0.17
Rapid Transit	45	0.009	0.10

Source: U. S. Department of Health, Education, and Welfare, Public Health Service, *Compilation of Air Pollutant Emission Factors* (Durham, N. C.: National Center for Air Pollution Control, 1968), p. 51.

[a]Based on emission factors for the uncontrolled automobile exhaust. The table shows the relationship between vehicle speed and the amount of air pollution generated from the vehicle.

[30:15-17]. It was also found in the study that commuters in cities are exposed to more pollutants than other Americans. It was concluded in the study that as one moves outward from the street line, there is a reduction in carbon monoxide concentrations [30:17]. Due to the traffic congestion problems of cities caused by the great concentration of vehicles, automobile emissions are highest. Tall city buildings prevent dispersion of these emissions and inversion conditions trap pollutants at the ground level. Serious conditions of air quality may thus result.

Summary

It has been determined that automobile pollution is mainly a problem of the American city due to their large concentrations of vehicles. Indications are that this problem will get worse, unless some action is taken to control vehicular pollution. In the next section of this chapter, pertinent air pollution legislation will be summarized and technological advances in the field will be discussed. These factors have tended to offset some of the side effects from automobile air pollution. In the final portion of this paper, the current and future air pollution problems of individual cities will be examined.

Forces at Work to Offset Automobile Air Pollution

Federal Legislation

Much has been accomplished in the 1960s in offsetting the side effects associated with the expanding output of fuels used in internal combustion engines. Legislation at the federal, state, and local levels of government has done much to abate air pollution. It has stimulated vehicle manufacturers to provide emission control devices for cars and to conduct more research in creating a more efficient engine and better control methods. Legislation has influenced the producers of fuels to provide for research in the treatment of gasoline and motor oil in order to lessen their polluting effects. Federal laws have stimulated state and local governments in the setting of air quality standards, and have provided for more research by state, local, and regional agencies. Legislation has also created clear lines of authority and responsibility for federal agencies in the field of air pollution. Government enactments have thus provided a good starting point in developing the required technology for prevention and control of air pollution [22:1-15].

As was shown earlier in this paper, the problem of automotive pollution is relatively recent and was caused by the tremendous growth in passenger car usage in the 1950s and 1960s (Table 8-2). As a result, there was a considerable lack of attention given the problem until recent years. This neglect of automotive pollution was attributed to all branches of government, private industry, and public apathy. The federal government took the initial step in leading the program to abate air pollution. Since most states and localities did not have great automotive pollution problems in the past, little or no action was taken in controlling air pollution. State legislatures would not authorize the funds required for research of the problem. The public was not aware of the potential health hazards that air pollution may create; therefore, there was a good deal of apathy toward needed legislation. As the air pollution problem increased and spread to areas previously with clean air and as pollution spread across state boundaries, the public became more concerned with the problem. Research linked air pollution with several diseases which further aroused society to the need for action [22:1-15].

In 1955, Congress amended the "Air Pollution Control Act" to provide for research and technical assistance in controlling and abating air pollution. This act reaffirmed the federal view that air pollution was a state and local problem and should be dealt with at those levels. A system of federal grants was established to states and localities.

In 1963, the "Clean Air Act" was passed. This act gave Congress the right to establish broad research programs and more authority to make recommendations on needed changes. This act was a milestone because it asserted federal responsibility in the field of air pollution and in the need to develop controls and standards of environmental quality. The act implied that the auto industry would have to share in the control of air pollution.

In 1965, the "Clean Air Act" was amended to provide for development of motor vehicle exhaust emission standards, limit emissions on 1968 model cars of hydrocarbons and carbon monoxide through the development of control devices and provide for more research on automotive pollution. The act also provided for the control of nitrogen oxides and aldehydes from diesel vehicles. It should be noted that the provisions of this act do not apply to vehicles manufactured prior to the 1968 model year. As a result of the amendment, crankcase and exhaust emissions are being controlled in part on the 1968 automobiles. No controls have yet been enacted for the prevention of carburetor and fuel tank evaporation, or the emission of nitrogen oxides [22].

It is yet to be proven how effective the controls imposed on the automobile will be. The Public Health Service has estimated that hydrocarbons will be controlled fully in the crankcase [28:17]. In addition, average reductions of about 50 percent for carbon monoxide and 70 percent for hydrocarbons are expected in the control of exhaust emissions on the 1968 model car [28:17]. The provisions of the amendment to the "Clean Air Act" have also given the Secretary of Health, Education, and Welfare authority to recommend standards for the future control of auto emissions. Proposed standards for 1970 have thus been developed which would require 90 percent control of carburetor and fuel tank evaporation of hydrocarbons, further control of carbon monoxide, and additional regulation of diesel vehicles [28:18]. More research is needed before the effectiveness of these standards can be evaluated. In 1966, Congress further amended the "Clean Act" to provide for more assistance to states and localities in air pollution research [22:14-15].

"The Air Quality Act of 1967" provides for a coordinated effort between government and industry toward development of air pollution standards and equipment. Air quality control regions were established in order to set regional standards of air quality. Other provisions of the act call for the establishing of enforceable ambient air quality standards, more research programs and federal grants, the registration of fuel additives with the federal government, studies on jet aircraft emissions, and economic incentives to industry [22:17-86].

This act thus provides the basis for future action by coordinating the program for clean air. It establishes the framework for the control of vehicular pollution at the national, state, and local levels and provides for the enforcement of the law by the Secretary of Health, Education, and Welfare.

Air pollution legislation has thus offset some of side effects from vehicle emissions. It appears that more research and eventual legislation is needed in the field. The Secretary of Health, Education, and Welfare in a report to the U.S. Senate has pointed out that

if more stringent national control is not imposed after 1970, vehicular pollution levels will reach a minimum during the late 1970s and then begin to rise in response to the ever-expanding numbers of motor vehicles. The current and proposed standards do more to keep the problem from getting worse than to solve it. More effective standards can be established only as the technology is developed to adequately cope with automotive emissions [28:19].

State Legislation

Since the problem of vehicular pollution is relatively recent, state legislatures did not act until the 1960s in attempting to control the problem. Generally, the federal government has influenced the states in creation of needed legislation. One exception is California, whose air pollution agency has pioneered in the study of automotive emissions and in the development of air quality standards.

Prior to the 1963 "Clean Air Act", only 14 states had enacted air pollution control legislation. By 1967, 31 additional state laws were passed or existing laws strengthened. During 1967, 39 state legislatures considered major air pollution control bills. Twenty of these legislatures adopted comprehensive air pollution control laws, and six others enacted amendments to improve existing laws. By 1968, twenty states had adopted standards for automotive emissions or ambient air quality. State budgets have more than tripled from 1963 to 1967 in controlling air pollution [28:33-34].

As polluted air flows from one state to another, an interstate air pollution problem is created. The solution to interstate air pollution involves cooperation between states. As of 1968, there were no formal interstate control programs in effect, although several are being proposed [28:34].

California has continuously led the nation in adopting air pollution control legislation. In 1962, California created the Motor Vehicle Pollution Control Board, which was mainly responsible for stimulating auto manufacturers to install blow-by control devices. These devices cut hydrocarbon emissions entirely from the crankcase. In addition, engine changes by the car producers, as required by the board, may eventually reduce total hydrocarbon emissions by 80 percent and carbon monoxide emissions by 60 percent on cars manufactured subsequent to 1965. It should be noted that these emission standards were adopted prior to federal legislation and were the basis for the development of federal standards for 1968 model cars. California also has developed standards for 1968 models sold within the state. Similar standards have been proposed by the Secretary of Health, Education, and Welfare on a national basis for the 1970 model cars [6:129-131]. Controls have not been imposed in California as well as the rest of the nation for emissions from used cars [37:66-69]. A highway inspection program, however, has been established. An effective statewide system for air measurement and monitoring has also been developed. It should be noted that California, especially Los Angeles, experienced an automotive pollution problem before the rest of the nation [6:129-131]. Table 8-16 indicates that California automobiles consume 10 percent of the nation's automotive fuels.

Automobiles in New York consume 6 percent of total United States

Table 8.16

Motor Fuel Consumption and Automobile Registrations by State – 1966
(thousands)

State	Motor Fuel Consumption (gallons)	Automobile Registrations
California	8031	8693
New York	4968	5514
Ohio	4146	4681
Pennsylvania	4039	4545
Texas	6123	4468
Illinois	4086	4124
Michigan	3725	3516
Florida	2574	2817
New Jersey	2534	2789
Indiana	2346	2070
Other States Combined	38339	35136
Total	80911	78353

Source: U. S. Department of Transportation, Bureau of Public Roads, *Highway Statistics–1966* (Washington, D. C.: U. S. Government Printing Office, 1967), pp. 2,31.

automotive fuels. The state has adopted a policy in general of following the federal government legislation rather than initiating new pollution control laws. Annual inspection is now required by law in the state of all motor vehicles, including examination of emission control devices. New York followed the example of California in 1963 by requiring crankcase emission control prior to federal legislation. In 1967, a statewide network of air monitoring stations was established [37:61-63].

Air pollution control legislation from other states has generally been stimulated by the federal government. Most of the major air pollution laws enacted by states are similar in requiring development of emission and air quality standards, an air monitoring program and more research in the field [28:33].

Local Legislation

The Secretary of Health, Education, and Welfare has noted that "nearly two-thirds of the 231 standard metropolitan areas are not served by significant air pollution control programs and these areas comprise 20 percent of the nation's population [28:35]. Activity, however, is progressing in the development of needed legislation by localities [28:35]. Los Angeles was among the first in the nation in the adoption of local ordinances against air pollution.

Los Angeles has perhaps the worst smog problem in the nation, caused mainly by automobile emissions [6:129]. Due to its adverse combination of weather, low wind speed, topography, and frequency of inversion, Los Angeles was especially oriented toward conditions of air pollution. Los Angeles was the first locality to develop standards of air quality and controls on automotive air pollution. Although the city has solved most of its industrial pollution problems of the air, vehicular pollution problems increased to a point where photochemical smog became a great annoyance to residents. A survey conducted of Los Angeles residents in 1956 showed that 74 percent of the people were bothered by smog [2:91].

Los Angeles began to clean up industrial pollution with the establishment of the Los Angeles County Air Pollution Control District. The district supervisors set out at first with the responsibility to clean up industrial pollution. Little, however, was accomplished in abating automotive pollution until state emission standards were established during the early 1960s. Los Angeles has continuously led the nation in expenditures for air pollution control and research (Table 8-18) [6:129]. The city has thus become a model to the entire nation in its efforts to control air pollution.

Chicago has followed the example set by Los Angeles in solving its air pollution problems. In recent years, Chicago has conducted more research on air pollution financed largely by federal grants. In 1962, an air resources management program was established with the goals of

determining the effects of air pollution on the health of Chicagoans, inventorying all potential sources of air pollution, improving the monitoring of pollutants in the atmosphere, improving the analysis of pollutants in the atmosphere, determining the transport of pollution and providing the public with a thorough understanding of air pollution [21:296-298].

This air resource program may do much for cleaning Chicago's air in the future.

St. Louis has established good air pollution control legislation and specifically has created emission control standards for the automobile. St. Louis was fortunate to have a study made of its air pollution problems by the U.S. Public Health Service [36:1-132]. The recommendations of this study were quickly enacted by state, county, and regional authorities. St. Louis is thus one example of how federal funds and research stimulated legislation at the state and local levels in abating air pollution.

Legislation in New York City has resulted in the setting of ambient air quality standards, establishment of an air monitoring network, and creation of the

Department of Air Pollution Control. This agency has been responsible for a great deal of the research on New York's air pollution problem. A complete inventory of emissions in the city has been published by this department [37:430-434]. A computerized system of air monitoring and evaluation is being developed for New York City.

Most other major cities are currently engaged in research of the air pollution problem in cooperation with the federal government (Table 8-18). In general, the cities mentioned have led other cities in developing legislation and policies which may lead to abatement of the automotive pollution problem.

The effectiveness of state and local laws in controlling air pollution is likely to depend upon standards of enforcement. In this respect, Los Angeles has shown the way to other cities and states wishing to control the quality of the environment.

Development of Emission Control Devices

With the establishment of the "Clean Air Act" in 1963 and with the anticipation of emission control legislation, the automobile manufacturers began to act on the problem. California was instrumental in stimulating the industry to develop the needed devices for emission control [7:54].

The main purpose of controlling the crankcase is to lessen hydrocarbon emissions. For the uncontrolled car, 25 percent of all hydrocarbons were emitted from the crankcase (Table 8-13). Crankcase control devices or blowby controls were developed by auto manufacturers. These devices operate on the principle of 'positive crankcase ventilation (P.C.V.), which involves recirculating the hydrocarbons from the engine oil pump to the combustion chamber. On 1968 model cars, standards for crankcase emission call for complete control of hydrocarbons [29:22]. Control devices for the crankcase are now used on most of the automobiles produced subsequent to 1963. Although the automobile industry installed the devices voluntarily, it is reasonable to suppose that it was the pressure of pending legislation which influenced the industry to act [30:35-36].

Two approaches have been developed by the automobile manufacturers for control of hydrocarbons and carbon monoxide in the exhaust system on 1968 model cars. Chrysler's 'Cleaner Air Package' involves controlling emissions through modifications in the automobile engine's ignition system and carburetor. As a result of these modifications, emissions are lessened in the exhaust system. The other three auto manufacturers use an air injection system to control exhaust emissions. This system involves the pumping of air into the exhaust manifold. The gases in the exhaust are directed toward the exhaust valves where the gases are burned, due to the extremely high temperatures in the exhaust [30:36-37]. Gases are thus burned in the exhaust before emission into the atmosphere. The effectiveness of these devices has not been fully evaluated. According to federal standards, the devices should reduce hydrocarbon emissions

70 percent and emissions of carbon monoxide in the exhaust by 50 percent [28:17].

The afterburner is a control device which limits hydrocarbon and carbon monoxide emissions from the automobile exhaust. The afterburner device burns unused gases in the exhaust by means of a direct flame. The afterburner proved to be ineffective in the control of exhaust emissions, and is currently not used by automobile manufacturers [30:40].

An exhaust control device which offers good potential for future development is the catalytic converter. During 1957 to 1964, automobile manufactures tried to perfect this device, but without success. The converter would work effectively when new; however, lead deposits would build up causing the device to become ineffective. When in good working order, the converter acts to convert exhaust gases through burning into harmless substances. The catalytic converter has been discontinued by automobile manufactures although research has continued. With the establishment of rigid federal emission standards, the catalytic converter is now being refined and improved. One possible application of the converter may be in the control of the emission of nitrogen oxides in the exhaust [30; 40-41].

An exhaust gas recirculating system for the control of nitrogen oxide emissions is currently under study. The National Center for Air Pollution Control and Esso Research and Engineering Corp. are attempting to develop this system. The system requires the recirculation of gases in the exhaust back through the engine intake system. This results in the reduction of the combustible mixture generated into the engine cylinders and the peak temperature, thereby reducing the formation of nitrogen oxides. One fault with the system is that it may cause a lowering of engine performance [28:22].

Evaporation control systems are being developed by Esso Research and Engineering Corp. and the Atlantic Richfield Corp. The Esso system employs a small charcoal box affixed to the fuel system vents. This device absorbs hydrocarbon emissions during selected phases of the driving cycle. These emissions are then regenerated into the automobile engine. The Atlantic Richfield system is similar but uses the crankcase in place of the storage box. Pressurized fuel tanks are also being developed by the automobile industry in controlling evaporation [28:22-23].

It appears that technological advances are being made in the control of automobile emissions. The research currently being conducted in the field is based on modification of the engine and the recycling of unburned gases. The Ford Motor Company has expressed the view that "major reductions in pollution caused by automobiles will have to come from radically new types of fume suppressors. [48].

Developments in the Measurement, Monitoring, and Inspection of Air Quality

The National Center for Air Pollution Control was established in 1967 as a branch of the Public Health Service. Its main functions are to establish air quality criteria and standards, conduct research and development in improving control technology, and inspect, measure, and monitor the air for purposes of abatement and control of air pollution. The monitoring and measurement of the air is necessary to aid in the enforcement of laws prescribing standards of ambient air quality [28:3].

An inspection laboratory has been established by the National Center for Air Pollution Control near Detroit. The purpose of this inspection station is to certify automobiles for production beginning with 1968 models, if found to be in compliance with federal standards. Both domestic and foreign manufacturers are required to submit vehicles for inspection [28:26].

The Detroit inspection laboratory may not provide a true account of automobile emissions under everyday driving conditions. The N.C.A.P.C. has thus authorized several studies in order to encompass driving habits of motorists, differences in vehicle maintenance, and possible disparities in vehicle production. In these studies, automobiles are generally kept under continuous surveillance and operated under simulated driving conditions [28:27]. In addition, the National Center for Air Pollution Control is attempting to provide for periodic inspection by state authorities under uniform conditions.

A properly designed air monitoring system should be capable of measuring both gaseous and particulate pollutants and providing data to show trends in pollution levels with time, seasonal variations, and meteorological changes, as well as the influence of topography, population density, fuel use, industrial activities, and other factors. Such a system is absolutely necessary to permit the intelligent planning of air conservation programs and to determine the interrelationships between source emissions and air quality levels [28:51].

In order to meet these goals, the National Air Sampling Network (N.A.S.N.) and the Continuous Air Monitoring Program (C.A.M.P.) were established.

The National Air Sampling Network consists of a system of manual air sampling stations whose purpose is to collect samples of specific pollutants for subsequent evaluation by the National Center for Air Pollution Control. At present, the N.A.S.N. monitors particulates, sulfur dioxide, nitrogen dioxide, oxidants, and aldehydes. Studies are proceeding toward the eventual analysis of hydrocarbons and carbon monoxide by air sampling stations [28:52].

The Continuous Air Monitoring System provides for the monitoring and evaluation of gaseous pollutants in major cities. Samples are gathered and tested simultaneously through use of specific monitoring instruments. Technological developments may eventually lead to the uniform sampling and evaluation of gaseous pollutants [28].

Carbon monoxide monitoring by C.A.M.P. is based on the infrared absorption method. One property of carbon monoxide as well as several other gases is that it absorbs radiation in the infrared region of the spectrum. By this method, carbon monoxide can be detected and measured [12:107]. The iodine pentoxide method is also used for carbon monoxide monitoring. This method involves reacting iodine vapor with an air sample. Carbon monoxide may thus be detected.

Hydrocarbon monitoring and measurement involves a combination of gas-solid and gas-liquid color analysis using a flame ionization detector. Atmospheric content of different types of hydrocarbons is thus determined by gas chromatography [12:120].

The monitoring and measurement of nitrogen oxides involves the gathering of air samples and subsequent analysis and evaluation of the samples in the laboratory. The air sample is mixed with prescribed gases and acids in testing for certain properties of nitrogen oxides [12:80,84].

Opportunities for Profit in
Abating Automotive Air Pollution

Although air pollution has been found to adversely affect the quality of the environment and has no known benefits to society, it has created certain opportunities for profit. Air pollution control is a relatively new technology which requires more research and development activities. This has resulted in the creation of new jobs and employment opportunities.

Automotive pollution control devices and techniques are currently being evaluated by auto manufacturers and the federal government on the 1968 model cars. If these devices are not proven effective, radically new pollution control systems will have to be developed [48]. This may result in greater opportunities for profit by independent automotive pollution equipment manufacturers. Profit opportunities also exist in the development of adequate air monitoring and measurement devices in order to meet the objectives and goals of the National Center for Air Pollution Control [28:51].

Projections of the Magnitude of the
Automobile Air Pollution Problem as
Related to Urban America

The American city faces a great problem in controlling air pollution.

With more than half the population living on less than one percent of the land, burning more fuel every year, it seems inevitable that some of these densely packed communities will literally overload the air with poisons that simply cannot be removed for days or even weeks. At that point a disaster of unbelievable proportions will occur; a disaster brought on by a shortage of breathable air. It is, also, inevitable that the air over our swarming cities and suburbs will grow worse unless drastic actions are taken immediately [6:74].

With the trend toward urbanization of our society and with the expansion of metropolitan areas into a huge megalopolis, emissions from the automobile may become more concentrated in cities. Major air pollution disasters have already occurred in the United States, such as in New York City and Donora,

Pennsylvania [39:3]. If air pollution problems are not corrected, it appears reasonable to assume that these disasters may continue to occur in the future.

Ten States Consume Almost Half of
Motor Vehicle Fuels

Table 8-16 indicates that ten states consume almost half of motor vehicle fuels, and account for about 45 percent of the automobile population. The state of California leads the nation in fuel consumption, accounting for approximately 10 percent of the total. Texas ranks second, consuming 8 percent of fuels. Vehicles in New York State consume 6 percent of the nation's transportation fuels. Ohio, Illinois, and Pennsylvania are next in rank, each state consuming 5 percent of total fuels. Since the impact of air pollution is mainly felt in the cities, fuel consumption data must be further evaluated by city.

In 1967, the National Center for Air Pollution Control ranked cities according to the degree of severity of their overall air pollution problems (Table 8-17). New York City was rated worst in the nation in controlling the quality of its environment. Chicago and Philadelphia were ranked second and third, respectively. The Los Angeles-Long Beach area was given the next adverse rating because it has a major problem in controlling the photochemical smog that envelopes the area. The industrial cities of Cleveland and Pittsburgh ranked fifth and sixth, respectively. Boston, Newark, Detroit, and St. Louis were ranked next according to the severity of their air pollution problems. Table 8-17 lists the air pollution ranking for 25 cities and metropolitan areas in all.

One indication of local efforts to fight the problem of air pollution is the total amount budgeted by a city or county. Los Angeles County ranks first in budgeted expenditures for air pollution control according to Table 8-18. New York City, with the nation's worst pollution problem, is second in budgeted expenditures. San Francisco ranks third, although it is not ranked among the 25 worst cities with problems in combating air pollution. Authorized budgets for Chicago rank the city fourth in the nation, although Chicago has the second greatest air pollution problem. It should be noted that the remainder of the air pollution control program budgets for cities are below $500,000, which indicates that cities may not be spending enough for air pollution control. For example, Philadelphia, which ranks third in the nation in air pollution problems, had authorized only $446,000 to combat the problem in 1967.

The Public Health Service, according to Table 8-17, has ranked cities according to their overall air pollution problems. As has been indicated on Table 8-3, motor vehicles contribute more to the creation of air pollution than any other source. The present and future impact of the automobile on American cities and major metropolitan areas, therefore, must be measured.

In order to evaluate the present impact of automotive pollution by city and project future emissions from the automobile, current and future emission control levels must be considered. These emission control levels were developed by the U.S. Public Health Service and are presented on Table 8-19. This table indicates that substantial reductions in total automobile emissions are expected

Table 8-17

U. S. Public Health Service Ranking of Cities with the Greatest Air Pollution Problems

City	Air Pollution Ranking
New York City	1
Chicago	2
Philadelphia	3
Los Angeles-Long Beach	4
Cleveland	.5
Pittsburgh	6
Boston	7
Newark	8
Detroit	9
St. Louis	10
Gary-Hammond-East Chicago, Ind.	11
Akron, Ohio	12
Baltimore	13
Indianapolis	14
Wilmington, Dele.	15
Louisville, Ky.	16
Jersey City, N. J.	17
Washington	18
Cincinnati	19
Milwaukee	20
Paterson-Clifton-Passaic, N. J.	21
Canton, Ohio	22
Youngstown, Ohio	23
Toledo, Ohio	24
Kansas City, Mo.	25

Sources: C. J. Sitomer, "California Wars on Smog," *Christian Science Monitor*, Dec. 4, 1968; "The Dirtiest Cities," *Time*, August 14, 1967, p. 27. The ranking of cities is based on data supplied by the National Center for Air Pollution Control, Cincinnati, Ohio.

Table 8-18

Summary of Air Pollution Control Program Budgets for Fiscal 1967 for Major U. S. Cities (thousands of dollars)

City or County	Fiscal 1967 Budget
Los Angeles County	$3,758
New York City	2,517
Chicago	1,163
Detroit	435
Philadelphia	446
San Francisco	1,195
Washington	78
Cleveland	277
Pittsburgh-Alleghany County	423
Newark	a
Boston	134
Houston	a
Minneapolis	67
St. Louis	252
Dallas	a
Paterson	a
Anaheim	a
Seattle-King County, Wash.	189
Cincinnati	a
Kansas City, Mo.	118
Atlanta	a
Miami-Dade County, Fla.	88
Baltimore	a
Denver	179
San Diego	a

Source: U. S. Senate, Committee on Public Works, *Air Pollution-1967, Hearings*, before a subcommittee of the Committee on Public Works, S. Rept. 780, 90th Cong., 1st sess., 1967, Part 4, p. 2353.

[a]Data are not available or the city does not have an air pollution control program.

Table 8-19

**Present and Future Automobile Emission
Control Levels** (lbs. per automobile per
year)

Air Pollutant	Uncontrolled Automobile 1963	National Standards 1968	Commercially Feasible 1970	Commercially Feasible 1975	Expected Ultimate After 1980
Hydrocarbons	520	180	60	20	10
Carbon monoxide	1700	750	500	250	120
Nitrogen oxides	90	90	40	15	10
Total	2310	1020	600	285	140

Source: U.S. Department of Commerce, *The
Automobile and Air Pollution: A Program
for Progress,* Part 1 (Washington, D.C.:
Government Printing Office, 1967), p. 22.

as technological advances are made in the field. Table 8-19 presents a breakdown of only the major automobile emissions in pounds emitted per year.

Table 8-20 summarizes data for the 25 largest standard metropolitan statistical areas for passenger cars, and U.S. Census Bureau population estimates in 1967. A statistical relationship has been established between these data; thus projections are derived for future passenger cars based on given projections of population for 1980 and 2000 by the Urban Land Institute [67:50-52]. Data for 1980 and 2000 population estimates and the statistical derivation of passenger cars for this period are presented on Table 8-21.

Air pollution for major emissions from the automobile is then projected on Tables 8-23 and 8-24 based on estimates by the Public Health Service of future emission control levels for the automobile (Table 8-19). The projections on Table 8-23 are based on the assumption that technological advances will be made in the field of air pollution, thereby reducing future emission control levels. The projections in Table 8-24 assume that 1968 federal standards will be in effect in 1980 and 2000. Technological advance and further government control are highly uncertain in the field of air pollution, thus present government standards are also being used to project future emissions.

Projections are also being made for 1967 emissions based on uncontrolled 1963 emission levels. These projections are being developed in order to determine the extent of current automobile pollution problems and for purposes of comparison with future projections. Table 8-22 summarizes 1967 data.

Data are presented in Table 8-20 for the metropolitan areas with the highest passenger car population. Approximately 34 percent of the nation's automobiles

Table 8.20

Twenty-Five Largest Metropolitan
Areas for Passenger Cars and Population Estimates for 1967 (thousands)

Standard Metropolitan Statistical Area	Passenger Cars at 1/1/67[a]	Rank	Provisional Population Estimate at 7/1/67[b]	Rank	Passenger Car Density[c]
Los Angeles– Long Beach	3365	1	6857	2	.49
New York	3082	2	11556	1	.27
Chicago	2355	3	6771	3	.35
Detroit	1750	4	4114	5	.43
Philadelphia, Pa.– N. J.	1607	5	4774	4	.34
San Francisco–Oakland	1342	6	3009	6	.45
Washington, D. C.– Md.–Va.	1008	7	2704	7	.38
Cleveland	910	8	2050	11	.44
Pittsburgh	890	9	2386	9	.37
Newark, N. J.	794	10	1889	13	.42
Boston	785	11	2542	8	.31
Houston	762	12	1788	14	.43
Minneapolis–St. Paul	743	13	1636	15	.45
St. Louis, Mo.–Ill.	712	14	2311	10	.31
Dallas	644	15	1405	16	.46
Paterson–Clifton– Passaic	584	16	1341	19	.44

Table 8.20 (*continued*)

Standard Metropolitan Statistical Area	Passenger Cars at 1/1/67[a]	Rank	Provisional Population Estimate at 7/1/67[b]	Rank	Passenger Car Density[c]
Anaheim–Santa Ana– Garden Grove, California	577	17	1231	23	.47
Seattle–Everett, Wash.	573	18	1262	22	.45
Cincinnati, Ohio–Ky.– Ind.	565	19	1361	17	.42
Kansas City, Mo.– Kans.	551	20	1214	24	.45
Atlanta	550	21	1289	21	.43
Miami	530	22	1114	26	.48
Baltimore	526	23	1990	12	.26
Denver	518	24	1090	27	.48
San Diego	510	25	1198	25	.43
Total	26233		58882		.45
Total in U. S. A.	78378		197000		.40
Percent	34		30		

[a]Source: *Spot Television Rates and Data* (Skokie, Ill.: Standard Rate and Data Service, January 15, 1968).

[b]Source: U. S. Department of Commerce, Bureau of the Census, *Population Estimates*, Series P–25, 11 (Washington, D. C.: Government Printing Office, December 5, 1967), p. 13.

[c]Passenger car density represents the ratio of passenger cars to population in 1967.

Table 8-21

Statistical Projections of Passenger Cars for Major Metropolitan Areas—1980 & 2000 (thousands)

Metropolitan Area	Population 1980[a]	Projections 2000[a]	Projected Passenger Cars (using regression equation $Yc=257.84 + .27x$)	
			1980[b]	2000[b]
Los Angeles[c]	12,744	23,462	6,245	11,496
New York[d]	13,806	17,688	3,985	5,034
Chicago	8,083	10,839	2,440	3,184
Detroit	5,500	7,990	1,743	2,415
Philadelphia	4,847	7,468	1,566	2,274
San Francisco-Oakland	5,332	7,694	1,697	2,335
Washington, D. C.	3,339	5,542	1,159	1,754
Cleveland	2,626	4,467	967	1,464
Pittsburgh	2,019	2,296	803	878
Newark[e]	2,258	3,018	868	1,073
Boston	3,111	3,646	1,098	1,242
Houston	2,263	3,860	869	1,300
Minneapolis-St. Paul	1,920	2,423	776	912
St. Louis	2,230	3,043	860	1,079
Dallas	2,625	3,982	967	1,333
Paterson-Clifton-Passaic[e]	1,627	2,231	697	860
Anaheim-Santa Ana-Garden Grove, Calif.[f]	2,093	3,160	823	1,111
Seattle	1,495	2,893	661	1,039
Cincinnati	1,436	1,829	646	752
Kansas City	1,307	1,690	611	714
Atlanta	1,573	2,429	683	914
Miami	3,092	5,788	1,093	1,821

Table 8-21 (*continued*)

Metropolitan Area	Population 1980[a]	Projections 2000[a]	Projected Passenger Cars (using regression equation Yc=257.84 + .27x) 1980[b]	2000[b]
Baltimore	2,098	2,750	824	1,000
Denver	1,407	2,227	638	859
San Diego	1,796	3,391	743	1,173
Total	90,627	135,816	33,462	48,016

[a]Source: J. P. Pickard, *Dimensions of Metropolitanism* (Washington, D. C.: Urban Land Institute, 1967), pp. 50-52. In order to reflect the trend toward increased urbanization and the growth of the megalopis, the S.M.S.A.'s have been redefined by Urban Land Institute to include adjacent areas.

[b]The regression equation is explained in Appendix E.

[c]Passenger car projections are based on a ratio of 49 percent of 1967 passenger cars to population (Table 8-20).

[d]Population projections are not made for these areas by Urban Land Institute. The population projections are thus based on U.S. Census Bureau growth rates from 1960 to 1967 as follows: Newark, 11.8 percent; and Paterson, 13.0 percent. On a twenty year basis, growth rates are 33.7 percent for Newark and 37.1 percent for Paterson.

[e]The population of the New York-Northeast New Jersey Consolidated Area is projected for 1980 and 2000 to be 19.255 million and 24.669 respectively. In order to conform to data on Table 4 which uses the S.M.S.A. for New York only, the projections were modified by applying the 1967 ratio of S.M.S.A. population to Consolidated Area population. This ratio is 71.7 percent.

[f]Population projections are not made for Anaheim by Urban Land Institute; therefore, used growth rates for metropolitan California of 70 percent from 1960 to 1980 and 51 percent from 1980 to 2000. These growth rates were applied to population data for 1960 as presented in the 1959 publication of *The Metropolitanization of the United States*. This work was published by Urban Land Institute and was also written by J. P. Pickard.

are located in 25 urban areas. These areas represent 30 percent of America's population. Automobiles are thus greatly concentrated in the cities and suburbs. One indication of the degree of concentration of vehicles is passenger car density, which is the relationship between passenger cars and population. According to Table 8-20, the Los Angeles-Long Beach area has the greatest number of passenger cars and the highest passenger car density (.49). Forty-nine automobiles are thus present in Los Angeles for every 100 people. New York City and its suburbs rank second in passenger cars; however, passenger car density is only 27 percent. New York City has a good urban transit system which may preclude the need for an automobile. Los Angeles has inadequate facilities for public mass transportation, thus residents have relied mainly on the automobile for travel [57:90]. It should be noted that vehicle density in the United States is 40 percent, but the density in the metropolitan areas as shown on Table 8-20 is 45 percent.

Table 8.22

**Projected 1967 Automobile Emissions
Based on Uncontrolled 1963 Emission
Levels** (thousands)

Standard Metropolitan Statistical Area	Passenger Cars at 1/1/67[a] (Thousands)	Projected 1967 Automoboile Emissions Based On 1963 Emission Levels[b] (millions of pounds)		
		Hydrocarbons 520 lb./year	Carbon Monoxide 1700 lb./year	Nitrogen Oxides 90 lb./year
Los Angeles-Long Beach	3365	1,750	5,720	303
New York	3082	1,603	5,239	277
Chicago	2355	1,225	4,003	212
Detroit	1750	910	2,975	158
Philadelphia, Pa.-N.J.	1607	836	2,732	145
San Francisco–Oakland	1342	698	2,281	121
Washington, D.C.-Md.-Va.	1008	524	1,714	90
Cleveland	910	473	1,547	82
Pittsburgh	890	463	1,513	80
Newark, N. J.	794	413	1,350	71
Boston	785	408	1,335	71
Houston	762	396	1,295	69
Minneapolis-St. Paul	743	386	1,263	67
St. Louis, Mo.-Ill.	712	370	1,210	64
Dallas	644	335	1,095	58
Paterson–Clifton–Passaic	584	304	993	53
Anaheim-Santa Ana–Garden Grove, Calif.	577	300	981	52
Seattle–Everett, Wash.	573	298	974	52
Cincinnati, Ohio-Ky.-Ind.	565	294	961	51
Kansas City, Mo.-Kans.	551	286	937	50
Atlanta	550	286	935	50
Miami	530	276	901	48
Baltimore	526	273	894	47
Denver	518	269	881	47
San Diego	510	265	867	46
Total	26,233	13,641	44,596	2,364

[a]Source: Table 8.20.

[b]Source: Table 8.19.

Table 8-21 summarizes projections of passenger cars for 1980 and 2000, which were derived by statistical methods. The population in most of the major metropolitan areas is expected to increase in 1980 and 2000, reflecting the trend toward increased urbanization [67:50-52]. In Appendix E, a relationship has been established between population and passenger cars. Therefore, passenger cars can be projected based on expected population for 1980 and 2000 (Table 8-21).

Table 8-22 presents data on the expected emission of hydrocarbons, carbon monoxide, and nitrogen oxides for 1967, based on uncontrolled 1963 emission levels on Table 8-19. Emissions are greatest for Los Angeles-Long Beach. New York ranks second in the nation, and the metropolitan areas of Chicago is ranked third in automobile emissions. In the 25 large metropolitan areas on Table 8-22, automobile emissions were assumed to be directly related to the number of passenger cars. Consideration was not given to driving conditions for individual areas.

Projections are made for 1980 and 2000 for automobile emissions in Table 8-23. The emission projections are based on passenger car data on Table 8-21 and future emission control levels presented in Table 8-19. When the results calculated on Table 8-23 are compared with 1967 emissions, it becomes apparent that expected advances in technology in the field of air pollution control may reduce the pollution from the automobile despite increases in the number of automobiles projected into the future. In 1967, the 25 metropolitan areas had passenger car stock of 26 million, according to Table 8-20. Car registrations are expected to rise to 33 million by 1980 in these areas and 48 million by the year 2000 (Table 8-20).

The increase in passenger cars projected for 1980 and 2000 may be more than offset by controls imposed on the automobile engine and exhaust. If expected technological improvements are enacted, automobile air pollution in the future will be greatly reduced and will not be as great a problem as in 1967. For example, the New York area has been projected to have total emissions of hydrocarbons in 1967 of 1.6 billion pounds, according to Table 8-22. In the year 2000, it is expected in this area that emissions of hydrocarbons may be reduced to 50 million pounds (Table 8-23). The Chicago metropolitan area in 1967 had projected emissions of carbon monoxide of 4 billion pounds, whereas in 1980 projected emissions may be reduced to 610 million pounds of this gaseous pollutant. It should be noted that all of the metropolitan areas on Table 8-23 may show substantial reductions in the expected amounts of pollutants in 1980 and 2000 from 1967. By 1980, an 81 percent reduction in carbon monoxide emissions may be expected. By the year 2000, a 96 percent reduction in hydrocarbon emissions and an 80 percent reduction in emissions of nitrogen oxides is deemed possible.

Table 8-24 projects emissions for 1980 and 2000 for various pollutants assuming that emission control levels remain the same as in 1968. The emission projections are based on passenger car data in Table 8-21 and future emission

Table 8-23

Projected Automobile Emissions for 1980 and 2000 Based on Expected Emission Control Levels (Millions of lbs.)

Metropolitan Areas	Projected 1980 Automobile Emissions Based on Commercially Feasible Emission Control Levels for 1975		
	HC^a	CO^b	NO^c
Los Angeles	125	1,561	94
New York	80	996	60
Chicago	49	610	37
Detroit	35	436	26
Philadelphia	31	392	23
San Francisco-Oakland	34	424	25
Washington, D. C.	23	290	17
Cleveland	19	242	15
Pittsburgh	16	201	12
Newark	17	217	13
Boston	22	275	16
Houston	17	217	13
Minneapolis-St. Paul	16	194	12
St. Louis	17	215	13
Dallas	19	242	15
Paterson-Clifton-Passaic	14	174	10
Anaheim-Santa Ana-Garden Grove, Calif.	16	206	12
Seattle	13	165	10
Cincinnati	13	162	10
Kansas City	12	153	9
Atlanta	14	171	10
Miami	22	273	16
Baltimore	16	206	12
Denver	13	160	10
San Diego	15	186	11
Total	668	8,368	501
Percent of 1967 Emissions (Table 8-22)	5	19	21

Source: Projections of future emissions were calculated from passenger car projections in Table 8-21 and emission control level data obtained from Table 8-19.

Projected 2000 Automobile Emissions
Based on Expected Ultimate
Emission Control Levels After 1980

HC^a	CO^b	NO^c
115	1,379	115
50	604	50
32	382	32
24	290	24
23	273	23
23	280	23
18	210	18
15	176	15
9	105	9
11	129	11
12	149	12
13	156	13
9	109	9
11	129	11
13	160	13
9	103	9
11	133	11
10	125	10
7	90	7
7	86	7
9	110	9
18	219	18
10	120	10
9	103	9
12	141	12
480	5,761	480
4	13	20

[a]Hydrocarbons.   [c]Nitrogen Oxides.

[b]Carbon Monoxide.

Table 8.24

Projected Automobile Emissions for 1980 and 2000 Based on 1968 Federal Emission Control Levels (millions of lbs.)

Metropolitan Areas	1980 HC^a	1980 CO^b	1980 NO^c	2000 HC^a	2000 CO^b	2000 NO^c
Los Angeles	1,124	4,684	563	2,069	8,622	1,035
New York	717	2,989	359	906	3,776	453
Chicago	439	1,830	220	573	2,388	287
Detroit	314	1,307	157	435	1,811	217
Philadelphia	282	1,175	141	409	1,706	205
San Francisco–Oakland	305	1,273	153	420	1,751	210
Washington, D. C.	209	869	104	316	1,316	158
Cleveland	174	725	87	264	1,098	132
Pittsburgh	145	602	72	158	659	79
Newark	156	651	78	193	805	97
Boston	198	824	99	224	932	112
Houston	156	652	78	234	975	117
Minneapolis–St. Paul	140	582	70	164	684	82
St. Louis	155	645	77	194	809	97
Dallas	174	725	87	240	1,000	120
Paterson–Clifton–Passaic	125	523	63	155	645	77

Table 8.24 (*continued*)

Metropolitan Areas	HC^a	1980 CO^b	NO^c	HC^a	2000 CO^b	NO^c
Anaheim–Santa Ana–Garden Grove, Calif.	148	617	74	200	833	100
Seattle	119	496	59	187	779	94
Cincinnati	116	485	58	135	564	68
Kansas City	110	458	55	128	536	64
Atlanta	123	512	61	165	686	82
Miami	197	820	98	328	1,366	164
Baltimore	148	618	74	180	750	90
Denver	115	479	57	155	644	77
San Diego	134	557	67	211	880	106
Total	6,023	25,098	3,011	8,643	36,015	4,323
Percent of 1967 Emissions	44	54	128	63	81	183

Source: Projections of future emissions were calculated from passenger car projections in Table 8.21 and emission control level data obtained from Table 8.19.

[a]Hydrocarbons.

[b]Carbon Monoxide.

[c]Nitrogen Oxides.

control levels presented in Table 8-19. When projected emissions on Table 8-24 are compared with 1967 emissions in Table 8-22, it appears that pollution generated from the automobile may be reduced 56 percent in 1980 for hydrocarbons and 46 percent for carbon monoxide. By the year 2000, the pollution problem may grow worse than in 1980 as the automobile population increases, and if there are no improvements in technology or government controls. In the year 2000, carbon monoxide emissions may be 81 percent of those in 1967 and hydrocarbon emissions may be 63 percent of 1967 data. Emissions of nitrogen oxides in 1980 and 2000 may be expected to increase from 1967. By the year 2000, emissions of this pollutant may grow by 83 percent.

Weather and Inversion Conditions
for Individual Cities

It has been determined that weather and inversion conditions may influence air pollution problems in cities. Inversions in cities trap pollutants at the ground level so that they cannot disperse. Table 8-25 lists inversion frequencies for the 25 cities corresponding to the metropolitan areas in Tables 8-26 to 8-24. The degree of air pollution may also be influenced by wind speed, precipitation, and air temperature. Data for these weather conditions is presented in Table 8-26.

In analyzing the data in these tables, it should be noted that Los Angeles has a very high inversion frequency along with low wind speed and precipitation. During the spring and summer months, inversions are present in the atmosphere 90 percent of the time at night. In view of the fact that automobile emissions are projected to be highest in Los Angeles and due to adverse weather conditions, the automobile air pollution problem may be worst in this city.

New York, which is projected to be second in automobile emissions, has more favorable weather conditions than Los Angeles. Inversions occur an average of 19 percent of the time; however, the city has strong 15 mile per hour winds which act to disperse inversion conditions. New York City also has a high rainfall, which further acts to lessen air pollution.

Chicago has a high inversion frequency during the summer months, thus air pollution conditions are probably worst during this period. Boston, which was ranked seventh by the Public Health Service on Table 8-17, has relatively low inversion frequencies along with favorable weather conditions for the dispersing of pollutants.

In projecting the impact of present and future automobile emissions on air pollution problems of cities, it is thus important to consider local weather conditions along with the influence of increased urbanization and the projected increase in the consumption of fuels.

Table 8.25

Percent Frequency of Inversion for Cities With Largest Passenger Car Population for 1967

City	Percent Frequency of Inversion–Daytime				Percent Frequency of Inversion–Nightime			
	Winter	Spring	Summer	Fall	Winter	Spring	Summer	Fall
Los Angeles	56	30	19	44	76	79	90	90
New York	14	16	19	26	*	*	*	*
Chicago	*	*	*	*	29	39	72	47
Detroit	*	*	*	*	27	40	63	47
Philadelphia	*	*	*	*	38	39	62	54
San Francisco	*	*	*	*	55	32	20	42
Washington	28	23	24	32	37	38	58	54
Cleveland	*	*	*	*	22	38	63	38
Pittsburgh	24	31	27	34	*	*	*	*
Newark	*	*	*	*	38	39	61	55
Boston	*	*	*	*	17	18	29	23
Houston	*	*	*	*	22	26	40	34
Minneapolis	*	*	*	*	35	30	46	36
St. Louis	37	27	34	44	*	*	*	*
Dallas	*	*	*	*	44	33	30	51
Paterson	*	*	*	*	*	*	*	*
Anaheim	*	*	*	*	*	*	*	*
Seattle	39	25	21	37	31	31	35	38
Cincinnati	*	*	*	*	31	38	69	50
Kansas City, Mo.	*	*	*	*	39	34	47	47
Atlanta	38	31	29	38	36	41	65	55
Miami	24	15	13	22	47	49	75	64
Baltimore	*	*	*	*	36	34	47	42
Denver	48	30	35	43	43	47	52	55
San Diego	57	28	17	44	86	82	94	94

Source: U. S. Senate, Committee on Public Works, *Clean Air, Hearings,* before a subcommittee of the Committee on Public Works, 88th Cong., 2nd sess., 1964, Part 2, pp. 906–919.

*Data not available.

Table 8.26

**Data on Weather Conditions for Cities
With Largest Automobile Populations**

City	Average Wind Speed		Degree Days	Precipitation (inches per year)
	miles per hour	*direction*		
Los Angeles	6	W	1,451	15
New York	15	NW	5,050	42
Chicago	10	SSW	6,310	33
Detroit	10	N	6,404	31
Philadelphia	10	SW	4,866	41
San Francisco	9	W	3,039	21
Washington	10	S	4,333	41
Cleveland	11	S	6,066	32
Pittsburgh	10	WSW	5,905	37
Newark	10	SW	5,252	43
Boston	13	SW	5,791	39
Houston	10	SE	1,276	45
Minneapolis	11	NW	7,853	25
St. Louis	12	S	4,469	38
Dallas	11	S	2,272	35
Paterson*				
Anaheim*				
Seattle	11	SW	5,275	34
Cincinnati	7	SW	4,870	39
Kansas City, Mo.	10	SSW	4,888	35
Atlanta	10	N	2,826	49
Miami	9	SE	178	56
Baltimore	11	WNW	4,787	43
Denver	10	S	6,132	14
San Diego	6	WNW	1,574	11

Source: H. M. Conway, ed., *The Weather Handbook* (Atlanta, Ga.: Conway Publications, 1963), pp. 19–101.

*Data not available.

Conclusion

Automobile air pollution will increase in our cities if efforts are not made at the present time to offset the problem. Fuel consumption from the internal combustion engine is expected to rise fourfold by the year 2000 from 1960 levels. For every gallon of fuel consumed, more pollutants are expelled into the atmosphere by the motor vehicle. As more emissions are generated into the nation's constant air mass, more air pollution will result. The expected increase in vehicle fuel usage indicates that more people will be affected by air pollution in the future unless more action is taken by the government and industry.

As population becomes more concentrated in cities and metropolitan areas expand in size, the air pollution in these areas will grow worse. By the year 2000, 85 percent of all Americans are expected to reside in urban areas with populations over 2,500, and almost two-thirds of the people will live in major metropolitan areas with populations over 50,000. In 1967, approximately 34 percent of the nation's automobiles were concentrated in 25 urban areas representing 30 percent of the nation's population. The trend toward urbanization of our society indicates that more and more Americans will be exposed to conditions of air pollution in the cities. One government survey conducted for Congress in the early 1960s indicated that 60 percent of Americans reside in areas with air pollution problems. As a result of the increasing urbanization of society, cars will become more concentrated in cities and more air pollution will be the result.

The motor vehicle, especially the automobile, contributes most of the carbon monoxide and hydrocarbons, and almost half of the nitrogen oxides to the atmosphere. Doctors have yet to determine the precise effects of automotive emissions on the human body over long periods of time. It is known, however, that auto emissions are harmful and adversely effect the quality of the environment. Hydrocarbon and nitrogen oxide emissions contribute to the formation of photochemical smog in the atmosphere. In 1966, 66 million tons of carbon monoxide were generated from motor vehicles, according to a Public Health Service survey. If automobile emissions are left uncontrolled as in 1966, it is expected that 213 million tons of carbon monoxide will be emitted into the atmosphere by the year 2000. Similar increases may be expected for other types of emissions if automobile pollution is no better controlled than in 1966. Control of emissions has improved, however, beginning with the 1968 model cars.

Adverse conditions of weather will further compound the air pollution problem. Periods of severe air pollution result mainly because of adverse weather conditions (such as the temperature inversion during a period of low wind speed) rather than a sudden increase in the total emission of pollutions generated into the atmosphere. The side effects caused by the inversion will intensify in the future as more and more emissions are discharged from the automobile and become part of a stagnant air mass. Air pollution episodes, thus, are expected to become more frequent and more severe in the future.

The air pollution problem will be compounded by the trend toward an increase in the average horsepower of the automobile and the average size of trucks. In general, as the average horsepower of the automobile increases, the amount of fuel consumption and resulting emission of pollutants increase, More energy must be expended by the automobile in fulfilling the requirements of a more powerful engine, thus, more gasoline must be used. Trucks of the future are expected to increase in size and will require more powerful engines. Increased emissions from the truck may, thus, be expected.

As cars become more concentrated in cities, greater traffic congestion will result. The Public Health Service has established a definite relationship between automobile speed and emission of pollutants. Cars which travel at low speeds in congested business districts of cities were found to emit the highest amount of air pollutants. On the other hand, as the average driving speed of the automobile increased, less pollution was generated into the atmosphere. In a test conducted by the National Air Sampling Network, it was proven that commuters in the central business district where driving speed was lowest experienced the greatest exposure to carbon monoxide. The automobile air pollution problem is, therefore, greatest in the central business districts of cities or other areas where large concentrations of vehicles are driving at low speeds. In the large cities, tall buildings prevent dispersion of emissions from the automobile and inversion conditions trap pollutants at the ground level. The average driving speed in cities of the future will decrease as more and more vehicles are concentrated in city streets. Americans who commute to work during rush hours may be exposed to serious conditions of air quality as traffic problems increase.

In 1967, the National Center for Air Pollution Control ranked New York City worst in the nation in controlling the quality of its environment. The cities of Chicago, Philadelphia, and Los Angeles-Long Beach were given the next adverse ratings. These cities will experience even greater air pollution problems due to the expected increase in the consumption of fuels.

The Los Angeles-Long Beach area has the greatest problem among major metropolitan areas in controlling automobile pollution. Los Angeles has the highest concentration of passenger cars in the nation. The area has inadequate facilities for public mass transportation, thus, residents have relied mainly on the automobile for travel. Passenger cars in the Los Angeles-Long Beach area will exceed 6 million by 1980, assuming that the present car density will remain unchanged. 1967 passenger cars in the area totalled 3.3 million. The air pollution problem in Los Angeles-Long Beach, caused almost entirely by the automobile, will, therefore, increase greatly. Los Angeles has traditionally led the nation in expenditures to abate air pollution.

New York City and its suburbs rank second in passenger car registrations behind Los Angeles-Long Beach, although the area is rated first in severity of air pollution. New York City has a good urban transit system, which may preclude the need for an automobile. Passenger car density in the New York area is only 27 percent compared to a national density of 40 percent and Los Angeles-Long Beach density of 49 percent. Almost 4 million cars are expected in the New York area by 1980, and approximately 5 million automobiles may be anticipated by the year 2000. This is compared to 3 million automobiles registered in New York City and surrounding areas in 1967. Automobile air pollution may be expected to increase in New York City; however, the severity of the problem will not be as great as in the Los Angeles-Long Beach area.

Much has been accomplished during the 1960s in offsetting the side effects associated with the expanding usage of fuels in internal combustion engines. Legislation has been enacted to control automotive emissions and regulate the quality of the environment. Emission control devices are currently in use on 1968 model cars. This is mainly due to the stimulus of federal legislation. Technological advances are being made rapidly in the development of more effective emission control devices for regulating carbon monoxide and hydrocarbon emissions in the exhaust. Federal standards in effect for the 1968 model cars are expected to cut hydrocarbon emissions two-thirds and carbon monoxide emissions 56 percent from uncontrolled 1963 levels. It will be several years before it can be determined if cars manufactured for 1968 will meet the federal standards. If it is determined that present emission control devices do not meet the objectives of the federal government in tests conducted over long periods of time, radically new devices will have to be created in controlling carbon monoxide and hydrocarbons in the exhaust. Present technological advances appear to indicate a trend toward redesigning the automobile engine to control exhaust emissions.

Automobile manufacturers have provided devices for the complete control of hydrocarbons in the crankcase. Uncontrolled crankcase emissions represented 25 percent of total hydrocarbons emitted from the automobile. Nitrogen oxide emissions in the exhaust and hydrocarbon evaporation in the carburetor and fuel tank, however, are basically uncontrolled. Emission control devices are currently being developed for possible use on the 1970 model cars. The principle of exhaust recycling is being applied to the control of nitrogen oxides. Catalytic converters are, also, being researched as possible control devices for nitrogen oxide emissions. Evaporation control systems are being developed which involve the catching of escaped gases from the fuel tank and carburetor and regenerating these gases into the automobile engine.

The effectiveness of emission control devices depends upon proper maintenance and the willingness of the automobile user to incur the cost of maintaining such devices. It has been estimated that the cost of control devices in the next fifteen years to the automobile user may amount to $2.5 billion. Of this amount, one billion dollars is expected to be spent on operating maintenance and $1.5 billion on capital outlays for equipment. Costs such as these must be weighed against the great social and economic costs to the American people if air pollution is left uncontrolled.

Technological advances are being made in the measurement and monitoring of air quality. In the future, it is expected that a complete air monitoring system will be established by the National Center for Air Pollution Control. At present, the air sampling and detection networks are incomplete and do not measure the air pollution caused by carbon monoxide and hydrocarbons from the automobile. It is essential for a complete air monitoring system to be operative so that the extent of vehicle air pollution can be evaluated on an individual city basis. The effectiveness of air pollution control legislation and technological advances can best be determined through proper monitoring and measurement of the air quality of cities.

If improvements in technology continue to progress as in the 1960s, air pollution conditions will grow better for American cities of the future despite expected advances in fuel consumption. The automobile air pollution problems of cities such as Los Angeles will lessen as older, uncontrolled vehicles are replaced by new cars having effective emission control systems. By 1980, few uncontrolled automobiles will be on hand, thus the average amount of emissions per automobile will decline. This decrease in the rate of emissions will more than offset the expected doubling of fuel consumption by 1980 from 1960. This is based on the assumption that present control devices will adequately control emissions in accordance with federal standards. If the present emission control devices are not proven effective over long periods of time, the American cities will experience deteriorating conditions of air quality and the air pollution problem will grow worse by 1980. If such conditions arise in the future, it may be deemed necessary to replace the internal combustion engine vehicle or greatly redesign the present automobile. Currently under study are the electric and steam-powered automobiles, which are being researched as possible answers to the future air pollution problems of the cities.

By the year 2000, radically new pollution devices will have to be created in order to offset the expected fourfold increase in fuel consumption from 1960. Air pollution in the cities, caused by the automobile, will grow worse by the end of the twentieth century unless great technological advances are made. The combined efforts of government, industry, and the American people is essential in order to solve the great air pollution problems facing the cities. It is apparent that hugh expenditures must be incurred in the future in meeting one of our nation's greatest problems.

The Crowded Skies and the Projected Increase in Air Traffic

Robert Graham

Since the beginning of the twentieth century there have been great advances in many fields as well as the development of new fields. As this century has progressed, the pace of these advances has increased very rapidly in some areas.

The field of aviation is an excellent example of this growth. Since the beginning of aviation, which did not occur until after the turn of the century, up to the present, there has been an almost unparalleled growth in both size and importance of the industry. Today, both commercially and militarily, aviation plays an increasing role.

It is difficult to imagine another field which, in the relatively short time since its birth, has grown at such a rapid pace and has affected, directly or indirectly, so large a segment of our population. As each year passes air travel becomes more important to our society. Aside from providing many thousands of jobs both in aircraft plants, airports and ancillary airport services, there is a greater number of people who fly to their destinations for both business and pleasure activities instead of relying on other modes of transportation.

Although the history of air travel is relatively short, since the end of World War II air travel has been an increasingly important part of American life as Table 9-1 shows. Each year there is an increase in air activity. Today we are beginning to realize that the increased use of air travel will bring problems associated with its use. The RFF projections show what levels may be expected in the future of air activity. In this way the problems that may be faced can be estimated and worked on today. Table 9-3 shows the level of air activity that is expected up to the year 2000.

In this chapter, the problems resulting from the increased use of air travel are evaluated and an attempt is made to forecast the extent to which these problems will cause undesirable effects and limit the extent of air travel growth. Because the present situation was generated by the existing level of air activity, an attempt is made to indicate how an additional increase will further complicate the situation.

Tables 9-1 and 9-2 show the increasing importance of aviation by the increased number of miles flown compared to the number of miles of surface transportation used in the past twenty years.

Thus, while air travel has consistently increased yearly, surface transportation has lost ground even though the population has been increasing steadily.

While this trend is expected to continue, the yearly increase of air travel is expected by many to become even larger in the future, due to a combination of many factors including increased affluence among a larger segment of the

Table 9.1

Historical Totals of Revenue Passenger Miles Flown (in billion miles)

Year	Total	Year	Total
1947	5.6	1954	19.6
1948	7.1	1955	22.3
1949	8.6	1956	25.5
1950	10.1	1957	28.1
1951	12.9	1958	28.5
1952	15.0	1959	32.4
1953	17.4	1960	34.6

Source: *Resources in America's Future,*
Table A5-6, pp. 646-647.

Table 9.2

Historical Totals of Revenue Surface Passenger Miles (in billion miles)

Year	Total	Year	Total
1947	56.3	1954	50.3
1948	57.4	1955	48.4
1949	58.4	1956	49.0
1950	53.9	1957	42.9
1951	57.8	1958	39.6
1952	58.7	1959	38.3
1953	55.9	1960	37.6

Source: *Resources in America's Future,*
Table A5-6.

Table 9.3

**Projected Revenue Passenger Miles to
the Year 2000** (in billion miles)

Year	Total
1970	66.6
1980	107.8
1990	160.7
2000	225.0

Source: *Resources in America's Future*,
Table A5–7, p. 648.

population, increased business trips by businessmen, and increases in the population itself. Therefore, the figures which have been projected forward to the year 2000 reflect the belief that these factors will cause the airline industry to gain in relative importance in the future and grow at an ever increasing rate.

A comparison of the trend of the RFF medium projection for the 1960s of commercial air travel with Federal Aviation Agency data for the same years shows a satisfactory degree of agreement (See Appendix A). Table 9-3 presents the RFF medium projection of Revenue Passenger Miles Flown for 1970, 1980, 1990, and 2000.

Resources for the Future, Inc. (RFF) based their projection on a number of assumptions. First, the projection takes for granted that airlines will acquire a larger share of the long-haul market at the expense of surface transportation. Second, the average citizen would be flying twice as much by air by 1980 as at present. Third, the number of revenue miles would be further multiplied by the increase in population up to the year 2000. These assumptions were considered realistic considering the present relationship of the airline industry to the remainder of the public transportation industry.

RFF believes that the aviation industry is presently in a transition stage which will result in aviation becoming a mass transportation industry. Two questions are raised in relation to the above assumption: first, whether the airlines would have a major share of the long-distance travel market or an overwhelming share, and, secondly, would airlines also make significant inroads into the short haul market?

It is believed that the answers to both of these questions depend on the fares and equipment in the airline industry and the influence of other forms of transportation.

As for equipment, the industry has been in a state of flux and RFF admits that answers are hard to reach. The industry does have the advantage of being able to draw upon the investment in military aircraft research and development.

The influence that other modes of transportation have on the airline industry depends on competition. Each industry competes for a larger share of the transportation market. The airline industry has some inherent advantages, such as speed and comfort, which are not matched by the other forms of transportation. However, a number of problems have developed in the past few years and may continue to grow in the future. The relative position of airlines compared to the remainder of the transportation industry depend on how the airlines are able to solve these problems in the near future. These problems and possible solutions facing the industry will be discussed shortly.

Difficulties Expected with the Increase in Air Traffic

As the volume of air traffic increases, a number of factors develop which present problems. Some are inevitable, but others result because our present air traffic methods are rapidly becoming outdated and surpassed, both by the continually advancing technology and by the sheer volume of air traffic that is increasing each year. It is important that solutions be found quickly so as to reduce the serious consequences that may result in the near future due to increased air activity. Not only has the increased volume of air travel resulted in outstripping the capacity of present facilities which, a few years ago, were considered adequate for the forseeable future, but the increasing size, capacity, and speed of new types of jets being produced have presented a new and more serious set of problems.

Due mainly to its larger size, the requirements for the newer jets result in need for additional runway, larger parking, and loading areas, as well as newer terminal procedures to process the much larger number of passengers that will be embarking or disembarking off each plane.

With the increased size of jets has come an increase in speed with many new models. These increased speeds allow airlines to deliver passengers to their destinations faster but also present difficulties due to these increased speeds. These newer jets enter landing patterns more quickly, and with more planes converging on airport approach patterns at higher speeds, the danger of midair collisions is increased. Thus, a greater margin of safety, such as not allowing as many aircraft into the approach patterns or requiring a greater amount of distance between planes becomes necessary to allow for possible corrective measures if they are needed.

Associated with this increased speed in airport approach patterns is the increased distances needed by modern jet aircraft in making turns and circling in holding patterns over airports during landing maneuvers. Due to increased speed, turns require a greater amount of airspace above each airport to be reserved for circling aircraft.

Although this is not serious in an area with only one airport, it is in the metropolitan areas which have a number of airports where this factor must be considered. In such areas as New York, Chicago, and Washington, D.C., which have two or more airports, it becomes important to make sure that aircraft destined for each airport are assigned a certain section of airspace which does not interfere with aircraft destined for the other airports in the vicinity. With the increased areas needed for larger jets to circle around airports, planes destined for the two airports may be forced to fly too close to each other if the airports are adjacent to one another.

Increased flying speed also results in increased landing speeds with the result that longer runways are needed by the newer jets, longer runways than many airports have available at present. In some communities it is possible to extend the runway length. However, in established communities, business and residential areas are already built up around airports and make it impossible to increase the length of runways substantially and allow for a sufficient safety margin for populated areas.

Linked closely with the need for increased runway length is the need for expanded airport facilities in general. With the advent of the Boeing 747, the Lockheed L-1011 and others, airports will be hard pressed to handle the tremendous influx of passengers embarking and disembarking with each flight. The capacity of the Boeing 747 is to be 400 and that of the Lockheed L-1011 will be 256-345. Thus, there will be a large number of passengers who will have simultaneous need of ticket counters, restaurants, luggage racks, and taxis. Present airport facilities are not adequate to accommodate this large number of people in such a fashion. With limitations of space in some airports it may be difficult to find solutions within the airport itself.

These large numbers of passengers entering and leaving the airport have added also to the number of cars on the roads in the vicinity of the airport. In the airport itself there is less of a traffic problem since such traffic is spread out during the day depending on plane arrivals and departures. Although there is an increase in activity between 5 − 8 P.M., such congestion usually does not take place until after leaving the airport. It is at this point where traffic congestion usually results in delays. In many surrounding communities, no provisions were made for airport traffic when roads were constructed. The result has been that traffic from the airport must merge with regular traffic in one place. During normal hours there is usually no delay. However, during rush hours when roads are used at near full capacity by commuters, converging airport traffic may often result in delays. In developed cities and suburbs, there may be very little undeveloped land available to widen roads. The buildup of the community itself may generate additional traffic that was not anticipated when the road was originally constructed. When added together these factors result in existing roads being used at a high rate of capacity. Thus, airport traffic may converge on a road which already has a large number of vehicles and result in continuous delays.

With the increased size and number of planes landing at airports, complaints from residents living near them concerning noise have increased. Because of the noise of aircraft landing and taking off, most people do not wish to live in the vicinity of airports. Since the larger jets have more powerful engines, the noise these engines emit is louder. With this increased noise level, living near an airport is made more uncomfortable because of this condition. Also, because larger jets require longer runway approaches a greater number of homes is affected.

The result has been that because of this increased noise and traffic in the area adjacent to the airport, local residents have usually expressed their resentment at any attempt to increase airport capacities or to build new airports in residential or business communities.

This community resentment compounds the problem because, according to the aircraft activity projection previously stated, even conservative estimates predict a threefold increase of air travel over 1960. Thus, not only are airport improvements needed to accommodate the new jet aircraft, but new airports will be needed simply to handle the volume of aircraft that will be in existence by the year 2000.

To sum up, lack of space, overcrowding, and lack of adequate facilities usually occur at large metropolitan airports where space is already at a premium. Because of limited space available to solve the already existing problems, the prospect of increase air traffic to these airports magnifies the importance of finding solutions in the very near future.

It appears that some form of governmental regulation will be unavoidable in the not too distant future. With the increase in the number of passengers using commercial airlines, a limit will have to be placed on flights. If not, passengers would demand so many flights at peak hours, delays would be intolerable and air safety itself would be impaired.

Main Areas Where Problems Occur

With air traffic activity showing a greater increase each year, the saturation point at many large airports is rapidly being reached. During the summer of 1968 delays occurred at nearly all metropolitan airports. It is in these airports where problems can be seen developing. For instance, Chicago's O'Hare Airport recorded a total of 553,093 airport operations for the fiscal year 1966 [1:34]. An aircraft operation refers to landing or takeoff of an aircraft. By the end of fiscal year 1967, there was an increase of 35,434, to a total of 588,527 aircraft operations [2:35]. This represented an increase in average daily aircraft operations of from 1,521 in fiscal 1966 to 1,613 in fiscal 1967, an increase of 92 aircraft operations a day. The figures for fiscal 1968 show a much larger increase. Total operations were 682,141 [37:36], for an average daily total of 1,869 aircraft operations, an increase of 256 operations a day. These figures show that, on the average, there were 78 aircraft operations- takeoffs and landings- each hour of the day. Of course, during the peak hours in the morning and evening the figure is actually much higher, and, in the early morning hours, much lower. Therefore, because of the great number of takeoffs and landings there is little room for error. Anything out of the ordinary such as fog or a delay in a takeoff or landing causes a slow down which then begins to back up other aircraft waiting to take off or land. Thus, one delay at O'Hare Airport could ultimately cause a tie-up of aircraft across the country destined for Chicago since each plane that is delayed causes each following plane to be off schedule until planes already waiting to land do so.

Weather conditions may have an adverse effect on schedules, especially if an airport is being used at a high degree of utilization initially. Fog, rain, or snow, for example, may cause takeoffs or landings to slow down. Once this occurs at a major metropolitan airport it is difficult to resume normal operations.

Individual airlines find it almost impossible to use equipment as efficiently as possible during periods of delay. Aircraft which are circling the field cannot be used for other flights, forcing the airline to use a reserve plane. If there is no reserve plane available that the airline could use at the particular airport, it is possible that an entire flight would be cancelled to allow the aircraft and equipment to catch up with the schedule [25:143].

The majority of air traffic flies between a number of main metropolitan areas. These areas form airport hubs and serve the largest metropolitan areas in the country. Presently, there are twenty-two airport hubs. Table 9-4 shows the total number of aircraft operations for each of these twenty-two airport hubs for fiscal years 1966, 1967, and 1968.

The large yearly increases which are observed in these airports point up the need to solve the existing problems faced by these airports before air traffic increases further. Already, overcrowding is causing its effect to be felt. In many large airports delays in arrivals and, to a lesser extent, in departures, are becoming commonplace.

New Procedures and Methods Designed
to Reduce Air Traffic Problems

Some of the difficulties facing the large metropolitan airports that have just been mentioned come mainly from the advanced technology of newer aircraft and the increased passenger capacity of these planes. Although the aircraft industry, as well as the government agencies involved, were somewhat unprepared for this large increase, steps are presently being taken to relieve the congestion around our larger metropolitan airports that are already experiencing delays due to overcrowding. Measures are also being taken to eliminate the difficulties being encountered by the older airports around metropolitan centers due to the advanced technology in the newer types of aircraft now in use.

The present amount of air traffic is already causing delays. Previously,

Table 9.4

**FAA–Operated Airport Traffic Control
Towers by Rank Order of Total Aircraft Operations**

Airport	1966	1967	1968
Chicago			
Midway	222,870	278,939	256,333
O'Hare	553,093	538,527	682,141
New York			
John F. Kennedy	421,810	451,533	481,092
La Guardia	275,279	316,246	352,289
Newark	240,695	242,989	271,158
Islip	284,174	319,304	293,098
Florida			
Opa Locka	500,218	596,949	622,539
Tamiami	300,288	382,211	300,288
Fort Lauderdale	292,674	451,910	495,130
Miami	398,669	441,156	444,544
Los Angeles			
LA International	400,284	437,777	534,234
Long Beach	422,186	499,724	488,627
Denver	368,097	436,105	443,128
San Francisco			
Oakland	295,823	343,967	436,080
SF International	284,736	298,908	341,229
Dallas			
Red Bird	139,731	191,747	189,803
Love	293,897	344,779	373,430
Addison	151,945	185,667	198,062
Atlanta	290,488	330,279	385,152
St. Louis	314,102	341,918	336,528

Table 9.4 (*continued*)

Airport	1966	1967	1968
Seattle			
Boeing	258,704	332,806	378,197
Seattle–Tacoma	125,197	128,955	152,347
Washington			
Washington National	318,961	318,241	341,899
Dulles	172,930	193,688	220,818
Cleveland	267,256	291,090	315,540
Kansas City			
KC International	172,672	199,009	221,625
Fair	247,930	281,187	305,878
Municipal	225,395	230,690	255,345
Detroit			
Detroit City	224,834	232,715	248,050
Pontiac	181,155		204,219
Wayne	208,895	279,763	297,342
Boston	243,448	265,475	296,976
Houston	250,842	269,090	286,382
Philadelphia	227,281	241,980	279,795
New Orleans	229,770	230,038	265,833
Pittsburgh	207,116	209,298	250,851
Minneapolis	184,429	250,762	245,500
Cincinnati	177,799	193,886	189,848
Las Vegas	165,408	180,772	193,935

Source: U. S. Department of Transportation,
Federal Aviation Agency, *FAA Air Traffic
Activity: Fiscal Year 1966, 1967 and 1968*
(Washington, D. C.: Government Printing
Office, 1966, 1967 and 1968).

statistics were given which stated that the projected amount of air traffic would approximately double by 1980 with much larger increases to the year 2000. The projected figures are restated below for convenience.

Year	Total Passenger Miles (In Billion Miles)
1970	66.6
1980	107.8
1990	160.7
2000	225.0

Thus, in the next thirty-two years, the skies in the vicinity of our large metropolitan airports will become even more crowded than at present.

Although this increase seems to be of overwhelming proportions in relation to the present level of aircraft and the congestion that is now present, new development in the industry are working to accommodate this increase in the future.

Presently, there are two measures being considered to ease the congestion being faced at this time. These measures are temporary in nature, designed only to alleviate present congestion until more permanent solutions can be implemented.

The airline industry has realized that they have an interest in this problem, and have suggested that the industry voluntarily reschedule some of the existing flights. Mr. Stuart Tipton, President of the Air Transport Association, said a voluntary schedule adjustment committee, representing the United States and foreign carriers, which met September 5, 1968, would attempt to work out a congestion reduction proposal. The effects would be felt approximately during November-December 1968, if the proposal was approved by the Civil Aeronautics Board.

During this period, the Federal Aviation Agency also proposed its own set of rules concerning the maximum number of planes that could land in an hour. The major difference that remained to be worked out was the number of aircraft each airfield could accommodate in an hour. The Air Transport Association set a 90 plane maximum in the John F. Kennedy Airport in New York City and a 70 plane limit at Newark and La Guardia Airports which also serve metropolitan New York. The Federal Aviation Agency set limits of 65-60-60, respectively, for these three airports. The reason for the difference between the two sets of figures was that the Air Transport Association based its figures on clear weather and the government figures were based on IFR (Instrument Flight Rules) weather. This is weather where visibility is less than in clear weather, limited by rain, clouds, fog, or snow. The Federal Aviation Agency also wanted O'Hare Airport in Chicago and National Airport in Washington, D.C. included in this plan [11:23].

These two measures are intended to keep the number of landings each hour to a safe limit. Although it may appear at first glance that this would lead to the point where passengers would not be able to get flights into New York and other metropolitan airports due to available aircraft being filled to capacity, newer aircraft have larger passenger capacity than ever before.

Larger Aircraft — Greater Passenger Capacity

There are a number of different aircraft being developed at present which have greatly increased passenger capacity. This will result in the same number of passengers being carried in fewer aircraft and reduce takeoffs and landings. This will work in connection with the rescheduling of flights to alleviate delays by having a maximum number of landings of new jets with increased passenger capacity and reduce to a minimum the number of passengers being forced to wait for other flights due to full aircraft. A pair of three-engine jets, which are called airbus types, the Douglas DC-10 and the Lockheed L-1011 are now being developed. The DC-10 will have a capacity of approximately 250 and the L-1011 will carry 256-345 passengers. Another jumbo jet in production at present is the Boeing 747, a four-engine jet with a capacity of 400 passengers which has undergone initial trial runs in February 1969.

These three jets are being considered by many knowledgeable people in the airline industry as very probably forming the backbone of the civil-airline fleet through the 1970s. Orders are already in for 443 planes at a total cost of 7.4 billion dollars [34:92].

Of course, these larger jets will require longer runways and larger waiting areas. Passengers will converge on restaurants, taxis, and baggage areas in greater numbers. Airport runways also will be utilized at maximum capacity during a continually increasing portion of a 24-hour day, due to the larger number of flights. Therefore, anything which tends to lessen the effectiveness and usefulness of airports or runways will be keenly felt.

There are a number of different solutions being proposed and tested that are designed to keep airports open and running at peak effectiveness.

Increasing Effective Airport Capacity

Presently the greatest congestion now being experienced is in the major metropolitan airports where unused space is already at a premium. Usually there is little room to expand in these airports. One proposed solution to this problem of lack of space has been put forward by Mr. Willis M. Hawkins, Vice-President of Science and Engineering at Lockheed Aircraft Corporation. He says:

If the auxiliary services and the 'waving goodbye' could take place at a satellite terminal far from the airport, and if passengers could arrive in chunks of from 40 to 60 per vehicle delivered directly to the airplane, expensive airport real estate could be reserved for use by the airport itself.

This satellite-airport concept has widespread support among many airport administrators, including Mr. Francis T. Fox, General Manager of the Los Angeles Department of Airports [33:96-97].

However, this will not result in anything but temporary relief. The main need was expressed in a statement released by the Federal Aviation Agency on November 11, 1968, which stated that the United States must build more than 800 new airports and improve almost 3000 existing ones within the next five years to relieve present congestion and accommodate future growth. These FAA figures include, for the first time, development of STOL-ports [35:4].

In existing airports, weather conditions frequently cause delays due to poor visibility or runway conditions. Some of these conditions, such as rain or snow, are unavoidable. Others can sometimes be eliminated. Fog, for instance, may cause delays due to poor visibility, especially for airports bordering on bodies of water. The Air Transport Association reported that a $100,000 fog dispersal test undertaken at Sacramento, California, in the winter of 1967-1968 proved successful enough to warrant an operational program during 1969. ATA stated that 70 percent of all seeding tests made when the airport was closed by fog produced successful results. Successful results means that the fog was dispersed in the vicinity of the airport allowing resumption of normal takeoff and landing operations. This process succeeds in cases of warm fog which comprises 95 percent of all fog. It is estimated that at present delays due to fog cost the airlines $75 million annually [21:37].

Related to the problem of fog is runway icing. During winter months, runways, at times, are forced to close because of extensive ice on landing areas. This results in delays and can be particularly serious in places such as Boston, New York, Chicago, and Minneapolis. The Dow Chemical Company has devised a solution designed to melt ice and add traction to runways. This deicing fluid is added to between 92-95 percent sand, depending upon conditions. The fluid melts the ice, allowing the sand to set on the runway. Tests have proven that the sand will remain on the runway in 175 mph winds. The test was conducted at Newark and John F. Kennedy Airports in the New York metropolitan area in February 1968 and showed further that this solution has no corrosive effect on metals and keeps the ice from reforming over a period of time. This has a twofold benefit. First, runways will remain open longer if large ice patches could be kept from forming. Second, this becomes even more significant when related to the newer, larger jets that will soon be in operation. Because of the extra runway length needed by these jets to land and take off, even small amounts of ice may become dangerous due to higher landing speeds. This solution may be applied to the runway and will eliminate ice on the entire length of it and eliminate the need for frequent runway checks during inclement weather [14:78].

Airports at Toronto, Canada, use a chemical fertilizer called urea to eliminate ice from runways. According to Mr. Keith J. Robinson, acting manager of Toronto International Airport, the fertilizer is applied by a spreader of the type used on farms and can clear an area 140 feet wide when the spreader runs at 20 miles per hour. Mr. Robinson stated that this solution has kept Toronto's runways free of ice for the past two winters [38].

A new lighting technique is being used at metropolitan airports since newer aircraft are using up a larger portion of available runway in landing and taking off and by cutting down the safety margin of extra runway length. Alternate rows of red and white lights are being installed warning pilots that they have only 3000 feet of runway remaining. When the pilot reaches the 1000 foot mark all lights become red [28:356].

More Effective Movement of Passengers
in the Terminal Area

With the increase in the number of passengers flying into airports, new ways need to be found to process these people more effectively and in larger numbers. In some cases, there is a little choice except to increase the amount of certain services, such as taxis and restaurants. In other cases, improvements are being made in the method by which passengers are processed onto the aircraft.

One such improvement involves the handling of passenger baggage. This method is based on a system of microwave transmissions and receptions. The baggage ticket has a builtin printed circuit which acts as an antenna. The transmitter, about the size of a pinhead, is designed to respond to a specific microwave frequency. The tailored ticket response can be keyed to a specific baggage destination. This system has been named the Spott System [5:32].

This and other improvements are becoming increasingly important as airports become more congested and larger numbers of people are boarding and disembarking from each aircraft. It is important that these airport operations become more evenly distributed and pressure taken off airport personnel. As one individual stated, once orderly airline terminals are beginning to resemble refugee camps. Airline employees have become so fatigued they are beginning to show signs of strain as inconvenienced passengers voice their complaints [25:43].

Rescheduling Air Traffic Off Peak Periods

As the number of flights increases, several metropolitan airports are attempting to discourage private aircraft from landing and taking off during the peak traffic hours of 8-10 A.M. and 3-8 P.M. The Port of New York Authority, which has jurisdiction over metropolitan New York's three airports, has increased the landing fee to $25 during these hours. Logan Field in Boston has set a minimum fee of $5 while National Airport in Washington, D.C., has set a minimum of $4 [22:23]. In this way it is hoped that if a major proportion of general aviation activity could be transferred to other hours in the day, there would be less congestion and room for more commercial flights.

This policy may act as a stopgap measure for a short time but the situation remains that congestion, which develops at metropolitan airports due to the number of aircraft converging onto the airport at once, causes flights to be delayed across the country. Of course, some delays are unavoidable. With the number of aircraft increasing annually, however, a great burden and heavy workload have been placed on the air traffic controllers. When the number of aircraft entering a certain airport area becomes too great for the number of air traffic controllers on duty, aircraft are held up to keep the number of aircraft at a safe level for controllers to handle. The FAA has taken steps to remedy this situation. On July 23, 1968, the Senate approved an increase of $15.75 million in the budget proposed for operation of air traffic centers and other facilities of the FAA. The money was earmarked for hiring and training 1,996 more air traffic controllers. The twofold purpose of this program is to eliminate delays due solely to insufficient numbers of air traffic controllers on duty relative to the number of flights, and to increase safety of all flights by lessening the number of individual aircraft each controller had to handle at any one time.

Improved Piloting – Greater Safety

There are a number of advanced technological systems now in the testing stage which are designed to further increase the air controllers effectiveness and increase air safety. The FAA is testing what is known as a localizer. This system would allow general aviation aircraft to approach 9,000 small airports in the country by instruments rather than through a controller. This would free the controller to concentrate on commercial aircraft and other duties and reduce the minimum spacing necessary between planes, which has been necessary to maintain safety levels [39].

An added improvement to the localizer which would further reduce danger in the vicinity of airports and also reduce the spacing required between aircraft is being developed by the National Aeronautics and Space Administration. NASA is developing a low-cost collision avoidance system for general aviation. The cost of this system has been projected to be about $1,000 per plane. There is also a collision avoidance system presently being developed for commercial aircraft. With these systems there will be less danger of accidents. The number of planes that can be in a given area safely will be increased. The benefit of this system is further increased because general aviation is not under constant control by ground personnel. This usually results in an added safety margin being allowed. With this collision avoidance system, the added margin of safety is less critical [15:61].

The present air traffic control system has come under criticism in recent times for being outdated. The localizer and collision avoidance systems are devices to modernize the traffic control system. Mr. Vernon I. Weihe, a consulting engineer, speaking to air transportation specialists on the present air traffic control system, stated that the system was essentially a hodgepodge of war surplus systems which had been reconfigured using modern components.

Mr. Weihe is in favor of an operational satellite navigation system for aircraft. He considers this an excellent improvement over the present system but states the biggest obstacle to the incorporation of this system is red tape. He stated the responsibility for this system would be spread between NASA, FAA, CAB, Federal Communications Commission, and the Departments of Defense and State [31:570].

This satellite navigation system is part of an area navigation system that is being developed by the FAA. High-ranking FAA officials believe area navigation systems will dominate the United States air traffic control systems in the 1970s because the current radar-based system imposes too heavy a work load on the controllers. Also, with the projected increase in air activity, the work load will increase even further. Area navigation systems now under development include course line computers, inertial platforms, and computers with pictoral displays. It is believed that these systems will be developed in the next few years and will become available for use at the twenty-two major airports where the heaviest congestion is expected [20:31].

One of these air navigation systems being tested employs a new Univac 1219 Computer. The test is being conducted in the New York metropolitan area at John F. Kennedy Airport. With this system, all aircraft going to La Guardia, Newark, and John F. Kennedy Airports will be controlled from this one room where the computer is located. This room is known as the New York Common IFR (Instrument Flight Rules) Room. It has been in operation since mid-July 1968. The shakedown period during which the system is to be tested was to last until late 1968 or early 1969. The computer is used in the alpha numeric (letters and numbers) portion of the New York Common IFR Room. The alphanumeric portion tracks all aircraft in the vicinity and automatically generates the display of flight information on the flight controllers radar scope in the form of alphanumerics. With this system the controller will be able to keep track of the location, identity, and altitude of up to 250 aircraft at any one time. A similar system which has been in operation in Atlanta since 1964 known as ARTS (Advanced Radar Traffic Control System) can control only 100 aircraft at any one time [18:63]. This will help alleviate delays by allowing more aircraft in the vicinity of the airport simultaneously.

In addition to technological advances, attempts have been made to aid the pilot in the plane itself. One experiment now being conducted concerns airborne displays. In the cockpit, an instrument allows the pilot to determine the present position and heading of the aircraft relative to a map of the area. This information has previously been shown on a number of different cockpit indicators; magnetic or directional gyro, manually settable course selective dial, course deviation indicators, to/from indicators, and DME counters [23:323].

A number of tests have been made designed to increase safety by reducing the pilot's workload through the combination of a number of different operations he must perform. This study is designed to discover relative values when different operations are combined. It is the objective of this operation to obtain the safest possible combination [24:282].

VTOL-STOL: Future Uses in Air Travel

Although all of the discussion so far has related to all commercial aircraft types, some points have had specific reference to the giant aircraft that are now in the planning stage and are ready to become operational in the next few years.

A problem arises in older airports usually in metropolitan areas. In some cases, due to construction around the airport, it is not possible or feasible to extend the runways so as to accommodate these large jets. Therefore, other possibilities are being investigated in order to use these older airports to maximum efficiency. The most promising possibility as well as the most radical is that of VTOL (Vertical Takeoff and Landing). There has been a good deal of research in this field and presently Ryan Aircraft Company plans to have a 500 mph VTOL business jet flying by late 1969. Mr. John Buin, Chief-of-Operations Research for Ryan, stated that this was a stopgap measure. He believes what is really needed is a practical, reliable full VTOL for airplane city-center to city-center transportation [19:15].

The National Aeronautics and Space Administration is presently planning a research program to expand VTOL technology. Plans are being drawn up for the purchase of a Lockheed XV-4B for research [16:50].

Plans have already been drawn up using the inertial guidance system of the Gemini spacecraft in VTOL. During a landing, the crew of a VTOL would ordinarily be required to handle five separate controls; thrust, elevator, lifting, ailerons, and rudders. The inertial guidance system will enable some of these functions to be done automatically. NASA expects to land a helicopter automatically by 1970 and flight test an advanced integrated landing system in a VTOL transport by 1972 [26:158].

Related to the VTOL is a type of aircraft which is already in limited service. This is the STOL (Short Takeoff and Landing) aircraft. NASA has been engaged in research in this field as well as VTOL and is planning on appropriating a de Havilland Buffalo to conduct experiments with STOL-type aircraft. The decision by NASA to go ahead with this research reflects their plan to concentrate on the type of aircraft to fill commercial aviation's immediate need for short haul intercity transport [16:50].

The degree of importance being placed on STOL aircraft and the measure of success it is expected to achieve by officials of NASA and the FAA is reflected in the fact that operational STOL-port guidelines have already been issued by the FAA. These guidelines set down specifications for STOL-ports to be built in the near future. In essence, the requirements call for runway length of at least 1500 feet and width of 100 feet. The runways will be designed to support aircraft weighing 150,000 pounds and have 150 feet of paved overrun at each end of the runway. There will also be a minimum of 1,000 feet of obstruction-free, clear zone at each end of the runway for landings and takeoffs. In conventional airports, specifications call for a runway of 6,000 feet in length, 200 feet in width, 200 feet of paved overrun, with an obstruction-free clear zone of 2,500 feet [30:390].

STOL proves to be a promising commercial possibility. The nation's first regularly scheduled STOL service began in the Washington, D.C. area in

September 1968. This service covered the three airports which serve Washington, D.C., Friendship Airport in Baltimore, Washington National Airport and Dulles Airport in Virginia [29:229].

The Robertson Aircraft Company of Washington is producing modifications which adopt present aircraft into STOL-type aircraft. These modifications are available for Cessna 172, 180, 182, 185, 205, 206, 210, and 337 models. Robertson has also developed a STOL aircraft, the Robertson STOL 182. The modifications involved were accomplished by a high-lift system which uses the existing ailerons as part of a full-span wing toiled edge. The total effect reduces stalling speed 20 percent and landing and takeoff distances 50 percent while increasing climb angle 60 percent [9:81].

There will be a practical test of the STOL aircraft between major cities in the near future. A French Breuguet 941 is being flown by Eastern Airline pilots between Boston, New York, and Washington, D.C. on courses which run parallel to existing commercial routes. The objectives of the program are (1) to establish flight operating procedures governing STOL operations; (2) to determine the feasibility of STOL operations; (3) determine overall cost and time savings of STOL operations; and (4) evaluate navigation and guidance systems for STOL operations [12:16].

Regulations Governing Speed and Altitude

Since the summer of 1968 when delays were experienced at a number of major airports due to overcrowding, the FAA has established new rules designed to separate commercial and general aviation and increase safety. A nationwide speed limit was set. Aircraft flying above 10,000 feet were required to fly faster than 288 mph. Another rule required all aircraft flying at 18,000 feet or above to be under positive control in the northeast section of the country extending from Kansas to Maine. Positive control means that aircraft could fly that high only when under constant supervision of FAA ground controllers, using radar and radio [32:55]. Ground controllers would assign the aircraft an altitude and compass heading which the pilot would be required to follow. Any change would require prior approval from the ground controller.

Research to Reduce Jet Noise

The giant jets of the future, designed to carry more passengers and fly at faster speeds, will add to a problem already being faced by present day aircraft. Jet noise has become serious in the vicinity of the airport, especially when aircraft are descending to land. Complaints from residents living near the airport or in the approach path to the airport have caused government officials to enact legislation designed to cut down aircraft noise. Towards the end of Spring, 1968, the House of Representatives passed HR #3400 authorizing the FAA administration to "prescribe and amend such rules and regulations as he might find necessary to provide for the control and abatement of aircraft noise and sonic boom [17:21]. In July, 1968, the Senate also passed the bill. The objective of the bill is to reduce noise by about 50 percent below the noise level of present aircraft. The reduced noise is to be achieved during flights one mile from touchdown, three and a half miles from the start of the takeoff, and one quarter mile on either side of the runway [8:24].

Unfortunately, some individuals, primarily pilots, believe that safety is being compromised because of the method to be used to reduce engine noise. The noise abatement law requires that pilots reduce engine power in the specified areas previously mentioned to reduce noise. Some pilots argue that under certain conditions such as turbulent air, an instrument or engine failure, or the attention of the pilot being momentarily diverted, the flight may be in danger. They state that because of the power reduction of the engines, there is no margin for error because the aircraft cannot be maneuvered at that power level and, therefore, if an emergency develops, the aircraft is in danger of crashing. During a meeting of the Airline Pilots Association a resolution was passed stating that the Association refused to accept or endorse noise abatement procedures which required maneuvers strictly for noise abatement purposes that they believed were hazardous, such as making turns below six hundred feet or taking off and climbing without sufficient speed for maneuvers [36:96-97].

NASA is also launching a quiet-engine program. The agency asked for bids on a new engine at the end of August 1968. The takeoff thrust rating of the new engine is to be 23,000 pounds. This is much larger than present engines but NASA has stated this engine will be applicable to all sizes of jet engines.

Further attempts have led the FAA to support a project to calculate the total amount of noise from aircraft at 29 representative United States Airports. The results of this survey will be used in future noise reduction programs. Airports have been selected to include a cross-section of those airports handling light, medium, and heavy aircraft traffic in both general and commercial aviation [27:61].

Although the programs presently being planned and those in actual operation are designed to help alleviate congestion and overcrowding of airports, because of the overwhelming increase that is expected in the next thirty-one years, these measures are, at best, short-term answers to a long-term problem. Washington officials are presently coming to the realization that what is needed is a long-term, permanent solution. In line with this decision Mr. Alan S. Boyd, Secretary of Transportation, revealed in June 1968 that the Nixon administration is planning on spending $1 billion for airport and air transportation improvements and new airports by 1973. This program is to be financed through charges on proposed users [13:16].

Conclusions

This increase in air activity that has already occurred and is expected to grow at an accelerated rate in the next thirty years is going to affect the urgency of solving this situation.

Below are the RFF projections previously stated with the year 1960 equaling 100.

Year	Total	Year	Total
1945	13.0	1970	192.2
1950	26.3	1980	311.6
1955	64.4	1990	464.4
1960	100.0	2000	650.3
1965	130.6		

The twenty-two major airport hubs account for a large percentage of air operations. These airports are already reaching or have reached the point of saturation. With the present level of congestion at these large airport hubs, there is little room for increased air traffic over present levels. During the summer months when there is an increase in air activity, delays become more apparent. Last summer, Kennedy Airport in New York and O'Hare in Chicago experienced delays of up to two or three hours. Thus, by 1970 there will be an additional increase in air traffic over the 1968-1969 levels further congesting these large airports. The congestion level may be partially offset by governmental efforts to transfer general aviation from peak traffic hours.

It is expected by that 1980 there will be approximately twice the amount of air traffic as in 1968. Very simply, the airports operating today cannot handle this load. Additional airports are part of the answer to this situation. However, locating airports in areas where they are needed is often difficult due to lack of suitable space.

Modernizing the present air traffic control system is also needed and would allow new airports to be built closer to one another with no loss in safety. This would permit airports to be constructed in areas close enough to metropolitan centers to enable commuters to be transported to and from the airports by rapid transit or mass transit relatively conveniently and quickly. Present day air traffic control systems cannot accommodate the number of aircraft expected to be present in the next thirty years and maintain the present safety level. Therefore, either airports are built far away from the metropolitan centers or the air traffic control systems are modernized. By 1980 the average plane landing and taking off at Kennedy or O'Hare is expected to have capacities of between five-hundred and eight-hundred people. Thus, if two Boeing 747 Aircraft or a Boeing 747 and a Lockheed 256 were to collide in midair, between 600 and 700 fatalities might result.

As previously stated, there are methods by which the air traffic control system could be modernized. The air navigation system employing the Univac 1219 Computer in operation at John F. Kennedy Airport could increase the number of aircraft that could be controlled from the ground to 250 with the same degree of safety achieved by the advanced radar control traffic system which can handle 100 aircraft at a time and has been in operation since 1964 in a number of cities, such as Atlanta.

If these systems are not modernized there will be a need for high-speed ground transportation from the metropolitan areas to airport locations which are reasonably convenient. High-speed trains appear to be the most likely solution to achieve this without disrupting the surrounding areas.

Cleveland has become the first city to provide a rapid transit system from the downtown terminal to the airport. The traveling time here has been cut to 20 minutes.

Short-run solutions to air congestion are the VTOL and STOL aircraft. With the increase expected in air traffic over the next 30 years, lack of air space in metropolitan areas will affect these types of aircraft as well as conventional types. Although these aircraft can land with much less space than conventional planes, the sheer number of aircraft present in the sky will be a self-limiting factor. There are no VTOL aircraft in service at the present time and only one STOL carrier serving the three airports in the Washington, D.C. area.

The main problem to be faced in the next 30 years is the number of aircraft which will be needed to accommodate the number of passengers desiring to fly and the total number of aircraft that can be accommodated in the relatively small air space of the airports. As the public desires more flights, the airline industry is developing newer, larger, more powerful aircraft with higher speeds and greater passenger capacity. These increased activities, however, also bring with them inherent problems of noise and passenger safety. Although larger aircraft are designed to reduce congestion they also bring with them increased noise levels which affect people living in the area of the airport. Noise abatement programs which are designed to lower the noise level also lower the plane's power level and in this way may effect its maneuverability, resulting in decreased safety margins. Each solution to one problem inherently creates others. The fact is that it will be practically impossible to satisfy the desires of the airline passengers for speedy traveling and proximity to major metropolitan cities. It appears almost certain that airports will have to be constructed further away from city centers as time goes on. Thus, the problem reduces itself to the fact that although advanced technology will allow more aircraft to enter the air space of present airports, the sheer volume will force an increasing number of aircraft to use more distant facilities. There will need to be an increased use of ground transportation, such as in Cleveland, to make transportation from the city centers to the airports themselves feasible.

10 The Social Costs of Surface Mined Coal

Robert F. Karsch

Much has been written about the future demand of the natural resources of the United States and the projected consumption of such. The major serious consideration has been given to whether or not the available resources are sufficient to meet our needs for the future. There does not appear to be a comprehensive study of offsetting costs of future resource consumption. The emphasis has been upon whether the needs can be met rather than what the social and economic costs will be. In the following pages there will be developed an analysis of what these costs will be for surface mined coal.

This chapter will set forth the basic assumptions upon which the projections of coal production, specifically surface mined coal, are based, what they are projected as being in the years between 1960 and the the year 2000 and what the social and economic costs will be in terms of disturbed acreage and the dollar outlays which may be necessary in order to restore the land to a useful or productive capacity. This is not intended to provide for changes in federal, state, or user reclamation policies but simply to investigate and project the magnitude of reclamation of the spoil banks associated with the surface mining of coal.

The most important use of coal is for the generation of electric power. This use accounted for half the 1960 demand for coal and is increasing in relative importance. RFF projects that coal for electricity generation will increase to two-thirds of total coal consumption by 2000, but trends in recent years suggest that this may understate the extent of the rise in this use. Coal companies have held down coal costs at the power plant by a combination of new transportation involving so-called "unit trains" and intensive mechanization, including that for surface mining of coal. As a consequence, coal has more than held its own in electricity generation, a rapidly rising market. Coal consumption in iron and steel and nonferrous metals production is projected by RFF to increase by 13 percent between 1960 and 1980 and by an additional 37 percent between 1980 and 2000. Use of coal by commercial firms and for export is projected by RFF to remain at a constant absolute level, while other uses, already minor by 1960, such as for residential heating and by railroads, are projected to decline to negligible proportions by 1980. (RFF assumed arbitrarily a constant level of export demand amounting to 40 million tons per year.)

However, overall demand for coal is projected to increase at a rapid rate, principally because of the burgeoning requirements for thermal generation of electric power. This is so despite the expectation that atomic fuels will make substantial inroads on the demand for fossil fuels by the electric power industry in the closing decades of the century.

Table 10.1

**Estimated United States Demand for
Bituminous and Anthracite Coal,
1970–2000, Inclusive** (production
figures in millions of net tons)

Year	1970	1980	1990	2000
High	644	864	1,040	1,328
Medium	516	630	658	718
Low	437	488	489	485

Source: *Resources in America's Future*,
Table A15-16.

RFF projections of United States demand for coal are presented in Table 10-1. Figure 10-1 is a graphic presentation of these projections. By utilizing a straight line interpolation between the 1960 figure of 436 million tons and the 1970 medium projection of 516 million tons an average annual increase of 8 million tons is derived. Based upon this interpolation, the 1966 and 1967 estimated demand would be 484 and 492 million tons respectively, as compared to the actual U.S. Bureau of Mines 1966 and 1967 production figures of 547 and 563 million tons, respectively. The actual figures for 1966 and 1967 compare quite closely to interpolated values for RFF's "high" projection. Figure 10-2 is a graphic presentation of this comparison. Because the "high" projection corresponds closely to the actual data for 1960 through 1967 the "high" projection will be used hereafter as the adjusted projected demand for coal through the year 2000. The straight line "high" projection to the year 2000 will be used for simplicity resulting in an annual increase in demand of 22.3 million tons.

Now that a projection of total coal demand has been derived it must be analyzed in terms of what portion is applicable to surface mining. The National Coal Association has published data made available by the U.S. Bureau of Mines. As can be seen from Table 10-2, anthracite coal has had an ever decreasing portion of total coal production and accounted for only 2.5 percent in 1966. Because of this and the fact that the U.S. Bureau of Mines' figures relative to surface mining apply only to bituminous coal, the analysis will proceed as if total production were of bituminous coal. Table 10-3 indicates coal production computed by this method. An analysis of the increase in the surface mining activity indicates that in the past 20 years, the percent of coal production attributable to surface mining has grown at an average rate of .58 percent per year. This is computed by dividing the increase from 1947 to 1967 by the 20

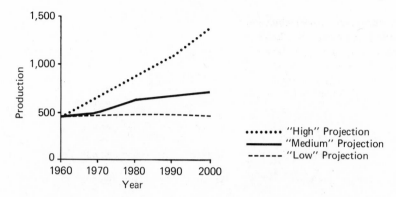

Figure 10-1 Projected United States Demand for Coal, 1960-2000, Inclusive (Millions of tons). Source: *Resources in America's Future* Table A15-16.

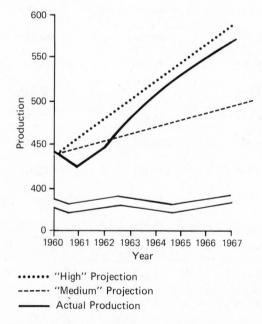

Figure 10-2 Comparison of Actual & Projected Coal Demand, 1960-1967, Inclusive (Millions of tons). Source: *Resources in America's Future,* Table A15-16; *Bituminous Coal Facts 1968*, p. 60.

Table 10.2

**United States Net Coal Production,
1947–1967, Inclusive** (thousands of
net tons)

Year	Bituminous Coal and Lignite	Anthracite Coal	Total Production
1947	630,624	57,190	687,814
1948	599,518	57,140	656,658
1949	437,868	42,702	480,570
1950	516,311	44,077	560,388
1951	533,665	42,670	576,335
1952	466,841	40,583	507,424
1953	457,290	30,949	488,239
1954	391,706	29,100	420,806
1955	464,634	26,200	490,834
1956	500,874	28,900	429,774
1957	492,704	25,338	518,042
1958	410,445	21,171	431,616
1959	412,028	20,649	432,677
1960	415,512	18,817	434,329
1961	402,977	17,446	420,423
1962	422,149	16,894	439,043
1963	458,928	18,267	477,195
1964	486,998	17,184	504,182
1965	512,088	14,866	526,954
1966	533,881	12,941	546,822
1967	551,000	12,000	563,000

Source: National Coal Association, *Bituminous Coal Facts 1968* (Washington, D. C.:
National Coal Association, 1968), p. 60.

Table 10.3

**United States Net Coal Production
Attributable to Surface Mining, 1947
through 1967, Inclusive** (millions of
net tons)

Year	Percent Surface Mined	Production by Surface Mining
1947	22.1	139.4
1948	23.3	139.5
1949	24.2	106.0
1950	23.9	123.5
1951	22.0	117.6
1952	23.3	108.9
1953	23.1	105.5
1954	25.1	98.1
1955	24.8	115.1
1956	25.4	127.1
1957	25.2	124.1
1958	28.3	116.2
1959	29.4	120.9
1960	29.5	122.6
1961	30.3	122.0
1962	30.9	130.3
1963	31.4	144.1
1964	31.2	151.9
1965	32.3	165.2
1966	33.7	180.1
1967	33.7	185.7

Source: National Coal Association, *Bituminous Coal Facts 1968* (Washington, D. C.:
National Coal Association, 1968), p. 58.

year time span involved. Using the least squares method of estimation the growth rate is .61 percent per year [20:700].

It is estimated that as of January 1, 1967 the United States had coal reserves recoverable by strip mining in the area of 108 billion tons [19:39]. Assuming that the projected rate of increase is correct, over 50 percent of the coal mined in the year 2000 will be by the surface mining method. The 108 billion tons of reserves available for strip mining in 1967 will be more than sufficient to cope with the increased production rates well past the year 2000. Figure 10-3 illustrates graphically the projected coal production and the number of tons to be recovered by surface mining based upon the least squares projection through the year 2000.

The largest reserves of coal recoverable by surface mining are located in Illinois, Kentucky, Montana, North Dakota, Ohio, Pennsylvania, West Virginia, and Wyoming. The reserves in these states range from 6 to 50 billions of tons [19:39]. With the exception of Montana, North Dakota, and Wyoming, these states were also the major producers of underground coal in 1965 [19:84]. With the major reserves recoverable by surface mining located in those states where the major production demand is, it does not appear that the projections will not be met because of lack of suitable reserves. If it becomes necessary to mine the Montana, North Dakota, and Wyoming reserves in significant quantity, transportation costs will become an important consideration. In addition to transportation costs, electrical generation and population demands will be discussed in a following section.

Thus far attention has been given to aggregate coal production and the portion attributable to surface mining with no attempt to localize the projections. It should be clear to the reader that aggregate projections are likely to be more accurate than the localized, or component, portions. It is for this reason that the localized projections will be treated in a separate section entitled Geographic Projections of Production.

Technological Causes for the
Increased Production of Surface Mined Coal

The projection just cited, dramatic as it may appear, is substantiated not only by the history of coal production in itself but also by the developments in technology in the production of surface mined coal. Over the years the production of coal has taken on many varied characteristics. These have ranged from the pick and shovel underground miner to the skilled operator whose equipment is equipped with radar or the operator whose 18.5 million pound machine standing 220 feet tall eats 180 cubic yards of earth every 55 seconds [19:28]. The 1950 daily output of a United States coal miner was about 6 tons as compated to 18 tons per day in 1966 [19:89]. What does all this mean with respect to the social costs of resource pollution and waste? The pollution problem as it relates to surface mining involves the unsightly and unproductive land acreage formed as a result of the foliage being removed, the scarring of the land surface and the acid condition of the soil and nearby waters which often

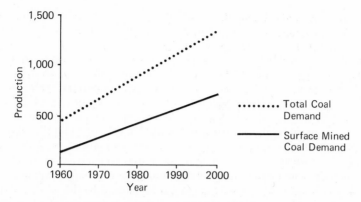

Figure 10-3 Adjusted Coal Demand & Surface Mining Projection, 1960-2000, Inclusive (Millions of tons). Source: *Resources in America's Future,* Table A15-16.

results from this method of mining. As with most pollution problems, it is almost impossible to measure these costs in terms of dollars. Vast areas of Kentucky, Illinois, or Ohio have had mile after mile of the land surface stripped clean and the coal deposits removed from below leaving many acres without any vegetation, growth, or protection from erosion.

The United States Department of Interior estimates that as of 1964, 153,000 acres of land had been disturbed by surface mining. Surface mining of coal accounted for 46,000 acres of disturbed land in 1964 [12:42]. Previous data indicate that some 157 million tons of coal was produced by surface mining in 1964 which indicates that roughly 3,400 tons of coal are surface mined for each acre of disturbed land. The United States Department of Agriculture further estimates that as of January 1, 1965, 1,301,430 acres of land had been stripped of its vegetation and soil coverage in order to obtain the deposits of coal beneath [12:110]. This indicates that up to and including the 1964 production, each 2,700 tons of surface mined coal resulted in an acre of disturbed land, suggesting that increased production standards has resulted in the increased output per acre. The stripping of the surface is only the beginning of the pollution and waste problems. The drainage patterns are altered and if not restored, subsequent rainfalls will result in landslides, pollution of the water beds, additional erosion and deterioration of esthetic values of the land. The United States Department of Interior estimates that if all the coal recoverable by the strip mining method were to be mined, it would result in spoil banks covering 42,000 square miles — an area larger than the state of Ohio [10:c16].

The pollution, or waste, resulting from surface mining is clearly a production problem for it results from the stripping of the land surface and not from input or consumption factors. Man has had little to do with the location of coal reserves for, like many other natural resources, their geographic location was determined millions of years ago. An illustration of the surface mining process may be the best vehicle to set forth exactly what is meant by pollution or wastes caused by surface mining. Stated in its simplest terms, surface mining of coal consists of removing the vegetation, topsoil, rock, and other material that lie above the deposits in order to recover the coal.

The actual surface mining of coal can take the form of area mining or contour mining. Auger mining is much the same as contour mining and is often classified as such [12:34]. In area mining an initial cut or hole is dug to the depth where the coal is located. This is the method used for mining on fairly flat land and usually to a depth of 30 to 40 feet. After the coal is removed, the area parallel to the hole, or strip, is cut and the earth, or overburden, is used to fill the original hole. This process continues until the entire area has been mined.

The method known as contour mining is used most commonly where the coal is located in hilly and mountainous areas. Mining of this nature follows the contour of the hillside as do many roads. A cut is made in the side of the hill to remove the coal. This cut is made along the side of, or around, the hill. The overburden is spilled to the downside of the hill and the coal is removed. A second cut is then made adjacent to the first cut but on the up-hill side of it. The overburden removed from the second cut is spilled to the downhill side and actually fills the first cut. This process continues until the removal of the overburden becomes too expensive a process for the amount of coal to be removed. This is usually when the overburden is 100 to 125 feet thick. This method is practiced most widely in the Appalachia region and its pollution and waste effects are more strongly felt than those of area strip mining [12:35].

The technological advancements in the design and production of surface mining equipment have made significant strides in coal recovery by this method. Surface mining output per man day is roughly 200 percent higher, overall recovery is 60 percent higher and operating costs are 25 to 30 percent lower than underground recovery methods [10:c2]. Continuing technological advancements have resulted in output per man day increasing from 15.6 tons in 1950 to 44.4 tons in 1966 as compared to an increase from 5.7 to 14.6 tons during the same period for underground mining [19:89]. It is evident then that the lower labor costs per ton of coal produced is a strong reason for the trend toward surface mining.

Increased production has been accompanied by continued improvements in the size and efficiency of earth moving machinery. The birth of the power shovel actually took place in England in 1796 when a 4 hp Watt steam engine was used to dredge for coal and had advanced to the 1965 stage when the Marion 6360 began taking 180 cubic yard bites of overburden out of the hillsides of Illinois [24]. The walking dragline has kept pact with the shovel developments of the 1960's as Bucyrus-Erie and Marion introduced new models. The Bucyrus-Erie models included a 2550-watt unit, which swung a 75 yard bucket from a 275 foot boom and Marion's draglines included the 8800, an 85 yard, 275 foot boom that began producing in 1963 [24]. Most of this newer equipment is powered by electricity with requirements in excess of 8,000 volts and machines currently on the drafting boards have capacities in excess of 200 cubic yards [10:c3].

The advances mentioned above have not only afforded increases in total production but have increased efficiency. Surface mining of coal in the United States has reached the point where 80 percent of the recoverable coal is extracted as compared to 50 percent for underground mining. It permits the mining of coal in areas of shallow overburden, multiple beds, and in badly faulted areas [10:c5]. When these advances in surface mining equipment are analyzed, the average cost of surface mined coal in 1966 was $1.41 per ton less than that of underground coal . . . $3.64 compared to $5.05 [19:37].

It has been assumed that coal production by surface mining will continue to increase relative to underground mining. As this trend continues, the increased number of acres disturbed by surface mining will become more of a problem. The presently existing spoil banks (2,040,600 acres as of January 1, 1965 as a result of all types of surface mining) still requiring reclamation and those to come about as a result of future surface mining impose a major threat to the beauty of the land and the utility of its resources [12:111]. About 95 percent of the acreage disturbed by surface mining is attributable to seven commodities: coal for 41 percent; sand and gravel for 26 percent; stone, gold, clay, phosphate and iron for 28 percent and all others accounting for the remaining 5 percent [12:42]. Surface mining in mountainous areas leaves spoil banks which may initiate landslides that devastate large areas and add silt to local drainage. Spoil banks are high in sulfuric acid content, due to the sulfur in coal and associated rock, and low in organic matter necessary to support plant life [10:c15].

The question which is asked next is what control does man have over the pollution and waste caused by the production or recovery process. As was pointed out earlier, man has little or no control over where the coal beds are located and he must meet competition by the least expensive production methods. Thus, the control which man has over the pollution and waste problems is that of reclamation. The extent and costs of such reclamation vary depending upon a number of variables which include, but are not limited to, the various laws of the states in which the mines are operated. Statistics for 1964 indicate that these costs range from $964 per acre for completely reclaimed acreage in West South Central states to $74 per acre for partial reclamation in the East South Central states [12:113].

The use and meaning of the term reclamation varies from state to state, depending upon specific laws. These requirements range from grading of soil, building access roads and covering refuse in Oklahoma to grading, planting, covering acid material with plant life supports, and removing or burying all refuse as required by Illinois [4:12].

Geographic Projections of Production

Previous discussions indicate that total coal production can be expected to increase continually and that estimates suggest production of 644, 864, 1,040 and 1,328 million tons in the years 1970, 1980, 1990, and 2000 respectively. Production attributable to surface mining in each of these same years is 35, 41,

47, and 53 percent, respectively. Data cited earlier suggested a 1964 surface mining coal output of 3,400 tons per acre. Assuming this ratio continues to hold, projected acreage disturbed in 1970, 1980, 1990, and 2000 will be 66, 104, 144, and 209 thousand acres, respectively. In summary, the 32 year period ending in the year 2000 will require a land area of 4.433 million acres in order to produce 15.071 billion tons of surface mined coal, if the projections are realized at the 1964 output ratio.

The major damaging effects of coal surface mining have been stated as the stripping of vegetation, causing acid soil and water conditions, and generally denying use of the land for productive and recreational purposes. Restoring the disturbed land involves a cost which is referred to as the cost of reclamation. This cost can vary greatly on a per acre basis as indicated in Table 10-4. Attention is focused on costs incurred in the Middle Atlantic, South Atlantic, East North Central and East South Central areas as they accounted for 89.7 percent of all coal produced from surface mine operations in 1965 as indicated in Table 10-5.

These data would be more helpful if more were known about (1) what portion of reclaimed acreage represented newly mined land; (2) the standards used to define partial and complete reclamation; and (3) whether or not the costs include any amounts attributable to federal services such as those which may be offered by the United States Army Corps of Engineers. Most states consider a return of the land to its condition prior to mining as being complete reclamation. Under this assumption it would appear that complete reclamation of acreage in areas where the land is naturally barren would only be considered partial reclamation in areas which were wooded or covered with foliage prior to mining. One such comparison would be that of the plain states to the eastern region of the nation. It is possible, however, to compare Tables 10-4 and 10-5 in order to achieve an appreciation of the manner in which various regions are pursuing the problem. It is interesting to note that the East North Central area produced almost twice as much coal as the second largest producing area while completely reclaiming more than three times as many acres as any other area. There could be numerous variables accounting for this such as the determination on the part of state authorities to enforce reclamation laws.

An estimate of reclamation costs for the various areas, based upon total production projections, must be made in order to obtain an idea of the overall problem facing the United States. In order to complete such an estimate it is necessary to determine to what extent this problem is localized. RFF Table A15-16 indicates that roughly 50 percent of the 1960 demand for coal was attributable to the generation of electrical power and that this figure will increase to 66 percent by the year 2000 which is in agreement with estimates by the United States Bureau of Mines [19:14]. The second largest user industry is iron and steel manufacturing, consuming about 15 percent of total coal production. The remaining amount is distributed among five users with no single one user having a significant portion. Thus it appears that the major changes in the geographic consumption pattern will depend heavily upon the demand for

Table 10.4

1964 Costs Attributable to Reclamation of Surface Mined Land in the United States

Area[a]	Complete Reclamation		Partial Reclamation	
	Acres	*Cost Per Acre*	*Acres*	*Cost Per Acre*
Middle Atlantic	4,343	$ 362.	1,763	$ 261.
South Atlantic	760	169.	1,788	97.
East North Central	12,476	192.	4,162	169.
East South Central	2,920	251.	2,431	74.
West North Central	987	91.	454	126.
West South Central	32	964.	304	221.
Mountain	13	49.	283	96.
Pacific	10	400.	-	-
Total acreage and average cost	21,541	$ 230.	11,185	$ 149.

[a]See footnote to Table 10.5 for names of states in each area.

Source: *Surface Mining and Our Environment, op. cit.*, p. 113.

electrical power generation. The demand for electrical power relates primarily on population density and industrial demand which in turn can be related to population factors. The iron and steel industries will be omitted from consideration due to their dependence upon other variables such as transportation routes of other minerals available and the relatively small portion of coal consumption attributable to them.

Table 10-5 indicated the geographic distribution of surface mined coal production for 1965. The Middle Atlantic, South Atlantic, East North Central and East South Central areas accounted for almost 90 percent of total production. Data for 1966 indicate that coal, as a percent of total B.T.U.

Table 10.5

1965 Production of Surface Mined Coal
in the United States (in thousands of
tons)

Area[a]	Production	Percent of Production
Middle Atlantic	23,767	14.5
South Atlantic	14,280	8.7
East North Central	72,245	44.0
East South Central	37,019	22.5
West North Central	8,426	5.1
West South Central	1,116	0.7
Mountain	7,484	4.5
Pacific	3	–
Total	164,340	100.0

[a]Following is the composition of geographical areas: Middle Atlantic: New York, New Jersey, Pennsylvania; South Atlantic: Delaware, Maryland, Virginia, West Virginia, North Carolina, South Carolina, Georgia, Florida; East North Central: Ohio, Indiana, Illinois, Michigan, Wisconsin; East South Central: Kentucky, Tennessee, Alabama, Mississippi; West North Central: Minnesota, Iowa, Missouri, North Dakota, South Dakota, Nebraska, Kansas; West South Central: Arkansas, Louisiana, Oklahoma, Texas; Mountain: Montana, Idaho, Wyoming, Colorado, New Mexico, Arizona, Utah, Nevada; Pacific: Washington, Oregon, California, Alaska; New England: Maine, New Hampshire, Vermont, Massachusetts, Rhode Island, Connecticut (Production negligible in New England).

Source: *Bituminous Coal Facts 1968*, p. 84.

equivalent used for electric power generation in these same areas, accounted for 83.7, 92.1, 81.8 and 76.5 percent, respectively [19:62]. Although heavy population centers exist in the New England and Pacific areas coal plays virtually no role in those areas in electric generation. New England is supplied almost 85 percent by water power while the remaining demand is supplied by nuclear power. More than half of the fuel used in generating electrical power for the Pacific area is oil. The balance of the power generated is attributable to natural gas and water power. The same source indicates that the West North

Table 10.6

Area Population Projections of Selected
Areas of the United States, 1965
through 2000, Inclusive (in thousands
of inhabitants)

Area	1965	1975	1985	2000[a]
Middle Atlantic	36,487	40,747	46,525	
(Percent)	18.8	18.3	17.6	16.7
South Atlantic	28,762	34,232	41,423	
(Percent)	14.8	15.4	15.7	16.4
East North Central	38,254	42,534	49,713	
(Percent)	19.7	19.1	18.9	18.3
East South Central	12,295	14,228	16,109	
(Percent)	6.6	6.4	6.1	5.8

[a]Data for the year 2000 is based upon a
straight line projection at the rate of previous interval changes.

Source: United States Bureau of the Census,

*Statistical Abstract of the United States,
1968*, 89th Edition (Washington, D. C.:
Government Printing Office, 1968), pp.
12-13.

Central, West South Central and Mountain areas each rely upon coal for less than
10 percent of their electrical power generation needs.

With 90 percent of present coal production centered in the Middle Atlantic,
South Atlantic, East North Central and East South Central areas, a more
meaningful analysis may be made from the data presented in Table 10-6. Set
forth in Table 10-6 are population projections for each of the four areas in
question. These four areas are estimated as having 59.9 percent of the nation's
1965 population and 57.2 percent of the population for the year 2000,
indicating little shift in population density. If the assumptions that electrical
power demand is a function of population and that coal demand is a function of
electrical power generation needs are true, it would appear that the total coal
production for these four geographic areas would maintain their proportionate

shares of total coal production. Although the overall population data for the four areas on a combined basis remains basically unchanged, the data for each area varies. Before discussing this point further, other factors should be considered.

Resources in America's Future indicates that as of 1958, electrical generation by use of coal relative to total generation sources, was declining slightly in the Middle Atlantic area. At the same time, gains in the percent of power generated from coal were being found in the East North Central and East South Central areas [19:285]. Other sources confirm that consumption of coal as a fuel for electrical power generation will continue to increase [15:25]. In addition, the East South Central area is maintaining above-average expansion in coal burning electrical generating plants [18:285]. Electric power generation by nuclear fuels and natural gas will probably be the major offset to expansion of coal burning generating stations. However, there are some authorities who question the adequacy of the resource bases of nuclear and natural gas fuels to meet future demand requirements [19:46].

Another major factor to consider is the transportation cost of coal. It is expensive to transport and is consumed as close to the source as possible. For example, statistics for 1965 indicate that it costs one cent per ton mile to ship coal and that the average length of shipment is 297 miles [19:96]. In addition, there is now emerging a trend to construct electrical generating stations at the mine site rather than to cope with transportation costs [25:f25]. Some power companies are attempting to cut transportation costs by ordering shipments in larger quantities in order to receive full train loads. Such unit trains, as they are known, cut transportation costs substantially.

Since it has already been established that there does not appear to be any inadequacies in the resource base of surface minable coal, attention can now be centered on adjusting the production data of Table 10-5 for projections through the year 2000. Adjustments will consider only the four eastern areas, for reasons previously outlined, which currently produce 90 percent of the surface mined coal. In the final analysis, the other areas will be projected as having the same market share as they currently do.

Middle Atlantic Area

Table 10-6 projects the Middle Atlantic area consisting of New York, New Jersey, and Pennsylvania as containing 18.8 percent of the nation's 1965 population and 16.7 percent of the the projection for the year 2000 — a net decline of 11 percent of its share of the nation's population. Although the Pennsylvania coal fields are available, it is assumed that nuclear power will continue to expand and that only 13 percent of the nation's coal output will be produced by this area in the year 2000 as compared to 14.5 percent in 1965.

South Atlantic Area

The projection of Table 10-6 indicates the South Atlantic area, consisting of West Virginia and the Atlantic seaboard south of New Jersey, as having 14.8 percent of the 1965 population and 16.4 percent of the projection for the year 2000 — an increase of 12 percent of its share of the nation's population. This, when considered in addition to a large coal resource base, would indicate an increase in total coal production to something in the area of 11 percent of the national production estimate.

East North Central Area

The projections of Table 10-6 indicate that the East North Central area, consisting of Ohio, Indiana, Illinois, Michigan, and Wisconsin, as having 19.7 percent of the 1965 population and 18.3 percent of the estimate for the year 2000 — a decline of 7 percent of its share of the national population. When viewed in the light of its substantial coal resources, a conservative estimate foresees 44 percent of the national coal output remaining in this area.

East South Central Area

This area, consisting of Kentucky, Tennessee, Alabama, and Mississippi, has a substantial reserve coal base and although the population projection indicates that it will have a 12 percent smaller share of the national population in the year 2000, new starts of coal burning power plants is above the national average. The net result would indicate that the East South Central area would continue to produce 22 percent of the nation's coal output through the year 2000.

Based upon the forgoing conclusions, Table 10-7 has been prepared to indicate how each of the coal producing areas of the United States are projected as sharing in the production of the 709 million tons of surface mined coal to be produced in the year 2000. Using the data presented in Table 10-4, these production estimates are converted into reclamation costs assuming that all land mined in the year 2000 is completely reclaimed in that year. The reader should be cautioned about the underlying assumptions upon which these estimates are based. A projection of this nature on a national or total production basis can be expected to be more accurate than the individual projections for the various geographic areas. It must also be realized that the coal produced in one area may be transported a few miles into another state and thus be consumed in another area. To attempt to project finite variables such as this would have no real application.

Other assumptions underlying Table 10-7 are that although technological advancements may permit more coal to be extracted per acre in future years, this may be offset by depleting reserves resulting in coal being mined at a lower

Table 10.7

Projected Disturbed Acreage and Reclamation Costs of the Surface Mining of Coal in the Year 2000 (millions of tons)

Area	Percent of Production	Production	Disturbed[a] Acreage	Cost Of[b] Complete Reclamation
Middle Atlantic	13	92	27,000	$ 7,047
South Atlantic	11	78	23,000	2,231
East North Central	44	312	92,000	15,548
East South Central	22	156	46,000	3,404
West North Central	5	36	10,000	1,260
West South Central	1	5	2,000	442
Mountain	4	30	9,000	854
	100	709	209,000	$30,786

[a]Based on a production rate of 3,400 tons per acre.

Source: Table 10.4, Table 10.5 and text material.

[b]These data are in thousands of dollars based upon Table 10.5.

output ratio in areas where concentrations are more dispersed. For this reason the production factor of 3,400 tons per acre is used throughout. In addition, the reclamation costs set forth in Table 10-4 are used without any adjustment for inflation, on the one hand, or technological changes on the other hand, resulting in lower reclamation costs.

It is interesting to note two factors at the conclusion of this section. Since coal production appears to be directly related to population, the most acreage is utilized in those areas where it is most needed for other purposes. Secondly, of the 22 states in which the surface mining of coal takes place, only eleven have specific laws relating to this problem. This problem will be discussed in the following pages.

Reclamation Technology and Restored Land

Previous projections indicate that one acre of land is disturbed for each 3,400 tons of surface mine coal produced and that, for the year 2000, 53.4 percent of the 1,328 million tons will be obtained by surface mining. It was also suggested that in 1970, 1980, and 1990, coal production by surface mining will result in disturbed acreage of 66, 104 and 144 thousand acres while the projection for the year 2000 foresees 209 thousand acres being disturbed. This acreage will be stripped of vegetation, the good soil will be buried and the contour of the land destroyed. The soil which is close the coal deposits is usually of an acid nature and will not support plant life. The result of this is that this acreage, unless reclaimed, will be deprived of productive use in terms of farm, recreational, and industrial capacities and will, in addition, be an eyesore to the nation.

Although the first state law regulating reclamation of surface mined acreage was enacted in West Virginia in 1938, first attempts at land reclamation date back to 1918 [21]. The passing years saw additional states enact reclamation and surface mining laws until early 1968 when 14 states had adopted such laws. Georgia and Kansas call for state boards to license and regulate surface mining and Montana authorized its Bureau of Mines and Geology to enter into contracts with coal surface mine operators [4:10]. However, the United States Congress has not yet found it necessary for the federal government to oversee such operations.

Federal legislation has thus far dealt with surface mining operations on government owned land only and has not moved into the private sector. Examples of this are the Materials Act of July 31, 1947, Section 402 — Reogranization Plan No. 3 of 1946; the Act of July 23, 1955, and the Statutes Relating to Particular Areas and Reservations [12:121]. The Forest Service, Department of Agriculture, has established the following policy in its Manual:

2842.1 — Strip Mining Policy — When the Forest Service has jurisdiction over mining methods, it will consider each application on its own merits. The determining factor is whether the long-term public benefit derived from the operation is greater than the damage to public land, water, and other resources and is in keeping with sound principles of overall resource management. Unless a mining operator can pay the costs of measures needed to prevent erosion and stream pollution and to rehabilitate and revegetate the surface, or otherwise restore the site to productivity, a permit is justified only in cases of national emergency [12:121].

The Senate Committee on Interior and Insular Affairs on April 30, May 1, and May 2 of 1968 held hearings on the proposed Bills — S.217, S.3126 and S.3132 which called for various means of regulating surface mining. S.217 — better known as the Lausche Bill — would permit the Secretary of the Interior to establish minimum reclamation standards for individual states and was restricted to coal. S.3126 also called for minimum standards but would give joint responsibility to the Secretaries of Interior and Agriculture and would apply to all surface mines. S.3132 recognized that equal requirements for all states would be impractical and provided that the Secretary of the Interior would review the laws of each state for approval. S.217 and S.3126 provided for Federal funds to reclaim land disturbed by surface mining in the past. The Bills did not reach the floor of the House [27]. Thus it appears that various state laws have been, and will continue to be, the major force affecting the reclamation, licensing, bonding, and resource extraction requirements. For example, a comparison of the requirements of Illinois and Oklahoma indicates that Illinois requires rather complete restoration of the disturbed land while Oklahoma provides simply for grading of the soil and covering of acid materials. Illinois is one of the best examples of what can be done with land reclamation. Studies indicate that as of June 1962 surface mining had resulted in 108,000 acres of spoil banks but that 44,000 acres had already been successfully reclaimed for agricultural purposes [16]. It also had 844 bodies of nonacid surface mine water, each of which was over one acre in size, to be used for boating, fishing, and swimming. Much has been said of the many camps, parks, clubs, lakes, and golf courses not existing on previous surface mined land in Illinois but only 28 percent of the surface mined acreage is being used for recreation. Klimstra has pointed out that not all surface mined land is needed for this purpose and far from all is adaptable for such. As of 1962, coal companies owned 62 percent, private individuals owned 28 percent and 10 percent was publicly owned [16]. Much of this land is now being put to industrial and profit making uses such as farming, tree farms, grazing land, and industrial parks.

Much of the surface mined acreage of the United States is put to these other uses. Onetime coal producing acreage in Ohio, Pennsylvania, and Kentucky is now producing lumber from trees planted some 40 years ago. The Great Canada Goose is being raised in three counties in Illinois and lakes formed as a result of surface mine operations in Ohio are being used as breeding grounds for fish to stock public lakes, rivers, and ponds. Farmers and fruit growers have also turned surface mined land into productive orchards, crop lands, and grazing pastures. Table 10-8 indicates the potential and alternative uses of surface mined land in the United States as estimated by the U.S. Department of Agriculture. A review of the table indicates that less than 50 percent is projected as being used for other than income producing ventures. The reader should take careful note of this trend toward utilizing the once unused land being put to money making use in addition to its initial coal producing capability. Making this possible have been the vast number of technological advancements in the area of soil conservation, fertilizer usage, plant and tree development and, of course, the equipment necessary to ease and make more economically feasable the cultivation of land. A good portion of this research work has been completed through university and agricultural service grants from state and federal governments.

A 1961 study of Pennsylvania reclamation techniques indicated that good timber crops could be grown on spoil banks. The study revealed that timber plantations yielded over 100 cubic feet per acre per year over the first 25 years [26:20]. Some trees grew better on spoil banks than on undisturbed land with pulpwood achieved in 20 to 25 years and saw logs in 30 to 40 years. By using poplar trees, this time is cut in half. A good portion of the Pennsylvania land has also been designed for wildlife production. Coalhaul roads constructed during

Table 10.8

Potential Uses of Surface Mined Land for Selected States (percent)[a]

Area	Crop Land	Past-ure	Range Land	Wood Land	Wild-Life
Arkansas	.3	6.2	14.7	44.4	15.5
Illinois	15.2	49.6	.9	27.3	39.8
Indiana	2.4	15.9		55.9	49.2
Kansas	1.3	14.7	20.5	24.2	32.1
Louisiana	.2	2.8		59.3	30.5
Michigan	3.3	7.0	.1	34.4	24.8
Missouri	.2	38.1	5.8	42.0	39.9
Nebraska	1.3	13.0	23.1	5.7	37.3
Oklahoma	.4	56.8	32.4	33.2	50.6
Pennsylvania	10.0	20.0		80.0	92.0
West Virginia	9.0	5.0		75.9	10.0

Area	Ponds	Farm-Forest	Build-ing	Other
Arkansas	10.0	6.8	1.1	1.3
Illinois	9.0	28.9	7.3	3.0
Indiana	12.7	47.5	12.9	6.0
Kansas	5.8	11.7	3.0	3.7
Louisiana	21.7	25.2	1.7	3.3
Michigan	5.6	12.3	3.7	13.6
Missouri	8.8	18.1	2.2	17.6
Nebraska	30.1	49.7	8.9	3.4
Oklahoma	10.4	25.6	14.1	1.7
Pennsylvania	2.0	12.0	13.0	5.0
West Virginia	.1	34.0	.5	.5

[a]Percentages exceed 100 percent due to multiple uses.

Source: *Restoring Surface-Mined Land*, p. 15.

mining operations open vast areas which were previously inaccessible. These areas which are too poor to support commercial uses are suitable for wildlife.

Among the technological advancements has been the recent experimenting with sprouting seeds in paper tubes slightly larger than a cigarette and setting out to plant the tubes at the age of six weeks, avoiding damage to the young roots [19:37]. These seedlings are of pine and can be planted throughout the growing season. Unlike the conventional seedling which spends a year in the nursery bed before being replanted, the "tubeling" stays in a restricted neighborhood which contains its own microclimate. Thus the initial shock of transplanting, which accounts for most seedling failures, is minimized. Experiments by land reclaimers in Ohio are aimed at protecting seedlings during shipping, planting, and the first summer of wind and sun. A method of coating the young roots with protective "kaolin clay" is being developed in order to keep the fine baby roots moist during these critical stages [28].

In addition to experiments with trees, Indiana, and Ohio have experimental sites for other types of growth projects. Indiana was the experimental area for growing black alder, technically known as *Alnus Glutenous*, first imported from Germany in the 1950s. It has a special ability to grow almost anywhere and to fix nitrogen in the soil. Experiments in Ohio have yielded a crop of crown vetch which, like black alder, fixes nitrogen in the soil but also has asthetic values in that it produces an orchid purple blossom. Various highway departments are now using crown vetch because of its thick fast spreading root system which builds top soil and stops erosion [29]. The Hanna Coal Company also uses reclaimed land, planted with crown vetch, to graze cattle on and later harvests it for hay. Peabody Coal Company also raises cattle on reclaimed land but has planted alfalfa. Peabody land yielded 35,000 bales of alfalfa and brome grass from one farm alone in 1967 [29].

The technological advances of strip mining have now combined with those of reclamation for an even newer trend. Coal deposits which could not be reached in 1950 are now able to be tapped because of more advanced equipment. In 1950 some 750 acres of surface mined land in Kentucky was reclaimed by planting various trees. The trees, which are now of a size that affords resale value for lumber, are being harvested. The land will then be remined, to extract coal which could not be reached the first time around, and planted with a crop of trees to be harvested at some future time [29].

Technological advancements have not only aided the surface mining of land but also the reclamation of the land. Advances have resulted in copter planting, hydroseeding, and seeding by airplane. The hydroseeder is a truck mounted water pistol which mixes seed, water and fertilizer and sprays the mixture over a wide area. This technique has proven quite successful in revegetating steep sloping mining areas such as those produced in contour mining. The use of the airplane for seeding is used on the Applachian slopes, similar to the method used for some time now by the crop dusters in the west. West Virginia recently used a helicopter to seed 5,333 acres of surface mined land in their biggest single seeding program [29].

In looking to the future it appears that colleges and universities are going to play an ever-increasing role in the reclamation of surface mined land. Ohio State University is developing information on the curricular offerings in institutions of higher learning for the education of students in the field of land management and reclamation [23].[7] Pennsylvania State University is actually engaged in formal research in surface mine spoil bank reclamation. Its research has gone through several phases resulting in the publication of guides for revegetating surface mine spoil areas. Current research involves experiments in those areas where the spoil banks are highly acid [30:11].[8]

Summary

In summary, the national and local governments, the coal industry and the public are taking an increasing interest in the reclamation of surface mined lands. This increase can be traced to a number of sources, including:

1. The history of surface mined lands and the general lack of reclamation guides.
2. Public pressures to retain the asthetic values of the land and environment.
3. The recent concern over natural resource consumption in future years.
4. The realization that spoiled acreage can be reclaimed and turned into income producing land.

Surface mining must be thought of as a result of social and economic evolution of our society. Some of the results of surface mining are undesirable and a means to diminish these undersirables must be found. Even though there are some who feel that, because the amount of acreage disturbed by surface mining is less than that consumed in any given year by road construction, there are more important land use problems, it does not follow that the question can be overlooked. Use of 4.433 million acres of land over a 32-year period for the production of one fuel source for our economy is far from a small problem. On the contrary, it is problem of major importance. This land cannot be left unproductive.

The use of 209 thousand acres of land in the year 2000 should be enough to tax the imagination. The fact that the problem is localized in a rather small portion of the total land of the nation creates an even greater problem. Of the 209 thousand acres projected as being disturbed in the year 2000, 188 thousand acres are east of the Mississippi River. This same geographic area, which covers far less than 50 percent of the nation's acreage, contains 59.9 percent of the population. The Middle Atlantic area, which includes coal-producing Pennsylvania, will have 27,000 acres of land disturbed in the year 2000 according to projections, West Virginia is the major coal producing state in the South Atlantic area and is projected to have 23,000 acres of land disturbed.

The East North Central and East South Central areas are unique in that they have many heavy population centers, and yet are projected to account for 138 thousand acres of disturbed land in the year 2000. Fortunately states such as Ohio, Indiana, Illinois, Kentucky, and Tennessee have made strides in reclamation procedures. However, unless steps are taken to find other fuels for electricity generation, the outlook for these two areas is far from good.

If legislation on a national scale is what is needed to assure the public that *all* disturbed acreage is reclaimed, then we should proceed along these lines. However, the movement should begin at the local level, for if implemented on a national scale, the desires of the local populations may not best be fulfilled. Prior to implementation of legislation which would be restrictive or costly, a positive approach should be studied. One such approach would be in the area of tax reforms. The current tax structure is filled with enough special concessions that a positive adjustment to reward those coal companies who strive to reclaim land would certainly be in order. This approach appeals to the writer far more than government grants and aid, for that type of reform is often shadowed by political concessions on the local level. To restrict output would serve little purpose for to do so would be (1) hiding from the problem; and (2) restricting productivity and national economic advancement.

11

The Environmental Effects of Surface Mining and Mineral Waste Generation

John A. Weisz

Since the early days of the pioneers prodigious withdrawals have been made from the rich storehouse of soil, waters, plants, and mineral deposits with which this country is blessed. In this process the land has been looted and ravished; and it is now apparent that this storehouse is not inexhaustible. Therefore, today a serious crisis is faced – the necessity not only to maintain the delicate balance between the requirements of the population and a shrinking resource base on the one hand, but also to avoid destroying the natural environment in the process [26:3].

The recent history of this country suggests that many resources were wrested from the land without regard to consequence. Forests were slashed without thoughts of reforestation or the effects of watershed dislocation; land was repeatedly planted for single crops until the essential growth elements of the soil were depleted; topsoil on hilly terrain was ruined due to improper cultivation methods. When the land could bear no more fruit, the pioneers moved onward to start the cycle all over again [26].

This wasteful attitude was apparent in another vital operation – the mining and processing of minerals. The accepted practice was, and still is to some degree, to mine as cheaply as possible the deposits that are accessible without regard to the resulting social costs involved – the silted streams, the polluted streams and the wasteland left by surface mining and mineral processing. The result, of course, has been the loss of valuable mineral resources and several million acres of productive land and water which have been left derelict [26].

Now, the nation's conscience is awakening and the problems of surface mining and mineral waste disposal are getting national attention. Government and industry both realize that something must be done to halt this prodigal waste of natural resources.

This chapter will describe the nature and significance of the problem as well as the steps being taken to alleviate it. An attempt will also be made to forecast the magnitude of the problem to the year 2000.

The Nature of Surface Mining and Related Solid Waste Problems

Simply stated, surface mining involves nothing more than removing the overburden that lies above a mineral deposit and recovering the mineral in question. In practice, of course, the procedures are somewhat more sophisticated.

Surface mining has definite advantages when compared to underground methods. First, it makes possible the recovery of deposits which, for physical reasons, cannot be mined underground. Second, it usually provides safer working conditions. Third, it usually results in a more complete recovery of the deposits. Fourth, it generally results in a lower unit cost for mineral production. Naturally, all mineral deposits cannot be surface-mined. The controlling factor is an economic one — the amount of overburden which must be removed to get at the mineral deposit. The overburden ratio (the ratio of thickness of overburden to thickness of deposit) has varying economic significance among operations, owing to differences in the characteristics of the overburden, type, and capacity of equipment used and the value of the mineral being mined. Nonetheless, this ratio is the factor that determines for the most part whether or not a mining venture can survive in a competitive market [26:33].

Before surface mining begins there is usually a prospecting or exploration stage, the purpose of which is to discover and measure the underlying ore body. Exploration techniques consist of either drilling to intersect deeper lying ore bodies, or excavating shallow trenches or pits to expose the ore. Because of their large numbers, these small excavations constitute a serious source of surface disturbance in some of the western states [26:33].

After an area has been explored and deemed suitable for mining, the mineral deposit is recovered utilizing one of the following methods: (1) open pit (quarry or open cast) mining; (2) strip mining (area or contour); (3) auger mining; (4) dredging; and (5) hydraulic mining.

Open pit mining is characterized by quarries producing limestone, sandstone, marble, and granite; sand and gravel pits; and large excavations opened to produce iron and copper. Because the ore bodies are relatively concentrated in an open pit operation, the overburden ratio is usually very small. Another characteristic of this type of mining is the length of time that the pit or quarry is in operation. Some open pits may be mined for fifty years or more; in fact, a few have been operating for more than a century [26:34].

Area strip mining is employed on terrain of a flat nature. Coal and phosphate mining account for a major part of the acreage disturbed by this type of mining. (The problems relating to the surface mining and processing of coal will not be discussed in this paper since they are adequately covered in another chapter of this volume.) An area stripping operation starts with the excavation of a long straight trench exposing a portion of a mineral deposit. Upon removal of the deposit within the trench, a parallel trench is dug with the new overburden being placed in the old trench and so-on to the limits of the deposit. The final cut leaves an open trench as deep as the thickness of the overburden plus the ore recovered, with the last spoil bank on one side and the undisturbed highwall on the other. It is not infrequent that the final cut is a mile or more from the initial one. Unless the entire area is graded, the effect produced is one of a gigantic washboard with alternating ridges and valleys [26:34].

Contour strip mining and auger mining are predominately used in the coal industry. These methods are employed where the terrain is mountainous or rolling and where area mining is not feasible.

Dredging operations utilize mechanical devices such as buckets, clamshells, and draglines mounted on floating barges or suction apparatus. Dredges are used extensively in placer gold mining and also in the recovery of sand and gravel from stream beds and lowlying land. Most of the sand and gravel produced by such operations is marketed but the dredging for higher priced minerals usually leaves a very high percentage of the mined material as waste which is left at the mine site [26:36]. Another type of mining which has been used extensively in the past for the recovery of high priced minerals, especially precious metals, is hydraulic mining; however, it has very little application today. (The method employed a powerful jet of water which eroded a bank of earth or gravel in order to get at the underlying deposit. This ore enriched overburden was fed into concentrating devices where the desired material was separated by specific gravity differences.)

Even though different methods are employed to varying conditions, there are basically four steps in the cycle of every surface mining operation. They are (1) site preparation — clearing trees, shrubbery and other obstructions from the area and building access roads and adjunct facilities, including areas to be used for the disposal of spoil and waste; (2) removal and disposal of the overburden; (3) excavation and loading of ore; and (4) transportation of the ore to a concentrator, processing plant, storage area or directly to market [26:37].

Surface mining has expanded rapidly since World War II; the principal reason for this being the development of larger and more complex earth moving equipment. Today's equipment includes bulldozers, loaders, scrapers, graders, and trucks of up to 100 ton capacity. There is presently a shovel that can handle 185 cubic yards in one bite and larger ones are being designed. Draglines of up to 85 cubic yard capacity are in operation and here too larger ones are on the drawing boards. In addition, there are rail cars, conveyor belts, overhead cable buckets, and pipelines for moving the overburden and ore beyond the reach of the basic excavating machines [26:39].

In addition to the deleterious effects of surface mining, the landscape may also be scarred by the huge quantities of solid waste generated from benefication and processing operations. This problem is encountered primarily in the production of iron ore, phosphate, copper, and coal. Moreover, the volume of solid waste generated per unit of recovery increases as technological advances permit economical mining and processing of ores of progressively lower grades.

Iron ore serves as an example of this. In the early days of the twentieth century the mining and development of iron ore was a rather simple matter. All one had to do was to explore the region for a suitable ore body and develop the underlying hematite or natural ores. These high grade ores are now rapidly disappearing, and the industry is relying heavily on the processing of the so called taconite ores (iron content 25 to 35 percent) which are found abundantly in Minnesota and elsewhere [21:68]. Because of its low iron content, this ore is usually put through a complex series of separating techniques. The steps involved include crushing, washing, concentrating, agglomeration by sintering, nodulizing, and pelletizing. These pellets which now usually contain 63 percent iron are then sent to the blast furnace for smelting [28:461]. Because of these separation techniques, huge quantities of waste material are produced.

The mining of phosphate presents another solid waste problem. Phosphate rock (ore), commonly called the matrix, is generally composed of one-third sand, one-third clay, and one-third phosphate. After the overburden is stripped, the matrix is recovered and put into large sumps where it is slurrified by high-pressure streams of water. This suspension is then pumped to the processing plant where it undergoes washing, flotation and drying. The residue remaining after this concentrating effort is composed of sand, clay, and phosphate of fine size. By far, the biggest solid waste problem is produced by the colloidal clay wastes called slimes. These slimes constitute over one-half of the total plant waste and about one-third of the mined matrix. They are presently disposed of by being pumped to gigantic settling ponds [21:51].

The production of copper generates tremendous amounts of solid waste. This is the case because of the relatively low initial yield of most copper ores. The process itself begins with an upgrading operation known as milling or concentrating. Large producers employ flotation methods for this purpose. The copper content after concentration is between 20 to 35 percent from an initial 2 percent. In the next step, which is smelting, the copper is taken from other elements of the crude copper ore; this product, called blister copper, is then refined either by fire or electrolysis, leaving additional slag. The Bureau of Mines estimates that there was more solid waste generated at copper mines in the United States during the period 1960-1963 than the total materials handled at mines producing ores of any other metal [28:276].

The Extent and Significance of Surface Mining and Related Solid Waste Problems

The factual and statistical information contained in this section, unless otherwise noted, was obtained from pp. 39 thru 64 of a unique study made by the Bureau of Mines [26]. The information was heretofore unavailable because mining companies do not publish these data.

In a survey conducted by the U.S. Bureau of Mines it was estimated that 3.2 million acres of land had been distrubed by surface mining in the United States prior to January 1, 1965. Included in this total are only those areas associated with actual excavations and overburden heaps. Additionally, 320,000 acres have been disturbed by mine access roads and exploration activities. Almost 95 percent of this total acreage can be attributed to but seven commodities: coal – 41 percent; sand and gravel – 26 percent; stone – 8 percent; phosphate – 6 percent; gold – 6 percent; iron – 5 percent and clay – 3 percent [26:39].

Since some of this land was disturbed by mining operations of the past, it is reasonable to assume that natural forces have played a part in reclaiming some of the scarred land. However, since people with differing points of view tend to define adequate reclamation differently, the total surface mined acreage still in need of reclamation can only be approximated. The Soil Conservation Service of the U.S. Department of Agriculture estimates that approximately one-third of the total acreage disturbed by surface mining has been adequately reclaimed — either by natural forces or by man's own effort. This means that the remaining two-thirds, or about 2.0 million acres, still require remedial attention.

There is no exact information on the annual increment to the disturbed acreage total; however, based on the data available, the U.S. Department of Interior estimates that 153,000 acres of land were disturbed by surface mining in 1964. Of this total, sand and gravel accounted for 60,000 acres (39 percent); coal for 46,000 acres (30 percent); stone for 21,000 acres (14 percent); phosphate and clay each 9,000 acres and all others accounted for 8,000 acres. As demand for minerals increases and the grade of mineral deposits available for exploitation decreases, this annual rate of disturbance is expected to rise. Indicative of this trend is the fact that surface mining production of all metals and nonmetals increased from 2.5 billion net tons of crude ore (including waste) in 1960 to 3.0 billion tons in 1965.

Having glanced at some of the aggregate statistics of surface mining, attention will now be focused on the particular impacts that these operations have on the environment. Included herein are aesthetic considerations, water and land pollution, soil erosion, and sedimentation problems.

Although, technically speaking, the pollution problems associated with surface mining pose a more serious threat to the environment, it is the aesthetic considerations which most deeply affect the nation's conscience. People are dismayed by the ugliness of land laid waste by surface mining. Many have often echoed the following paraphrased excerpts from *Derelict Land*:

Our derelict acreage is made up of tens of thousands of separate patches. In some regions they are often close together. Where one acre in ten is laid bare, the whole landscape is disfigured. The face of the earth is riddled with abandoned mineral workings, packed with subsidence, gashed with quarries, littered with disused plant structures and piled high with stark and sterile banks of dross and debris, and spoil and slag. Their very existence fosters slovenliness and vandalism, invites the squatter's shack and engenders a derelict land mentality that can never be eradicated until the mess itself is cleared up. Dereliction, indeed, breeds a brutish insensibility, bordering on positive antagonism, to the life and loveliness of the natural landscape it has supplanted. It debases as well as disgraces our civilization [26:52].

The Bureau of Mines reported that nearly 60 percent of the more than 690 surface mine sites examined could be observed from public-use areas. These sights were considered unsightly or even repellent when contrasted with the greener surroundings. The sites in arid or desert areas are not objects of much public concern, partly because of the sparse population and also because the sites are somewhat similar to the surrounding areas.

At one-third of the sites visited, the areas were being used by the public to discard garbage, rubble, junked vehicles and construction materials; however, in the majority of cases no abandoned structures or equipment had been left on the site of the operation.

The land pollution problem at surface mining sites is indeed a serious one. At only 25 percent of the sites observed by the Bureau of Mines was the spoil material considered suitable for agricultural use. Where excessive stoniness was reported (at about 20 percent of the sites) the possibility of getting a quick cover was hampered by the rapid runoff and lack of soil. Most of the remaining 55 percent could be receptive to tree or herbaceous type plantings if climatological conditions are favorable.

Serious erosion problems were found at about 40 percent of the sites visited. Sediment deposits were found in 56 percent of the ponds and 52 percent of the streams on or adjacent to the sample sites.

Although the surface mining industry is not the major contributor to water pollution on a national basis, there are many areas especially in Appalachia, where it is a serious source of pollution. The polluted water may be too acid, too alkaline, or contain excessive concentrations of dissolved substances such as iron, manganese, and copper.

The most serious type of water pollution encountered in surface mining is that of acid mine drainage. This form of pollution is encountered chiefly in the coal industry where the sulfur bearing coal comes into contact with surface runoff and the sulfuric acid which is formed pollutes nearby rivers and streams. A similar problem arises when salts of metals such as zinc, lead, arsenic, copper, and aluminum enter adjacent streams. Even in minute concentrations, these salts are toxic to fish, wildlife, plants and aquatic insects. Another deleterious effect is caused by the undesirable slimy red or yellow iron precipitates (yellow boy) in streams that drain sulfide bearing coal or metal deposits. The Bureau of Mines survey team reported that of the streams receiving direct runoff from surface mine sites, 31 percent contained noticeable quantities of precipitates. At 37 percent of the streams adjacent to mining sites, water discoloration was observed, suggesting chemical or physical pollution.

From the point of view of total acreage disturbed, coal, sand and gravel, stone and phosphate surface mining are the most significant contributors. Iron and copper surface mining also warrant attention because of the sheer massiveness of their operations.

Sand and gravel pits have accounted for approximately 26 percent of the total acreage disturbed by surface mining prior to 1965 and for approximately 40 percent of the 1964 total. The pits themselves are usually located in or near urban areas. They are not usually a source of chemical pollution, and most of the fine-grained material produced can be retained in the mined area or settled out in basins or ponds. Operations located in or near streams have significantly contributed to sediment problems. Wind-blown dust, unsightly appearance, and noise are problems of this type of mining. In addition, the precipitous banks of these pits which are subject to slides are safety hazards.

Stone quarries, unlike sand and gravel pits, are widely distributed. They may be steep-wall pits excavated downward from level terrain or workings that are driven horizontally into a hill or mountainside. Chemical pollution is rarely a problem in these quarries and erosion and sedimentation frequently can be controlled with minimum effort. The steep walls of these quarries are often quite hazardous, and the clifflike highwalls may be regarded by many as unsightly.

Phosphate is mined principally in the wetlands area of Florida and to some degree in the West. The Florida operations involve typical area strip mining practices with long trenches and piles of overburden. Because these sites are typically in remote areas, the mining operations, except for the possible loss of the wetlands for wildlife use, are not considered as seriously detrimental to the environment.

Iron ore pits usually extend over vast areas and reach considerable depth. It has been estimated that the giant Messabi Range in Minnesota which is 120 miles long and three miles wide will within a hundred years become an enormous canal or lake. The minerals involved are chemically inert and the terrain is flat; thus the mining operations cause little or no water pollution. There are steep highwalls in many places that are dangerous and impede the movement of wildlife and humans. There are tremendous piles of low grade ore that dot the countryside. Depending on one's viewpoint, they may be considered unsightly or attractive features in an otherwise monotonous landscape.

Copper pits are large amphitheaterlike openings, few in number, and generally found in arid or semiarid regions of the West. Some of them are a mile or more in diameter and hundreds of feet deep. The ampitheater effect is achieved by the cutting of giant steps, or benches, having heights and widths exceeding 50 feet. Alongside these pits and occupying a larger area are piles of overburden and processing wastes. These piles are frequently the source of dust and sediment. Because rainfall is limited in most of the copper mine states, the exposed sulfide ores do not pose a chemical pollution problem. However, when these piles are leached to recover copper content, water pollution can become acute.

The processing wastes mentioned above are part of a serious problem in the mineral industry. All told, the mineral industries created one billion tons of solid waste in 1965, in the form of mine waste, mill tailings, washing plant rejects, processing plant wastes, and smelter slags and rejects [21:7]. Excluded from this figure is the overburden from surface mines.

Nearly 80 percent of this one billion tons of waste was generated by eight industries. In descending order of magnitude they are: copper, iron and steel, bituminous coal, phosphate rock, coal ash, lead-zinc, alumina, and anthracite coal [21:7]. Table G-11-3 gives the total breakdown by industry and classification of waste. The total accumulation of solid waste as of 1965, from basically the same sources, was 19 billion tons [21:7].

These wastes can be generally classified into three groups: (1) those which have economic value in spite of their social costs; (2) those which pose social costs but are worthless; and (3) those which are worthless yet pose few social costs.

Included in the first group are iron mine or washing plant rejects with a substantial percentage of iron but not immediately marketable because of technological and economic problems. Also included are those slag heaps and slack piles which have no significant material content but are important because their structural characteristics make them excellent construction aggregates [21:8].

In the second category are those dumps which impair public health and safety, such as the burning culm banks in the anthracite area and tailing ponds which generate dust near populated areas, pollute water, or which offer a potential hazard with respect to their containment. Also in this category are those wastes which because of their location retard development; that is, they prevent land use for other purposes. And still others pose an aesthetic problem — especially those of substantial volume or lateral extent located near urban centers or primary road systems [21:8].

The third category includes those wastes which are of small volume and which are remote from population centers.

As of 1965, 60 percent of the wastes, by weight, fell into the potentially valuable category, 37 percent fell into the second grouping, and 3 percent fell into category three [21:8].

The Problem Tomorrow

Now that the major problem areas have been defined, the next step is to forecast the amount of land which will be disturbed by surface mining operations of the future. Also of interest is the amount of solid waste which will be generated.

As a basis for these projections, a study made in 1962 by Resources For The Future, Inc. (RFF) [1] was employed. This study attempted to project to the year 2000 the demand and supply of natural resources in the United States. The authors of the study made three projections for each resource; a low projection, a medium projection, and a high projection.

The methodology used in making the surface mining projections was to ascertain from current production statistics which one of the three RFF projections best fit the production trend of the commodity in question and then to use this projection along with a ratio of land disturbed to tonnage produced to determine the annual increment of disturbed acreage in the year 2000.

The solid waste projections were obtained from a study made by the U.S. Bureau of Mines; a study which used basically the same methodology as described above.

As was mentioned earlier, the major contributors to the disturbed annual acreage total, besides coal, are sand and gravel, stone, and phosphate. Since demand for these minerals is expected to increase significantly, the amount of land disturbed by the surface mining of these minerals will also rise.

Sand and gravel, as well as stone are utilized primarily in the building construction industry, and particularly as aggregates for the batching of

Table 11.1

Historical and Projected Use of Construction Aggregates

Year	Aggregate (bil. ton)
1950	0.55
1955	0.88
1960	1.13
1970	2.26
1980	3.83
1990	5.97
2000	9.00

Source: *Resources in America's Future*, p. 632, Table A4-10.

concrete. The RFF did not make demand projections specifically for these two items but they did make one for construction aggregates, and from this series the needed projections can be evolved. Table 11-1 shows the pertinent RFF series for construction aggregates. Using this series as a proportionate basis and published historical data for sand and gravel, as well as stone, Table 11-2 was constructed.

Using the 1964 disturbed acreage statistics quoted in the previous section and 1964 production figures [25:50], the following ratios may be developed:

$$\text{Stone} \quad \frac{21{,}000 \text{ Acres Disturbed}}{.725 \text{ bil. Tons Produced}} = \frac{29 \text{ Acres}}{\text{Mil. Tons}}$$

$$\text{Sand and Gravel} \quad \frac{60{,}000 \text{ Acres Disturbed}}{.869 \text{ bil. Tons Produced}} = \frac{69 \text{ Acres}}{\text{Mil. Tons}}$$

These ratios indicate the number of acres disturbed per unit of production utilizing current technology. Assuming that there will be no radical change in the methods presently used for the surface mining of these minerals, disturbed acreage projections were determined. The method was simply to multiply the acreage ratio by the projected demand from Table 11-2 for the commodity in question. Additionally, cumulative totals were obtained by averaging ten-year

Table 11.2

Historical and Projected Use of Stone,
and Sand and Gravel

Year	Stone (bil. tons)	Sand and Gravel (bil. tons)
1945	0.15	0.20
1950	0.25	0.37
1955	0.47	0.59
1960	0.62	0.71
1965	0.78	0.91
1970	1.23	1.42
1980	2.08	2.40
1990	3.24	3.74
2000	4.90	5.65

Source for historical data: U. S. Department
of Interior, *Study of Strip and Surface Mining in Appalachia* (Washington, D. C.:
Government Printing Office 1966), p. 50,
Tables 5 and 6.

interval statistics and multiplying these figures by ten. The results are shown in
Table 11-3.

It will be observed that the annual increment of disturbed acreage in the year
2000 for stone, and sand and gravel is projected to be 142,000 disturbed acres per
year, and 390,000 disturbed acres per year, respectively, as compared to 1964
totals of 21,000 for stone and 60,000 for sand and gravel. This is more than a
sixfold increase. In addition, a cumulative total of 2,430,000 acres will have
been disturbed between the years 1970 and 2000 by the surface mining of stone,
while 6,670,000 acres will have been similarly disturbed by the mining of sand
and gravel.

The major portion of this disturbed acreage will occur in or near urban
centers where construction activity is the heaviest. This is the case because these
minerals have a very low value per unit of volume and, therefore, are mined as

Table 11-3

Projected Annual and Cumulative Disturbed Acreage Statistics for the Surface
Mining of Stone and Sand and Gravel

	Stone		Sand and Gravel	
Year	Annual Increment (Acres/Year)	Cumulative Total (Acres)	Annual Increment (Acres/Year)	Cumulative Total (Acres)
1970	36,000		98,000	
		480,000		1,315,000
1980	60,000		165,000	
		770,000		2,115,000
1990	94,000		258,000	
		1,180,000		3,240,000
2000	142,000		390,000	
Total		2,430,000		6,670,000

Source: "Annual increments" computed by multiplying annual output projections of Table 11-2 by appropriate disturbed acreage ratio, for stone — 29 acres per million tons output, and for sand and gravel — 69 acres per million tons output.

close to application points as possible to reduce costly transportation expenses. Because land prices are typically at a premium in urban centers, stone, and sand and gravel sites are often voluntarily reclaimed and sold at a premium [26:52].

Since the dimensions of the forecasted disturbed acreage totals are quite large, an attempt will be made to pinpoint the major problem areas. Assuming that construction activity is more or less directly proportional to population extent, it can be seen that the large urban areas will bear the brunt of the problem. The Urban Land Institute has estimated that 70 percent of the United States population in the year 2000 will be living in 223 urban areas. In addition, roughly 60 percent of this group (or 42 percent of the total United States population) will be living in the 25 most populated areas [2:53]. Table 11-4

Table 11.4

Projected Population of the Twenty-Five Most Populous Urbanized Areas in the Year 2000

Urbanized Area	Population (000)
New York–Northeastern New Jersey	24,669
Los Angeles	23,462
Chicago–Northwestern Indiana	10,839
Detroit–Pontiac–Ann Arbor	7,990
San Francisco–Oakland–San Jose	7,694
Delaware Valley	7,468
Miami–West Palm Beach	5,788
Washington	5,542
Cuyahoga Valley	4,467
Dallas–Fort Worth	3,982
Houston–Galveston	3,860
Boston	3,646
San Diego	3,391
Connecticut City	3,198
Saint Louis	3,043
Seattle–Tacoma	2,893
Baltimore	2,750
Phoenix	2,630
Atlanta	2,429
Minneapolis–Saint Paul	2,423
Pittsburgh	2,296
Denver	2,227
Milwaukee	2,188
Tampa–Saint Petersburg	2,007
Cincinnati	1,829

Source: J. P. Pickard, *Dimensions of Metropolitanism* (Washington: Urban Land Institute, 1967), p. 52, Table S-6.

Table 11-5

Historical and Projected Use of
Phosphate Rock

Year	*Phosphate Rock (mil. tons)*
1960	20.0
1970	32.0
1980	52.0
1990	85.0
2000	138.0

Source: Phosphate rock production, 1960 - U. S. Department of Commerce, Bureau of the Census, *Statistical Abstract of the United States*, (Washington, D. C.: GPO, 1968), p. 666. Projections for subsequent years shown calculated on assumption of 5 percent annual rate of increase as assumed in *Resources in America's Future*, op cit, p. 328.

shows the projected population figures for these 25 areas and accordingly pinpoints those areas where urban planners should be most concerned.

The third commodity which has contributed significantly to the disturbed acreage total is phosphate. The RFF projects that on the average demand for phosphate will increase roughly 5 percent per annum, based on projected farm outlays for fertilizers, and likely trends in growth rates for various nutrients [1:328]. Based on a 5 percent increase and beginning from 1960 production statistics, Table 11-5 was constructed. This table shows the projected demand to the year 2000 for phosphate rock.

Using the same methodology as was employed for stone, and sand and gravel, a disturbed acreage ratio was calculated utilizing 1964 acreage and production statistics [30:666]. The results follow:

$$\text{Phosphate Rock} \quad \frac{9{,}000 \text{ Acres Disturbed}}{25.7 \text{ mil. Tons Produced}} = \frac{350 \text{ Acres}}{\text{Mil. Tons}}$$

Once again assuming that there will be no radical change in the methods presently used for the surface mining of phosphate, Table 11-6 was constructed. This table, which shows disturbed acreage projections, utilizes the same methodology as was employed for the stone and sand and gravel acreage projections.

The projected annual increment of 48,000 acres for the year 2000 represents more than a fivefold increase from the 1964 figure of 9,000 disturbed acres.

Table 11-6

**Projected Annual and Cumulative
Disturbed Acreage Statistics for the
Surface Mining of Phosphate**

Year	Annual Increment (Acres/Year)	Cumulative Total (Acres)
1970	11,000	
		145,000
1980	18,000	
		240,000
1990	30,000	
		390,000
2000	48,000	
Total		775,000

Source: Projected phosphate rock use from
Table 11-5 multiplied by disturbed acreage
ratio of 350 acres per million tons (see text)
to calculate projected annual increments.

Additionally, the cumulative projection of 775,000 disturbed acres is roughly
four times the total amount of land disturbed through phosphate surface mining
to date.

The major impact of this vast increase in disturbed acreage will be felt in
Florida. This state presently produces approximately 85 percent of the United
States total, and indications are that this trend will continue [26:47]. The RFF
study indicates that Florida has about 50 percent in excess of the reserves
necessary to meet demand requirements to the year 2000 [1:486]. Other states
which presently mine phosphate rock and can therefore be expected to witness
an increase in disturbed acreage are Idaho, Montana, Wyoming,and Utah.

The effects of phosphate mining have been remedied to some degree by
reclamation programs voluntarily entered into by mine owners. These programs,
which have received much critical acclaim from mining and conservation people,
have developed surface mined land for citrus groves, building sites, parks, and

other uses [26:54]. If these programs are continued in the future the deleterious effects of the projected increase in disturbed land will be greatly reduced.

The method employed here in projecting the future acreage of disturbed land is clearly highly simplified, perhaps oversimplified. It is doubtful, however, that any more highly refined technique could be justified by the improvement in accuracy that might be achieved. The fact is that any projection of the amount of land to be disturbed in surface mining construction materials and phosphate rock will overstate unavoidably the magnitude of the resultant reclamation problem, or, put differently, the amount of land that is likely to remain in a disturbed condition for any considerable length of time after mining. It has been noted that the bulk of the acreage disturbed in surface mining construction materials is likely to be near urbanized areas where the demand for land for other uses is high. Likewise, land values are high in most of Florida which will be the site of most of the expansion in phosphate rock mining. The reclamation of such high value land for other purposes after mining is completed may be expected to follow as the more or less inevitable consequence of the operation of economic forces. Accordingly, the projections presented here should not be regarded as forecasts of the amount of land likely to remain in a disturbed condition.

It does not follow that the projections contained in this chapter are therefore valueless. On the contrary, they are exceedingly useful in indicating the magnitude of the problems that must be dealt with if development is to proceed most efficiently. It would seem evident that if the surface mined lands considered here are virtually certain to be restored in due time to usefulness because of the operation of economic forces, that it would be desirable to facilitate such restoration by planning in advance of mining for the ultimate nonmineral use of the land. Thus, the design of sand and gravel pits and stone quarries located near urban centers could be planned with an eye to the eventual urban use of the land. This might be done, as well, with phosphate mines in Florida.

In addition to the projected increases in disturbed acreage due to surface mining, the increased generation of solid mineral waste is also a serious problem.

Using basically the same methodology as the RFF, the U.S. Bureau of Mines has made independent projections relating to the future magnitude of the solid waste problem. (See Table 11-7.) As an added refinement to their projections, the Bureau has attempted to take into consideration technological change factors and accordingly has computed ratios that reflect the hypothesized technological states of nature of the future time period in question.

It will be observed from Table 11-7, that the largest contributors to the solid waste problem are the copper and iron ore industries. The tonnage of solid waste generated by these two industries in 1965 was over 63 percent of the United States total. The projected totals for 1980 indicate a 57 percent figure.

It is difficult to estimate accurately copper reserves in the United States because the industry is dominated by six companies and they tend to limit the quantity and quality of available statistical information. Therefore, those

Table 11.7

U.S. Production of Minerals and Related Solid Wastes, 1965 and 1980[a]

Industry	Marketable Production (Thousand short tons) 1965	1980	Annual rate of growth 1965–1980 (Percent)	Total Solid Waste (Thousand short tons) 1965	1980	Ratio of waste to marketable production 1965	1980
Anthracite Coal[b]	14,865	12,996	−.9	2,000	3,509	.134	.27
Bituminous Coal[b]	332,200	517,554	+2.3 −3.0	99,600	207,022	.3	.4
Copper[c]	1,400	1,803	+1.7	466,700	787,550	333.4	436.8
Iron Ore	98,400	130,498	+1.9	233,877	365,394	2.4	2.8
Lead–Zinc	912	1,695	4.2	20,311	83,055	22.3	49.0
Phosphate Rock	26,400	54,104	+4.9	68,308	167,722	2.6	3.1
Other	1,916,372	3,210,575	+3.5	230,000	385,269	.12	.12
Total	2,390,549	3,929,225	+3.4	1,120,796	1,999,521	.37	.51

[a]Excluding petroleum and gas.
[b]Clean coal only.
[c]Recoverable content of ore.

Source: IIT Research Institute, Proceedings of the Symposium: Mineral Waste Utilization (Chicago, Ill., 1968), Table 3, p. 10.

estimates which have been made are in a certain sense incomplete since they pertain to deposits which have been measured or indicated, but not inferred [1:452].

Copper reserves have increased primarily in two ways: (1) new deposits have been located; and (2) the specifications for suitable ore have been reduced. Study of recent reserve history in the United States reveals that extension of reserves has come about mainly through successful development of poorer portions of known copper fields. Such extension often results in a change from underground to open pit mining and subsequent reduction in cost [1:453].

Those estimates which have been made put copper reserves in the United States at not less than 40 million tons and perhaps as much as 50 million tons. The RFF states that at medium rates of domestic demand such reserve statistics would support domestic consumption only through the late 1970s. Consequently, the United States will find itself dependent on foreign sources. At present, foreign ore supplies some 30 percent of all cooper ore refined in the United States [1:455].

Iron ore imports are also on the rise. At the end of World War II, American imports were only four percent of the nation's iron ore consumption, whereas in the late 1950s this figure had approached 30 percent. It is speculated that the bulk of future growth of American consumption is likely to be met by foreign sources. By the year 2000, it is estimated that imports might fill over 75 percent of domestic demand. At that time it is assumed that Lake Superior ore deposits, other than taconite, would be exhausted or nearing exhaustion and that substantial developments would have been made into both small deposits elsewhere and into magnetic taconite reserves [1:435].

Although a switch from domestic to foreign sources would reduce the annual increment of surface-mined disturbed acreage for the industries in question, the problems of solid waste generation would still prevail. This is the case because all indications are that only crude ore will be imported and not the finished product. Therefore, the ore would still be refined in the United States, generating a good deal of mineral waste. The overall problem would improve, however, because that category of solid waste known as mine waste (the unsorted material that is removed when the ore is excavated) would be substantially reduced. Mine waste contributes significantly to the domestic mineral waste totals.

Answering the Challenge

Having taken a broad look at the surface mining and mineral waste disposal problem in the United States, attention will now be focused on those forces in existence which might offset some of the deleterious effects discussed previously. The concept of land reclamation is perhaps the most important aspect in this regard; also to be considered are those beneficial effects which enter into the surface mining and solid waste picture.

It should be noted that solutions to the surface mining problem will not come from those same technological advances which are so important to the other types of environmental problems herein discussed. The surface mining of minerals inherently disturbs the land, and there is no conceivable technological breakthrough which would diminish this effect. As a matter of fact, as lower and lower grades of ore become economically feasible to process, the amount of land disturbed will increase. Therefore, some other solution must be found. The answer lies in land reclamation and rehabilitation.

In its report to the nation, and as noted earlier, the U.S. Department of Interior points out that as of January 1965, there were some 3.2 million acres of land disturbed by surface mining in the United States. The Soil Conservation Society of the Department of Agriculture considers one-third of this total adequately reclaimed and in need of no further treatment [26:74]. This then leaves approximately 2.0 million acres to be reclaimed, of which 800,000 were mined for coal, 400,000 for sand and gravel, and the remaining 800,000 for stone, phosphate, iron, gold, and other minerals [26:81].

In discussing reclamation programs, it is important to distinguish between reclamation of existing disturbed areas and reclamation of land disturbed by present and future surface mining operations. It is generally conceded by those in the field that the only way in which the 2.0 million or so existing acres of disturbed land will be effectively reclaimed is through a federally sponsored program. This is the case because it would certainly be unjust to have an individual or a state assume the financial burden of reclaiming land which might have been disturbed fifty or more years ago — when reclamation was not at all a familiar concept. The Department of Interior estimates that the cost of basic reclamation for these 2.0 million acres would be 750 million dollars [26:82]. They define basic reclamation as the minimum effort required to correct undesirable on-site and off-site conditions caused by past surface mining. This would include the alleviation or prevention of erosion, acid discharge and other related physical or chemical aftereffects [26:81].

Once basic reclamation has been completed, the next desirable step is that of land rehabilitation. This involves the development of derelict land for specialized uses. The Department of Interior feels that the 2.0 million existing acres of disturbed land could be rehabilitated for one or more of the following purposes: cropland, occupancy, forests, pasture, pond-lakes, rangeland, recreation, streams, and wildlife. The estimated cost for this additional work is 450 million dollars [26:84]. At the present time, such a reclamation and rehabilitation program is only on the drawing boards. It is tentatively planned as a twenty year program and is likely to be introduced in Congress in the near future [23:35].

Having dismissed these 2.0 million acres as unlikely to be reclaimed presently, what of the 150,000 acres which are being disturbed annually by present surface mining operations? It is estimated that only one-third of this annual total is being reclaimed [23:37]. Every state in the union has some surface mining activity within its boundaries but only 14 states have laws relating to the conduct of this mining and the reclamation of disturbed acreage. In addition, five of these state laws pertain to the mining of coal only [23:37].

Due to the apparent laxness on the part of industry and state governments to reclaim surface-mined areas, the federal government has proposed a bill which would give the Secretary of the Interior power to require all states to submit reclamation plans which he could accept or reject. In addition, the Secretary would be empowered to enforce these plans if the states were not doing so. The bill, which is entitled S. 3132: A bill to provide for the cooperation between the Secretary of the Interior and the States with respect to the future regulation of surface mining operations, and for other purposes, is presently before the Senate Committee on Interior and Insular Affairs, where it is being met by vigorous opposition from industry groups and state administrations.

The argument against federal legislation is a strong one. First of all, many mining firms and reclamation associations are already giving increased attention to the problem. Their results have been quite impressive. Additionally, the economic impact of such a program might be too great a handicap for many marginal producers.

In the private sector, reclamation associations have been formed in a number of states with professional staffs to aid in restoration work. Individual firms, along with these associations, have restored many disturbed acres, conducted demonstration projects and experimental revegetation, carried on a good deal of research and in general have promoted effective conservation treatment of surface-mined land. For example, the National Sand and Gravel Association's member firms claim that they had rehabilitated 52 percent of the acreage that they had surface-mined in 1965, compared with 25 percent in 1963. In Florida, where 85 percent of domestic phosphate rock is mined, mine operators were reported to have voluntarily restored 75 percent of the land disturbed from 1961 to 1966. In cases where the mining operations are near urban centers, many phosphate mining companies make plans before mining for later development of the site for residential, commercial, or recreational purposes. Furthermore, surface-mine operators in 22 states have formed the "Mined Land Conservation Conference" to promote restoration of mined land for useful purposes [23:78].

The economic impact of any federally proposed reclamation program is also an important consideration. The concern of the mining industry about this impact has been clearly presented by Mr. Joseph Abdnor, representing the American Mining Congress, at the hearings before the Committee on Interior and Insular Affairs:

Certainly such reclamation is a cost factor and, if reasonable, a legitimate and fully accepted one by the mining industry. The mining industry should not, nor should any other segment of our society ruthlessly destroy beneficial environmental conditions. But the economic impact of the legislation before you must be recognized. The problems of maintaining appropriate environmental quality are such as to require the most delicate balancing of interests — interests that include the public's vital need for mineral resources. One of the major objections to the legislation is that, in its approach, it does not make clear the necessity for reasonableness. It fails to reflect a proper regard for practicability and economic feasibility. It exposes mining operations to the imposition of arbitrary requirements by government officials responsible for issuing permits under law. In our judgment, the placing of federal controls over surface mining . . . could easily become such an economic burden to the domestic mining industry as to seriously weaken it as it faces a dangerous competitive situation in relation to foreign mineral resources [23:99].

There are, of course, situations in which reclamation might not be practical nor even desirable. Certainly, no one would seriously consider requiring mining companies to fill in the huge open pits which are characteristic of many stone, copper, and iron operations. Also, the huge piles of mineral waste at these sites might prove valuable in the future. A case in point is the vast iron range in Minnesota, parts of which were mined and then abandoned in the 1920s leaving large piles of low grade ore which were at the time uneconomical to process. With the advances in technology and the high demand for steel brought about by the war, these low grade ores were processed; principally because mining costs were negligible [23:173].

Although mined land reclamation has become a popular theme, the problems of mineral waste disposal have not attracted much legislative or industry attention. Part of the reason for this, undoubtedly, is the fact that much of the problem occurs in sparsely populated areas of the West and the Midwest. Also, that category of solid waste, known as mine waste, is usually considered part of any mine reclamation work. On the brighter side, one finds the activities of the National Slag Association. This group is constantly trying to find new uses for slag and other mineral processing wastes. Unfortunately, the relatively low value per unit of volume of these mineral wastes as well as the extremely high transportation costs involved in their shipment usually preclude their employment.

As was mentioned earlier, not all effects of surface mining are harmful. Indeed, there are a few beneficial ones. Flood control is one such effect. When massive rocks are fragmented during surface mining operations, the residual piles of overburden contain considerably more void space than existed in the undisturbed rock. The danger of floods is thereby diminished because a significant portion of the rainfall is trapped in depressions where it sinks into the earth to augment ground water supplies rather than running off rapidly to nearby streams. Also, because water stored in the banks moves slowly, drainage will continue for a long time and, therefore, streams near surface-mined areas often maintain a longer sustained flow during dry weather than those draining undisturbed ground [26:64].

In the western states, some surface mines have exposed ground water sources and have, therefore, made water available where none existed before. At some mountainside operations, open pits have impounded surface runoff from torrential rains, thereby minimizing the sediment load of streams draining the area as well as effecting considerable ground water recharge [26:64].

Another beneficial effect occurs through public utilization of mine-access roads. When these roads are properly maintained, they can be used to promote the multiple-land-use potential of extensive areas. The roads provide accessibility for fire protection, recreation, and management activities. Their existence can

mean the difference between use and isolation. Because they were constructed to facilitate the movement of heavy materials, most access roads are of a quality that can be converted to public use at little additional expense. This is advantageous in many areas where tourism could be encouraged [26].

Tourism is indeed an important beneficial effect of surface mining. Many large open pit operations have invited the public to view their facilities. Guided tours, where practical, have been instituted. In the summer of 1967, 80,000 tourists visited the Hull-Rust mine, the largest open pit iron mine in the world [23:166].

Conclusion

Having looked at the problems of surface mining and mineral waste generation in perspective, it is now possible to summarize the relevant data and to draw conclusions.

Prior to January 1, 1965, surface mining activities in the United States had disturbed some 3.2 million acres of land. Chiefly responsible for this disturbed acreage were the coal, sand and gravel, stone, and phosphate mining industries. Of this total, 2.0 million acres are considered in need of reclamation and rehabilitation.

The projected increase in this disturbed acreage total is staggering. It is estimated that the cumulative total land area which will be disturbed between the years 1970 and 2000 by the sand and gravel, stone, and phosphate mining industries will be 10 million acres. Additionally, as technological advances in mining and processing methods are developed, it is conceivable that other minerals will be surface mined to a greater degree and will add to the projected total.

The question of course is: "What can be done about it?" The answer has two parts. The first concerns itself with the existing 2.0 million disturbed acres, and the second with future mining operations.

For reasons pointed out earlier, the existing 2.0 million acres of disturbed land are unlikely to be reclaimed unless it is done through a federally sponsored program. Such a program is presently being drawn up within the U.S. Department of Interior and hopefully will be submitted to Congress in the near future.

As for future surface mining activities, it seems clear enough that the sheer magnitude of the projected disturbed acreage totals should inspire responsible reclamation and rehabilitation programs. Fortunately, some of this responsibility has already been acknowledged by the industries involved. However, imposed legislation might be necessary if industry fails to meet the challenge satisfactorily.

In spite of the seemingly pessimistic projections concerning the magnitude of future disturbed acreage, there lies a clear opportunity for urban and regional planners to aid in the development of this disturbed land for useful purposes.

This is brought about by the fact that much of the land disturbed for the mining of stone, and sand and gravel is located in or near urban centers where land values tend to be high. Phosphate is mined principally in Florida, where land values are also high. The prospect of financial gain will certainly induce the mine owner to plan for the future nonmineral use of his land, and if properly coordinated, these reclamation plans could greatly enhance the aesthetic and economic development of a regional or urban area. Before mining even starts, the land in question could be designated for many different uses, such as parks and lakes, industrial sites, and housing projects. By making these plans beforehand, the mining process itself could be designed to best effectuate this development.

As in the case of existing surface mined land, the 19 billion tons of accumulated mineral waste are also unlikely to be dealt with unless the federal government sponsors a reclamation program for this purpose. This is the case because the problem occurs chiefly in the sparsely populated areas of the West and Midwest where relatively few people witness the deleterious effects involved.

The U.S. Bureau of Mines estimates that by 1980 the annual generation of mineral waste will have doubled from the 1965 figure of 1.1 billion tons. This would indicate a cumulative total of approximately 25 billion tons for the fifteen year period. It seems certain that only legislation and perhaps federal funding can provide answers to this problem. The economics of the situation clearly argues against much voluntary reclamation on the part of industry.

The long-term projections for mineral waste generation are beset by two opposing forces. On the one hand, there is the trend toward the processing of progressively lower grades of ore as technology evolves and thereby makes this economically viable. This process naturally leads to an increase in waste generation. On the other hand, there is the trend toward the importation of more and more copper and iron ore. Since these two industries provide more than one-half of all waste generated, as imports of these minerals increase the total generated waste will decrease.

In conclusion, it has been shown how both surface mining and mineral waste generation affect the environment. Projections have been made which attempt to outline the magnitude of the problem in the future. The prospects for attacking the surface mine problem seem bright due to a combination of increased public awareness and the potential economic gains associated with voluntary reclamation. The prospects for attacking the mineral waste problem seem much less bright precisely because the above two conditions are absent.

12 Solid Waste Disposal Problems Arising from the Projected Output of Containers

N. Russell Wayne

Concern about the erosion and adulteration of our natural resources has, for the most part, centered itself about air and water, our most precious commodities. The air we breathe, more vital than all else for the preservation of the human breed, has gradually been transformed from its original state of purity by the increasing presence of microscopic foreign bodies. In major urban areas, deleterious emissions from industrial facilities, motor vehicle transport, public utilities and the like, attendant to the growth of our modern society, have poisoned the air to such a degree that it has become a potential source of danger to life. Often, the concentration of pollutants is so dense as to infect the surrounding environment, both externally and internally.

Our water supply has been similarly afflicted. Rivers, which yesterday were as pure as the rain, have become the victims of an increasing level of waterborne freight and a mounting total of urban sewerage. Bodies of water which once were fit for human intake have become graveyards for garbage. Even our underground sources are being contaminated as pollutants seep down through the earth from open dumps and landfill sites above. To the present, our attention has been devoted mainly to the two vital elements, air and water, yet there is a third area, solid waste, equally deserving of our interest.

Solid waste, commonly known as garbage or refuse, is what for years we have calmly thrown away, confidently believing that by some miracle it would be collected or disappear. When the land was young, it was wide open and unspoiled, dotted infrequently by signs of debris. Yet as the population grew, the spoilage grew. Cities, which had heedlessly persisted in using barren land areas for garbage dumps, found that land was becoming far too dear to be used so unproductively. And that was if it was to be found at all.

A significant portion of the solid waste problem stems from packaging residues, specifically, containers. Tin cans, glass and plastic bottles, paperboard cartons, and wooden crates, are thrown away in massive numbers, never to be used again, though in certain instances only minor reprocessing would be required for them to be suitable for a second use. But the fact of increased overall container output is only one facet of the problem. Another is the rise of the one-way, no-deposit, no-return beverage bottle. This outgrowth of the throw away spirit is punctuating the countryside from coast to coast, incurring a mammoth litter collection bill. All told, the total cost of disposing of United States packaging wastes is now believed to be in the area of $500,000,000 [25:103]. Of this total, about seventy-five percent is spent for collection [25:103]. But even when the garbage has been collected, a formidable task is still at hand. New container forms do not take readily to attempts at their destruction.

Continually, industry has demanded containers which are cheaper, lighter, and stronger, yet fit for a wide variety of uses. Though designers have met success in fitting this order, they have, in the process, compounded the waste disposal problem. Containers have been developed which are so durable and strong that they severely frustrate most efforts to dispose of them through traditional methods of solid waste processing. Plastics and glass, highly resistant to incineration and compaction, will live for years underground with virtually no change in their physical characteristics. Aluminum, used for beverage containers, does not rust away as did its predecessor, the tin can. Research, apparently, has succeeded all too well.

By the year 2000, if present trends continue unabated, we will be confronted by a mass of container waste which will be even less responsive to existing disposal methods. Clearly, research efforts must be expanded, not only to find new methods of disposal, but to develop containers which lend themselves more readily to natural degradation. The ultimate solution, however, according to one group, would be a closed system wherein wastes are continually recycled for second and later uses. (In Houston, researchers are planning a "closed loop" wherein all water and solids will be reused. Ferrous metals will be removed; rags, paper, plastics, and aluminum, wood and rubber, will be reprocessed; organics will be cooked and deodorized to make fertilizer.)

This chapter will discuss the impact of packaging on the overall solid waste problem. Initially, the 1960 study on resource consumption by Resources for the Future will be considered. Then, trends in technology and consumer philosophy will be evaluated. Finally, a projection of the magnitude of the solid waste problem for the year 2000 will be presented.

Resource Consumption for the
Production of Containers

As in other chapters of this study, the output projections of Resources for the Future (RFF) are used to suggest the magnitude of future container disposal problems. Before examining those projections, however, it is interesting to see what the recent trends in container materials have been. For purposes of this discussion, the emphasis will be placed on types of containers which make up the bulk of urban refuse. Thus, the category "miscellaneous metal containers," which is largely comprised of industrial containers, will not be considered. Table 12-1 sets forth historical data on resource consumption for the production of containers for the period 1948 to 1960.

From the data given in Table 12-1, certain trends are apparent. The use of plastics in packaging has increased almost 150 percent in the decade from 1950 to 1960, more than twice the rate of growth of any other container material. While the absolute percentage of plastics usage remains small (in proportion to the total of all container materials used), the sharp upward trend is likely to be maintained to the end of the century (as illustrated in Table 12-2). The

Table 12.1

Historical Data on Resource Consumption for Production of Containers[a]

	Metal Plate used in cans (mill.tons)	Lumber used in boxes and crating (bill.bd.ft.)	Shipments of glass containers (mill.gross)	Paper used in containers and packaging (mill.tons)	Plastics used in containers and packaging (mill.tons)
1948	3.25	3.99	94	11.51	n.a.
1949	3.28	3.78	87	10.81	n.a.
1950	3.89	4.29	105	13.17	.36
1951	3.80	4.51	112	14.03	.41
1952	3.84	4.69	111	13.13	.40
1953	4.08	4.41	124	14.60	.46
1954	4.14	4.09	122	14.40	.55
1955	4.48	4.21	134	16.22	.64
1956	4.79	4.54	138	16.93	.70
1957	4.59	4.01	140	16.39	.71
1958	4.76	4.23	140	16.53	.75
1959	4.95	4.34	150	17.95	.85
1960	4.82	4.09	156	17.99	.89

[a]Wherever possible, data are given in similar measures. With lumber and glass, however, this was not possible. This is not believed to be critical since the evaluation deals largely with trends.

Source: *Resources in America's Future,* Tables A7-3, A7-5, A7-7, A7-9, pp. 693, 696, 698, 700.

Table 12.2

**Projected Data on Resource Consump-
tion for Production of Containers**

		Metal plate used in cans (mill. tons)	Lumber used in boxes and crating (bill. bd. ft.)	Shipments of glass containers (mill. gross)	Paper used in containers and packaging (mill. tons)	Plastics used in containers and packaging (mill. tons)
	L-	5.59	3.00	194	24.42	1.61
1970	M-	6.26	5.70	220	26.53	2.03
	H-	7.15	7.90	253	29.55	3.54
	L-	6.40	2.10	239	32.03	2.61
1980	M-	7.70	6.60	311	38.16	3.82
	H-	9.58	10.90	400	46.94	9.11
	L-	5.89	1.60	290	41.20	3.44
1990	M-	8.70	7.20	424	54.15	5.81
	H-	12.63	14.00	622	73.62	17.08
	L-	5.72	1.30	339	52.10	4.18
2000	M-	9.76	6.70	570	75.81	8.04
	H-	16.06	16.50	950	114.00	28.31

Source: *Resources in America's Future*,
Tables A7-4, A7-6, A7-8, A7-10, pp. 694,
695, 697, 699, 701.

significance of this trend is that special problems arise with respect to disposal of plastic containers. This, however, will be discussed in the next section, dealing with technological trends.

The trend in glass container production is also of interest. In Table 12-1, a leveling in the mid-1950s is noted; there is a renewed uptrend at the end of the decade. This, it is believed, was largely the result of the introduction of improved disposable beverage containers in 1959. According to recent data, this strong rise is continuing. With respect to the question of waste disposal, glass containers also pose special problems.

It is significant that in the three other categories, metal, wood, and paper, for which waste disposal considerations are least troublesome, the rate of absolute increases is moderating. Metal cans and wooden crates and boxing, in fact, have shown minimal growth in recent years.

Projected Data

Are these historical trends likely to persist through the end of this century? Table 12-2 sets forth RFF's projections for resource consumption for the production of containers through the year 2000. These projections indicate RFF's belief that most of the trends now in evidence can be expected to continue. The sharpest gains can be anticipated in the area of plastics. Paper, which currently is displaying a leveling trend, will see accelerated consumption as the demand for new forms of paperboard grows. Wooden boxes and crating, on the other hand, will continue to lose ground relatively.

Clearly, the most significant projection in this table is the envisioned growth in the use of plastics. It is important because the rising use of plastics will necessitate the development of new disposal techniques. Plastics do not lend themselves to incineration since they leave a residue which clogs the incineration apparatus. And, similar to glass, they can remain buried for years without any physical decomposition. While plastics account for only a small fraction of container production currently, Table 12-2 indicates that they will comprise a substantial share by the year 2000.

Accuracy of the RFF Projections To Date

Table 12-3 presents estimated and actual data on resource consumption in four categories of containers for 1965 and 1966. The series on plastics was omitted since the aggregate figures used by RFF were based partially on unpublished data of the Business and Defense Services Administration which are no longer available.

With respect to lumber, the projection estimates were almost exactly in line with the actual figures reported. In glass container shipments, RFF's estimates were also reasonably accurate. The actual number of glass containers shipped fell about halfway between the medium and high projections. Tonnage for metal plate and paper, however, was below the level which RFF had anticipated. In 1965, actual metal plate tonnage was five percent below the low projection for that year. In 1966, however, the error was less than two percent. This trend suggests that by 1970, the actual figures for metal plate tonnage are likely to be within the projected range. The reason for the lower-than-expected metal plate consumption in 1965 and 1966 was competition within the can industry which stimulated the development of lighter cans. The reduction in weight has been spurred by the use of thinner-gauge steels and by a growing proportion of

Table 12-3

Resource Consumption Data for 1965
and 1966, Estimated and Actual

			Metal plate used in cans (mill. tons)	Lumber used in boxes and crating (bill.bd.ft.)	Shipments of glass containers (mill.gross)	Paper used in containers and packaging (mill.tons)
		L-	5.19	3.50	173	21.19
Projection Estimates[a]	1965	M-	5.52	4.90	186	22.24
		H-	5.95	5.80	203	23.75
		L-	5.27	3.40	177	21.83
	1966	M-	5.66	5.00	192	23.09
		H-	6.19	6.20	213	24.91
Actual	1965		4.95	4.90	198.1	19.52
	1966		5.19	5.06	206.3	20.09

[a]Estimates were extrapolated from the 1970
RFF projections in Table 12-2 by simple
linear trend.

Source: Metal plate — U. S. Department of
Commerce, Business and Defense Services
Administration, U. S. Industrial Outlook,
1968 (Washington, D. C.: Government
Printing Office, 1967), p. 121. Lumber —
National Forest Products Association,
Forest Products Industry Facts, 1966
(Washington, D. C.: National Forest Pro-
ducts Association, 1967), p. 21. Glass and
Paper — U. S. Department of Commerce,
Business and Defense Services Administra-
tion, Containers and Packaging, Quarterly
Industry Report, October, 1967
(Washington, D. C.: Government Printing
Office, 1967), p. 9. U. S. Department of
Commerce, Business and Defense Services
Administration, Containers and Packaging,
Quarterly Industry Report, October, 1968
(Washington, D. C.: Government Printing
Office, 1968), p. 9.

aluminum cans. As a result, though the unit volume of cans produced has risen
substantially, a much lesser gain in tonnage has been recorded. In the paper
container field, a similar situation has prevailed. Many more paper containers are
being produced, but the rate of resource consumption is not increasing as
quickly as the gains in unit volume. For both these categories, RFF has
anticipated the trends. While the actual results for 1965 and 1966 fell outside
the anticipated range, the RFF projections through the year 2000 will be

Table 12-4

**Domestic Shipments of Bottles for
Beer and Soft Drinks** (millions of gross)

	Beer			Soft Drinks		
	Total	*Returnable*	*Non-Ret.*	*Total*	*Returnable*	*Non-Ret.*
1948	7.7	4.1	3.6	7.8	7.8	—
1949	5.0	2.0	3.0	5.3	5.2	.1
1950	6.4	3.2	3.2	6.5	6.3	.2
1951	14.3	4.5	9.8	6.6	6.4	.2
1952	10.5	2.3	8.2	8.3	7.9	.4
1953	11.6	2.9	8.7	9.9	9.0	.9
1954	9.9	2.1	7.8	7.3	6.3	1.0
1955	10.5	2.4	8.1	9.7	8.5	1.2
1956	10.7	2.5	8.2	10.4	9.2	1.2
1957	10.8	2.3	8.5	9.7	8.5	1.2
1958	11.3	2.7	8.6	9.9	8.6	1.3
1959	13.0	3.0	10.0	11.3	9.8	1.5
1960	16.5	3.0	13.5	11.5	9.8	1.7
1961	22.0	2.6	19.4	12.1	9.3	2.8
1962	26.2	2.5	23.7	14.2	10.9	3.3
1963	29.4	2.7	26.7	16.2	12.3	3.9
1964	33.3	2.9	30.4	17.7	13.3	4.4
1965	36.1	3.5	32.6	20.3	13.3	7.0
1966	38.9	4.0	34.9	27.1	13.4	13.7
1967	44.5	4.4	40.1	38.2	13.3	24.9

Source: Tabulated from data in U. S. Department of Commerce, *Current Industrial Reports*, series M-32G, and published in Glass Container Manufacturers Institute, *Glass Containers 1967* (New York: Glass Container Maunfacturers Institute, 1968).

retained intact for purposes of this discussion since the trends are the focal points of this evaluation.

No scarcity of resources is likely to hinder the upward trends suggested by the RFF projections. On the question of waste disposal, the shifting utilization of resource materials expected to occur is more important than resource sufficiency. New waste disposal techniques will have to be developed to handle the container materials expected to receive increased usage in the future.

Packaging and Society

The Impact Of Rising Affluence

The European tradition of quality and durability seems to be lost in the American climate. As a result of their rising standard of living, people in the United States throw away more than twice as much as Europeans [32:3].

Packaging and the solid waste problem are closely linked in public view, and this is with good reason. Discarded packages are visible all around us. It is impossible to stroll through city streets, drive in the country, walk in a park, or ride a boat on our rivers and lakes without encountering the tell-tale signatures of our affluence; discarded cans and bottles, cigarette packs and paper sacks, and similar objects. It is not surprising, therefore, that packaging materials are placed high on the list of items which create aesthetic blight [27:3].

Why build a product that will last for years when a program of planned obsolescence will pave the way for a vastly higher level of manufacturing output by designing products with a limited life span? Obviously, the latter makes more business sense, at least in the opinion of most domestic producers. Make a cheaper product that will wear out quickly and thereby maintain a constant demand. This is the surest way to increased profits. For what other purpose does a business exist?

In Aldous Huxley's *Brave New World,* the dictator of the utopia, Mustapha Mond, comments:

We don't want people to be attracted by old things. We want them to like the new ones. [35:262].

Vance Packard, in *The Waste Makers,* mirrors Huxley's earlier thoughts:

Residents of the United States were discarding, using up, destroying, and wasting products at a rate that offered considerable encouragement to those charged with achieving ever-higher levels of consumption for their products [36:42].

In this country, the prevailing philosophy has been to throw away, wherever that option has been available. Over the years, the tin can has been a prime candidate for the trash pile. Rusting away as it did after a short time, it was ideally suited to that end. Other types of containers, however, traditionally were fed back into the production cycle. Glass containers were delivered by the neighborhood milkman, used, and returned for sterilization and numerous additional trips to consumers. Recycling was also quite important with respect to soft drink and beer containers. But, within the last decade that importance has diminished considerably.

The Trend Toward Disposability

No-return bottles are a relatively recent development. They were introduced in the mid-1930s but gained only a small share of the packaged beer market until 1959 when a new compact design was introduced. This new no-return bottle was accepted readily by consumers across the country. The consumer bought no-return bottles in steadily increasing numbers during the years that followed. As a result, the glass container industry produced nearly five times as many nonreturnable containers for the beer industry as it did nine years before [28:30].

From the beginning in 1959, the second generation non-returnable bottle has been an outstanding success, much to the dismay of waste disposal authorities. In 1959, disposable beer bottles accounted for 77 percent of total beer bottle output. Eight years later, disposables were more than 90 percent of the total. Even more striking, nonreturnable soft drink bottles accounted for less than 13 percent of the total soft drink bottle output in 1959, but in 1967 nonreturnables were almost two-thirds of the total. Over the past few years, virtually all of the gains registered in soft drink container output have been in nonreturnables [28:45]. Table 12-4 illustrates these trends over the past twenty years.

The sharply increased proportion of disposable beverage containers is distressing. As the result of this trend, an additional 55,000,000 gross bottles annually are now heading straight for waste disposal channels, markedly magnifying the burden of getting rid of them. Also, to a certain extent, consumers are no longer bothering to return returnable bottles. Most important, the rising proportion of disposables has seriously compounded the problem of littering.

The Littering Problem

Tin cans, glass and plastic bottles, paperboard cartons, and wooden crates, are thrown away in massive numbers, never to be used again. A disturbingly high percentage of these containers clutter the sides of our highways, spoil our recreation areas, and inhabit a host of other places. The extent of the litter problem is far greater than one would suspect. In a survey conducted by John E. Evans, Assistant Director of Public Affairs for the Glass Container Manufacturers Institute, an average of over 2,500 pieces of litter were found in five different one-mile stretches of highway in various parts of the country [14:163]. A similar study conducted along a one-tenth mile section of highway in southern New York tallied a total of 362 pieces of assorted litter [14:163]. George Stewart in *Not So Rich As You Think* relates that 20,000 cans were counted along a one mile shoulder of road less than fifty miles from San Francisco [18:120]. These figures are even more significant when measured against the cost of collecting this rubbish. The Michigan State Highway Department calculated the cost of litter removal at about 32¢ per item [14:163]. Another study pegged the cost between 60¢ and 90¢ for each item [25:104]. Multiply these estimates by the number of trash items marring the countryside and the result is a garbage bill running well into the millions of dollars. Keep American Beautiful, Inc., an organization devoted to the prevention of litter, estimates that litter cleanup costs United States taxpayers about $500,000,000 a year. Of this, $100,000,000 is spent for litter removal from highways.

Clearly, the responsibility for the spreading litter problem must be borne by both the container manufacturers and the consumer. Manufacturers, seeking to pass on costs quickly to the consumer and eliminate the recycling phase, favor the nonreturnable container. The consumer, willing to pay the slightly higher price and often too busy to be bothered returning many-trip versions, evidences a similar feeling. But William Foster, editor of American City Magazine, thinks that producers are the major offenders:

I hold that the handy six pack and the non-returnable bottle have done more to despoil the landscape than any single object other than the neon sign, and that they have robbed the taxpayer of so much money through the cost of picking up and disposing of the empties that they make Boss Tweed look like Calvin Coolidge [32:4].

But, one might say, the producer is merely adapting his output to meet the desires of the consumer. Does supply create its own demand, as Say suggests, or is the opposite really the case? An editorial in *Time* supports the latter view:

... the modern American is not bothered by the waste of materials. What concerns him is time — his time. In the abundant U.S. economy, materials are relatively cheaper than labor. If something he can buy and throw away can save an American time, he does not feel it is a real waste [6:56-57].

Not only is littering a troublesome and costly nuisance, but it creates a potential danger to life and property. Every twelve minutes a home is destroyed or damaged by a fire starting in rubbish or litter. In one year, an estimated 130 persons lost their lives in litter-fed fires. (A major portion of the data on the littering problem was derived from informational pamphlets prepared by Keep America Beautiful, Inc.)

The Cost Factor

Consumers have given convenience packaging their wholehearted endorsement. The popularity of disposable containers has been such that consumers have been

Table 12.5

Bottle Costs

	Non–Returnables			Returnables	
Size	*Cost per Gross*	*Weight of Glass*	*Size*	*Cost per Gross*	*Weight of Glass*
10 oz.	$4.26	7 oz.	10 oz.	$9.00	15 oz.
12 oz.	4.74	8-1/2 oz.	12 oz.	9.00	15 oz.
16 oz.	5.37	10-1/2 oz.	16 oz.	9.40	16 oz.
28 oz.	9.28	16-1/2 oz.	28 oz.	14.41	28 oz.

Source: *Soft Drink Industry Annual Manual,
1968-1969* (New York: Magazines for
Industry, Inc., 1968), p. 22.

willing to pay a premium for the convenience of throwing away a container, rather than holding on to it and returning it to the store. Most of the added cost of nonreturnables has been passed on successfully to the consumer. (Added cost, in this context, means increased expense per trip. Since the cost of returnable bottles is amortized over many cycles, their effective cost to the consumer is lower than that of nonreturnables.) Similarly, the philosophy of disposability has become so deeply ingrained that consumers are increasingly willing to forfeit their deposits and throw away returnable containers as well.

Returnable bottles, as noted in Table 12-5 below, cost almost twice as much as nonreturnable bottles. But, over fifteen or twenty trips to the consumer, the per trip cost of the returnable is only a fraction of the cost of the disposable unit which must be paid for at one time. Recycling, which consists mainly of collection and washing, incurs only a minimal additional expense [24].

Two points are readily apparent. From the standpoint of economics, it is obvious that the cost of producing nonreturnable bottles is far lower than the cost of producing returnable bottles, owing to the reduced glass content. Second, since about forty percent less glass is used in the nonreturnable units, this tends to offset partially the huge increase in overall container output which must be coped with in the waste disposal phase.

Table 12-6 provides the base for an actual cost comparison as measured per trip.

Based on the figures in Tables 12-5 and 12-6, it is found that the per trip cost of a typical returnable 10 oz. soft drink bottle is .39¢ compared with 2.96¢ for a nonreturnable unit of the same size. Similarly, the cost of a 12 oz. easy open soft drink can is about 4.25¢ [37:22]. Since most of this added expense is incorporated in the selling price, the consumer is paying dearly for his laziness. Too, since sixteen to nineteen disposable bottles are needed to replace one returnable bottle, the expense of litter collection has increased exponentially.

Table 12.6

Trippage Factors for Bottles (number
of trips per bottle)

	Soft Drinks	*Beer*
1967	16	19
1966	16	23
1965	17	27
1964	17	31

Source: Glass Container Manufacturers Institute, *Glass Containers 1967* (New York: The
Institute; 1968), p. 7.

Technological Trends Affecting the Solid Waste Problem

Present and Projected Trends

Traditionally, packaging has concerned itself with containers only during their period of use. It has thus developed containers that tend to be precisely the opposite of what sanitation departments would like: packages that are readily burned, compacted, dissolved by water or rapidly degraded by exposure to the elements.

As a matter of fact, packages are getting stronger, more resilient, more complex, larger (which means more packaging material is required for the same amount of product) and above all, more durable. For example, flame retardants and ultraviolet-light stabilizers are added to many plastics and these additives increase resistance to disposal [25:103].

The difficulties confronted by waste disposal authorities vary according to the type of material being dealt with. Clearly, in the collection phase, it makes little difference whether the garbage can contains empty beer bottles or used soda cans. Yet, in the disposal phase, there is often a significant difference. It is obvious that paper bags will succumb more readily to incineration than will glass bottles. Indeed, paper is the most readily disposable of all packaging materials. In ascending order of disposal difficulty, the other major materials are: wood, plastics, metal, and glass. Metals and glass rank equally on this score.

The type of material, to some extent, determines the disposal method to be used. Paper and wood are ideally suited to incineration. Other materials, however, require the use of other methods. Frequently, this means open dumps or sanitary landfills. Herein lies another problem. Owing to the scarcity of land available for waste disposal, it is usually necessary to deposit waste until it accumulates to a substantial depth (varying according to the type of terrain). With these disposal methods, it is expected that the elements will facilitate the process of natural degradation. But, according to one authority:

No material buried more than three to five feet deep will degrade readily; there normally is not enough oxygen at that level [33:p.1].

Natural degradation, if it does occur, is likely to take place in paper, wood, or tinned containers only. Paper and wood will decompose. Tin cans will rust away. But neither of these processes will occur unless the containers are within several feet of the surface. With other container materials, little physical change will be evident, regardless of the environmental condition.

Aluminum, glass, and plastic containers are virtually indestructible and persist for decades [27:p.7].

Yet, if difficulties are experienced with disposal by landfill, they are even more apparent with incineration. Plastics, which are likely to show the greatest increase in use through the end of the decade, create special problems. Where plastic containers comprise a substantial portion of the waste to be burned, they leave an inert residue which must be hauled away and dumped. Similar problems are caused by metals and glass.

On balance, as projected by RFF, those materials which pose the greatest disposal difficulty are likely to show the largest gains in consumption by the year 2000. In the area of metals, the tin can (long considered the ideal container by waste disposal authorities since it degrades naturally within a relatively short period of time) is to give way, in small measure, to aluminum, a substance far harder to eliminate. Owing to the sharply increased use of disposables, glass, another difficult material to dispose of, is also expected to experience sizable gains. Very moderate growth, on the other hand, is likely for wooden containers. Perhaps the only encouraging trend, from the waste disposal standpoint, will be the higher consumption of paper.

Observed External Effects

Resource Waste. Notwithstanding the conclusion of RFF that there will be sufficient raw materials to meet the projected demands for containers, the trend to convenience packaging, eliminating as it does the need to return containers to the production cycle, is accelerating the rate at which solid waste is being created. This is primarily true with respect to disposable glass and metal containers for soft drinks and beer. As noted in Table 12-6, a returnable bottle usually makes sixteen to nineteen trips to the consumer during its life cycle. This means that 16 to 19 nonreturnable bottles must be produced to replace each recyclable unit. While disposables generally consume about 40 percent less raw materials, the gain in materials consumption projected is still close to 1,000 percent overall.

Decreasing Amount Of Urban Landfill Space Available For Waste Disposal. The major portion of our solid wastes is deposited in open dumps, a technique not considered acceptable by most sanitation authorities. Open dumping is considered unacceptable since little or no processing of the waste matter takes place. Since the wastes are untreated, they are likely to infect the surrounding environment. Sanitary landfilling, on the other hand, is a preferred method. By this process, solid wastes first undergo compaction, reducing their volume by 50 percent or more, and are then distributed evenly over the specified area; finally, they are covered by a layer of soil. Landfilling utilizes refuse materials to reclaim barren or otherwise unusable land areas. The difficulty which has arisen with respect to landfills is that, in many areas, the amount of nearby landfill space is rapidly being exhausted, necessitating either long distance transportation of the refuse or a shifted emphasis to other methods of disposal.

Adulteration Of The Surrounding Environment Caused By The Presence Of Solid Waste. Open garbage dumps are enemies of the environment. They allow disease to fester within, they filter their germs down through the ground, contaminating underlying water tables, and they provide a continual fire hazard to surrounding areas. In uncontrolled, unsupervised open dumps, spontaneous combustion takes place with surprising regularity.

Under a $68,900 grant by the U.S. Public Health Service, Drexel Institute of Technology is constructing two artificial landfills which will simulate the conditions at the center of a large sanitary landfill. A wide range of weather conditions will be reproduced. Changing weather conditions within the fill will be automatically recorded; soils, gases and water from wells installed in the area will be regularly sampled and analyzed. The findings of the study will make it possible for engineers to predict the movement of moisture through sanitary landfills in advance of construction. They will provide a basis for determination of the safety of landfills in other parts of the country [12:48].

Control Aspects

Is The Problem Of Container Waste Disposal Controllable? The answer to this question depends largely upon the angle of attack. In other words, is the emphasis to be placed primarily on development of new disposal techniques or will efforts be made to minimize the quantity of containers being transferred from the production cycle? Clearly, efforts along both these lines will be required.

Perhaps the cost of specially designed containers (to increase merchandising appeal) will continue to rise until the consumer realizes that he is paying far more for the package than for its contents.

All this packaging and disposing were not a free dividend to the consumer. In some instances the package was costing ten times as much as the product inside. Salt coming in small throwaway containers costs seventeen times as much as salt by the pound. The metal aerosol can with squirt mechanism and chemical propellant adds at least a third to the cost of getting a topping for a sundae.

By the time Americans finish paying for all the inviting packaging they are induced to buy, the annual bill is twenty-five billion dollars [36:45].

Or perhaps controls will not be invoked by the consumer, but by the legislatures to curb the mounting waste totals. Regardless of the source of action, the problem would appear to lend itself to control. The more important question is when will that control be exercised?

To What Degree Are Waste Management Techniques Effective? Open dumping, the oldest and most widely used disposal technique, is effective only in that it removes garbage from the immediate vicinity. At the same time, the land thereby used is no longer fit for any productive purpose. In urban areas, the decreasing amount of land available suggests that the open dump method will be playing an increasingly less important role in the years ahead. Sanitary landfills are facing much the same consequences. Incineration, the other commonly used method, is effective so long as the solid wastes are flammable. However, even after the process has been completed, some solid residue often remains where glass, metals, or plastics had been present in the waste being treated.

Indeed, current waste management techniques are effective in disposing of the bulk of solid wastes now encountered. But, in the years to come, landfill disposal, especially in the case of urban areas, will no longer be a feasible alternative. Thus, by necessity, incineration will play an increasing role. Other disposal methods will have to be developed. Already, Europeans have begun a new trend by using incinerators as power plants. A Japanese firm is producing machines which compact garbage into building blocks. Certain United States firms are developing plastic containers which degrade naturally. These are just several of the new methods being explored. (The following section contains a full discussion of these and other new developments.)

Disposal Methods: Present and Projected

Landfills

Disposal in a landfill site takes a variety of forms depending on the method used to disperse the waste matter and the degree of supervision given to the operation. At one end of the spectrum is the open dump to which garbage is simply carted and dumped. Wastes are deposited in an uncertain fashion and no supervision is provided. At the other end is the sanitary landfill wherein wastes are evenly dispersed, compacted, and covered at least once daily by a layer of soil to minimize adulteration of the surrounding environment and eliminate the hazard of fire.

This type of waste disposal has been favored by sanitation authorities since it required the least effort. For open dumps, several large trucks were usually sufficient to service a small community. With sanitary landfills, a few bulldozers (to compact the waste) and additional personnel to supervise the operation were also necessary. But with land sites becoming increasingly scarce, planners have had to become more imaginative in their disposal programs.

Recently, the New York City Sanitation Department was negotiating with several railroads about the possibility of transporting garbage to distant points where it might be needed as landfill. One possibility suggested was the old anthracite area of Pennsylvania where refuse could help erase the ugly scars of abandoned strip mines. But, it was thought that all such mines could be filled in a matter of years [2:6/19/67, 37]. Similarly, officials of nearby Westchester County proposed shipments of compacted garbage by train to low upstate areas for use as a sanitary landfill [2:5/7/67, 55]. But the most unique approach has come from Dupage County, Illinois, which built a garbage mountain. The mountain is 118 feet high, covers 39 acres at the base and 3 acres at the top. It is composed of 800,000 cubic yards of garbage and 900,000 cubic yards of clay. Originally a gravel pit, the mountain is now used for skiing and toboganning [2:9/14/67, 19].

Whatever the approach, however, the landfill technique has been preferred due to its cost advantage. Recent estimates have placed the cost of disposal in a landfill at $1.13 a ton over the next decade. Incineration (with proper fly-ash controls installed to minimize dispersion of harmful particulates into the surrounding air) would cost about $5.25 a ton. Composting, whereby waste is reprocessed for later use as agricultural fertilizer, would cost $3.50 a ton. In addition, the landfill technique enables urban areas to reclaim a substantial amount of otherwise unusable land [10:103].

In virtually all cases . . . the value of the land so filled and the extent to which it may be subsequently developed is at least equal and probably greater following completion of sanitary landfill operations than before. . . . [10:103].

Incineration

Incineration seems the only practical answer to mounting refuse-disposal problems in heavily urban parts of our nation, which are the areas of greatest growth [9:121].

Traditionally, incineration often meant nothing more than burning of wastes. Garbage was delivered and fed to the flames. Usually, because little or no consideration was given to potentially hazardous by-products, black soot was allowed to belch freely from the smoke stacks and fly ash descended upon the surrounding land areas. But as a result of the increasing emphasis on air pollution controls, the traditional image is quickly being obliterated.

New York City has engaged in a $25,000,000 program to equip all 46 furnaces of its eleven incinerators with electrostatic precipitators. These devices will be the first of their kind used in the United States though they are common in Europe. They trap more than 95 percent of the particulate matter which would otherwise be emitted into the surrounding air [8:40].

Electrostatic precipitators perform their function by charging the particles in the gas stream outflow of an incinerator by passing them through the corona of a high voltage conductor. The charged particles then pass polarized plates which pull them out of the stream. These plates are shaken at regular intervals and the accumulated dust falls into hoppers below [9:124].

In addition to purification of the gas emissions, however, sanitation authorities are developing methods to utilize garbage as a fuel to produce steam and electricity. While garbage is far less efficient than other commonly used fuels, there is so much of it that it can hardly be overlooked as a power source. Elmer R. Kaiser, a senior research scientist as New York University's School of Engineering notes that 2½ pounds of garbage equals a pound of coal; he estimates that half of New York City's waste output may be usable fuel [2:2/13/67, 1].

Still, the United States is far behind Europe on this score. Europeans, in certain instances, were led to this approach after needs for additional power sources and alternate methods for trash disposal were required.

A plant in Rosenheim, Germany, is typical of this new concept. The solid wastes, transported by ordinary garbage vehicles, are dumped onto inclined burners where they are incinerated. Thereafter, the metal objects are removed by belts and shakers and sold for scrap. The entire process is quite clean; 98 percent of the dust particles from the incineration are removed from the smoke by filters in the stacks. From this waste is derived steam and electricity [7:82].

In Munich, Germany, the method is being used on a much wider scale. The city, with a population of 1,300,000, turned to trash-burning for another reason: its coal-burning power plant was emitting an excessive amount of sulfur-oxide-bearing smoke. This problem, plus the diminishing amount of dumping area available, caused Munich to construct a trash-burning power plant. The plant burns 1,500 tons of trash daily, about 80 percent of the household and commercial debris of the city's population. The facility differs from the Rosenheim plant in that it is a hybrid: both trash and coal are used as power sources. This is for good reason. Trash, as noted previously, produces substantially lower output than coal and is subject to delays in delivery. The coal-burning capability of this plant insures uniformity and continuity of power output [7:84].

In the trash-burning approach, the world leader is Paris, France, where four huge plants produce steam from the incineration of almost 1½ million tons of garbage annually, half of the city's total output. Revenues from the sale of steam recoup about one-third of the operating costs of the system [7:84]. The plant at Issy-les-Moulineaux, the largest of the four, converts 1 ton of garbage in its boiler ovens into 1.8 to 2 tons of steam. (Steam is sold by weight.) Steam is fed into a first group of turbo-alternators that produce electricity or is used directly for heating purposes [2:2/13/67, 29].

The Issy plant employs a high degree of sophistication.
Television cameras monitor all important plant operations, and electrostatic precipitators clean the gases well enough to pass any U. S. Air-pollution codes. [13:40].

Clearly, incineration seems destined to be the most important waste disposal technique over the coming decades. With the incorporation of electrostatic precipitators and other types of filtering equipment, incinerators will no longer serve merely to exchange one form of environmental pollution for another. With a new emphasis on salvaging garbage for use as a power source, a positive benefit will be obtained while the residues of society's consumption are eliminated.

Composting

Composting is a process whereby solid wastes are converted into soil fertilizer. Costing about $3.50 to process a ton, as noted earlier, this method depends for its success on the development of a market for the sale of compost. Due to the fact that compost has a significantly lower fertilizer value than other types of fertilizers, manure particularly, and due to its relatively high cost, a strong market for its sale has not developed [10:103]. With respect to disposal of container waste, this method is unsuitable since it deals with organic matter.

Pulverization

Pulverization is less widely used. In Wiesbaden, Germany, sanitation authorities have constructed plants which smash up solid wastes into a granular compact pulp, reducing volume by 50 percent. The dense residue is then dumped into a big pit. This technique is currently being employed in more than twenty towns in Britain and on the continent [7:86].

Compaction

Compaction is a method whereby solid wastes are compressed to a fraction of their original volume. As more commonly used, compactors have been installed in a number of residential buildings where they have taken the place of incinerators. Collected waste is compacted and then hauled away to landfill sites. A more interesting development, though, is the use of giant compactors to produce dense cubes or bricks for construction purposes. In Chicago, a pilot model compactor will compress refuse into cubes that may eventually be used to fill low lake shore property [5:58]. A similar unit produced by Tezuka Kosan, a Japanese firm, has been proposed for an even more ambitious project. The suggestion was that a fourth jetport for New York City be built on an artificial island of garbage off the northern New Jersey coast. This plan would utilize Tezuka Kosan's converter. The hydraulic pressure compacter compresses baled refuse under immense pressure and encases the resultant solid material in asphalt, cement, or vinyl sheeting. Blocks can be made any shape, with interlocking if desired. When enclosed in iron, they can be welded like steel plates. Standard-size plates weigh two tons each. Bacteria present are killed by the lack of oxygen. The process is 50 to 75 percent cheaper than incineration (less than 50¢ a ton) and creates no smoke. The units range in size from a $228,000 model which handles 150 tons daily to a mammoth $5,600,000 compressor which handles 3,000 tons daily [2:2/2/68, 39].

Naturally-Degrading Containers

For the standpoint of waste disposal, the tin can has been an ideal container since it will rust away quickly after being exposed to the elements. But, other types of self-degrading containers are being developed.

The Swedes have one, made of plastic, paper, metal foil, about a tenth the weight of a glass bottle. If the litter-happy Swede throws it into a trash can and it winds up in the local incinerator, it burns. It does not slag and damage the incinerator grates or linings [4:6]

About a year ago, another group of Swedes developed a plastic beer bottle which was supposed to dissolve after two years' exposure to the elements. However, Warby Breweries, the developer, has postponed its use in order to further study the effects of burning on polyvinylchloride, the plastic of which the bottle is made. Possible harmful effects of incineration are suspected [3:34].

Another Swedish company, Rigello Pak, has developed a lightweight beer container made of laminated paper and plastic which can be burned. Under prolonged exposure to the elements, this container will disappear, but that period is believed to be in excess of two years. [3:34].

Domestic producers such as Dow Chemical, Continental Can and Eastman Kodak are working on development of similar containers. Others are known to be experimenting with water-soluble plastics and glass [25:106].

Production Of Combustible Fuels

Pan American Resources, an Albuquerque, New Mexico firm, has developed a converter which turns waste packaging materials into combustible gas and charcoal. The machine, being tested at a Ford Motor Company assembly plant in

San Jose, California, distills wastes in a superheated (to about $1,500°$ Fahrenheit) cylinder to produce combustible fuel. Part of the end product is used internally and the remainder is sold for thirty dollars a ton to outside consumers [25:106].

Other Proposals

Several other interesting approaches have been proposed. One group of researchers has suggested an incinerator ship which would burn refuse at sea and dump the ashes into designated areas of the ocean. Also, a method is being developed to accelerate the disintegration of paper products (which comprise about two-thirds of United States household refuse) from several months to a few days [7:86].

To the extent that any of these methods do nothing more than utilize less convenient dumping sites, they would appear to contribute little to solution of the solid waste problem. This area, too, must eventually diminish. Ideally, the solution should eliminate the waste in physical terms; hopefully, the method would produce some positive benefit at the same time.

In the area of legislation, there have been only a few significant developments.

A Projection of the Magnitude of the Solid Waste Disposal Problem in the Year 2000

The National Problem

The rise in solid waste output in the United States over the next 30 years will be largely dependent on the rate of population increase and on the growth in personal consumption expenditures. These figures will serve as working tools to illustrate the overall magnitude of the national solid waste disposal problem. For clearer significance, they should be considered with special regard for the urban areas, where the difficulties of resolution are likely to be far greater. Table 12-7 following sets forth projections made by RFF for the series: population, personal consumption expenditures—aggregate, and personal consumption expenditures — per capita.

As a preface, we must be mindful that population projections are notoriously undependable; the best efforts of demographers are none too good. Nevertheless, the RFF projections (based on projections made by the Bureau of the Census for the period up to 1980 and on unpublished data compiled by that agency for the following two decades) are probably as reasonable as any. At least through 1970, RFF's medium population projection appears on target. United States popula-

Table 12.7

Projections: Population and Personal Consumption Expenditures, Aggregate and Per Capita

		1970	1980	1990	2000
	Low	202	226	249	268
Population (mill.)	Medium	208	245	287	331
	High	223	279	349	433
	Low	448	610	819	1,070
Pers. Cons. Exp., Aggregate (1960–$mil.)	Medium	462	662	944	1,320
	High	495	753	1,150	1,730
	Low	2,110	2,450	2,840	3,300
Pers. Cons. Exp., Per Capita (1960 dollars)	Medium	2,220	2,700	3,290	4,000
	High	2,290	2,880	3,620	4,550

Source: *Resources in America's Future*, Tables A1-2, A1-25, A1-27, pp. 517, 551, 556.

tion as of February, 1969 was 202.4 million, up from 200.4 million in February, 1968. At this rate of increase, the actual United States population may fall just short of the 208 million projection made by RFF for 1970. [22:5-12]. For the purpose of further discussion, let us assume that this projected series will be fairly accurate through the close of the century. Thus, the medium projection suggests an overall population increase of 59.1 percent, about 1.2 percent compounded annually. This is in line with historical experience. For personal consumption expenditures, though, we seem to be running close to RFF's high projection. The annual rate of personal consumption expenditures as of fourth quarter, 1968 was $546.8 billion [22:9]. Using a price deflator (117.5), 1960 constant dollars for this series were $465.3 billion. Thus, to reach the RFF high projection for 1970, an actual increase of 3.2 percent will be required. This rate seems likely. Let us assume that this trend, too, will continue. If this be the case, aggregate personal consumption expenditures will increase 249.5 percent over the next 30 years. Combining these figures, then, per capita personal consumption expenditures are expected to rise from $2,380 (1960 dollars) in 1970 to $5,227 (1960 dollars) by the year 2000, an increase of almost 120 percent. (Note that these computed per capita personal consumption figures are substantially above RFF's high projections for this series.) Regarding the problem of container waste disposal, this is the key figure. For 1970, based on estimates made by the Midwest Research Institute (in preparation for a forthcoming federal study of the solid waste disposal problem), packaging materials tonnage is likely to be in the area of 52.5 million tons; per capita packaging consumption (based on the medium RFF population projection for 1970) would be about 504 pounds annually [27.4]. The MRI anticipates that in the decade ending in 1976, the average annual increase in packaging consumption will be about 3.3 percent [27:4]. This is an increase fifty percent greater than that expected in per capita personal consumption expenditures. (RFF projects the aggregate PCE to increase at an annual rate of about 2 percent for its medium forecast; its high projection uses a 2 1/4 percent annual factor.) The question, then, is what sustained rate of growth can be expected in the consumption of packaging materials to the year 2000. There is a conflict of opinion on this matter. In 1965, the National Academy of Sciences saw a continuing annual increase of 4 percent [2:6/19/67, 39]. In this forecast, no time period was specified. New York City sanitation authorities, on the other hand, project an average annual increase in the volume of trash output of 3.5 percent over the next twenty years [16:27]. Still, this rapid rate will probably moderate as the rush to disposables slows and a trend to recycling (hopefully) takes hold. For the purpose of this discussion, it is assumed that solid waste output will increase at least as fast as aggregate PCE, but somewhat slower than the current 3.3 percent annual rate. The calculations are as follows:

Thus, relative to the medium projection in Table 12.8, we can expect a 29.6 percent rise in per capita packaging materials consumption to yield an increase of almost 110 percent in aggregate packaging waste output by the year 2000. These projections, however, are only an indication of the trend anticipated. Widespread adoption of recycling or an even greater increase in the proportion of disposables could alter them significantly. Nevertheless, all possibilities and probabilities considered, these projections appear to be a reasonable starting point. To gain their full importance, they must be considered with regard to the cities, where the waste disposal problem is most critical.

The Problem As Faced By The Cities

Urban areas, with high population density, are faced with the most difficult waste disposal problems. Most cities are heavily dependent on incineration and sanitary landfills (and open dumps) as avenues of elimination for their mounting solid waste totals. But, incineration, which takes place within the urban area, is often a flagrant air polluter. In many instances, the disposal of solid waste by incineration is not an elimination but in fact is an exchange of one environmental affliction for another. However, great strides are being made in

Table 12.8

Projection of Packaging Materials
Consumption

		1970	1980	1990	2000
	Low	- -	62.8	76.5	93.3
Aggregate (mill. tons)	Medium	51.5	65.9	84.4	108.1
	High	- -	69.2	93.0	125.0
	Low	- -	513	533	564
Per Capita (pounds)	Medium	504	538	588	633
	High	- -	565	648	755

Source: Calculations were based upon an extrapolated estimate of the Midwest Research Institute for 1970. Projections for the years 1980, 1990, and 2000 were based on annual growth from the 1970 base of 2 percent, 2-1/2 percent, and 3 percent, respectively. Computation of per capita consumption are based upon the RFF medium population projections.

this area and modern incineration practice has reduced the airborne effluent considerably. The bigger problem is the shrinking availability of land sites for disposal. Often, disposal sites are in peripheral areas, sometimes miles away from the city itself. As space is exhausted, the time and cost of waste transportation becomes increasingly important. Eventually, the point is reached where long distance movement becomes economically infeasible. As a result, the role of land disposal sites is likely to become less important in the future.

In 1957-58, the average member of a household in the U.S. threw away about four pounds of trash daily [19:668]. Today, the rule-of-thumb for per capita trash output is 5.4 pounds [15:31]. Based on the data in Table 12-8, per capita daily consumption of packaging materials in 1970 will be about 1.4 pounds daily. This is equal to about 26 percent of the present solid waste total. It should be noted, however, that sanitation authorities make little or no distinction between packaging waste and other types of solid waste. Their concern is mainly whether or not the waste generated is combustible and suitable for incineration. On this point, see Figure 12-1 for a projection of combustible vs. noncombustible waste to 1990 in California. Thus, the data on packaging as a component of the solid waste total are largely academic. The more important figure is the overall solid waste total. A survey of five major United States cities disclosed the per capita waste output totals as shown in Table 12-9.

This study, performed over ten years ago, demonstrates a wide range of per

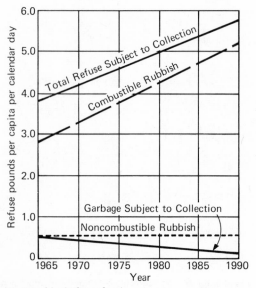

Garbage: residuals from food
Refuse: garbage and residuals from durable and nondurable goods
Combustible Rubbish: paper, plastics, cartons, boxes, barrels.
Noncombustible Rubbish: aluminum foil, tin cans, glass.

Figure 12-1 Projection of Refuse Production Trends. Source: Aerojet-General Corporation, *California Waste Management Study,* a report to the State of California, Department of Public Health, Report No. 3056 (Final), Azusa, Calif., August, 1965.

capita waste output. Interestingly, in the decade following, the figures have changed drastically. The average Californian's daily solid waste output is now 6.5 pounds, well above the 1957-58 level for either Los Angeles or San Francisco [15:31]. The average New Yorker's daily solid waste output is now about six pounds, sixty-five percent above the 1957-58 level [16:27].

Two years ago, former New York City Sanitation Commissioner Samuel J. Kearing stated that the city's landfill sites will be exhausted by 1975 [2:2/20/67, 27]. At that time, according to Kearing, the city's six million tons of annual garbage would fill Yankee Stadium a mile high. The Regional Plan Association, in its March, 1968 report on waste management said:

The problem can be illustrated by consideration of solid waste accumulation (requiring disposal) in the period from 1965 to 2000 for the five boroughs of New York City ... assuming no reclamation or salvage of the generated solid wastes, with about 28 percent and 12 percent of the generated wastes handled in municipal and on-site incineration respectively, and with the remainder of the generated wastes plus the incinerator residue going directly to landfill, the total volume of compacted solid wastes to be disposed of over that period would be about 500,000 acre-feet. If this volume were disposed of in Central Park, it would cover the total area of the park to a depth of about 600 feet (assuming vertical sides) [31:51].

Table 12.9

Total Refuse Collected in Five U. S.
Cities, 1957–58

Cities	Pounds per capita per day
Los Angeles, California	4.61
Washington, D. C.	4.36
Seattle, Washington	3.75
New York, New York	3.63
San Francisco, California	3.18

Source: Aerojet-General Corp., *California Waste Management Study*, a report to the State of California, Department of Public Health, Report No. 3056 (Final), Azusa, Calif., August 1965.

New York City's population of 8 million persons is generating solid waste at the rate of 19,000 tons a day [16:23]. Assuming a 3.5 percent increase annually in per capita output, a total of almost 55 million tons of solid waste will have to be reckoned with between now and 1975. Since about half of the solid waste total is incinerated [2:12/24/68, 22], that leaves no more than 27.5 million tons that could be sent to landfills such as the massive Fresh Kills operation of Staten Island [2]. Additional land space may be obtained by the use of abandoned strip and underground mines. Admittedly, this is only a short-run solution, and one involving substantial transportation costs. After 1975, New York City will have a minimum of 8.5 million tons of solid waste annually which will have to be disposed of by either sharply increased incineration or alternate disposal techniques. Note, too, that the city's sanitation authorities project little change in the area's population over the next twenty years [16:27].

Most demographers suggest that increasing urbanization will be manifest as a larger size of existing cities, but the actual population density of these cities probably will not increase substantially. The trend is likely to bring with it a rise in the megalopolis, the multicity, rather than an ad infinitum continuation in the growth of presently-defined urban areas. The suburbs of today will be annexed to the cities and new suburbs further from the heart of the cities will spring up. Currently, about 70 percent of the nation's population lives in urban areas. By the year 2000, city inhabitants are expected to account for ninety percent of the total [34:2].

Of the states, highly urbanized California is the leader in annual production of refuse. Currently, The Golden State is producing 22.9 million tons of solid waste yearly. Uncompacted, this garbage total would form a mass 100 feet wide and ten feet high, stretching the length of California, from Oregon to the Mexican border. That state, in addition to being the leader in total waste output, ranks very high in terms of per capita output. Whereas across the country the average person generates about 5.4 pounds of solid waste daily, Californians produce 6.5 pounds of garbage every day. What do they do with it? Again, the critical question is the availability of land. In California, 27 percent of the total waste output (including industrial and farm waste) is sent to disposal sites. In actuality, disposal sites are used primarily for urban refuse. Though only about one-fourth of all solid waste is sent to landfills and dumps, the major portion of urban refuse is disposed of in this way. Over half of these sites are primitive uncontrolled open dumps. Those sites which would qualify as sanitary landfills comprise less than ten percent of the total. (In a site which qualifies as a sanitary landfill, the compacted refuse is covered daily.)

Presently, California devotes a total of 56 square miles for disposal sites. Open burning dumps, which account for about one-third of that area, receive less than six percent of the state's garbage total. Sanitary landfill sites, on the other hand, though they occupy only about nine percent of the land space, receive 63 percent of the refuse total.

The state has a total remaining capacity of about 25 square miles (45 feet deep) in its existing disposal sites. Over one-fourth of this area is likely to be filled by 1973. Within 20 years, 630 of the 716 general disposal sites will be filled, according to latest estimates. And, as of now, only 86 replacement sites are planned. In California, as in New York, it appears that new methods of waste disposal will be required if the mounting total of garbage is to be kept under control. (Virtually all of the data about the California waste problem was obtained from the article "State Produces 71.5 Million Ton Mountain Of Refuse Every Year" cited fully in footnote 15).

Availability Of Data Relating To
Special Urban Problems

'To anyone who has attempted to solve the solid waste management problem, one fact is evident: little reliable information on solid wastes is available.' This view expressed by Ralph J. Black, deputy chief, Solid Wastes Program, U.S. Public Health Service, could not be more to the point [11:6].

To the extent that data on waste output are available, they refer to gross output of all solid waste. In no case have any sources contacted disclosed special information with regard to the solid waste generated by the mounting consumption of containers. Thus, many of the conclusions drawn about the problem of container waste are necessarily dependent upon the use of estimates.

For this reason, the present discussion is heavily influenced by the studies conducted by the Midwest Research Institute [MRI]. The MRI is preparing a major study on the impact of packaging materials output on the solid waste problem. This study, authorized by the U.S. Public Health Service, will be published under federal auspices. In the absence of any other pertinent data on the packaging waste component, the MRI estimates stand as the foundation of the projections set forth herein.

With regard to data on solid waste generally, the task is somewhat simpler, though as Mr. Black has stated, this information is scanty and often unreliable. Nevertheless, what little there is available gives a starting point and serves to indicate the direction of change. Since overall solid waste totals are available, it is possible to formulate estimates about the size of the component contributed by containers. Still, since the problem of container waste disposal is in most cases not differentiated from that of solid waste generally the aggregate solid waste figures are an adequate working tool.

Ideally, the waste component contributed by containers should be measured by volume. In virtually all cases, however, both in terms of production and consumption totals are expressed by weight. Thus, this discussion necessarily considers the container waste problem in terms of weight generated.

A Proposed Ratio For Container Waste Output

Given projected data on personal consumption expenditures and on consumption of packaging materials, it is possible to construct a useful output ratio. The ratio suggested is the output of packaging materials in pounds per dollar of personal consumption expenditures. In Table 12-10 following, that ratio is set forth as a series of waste output coefficients.

Table 12-10

Coefficients of Container Waste Output
(pounds of container waste per dollar of PCE)

	1970	*1980*	*1990*	*2000*
Low	.239	.220	.207	.198
Medium	.237	.199	.179	.163
High	.220	.187	.162	.144

Source: Calculations were based upon the medium projections for packaging materials consumption set forth in 12-8 and the Low, Medium, and High projections of per capita personal consumption expenditures set forth in Table 12-7.

From this table, we note a trend toward a declining ratio of waste output as the level of personal consumption expenditures increases, which might be explained in part by the assumption that future containers will be lighter and more costly (in absolute terms) than those of today. Both of these trends are apparent at present.

Factors Influencing The Output Ratio

Of the two components of the waste coefficient, the less reliable is apt to be the projection of packaging materials consumption. For the purpose of forecasting, annual increases between two and three percent have been used on the premise that the current 3.3 percent annual rate of growth is likely to moderate. One factor in this projected moderation is likely to be a wider adoption of recycling. By the year 2000, it is expected that recycling will be an important factor in control of the solid waste total. However, if this expectation is not fulfilled, the actual waste output total could be markedly higher than that projected. Another factor which will influence the ratio significantly is the relative proportion of various container materials. If the use of plastics grows faster than anticipated, the weight of an average container could be much less than expected. However, plastics still account for only a tiny portion of the overall container output so even a huge increase may not have much impact. The projections herein formulated are predicated upon a continual trend both toward less material per container and to the adoption of other substances which are still lighter. Thus, the conclusion that container waste totals will grow at least two percent, but no faster than three percent annually seems reasonable.

Conclusion

The mounting total of container waste in the United States stems from industry's continuing competition for consumer approval. A distinctive package serves as an effective marketing tool in achieving product differentiation. The need for product differentiation has placed special importance on the role of the container in the marketing process. Glance along the shelves of any store counter and marvel at the seeming diversity of product offerings. Yet, if the wrapper is removed, the consumer would be hardpressed to make a buying decision.

Product differentiation is not the only aim of the container industry. In 1959, a fullscale campaign was begun to save the consumer the annoyance of returning empty soft drink and beer bottles to the neighborhood grocery store. Through the introduction of nonreturnable containers, most of the costs of the improved units were passed on directly to the consumer in one cycle. Using bottles with substantially reduced glass content, producers were able to effect a proportionate cost reduction, without impairing the bottle's functional value. As a result of this cost reduction, these new bottles bypassed the recycling phase and headed straight for the trash basket. From the producer's standpoint, apparently, it made more sense to tie up all loose ends at once than to amortize costs over as many as two dozen cycles.

As a result of these efforts, the disposable container has become a key component of current merchandising programs. Clearly, the consumer's response has been overwhelming. Is this trend likely to continue? Can it be supported by the existing supply of raw materials? Resources for the Future, in its 1960 study, answered this question in the affirmative. But the question, as noted earlier, is less that of resource availability than it is of shifting resource utilization. Obviously, wooden and paper containers pose little difficulty in terms of waste disposal. Plastics, on the other hand, require special disposal techniques. It is significant that those resources which are projected to experience the greatest increase in consumption to the year 2000 are the most difficult to eliminate. Plastics, with the highest anticipated growth rate, do not take readily to incineration. Yet, from all present indications, incineration is expected to be the predominant method of solid waste disposal in the coming decades. Metal cans, too, are undergoing an interesting metamorphosis. Traditionally, the metal can was made of steel or a tin-steel combination. After use, it invariably found its way to a convenient dumping ground and rusted away after prolonged exposure to the elements. But this has changed. Aluminum, a lighter and more costly material, is being used for an increasing percentage of overall metal can output. What happens to aluminum cans when they are exposed to the weather? Virtually nothing. With respect to all types of biodegradable containers, the picture has changed significantly. In most cases, a biodegradable container will not degrade unless it is exposed. Yet, the present trend is away from primitive open dumping toward supervised sanitary landfills in which garbage is deposited in layers and is regularly covered by soil. But, since waste products in sanitary landfills are buried well below the surface, preservation, not degradation, often takes place.

The sanitary landfill-degradation paradox, however, is becoming a moot point because major urban areas are rapidly running out of landfill space. Within a decade, landfill alternatives will have been exhausted for both New York and Chicago. For other cities, the time factor may not be much greater. In most instances, incineration will become the prime solid waste disposal technique. But, incineration of the future may be markedly different.

Historically, incinerators have been only partially successful in curbing environmental pollution. Solid waste was not eliminated, but was exchanged for an adulteration of the surrounding air by the emission of harmful particulates. Often, incinerators cast a dark shadow of dust over the adjacent territory. Now, with a heightened emphasis on clean air, the situation is changing. Advanced filtration techniques are being utilized to bring down the emitted residue to a minimal fraction of the level which had previously been considered normal. Too, in certain European cities, sanitation authorities have begun using garbage as a fuel source to supply power. This trend, which is slowly taking hold in the United States, offers a happy medium. Not only is the undesirable side effect eliminated, but a positive benefit is obtained. Indeed, this avenue seems destined for heavy traffic.

Compaction of garbage and use of the resulting dense product for land reclamation and for construction purposes also offers an interesting route. Regardless of whether the solid waste total is large or small, it will always exist in some measure. It would seem far better to develop methods which would convert these waste products into some material suitable for future use.

By the year 2000, landfill-type disposal will play a diminished role in the overall waste disposal program; for the larger cities, it will no longer be a feasible alternative. Clean-burning incinerators will produce electricity and will supply steam to heat houses. Giant compactors will condense huge bales of garbage into dense blocks which will be used to convert large areas of marginal land into useful territory; they will also be used for more standardized types of construction projects. The resistance of the container industry is apt to be overcome and efforts to make the used containers more amenable to disposal techniques may be expected to develop. Containers which eventually enter the waste channels will lend themselves more readily to destruction. Others may be designed to disintegrate after a given period of time. Still, all these efforts will be directed to waste disposal, but, as many authorities have indicated, the ultimate solution must be recycling. Perhaps the best summary was a statement by Mr. Alexander Rubin, Jr., Assistant Commissioner of Health for Air Resources of New York City at the Fourth Annual Symposium on Air and Respiratory Diseases.

In my opinion, the answer is to shift the emphasis away from waste disposal and turn instead to waste prevention. We must find ways to salvage and reuse bottles, cans and paper products; and most important, we must develop new packaging methods that will minimize rather than increase the mess around us. [2:11/11/68, 92].

13 Problems in the Disposal of Solid Waste from Durable Goods

Kevin F. Frain

During the past few decades, the United States has experienced a rapid expansion in the production sector due to increases in productivity, real wages, and population. The side effects of the production process during the same period have often been overlooked or neglected, while a connection between affluence and the various types of pollution has not been recognized. One of these pollution areas is solid wastes. The purpose of this chapter will be to examine the problems of disposal of solid wastes from durable goods for both the present era and the next 30 years.

The increase in solid waste generation can be defined as a social cost that accompanies the expansion of our economy, a cost that only recently has been viewed as potentially sizable and troublesome. It is relatively simple to appreciate the present day problems of solid waste disposal. An accurate realization of the difficulties that are likely to be present in the year 2000 is not as easily attained. Two factors, namely, the extent of production and the technological advances in disposal methods, will determine the extent of the problems in the years ahead.

This chapter is concerned with the disposal of wornout and obsolete durable goods. RFF found that the percentage of personal consumption expenditures spent on various categories of consumer durables was remarkably stable over the past few decades. In looking ahead through the decades to 2000, RFF concluded that the percentages spent on such categories as furniture and furnishings, passenger cars, and tires, and batteries, would remain substantially stable, but that the percentage spent on household appliances would increase slightly and that on books, toys, and sporting equipment substantially as average personal incomes rose [34:546]. Applying these percentages to the personal consumption expenditure projections derived in accordance with the assumptions and methodology set forth in Chapter 1, RFF arrived at the projections of aggregate personal consumption expenditure by type of product presented in Table 13-1. A check of actual consumer expenditures on these categories of durable goods during the mid-1960s against interpolated values of the RFF projections revealed that the latter were generally low, especially with respect to passenger cars (see Appendix A). However, the RFF projections are believed to furnish an adequate foundation for a look ahead at the volume of consumer durable goods requiring disposal. It was felt that because of their small bulk certain classes of consumer goods presented no disposal problem and these classes were ignored; they were: tableware and utensils, jewelry and watches, and opthalmic goods. Military products are also classified as durables but their disposal is usually a function of government.

Table 13-1

Historical and Projected Aggregate Personal Consumption Expenditure by Type of Product, 1950–2000 by Selected Years at 1960 Prices (in billions of dollars)

	1950	1955	1960		1970	1980	1990	2000
				L	9.0	9.8	10.6	11.8
Furniture and	6.5	7.8	8.3	M	12.5	17.9	22.5	35.6
Furnishings				H	14.4	23.3	38.0	60.6
				L	9.9	13.4	18.0	23.5
Household Applicances	6.9	7.5	8.4	M	13.4	23.2	36.8	56.8
				H	17.3	33.9	63.2	112.4
				L	22.0	28.7	36.9	46.0
Passenger Cars	12.8	17.3	15.8	M	23.1	33.1	47.2	66.0
				H	27.7	48.2	84.0	140.1
				L	3.6	4.6	4.9	6.4
Tires and Batteries	2.6	2.7	2.8	M	4.2	6.0	7.6	10.6
				H	5.9	10.5	16.1	24.2
				L	4.5	6.1	8.2	10.7
Books, Toys and	1.7	2.4	3.5	M	5.5	9.3	15.1	23.8
Sporting Equipment				H	6.9	13.6	25.3	45.0

Source: *Resources In America's Future*, Table A1-27 p. 556 (Baltimore: John Hopkins Press 1964), Hans Landsberg, Leonard Fischman and Joseph L. Fisher.

It is not expected that shortages of natural resources will interfere with the realization of projected increases in output of consumer durable goods.

In recent years, Americans have become more conscious of the appearance of our countryside, highways and local neighborhoods. The beautification program of Mrs. Lyndon Johnson provided impetus towards greater public concern with properly managed waste disposal. Still, the problem continues to demand attention.

The automobile has been foremost in degrading the appearance of various communities as auto junk yards and abandoned automobiles serve as eyesores and a general nuisance. Obsolete appliances, discarded furniture, and old automobile tires have also contributed to the situation by migrating into vacant lots and wooded areas unauthorized and unsuitable for dumping. These unsanctioned dumping grounds often serve as a breeding place for rats and harmful insects and become perilous playgrounds where injuries to children are common.

Air pollution from incineration of durable goods continues to plague many large cities. Since burning of automobile bodies is a necessary step in the recycling process, the problem cannot be easily sidestepped. Burning of plastics represents a two sided problem, since the residue from the product has a damaging effect on the incinerator components.

As noted in the preceding chapter, the shortage of available land for sanitary landfill in and around major cities has in recent years become more pronounced. Property in areas such as New York, Chicago, and Philadelphia is scarce and costly. In addition, communities are reluctant to sell land to more densely populated towns for sanitation and landfill operations; Brookhaven in Suffolk County, New York, recently refused to sell land to neighboring Islip Township with the comment that "we don't want any outsiders dumping their garbage here" [28:15].

Closely tied to the problems of disposal of solid waste is the cost factor. Land, incinerators, and sanitation workers all require funding which at present is $3 billion a year in the United States. The implications of rising cost become increasingly obvious, when we consider that each day 800 million pounds of waste is generated and this is expected to triple by 1980 [27].

The most obvious reasons for the inevitability of the side effects previously outlined in this section are the increases in population and urbanization. As RFF points out, domestic population could double by 2000, while more than 90 percent of the population will be urbanized. Added to these factors that imply increased production, are increases in productivity, increases in real income, increases in leisure time, conspicuous consumption, and an attempt to keep pace with our neighbors, all of which increase demand for certain products and ultimately generate waste.

Recent movements to the suburbs has stimulated homebuilding which in turn increased the demand for home appliances, furniture, garden tools, and the second car. Even within existing households the demand for certain durables has plenty of room for expansion; only 7 percent of all households own dishwashers, only 10 percent have food waste disposers and only 20 percent clothes dryers [34:150]. Projections for a shorter work week and earlier retirements will also affect demand for durables specifically in the do-it-yourself and recreation areas with power tools and sporting equipment, just two categories that will expand. It becomes evident that we have developed a chain of events that can be traced to the advances made in technology, from the gathering of raw materials to the methods utilized in the production process; thus we have more products to distribute among more people that will eventually result in greater disposal problems.

Another of the factors relating to the question of waste disposal is the concept of planned obsolescence. Perhaps this should be considered a social influence, in any event it is instrumental in creating some of the side effects associated with the problem. Planned obsolescence results from the use of inferior materials or the failure to use better available materials of similar cost, and unnecessary style changes. Frequently it is the manufacturers intention that a particular product be shortlived in utility so that another may be sold in its place. Sir Geoffrey Vickers refers to this process as the self-exciting system where "producers must innovate even when they cannot improve, in order to replace good products in which they have barely recovered their tooling costs. No one benefits but no one can stop" [39].

A Look at Present and Projected Side Effects
Associated with the Current and
Anticipated Output of Certain Durable Goods

Locating the Problem

The production projections of RFF are especially important to this section. They provide a basis upon which a formulation of the degree of unfavorable side effects can be made. As was discussed earlier, the projections through 1968 were reasonably accurate; however a note of caution is necessary, especially when one considers the inability of previous economists and demographers to adequately forecast future trends. Like the authors of *Resources In America's Future*, the author of this chapter runs the risk of inaccurately estimating the potential side effects of increasing durable goods production. Nevertheless, attempts must be made.

While production and population will weigh heavily upon the outcome of projected diseconomies, problems of waste disposal of durable goods will also depend on population concentration. It is understandable that New York City experiences more difficulty with solid waste disposal than Bangor, Maine, or Fairbanks, Alaska, and this may be expected to continue. The shortage of available land for waste disposal in New York City is already a major consideration and by 2000 little if any space will be available for sanitary landfill. Similar situations exist in most major metropolises and some smaller cities that have experienced recent rapid growth have been caught completely unprepared to handle the large volume of waste.

Future population trends point to increasing urbanization. This movement is likely to affect the suburbs surrounding major cities. The resulting pattern will be suburban sprawl making it difficult to distinguish where the city ends and the suburbs start. This situation will not alleviate the problems of the cities, but it will mean added difficulties for the neighboring counties. Westchester, Bergen, Nassau, and Suffolk counties outside New York City are already in this stage. Secondary size cities such as Richmond, Virginia; Atlanta, Georgia; and St. Petersburg, Florida may increase at a faster rate than the rest of the country, while specialized areas, especially those that cater to the retirement group, must have the foresight to anticipate future needs. It is also expected that the West Coast will grow faster than the rest of the country. Thus, we can anticipate an occurence in this area of many of the side effects that presently characterize the East Coast.

A further point concerning population concentration is that small areas often lack the financial and technical means that are available to the larger cities for dealing with waste disposal. To circumvent this lack and to insure greater cost efficiency, it will become necessary for certain communities to pool their resources in unified waste management programs, otherwise smaller communities may find themselves overwhelmed by solid waste disposal problems for which they are unprepared financially.

Quantifying the Problem

Disposal of solid wastes has become a big business in the United States where the estimated yearly expenditure in this field is $3 billion [17:3]. This amount is probably divided equally between government spending and fees paid to private carting jobbers. To partly explain this expenditure the Public Health Service estimates that in a typical year, "Americans throw away over 30 million tons of paper, 4 million tons of plastics, 48 billion cans and 26 billion bottles." Agricultural wastes have been estimated to contribute 1 billion tons per year to the solid waste disposal problem while the actual industrial contribution is unknown [17:3].

The Regional Plan Association which is concerned primarily with an extended New York metropolitan area reported that waste generation in the study area during 1964 was 17.4 million tons of solid waste. A survey by the National Research Council pegs daily waste generation at 4.5 pounds per person in 1965. New York City reports a growth in accumulation of 2.5 percent annually since 1960 while other cities average 2 percent [10:46]. Regional Plan Association has also stated that if present population trends continue, then in their study area, given the same per capita generation annual wastes will be 28.4 million tons by the year 2000 [10:56].

Localizing the Cost

A 1962 United States Census of local government, revealed that 79 percent of all sanitation expenditures other than sewage are accounted for by the standard metropolitan statistical areas, which contain only 63 percent of the population [19:192]. California, Illinois, New York, Ohio, and Pennsylvania account for 50 percent of total expenditures while Florida, Michigan, Massachusetts, New Jersey, and Texas are responsible for 20 percent. Thus ten states spend 70 percent of the national total on waste disposal [19:189].

Table 13.2 presents the expenditure for sanitation other than sewage for 30 selected cities. The average per capita expenditure for this group in 1965 was $8.94. In accepting the individual values and the per capita average for these cities, it must be recognized that different methods of accounting and organizational structures tend to make city by city comparisons unreliable. Nevertheless, the 30 cities when taken as a whole do provide valuable information.

If we accept four pounds of refuse generation daily as the per capita average, then the cost per ton of handling refuse is $14. If refuse generation per person increases to 5.9 pounds daily by 1985, as has been projected (see Figure 12-1) the annual per capita cost would increase to $12.74. Most authorities estimate that public expenditures on sanitation other than sewage represents only 50 percent of the total. If this is correct then all of the aforementioned per capita cost statistics would have to be doubled to arrive at the true total cost.

Other Cost Factors

It is estimated that the collection of waste and rubbish accounts for 80 percent of total disposal costs. The remaining 20 percent is concerned with the actual disposition of waste and the capital costs involved in land and facilities.

Current capital investment in the refuse collection and disposal field amounts to $170 million annually. The capital requirements for refuse collection and disposal for the period 1965-75 are estimated at $2.42 billion in 1965 dollars. Of this amount, $1.42 billion will go for collecting equipment and storage, $340 million for sanitary landfills and $660 million for incineration [19:201]. In 1965, 35-36 percent of communities financed collection and disposal of waste through service charges, 50-52 percent through general taxes and 12-15 percent through a combination of both methods [19:199]. Future methods of financing waste disposal will depend on local communities and their elected representatives.

Projected Side Effects of
Automobile Disposal

Automobile production is expected to triple from the present $23 billion to $66 billion annually by the year 2000. In 1960 there were 59 million user

Table 13-2

**Expenditures of Selected Cities for
Sanitation Other Than Sewage, 1964-65**
(in thousands of dollars)

City	Expenditures	Population 1965 (est)[a]	Per capita expenditure
Montgomery, Alabama	933	144,741	6.45
Anchorage, Alaska	572	47,650	12.00
Phoenix, Arizona	4,899	472,986	10.35
Los Angeles, California	19,541	2,669,899	7.32
San Francisco, California	2,785	797,320	3.49
New Haven, Connecticut	629	163,755	3.84
Wilmington, Delaware	977	103,205	9.47
Washington, D. C.	8,945	822,780	10.87
Miami, Florida	3,902	314,147	11.24
Chicago, Illinois	31,549	3,823,785	8.25
Indianapolis, Indiana	1,578	512,929	3.08
New Orleans, Louisiana	4,705	675,844	6.96
Baltimore, Maryland	6,174	1,011,328	6.10
Boston, Mass.	5,154	750,881	6.86
Detroit, Michigan	16,661	1,798,745	9.26
Minneapolis, Minnesota	1,637	520,053	3.15
St. Louis, Missouri	3,049	807,778	3.78
Newark, New Jersey	4,559	436,421	10.44
Hempstead, New York	354	37,308	9.40
New York, New York	112,678	8,381,196	13.44
Cincinnati, Ohio	3,785	541,246	6.99
Cleveland, Ohio	8,624	943,505	9.14
Portland, Oregon	987	401,372	2.46
Philadelphia, Penn.	18,956	2,802,905	6.76

(*continued*)

Table 13-2 (*continued*)

City	Expenditures	Population 1965 (est)[a]	Per capita expenditures
Pittsburg, Penn.	6,322	650,765	9.71
Memphis, Tenn.	5,016	535,831	9.36
Dallas, Texas	5,227	732,019	7.14
Houston, Texas	4,112	1,010,461	4.07
Seattle, Wash.	3,965	599,982	6.61
Milwaukee, Wisconsin	9,349	798,405	11.70

[a]The total population of the United States increased 7.69 percent from 1960 to 1965. Since it was not possible to obtain a reliable city-by-city population breakdown for 1965, the percentage increase of the entire population was applied to each city to arrive at an estimated figure for 1965.

Source: U. S. Bureau of the Census, *County and City Data Book*, 1967 (A Statistical Abstract Supplement) (Washington, D. C.: U. S. Government Printing Office, 1967), pp. 473-553.

operated vehicles. In 2000, if the high projection of RFF proved valid, there would be more than one car per person or 372 million automobiles in the United States. If these statistics seem unbelievable, the middle projection would still provide for 243 million vehicles by 2000 or four times the number presently on the roads.

Car ownership is correlated with income and higher income families tend to live in urban areas. Thus, it would appear that those areas already overcrowded with automobiles can expect more congestion in the years ahead.

The history of the 65 percent growth from 1940 to 1960 in the stock of user operated automobiles in the United States is shown in Table 13-3, together with the RFF projections of massive increase to year 2000. It will be noted that much of the past growth in the vehicle stock has been attributable to a decline in the number of people per car. With more cars per family there is less incentive to retain in service vehicles that are worn or out-of-date and the rate of retirement rises.

It is not suprising that the number of cars scrapped or abandoned annually has increased as the stock of motor vehicles has risen, and it is reasonable to expect this trend to continue if RFF projections are realized. These trends are reflected in Table 13-4 which presents historical data and RFF projections of number of automobiles scrapped or abandoned.

The average automobile that is junked or abandoned is 10.5 years old and is today usually devoid of any tangible value [4:E-6]. In a sense, the relatively young age of the automobile reflects the degree of affluence that char-

Table 13-3

Historical and Projected Total Stock of User Operated Vehicles Selected Years, 1940-2000 (in millions)

1940	1960		1980	2000
		L	114 (1.3)	199 (.94)
36	59	M	120 (1.3)	243 (.85)
(3.3)[a]	(1.9)	H	144 (1.1)	372 (.65)

[a]Figures in parenthesis indicates the number of people to each car.

Source: *Resources in America's Future*, p. 137.

Table 13-4

Historical Data and Projections of Number of Automobiles Scrapped or Abandoned, 1950-2000, by Selected Years (in millions)

1950	1955	1960[a]		1970	1980	1990	2000
			L	5.9	7.5	9.4	11.5
2.7	4.0	5.0	M	6.7	9.6	13.6	19.5
			H	8.3	14.9	27.8	54.7

[a]The Automobile Manufacturing Association estimates 4.2 million in 1960 and 6 million in 1966, *New York Times*, Oct. 27, 1968; p. 46.

Source: *Resources In America's Future*, p. 132.

acterizes the nation, since most other countries retain their cars for longer periods. If an aged car happens to break down on the road, the owner often finds his least expensive alternative is to remove the license plates from the vehicle and abandon it. Thus he escapes a towing charge that could exceed the value of the automobile. If an automobile is driven to a junk yard, the body of the car is likely to remain indefinitely until the price of scrap increases.

Table 13-5 lists the number of automobiles abandoned in selected cities during the past several years. Most cities reported that they distinguish between cars towed away for parking violations and those actually abandoned. Some cities only estimate the number of abandoned cars. Thus, in evaluating the statistics in Table 13-5 it should be recognized that accurate city by city comparisons are difficult to formulate.

It is difficult to estimate the total number of abandoned cars in any year. Since many of the cities questioned on this problem failed to respond, it seems probable that a large number of municipalities lack statistical data in the area.

If it were assumed that the number of cars abandoned annually in major cities would increase in proportion to the projected production increase of automobiles, then in 2000, there would be 90,000 cars abandoned in New York City, 60,000 in Philadelphia, and 48,000 in Detroit.

The potential cost of removing these vehicles from public streets would be tremendous. Even if it becomes possible to insure the movement of the automobiles into junk yards, the economic problem of salvaging continues to be a factor. At current prices not all auto hulks can be used as open hearth or oxygen process scrap because of the presence of contaminants such as cooper (30 pounds per car), lead (30 to 40 pounds per car), aluminum (30 to 90 pounds per car), and zinc (30 to 45 pounds per car). Thus the number of automobile bodies is greater than the existing demand for the commodity [5:671].

To climax the projected side effects in this area the impact of the increased use of plastics which already accounts for forty pounds in the average car must be considered. Incineration of automobiles, as mentioned previously, is a necessary step in the scrapping process. The Battelle Memorial Institute has conducted a study of this process and has found that plastics corrode incinerator parts and clog incinerators [30:64]. Since it is often difficult to remove the plastics prior to incineration the difficulties in this area becomes self-evident.

Problems of Disposal Relating to Other Bulky Items

Many of the projected diseconomies for automobiles that were discussed in the previous sections will also apply to major appliances, furniture, and tires. Still there are some specific problems in respect to these categories.

Many municipalities provide for the removal from private homes of bulky junk and refuse at considerable cost to the local sanitation department. This service can hardly be discontinued since there is no way for the average person to haul an obsolete washing machine to the city dump. What is

Table 13-5

Number of Automobiles Abandoned
Annually in Selected Cities, 1963-1968

City	1963	1964	1965	1966	1967	1968
Chicago	21,944	20,741	21,212	21,858	22,000	
Detroit		6,662	9,492	12,605	15,341	
Houston			10,200	11,000	12,400	14,500
Indianapolis			1,496	2,232	2,917	3,605
Minneapolis	684	934	966	1,476		
New Orleans[a]						4,607
New York					25,000	30,000
Philadelphia	5,458	10,520	12,341	16,000	20,000	
San Francisco			4,479	5,137	4,876	5,659

[a]New Orelans reported a total of 15,470 abandoned cars from April 1, 1966 to March 31, 1969.

Source: The statistics obtained from responses to inquiries sent to selected major cities. Several cities, including Los Angeles, Washington, D. C., and Memphis, responded that they did not compile statistics of this nature.

surprising is the fact that many people fail to take advantage of this disposal service and instead, manage to cart the broken television sets or old mattress to a nearby vacant lot.

When the bulky items are picked up by the local sanitation departments, the problem of disposal is only beginning. While automobiles can be recycled, usually television sets will not be used at all. "They consist of glass, plastic and various metals interlaced in such intricate fashion that they cannot be economically separated" [7:100]. Washing machines, dryers, and old furniture also fall into this category, where reclamation, except for charitable purposes, is unprofitable. Thus, we are forced to dispose of much of this bulk in landfill operations and again land shortage becomes an obstacle.

Nobody wants automobile tires. Service stations and department stores are usually the recipients of old tires, but frequently their carting services refuse to handle them. Except for a small percentage that are recapped, tires are not recycled. They create noxious smokes when burned and when buried in landfill operations often rise to the top after a period of time. About the only useful products derived from tires are rubber door mats and cushions for the sides of tugboats and docks.

To underscore the extent of future side effects that can be expected, it is helpful to reflect on the case of books and the large number of acquisitions that modern libraries must make to keep pace. Rarely if ever are the books thrown out. Instead they are retained along with the countless volumes of newspapers, periodicals, and governmental publications and when the collection becomes too large a new building is erected to house the ever expanding literary treasure. According to George Stewart the ancients had it much better: "Their papyrus went to pieces in less than a hundred years. Unless someone took the trouble to copy a whole book into new papyrus, that work vanished" [7:100].

Countervailing Forces Offsetting Side Effects Associated with Expanding Output of Durable Goods

The problem of solid waste disposal concerns all levels of federal, state, and local government. This concern is manifested more in certain localities than others depending on the concentration of the problem. Nevertheless, as population density shifts to new areas, the question of solid waste disposal begins to involve most city planners and legislators.

Federal

The federal government has responded to the problems of solid waste by passing the "Solid Wastes Disposal Act" in Oct. 20, 1965. The objectives of this legislation are twofold: (1) to initiate and accelerate a national research and development program for new and improved methods of proper and economic solid waste disposal; and (2) to provide technical and financial assistance to appropriate agencies in the planning, development, and conduct of solid waste disposal programs [17:3]. Appropriations under the Solid Wastes Disposal Act are handled by the Public Health Service in the Department of Health, Education and Welfare, and the Department of Interior. Grants to states and organizations are usually on a matching basis but can account for two-thirds of total costs. Funds available from the Department of Health, Education and Welfare were $60.2 million and $32.3 million from the Department of Interior through 1969. Some of the grants thus far, that apply to the disposal of durable goods include "Sanitary Landfill Investigation," "Incineration of Bulky Municipal Refuse," and several studies in the area of solid waste management [15].

State and Local

Inquiries were sent to numerous state and local authorities concerning solid wastes legislation. Surprisingly, many municipalities have failed to act in the solid wastes area to date. The cities and states that have passed or adopted regulations have concentrated their efforts on a few specific areas.

Practially all political subdivisions prohibit open burning of rubbish. In many major cities, including New York, laws have been passed controlling use and types of incinerators. Sanitary landfill procedures have been spelled out in great detail for most areas and this is often the only type of disposal permitted in a specific location. Dumping laws exist in most towns where pickup service is provided or where certain areas are designated as dumping grounds for junk. In some cities removal of doors from discarded washing machines and refrigerators is required.

Automobile disposal has received much legislative attention recently. As with sanitary landfills, zoning laws usually regulate the location of auto junkyards and require the area to be enclosed by a high fence. The abandoned automobile is also responsible for several new laws which generally prohibit the abandoning of vehicles on public or private property. Most cities have 24-hour parking ordinances; however this fails to deter the person abandoning an automobile and enforcement to date has been a problem. Most cities provide for abandoned cars to be held for a specified time and then sold at auction. Unfortunately, the value of these abandoned cars is usually inadequate to meet the towing and storage charges. Maryland is attempting to facilitate the movement of abandoned and junk cars to the scrap dealers. Thus Governor Mandel has asked that the state legislature authorize a $10 bounty, financed through an increase in the automobile registration fee, to be paid to any citizen or auto wrecker that delivers a car to a scrap dealer [38]. Recently Governor Rockefeller of New York approved a bill that, "gives municipalities a means of recovering the cost of removing abandoned vehicles by making the last registered owner liable for the towing charge" [36:13].

Technological

Sanitary Landfill Procedure: The oldest method of waste disposal involved the dumping of trash on the ground at a convenient location. For years, this primitive disposal process was viewed as a simple and inexpensive method of dealing with wastes. At present, land dumping is still used extensively and New York City continues to dispose of half its waste products in this manner. However, the attitude of neglect that once characterized this process has been transformed by a consideration of its sanitary effects on the environment.

The experiences of cities like New York and Chicago and the United States Army with sanitary landfill has influenced many other municipalities to use the process. "By the end of 1945 almost 100 cities in the United States had adopted it and by the beginning of 1960 more than 1,400 cities were reportedly using it" [2:87].

Usually sanitary landfill provides for the burying of refuse in layers in an open trench with each layer covered by two feet of dirt. Technological advances in sanitary landfill concern the type of fill used to minimize odors and eliminate rodents, rats, and other pests. The United States Bureau of Public Roads recommends use of a sandy loam that is devoid of rocks, tree roots, and clay, the presence of which results in cracking in the cover allowing for gas odors to escape and for insects to reach the waste products two feet below. Use of compressing machines and natural processes result in the organic breakdown of the waste product and in its being reduced to one-sixth of its original volume [24:38].

It may be noted that bulky objects such as most of the durable goods with which this chapter is concerned present special problems for sanitary landfill operations.

Because of the shortage of available land for sanitary landfill, several novel solutions have recently been advanced. The Massachusetts Institute of Technology has recommended using highway right of ways for landfill to build up shoulders and reduce accidents [29].

Incineration: Incineration continues to serve as a method of disposal for trash and garbage, however its application to solid waste from durable goods to date has been negligible. Bulky items such as automobiles, furniture, and appliances could not be handled by incinerators even for their nonmetalic parts. Recently, Dr. Elmer Kaiser of New York University has been working with an incinerator capable of handling bulky objects and along with Norman W. Wagner, supervisor of sanitation for Stamford, Conn., has designed a multipurpose incinerator that can process 200 tons a day of furniture, tires, plastics, and nonmetalic parts of automobile bodies [24:42].

In automobile scrapping, incineration is necessary once a car has been stripped to eliminate undercoating and lead. Certain refinements in this area have developed that enable the recovery of desirable metals during incineration. Tezuka Kosan, a Japanese firm, presently operates a crushing and cooking facility for this purpose.

The system called Carbecue burns off non-metalic material, melts non ferrous metals out of the scrap, and bales the ferrous metal that remains. Each car passes through a furnace, three cars at a time. In 900 C, the cars heat up. First lead, then aluminum, and finally copper drip out for collection on a conveyor belt as their melting points are reached. All this takes only 8 minutes [24:40].

A new American technique for burning automobiles was recently developed (U.S. patent 3,367,769). Unwanted non-metallic materials are burned off during the melting process.

The cars are squeezed together and loaded into a furnace having a fuel-oil fire at the bottom. The iron melts in a low-oxygen condition to hold back oxidation. Further up in the stack, the partially burned, escaping gases are ignited in normal air. The heat from the combustion burns out most of the remaining non-metallic components [23:34].

There is little doubt that incineration can serve as a practical method of disposal for the future. In some areas such as Indianapolis where the water table is very high, local officials feel that incineration is the only available long range alternative. Still, cost will be a determining factor. The Battelle Memorial Institute estimates that it costs $7 to $9 to burn a car in an incinerator as compared with $4 for outside burning [4:E-6]. A survey of light incinerators completed during the past few years indicate an average construction cost of $4,500 per ton capacity in a 24-hour period. The cost increases to $5,000 to $7,000 per ton when the latest air pollution control devices are added. If heat recovery systems are included the costs range from $8,000 to $10,000 per ton capacity in a 24 hour period [19:195].

Sea Disposal: Disposal at sea of certain obsolete durable goods and other forms of trash has in the past few years been receiving more attention. Dumping of compressed and unaltered automobiles and appliances has already been tried. Boston is studying a plan to convert a ship into a mobile incinerator that would carry ashes far out to sea for disposal. Dr. Robert A. Arb, of the Franklin Institute Research Laboratories in Philadelphia has suggested installation of a pipe line network to serve major cities and dump waste eight miles out at sea [29].

Historical data indicates that sea disposal can have certain drawbacks. First is the question of the high cost of transporting solid wastes out to sea. Secondly, ocean bordering cities such as San Francisco and New York have dumped garbage at sea only to have it drift back to shore and pollute beaches. While the disposal of dense bulky items at sea would not likely result in pollution of shore lines, further studies in this area are continuing. A team of University of Rhode Island scientists, "are using an electronic computer and a small submarine in experiments to find answers to questions about the effects on marine life of certain types of sea disposal" [22:95].

Compaction: Several foreign and domestic companies have recently been experimenting with the compaction of solid wastes and garbage. Tezuka Kosan Ltd. has been involved in compression of wastes for several years and claims to have spent $3 million on research and development in this area. It describes the way its 30,000 ton compactor takes care of disposal problems as follows:

1) There is no need to sort wastes. Plastic bottles or refrigerators are crushed down to 1/10 of their original volume.
2) Since there is no incineration there is no air pollution.
3) The wastes are compacted into sealed blocks.
4) Aerobic and anaerobic bacteria, sealed into the blocks, are eventually killed, thus eliminating a health hazard, which sometimes results when waste is disposed of in landfill [20:55].

Chicago is presently operating a $1.5 million compaction press supplied by Tezuka Kosan Ltd. to test its practicality. The city is considering using the compressed waste blocks as landfill for a proposed Lake Michigan airport.

American Manmax Corp. of Port Jefferson, New York, is a domestic company that has entered the compaction field. Currently the company is conducting talks with Suffolk County, New York, concerning the cost of the shredding and compaction of wastes [28]. An engineering firm, Korblock Corp. of Hornell, New York, has established a process for making lightweight concrete building blocks that are molded around compacted automobile scrap. Structure-strength tests carried out at Lehigh University show that these blocks can bear as heavy a load as standard concrete blocks [23:34].

Beneficial Side Effects

Thus far, the side effects of increased production outlined in this paper have been primarily negative. Fortunately there are methods of converting many of these side effects into productive and useful measures through imagination and innovation.

Perhaps the most publicized beneficial side effects of waste disposal are the landfill and land reclamation projects. DuPage, Illinois, has through a 2-year landfill project created a 118 ft. ski slope. The dirt used to cover the 800,000 cu. yards of garbage necessary for the slope was dug in such a way as to create a lake. Evanston, Illinois, has created a hill with a toboggan run and San Bernadino County in California used landfill to create a flood control levee 1,400 feet long and capped with concrete along the Santa Anna River [27]. In New York City, Flushing Meadow Park the site of the two worlds fairs was reclaimed by landfilling while Great Kills Park in Staten Island was created with 15 million cubic yards of solid waste [10:61]. Potential uses of landfill for recreational and industrial purposes appear limitless and should provide engineers and city planners with ample opportunity for innovation.

The recent interest in compaction of waste products has served to introduce the usage of building blocks as a by-product of the process. Tezuka Kosan Ltd. has already built a two story building from compressed blocks of waste materials that have been covered with concrete sheets. Different types of coating are available for the blocks so that they might be used for ocean dumping, landfill, shore protection, or flood prevention [20:55].

In western Europe, the heat and power from incineration has in some cities been transformed into useful purposes. Thus far in the United States, because of the low cost of fossil fuels, little has been done in this area. The Office of Solid Wastes is working on a new method of using heat from incineration to generate steam. "Waste heat from combustion is transmitted directly to a gas turbine, and thereby generates electric power" [23:83].

Recently the town of Hempstead in Nassau County, New York, gave a new twist to sea disposal. Since fishing is usually better near sunken ships, an artificial reef or fish haven was created by sinking obsolete barges loaded with concrete pipe. The idea has rendered fruitful results for fishermen. It appears likely that similar benefits might be obtained from a reef created with automobile bodies and old appliances.

Conclusions

The purpose of this chapter has been to outline the expected side effects of mounting industrial production of durable goods and possible counteracting forces. Comparing the projections for durable goods of *Resources In America's Future,* with the actual results to date tends to support the inevitability of these side effects. Sufficient quantities of raw materials and an economy responsive to the demands of an expanding and more affluent population makes it likely that the volume of such solid waste requiring disposal will continue to mount.

A Waste Management Program

Given the conditions that accompany increased output, how is man supposed to deal with the wastes crisis? Planned obsolescence and a decreasing emphasis on product durability appear to rule out control at the point of production. Instead, cities and communities must take the initiative. Certain guidelines and specific regulations relating to the disposal of solid waste must be formulated. To establish control, a solid waste management program should be the starting point.

Once a waste management program begins to function, each community should examine its own particular position. Patterns of population and supply of suitable land will help determine initial plans. Existing alternatives including land reclamation and the building of recreation areas through sanitary landfill should be evaluated. Attention can be directed to newer disposal methods such as the compaction process that yields solid waste building bricks and saves on landfill space. Preliminary planning should include the study of possible areas of cooperation among neighboring communities. High costs might make mutual use of personnel, equipment, collection systems and landfill sites desirable. In some areas, county or citywide integrated disposal systems might help to lower costs further.

A waste management program should also formulate a plan of action to meet possible future circumstances. Provisions for securing landfill sites in anticipation of rising land values and adequate funding of research and development are two areas that merit this early consideration. Studies in the field of incineration, concentrating on advanced air pollution controls and power conversion capability are needed. The effects of sea disposal on marine life should also be considered.

The Ultimate Solution: A Disposal Tax?

Most methods that are advanced for dealing with the solid waste disposal problem involve high costs. As a necessary step in waste management, funding must be considered. Present systems for financing waste disposal draw on service charges and taxes which undoubtedly will be continued. However, future capital expenditures on equipment and facilities may necessitate other types of support. One alternative is the disposal tax.

A disposal tax on certain durable goods has been proposed by several lawmakers during recent years. The administration of such a policy would call for a premium to be included in the original price of a product. The tax when collected would be placed in a special fund for eventual use in financing the disposal of the product. In the field of automobile disposal such a measure may be the only answer since most scrap processors are finding it increasingly difficult to make a profit.

The future of disposal taxes will depend on the speed with which technology enables us to solve the solid waste problem. Its eventual usage seems certain if the side effects of production continue to exert substantial offsets to the benefits that accompany affluence.

14 The Harmful Side Effects of Pesticide Use

Thomas Sassi

In his quest to attain mastery over his environment man's ingenuity has opened wide panoramas of progress. As man manipulates the environment to serve his interests it is increasingly evident that the ecological ramifications of these changes may pose serious threats to man's long run well-being.

History provides no more dramatic struggle than the effort to provide enough to eat for the human race. It is a problem which to date remains clearly unsolved on a global basis but is ironically, only a faint memory in the minds of most of the citizenry of this rich land. While the problem on a global basis may be more a question of distribution than production, it is to the question of production that this chapter will be addressed given the total ramifications of our production processes and particularly the ecological implications and dangers to man stemming from the use of pesticides as an aid to environmental control.

The threat to our environment resulting from the use of pesticides is sinister and often subtle. The nature of the danger stems from the highly toxic properties of the synthetic organic pesticides employed as an aid to production. The toxic nature of the pesticides combined with the phenomenons of persistence, potentiation, and the impact upon the chain of life represent the salient dangers to man and his environment. This chapter will endeavor to explore the questions which have been raised concerning pesticides. Moreover, an effort has been made to present scientific evidence relative to each of the suspected danger areas.

The fundamental question is whether or not the benefits of pesticide use are large enough to warrant its use given the increasing volume of evidence which suggests that the dangers to man, animals, and the environment may be so grave as to question the wisdom of our reliance upon pesticidal controls.

It has been over five years since Dr. Rachel Carson published her book *Silent Spring*. Her work represented the first major public disclosure of the dangers of DDT and other persistent pesticides. Her thesis was attacked by many scientists who believed that the evidence did not unequivocally support her assertions. Senator Gaylord Nelson of Wisconsin believes that Dr. Carson may have understated her case. Senator Nelson's views concerning the extent of the problem are suggested by the tone of a recent public statement.

Massive accumulating evidence supports her (Dr. Carson's) thesis at every point. Dangerous environmental contamination is occurring at a rapid and accelerating pace. We are literally heading toward environmental disaster. It is no longer the question — will it happen? It is happening now. The question is — will we temporize with this issue until it is too late?

Until, in fact, the land, the water and the air are polluted and all the living creatures in it are dangerously compromised [27].

It is the intent of this chapter to reexamine much of the material previously presented by Dr. Carson. Additionally, research studies, laboratory experiments, and real world situations are reviewed and evaluated in an effort to appreciate the nature of pesticidal pollution.

The Nature and History of Synthetic Organic Pesticides

History

Essentially, pesticides have been developed as a chemical means of eliminating from the environment undesirable biological species which represent a threat to the short run interests of man at a given time and place. The pesticide industry of today is a by-product of the Second World War. As scientists worked to perfect the sinister science of chemical warfare it was learned that many of the chemicals were also lethal to insects. Prior to this time, pesticide use was relatively limited and the pesticides employed were inorganic.

The advent of synthetic organic insecticides brought as a concomitant to their advertised effectiveness a great range of problems which may threaten many forms of life on this planet beyond the immediate victims intended. The synthetics differ sharply from the simpler inorganic insecticides of prewar days. The prewar insecticides were derived from minerals and plants which are the products of nature. Compounds of arsenic, copper, lead, manganese, zinc, pyrethium from dried Chrysanthemums, nicotine sulphate, and rotenone from leguminous plants previously provided the basis of most prewar pesticides.

What sets the new synthetics apart is their enormous biological potency. They have immense power not merely to poison but to enter into the most vital processes of the body and change them in sinister and deadly ways . . . They destroy the very enzymes whose function is to protect the body from harm, they block the oxidation processes from which the body receives its energy, they prevent the normal functioning of various organs, and they may initiate in certain cells the slow and irreversible change that leads to malignancy [14:16-17].

The Nature of Synthetic Organic Pesticides

Synthetic pesticides fall largely into two major groups, DDT (dichloro-diphenyl-trichloro-ethane) which are known as the chlorinated hydrocarbons and the organic phosphorus insecticides such as malathion and parathion. The common link between all of these synthetics is that they have as their base atoms of carbon, which is the indispensable building block of the living world. Carbon has the faculty of uniting with other carbon atoms and linking with atoms of other substances in an apparently inexhaustible number of permutations [14:17-19].

The two major factors which loom as a threat to living things are that the synthetic pesticides are enormously toxic and their manmade structure renders them immune to decomposition by the biological processes of living organisms [20:400].

The side effects arising from the use of synthetic organic pesticides present a broad range of problems with serious ramifications in many areas of the ecological system. The use of pesticides on the present scale is relatively new and the effects of their use are at issue among many experts in the field of entomology. The known danger areas may be discussed under these major headings:

1. The lethal nature of synthetic pesticides.
2. Chemical reactions with other substances, other pesticides, and potential synergism.
3. The inability of living things to breakdown the synthetics and bodily storage.
4. The implications to the food chain and the chain of life.
5. Residues and the means of transmission.

The Lethal Nature of Synthetic Pesticides

DDT is probably the most widely known pesticide. It is a powerful chemical agent which may cause substantial harm to those exposed to even very small doses of it. In animal experiments, 3 parts per million of DDT has been found to inhibit an essential enzyme in heart muscle; 5 parts per million has resulted in the disintegration of liver cells [28:614-622].

The lethal effect of synthetic pesticides is dramatically illustrated when one considers that dieldrin, for example, is about five times as toxic as DDT when absorbed through the skin in solution [20:891-912]. The most toxic of all the chlorinated hydrocarbons is endrin. Endrin is five times as toxic as dieldrin and when contrasted with DDT its extremely noxious nature is strikingly apparent. It is fifteen times as poisonous as DDT to mammals, 30 times as poisonous to fish, and 300 times as poisonous to many birds [26:10].

The organic phosphorous group on the other hand destroys critical enzymes in the body of its victim. Parathion is one of the most lethal of this group and is also used in great abundance. In 1962 seven million pounds of parathion were applied to the fields of the United States by hand sprayers, motorized dusters and blowers, and by airplane. "This amount of parathion is enough to provide a lethal dose to 5 to 10 times the world's population" [14:30]. Fortunately, parathion residues are relatively short lived. Hence, humans are not exposed to the full toxic impact of parathion. However, there are records which indicate that the level of residue and the threat to the users of the product are significant. California has reported over 200 cases annually of accidental parathion poisoning [14:29].

It is apparent that there is considerable danger to many forms of life arising from the use of various pesticides. However, the danger is further accentuated when one considers the combined effect of two or more of these chemicals. For illustrative purposes, consider the organic phosphate malathion. Malathion has been widely used in household insecticides, mosquito sprays, and in massive sprayings such as that in Florida when nearly one million acres were treated in an effort to eradicate the Mediterranean fruit fly. Malathion is advertised as a safe insecticide. It is safe because the mammalian liver renders it relatively harmless. Detoxification of malathion is accomplished by one of the enzymes in the liver, but what if something interferes with this enzymes activity? In this event, the mammal in question receives the complete toxic impact of the poison [14:30-32].

Potentiation

A remarkable feature of the pesticide syndrome is the synergistic toxic effect which occurs when certain pesticides are combined. It has been learned that when malathion and certain other organic phosphates are combined a toxic effect up to 50 times as severe as would be predicted on the basis of adding together the toxicities of the two occurs. Moreover, this effect may be achieved even if the two agents are not assimilated at the same time [14:31].

This phenomenon has serious implications. If residue levels are established based on human tolerance levels of specific pesticides and if at some point from production to consumption of the food commodity it comes in contact with another agent which reacts synergistically with it, the toxic impact to the consumer may be above assumed safety levels [16:488-96].

Similarly, some scientists believe that drugs used by people for various ailments may be altered in such a way as to produce harmful effects upon the user due to the presence of pesticides stored within the person's body. The results of laboratory experiments suggest that tranquilizers derived from phenothiazine should be avoided if the recipient is exposed to parathion due to the increased toxicity resulting from their combination [30:1260-1261].

Bodily Storage of Pesticides

Another characteristic of the pesticides syndrome is the propensity of ingested pesticides to be stored within the bodies of living creatures exposed to them. The evidence regarding the bodily storage of pesticides in man and animals is growing at an alarming rate.

According to a 1966 study by the U.S. Public Health Service, the average American has gathered 12 parts per million of DDT in his human fatty tissues, as well as .15 of a part per million of dieldrin. Infants now receive .08 of a part per million of DDT in the milk from nursing mothers [27].

Wayland J. Hayes Jr., M.D. and his associates performed a detailed study of the storage of DDT and DDE in people with different degrees of exposure to the chemicals. Using scientific methodology they broke the samples taken down into groups representing varying degrees of exposure to the chemicals. After completing the stratification they examined the adipose tissue of the subjects. The findings of the study are detailed in Table 14-1. It was found that the storage of DDT and DDE varies according to the dietary habits and occupational exposure of individuals. The analysis of 10 samples of human fat tissue collected and sealed before the advent of DDT in this country failed to develop a color typical of DDT or DDE when tested. Abstainers from meat stored on the average about half as much DDT and half as much DDE as persons in the general population who stored an average of 4.9 parts per million and 6.1 parts per million of the two pesticides, respectively. Persons in the general population with significant environmental exposure (group 4) stored on the average 6.0 parts per million of DDT while those with little or no environmental exposure (group 3) stored an average of 4.9 parts per million of DDT. Although the difference was small it was statistically significant at the 0.02 level of significance.

Agricultural occupational exposure caused a much more marked increase in the storage of DDT derived material. The increase above the general population level was especially marked in persons who had occupational exposure within a year (group 6). These people stored DDT at an average concentration of 17.1 parts per million.

The fact that environmental exposure results in extremely high quantities of pesticides being stored in human adipose tissue gives tacit testimony to the assertion that one does not have to ingest a pesticide to have it stored in one's body. Storage may result from contact on the skin or through the respiratory processes [20:400-403].

No one questions the fact that pesticides are being stored within the human body. However, few people are aware of the dangers such storage represents.

The range of proven storage is quite wide and, what is even more to the point, the minimum figures are above the level at which damage to the liver and other organs or tissues may begin [14:22].

In addition to the storage of pesticides in the bodies of humans is the similar impact that the pesticides have had upon animals. Samples of various species of wildlife have revealed substantial amounts of pesticidal chemicals within their fat tissues. This fact has serious implications to man as shall be seen in the section concerning the chain of life.

The National Wildlife Federation recently reported that about 75 percent of

Table 14.1

Storage of DDT and DDE in the Fat of People in the United States as Determined by Degree of Dietary, Environmental, and Occupational Exposure

Exposure Group Description	no. cases	Value and Unit[a]		DDT Tissue	DDT Extract	DDE Tissue	DDE Extract
Died before DDT	10	Range	ppm	Not greater than reagent blanks			
Abstainers from meat	16	Range	ppm	0-7	0-10	0-9	0-12
		Mean	ppm	2.3	3.5	3.2	4.9
Eat Meat	12	Range	ppm	0-7	0-10	0-8	0-12
		Mean	ppm	2.1	3.3	2.8	4.3
Eat Meat	4	Range	ppm	2-5	3-6	2-9	4-12
		Mean	ppm	2.8	4.0	4.5	6.8
General Population	61	Range	ppm	2-12	3-22	2-13	3-25
		Mean	ppm	4.9	6.8	6.1	8.6
People with heavy env. exposure	110	Range	ppm	2-14	2-18	2-25	0-34
		Mean	ppm	6.0	7.9	8.6	11.0
Agricultural applicators total	30	Range	ppm	3-37	6-48	4-58	4-95
		Mean	ppm	14.0	20.5	19.0	27.3
Heavy exposure More than 1 year	11	Range	ppm	4-16	6-46	4-21	10-39
		Mean	ppm	8.8	16.1	13.4	22.4
Heavy exposure Within last year	19	Range	ppm	3-37	9-48	4-58	4-95
		Mean	ppm	17.1	23.1	22.3	30.2

[a]ppm - parts per million

Source: Wayland Haynes, et al., "Storage of DDT and DDE in People with Different Degrees of Exposure to DDT," *AMA Archives of Industrial Health*, vol. 18 (Nov. 1958), p. 400.

the specimens of fish, birds, and mammals collected from various parts of the world including the Arctic and Antarctic regions contained DDT. California marine scientists examined several hundred samples of fish and shellfish from the Pacific, from both salt water bays and the open sea. They found that 396 of the 400 samples analyzed contained measurable DDT residues. In Wisconsin, pesticide residues including DDT and dieldrin have been found in everyone of more than 2,600 fish samples taken from 109 of the states lakes and inland waterways. The amount of residue appearing in each of the various samples seems to be directly related to the intensity of pesticide application in any given area. The concentration of DDT ranged from .02 to 16.2 parts per million for the whole fish and from .22 to 534.6 parts per million in the adiopose tissue of the fish [27].

The problem of bodily storage of pesticides is accentuated by the tendency of all hydrocarbons to build up in the body in a cumulative fashion. This characteristic has serious implications. Even if residue levels are maintained within legal standards one may postulate that over a period of time there is the distinct possibility that the level of pesticidal chemicals stored within one's body may reach a dangerous level. Laboratory experiments have shown that a diet containing 2.5 parts per million of chlordane may eventually lead to storage within the body of 75 parts per million [15:283].

The Chain of Life

Another characteristic of the pesticides syndrome is the manner in which concentrations of stored pesticides are passed along the food chain and the chain of life. This phenomenon has been thoroughly documented and is disputed by no one to the writer's knowledge. The aspect of the problem which is more startling and has not been unequivocally proven is the intensification of pesticide concentrations as one moves up the food chain and the chain of life. The transfer of residues from one organism to the next along the food chain is serious, the magnification of the storage level from one organism to the next has cataclysmic overtones. The intensification of concentrations of pesticides has been observed and the characteristics of the process were the following.

Hay containing residues of 7 to 8 parts per million, may be fed to cows. The DDT will turn up in the milk in the amount of 3 parts per million, but in butter made from this milk the concentration may run as high as 65 parts per million [14:22].

Milk and butter are staples of the American diet. The impact of the passage of residues along the food chain represents a threat to the health of the citizenry of this nation. The importance of this matter is increasing since DDT is now being used to control insect pests of alfalfa; mosquitoes in permanent pastures; the European corn borer on corn; the pea weevil and pea aphids on peas, and in numerous other situations where the treated plants are fed to cattle. The findings of a study done by Ray F. Smith, W. M. Hoskins, and O. H. Fullmer illustrate the problem further.

Up to 36 parts per million of DDT have been reported in the milk of cows that had grazed on DDT sprayed pasture or fed on DDT sprayed meal containing 184 parts per million DDT residue . . . A Jersey cow fed 24 grams per day for 5 months had 44 parts per million DDT in her milk at the end of the feeding period, 15 parts per million 1 week after feeding of DDT was discontinued and 7 parts per million 3 weeks later. Five cows receiving pea silage containing about 100 parts per million DDT for approximately 4 months had 15.6 parts per million DDT in their milk [32:759].

The impact upon the milk and butter of dairy cows may be amplified because in addition to the quantities of pesticides ingested during feeding cows are exposed to pesticides from other sources. Ponds of water from which cows drink are often exposed to insecticidal sprays. Moreover, cows are often sprayed for insect control directly and since they have the habit of licking themselves increased dosages of chemicals ingested and stored within their bodies may result.

The previous data demonstrated the nature of the effect upon the food chain as manifested under laboratory conditions. The following is a description of what occurred in a real world situation. In an effort to exterminate a troublesome breed of gnats, DDD was applied to the water of Clear Lake in California in a concentration of 1/50 part per million. The death of many greber stimulated inquiries and the dead birds were found to have DDD concentrations of 1,600 parts per million. When an effort to explain this phenomenon was made and the food chain reconstructed it was found that there was a progressive increase in the concentration of DDD as one moved up the food chain. Plankton were found to contain 5 parts per million of the insecticide which was 25 times the concentration ever reached in the water; plant eating fish had accumulations of 40 − 300 parts per million; carnivorous species had concentrations as high as 2,500 parts per million. Moreover, even after the condition was discovered and pesticide application discontinued the effects of the treatment were still evident upon the creatures of the lake. Although the water no longer contained traces of DDD two years after the last application of DDD, plankton still contained concentrations of as much as 5.3 parts per million of the pesticide. Hence, the poison had permeated the fabric of life within the lake [21:91-106].

Although no one is in a position to say exactly what levels of pesticide concentration in foods may prove dangerous over the long run the nature of the problem is clear. It begins with chemical agents which are extremely toxic, which have the characteristic of being stored in the tissues of living things. Moreover, it has been shown that in combination the chemicals may yield a synergistic impact upon the recipient of more than one of the agents. This phenomenon in conjunction with the problem of potentiation as one moves up the food chain represents the most difficult aspect of the problem to evaluate and deal with.

The Balance of Nature

It has been suggested that an important aspect of the pesticide syndrome is its effect upon the balance of nature [25:3-15]. When an area is treated for the purpose of pest control the pest may or may not be eliminated. If it is eliminated an extraordinary thing may happen. The balance of nature may be upset with the result that the insects upon which this creature was either a predator or a competitor for food may, due to the absence of natural enemies, be unleashed in great abundance [29:403]. A second alternative outcome is that the intended victim is immune to the pesticide employed, but its natural enemies are not [12:149-155]. In this instance, the intended victim is free of natural restraint and may multiply prodigiously. Insects are generally only considered serious pests when their numbers threaten the interests of man at a given time and place. The introdction of pesticidal chemicals into a given environment may under the hitherto described circumstances create a pest problem of substantial magnitude [3:1-7].

Persistence

The tendency of pesticides to maintain their potency over long periods of time within soil is referred to as persistence. This characteristic represents a danger in and of itself as well as a potential source of potentiation in the event of future application of pesticides. The United States Department of Agriculture has examined the question of persistence and found that the evidence supports the concern over persistence. The percent of various insecticides remaining in the soil after 14 years was Aldrin (purified) 40 percent; Aldrin (nonpurified) 50 percent; Dieldrin 35 percent; Chlordane 40 percent; Heptachlor 12 percent; Toxaphene 50 percent or more [2:172].

The problem of persistence and the implications it suggests will be discussed in the next section of this chapter.

The Dangers to Man and His Environment

Residues

Residues of pesticides on crops that are shipped in interstate commerce are subject to government limitations, however, the real significance of the residues lies in the amount actually ingested by animals and humans. Data on the amount of residues on food as it is shipped does not give a clue to the amount which may be ingested and stored within the body of the recipient. However, the presence of residues certainly means that consumers of food are going to be exposed to varying amounts of poisonous chemicals.

A study of food samples from 18 markets consisting of 82 foods collected from 3 different geographical areas of the United States showed the following. The existence of residues of chlorinated organic pesticides was confirmed in 129 samples. Twenty-five different residues were found in the samples examined.

The most common were DDT, DDE, and TDE, with maximum values of .15, .22, and .053 parts per million, respectively, in various dairy products. These same pesticides were found in meat, fish, and poultry in quantities of .86, .92, and .25 parts per million of DDT, DDE, and TDE, respectively [22:1-3].

A similar examination by the Food and Drug Administration found pesticide residues in excess of legal limits in about 5 percent of the samples which they examined in 1964. The findings of this study are shown in Table 14-2.

Pesticide residues on food commodities have resulted in seizures of these commodities by the Food and Drug Administration. A summary of the commodities seized is presented in Table 14-3.

Pesticide residues are also found on tobacco leaves and ultimately within the finished tobacco products. Tables 14-4 and 14-5 reflect the findings of the department of agriculture investigation. Residues on tobacco products contribute to the total exposure to pesticides received by users of these products.

The environment contains numerous sources of exposure to pesticides. It has been shown that residues are passed along the chain of life. They are present on food and tobacco products. Moreover, they may be found in the air man breathes or the water he drinks. Hence, it is extremely difficult to quantify the degree of environmental exposure any given individual is subject to. This fact viewed in light of the synergistic action of certain pesticides makes the establishment of acceptable residue levels for food products a perplexing task.

Persistence and The Spread of Residues

Given the problem of persistence and the tendency of living things to absorb and store varying levels of pesticides one wonders whether or not the persistence in conjunction with new applications may produce serious ill effects and perhaps synergism. If synergism occurs within the soil the phenomenon of seedling uptake may represent a more serious danger in terms of the contamination of food crops. Seedling uptake is a process whereby crops growing in the soil absorb chemical elements from the soil. This process results in food products which have foreign chemical agents as an integral part of their biological configuration. This suggests that the amount of pesticidal chemicals consumed by those who eat these products will be in excess of the residue levels on the product. Table 14-6 illustrates the degree of seedling uptake in 4 agricultural commodities treated with 4 different pesticides.

The Spread of Pesticide Residues

Pesticide residues are spread in numerous ways. They may be carried by the wind, transported by insects and animals which have come in contact with them, or they may be spread by surface and ground waters. The spread of pesticide residues by rain and ground water is illustrated by the results of a Department

Table 14.2

Samples Examined for Pesticide
Residues by the Food and Drug Administration During February 1964

Commodities	Examined	Illegal Residues Detected
Manufactured dairy products	2,683	131
Shell eggs and egg products	717	51
Fish and shellfish	410	65
Manufactured animal feeds	1,002	32
Vegetable oils	340	0
Raw agricultural products	22,458	794
Fluid milk	4,352	315
Dietary and baby foods	252	4
Fish liver oils	185	0
Miscellaneous manufactured foods	279	36

Source: U. S. Senate, Hearings before the
Subcommittee on Reorganization and In-
ternational Organizations, 88th Congress,
Second Session, p. 1002.

of Agriculture study. It was found that runoff from a watershed receiving 5 pounds per acre of dieldrin contained 3,000 parts per ton as compared with 40 parts per ton from an untreated watershed. Moreover, rainfall collected in the treated areas contained concentrations of dieldrin [2:174].

Although the treated lands yielded runoff containing over seventy times that of the untreated land there was an appreciable amount of dieldrin present in the untreated lands runoff. Hence, the untreated lands runoff had been contaminated either as the result of groundwater movement, rainfall, the prevailing winds, or a combination of these elements. The magnitude of the problem is emphasized when one considers that over 103 million acres of land were treated for insect and weed control alone in the United States in 1964 [1:12].

One may speculate that farm lands which are subject to intensive applications of pesticides, many of which are persistent, will over time become increasingly impregnated with various pesticides. This effect may be supplemented by amounts of pesticides deposited by rain, wind, and groundwater. Given the phenomenon of seedling uptake one may envisage crops containing very high

d Commodities Based
sticide Residues in 1964

District	Product	Volume of commodity	Pesticide residue
Atlanta	Cabbage	534 crates, 50 lbs. each	Toxaphene
Dallas	Carrots	1,143 boxes, 48 lbs. each	Endrin
Dallas	Carrots	182 boxes, 75 lbs. each	Endrin
Dallas	Wheat	129,000 lbs.	Mercurial compound
Dallas	Parsley	400 crates	Endrin
Dallas	Shell eggs	29 cases	DDT and DDE
Denver	Alfalfa hay	450 bales	Toxaphene and DDT
Denver	Alfalfa hay	450 bales	Dieldrin
Los Angeles	Alfalfa hay	18 tons	DDT and DDE
San Francisco	Alfalfa hay	158 tons	DDT, DDE, DDT, and Heptachlor
Detroit	Bibb lettuce	10 crates	Endrin
Kansas City	Potatoes	20,800 lbs.	Aldrin and Dieldrin
New Orleans	Potatoes	15,500 lbs.	Aldrin and Dieldrin
New York	Cauliflower	476 crates	Endrin
San Francisco	Broccoli	594 boxes	Endrin
Seattle	Flour	50 bags, 25 lbs. each	Lindane and Methoxychlor
Denver	Cheese	48 cases, 48 lbs. each	Dieldrin
New Orleans	Cheese	13,000 lbs.	DDT
San Francisco	Frozen broccoli	1,266 lbs.	Endrin

Source: U. S. Senate, Committee on Government Operations, *Interagency Coordination in Environmental Hazards (Pesticides)*, 1963, 88th Congress, 1st Session, pp. 1003-1004.

Table 14.4

Pesticide Residues Found on Tobacco
Leaves in a 1962 Auction Market

| Type of Tobacco and Area | Residues p.p.m.[a] | | | | | |
| | DDT | | TDE | | Endrin | |
	Mean	Maximum	Mean	Maximum	Mean	Maximum
Flue Cured[b]						
Florida	2.50	4.5	18.83	60.0	2.13	5.1
Georgia	7.90	32.0	35.85	58.0	1.21	1.8
South Carolina	10.44	27.5	31.19	60.0	1.22	2.7
North Carolina						
Eastern Belt	4.65	15.0	2.80	7.0	2.40	3.1
Middle Belt	4.80	22.0	7.20	18.0	0.75	2.1
Old Belt	3.00	10.0	4.30	20.0	0.49	1.1
Cigar Wrapper[c]						
Florida		216.0		10.0		7.8
Check Tobacco	0.0				0.5	

[a] p.p.m. parts per million.

[b] Composite sample (100 leaves) from 95 growers.

[c] Ten flue cured tobacco samples (50 leaves sample) from each area.

Source: U. S. Senate, Hearings before Subcommitttee on Reorganization and International Organizations, 88th Congress, Second Session, p. 1600.

levels of pesticides within the fabric of their structure as the years go by and the volume of pesticides applied directly or indirectly to the soil increases. This is, of course, conjecture, but in light of the empirical evidence it is not impossible.

Pesticide Residues in Human Fat and Milk

It is apparent that man is continually being exposed to numerous potential sources of pesticide poisoning. However, the degree of exposure has to date had no serious measurable detrimental effect upon the citizenry. However, no one is

Table 14.5

Pesticide Residues in Cigarettes

Brand No. Cigarettes	Type 1 carton each	DDT (ppm)	TDE (ppm)	Endrin (ppm)
1	regular	2.0	12.0	0.5
2	regular	3.0	17.0	1.0
3	regular	4.0	18.0	0.5
4	regular	4.0	18.0	1.0
5	filter	3.0	14.5	0.5
6	filter	4.0	16.5	1.0
7	filter	6.0	21.5	2.0
8	king	3.0	20.0	0.5
9	king	4.0	23.0	0.5
10	king	5.0	23.0	1.0

Source: U. S. Senate, Hearings Before Subcommittee on Reorganization and International Organizations, 88th Congress,
Second Session, p. 1601.

in a position to state that this fortunate circumstance will continue in the future as more and more pesticides are employed and the element of time has the chance to enter the picture.

The result of an analysis of 75 samples of human fat and milk are presented in Tables 14-7 and 14-8, respectively. Table 14-7 illustrates the number of cases in which DDT was found in each of six ranges of concentration. Approximately one-fourth of the specimens examined contained no DDT, or only traces (0.1 to 1.0 parts per million). The two values in the high concentration range were 26 and 34 parts per million, and strangely enough the latter accumulation was present in an infant. The average for all samples was 5.3 parts per million. Males and females were equally represented in the sample and no significant difference between the sexes was observed at the .05 level of significance.

Table 14-8 shows the range of concentration of DDT found in 32 samples of

Table 14.6

Seedling Uptake of Chlorinated Insecticides from Soils[a] (in parts per million)

	Soybeans	Wheat	Soybeans	Corn
Endrin	.024	.070	.045	.067
Dieldren	.024	.058	.019	.017
Heptachlor	.040	.046	.150	.208
DDT	.005	.036	.007	.003

[a]The soil was treated with 0.5 parts per million of various insecticides.

Source: U. S. Department of Agriculture and Cooperation, *Progress Report on Pesticides and Related Activities* (Washington, D. C.: Government Printing Office, 1967), p. 191.

Table 14.7

Range of Concentration of DDT in 75 Samples of Human Fat

Range, p.p.m. of DDT	Cases
0.0	15
0.1 - 1.0	7
1.1 - 5.0	21
5.1 - 10.0	21
10.1 - 20.0	9
Over 20.0[a]	2

Average concentration = 5.3 p.p.m.

[a]Actual values were 26 and 34 parts per million.

Source: Edwin P. Laug, et al. "Occurence of DDT in Human Fat and Milk," *AMA Archives of Industrial Hygiene and Occupational Medicine* Vol. 3 (1951), p. 246.

Table 14.8

Range of Concentration of DDT in 32
Samples of Human Milk

Range, p.p.m. of DDT	Cases
0.00	2
0.01 – 0.05	3
0.11 – 0.15	13
0.16 – 0.20	2
Over 0.20[a]	4

Average concentration = 0.13 p.p.m.

[a]Actual values were 0.25, 0.28, 0.42, and 0.77 parts per million.

Source: Edwin P. Laug, et al., "Occurrence of DDT in Human Fat and Milk," p. 246.

human milk. The average concentration for all 32 specimens was 0.13 parts per million. This concentration of DDT is of the same order as that found in the past in a number of market milks analyzed by the Food and Drug Administration. The four samples of milk in the high concentration range showed concentrations of .25, .28, .42, and .77 parts per million. In none of these cases could the high values be correlated with any unusual known exposure to DDT.

This study demonstrates that DDT occurs in human fat and milk presumably as the result of the widespread use of DDT with the consequent contamination of important foodstuffs and the water people drink.

The Threat of Cancer and Mutation

Studies have shown that certain pesticides are capable of altering the genetic makeup of certain exposed organisms. Little attention has been paid to this matter; however, there is information available which illustrates that a number of pesticides have caused changes in vital cell processes ranging from slight chromosome damage to gene mutation with consequences extending to the ultimate catastrophy of malignancy.

Mosquitoes exposed to DDT for several generations turned into strange creatures called gyandromorphs part male and part female [11:607-612]. Mutations occurred in fruit flies the classic subject of genetics experiments when subjected to phenol [24:453-484].

Plants treated with various phenols suffered profound destruction of chromosomes, changes in genes, and had a large number of mutations. The herbicide 2,4-D has produced tumorlike swellings in treated plants. Chromosomes become short, thick, and clumped together. Cell division is seriously retarded. "The general effect is said to parallel closely that produced by X-rays" [13:274-283].

The findings of large residues of DDT in the gonads and germ cells of birds and mammals is strong evidence that the chlorinated hydrocarbons, at least, not only become widely distributed throughout the body but also come in contact with genetic material [14:207].

The area of mutation may indeed represent the most serious long range threat to man and the environment. The state of knowledge is not adequate to make any predictions or judgments concerning the impact of the problem in the future.

Investigations by the Department of Agriculture has indicated that about 100 herbicides should be classified as mutagenic [2:180].

Almost all chemicals caused a slight increase in the mutation rate in several test organisms. For example, in one test system the spontaneous mutation rate is at the relative value of .05 percent while the known mutagen 5-bromouracil, increases the rate of mutation to 3.0 percent. Some of the herbicides have caused apparent increases as high as 0.3 percent [2:179-180].

The organochlorine pesticides have been used extensively. They have proved efficacious and have lower acute toxicities than many other pesticides. However, they have produced tumorigenic effects on test organisms. Moreover, even at relatively low doses they have effects on liver enzyme systems [36:13].

All of the sources consulted and cited by the writer suggest that more information is needed concerning the mutagenic and carcenogenic effects of certain pesticidal chemicals. However, many studies including those cited in this chapter have shown that under certain circumstances mutagenic or carcenogenic effects have resulted due to exposure to particular pesticides. Given these findings and the appreciation of the fact that there is much remaining to be learned it would appear that the prudent course of action would be away from massive reliance on pesticidal chemicals as a means of environmental control. The section of this chapter dealing with bioenvironmental controls suggests that there is a safe and effective alternative to our sole reliance upon pesticidal controls. All of the evidence presented to date suggests that although pesticides may not have been proven unequivocally dangerous there is at the very least reason to view them with suspicion. This being the case, it would appear to the writer to be nothing more than common sense to reserve the use of pesticidal chemicals to those situations which cannot be dealt with in any other manner.

All this is not to say there is no insect problem and no need of control. I am saying, rather, that control must be geared to realities, not to mythical situations, and that the methods employed must be such that they do not destroy us along with the insects. . . . It is not my contention that chemical insecticides must never be used. I do contend that we have put poisonous and biologically potent chemicals in the hands of persons largely or wholly ignorant of their potentials for harm. We have subjected enormous numbers of people to contact with these poisons, without their consent and often without their knowledge. If the Bill of Rights contains no guarantee that a citizen shall be secure against lethal poisons distributed either by private individuals or by public officials, it is surely only because our forefathers, despite their considerable wisdom and foresight could conceive of no such problem [14:9-12].

Tolerance Levels for Human Intake
of Various Pesticides

The World Health Organization has developed tolerance levels for the amounts of various pesticides in common usage which may be consumed on a daily basis by humans without danger. The study points out that the levels they have established are based on research to date and are subject to change as the state of knowledge concerning this matter increases.

The acceptable daily intake of a chemical is the daily intake which, during an entire lifetime, appears to be without appreciable risk on the basis of all the known facts at the time [36:22].

The term appreciable risk as used by the World Health Organization is taken to mean the "practical certainty that injury will not result even after a lifetime of exposure" [36:23].

As the World Health Organization points out these tolerances are not infallible. At best they provide rough guidelines for determining whether or not a given residue level on a given commodity is known to be dangerous. The difficulty of establishing levels which are absolutely safe is compounded by the unknown effect time may play on concentrations of pesticides stored in one's body. In a previous section of this chapter documented evidence was presented which showed the mutagenic and carcenogenic effects of certain pesticides. This phenomenon requires time on the order of generations to manifest its effects. Similarly, the synergistic reactions which certain pesticides have when they come in contact with other pesticides or other chemicals has been shown to have serious implications.

Beyond these two questions which cannot be adequately answered at this time is the fact that today people are in many cases being exposed to pesticides in concentrations which exceed the recommendations of the World Health Organization [22:103]. For example, DDT and DDE residues have been found on food commodities at the levels of 0.862 and 0.915 parts per million respectively. The practical residue limits for DDT or any combination of DDT, DDD, or DDE has been established by the World Health Organization at 0.2 to 0.005 parts per million (Table 14-9). Of course there are more flagrant examples of pesticide concentrations in food commodities. In Wisconsin a sample of

Table 14.9

Summary of Recommended Acceptable Daily Tolerances and Practical Residue Limits

Compound	Maximum Acceptable Daily Intake (mg./kg. body-wieght)[a]	Tolerances (ppm)[b]	Practical Residue Limits (ppm)[b]
chlordane	0.001	0.1 - 0.3	0.1
DDT (or any combination of DDT, DDD, or DDE)	0.01	1.0 - 7.0	0.2 - 0.005
dieldrin	0.0001	0.1 - 0.05	0.2 - 0.005
heptachlor	0.0005	0.1	0.2 - 0.005
lindane	0.0125	3.0 - 0.5	0.7 - 0.004
malathion	0.02	3.0 - 8.0	(None given)
MGK 264	None recommended	None recommended	None recommended
parathion	0.005	1.0 - 0.5	(None given)
endosulfan	None recommended	None recommended	None recommended

[a]Mg./kg.-miligrams of the chemical per kilogram of body weight

[b]Ppm - parts per million

Source: United Nations, World Health Organization, *Pesticide Residues, Report of the Joint Meeting of the FAO Working Party and the WHO Expert Committee* (WHO Technical Report Series No. 391), 1968, pp. 29-36.

2,600 fish were found to contain concentrations of DDT ranging from .02 to 16.2 parts per million for the whole fish and .22 to 534.6 parts per million in the adiopose tissue (27).

Hence, the inhabitants of this planet are being exposed to levels of pesticides which in the view if eminent authorities are in excess of safe levels. Moreover, these same experts suggest that even the safe levels may be suspect given the long-run aspect of the problem and a lack of knowledge in this regard.

Again the evidence suggests that it is imprudent to place primary reliance upon pesticidal chemicals as a means of environmental control. Given the irretrievable consequences which may result from their use, it is evident that a shift from pesticidal to bioenvironmental control of pests is in the best interests of the citizenry.

National Ban on the Sale of DDT Proposed

Senator Gaylord Nelson of Wisconsin has proposed legislation which would prohibit the interstate sale or use of DDT. The bill deals exclusively with DDT and makes no reference to other pesticides. The Senator also plans to introduce legislation which if adopted would establish a national scientific commission to study all pesticides and establish firm regulations for their use.

The proposal of this ban corresponds to an increased public awareness of the problem. This awareness is in part due to the nationwide news coverage received by the recent hearings concerning pesticides in Wisconsin. Moreover, recent articles in such newspapers as *The Wall Street Journal* and *The New York Times* have presented the facts to the public on a broader scale than has ever before been achieved. Although a national ban remains a question with which the Congress must deal, three states have already banned the use of DDT. These states are Arizona, Michigan, and Wisconsin [34]. With so many pollutants and pesticides altering the environment, the time has come to err on the side of caution. Other states and ultimately the nation should follow the example of Arizona, Wisconsin, and Michigan. The evidence has been presented time and again, the problem is too serious to delay action any longer.

The sex hormones affected in rats by the DDT activated enzymes are the same ones found in man. The amount of DDT needed to produce the effect is within the range of DDT found in human fat . . . thus, if one can extrapolate data from test organisms to man then one would say that the change in these enzymes probably do occur in man [35].

Action should not be delayed until conspicuous serious damage is done. In Michigan, the ban on DDT came only after a million coho salmon were killed as the result of pesticidal poisoning and the authorities declared that "irreparable contamination" of the lake region was imminent [33].

A Safe Alternative to Pesticidal Control

Bioenvironmental pest control involves the reduction of pest populations to tolerable density levels by the manipulation of the pests environment, physiology, genetics or behavior, or by employing a combination of these means.

For certain pests there are no immediate prospects for the development of effective bioenvironmental controls. Many conventional pesticides are currently indispensable for maintaining current food and fibre production as well as the health of man and animals. Moreover, all pesticides are not persistent and are not highly toxic to man and other warm blooded species and, in general, do not represent serious threats to the environment.

An effort to formulate and implement a well-coordinated and diversified control program is being made among many of our Federal agencies. Numerous avenues of research and development can be followed to reduce pollution hazards without sacrificing agricultural productivity.

It is estimated that thorough application of our present knowledge of pest suppression through integrated control programs could result in certain cases in an immediate reduction of pesticide pollution to about one half of existing levels. A further major reduction in pollution can be made through the development of bioenvironmental methods for the 100 major pests of plants and animals in the United States. These developments would free the grower from the costly routine treatment schedule and place him on a treat when necessary basis [9:234].

Bioenvironmental Methods of Pest Control

The development of bioenvironmental controls is not an easy task. The numbers and complexity of the various species present an awesome problem to the advocates of this approach. It is apparent that no single method will be satisfactory for dealing with all of the species in such a diverse group. There are numerous approaches to the problem and some of the more significant methods are discussed in the following pages.

Parasites and Predators

One of the most important causes of animal and insect mortality is the impact of parasites and predators. The deliberate use of these natural enemies to reduce the numbers of undesirable creatures in a given area is a form of biological control.

All species of insects are attacked by parasites and/or predators. Most are kept in check through this natural process with only 1 percent of the total exceeding the threshold at which they are considered pests. Natural enemies are sometimes destroyed by the use of pesticides in a nonselective manner resulting in a new candidate to the rank of pest.

The use of natural enemies in this country dates back the to the nineteenth century. Early efforts were limited but highly successful, for example:

The Vedalis beetle was introduced to California in 1888-1889 and quickly provided complete control of the cottony-cushion scale, for which no other effective control was known, thereby saving the California citrus industry from extinction. This control continues unabated today, 76 years later [9:234].

The Sterile Insect Release Method

The sterile insect release method provides a new principle of control which may change the whole concept of insect control. Insects may be sterilized by means of gamma radiation or by application of chemosterilants. The process of releasing sterile insects to compete with other insects for mates has the ultimate effect of reducing the numbers of the species.

The male sterilization technique was developed by Dr. Edward Knipling and his associates. Dr. Knipling is the chief of the United States Department of Agriculture Entomology Research Branch. After many years of work a major experiment was conducted in August 1954.

Screw-worms reared and sterilized in an Agriculture Department laboratory in Florida were flown to Curacoa (an island in the Caribbean) and released from airplanes at the rate of about 400 per square mile per week. Almost at once the number of egg masses deposited on experimental goats began to decrease as did their fertility. Only seven weeks after the releases were started all eggs were infertile. Soon it was impossible to find a single egg mass sterile or otherwise. The screw-worm had indeed been eradicated on Curacoa [39].

Although this experiment was a great success the application of this technique on a large scale remains a difficult problem for many varieties of pests in many locations. Experiments are being conducted to determine the feasibility of introducing chemosterilants into the pests environment. This approach would eliminate the necessity of raising and releasing sterile males into an area threatened with a pest problem. The Department of Agriculture is continuing its work in this area, some recent remarks by a Department spokesman indicate the possibilities of this approach:

Recently, we demonstrated eradication of the melon fly a relative of the Mediterranean fruit fly in an experiment on the islant of Rota, demonstrating for the first time that a multiple-mating inset can be eradicated in this manner.

And work is underway on such insects as the boll weevil, the pink bollworm, the tobacco budworm, and a number of others.

We think that this method can be an important aid in combating some of our major insect pests and, of course the method is highly specific [4:1075-1076].

Insect behavior is governed by their internal physiological condition and their response to external stimuli. Physical and chemical stimuli play major roles in three aspects of their behavior. Those aspects are breeding, mating, and oviposting. The behavior of the insect in finding a mate, having attained the necessary physiological conditions, and in copulating after the mate has been selected is regulated by chemicals, sounds, and various electromagnetic radiations. Studies of the specific circumstances and elements surrounding the habits of many insects have been made and the chemicals synthesized in a few cases.

An outstanding example of the practical application of attractants in insect control is found in the recent eradication of the Mediterranean fruit fly from Florida. The principle method used was the distribution of a protein hydolysate bait containing malathion. In this case, the distribution of the bait was widespread. The distribution was accomplished by airplane, but the attractiveness of the bait made possible the use of a nonpersistent insecticide and provided eradication with a much smaller quantity of insecticide than would have otherwise been possible [9:244].

The principle advantages generally attributed to biological controls are (1) that once effected control is relatively permanent; (2) they have no undesirable side effects such as toxicity, or environmental pollution; and (3) the cost in relation to the savings they effect are low.

There are three basic kinds of biological controls: conservation, introduction, and inundation. The conservation effort involves the appreciation of the conditions under which natural enemies will survive as well as the use of highly selective pesticides as a measure of last resort. The introduction of natural enemies into an area threatened by an abundance of a given pest requires a thorough understanding of the specific principles of predation and parasitism applicable to a given species. If this understanding can be achieved, it is then possible to introduce a natural enemy or parasite into an area which has a pest problem and by so doing reduce or eliminate the problem [9:234]. The process of inundation is the same as that described in the introduction of natural enemies approach. The difference is in the intensity of the introduction and the goal of complete destruction of a pest population [9:234].

Pathogenic Control

It is only in the last two decades that there has been significant research devoted to the diseases of insects and the possibility of using such knowledge as a means of pest control.

Some outstanding examples of insect pest control by means of microorganisms include the Japanese beetle (milky disease) and the European spruce sawfly (virus disease).

The milky disease of the Japanese beetle is caused by a bacterium, and infection occurs when the beetle grubs ingests the bacteria. The mechanical dissemination, mainly on turf, of commercially produced spore dusts of this bacterium throughout the northeastern part of the United States, has resulted in permanent control within three years [9:236].

The advantages of microbal control include (a) the generally harmless and nontoxic nature of insect pathogens for mammals; (b) the high degree of specificity of most pathogens, which tends to protect beneficial insects and mites; (c) the compatibility of many pathogens with many pesticides enables the two to be used concurrently; and (d) the high versatility of pathogens in so far as methods of application are concerned.

Some of the difficulties of microbal controls include (a) the need for exact timing in the application of the pathogen with respect to the incubation period of the disease; (b) the need to maintain the pathogen in a viable condition until the pest is contacted; (c) the difficulty of producing some pathogens in large quantities at a low cost; and (d) the requirement of some pathogens for favorable climatic conditions to infest the pest species. It is apparent that further research is needed in this area, but it is heartening to note that a shift in emphasis has begun to take place. This is indicated by a statement made before the United States Senate by a spokesman of the Department of Agriculture.

Two thirds of our present total research effort on insects is aimed at finding ways to control insects biologically, developing highly specific chemicals, and studying the life cycles of pests in the hope of being able to interrupt these cycles on a mass scale [4:1091].

Environmental Manipulation

Pest problems are created by environmental conditions which favor the pest. Changing the environment may make it less favorable to the pest and hence serve to control or reduce their rate of reproduction as well as shortening their life span. Environmental manipulation for pest control includes plant spacing, species diversity, timing, crop rotation, plant hormones, water management, fertilization, soil preparation, and sanitation.

Preliminary research has indicated that insect damage to crops can be reduced through changing the spacing of plants. The relative rate of growth of a plant and the behavior of the pest in searching for food may be affected. Diseases of pests may also be enhanced by the manipulation of spatial patterns. Similarly, the alternative of placing plants far apart may hinder pests in finding their host plants.

The maintenance of the diversity of the landscape is also a significant means of holding a pest population in check. Plant diversity supports greater animal diversity which in turn serves to maintain the balance of nature. Although this approach may be incongruent with modern agricultural techniques, it may be adaptable as a supplemental part of an integrated pest control program to be employed on the fringes of croplands [4:238].

The timing of planting of crops may also serve as a means of pest control. If the plants are planted so as to have their most susceptible stages of development coincide with a low ebb in the seasonal abundance of the pest, damage to crops may be held down. This approach is limited to those varieties of crops whose growing seasons and dispositions allow for such flexibility given the limitations of climate. Some examples of effective use of this technique include the control of the pickleworm, which is controlled in pickling cucumbers by growing the crop in the spring before the annual invasion of the pest from areas along the Gulf coast where it is endemic. In much the same manner, the clover midge boll weevil and pink bottworm are controlled in many areas of the nation.

Use of this technique alone can reduce the population of these pests by one generation each year [4:238].

Crop rotation may also serve as a deterrent to insect ravages. For example northern and western corn rootworms which lay their eggs in the soil during the summer and late fall and hatch about the time the corn emerges the following spring may be controlled reasonably well by not planting corn for two successive years. A rotation in which oats or some leguminous crop follows corn provides food plants which are unsatisfactory to the hatching larvae.

Mosquitoes whose larval stages are spent in water are effectively controlled in many cases by making small changes in the water level of the impoundent to allow more effective predation by fish such as Sambusia. Moderate adjustments in the time schedule of flooding and draining irrigated fields can reduce mosquitoes breeding greatly by rendering oviposition sites unsatisfactory. Draining rice rields at the proper time and withholding further irrigation until the soil has dried to a point beyond which the crop would suffer from water stress has been used successfully for more than 40 years as the only method for control of the rice water weevil [4:239].

Geneticists are working on techniques which alter the genetic makeup of the species which it is desired to control. Work has been done in the areas of lethal genes, male-producing genes, plant-pest gene complexes, and insecticide unfavorable gene complexes. To date there have been considerable advances in these fields, but as a practical means of pest control these techniques are still in the experimental stages of development.

It appears that bioenvironmental controls offer an alternative to pesticidal controls. Although they do not represent a panacea for all of our problems at present, they offer a beginning for the future. A prudent course of action is the adoption of those bioenvironmental methods which have already proven practical and efficacious, while continuing the research effort to perfect those methods which are still in the experimental stage.

The Economics of Bioenvironmental and
Pesticidal Control of Pests

In an effort to compare the effectiveness and the relative cost of the two methods of pest control, a study of the activities in California was undertaken. California is atypical in that it invests the greatest part of its resources in research on biological pest control. In fact, its expenditures are almost equal to those of all other states combined. California produces over $3.7 billion per year in agriculture products with about one-third of its population being engaged in the industry at varying levels of activity.

The cost of pesticidal control is higher than that of biological or bioenvironmental control.

The result is that pesticidal control as an economic proposition without consideration of possible undesirable effects is only about 1/6 as attractive as biological control [4:269].

Table 14.10

Number of Major Pests in California Forestry and Agriculture

Pest	Number
Insects, mites, and other athropods	107
Weeds	61
Plant diseases	30

Source: U. S. President's Science Advisory Committee, Environmental Pollution Panel, *Restoring the Quality of Our Environment* (Washington, D. C.: The White House, 1965), p. 268.

Table 14.11

The Relative Cost of Pesticidal vs. Biological and Bioenvironmental Controls

Type of control	Research and development	Retail and application costs
Biological Control	$800,000.	$300,000.
Other Bioenvironmental controls	$325,000.	$2,237,000.
Pesticide Controls	$13,250,000.	$230,000,000.
Total	$14,375,000.	$232,637,000.

Source: U. S., President's Science Advisory Committee, Environmental Pollution Panel, *Restoring The Quality of Our Environment* (Washington, D. C.: The White House, 1965), p. 268.

Great benefits have been reaped by mankind in terms of production of food commodities as the result of the application of pesticides. Those benefits have enabled man to grow and prosper. However, the environmental threats associated with the use of pesticides have begun to cast a cloud of suspicion as to the wisdom of massive reliance upon pesticides given the long-run ecological implications which the mounting evidence suggests for the future. Vast amounts of time, money, and energy have been and are continuing to be spent in an effort to fully appreciate the nature and scope of the pesticide syndrome. Although the knowledge to date is inconclusive, we are looking in the right places and one has the impression that in time the dangers will become less mysterious and hence pose less of a threat as they are understood and a change in emphasis begins to take hold. With the growing store of knowledge in entomology, one may speculate that the growing trend toward bioenvironmental controls will be the wave of the future. One can envision the selective use of specific, nonpersistent pesticides in appropriate situations with the main burden of control being achieved by means of bioenvironmental procedures.

If we fail to move in this direction no one can predict the extent of the environmental pollution we risk. The known and suspected dangers to man and his environment have been presented in an effort to focus attention on the problem and point out the seriousness of the consequences which are being risked by our massive reliance upon pesticidal chemicals.

If we continue to rely on pesticides as our prime means of pest control, what will be the consequences in twenty or forty years? No one can answer this question, but the amounts of pesticides we are employing currently, as well as what will be used in the future if we do not shift our emphasis, cannot be assumed to be without adverse effect given what is known about them.

Pesticide Production and Projections

It has been shown that there is grave concern in many quarters concerning our current use of vast amounts of pesticidal chemicals. In an effort to place the problem in a perspective, one must appreciate the amounts of the various pesticides which are currently being employed in this country. These figures should be viewed in light of the preceeding pages which reported the various serious dangers involved with their use.

Pesticide production and use is related to a variety of variables. It is dependent upon the cropland under cultivation, the acreage required for grazing, weather conditions, the perceived potential threat from plant and animal predators, the crop yield expectations from cultivated acreage, and ultimately, upon the population of the nation which determines the demand for the produce in question. Since there are so many variables to be considered, it is apparent that no single projection beyond a five-year period will have a great deal of validity. Hence, in an attempt to appreciate the scale of pesticide production in the years 1980 and 2000, an effort to project the scale of

based upon various alternative sets of assumptions has been
The work of RFF has been used as the basis of the projections
this text [37].

F projected the acreage requirements for crops and pasture in the
years anead. Their projections are shown in Table 14-12. Their model presents
low, medium, and high projections for acreage requirements which are combined
with low, medium, and high demand requirements. Hence, the state of demand
and the level of technology and productivity have been incorporated into their
model.

Working from their projections of land requirements, an effort has been made
to correlate the amount of pesticides which may be utilized at the various levels
of production anticipated. In so doing, the assumption has been made that
entomology will not provide any revolutions resulting in the displacement of
pesticides as the major deterrent to the destruction of pests.

In 1964, approximately 35 percent of the acreage harvested on which corn,
small grains, and cotton were harvested was treated with pesticides (Table
14-16). Using the RFF projections (Table 14-12) for these commodities
and the acreage required for each based on various sets of alternative
assumptions, the projections for acreage to be treated in the future are
calculated and presented in Table 14-17.

In 1964, 103 million acres were treated for weed, insect, and fungus control
in the United States (Table 14-13). To achieve this level of application, over 692
million pounds of pesticides were sold in the United States in 1964
(Table 14-14). This is a rate of slightly over six pounds of pesticides per acre
treated. If this rate of application is similar in the years 1980 and 2000, the
amount of pesticides required in these years may be calculated. These
calculations are presented in Table 14-18.

It is estimated here that the sales volume of pesticides in the United States in
the year 1980 will lie within 672 to 936 million pounds. Simiarly, the estimate
for the year 2000 ranges from 684 to 1,350 million pounds of pesticides. If the
upper projection is correct for 1980, pesticide production will have increased by
35 percent over the 1964 figure. If the lower projection is more accurate,
pesticide production may in fact remain at about the same level it was in 1964.
If the upper projection for the year 2000 is accurate, pesticide production will
have increased by about 95 percent over the 1964 figure. If alternatively, the
medium projections for 1980 and 2000 are more appropriate given the state of
reality at that time, an increase of 34 and 43 percent, respectively, may be
anticipated in those years.

The fact is that it is clearly infeasible to project pesticide production on the
basis of past rates of usage and economic forecasts of the volume of crop output.
The economic forecasts, though notoriously hazardous, are not the weak links in
predicting the future of pesticides. Rather, it is evident that public opinion
concerning the possible harmful side effects of their use will be decisive.

Actually, the estimates advanced in this study and contained in Table 14-18
are conservative compared to the prognostications advanced by some authorities
in recent months.

Table 14.12

**Projected Acreages Required for Crops
Under Different Demand and Yield
Assumptions** (million acres)

Commodity	1960	Demand yield assumption	1970	1980	2000
Feed grains	133.6	HL[a]	113.5	116.3	112.9
		MM[b]	102.6	109.6	124.6
		LH[c]	105.6	115.3	154.9
Wheat, cotton,	287.0	HL[a]	278.0	294.0	303.0
soybeans, and hay		MM[b]	266.0	296.0	346.0
		LH[c]	264.0	296.0	383.0
Total cropland	313	HL[a]	303.0	319.0	328.0
required		MM[b]	290.0	323.0	378.0
		LH[c]	288.0	323.0	416.0

[a]HL - High demand low yield assumption.   [c]LH - Low demand high yield assumption.

[b]MM - Medium demand medium yield
assumption.

Source: *Resources in America's Future*, pp. 979-980.

Last year, sales of pesticides increased 12 percent of the previous year and, by 1985, it is estimated that they will increase another sixfold [27].

This statement by Senator Gaylord Nelson of Wisconsin is meant to express his alarm at this prospect, an alarm which has led him and other goverment officials to exert increasingly effective constraints on the uninhibited use of synthetic chemical pesticides. The latter tendencies rather than freely operating economic forces will determine future levels of chemical pesticide production.

Summary

The preceding pages have presented the most serious aspects of the pesticide syndrome. It has been established that there are real dangers to man, animals,

Table 14.13

**Pest Control by Type of Crop: Acreage
Treated in the United States, 1964**
(million acres)

Crop and purpose of treatment	Acreage treated	Percent of total
Insect and fungus control		
Grain	16,260	42.7
Cotton	8,285	21.3
Fruits and nuts	3,296	8.5
Hay crops	2,273	5.8
Vegetables	1,972	5.1
Seed crops	6,475	16.1
Total	38,924	100.0
Weed control		
Corn	27,130	42.1
Small grains[a]	21,107	32.7
Cotton	4,046	6.3
Pastures	3,688	5.7
Other	8,527	13.2
Total	64,500	100.0

[a]Includes wheat, oats, barley, rice, rye, proso millet, safflower, flax seed, and buckwheat.

Source: U. S. Department of Agriculture, *The Pesticide Review* (Washington, D. C.: U. S. Government Printing Office, 1967), p. 14.

Table 14.14

**Sales Volume of Synthetic Organic
Pesticides in the United States**
(1,000 pounds)

Use	1963	1964	1965
Fungicides	93,625	95,956	105,938
Herbicides	122,872	152,027	183,444
Insecticides, fumigants, rodenticides, and soil conditioners	435,334	444,772	472,863
Total	651,471	692,355	762,745

Source: U. S. Department of Agriculture, *The Pesticide Review* (Washington, D. C.: U. S. Government Printing Office, 1967), p. 2.

and the general quality of the environment stemming from our massive reliance upon pesticidal chemicals as a means of entomological control. It has been shown that (a) pesticides are enormously toxic; (b) they are persistent in the soil; (c) they are present in the air and water; (d) they are stored in the bodies of man and animals; (e) bodily storage has resulted in various carcenogenic and mutagenic effects upon test organisms; and (f) there is the imponderable question of synergism and the potential long-run prospect of increased danger given the effect on the chain of life. It has also been shown that there is another road which we may follow. This road involves the shift in our massive reliance on pesticides to the proven techniques of bioenvironmental control where practical. Such a shift would reduce the dangers of pollution and give us time to understand the problem more fully. In light of all that is known about pesticides, it seems prudent that we shift the burden of proof and that we rely on absolutely safe methods of control until it can be proven unequivocally that there is safety in massive reliance upon pesticides.

Table 14.15

Breakdown of Pesticidal Chemical Production in the United States, 1964–1966 (1,000 pounds)

Chemical	1964	1965	1966
Fungicides			
Copper napthenate	1,897	3,268	3,201
Copper sulphate	41,816	47,272	41,504
Ferbam	1,838	2,384	1,379
Mercury fungicides	1,138	1,602	1,035
Nabam	2,251	2,489	2,053
Penachlorophenol (PCP)	36,901	39,965	43,262
2,4,5 - Trichlorophenol	4,790	4,003	5,958
Zineb	6,664	5,075	4,721
Other organic fungicides	48,352	44,969	63,818
Total	145,647	151,027	166,931
Herbicides			
2,4 - D Acid	53,714	63,320	68,182
2,4 - D Acid esters and salts	54,366	63,360	72,522
DNBP	4,146	4,619	(not available)
DNBP ammonium salt	55	59	85
Phenyl mercuric (PMA)	495	588	502
Sodium chlorate	35,000	32,000	32,000
2,4,5 - Tacid esters and salts	12,963	13,516	18,059

Table 14.15 (*continued*)

Chemical	1964	1965	1966
Herbicides			
2,4,5 - Tacid	11,434	11,601	15,489
Other organic herbicides	87,046	105,861	148,765
Total	196,238	220,003	271,933
Insecticides, fumigants, and rodenticides			
Aldrin - toxaphene group	105,296	118,832	130,470
Calcium arsenate	6,958	4,192	3,000
DDT	123,709	140,785	141,349
Dibromochloropropane	5,314	3,433	8,722
Lead arsenate	9,258	7,098	7,000
Methyl bromide	16,994	14,303	16,345
Methyl parathion	18,640	29,111	35,862
Parathion	12,768	16,607	19,444
TEPP	669	(not available)	(not available)
Other organics	163,715	167,368	199,404
Total	463,321	501,729	561,596
Grand total	805,206	872,759	1,000,460

Source: U. S. Department of Agriculture, *The Pesticides Review* (Washington, D. C.: U. S. Government Printing Office, 1967), pp. 3-4.

Table 14.16

Acreage Treated for Pest Control in the United States, 1964

Crop	Acres Harvested	Acres treated
Corn	63,515,151	27,130,711
Small grains[a]	83,624,139	21,107,303
Cotton	13,913,478	8,285,994
Total	161,052,768	56,524,008

[a]Includes wheat, oats, barley, rice, rye, proso millet, safflower, flaxseed, and buckwheat.

Source: U. S. Department of Agriculture, *The Pesticide Review* (Washington, D. C.: U. S. Government Printing Office, 1967), p. 15.

Table 14-17

Projected Acreage to Be Treated with Pesticides in 1980 and 2000 (million acres)

Projection model	Projected acreage to be harvested		Projected acreage to be treated with pesticides	
	1980	*2000*	*2980*	*2000*
Low	319	328	112	114
Medium	323	378	113	133
High	445	645	156	225

Source: *Projected acreage to be harvested -* Hans H. Landsberg, Leonard L. Fischman and Joseph L. Fisher, *Resources in America's Future* (Baltimore, Md.; Johns Hopkins Press, 1963) Table A 18-9. The projection model designated Low here is described by RFF as follows: "The Low-Low model minimizes acreage requirements by combining Low demand, High feed efficiency, High use of concentrates with High crop yields." The model designated here as High is described by RFF as follows: "The High-High model maximizes acreage requirements by combining High demand, Low feed efficiency, and Low use of concentrates with Low crop yields." The model designated here as Medium "is based on Medium assumptions for both demand and yields." *Projected acreage to be treated with pesticides -* Figures under this heading are derived by multiplying the appropriate figures under "Projected acreage to be harvested by 35 percent, the percentage of harvested acreage found to be treated with pesticides in Table 14-16.

Table 14.18

Projected Sales Volume of Pesticides in the United States for 1980 and 2000
(in millions)

	1980		2000	
Projection model	Projected acreage to be treated[a]	Projected sales of pesticides (pounds)	Projected acreage to be treated[a]	Projected sales of pesticides (pounds)
Low	112	672	114	684
Medium	155	930	166	996
High	156	936	225	1,350

[a]Compiled in Table 14.16.

Source: *Resources in America's Future*, p. 979-980; and U. S. Department of Agriculture, *The Pesticide Review* (Washington, D. C.: U. S. Government Printing Office, 1967), p. 14.

15 Eutrophication and Nutrient Sources

Robert J. Butscher

Introduction

Definition

Nutrient enrichment of waters is part of the natural geological process in the aging of a lake. This process is referred to as natural eutrophication. The meaning of eutrophication comes directly from the Greek *eu* meaning "well" and *trophein* meaning "to nourish" [36:4]. The influx of mineral nutrients to a lake is necessary to the biological growth of aquatic life that serve as food for fish, shellfish, and crustaceans which are then harvested by man. In fact, all plant and animal life require mineral nutrients to grow and reproduce.

This water enrichment process, however productive to necessary aquatic life, controls the life of the lake. If the flow of nutrients (primarily nitrogen and phosphorus) is accelerated the life of the lake can be adversely affected. Excessive growths of algae and other aquatic forms may occur as a result of overfertilization. It is only when such enrichment causes these phenomena that the term "eutrophication" is used to identify and classify a type of water pollution.

The effects of eutrophication also occur, in varying degrees, in rivers and estuary areas. This chapter will concentrate on lakes and other stillwater bodies.

Natural Eutrophication

In general, as a lake ages naturally it undergoes change and a process of maturation takes place. The original state of a lake is classified as oligotrophic. The water is blue or greenish-blue, clear and transparent, and its content of phosphorus compounds is so low that the development of phytoplankton and littoral plants is slight [16:299]. Dissolved oxygen is abundant.

Tributaries and wind carry dead leaves, pollen grains, insects, excrement from forest animals, and other organisms to the lake. These organisms decompose in the water, releasing fertilizers which can result in the increased development of plankton and shore algae. As fertility increases, so does biological production. The lake becomes greener from the proliferation of single-celled algae and tends to absorb more solar radiation and reflect less. This creates higher temperatures that speed the biological process. Thus the process of enrichment tends to be self-accelerating [22:4].

Other natural sources of algal growth materials are air and rain which contain nitrogen and phosphorus. Rain tends to wash the atmosphere. Water plants and animals die and release fertilizers. Muds at the bottom of lakes contain nutrients and runoff from natural, uncultivated land provide additional amounts.

Man-generated Sources of Nutrients

In the last several decades, especially the past several years, scientists and engineers are learning that lakes can be excessively and unintentionally enriched. The natural eutrophication process is being accelerated as a result of intense urbanization and changes in agricultural methods. The discharge of effluent from sewage plants which have partially treated human waste as well as the discharge of raw sewage directly into lakes and streams, all contribute to a buildup of nutrients in the receiving water bodies. The use of detergents represent a distinct source of phosphorus and a separate problem. Industrial effluents also contain nitrogen and phosphorus. Runoff from urban lands carry pet excrement and nutrients in other forms.

Agricultural sources of nutrients include both chemical fertilizers and animal wastes. Manure has been found to be a very significant contributor in local regions. Nitrogen in fertilizers can leach through the soil and is carried to lakes by ground water. Both nitrogen and phosphorus are carried by erosion.

The amounts of nitrogen and phosphorus reaching waters that can be attributed to man-generated and natural sources are as yet largely unknown. This chapter will attempt to evaluate and project the effects of the various nutrient sources. The nutrient sources that directly contribute to eutrophication are fertilizers, livestock, detergents, and urban and industrial wastes. The effects of accelerated eutrophication and the forces tending to offset it are then discussed, concluding with a forecast of the magnitude and impact of future eutrophication trends.

Projections of Nutrient Contributing Factors by RFF

Classification of Such Factors

As previously noted, the process of accelerated enrichment and its effect on America's lakes has been as a direct result of man's activities. The greater use of water by the population, agriculture, and industry (including power plants) has increased the influx of nutrients, fostering algae growth in both large and small lakes and other water bodies. RFF states that "by far the larger proportions of water used for industrial, steam-electric, and municipal purposes are returned to water courses" [2:261]. For purposes of classification the projections of these activities have been grouped into three broad categories: (1) urbanization and associated activities; (2) chemical fertilizers and livestock production; and (3) industrial water use and heat dissipated in electric power generation.

RFF have amassed various historical values and projections to the year 2000 which can be utilized to trace both recent and future trends in these activities.

Intense urbanization and associated activities: Intense urbanization has been pointed to as a major source of nutrient material. The most important being plant nutrients in the form of nitrogen and phosphorus. Both of these elements are found in human excreta and phosphorus is a base material in household detergents. Three series compiled by RFF are immediately relevant to the effects man's numbers are having on the output of nutrients. Human waste is increasing directly with the increase in population. This fact is further emphasized by the increased use and discharge of fresh water by municipalities, especially in the East where the density of population is the greatest. The use of detergents is also on an upward trend.

Table 15-1 portrays these three series to the year 2000. Historical values are given for the last 20 years (where possible) and future estimates are presented as low, medium, and high projections. The first shows total population for the United States. The second reflects total municipal water withdrawals in the East destined for discharge into fresh water. The third displays synthetic detergent production. Each of the series show a consistent increase.

Output of chemical fertilizers and livestock production: In some areas of the country, especially in the midwest, agricultural activities including the use of chemical fertilizers and the raising of livestock have increased tremendously in recent years. The indications are that such increases will continue in the future.

Chemical fertilizers are being used in increasing amounts. Modern technology and the low cost of nitrogen (see section on effects of eutrophication) has permitted more extensive application of nitrogen and phosphorus to encourage crop production. Crops, however, do not absorb all these nutrients. Large quantities remain in or on the soil and are carried to water bodies as a result of leaching, runoff after rainstorms or by irrigation waters.

In recent years, it has been found that it is more economical to feed cattle, hogs, and poultry in concentrated feedlots. Large numbers of animals are held and fed on relatively small areas of land. Huge quantities of manure from such livestock and poultry accumulates on the land surface and are carried to water bodies following rainstorms or by percolation.

Three series compiled by RFF show increases in use of fertilizers, irrigation trends, and growth of livestock production. Table 15-2 presents these three series. Historical values and future projections are given. The first series shows farm outlays on fertilizers and lime. The second gives total return flow of fresh water used in irrigation in the West. The third displays the demand for animal products as produced. This series is in three parts: (1) cattle and calves, (2) hogs, and (3) commercial broilers. Again, each of the series show a consistent increase.

Table 15.1

Historical Values and Low, Medium, and High Projections of Population, Municipal Water Withdrawal, and Detergent Production

	1945	1950	1955	1960		1970	1980	1990	2000
Total population (in mill.)[a]		151.7	165.3	179.9	L	202	226	249	268
					M	208	245	287	331
					H	223	279	349	433
Municipal water withdrawal in the East destined for discharge into fresh water (mill. gal. per day)[b]			5,397[d]	6,119	L	6,875	7,624	8,281	8,273
					M	7,380	8,958	10,673	12,480
					H	8,175	10,758	13,965	17,705
Synthetic detergent production (mill. lbs.)[c]	150	1,443	2,704	3,970	L	5,250	6,330	6,970	7,500
					M	5,410	6,860	8,040	9,270
					H	5,800	7,810	9,770	12,100

[a]Source: Table A1-1, pp. 516-517.
[b]Source: Table A14-1, pp. 824-825.
[c]Source: Table A17-11, p. 967.
[d]For year 1954.

Source: *Resources in America's Future,* as listed in footnotes.

Industrial Water Use and Heat Dissipated in Electric Power Generation: The effluents of many industries contain nitrogen and/or phosphorus. A list of just a few include most of the major industries, namely, basic chemicals, textile mills, petroleum refining, sugar refining, and paper and allied products. State Senator Krueger of Wisconsin indicated that nine percent of the phosphates produced are used by industry in processing metals or in producing products such as insecticides and gasoline additives [7:2].

Thermal pollution resulting from the discharge of heated water by electric power companies (and also certain industries) affects the ecology of the water-receiving body. Of particular importance in this paper is that heated water accelerates the production of algae.

Two series prepared by RFF and presented in Table 15-3 are helpful in evaluating quantitatively the contribution of industrial and power plant effluent. The first shows fresh water used by the chemical industry; and the second, portrays total heat measured in B.T.U.'s (British Thermal Units) dissipated in thermalelectric power generation. The chemical industry was selected as an example of a water-using industry (although others would have served as well) primarily because it is the largest water user.

RFF Projections and the
Adequacy of the Resource Base

The process of eutrophication is a complex one and not subject to precise quantitative study. Insofar as this chapter seeks to suggest the magnitude of the factors contributing to the increase in eutrophication of United States waters, it will do so by reference to RFF projections of output as in other chapters. Insofar as the series of most interest for this chapter are concerned, a comparison of the RFF projections with recorded statistics through the mid-1960s indicates that the projections are reasonably close to the mark. The rate of population increase is the principal determinant of the contribution of human sewage to eutrophication since present treatment methods do not remove plant nutrients. The population projections used by RFF were within 1/2 of one percent of the actual figures. RFF underestimated the level of farm outlays on fertilizers during the 1960s by about 10 percent. On the other hand, RFF overestimated by about 8 percent the amount of the increase in synthetic detergent production. However, both synthetic detergent production and farm fertilizer outlays increased very substantially as expected by RFF. (See Appendix A.) There is no reason to suppose that the medium projections of RFF will overstate markedly the rise in the output of products which contribute to eutrophication.

Nor is there any reason to suppose that a shortage of the chemical constituents of fertilizers or detergents will interfere with the realization of the RFF output projections.

Table 15.2

**Historical Values and Low, Medium, and
High Projections of Fertilizers, Irrigation
Water, and Livestock Production**

	1945	1950	1955	1960
Farm outlays on fertilizers and lime (bill. 1960 dollars)[a]		1.03	1.23	1.46
Return flow of fresh water used in irrigation in the West (mill. gal. per day)[b,d]			34,792[e]	39,453
Demand for animal products as produced (bill. lb. livewt.)[c]				
cattle and calves	19.6	20.7	27.9	28.6
hogs	18.8	19.8	19.5	20.0
commerical broilers	1.11	1.94	3.35	6.02

	1970	1980	1990	2000
L	1.5	1.8	1.9	2.1
M	2.0	2.7	3.5	4.3
H	2.4	3.6	4.3	7.6
L	38,491	36,567	36,642	33,680
M	38,491	38,888	41,673	44,354
H	38,491	39,314	45,243	53,118
L	34.1	39.8	43.9	47.2
M	39.6	50.6	60.6	69.8
H	44.1	60.4	78.9	99.4
L	24.5	28.2	31.1	33.6
M	24.5	30.5	37.9	44.3
H	29.5	37.3	49.3	62.0
L	8.2	9.9	11.0	11.8
M	7.1	9.2	10.8	12.4
H	6.7	8.6	10.8	13.6

[a]Source: Table A1-30, pp. 578-79.

[b]Source: Table A14-4, pp. 823-33

[c]Source: Table A12-1, p. 782.

[d]Derived by subtracting total depletion of water from total water diverted for irrigation.

[e]For year 1954.

Source: *Resources in America's Future*, as listed in footnotes.

Table 15.3

Historical Values and Low, Medium,
and High Projections of Chemical
Industry Water Use and Heat Dissipated

	1954	1960		1970	1980	1990	2000
Fresh water used in the chemical industry (mill. gal. per day)[a]			L	25,336	33,453	43,661	55,714
	12,305	19,432	M	31,116	47,104	69,734	102,818
			H	41,201	76,129	137,009	242,778
Heat dissipated in thermal–electric power generation (quadrillion (B.T.U.)[b,c]			L	8.44	11.93	15.09	19.00
	4.52	6.51	M	10.27	16.30	22.65	31.31
			H	13.72	23.32	34.86	51.95

[a]Source: Table A14-3, p. 827.

[b]Source: Table A14-2, p. 824.

[c]Derived by multiplying thermal-electric
utility output by heat rates assumed in

B. T. U. (British Thermal Unit) per Kwh.

Source: *Resources in America's Future*, as
listed below in footnotes.

**Effects of Eutrophication Associated with
Increased Amounts of Nutrients**

Accelerated Eutrophication

Lake waters have substantially less movement and replacement than other bodies
of water and as a result are more susceptible to the process of eutrophication.
The enormous increase in manmade nutrients in recent years has tremendously
accelerated the usually slow process of natural eutrophication. This increase in
the influx of nitrogen and phosphorus to lakes has been directly and

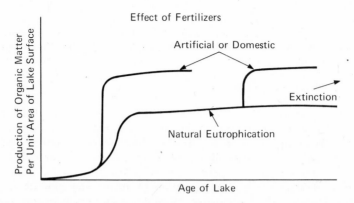

Figure 15-1 Hypothetical Curve of Eutrophication: The effect of artificial fertilization on the process of natural eutrophication. Source: Gerard A. Rohlich, *"Eutrophication"* (paper presented at the 41st Annual Convention of the Soap and Detergent Industry, New York City, January 25, 1968) p. 9.

substantially stimulated by the ever-increasing output of nutrients from sewage plants, raw sewage, detergents, industrial effluents, chemical fertilizers, and manure. These nutrients fertilize algae and aquatic weeds which clog and degrade the waters. Eventually swamps are produced and the lake is destroyed [5:5]. The natural process of enrichment is contrasted to the accelerated changes that occur as a result of man's activities in the hypothetical curve of eutrophication below (Figure 15-1).

The overfertilization of lakes encourages prolific growths of algae mosses and other aquatic vegetation. Blue-green algae has received most of the attention of scientists and engineers. One major reason for this recognition is because blue-green algae tends to bloom and float as large mats concentrated on the surface. Mats of algae over a foot thick covering several hundred square miles have been reported in Lake Erie [32:46]. Rooted vegetation grows in from the lake's shore. Areas of the lake become densely weed choked. Fish species change from valuable sport fish to rough fish such as carp.

The lake may become so filled with algae that it cannot survive. The algae dies and decays. Through biological degradation the decaying aquatic vegetation exerts a dissolved oxygen demand just above the bed of the lake and in the surface water near the shore [16:302]. Decomposing dead algae and other water plants deprive fish of oxygen, causing extensive fish kills.

A recent report of the Committee on Government Operations prepared by the National Resources and Power Subcommittee describes the results of a study made by the University of Michigan as follows:

Algae produce oxygen through photosynthesis and thereby increase the ability of lakes and streams to assimilate wastes. However, death and decay of large quantities of algae impose an additional load on the ecological system since oxygen is no longer produced by the algae but is required to degrade the algal cell material. After degradation, the inorganic nutrients are released back into the water; this tends to make the process self-perpetuating. Aquatic vegetation, particularly phytoplankton, is essential in the food chain, and an increase or decrease in the production of algae can induce subsequent imbalances in more highly developed species including fishes [5:6].

Algae is most prolific in the summer when such plants enjoy the benefit of sun and warm temperatures. It is also during this period that stratification occurs in lake waters. The water in the lower part of the lake (below the thermocline or line of stratification) remains stagnant with little mixing and is of essentially uniform temperature. Since this water is not subject to wind action, dissolved oxygen which is depleted by decomposition of plants and animals is not restored. The water over the thermocline, called the epilimnion, is warmer and is subject to wind action. In the fall when the temperatures of both layers become uniform, the period of overturn commences.

Thermal pollution has a direct effect upon this natural cycle. Heated water will cause the summer stratification of the lake to start sooner and last longer into the fall. The lake's growing season will be extended at both ends with a higher rate of biological production [22:5]. The effects of eutrophication are thus further accelerated by discharges of heated water.

The effects of eutrophication are not confined solely to lakes. As a result of unintentional or uncontrolled fertilization, irrigation systems, farm ponds, and reservoirs are similarly affected. Eutrophication is also a problem in estuaries, such as Boston Harbor, San Francisco Bay, San Pablo Bay, and Long Island waters.

Eutrophication is being recognized as one of the day's most urgent water pollution problems, and unless it is understood and controlled many of America's water resources may become fouled or destroyed completely. Floating algae scum are a nuisance to those who use the water commercially or for recreation.

Excessive algae growths in a lake cause the value of surrounding shore line property to decrease. Commercial fishing has been significantly curtailed in such waters as Lake Erie. Algal growth imparts undesirable tastes and odors to water supplies. Nearby industrial users who depend on the lake must filter the water to remove the algae, a costly step. "Eutrophication is a major cause of overloading, nuisance, and ultimate failure in raw sewage waste disposal ponds, and in receiving ponds for primary activated sludge, and trickling filter effluents" [28:965-66]. When algae mats accumulate in tertiary waste disposal ponds, the volume of effluent that can be handled is sharply reduced.

Algae interferes with the recreational use of the lake. Water sports, such as swimming, fishing, boating, and other water activities decline sharply. Certain species of algae are jellylike and entangle in a swimmer's hair and on his body. A slime is formed on the beach. Boat propellers and fishing lines get fouled in the vegetation. The dying off and rotting away of algae on the shoreline produces hydrogen sulfide. Decomposition of organic debris in the bottom muds produce offensive odors. And, blue-green algae may be toxic.

Paul R. Gorham at a 1962 water pollution symposium, presented case histories of death and other toxic effects resulting from concentrations of blue-green algal blooms [16:37,42]. He recited accounts of the death of livestocks, pets, waterfowl, and other animals. He also pointed out the potential hazard to public health. Algae can cause gastritis and allergies.

Specific Lakes Discussed

No lake is too large or too small to escape eutrophication and its effects. Some of the more popular lakes currently receiving attention are the Great Lakes, Lake Tahoe, and Lake Washington, among others. But other smaller, less known lakes are eutrophic and are causing extreme problems in areas surrounding these lakes. Onondoga Lake at Syracuse, New York, is one prime example.

To discuss Lake Erie, one of the Great Lakes, and Lake Tahoe in the same context may seem absurd. Lake Erie in some of its worst sections is like an open sewer. Lake Tahoe throughout its length and breadth is a lake as pure biologically as a mountain stream. But, Tahoe, better than Erie, exemplifies the process of eutrophication; i.e., the overrapid growth of vegetation due to excessive fertilization. Erie is a near hopeless case where biological pollution combines with excessive algae growth to accelerate the dying of this lake. But Tahoe, despite its biological purity, is experiencing rapid growth of algae which is turning its waters once famous for their sharp blue hues to a pale sickly green, even though no biological pollution has yet resulted. It is simply that the effluent from the growing population, attracted by the blue waters of the lake, is feeding the lake an overdose of plant nutrients, even though biological pollutants are removed by natural processes. In due time, continuing decay of algae in Tahoe, which uses up dissolved oxygen, could threaten biological pollution as well, if nothing were done.

The Great Lakes: Alfred M. Beeton of the U.S. Bureau of Commercial Fisheries applying various criteria used to evaluate the stages of eutrophication has classified the five Great Lakes [20:240-53]. He classifies Lakes Huron, Michigan, and Superior as oligotrophic on the basis of their biological, chemical, and physical characteristics. Lake Ontario, although rich in nutrients, is mesotrophic (meaning partly eutrophic) because of its large area of deep water. Lake Erie is eutrophic. It is the shallowest lake with a mean depth of 17.7 feet. Criteria used in classifying lakes are abundance of plankton, transparency, chemical characteristics, sediment types, distribution of dissolved oxygen, productivity, and fish populations. For example, Beeton classifies a lake as eutrophic if its mean depth is less than 20 feet, transparency is low, total dissolved solids exceed 100 parts per million (p.p.m.), and the oxygen level is less than 70 percent saturation in the hypolimnion (water in the lower part of the lake).

Lake Ontario although classified as mesotrophic has the physiochemical characteristics of being eutrophic. It should be noted that the main inflow to Lake Ontario is from Lake Erie via the Niagra River. Lake Michigan has a high content of dissolved solids (150 p.p.m.) and a low transparency of 6 on the Secchi disc (an instrument which measures light transparency). These characteristics indicate a trend to mesotrophy. Both Lakes Michigan and Ontario would be eutrophic except for large volumes of deep water. Data also indicated a progressive increase in the concentration of various major ions in all lakes except Lake Superior. Over the years plankton species have changed in Lake Michigan and also in Lake Erie. Fish populations have also changed in Lake Erie.

Beeton presents a chart (Figure 15-2) which shows changes in total dissolved solids since 1900.

It is interesting to note the increases experienced in Lakes Erie, Ontario, and Michigan; while Lake Superior has a slight downward trend. The sharp increases noted after 1910 relate to the population growth in the lakes' drainage basins which increased sharply after that year. Man's activities have clearly accelerated the rate of eutrophication. The greatest acceleration, as noted, has been in Lakes Erie, Ontario, and Michigan; and those lakes have had the largest population growth within their drainage areas.

Lakes Cayuga and Seneca: Of the several Finger Lakes in Central New York, the most important are Cayuga and Seneca. These two lakes are important water resources for the two cities located at the southern end of each lake, Ithaca and Watkins Glen, as well as surrounding industry. Both lakes suffer a proliferation of blue-green algae during the warm summer months which affects water supplies to the cities and local industry. Recreational activities have declined.

A recent study concluded that both lakes are fertile and should be considered eutrophic [37:1-24]. The transparency of both lakes is low, approximately seven feet during the month of July. The lakes have been getting progressively less transparent over the years. Water temperatures have remained rather stable. Tests of dissolved oxygen indicate a progressive general decrease through the summer months. This could be due to increased biological oxygen demand resulting from the death of the early summer plankton population. Both lakes support farily large crops of algae. Tests also showed that the level of nitrogen in Cayuga Lake is greater than in the Wisconsin lakes which have been studied and are considered eutrophic. Seneca Lake was slightly less so. Sources of nitrogen and phosphorus, in order of importance, were from runoff from cleared agricultural land, sanitary sewage from public and institutional sewage systems, runoff from forest areas, and precipitation.

Lake Mendota and the Wisconsin Lakes: The Lake Mendota watershed in Wisconsin is primarily cropland. The major crops raised are corn and oats. Urban land occupies a very small percentage of the watershed. However, the annual contributions of total nitrogen from municipal and industrial waste water during 1966 amounted to 47,000 pounds and total phosphorus 17,000 pounds. Rural

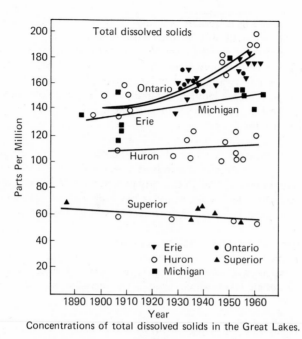

Concentrations of total dissolved solids in the Great Lakes.

Figure 15-2 Dissolved Solids in the Great Lakes. Source: Alfred M. Beeton, "Eutrophication of the St. Lawrence Great Lakes," *Limnology and Oceanography*, X (April, 1968), p. 243.

runoff contributed 52,000 pounds of nitrogen of which approximately 45,000 pounds were derived from manure. Of the 20,000 pounds of phosphorus entering the lake annually from rural sources, 15,000 pounds were attributed to manure [18:23-24]. The eutrophic state of Lake Mendota has been under study for several years.

Schraufnagel in summarizing nitrogen and phosphorus quantities that reach Wisconsin surface waters concluded that ground water contributed the most nitrogen (18, p. 1). Municipal treatment plants are the largest source of phosphorus and second largest nitrogen contributor. Manured lands were classified next followed by natural precipitation. He concluded that in Wisconsin chemical fertilizers do not appear to be significant.

Lakes Washington and Tahoe: Lake Washington located in the state of Washington is a large, relatively unproductive lake, which recently has shown symptoms of enrichment. The lake is evidencing progressive deterioration, and is producing denser populations of blue-green algae, noticed for the first time in 1955. Such populations of algae are a notorious nuisance to the surrounding community. The nutrient source which encouraged the eutrophic state of the lake was sewage received in increasing amounts each year [23:47]. Lake Tahoe in the Sierra Nevada mountains of California has a similar history.

Corrective action has been taken by the communities around both lakes. Changes in the sewage system now divert all the effluent and raw sewage from Lake Washington. Tertiary treatment of waste water effluent is currently being practiced to lower phosphorus input into Lake Tahoe. Sewage flow is also being diverted to a watershed draining away from the lake in order to help preserve the fine quality waters of Lake Tahoe.

Onondoga Lake at Syracuse: This small urban lake is eutrophic. It adversely affects the health and welfare of thousands of persons and is a blight on urban and industrial development. The entire urban community suffers from the problem it created. Onondoga Lake at Syracuse, New York, is five miles long, and one mile wide. The lake received untreated sewage for years. Industrial wastes also entered the lake.

The lake water is unfit for drinking, swimming, and boating. It has an unpleasant odor and is losing its utility for industrial use. Restoration is underway, but is expected to involve a three-year program. This lake typifies the problem of small urban lakes which have been degraded by eutrophication [5:19-20].

Other lakes: Partially treated sewage from Minneapolis and St. Paul is carried downstream in the Mississippi River to Lake Pepin where algae thrive on these sewage nutrients.

Cochran Lake in northern Wisconsin has in the last ten years deteriorated rapidly as a result of seepage from the septic tanks of just a few summer cabins on its shores. "It now looks like a 300 acre caldron of pea soup" [26:14-15].

The Natural Resources and Power Subcommittee report included a partial list of lakes undergoing rapid eutrophication. Lake Zoar in Connecticut, Fox Chain O'Lakes in Illinois, Sebasticook in Maine, Shagawa in Minnesota, and Klamath in Oregon were included. The report further stated that "there are hundreds of small lakes with eutrophication problems [5:5-6].

The lakes selected for discussion, although perhaps appearing to be randomly selected, clearly indicate that eutrophication is a national problem. Lakes throughout the United States have become increasing fertile, some as a direct result of chemical fertilizers, especially in the West. Because of sewage and industrial effluent, other lakes in the East have become eutrophic.

Influence of Technological Trends

The effects of accelerated eutrophication are inevitable as long as nutrients continue to pour into our lakes. The primary source of plant nutrients to some lakes can be correlated to increased agricultural activities while other lakes have received increasing amounts of nitrogen and phosphorus from urban activities.

Modern technology has inadvertently contributed to this acceleration of the aging of lakes. And, it is apparent that the increased quantities of nutrients found in America's lakes can be related to the production of fertilizers and detergents, technological changes in animal feeding, or as a result of human and industrial wastes.

The pollutant effects of fertilized land drainage and sewage discharges are becoming more pronounced. The specific technological and nontechnological conditions which have intensified and magnified the problem of eutrophication are (1) fertilizers are more widely used than ever before; (2) detergents with a phosphate base have revolutionized the soap and detergent industry in the last 25 years, all but replacing fat-based soap; (3) feedlot feeding of animals has created increased concentrations of animal excrement; (4) increased production has increased industrial effluent containing nitrogen, phosphorus, and other nutrients; and (5) concentrations of populations in urban areas with large sewage plants and increased paved areas which offer ready channels for transmission of pollutants to water courses has further added to the increase in plant nutrients.

Chemical fertilizers: Due to improved methods of application and the low cost of nitrogen fertilizer, the use of chemical fertilizers to encourage crop growth has sharply increased in recent years. According to the Department of Agriculture, fertilizer use has increased from 8 million tons in 1940 to over 35 million in 1966, and the percentage of nitrogen in a unit of fertilizer has increased from 4.9 percent to 10.9 percent. Phosphoric oxide content in a unit of fertilizer has increased from 10.7 percent to 12.1 percent [9:602]. Modern technology and research has demonstrated that the increased use of fertilizers has contributed directly to increased crop production. Corn production is a prime example.

A second contributor to agricultural runoff has been increased irrigation. Modern methods of water control and irrigation techniques have not only permitted more acres to be irrigated but also to increase the amount of water brought to the land irrigated. More efficient pumps, spraying equipment, and the lining and covering of irrigation ditches have made irrigation more effective.

Detergents: The substantial increase in the use of detergents in recent years, with their high phosphorus content, has contributed significantly to nutrient problems. After World War II the soapmaking industry experienced a revolution in its raw material base. By 1950 one-third of all soap products consisted of detergents, and by 1960 the revolution was complete; synthetics had conquered all but 24 precent of the market [2:319]. Soap production based on traditional fats and oils had dropped to less than one-third its 1940 level by 1960.

This general upheaval has been complemented by continual changes in the industry. There has been a rise in the use of washing machines, a transition from soap bars to flakes to powders and to liquids. There are few fields where the rise can equal that of synthetic detergents.

Feedlots: In some areas of the country, animal feedlots are considered a prime contributor of pollutants in the form of excrement. Specifically, in the Midwest there are numerous feedlots on small watersheds where animal concentrations are extremely high. Such large-scale operations provide greater flexibility in the kinds and sources of rations used and permit the application of more effective veterinary care. Additives, such as minerals, urea, vitamins, and hormones can be more easily administered. Hogs are similarly fed on such feedlots.

Heavy slugs of animal wastes are flushed into streams or lakes following rain storms. The volume of stormwater, however, is not sufficient to dilute the nutrient content of the wastes. The magnitude of the problem is evidenced "by estimates that, in terms of standard BOD (biochemical oxygen demand), U.S. farm animal waste production is 10 times greater than U.S. human sewage" [10:II, 197].

Growth in industry and power generation: An assessment of the volume and pollutant characteristics of industrial wastes has not been made except in connection with specific localized problems [10:2, 62]. Thus, how much algae growth material is attributed to industry is largely unknown. However, it is definitely known that the industries requiring large plants use most of the water and produce most of the wastes. Such large industries as the chemicals, paper and allied products, sugar refining, and primary metals discharge either nitrogen or phosphorus or both. Detergents are extensively used in metal and food processing, and in dairies and meat-packing plants.

Since the late 1950s the fuel used in electric generating power plants has shifted from fossil fuels to nuclear energy. This has been a most significant change in the industry, and the conversion is expected to continue. Nuclear-fueled plants require more cooling water per megawatt of output than do conventional fossil-fueled plants. By 1980 the annual cooling-water needs of the electric industry may exceed one-sixth of the total supply of runoff water. For example, the proposed Cayuga nuclear plant will add 6 billion B.T.U. per hour to the water, compared to about 1.3 B.T.U. per hour for the present plant [22:4].

Urbanization: Changes caused by increasing population must also be considered. The effects of population increases in urban areas have aggravated the problem of eutrophication. Some of our major cities are located directly on lakes or rivers. Chicago, Gary, and Milwaukee are on Lake Michigan. Detroit and Cleveland are on Lake Erie. Effluents from Rochester and surrounding Monroe County which are discharged into Lake Ontario contain sufficient phosphates to support 4 million tons of algae per year [5:5]

To meet the needs of expanding populations large sewage disposal facilities have been required. Such waste treatment facilities while capable of reducing waste load by biological degradation create other effects. Residual products of organic waste degradation are plant nutrients nitrogen and phosphorus. The greater the quantity of sewage, the greater the quantity of plant nutrients.

Continuing urban development will reduce the land area available for water percolation. Paved areas encourage runoff. Pet excrement and other nutrient sources are carried off to the water bodies with each rain.

Projection of Eutrophication Associated with Anticipated Increases in Nutrient Output

Measures of the Relative State of Eutrophication

There exists today no universal agreement on the basis for classifying lakes as oligotrophic or eutrophic. For example, Beeton reports that Lake Erie "has been called oligotrophic, mesotrophic, and eutrophic by various investigators over the past 30 years" [20:241]. Limnologists freely use these terms, but there exists considerable disagreement on precisely what each term means. Various physical, chemical, and biological criteria have been used to classify lakes: species and abundance of plankton, intensity and frequency of algae blooms, transparency of the water, types of organisms, levels of dissolved oxygen, and changes in fish populations.

Although concentrations of nitrogen and phosphorus are the prime factors in accelerated eutrophication and excessive algae, other factors contribute to the growth of algae. Manganese, cobalt, and vanadium are known to be required for optimum algal growth. Hormones and vitamins stimulate the growth of algae. Zinc and especially iron may control the level of primary productivity in Lake Tahoe [27:1453]. Although these elements are recognized as necessary material for algae growth, little is known on how much of these elements can be present and the water still remain free of excessive algae growths. Scientists have yet to determine the relative effect of these elements, their sources, and how much control is necessary to regulate their effects.

Difficult to Establish a Quantifiable Measure of Eutrophication

It is apparent that measures of the relative state of eutrophication are far from perfect. The meaning of terms used are not consistently applied. The factors of algae growth are many and their individual contributions are largely unknown. These problems make any projection of eutrophication associated with anticipated increases in nutrient output extremely hazardous, if possible at all.

Dr. Rohlich of the University of Wisconsin highlighted this lack of quantifiable data in a paper presented at the 41st Annual Convention of the Soap and Detergent Association on January 25, 1968:

> Despite the unprecedented activity in the last decade, directed toward an understanding of the enrichment process and the measurement of changes which occur in lakes and streams, there is not yet a simple relationship between the maturing process and the amount of nutrients present or entering the receiving body of water or to other variables in the terrestrial and aquatic environment [36:3].

The interrelationships of the various factors which affect the metabolism of a lake are very complex. It is extremely difficult to understand much less evaluate factors, such as geographic location, drainage area, climate, nutrient input, and the many other variables that influence the trophic nature of the lake. Figure 15-3 suggests the interrelationships of factors affecting the metabolism of a lake.

Advances to overcome difficulties: Although the state of the art in providing necessary quantitative data in order to make projections is sketchy, certain advances to overcome these difficulties have been made. Based on flow data from inlets and outlets some methods have been developed to measure the amounts of nutrients entering, retained, and leaving the lake. Detailed studies of the Wisconsin lakes have been completed [18:1-24]. Quantitative estimates were made of the annual contribution from each of the various nutrient sources. This study indicated that most of the nutrients were from rural runoff. Similar studies were and are being made at other lakes.

In 1955 Edmondson et al. measured the accelerated rate at which Lake Washington was receiving treated sewage [23:47-48]. They noted that observed eutrophication in the lake could be directly attributed to sewage plant activities. They forecasted that if the then present rate of enrichment was to continue the lake would develop serious algae blooms. In less than ten years the problem was so acute the state had to take direct action by diverting the sewage away from the lake to another watershed.

Recently attention has been given to the relationship of a watershed to its receiving body of water in order to evaluate eutrophication potential. If a watershed is large in relation to the lake and is heavily populated, eutrophication is inevitable.

In January 1968 the Joint Task Force on Eutrophication (formed by the Department of Interior) announced that it will develop a standardized procedure to determine the algal growth potential (AGP) of various chemicals and waters.

The proposed procedure would be designed to (1) anticipate the effect on algal production of introducing various nutrients; (2) determine the extent to which nutrient levels must be reduced in a body of water to remedy eutrophication; (3) determine at what point along the time scale of progressing eutrophication a body of water lies; (4) evaluate the effectiveness of waste treatment processes in removing elements that support or stimulate the growth of algae; and (5) be adaptable for special problem purposes [33:1/68, 1].

415

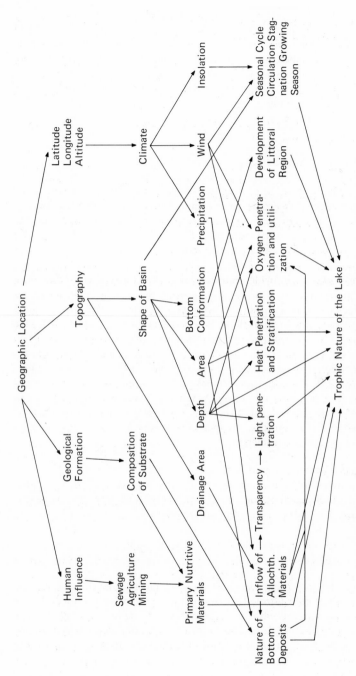

Figure 15-3 Factors Affecting The Metabolism of a Lake. Source: Gerard A. Rohlich, *"Eutrophication"* (paper presented at the 41st Annual Convention of the Soap and Detergent Industry, New York City, January 25, 1968), p. 10.

This concept of AGP is not new. Oswald and Golueke in 1960 conducted laboratory tests of algal growth materials [28:964-75]. They defined AGP as the dry weight of algae which will grow in a given water sample when no factor other than the nutrient being tested is dissolved in the water. The objective being to determine which nutrient sample is limiting to growth. Two to three months may be required to obtain a complete evaluation. The authors considered the AGP test as a useful common denominator for comparing the eutrophic tendency of various waters.

Projected Increases in Nutrient Output

As had been indicated above, it is virtually impossible to establish a quantifiable ratio of eutrophication (projected) to anticipated increases in nutrient output. Projections of total nutrient load to the year 2000 are possible, however, for certain sources of man-generated nutrients. The assumption that nitrogen and phosphorus are the prime plant nutrients is made.

One estimate of total nationwide nutrient load: Relatively few studies have been made to determine how much algae growth material is contributed by individual sources. F. Alan Ferguson of Stanford Research Institute compiled total nationwide nutrient contributions from various sources [24:189-90]. He acknowledges that due to the paucity of data some of his estimates are gross extrapolations and may be subject to considerable uncertainty. However, his estimates serve two purposes. First, they offer a comparison with figures computed in this paper. Second, they emphasize the tremendous impact man has had on his environment (see Table 15-4). As much as 80 percent of the nitrogen and 75 percent of the phosphorus may come from man-generated sources. Of the total man-generated sources, 51 percent of the nitrogen comes from fertilizers and 33 percent from sewage.

Projections based on tables: Based on projections made in Tables 15-1 to 15-3 or from other sources, as defined, estimates of nutrient output to the year 2000 are attempted. In each instance the amount of nitrogen and phosphorus output is computed using the medium projection in the tables.

Population

Oswald and Golueke indicated that "due to predicted population increase and shifts of population to concentrated areas, the rate of eutrophication will double in the next 25 years and redouble near the turn of the century" [28:964]. The authors further state that in 1965, 70 percent of the population lived on less than 2 percent of the land; and that most of the populated areas were near water bodies [28:967].

Table 15.4

Approximate Quantities of Algal
Growth Materials from Sources
Either in or Entering United States
Surface Waters

	Nitrogen		Phosphorus	
Sources	Quantities (mill. lb. per year)	Percent	Quantities (mill. lb. per year)	Percent
Natural	1,035-4,210	21-51	245-711	26-41
Man-generated:				
Domestic sewage	1,330[a]		137-166[a]	
Washing wastes			250-280[a]	
Runoff from				
Urban land	200		19	
Fertilized land	2,040[b]		110-380	
Land on which animals are kept	410		170	
Industrial	n.a.		n.a.	
Total man-generated	3,990	79-46	686-1,015	74-57
Total	5,025-8,200	100	931-1,726	100

[a]Data based on the assumption of 30 percent removal of nutrients in treatment plants.

[b]Estimated.

Source: F. Alan Ferguson, "A Nonmyopic Approach to the Problem of Excess Algal Growth," *Environmental Science and Technology*, II (3) (March, 1968), Tables 2, 4-5, pp. 191-192.

Projections of nitrogen and phosphorus output in human waste are computed in Table 15-5 by applying the per capita output of nitrogen and phosphorus content in excreta to population figures. In the Wisconsin study, the annual per capita output of nitrogen was estimated to be 10 pounds, and of phosphorus 3.5 pounds. However, it was also indicated that 3.17 pounds per year of phosphorus

Table 15.5

Projection of Nitrogen and Phosphorus in Human Waste

	1960	1970	1980	1990	2000
Medium projection of total population[a] (millions)	180	208	245	287	331
Total nitrogen[e] (mill. lbs.)	1,800	2,080	2,045	2,087	3,331
Total phosphorus[f] (mill. lbs.)	216	250	294	344	397
Urban population[b] (millions)	128	160	195	240	280
Total nitrogen[e] (mill. lbs.)	1,280	1,600	1,950	2,400	2,800
Total phosphorus[f] (mill. lbs.)	154	192	234	288	326
Lake Erie basin[c] (millions)		13[d]		18	
Total nitrogen[e] (mill. lbs.)		130		180	
Total phosphorus[f] (mill. lbs.)		16		22	

[a]From Table 15.1.

[b]Estimated from: *Industrial Incentives for Water Pollution Abatement*, Report for the U. S. Department of Health, Education, and Welfare, Public Health Service, Howard N. Mantel of the Institute of Public Administration (New York, 1965), Figure 1, p. 7.

[c]*Water in the News*, published by the Soap and Detergent Association (New York, November, 1968), p. 4.

[d]Actual 1968 population.

[e]Nitrogen content of excreta estimated at 10 pounds per capita.

[f]Phosphorus content of excreta estimated at 1.2 pounds per capita.

was attributed to phosphates in detergents. The Wisconsin study referred to an earlier work which indicated that prior to the heavy use of detergents phosphorus in sewage was estimated to be 1.2 pounds per year per capita [18:32-36]. As the projection of phosphates in detergents is to be considered separately, the figure of 1.2 pounds per year is used in the projections of human waste.

In order to portray the magnitude of the quantity of nitrogen and phosphorus in excreta three projections were made. The first projection of nutrient wastes for the total population was given to show the gross amount of total wastes. It is recognized that only some portion (the exact amount largely unknown) of these nutrients will be discharged into fresh water bodies. The second projection for urban population is important when one considers that most of the populated areas are near water bodies, as was previously mentioned. Again, only some portion will be discharged into fresh water. In the year 2000 the nitrogen output of urban areas will have increased over 1.5 billion pounds and the output of phosphorus in excreta will have increased 172 million pounds, or an increase of almost 120 percent in forty years.

The third series projects an estimated increase in nitrogen and phosphorus output of 50 million pounds and 6 million pounds, respectively for the Lake Erie Basin alone. The represents almost a 40 percent increase in twenty years.

Detergents

Total detergent output is given in millions of pounds in Table 15-1. The medium projection was again used. Various estimates of the phosphate content of detergents have been given in the literature. Some estimates of phosphate content in modern detergents ranged to a high of 50 percent. Mr. E. Scott Pattison, manager, Soap and Detergent Association, in a letter to the Natural Resources and Power Subcommittee of the House Committee on Government Operations wrote that "Generally speaking, a heavy duty synthetic detergent will contain about 40 percent phosphate, because this amount is essential to do an adequate washing job [5:10]. This figure is used in the projections below.

Table 15-6 clearly indicates that the amount of phosphorus used in detergents is likely to increase over 130 percent in the forty years after 1960. This increase is due to two factors. Per capita production of detergents are projected to increase from 22 pounds in 1960 to 28 pounds in 2000 [2:Table A17-11]. The second reason for this growth in total detergent consumption is related to expected increases in total numbers of people using detergents.

These projections represent total production of phosphate based detergents. Again, it should be recognized that not all of this phosphorus will reach fresh water bodies through sewage systems or by ground percolation.

Table 15.6

Projection of Phosphorus in Detergents

	1960	1970	1980	1990	2000
Synthetic detergent production[a] (mill. lbs.)	3,970	5,410	6,860	8,040	9,270
Total phosphorus[b] (mill. lbs.)	1,588	2,164	2,744	3,216	3,708

[a]From Table 15.1.

[b]Estimated 40 percent phosphorus content per unit of weight.

Table 15.7

Projection of Nitrogen and Phosphorus in Chemical Fertilizers

	1960	1970	1980	1990	2000
Farm outlays on fertilizer and lime[a] (bill. 1960 dollars)	1.46	2.0	2.7	3.5	4.3
Total nitrogen[b] (mill. lbs.)	7,000	11,600	15,660	20,300	24,940
Total phosphates[c] (mill. lbs.)	6,000	8,200	11,070	14,350	17,630

[a]From Table 15.2.

[b]The 1960 fertilizer and lime expenditures were for 7 billion pounds of nitrogen. Each 1.0 billion dollars purchased 5.8 billion pounds (or 5,800 million pounds).

[c]These expenditures were also for 6 billion pounds of phosphates. Each 1.0 billion dollars purchased 4.1 billion pounds (or 4,100 million pounds).

Computations in (b) and (c) were derived from *Resources in America's Future*, pp. 328 and 486.

Fertilizers

Farm expenditures on fertilizers and lime is given in Table 15-2. These figures, however, are in dollars of expenditures and not in quantities of nitrogen and phosphorus. The RFF study does not give a quantitative series for these two elements. The study does, however, give some useful figures from which quantities of phosphorus and nitrogen can be derived for the years 1970 to 2000 (Table 15-7).

It appears from this table that total nitrogen/phosphate fertilizer consumption will triple in the forty-year period if the projections in *Resources in America's Future* prove sound. The magnitude of these projections (17 billion pounds of phosphorus and 25 billion pounds of nitrogen in the year 2000) demonstrate the impact that fertilizers may have on the continuing problem of accelerated eutrophication. Again, only some portion of these nutrients will reach the waterways.

Feedlot Pollution

Animal manure from feedlots is becoming an increasingly important problem. One cow excretes 17 pounds of phosphorus annually, over eightfold that of humans. The number of cattle held in a feedlot concentration may range up to 30,000 head. A quick calculation indicates that the annual output of phosphorus from one feedlot of this size is over a half million pounds. Cattle held in feedlot for fattening may produce double the average annual quantity of waste.

The projection below of phosphorus in animal wastes is based on the demand for animal products measured in liveweight and the weight of phosphorus in various animal excreta (Table 15-8).

The trend in phosphorus output from animals is apparent. By the year 2000 more than a twofold increase will have occurred. The effects of animal pollution are more acute in local areas where the animals are held in large feedlot concentrations.

Industrial Wastes

Quantitiative estimates of nitrogen and phosphorus output from industrial effluent can not be made. As was previously pointed out, the difficulties are due largely to data deficiencies.

It is of some interest to compare the conclusions of the table derived from Ferguson's article (Table 15-4) to those computed on the preceding pages. One caution should be mentioned regarding the figures to be used in this comparison.

Table 15.8

Projected Phosphorus in Animal Wastes

	1960	1970	1980	1990	2000
Demand for animal products (bill. lb. livewt.)[a]					
cattle and calves	28.6	39.6	50.6	60.6	69.8
hogs	20.0	24.5	30.5	37.9	44.3
commercial broilers	6.02	7.1	9.2	10.8	12.4
Total phosphorus output[b] (mill. lbs.)[c]					
cattle and calves	486	673	860	1,030	1,187
hogs	900	1,102	1,373	1,706	1,994
commercial broilers	181	213	276	324	372

[a]From Table 15.2.

[b]Annual excretion of phosphorus per 1,000 pound weight: cow - 17 pounds; swine - 45 pounds; poultry - 30 pounds.

[c]Calculation derived from: U. S. Department of the Interior, Federal Water Pollution Control Administration, *The Cost of Clean Water*, II, 1968, Table III-16, p. 220.

The figures from the tables computed are those projected for 1970 and the figures derived from Ferguson's article represent his conclusions as of 1967 (see Table 15-9).

It is quite evident that some wide differences exist. One explanation lies in the fact that Ferguson attempted to estimate nutrients entering surface waters, whereas the quantities computed in this chapter represent totals generated. A second explanation is that gross errors may exist in either of the conclusions.

The projections computed for the various sources are, admittedly, probably far from exact, but they do indicate that the trend of nutrient output is definitely spiraling upward. It is evident that the rate of eutrophication with the resultant deterioration of America's lake waters will continue to accelerate due to the ever-increasing outpouring of nutrients.

Table 15.9

Comparison of Ferguson Table to Those
Computed

	Nitrogen (mill. lbs.) per year)		Phosphorus (mill. lbs.) per year)	
	Ferguson[a]	Computed[b]	Ferguson	Computed
Domestic sewage from human waste	1,330	1,600[c]	137-166	192[c]
Detergents			250-280	2,164
Fertilized land	2,040	11,600	110-380	8,200
Animal wastes	420	n.a.	170	1,988[d]

[a]Data as of 1967 from Table 15.4.   [c]Output of nutrients from urban population.

[b]Projected quantities for 1970.   [d]Sum of cattle and calves, hogs, and broilers.

**Forces Tending to Offset
Accelerated Eutrophication**

Pollution Control and Government

The Federal Government enters the water pollution control field on several levels: (1) to provide support for research to discover new and better methods of waste disposal; (2) to provide technical services to the various states; (3) to make grants to the states for research; (4) to make construction grants for new disposal facilities; and (5) to enforce pollution controls on interstate waters [4:63].

To date, no Federal legislation has been passed which directly controls or regulates the inflow of nutrients to America's lakes and other waters. Existing water pollution legislation regulates water practices which relate to the more widely recognized water pollutants, such as effluents containing toxics, other chemicals, raw sewage, bacterial problems, oil pollution, waste from watercraft, dissolved oxygen losses, and causes of fish kills.

Several important bills have been passed in recent years which attempt to control or regulate practices which cause the discharge of water pollutants into lakes and streams. In 1954 the Watershed Protection and Flood Prevention Act was passed. This was followed by the Federal Water Pollution Control Act. Two important amendments to this act were subsequently passed. First was the Water Quality Act of 1965, followed by the Clean Water Restoration Act of 1966. One objective of these laws is to establish standards to which the pollutant content of municipal and industrial effluent could be compared. No standard has been set for permissible levels of nitrogen or phosphorus in such effluents. Another objective is to provide for additional funds to help local and state governments meet the problems of eutrophication.

Federal support for research and demonstration programs to help solve the problem of eutrophication has been minimal. For example, in fiscal year 1966, the Federal Water Pollution Control Administration devoted only $150,000 to eutrophication research. This was increased to $2.5 million for fiscal year 1967 and estimated funding for fiscal year 1968 is $3 million [5:3].

Eutrophication as a national problem has only recently received Federal attention. The interest that has been generated has come about as a result of the Committee on Government Operations and such agencies as the Department of the Interior and the Department of Agriculture.

The Natural Resources and Power Subcommittee of the Committee on Government Operations has pointed out that the FWPCA did not in its May 1966 "Guidelines for Establishing Water Quality Standards for Interstate Waters" suggest that water quality standards provide for the control of phosphates. The committee recommended that FWPCA should require all state water quality standards to include provisions for controlling phosphate levels. The committee also suggested broadening the Watershed Protection and Flood Prevention Act to include water quality management which would provide reservoir storage for controlled releases of water to dilute nutrient enriched waters. Other recommendations were primarily aimed at prodding the various government agencies into action [5:4-5].

The need for establishing water quality standards is also receiving attention at the regional and local level. Professor Hines suggests that in addition to quality standards the waters should be classified with respect to the uses for which the waters may be suitable [4:59]. He further suggests that these standards and classifications should be discretionary with the individual state's control commission.

State legislators have been slow in facing the problem of eutrophication. Maryland was the only state as of July 1967, to enact comprehensive legislation for countywide water and sewer planning in each local jurisdiction of that state. Another state in the forefront is Virginia. That state's water control board must rule on the adequacy fo all new waste disposal plants. Last November bond issues were presented before voters of several states to provide municipalities with sorely needed aid for water cleanup. Many of these issues were accepted. However, Illinois voters turned down a $1 billion natural resources development bond act.

Administrative Action

Several Federal agencies are directly concerned with the problem of accelerated eutrophication. Those most concerned are the Departments of Interior; Health, Education and Welfare; Agriculture; and Housing and Urban Development. There appears to be a need to expand and coordinate the programs of these several agencies.

The Department of Interior has the most comprehensive program. Its objectives are to remove the phosphorus content in treated sewage water, build new sewers, enforce and strengthen new laws, build drains and dams to control agricultural pollution, find a replacement for the septic tank system, and accelerate research.

In August 1967 the Department of Interior formed with the Soap and Detergent Association and its industry member the Joint Industry-Government Task Force on Eutrophication. Members of the Department of Agriculture and representatives of agricultural industries joined the Task Force in April 1968. The Task Force's function is to (1) recommend cooperative industry-government programs; (2) investigate proposed solutions to the complex and incompletely understood problems of eutrophication; and (3) consider all contributing factors and their effects.

The National Eutrophication Research Program's center is located at FWPCA Pacific Northwest water laboratory in Oregon. Their stated objectives are to develop technology to save lakes and other waters from accelerated aging and to develop economically feasible ways to prevent and control eutrophication.

The Lake Michigan Conference was specifically held to recognize and tackle the growing problem of eutrophication. The report warned that unchecked pollution could turn Lake Michigan into another Lake Erie. Lake Michigan is presently showing signs of eutrophication, especially in the inshore areas. Conferees were representatives from Federal agencies and from the states of Illinois, Indiana, Michigan, and Wisconsin. Corrective measures recommended at the conference include biological treatment or its equivalent for the removal (by July 1972) of phosphorus and other nutrients from municipal and industrial effluent. Municipalities are to provide waste treatment to achieve 80 percent removal of phosphorus. Adjustable sewage overflow devices are to be installed [33:3/68, 4].

The attendees at the Lake Erie Conference were representatives from the FWPCA and the states of Pennsylvania, Indiana, Michigan, New York, and Ohio. This most recent conference, held during June 1968, was primarily a progress review of the implementation of prior recommendations. The conclusion was that all programs were moving forward. The Lake Erie Conference also recommended 80 percent removal of phosphorus.

Technological Effort to
Control Nutrient Sources

When a deep, unproductive lake has been made productive by wastewater discharges (as opposed to natural sources), it can be expected to return toward its original condition only when relieved of such effluent. It is generally agreed that control of accelerated eutrophication is best achieved by preventing the nutrients from entering the water body. There are three primary methods for limiting nutrient output into watercourses: (1) remove the nitrogen and phosphorus at the source; (2) divert the nutrient rich waters from the receiving body; and (3) dilute the effluent.

In general, primary treatment removes no soluble phosphate from sewage water and removals by conventional secondary treatment vary from 10 to 75 percent depending on operating and design conditions. Various process modifications and additions to conventional sewage treatment systems have been considered in recent years, such as oxidation ponds or a tertiary treatment process, sand filters, chemical precipitates and coagulants, harvesting, and the activated sludge process.

The technique of diverting nutrient-rich waters from the normal receiving body has been successfully tried in some cities. Sewage effluent from metropolitan Madison is diverted around Lakes Waubesa and Kegonsa and discharged through a 5.1 mile, 54 inch concrete pipeline into Badfish Creek. The communities around both Lakes Tahoe and Washington divert the sewage effluent away from the lake. This technique is not new — Chicago reversed the flow of the Chicago River away from Lake Michigan and into Mississippi River waters around the turn of the century. Diversion does not eliminate nutrients, rather it may place the problem somewhere else.

Little has been done by the agricultural industry to control that industry's contribution to accelerated eutrophication, although there has been much talk of what might be done. Senator Krueger suggests that "through research we can seek to develop less persistent forms of fertilizers which are absorbed more rapidly by the soil and crops" [7:2].

Strip cropping and contour farming have been suggested to reduce or impede the rapid runoff of water which carries phosphates. Manure used as a fertilizer is a separate problem, especially when the manure is placed during the winter months on frozen land. "Liquidization of winter manure and storage until spring may prove to be an effective measure" [18:2].

There is very little written on what industry in general is doing to correct its contribution to the problem. In fact, methods of measuring nutrient contributions from industry are sorely needed. The detergent industry which is credited with using most of the phosphorus that does not go into the making of fertilizers is, however, attempting to find a substitute for the phosphates in synthetic detergents.

Recovery of Eutrophic Lakes

Several techniques have been tried to reverse the trend of eutrophication in a lake. Some have met with success, others enjoyed not as much success. Several of the techniques tried are dredging, harvesting weeds and algae, diverting nutrient poor water into a lake, drawing nutrient-rich water out of the lake, aeration, and chemical means.

Dredging and disposal of lake bottom deposits and harvesting and disposal of algae have been tried in several lakes. The technique generally used is to dredge only the upper two or three inches of bottom deposits. Phosphorus concentrations occur in only the upper two inches of bottom sediments. Algae is harvested from the surface waters and from along the shore. The removal of bottom deposits and algae have been beneficial in reducing the nutrient load in specific lakes.

Green Lake near Seattle is a natural eutrophic body of water plagued by blooms of blue-green algae in the summer. To keep algae below nuisance levels large amounts of nutrient-poor city water is diverted into Green Lake for dilution purposes. Results have been a partial control of the lake's eutrophication [27:1457].

Another technique is to draw nutrient-rich, oxygen-poor water from the lake and discharge it into the lakes outlet. Aeration by using compressed air has been used with some success in small lakes.

Carbon black has been tried successfully on small lakes. This element is employed to exclude light necessary for algae growth. Algicides have been used to kill algae. However, its use must be with great care and the chemical selected must not be toxic to fish and fish food organisms.

Drs. Echelberger Jr. and Tenny of the University of Notre Dame have experimented with an air pollutant to improve water quality. Fly ash, a coal and oil fire waste product, can eliminate up to 90 percent of the pollutants found in fresh water lakes. An experiment conducted in Stone Lake, Michigan, which is eutrophic as a result of deposits of raw sewage in its waters for 30 years, indicated that after treatment with fly ash, the murky waters cleared and there was a decline in organic and inorganic phosphates contained in the water [33:9/68, 2].

Beneficent Effects

Several beneficent effects have been derived from the growth of excessive algae as a result of nutrient enrichments. Algae is a source of protein that may be fed to animals and possibly humans. The nutrient content in algae may make harvested algae or the sewage effluent a rich fertilizer. Artificial seeding of lakes with nutrients has been found to increase fish productivity.

Algae stripping is presently being tested by the Interagency Agricultural Waste Water Treatment Center near Firebough, California. Under controlled conditions algae is being grown and harvested. Benefits associated with this activity are the purifying of the water discharged and yielding a salable crop. The potential market for this harvested algae is feed for livestock and poultry. Algae can be a substitute for fish meal because of its high protein content. Algae contains xanthophyll which adds color to egg yolks. The center has approached the United Nations suggesting the use of algae as a high protein food supplement for human consumption [33:10/68, 4].

Two problems exist. The first is that there is not now a durable and lucrative market for sewage-grown algae, and if one is not found, the algae is still a waste product to be disposed of. The second centers around handling problems. Ponds designed to produce algae involve the handling of large volumes of liquid in order to recover a small amount of product.

Algae content is high in nutrients and as such may serve to provide a fertilizer for farming. The Metropolitan Sanitary District of Greater Chicago last summer conducted an experiment using digested sludge. Marketable crops of corn and soy bean were grown successfully on land treated with controlled applications of the sludge. One problem was noticed. The application rates supplied nitrogen in amounts greater than those used by the crops. Therefore, nitrate levels in drainage waters were increased [33:12/68, 4].

Fertilizers are organic and inorganic and include animal manures, leaves of land plants, and chemical fertilizers. When added to a pond or lake they accelerate the growth of plankton, aquatic insects and worms which in turn serve as food for fish. Knowledge of this cycle has served to provide countries such as Japan, China, and India with a basic and desperately needed food source, fish. To a limited extent this concept has been tried in the United States. Farmers are raising such desirable sport fish as bass by fertilizing their ponds encouraging the food cycle.

Forecast and Concluding Remarks

Summary Comments

Enormous increases in manmade nutrients in recent years have tremendously accelerated the usually slow process of eutrophication. Oswald and Golueke conclude that "eutrophication is a problem which must be considered in any watershed having inland receiving waters and a population" [28:969]. A large population imports into the watershed which it occupies a vast amount of food and fertilizers. Fertilizers run off into streams and lakes. Food is turned into nutrient-rich waste by both humans and animals. Such waste is then deposited directly or indirectly into surface waters accelerating the growth of algae.

The overall increases in these factors which are threatening America's lakes was demonstrated in the tables presented earlier in this paper. Quantities of nutrients from each of several sources were projected to the year 2000. Table 15-5 indicated that nitrogen and phosphorus in human waste will increase almost 120 percent in the 40 years from 1960. A 130 percent increase in total phosphorus waste as a result of detergent use was projected in Table 15-6. Increases in the amount of phosphorus output to the year 2000 may more than double as a result of animal waste as indicated in Table 15-8.

However, the most significant increase in the output of both nitrogen and phosphorus may occur as a result of the use of chemical fertilizers. The use of such fertilizers will triple by the year 2000 (Table 15-7). Nitrogen used in fertilizers is projected at 24,940 million pounds and phosphorus at 17,630 million pounds by the year 2000. These quantities far exceed the nitrogen and phosphorus output of the other three sources combined.

The significance of these figures is not in their numerical value but in the fact that while nutrient output is increasing, the area of surface water receiving such nutrients remains constant. Therefore, the ratio of nutrient output to area of surface water increases in direct proportion to the output of these threatening factors. Unless major corrective changes are implemented in the next 30 years to control (by diversion or removal) the everincreasing outpouring of nutrients into America's lakes, the water pollution phenomenon known as eutrophication will accelerate and bring to ruin many of the country's fresh water lakes.

Future Considerations

Lake rehabilitation and preventive controls will not likely evolve from any single formula. The problem is complex and each natural body of water is unique in the balance of properties that control productivity and the population density of algae. Many questions have yet to be answered before controls will be meaningfully effective. What causes nuisance algae growth? How can they be controlled? Which variables to study? What are the relationships of the various factors to each other and with the environment in which they live?

Before these questions can be answered with a reliable degree of accuracy, systematic studies of the variables over an extended period of time are necessary. Nutrient surveys to identify sources and to single out sources subject to control are required. Additional tests are necessary to evaluate the effectiveness of new methods and techniques of nutrient removal from sewage. Long-term studies on the relationship of nutrient influx to excessive growth of aquatic plants should be carried out. Scientists and engineers should study the effects of various corrective actions on water quality, and also search for possible beneficent uses for algae which is rich in protein and plant nutrients. Such studies it is hoped will provide answers necessary to develop effective controls to prevent excessive algae growth and to limit the quantity and sources of nutrient output.

Unless effective controls are developed to anticipate and prevent the problems of eutrophication, America's lakes may rapidly be destroyed. In Oswald and Golueke's article on eutrophication trends, they state that:

eutrophication is one of the day's most urgent problems in water pollution and that unless it is understood and controlled in the next few decades, many of our most valuable natural water resources will be seriously, if not irrevocably, impaired or completely lost [28:964].

16 Summary of Findings

Alfred J. Van Tassel

The magnitude of the obstacles that must be overcome if the quality of the environment is to be maintained tends to increase as the nation's output rises. This central conclusion of the present study is not equivalent to a gloomy forecast of an inevitable increase in the extent of pollution of the nation's air, water, and land. Rather, technological advances in most areas tend to reduce the amount of pollution associated with a given output. Legislative enactments give promise of enforcing more effective pollution control measures, and also tend to speed the development and application of new techniques in this field. Nevertheless, this qualification does not invalidate the view that at any given point in time and stage of development of pollution control techniques, the amount of skill and effort that must be expended to hold the line will be roughly proportional to the scale of output. If the projected quadrupling of GNP between 1960 and 2000 has validity, the battle promises to be a hard one.

A second general conclusion that emerges from the study is that pollution problems and solutions are inextricably interconnected in a complex web of interdependencies. The amount of air pollution involved in the generation of electric power may be reduced by substituting atomic for fossil fuels, but only at the expense of exacerbating thermal pollution and creating new tasks in the safe disposal of atomic wastes. Or, air pollution may be reduced by putting exhaust gases from industrial processes through scrubbing towers, but this may amount to no more than the substitution of a problem in water pollution for one in air pollution.

Pollution problems manifest themselves not in some abstract nation as a whole, but in specific localities. In general, the impact of pollution is likely to be greatest in the most populous and industrial areas — scarcely a conclusion pointing to an easy road ahead for an increasingly urbanized and industrialized America.

These general conclusions are nowhere better illustrated than in the four Chapters — 2 through 5 — which deal with various aspects of water pollution. Pollution of a stream or lake may begin with the discharge of untreated or incompletely treated municipal sewage. This will frequently mean the introduction of disease-causing bacteria, but whether or not this will create a serious source of danger will depend on two factors: (a) the degree of dilution — sufficient dilution, for example, through powerful tidal movements in an estuary, may be enough to remove the danger; and (b) the amount of dissolved oxygen in the water will determine the rate and extent to which foreign materials (pollutants) are burned up, figuratively speaking. The dissolved oxygen in a body of water is its first weapon in combatting pollution and it is in the reduction of the precious supply of this defense that the effluents of industrial plants most frequently exert their principal polluting effects. The untreated discharge from a paper mill, for example, has a voracious appetite for oxygen. It has been estimated that one large Southern paper mill on the Coosa River pours into the stream wastes equivalent in oxygen demand to untreated sewage from a city of 200,000 persons. When such a stream is drained in this fashion of its dissolved oxygen, the first biological pollutant that enters the stream is free to multiply rapidly to dangerous concentrations.

This latter consequence will be accelerated if the stream is subject to thermal pollution as it might be if water from it is used for cooling purposes. The effect on pollutants is twofold: (a) the dissolved oxygen content is reduced because the solubility of oxygen in water decreases as its temperature increases; and (b) reproduction rates for bacteria and life processes in general are accelerated as temperatures rise. Thus, the most serious water pollution is likely to arise in those streams or other bodies of water which receive the effluents of industrial plants, plus municipal sewage, and are heated by use for industrial cooling purposes.

This latter — thermal pollution — may seriously exacerbate biological pollution, and is expected to become a more serious threat because it is associated especially with electric power production. The projection of future power production is one of the most steeply rising curves in the RFF series. Moreover, an increasing portion of the total is expected to be generated using atomic fuels, and the waste heat which must be dissipated is higher per KWH generated in atomic than in fossil fuel plants.

Aspects of water pollution are dealt with in Chapters 2 through 5 of the present volume. In Chapter 2, Robert Gordon finds reason for hope that the paper industry will be able to come close to holding the line on its contribution to water pollution during the remainder of the century despite a nearly fourfold increase in projected output. This is based largely on the demonstrated fact that it is economically feasible in plants employing the most modern technology to eliminate almost entirely the water pollution associated with paper production. The Federal Water Pollution Control Administration estimated that in 1963 the plant typical of today's average technology generated a biological oxygen demand (BOD) per ton of product that was about one-third less than the average for plants employing the older production methods, while plants characterized by newer technology had a BOD ratio only forty percent that of the older. The newer plants have higher capacities than the older plants and it is not unreasonable to suppose that an increasing portion of the total output will come from paper plants which add little to the pollutional burden of the streams on which they are located.

While this generally optimistic assessment is justified by the examples of what is technically feasible in the best practice, it requires some qualification in the opinion of the editor. High standards of pollution control in paper production, while never costless, are within reach for a new plant starting from scratch. Then the addition to total investment required for effective pollution reduction is relatively modest compared to the heavy outlays required to bring an old plant up to anything approaching the same level. Accordingly, a prudent investor in a new plant (with one eye on policies of government regulatory agencies) is likely to opt for a high level of pollution control from the beginning, but the same investor might resist strenuously government efforts to impose similar standards on older facilities. Robert Gordon has assumed a steady reduction in the BOD of the paper mill effluent per ton of product in the remaining years of the century as well as a shift of an increasing proportion of output to mills employing newer technologies. These assumptions do not appear unreasonable, but even so the increase in output is such that the BOD of the total paper mill discharge is projected by him to be forty percent above the 1960 level in 1990, scarcely a reassuring estimate.

Moreover, the burden of water pollution associated with paper production is likely to be much heavier in the older producing regions than the new. The increase in the number of new plants in the older producing regions of the northeast, middle Atlantic and north central states is much smaller than the increase in the southern and far western states. Senator Muskie of Maine, whose efforts to clean up the Androscoggin River have met with resistance, can testify that the route to pollution control involving rehabilitation of older mills is a slow and painful one indeed. Communities in the older regions concerned about loss of business to the new may not be disposed to put the necessary pressure on the industry.

In Chapter 3, Thomas B. Christman examines the water pollution problems associated with steel production, petroleum refining and the conglomerate known as the chemical industry. As in the paper industry, technological advances are expected to reduce the amount of pollution associated with a unit of output in the petroleum and steel industries. However, in the steel industry, unlike the paper industry, plants with more advanced technology have larger water requirements per unit of product. The volume of waste-water per unit of output in steel mills was estimated by the Federal Water Pollution Control Administration to be more than a third higher in advanced mills as compared to typical ones and the change from old mills was even more pronounced. In the petroleum industry, on the other hand, both the amount of pollution thrown off and water usage were estimated to be dramatically lower for advanced refineries compared to typical and for the latter class compared to older.

Using the high projections of RFF and the pollutional loads per unit of output estimated by FWPCA, Mr. Christman computed projections of pollution in the three industries under study in his chapter. For the steel industry and especially for the chemical industry, the resultant quantity of pollution projected for the year 2000 is, as Mr. Christman put it "staggering." When account is taken of expected technical advances in the steel industry, the projected quantity of pollution generated is markedly reduced. Still more striking reductions in projected pollution for both the steel and the chemical industries result if RFF's medium rather than high projections are employed in the computations. In petroleum refining, where projected pollutional loads were modified both by use of RFF's medium projection and allowance for technical advances which reduce pollution, the projected increases in waste loads were much more modest. It is difficult, however, to avoid Mr. Christman's central conclusion concerning the projected impact on the three industries: "... it appears sufficient to say that the overall quality of the waters will deteriorate approximately in proportion to the increase in output unless there is a marked acceleration in antipollution progress."

Much of the progress that has been made in reducing industrial pollution, especially of the air, has been associated with by-product recovery. The recovery and reuse of gases from coke ovens and blast furnaces, recovery of acids from spent pickling solutions and suspended solids in the blast furnace gas washer, are examples from steel. Reprocessing of waste oils and recovery of sulphur combat pollution in petroleum refineries. Recovered sulphur was estimated to be worth $40,000,000 to refineries in 1966.

The chemical industry is too variegated to be subject to easy generalization, but it can be said that much of its waste cannot be utilized profitably at the present time. The search for possible uses is sure to be intensified by the adoption of anti-pollution legislation and regulations.

In Chapter 4, Charles H. Weidner looks at the present and future magnitude of the problem of mass sanitary sewage disposal; i.e., the sewage effluent which is transported to a central treatment or discharge point by means of a sewer system. The population served by sewers is almost exclusively an urban population and this portion of our population is expected to increase in relative importance in the remainder of the century.

The technology of the treatment of sanitary sewage represents perhaps the oldest and most highly developed facet of pollution control. It is technically feasible to achieve any degree of purification of sewage effluent, required by the intended use, but always at a cost. Until recent years most municipalities located near the ocean or a stream have been content to give their sewage minimum treatment before discharge to the water. Such a disposal method relied heavily on two forces for purification: (a) dilution of the sewage; and (b) the ability of the water to destroy the biological pollutants by oxidation and thereafter to restore its dissolved oxygen content, usually entirely by natural means. The amount of dilution will depend on rate and dependability of stream flow and will vary widely from one river basin to another. The ability of the water to restore itself will depend largely on the extent of competing demand for dissolved oxygen, such as from industrial sources of pollution.

The mighty Ohio River, draining a humid area, would appear to carry enough water to meet all needs, but is so beset by sources of industrial pollution that it is easy prey to pollution by sewage. Moreover, water is so taken for granted as a free good in the Ohio Valley that there is little disposition to pay money for its reclamation. On the other hand in the Southwest, where water is in chronic short supply, the recovery of water from sewage effluent for agriculture, recreational, and even drinking purposes appears more and more feasible economically. Water here may be regarded as a by-product of sewage treatment and a highly valuable one in arid and semiarid areas. Other efforts to recover by-products from sewage such as the production of fertilizer have not so far proven sufficiently rewarding to defray the cost of sewage treatment. Recent experiments which use atomic waste to irradiate sewage give promise of producing a fertilizing compost that is both sterile and concentrated. Such a use would not provide an outlet for any considerable amount of atomic waste, but it might be a substantial impetus to by-product use of sewage.

Further aggravating the water pollution problems arising from the combined action of industrial and sanitary sewage discharges, especially in the highly industrialized areas, is a threat whose major impact is yet to be felt. Electric power generation — one of the most rapidly rising of the projected output curves — is expected to increase by about half in each ten year period from 1960 to 2000 to a level five times that at the beginning of the period. Moreover, an increasing portion of this rising total will be generated by methods that usually result in the discharge of large quantities of heated water into the nation's waterways. This thermal pollution — one of the most recently recognized types of pollutant — may arise in a variety of ways, but electric power generation is a prime and growing source. Thermal pollution from electric power generation is the subject of Chapter 5 by J. D. Crespo.

Thermal pollution may have direct effects in driving various forms of aquatic life out of heated waters, and sometimes even killing them. More important, perhaps, is the synergistic effect of raising the temperature of water already polluted from industrial and municipal sources. Thermal pollution aggravates the general problem in two ways: (a) by driving oxygen out of solution; and (b) by accelerating all life processes, including the multiplication rate of biological pollutants.

There are few remaining opportunities for expanding hydro power capacity so most of the projected vast increase in power generation will have to come from thermal plants. Moreover, the amount of power generated from nuclear fuels which was negligible in 1960 is expected to account for nearly a fifth of the total in 1980, over a third in 1990, and over half in 2000. Nuclear power generation in 2000 is projected to be over sixty-seven times that of 1970. The thermal efficiency of nuclear power plants is much lower than that of those using fossil fuels and so the amount of heat to be dissipated will increase faster than electric power generation as a whole. Progress in thermal efficiency for all types of generators may be expected, but is unlikely to be sufficient to reverse these conclusions.

Cooling towers which are unsightly and expensive to construct offer one solution. Cooling ponds require large areas and are not always feasible. Experiments have been undertaken to make use of heated waters, for example to speed the growth of shellfish. But such uses require that the water used for cooling be pure. Utilities are always under public scrutiny and run the risk of being blamed for the pollutional sins of others. Even though the quality requirements for cooling water in power plants are not high, the utilities nevertheless have a substantial interest in seeing to it that the nation's waterways are cleaned up to the maximum extent possible.

There can be little doubt that the most disturbing aspect of water pollution problems, especially in the highly industrialized parts of the nation, is the way in which various forms of pollution interact to compound the difficulties. If the only type of pollution to be dealt with was from sanitary sewage there would be little cause for concern. Population — the prime determinant of the amount of sewage requiring disposal — will certainly grow at a much lower rate than output of goods and services. Moreover, the technology for thorough treatment is well known and more intensive use could be made of it as soon as more resources were made available. Local governments may be more resistant to federal regulation than industry, so that occasional discharge of undertreated sewage may be expected for some time after water pollution control is well developed. But simple dilution would minimize the impact of such occasional transgressions in the absence of extensive industrial waste pollution.

With respect to the latter, the logical implications of the output projections developed by RFF are difficult to ignore. There is at present no reason to suppose the projections are necessarily too high. Thus far, they have tended for the most part to understate the increase in output that has occurred. Unless there is a radical change in the nature of the postwar economy occasioned by a major depression, a general war or an overall reevaluation of national goals, output will continue to rise at approximately the projected rate. Under such circumstances, the progress in industrial water pollution control will have to be very rapid indeed if the nation is to hold the line in the industrialized sections of the country even at present unsatisfactory levels. Since industrial sources of both thermal and oxygen-demanding pollution are greatest in urban areas which are also the centers of greatest population growth, there are likely to be frequent situations of synergistic interaction among pollution sources.

The Interior Department has recently given notice of its intention to enforce vigorously federal legislation against water pollution. The Department notified two steel companies, a mining company, and Toledo that they were charged with causing water pollution and invited them to appear at hearings. If they are found guilty of the charges and fail within 180 days to institute a satisfactory program to eliminate pollution the Interior Department plans to bring suit [1].

Chapters 5 and 6 of the present volume dealing with thermal pollution and atomic wastes both find their justification in the expectation of a vast expansion in the generation of power from nuclear fuels. If atomic power proves to be of slight importance, there will be no problem of thermal pollution and certainly no difficulty in disposing of the atomic wastes. According to Jack Gordon, who prepared Chapter 6, there will be no problem in disposing of atomic wastes from power production, even if atomic plants increase in importance to the extent projected by RFF. That organization expects over fifty per cent of electric power in the United States to be generated from atomic fuels by 2000.

Atomic power has been hailed by many as a way of easing, if not eliminating, air pollution in our cities. Certainly, if all the increase in electric power production projected to 2000 were to come from fossil fuels, the contribution to air pollution might be considerable. However, there were some who feared we might be trading one form of pollution for another more dangerous if atomic wastes left from the use of atomic fuels in power generation proved difficult to dispose of with safety. Experience thus far is no guide, it might be argued, since atomic power production has just begun.

Mr. Gordon presents a persuasive argument for the position that there will be no obstacle to the safe disposition of the resultant atomic wastes, even if expansion is at the rate projected by RFF. In part, this is because means have been found to reduce drastically the bulk of atomic waste generated per ton of processed fuel. In terms of aqueous wastes, the volume per ton of processed fuel has been reduced from 2,000 gallons in 1940 to 1,400 in 1950, to 1,000 in 1960, and to 300 today. Further, concentration by solidification may reduce the volume of waste per ton of processed fuel to 2.5 cubic feet.

Accordingly, Mr. Gordon concludes that storage facilities by tested and proven methods appear to be adequate even at year 2000. Total accumulation of high-level aqueous wastes from now to year 2000 will add only 200 million gallons to the 600 million gallons accumulated since 1939, primarily from military plutonium production plants. The costs of such safe disposal of atomic waste do not constitute a competitive handicap for nuclear fueled plants.

Mr. Gordon concludes his essay with this statement: "The industries associated with nuclear production are harvesting the fruits of a waste management science that was well conceived, is well implemented, and assures a bright future of growth, expansion and safety."

Sheldon Novick of Washington University, St. Louis, takes a dimmer view of the atomic power program, although he does not contradict Mr. Gordon's judgment on the safety and adequacy of ultimate storage facilities for the atomic wastes arising from spent reactor fuel. However, in his book, *The Careless Atom,* Mr. Novick raises many questions concerning dangers involved in transporting atomic wastes for reprocessing and from disposition of tailings from uranium, a subject which lay outside Mr. Gordon's field of study. Mr. Novick also seriously questions the necessity for the projected expansion in output of atomic power, its economic justification and the safety and desirability of reactor operation in general [2].

As noted, one of the most appealing aspects of power generation from atomic fuels is the promise it offers of easing the air pollution that besets our major cities. The appearance of our cities, to say nothing of the health of our people, is impaired by the rising clouds of pollutants. To be sure, the major cause of the most serious air pollution in the United States is the automobile, but there is no doubt either that thermal electric power generating stations burning fossil fuels are frequently substantial contributors to air pollution. It has been noted that the curve of thermally generated electric power is expected to continue to rise with particular rapidity. Moreover, the electric automobile – the most widely discussed cure for automotive air pollution – would require the generation of vast additional kilowatts. The electric automobile might make a substantial dent in urban air pollution only if the electricity needed to power it was generated in new rural stations or by atomic fuels. Because the pollutants released to the air would be so heavily diluted by clean, free-flowing country air, fossil power plants located well away from cities would not contribute significantly to urban air pollution any more than atomic power plants would. Looked at in this light, atomic power plants would offer decisive advantages over thermal plants only if they were close enough to the cities to reduce substantially the power losses in transmission. One may ask if atomic power plants close to major cities actually offer a realistic alternative. The danger of accidents in power plants using atomic fuels may be very real or exclusively a product of overheated imaginations. The difference in end results will be unimportant if the public becomes convinced that the risk is not worth it.

In sum, this dilemma argues strongly in favor of a high priority for research directed toward lowering the power losses and hence the costs of long distance transmission. One phase of this research might be to seek means of transmission less destructive of the beauty of the landscape than present high tension lines. Success in reducing transmission costs would pave the way for safe utilization of atomic power to the fullest and pollution-free expansion of thermal power generation.

As noted earlier, the main cause of urban air pollution is the automobile. In Chapter 7, Norman Wesler examines the amount of urban air pollution associated with the combustion of fossil fuels for all purposes except the operation of internal combustion engines. Much the most important of these uses is for power generation for which coal is far and away the leading fuel. Although coal is expected to lose its ascendancy as an energy source for thermal power generation to atomic fuel by about 1990, the absolute amount of coal used for power generation is projected to continue to increase in each decade to 2000.

Coal consumed in generating power has no doubt contributed significantly to urban air pollution. Even with highly efficient fly ash control equipment, the amount of particulate discharged into the atmosphere is still enormous because of the huge amount of coal burned. Using emission factors issued by the U.S. Public Health Service, and assuming the average degree of fly ash control then in use, Mr. Wesler estimated that United States power plants discharged 2.6 million tons of particulate matter into the atmosphere in 1960 from the cumbustion of coal. Consumption of coal by the industry is increasing so rapidly that even if there was universal adoption of a level of control regarded as good in 1960, this figure would be increased to 2.84 million tons in 1980. However, if it is assumed that equipment of 99 percent collection efficiency were adopted by 2000, there would be a reduction to about .9 million tons, even if coal consumption in that year by electric power stations rose to 220 percent of the 1960 level as projected.

While smoke and suspended particulate matter are a highly visible nuisance, the sulfur dioxide and other sulfur oxides formed in coal cumbustion represent a more serious threat to health. Again using emission factors developed by the

U.S. Public Health Service, it appears that nearly 8.6 million tons of sulfur oxides were discharged into the atmosphere by plants generating electricity in the United States in 1960. Assuming no improvement in pollution control, the comparable figures for 1980 and 2000 would be 16.3 and 19.3 million tons, respectively.

These data are impressive, principally as a further demonstration of the effect of increasing output on the potential volume of pollutants. Because fuel consumption is highly concentrated in electric power generation and because public utilities are especially subject to scrutiny, it is entirely reasonable to suppose that the pollution actually reaching the air could be and will be held to a fraction of the above figures. For example, the highest collection efficiency assumed above for particulate matter is ninety-nine percent, whereas the best practice today achieves 99.9 percent collection. Universally applied to power stations, the projections of particulate matter generated would be cut to a tenth of the figures given. Moreover, very high stacks and correspondingly high dilution ratios are economically feasible for power stations.

Both particulate and sulfur oxide emissions may be reduced to acceptable levels by a process which recovers sulfuric acid. The Monsanto Company has developed a process which it claims permits the use of low cost, high sulfur fuels with particulate and sulfur oxide emissions reduced to acceptable level and much of the cost of pollution abatement offset by recovery of sulfuric acid. Sulfur dioxides are converted by catalytic oxidation to sulfur trioxides and fly ash and other particulates are eliminated in the passage of the resultant gases through scrubbing towers where the acid is formed. Although such a process permits use of low cost, high sulfur fuels, it is only economically feasible in such installations as a power plant where volume is high and enough acid is recovered to make by-product disposal worthwhile. The U.S. Bureau of Mines concluded that disposition of by-product acid presented too many problems and developed a sulfur oxide removal process yielding elemental sulfur as a by-product. Sulfur, the Bureau held, could be easily and inexpensively stored and transported. By-product recovery is most likely to be worthwhile where the volume generated is sufficiently large to make disposition worthwhile. Such a condition is most likely to be realized by a large central power station or a major industrial user.

The steel industry, which is by far the leading fuel consuming manufacturing industry, draws much of its coal from its own mines and much of this is low sulfur content suitable for use in making coke. The steel industry uses over sixty percent of the nation's output of low sulfur coal. The relatively clean skies of Pittsburgh is testimony to the effectiveness with which the steel industry can control air pollution, and Mr. Christman in Chapter 4 found that much of the industry's contribution to water pollution arose from the blast furnaces' gas washers.

Residential and commercial combustion of coal was less than ten percent of total consumption in 1960 and, together with railroads, is expected to decline steadily to about one percent of the total in 2000. However, residential and commercial consumption of fuel oil was by far the most important use of petroleum for other than internal combustion engines and has been a major contributor to urban air pollution. In 1960, residential and commercial consumers accounted for almost two-thirds of the consumption of oil aside from internal combustion engines.

Moreover, a large and growing percentage of the fuel oil burned in the populous eastern and central states is the low cost, high sulfur residual oils. For example, in 1965, these two regions consumed nearly two-thirds of the residual oil with a sulfur content greater than two percent. In 1964, the New York metropolitan area alone consumed 113 million gallons of residual oil for which the average sulfur content was 2.4 percent. Since then New York and other communities have enacted antipollution laws prohibiting the use of high sulfur oils. The New York law which was scheduled to go into effect October 1, 1969 confronted a major technical hitch according to the *New York Times* [3:9/23/69, 28]. The sweet low sulfur oils did not flow through equipment as easily at ordinary operating temperatures as had the sour or heavily sulfurized oils. This did not affect the small homeowner who had used the diesel type of lighter residual oil for years. Nor did it affect such major consumers as the utilities who had installed the expensive equipment needed to keep the oil at free flowing temperatures. But many factories, large apartment houses, office buildings, and institutions were not similarly equipped. The same account reported that refineries were "spending hundreds of millions of dollars to rush the desulphurization plants to completion."

The burning of fossil fuels for power generation, space heating and in industry accounted for twenty-four million of the twenty-six million tons of sulfur dioxide discharged into the United States atmosphere in 1966 and ten million of the twelve million tons of particulates in the same year. But this source of pollution was dwarfed by motor vehicles which in 1966, emitted sixty-six million tons of carbon monoxide alone as well as twenty million tons of other pollutants. Some considerable part of this was released to country air and created no important pollution problem. But a large and growing proportion of this pollutant release was in the cities which were homes for a rising fraction of the population. Air pollution from combustion of fossil fuels in internal combustion engines is examined by Alan Thierman in Chapter 8.

Air pollution by the automobile has been strictly a problem of the period since World War II. It is hard to realize that there were only twenty-six million automobiles in the United States in 1945. By 1956 this number had doubled and in the following decade another twenty-six million cars were added to the nation's stock for a total of seventy-eight million in 1966. RFF expects this growth to continue although its medium projection underestimated the sharpness of the rise during the 1960s. The RFF medium projection foresees 120 million United States passenger cars in 1980 and over 240 million in 2000.

The projection of gasoline consumption follows a similar path, but there is reason to suppose that this somewhat understates the rise. This is so principally because the movement to the cities has coincided with the upsurge in car ownership and the two are expected to continue to move together. Efficiency in combustion of gasoline is markedly lower in the stop-and-go traffic of the city than on the open road, and hence pollution per gallon of gasoline burned is likewise higher in the city, exactly where it will do the most harm.

If the trends in gasoline consumption in the cities were to follow the RFF projections without improvement in automobile pollution control, it is not alarmist to suggest that a number of our cities would literally choke to death when weather conditions were unfavorable. Los Angeles and New York have already come near doing so on a number of occasions. Fortunately, there has been widespread awareness of the problem and this has led to legislative enactments which had begun to change the automobile pollution picture by 1968. By federal statute, all automobiles sold in the United States in 1968 and subsequent years are to be equipped with emission control devices capable of reducing the amount of unburned hydrocarbons discharged to the atmosphere by almost two-thirds and the carbon monoxide formed by fifty-six percent. Even more striking improvements in completeness of automotive combustion are foreseen and believed to be commercially feasible by the 1970s. Mr. Thierman demonstrates that even the 1968 federal standards of emission controls come into general use by 1980, it will largely offset the increase in pollution resulting from the rise in the number of automobiles projected to be in use by that date. With respect to pollution due to unburned hydrocarbons and carbon monoxide, the situation would be improved by 1980 relative to 1967 in all 25 of the leading metropolitan areas. Looking ahead to 2000, a similar result would follow from adoption of the 1968 federal emission controls in all cities except Los Angeles, where the anticipated increase in number of cars would overcome pollution control improvements.

The devices required to meet 1968 federal standards of emission control do not reduce the amount of nitrogen oxides emitted. These are the gases that react with other constituents to form the brownish haze known as smog which has so plagued Los Angeles. Since the number of cars in each of the principal metropolitan areas is projected to increase from the present to 2000, nitrogen oxide pollution would grow worse in these areas if nothing better than the 1968 control devices were adopted.

As noted, much more effective controls (which would also reduce nitrogen oxides) are expected to be commercially feasible by the 1970s. Finally, the ultimate emission control levels projected for after 1980 are hoped to reduce unburned hydrocarbons to a fiftieth of those released by the uncontrolled exhaust of 1963; comparable fractions for carbon monoxide and nitrogen oxides would be one-fourteenth and one-ninth, respectively. Mr. Thierman demonstrates that if the level of controls believed to be commercially feasible by 1975 were uniformly adopted by 1980 and the ultimate controls likewise in general use by 2000, the result would be a decisive reduction in the volume of all three types of automotive pollutants entering the air of all the leading metropolitan areas. On this basis, Mr. Thierman reaches the cautious conclusion that: "If improvements in technology continue to progress as in the 1960's, air pollution conditions will grow better for American cities of the future, despite expected advances in fuel consumption." He recognizes that this depends on the assumption that pollution control devices will prove as effective as expected, will be maintained in good working order, and will continue to improve. This requires a good deal of faith in technological ingenuity since the devices Mr. Thierman relies on for his final projection have not even been designed yet. Moreover, it has been noted that there has been a recent trend to cars of higher horsepower, which, other things being equal, means higher emissions. Also, with increasing urbanization cars will be subjected more of the time to stop-and-go driving in which pollution rates are highest.

In fact, if one considers the present state of affairs with only about seventy-eight million passenger cars in the nation, the prospect of about 169 million crammed into the roads and streets of 1990, or the still more appalling 244 million projected to 2000, must raise fundamental questions about the projections themselves. Surely, any such stock of cars as 169 or 244 million would create such massive traffic jams that no amount of emission control devices, no matter how ingenious, could prevent serious air pollution by internal combustion engines. The more basic question is whether consumers would continue to buy cars in a lemminglike drive toward such a disastrous fate.

With respect to air pollution, appearances are sometimes deceiving. Anyone seeing the smoking exhaust of a large diesel truck would conclude that this vehicle is one of the most serious contributors to air pollution per gallon of fuel burned. Actually, diesels are worse than ordinary internal combustion engines with respect to particulates, nitrogen oxides and sulfur oxides, but since they ingest large quantities of air, diesels emit only about a fortieth of the carbon monoxide and about two-thirds of the hydrocarbons thrown off by the usual engine. Similarly, jet planes take-off, trailing clouds of black smoke, but the actual volume of pollutants emitted constitutes a negligible addition to that created by the automobile.

Jet planes may not add significantly to air pollution, but aviation nonetheless has its pollution problems that have many points in common with those in other areas. Most notable is the fact that the airline industry has few difficulties that couldn't be solved by dilution, i.e., more sky or landing field per plane. But a burgeoning demand offers few opportunities for solution by dilution. The pollutional impact of crowded skies does not make itself felt evenly throughout the country, but is concentrated in the nation's 22 major airports.

At these major airports, and especially at such crucial hubs as Kennedy, O'Hare, Washington National, and Los Angeles, at certain popular hours planes must wait in long lines for take-off or — more dangerous and more aggravating — be stacked-up in holding patterns in the vicinity of the field waiting for a chance to land. The burden of these activities falls most heavily on the tension-ridden shoulders of the Federal Aviation Agency's traffic controller who is responsible for guiding the incoming and outgoing flights of a number of planes. The traffic controller follows the actions of his wards by observing the blips dotting the faint luminescence of a radar screen. The strain of this responsibility has found outlet in recent years in protests and job actions by these men who carry the fate of so many in their hands.

A period of drought may render critical a water pollution problem that would be eased by dilution at other times. Bad flying weather has a comparable effect on airline operations, as each plane requires more space to navigate with safety. With perverse irony, bad weather jams more planes into the skies as landings are delayed and planes are forced into holding patterns.

New and better equipped airports with sophisticated electronic systems are needed to fill the gap, but long lead times are required for such facilities. Officials appear to have declined to heed the logic of the projections of expanded air travel.

The jumbo jets scheduled to take over a large part of the flying job in the next few years will account for more passenger miles with fewer take-offs and landings thereby effecting a sort of dilution. The difficulty is that the large jets require longer runways than are available at many airports. Moreover, the massive planes will put a massive strain on all airport facilities, most notably for baggage recovery, already a source of major delays.

In Chapter 9, Robert Graham discusses the measures that the airlines and the responsible government agencies have summoned up to deal with this host of interlocking problems. Passenger miles flown in the United States showed a nearly tenfold increase from 1947 to 1967 when a 55.9 billion mile mark was reached. This was consistent with RFF projections which call for a further increase of nearly as much to 107.8 billion miles in 1980, followed by a further more than double increase to 225 billion miles in 2000. In the discussion of air pollution from automobiles earlier in this chapter, it was suggested that the problem might solve itself in part because the projections would not, in fact, be realized because of the onerous driving conditions attendant upon the very growth itself. Considering the slowness with which action is being taken to expand aviation facilities, the same sort of question might arise in this sphere.

In Chapters 10 and 11, Robert F. Karsch and John A. Wiesz examine the impact of surface mining on the American landscape and the likely scope of such operations in the future. In the literature on the subject, the land left by surface mining, always scarred and sometimes ravaged, is usually described as disturbed. This is a euphemism on a par with shaken-up, a term used by announcers of football games to describe an injured player who is frequently in an obvious state of near concussion and physical shock.

Mr. Karsch considers surface mining of coal which has accounted for roughly forty-one percent of the 3.2 million acres of disturbed land still unrestored in 1965. Mr. Weisz discusses surface mining of other minerals, centering attention on construction materials (stone, sand, and gravel) and phosphate, which together account for forty percent, of the unrestored disturbed land, or almost as much as coal.

In earlier chapters, the automobile was cited as the principal contributor to urban air pollution. The petroleum industry has expanded along with automobile usage, as has the chemical industry which relies so heavily on petroleum derivatives for its raw materials; both industries were among the major sources of industrial water pollution. So pervasive is the influence of the automobile on the shape and pattern of American life that it is difficult to know where its influence stops. It is not entirely coincidence that the post World War II years that saw the most rapid burgeoning of automobile production also witnessed the rise to major importance of the strip mining of coal. In this period, oil displaced coal almost entirely as a fuel for railroads, and, with natural gas, took over space heating, another major traditional use for coal. In the fight to retain the electric power market the only remaining major outlet, a reduction in delivered cost of coal was crucial. Underground mine mechanization and a revolution in the techniques of mine to power plant transport were two of the weapons used by the coal industry in this struggle: surface mining was another factor that helped to triple average coal output per man-day between 1944 and 1964 [4:85].

The output of other minerals obtained by surface mining also soared during the postwar years. For example, output of stone increased five times from 1945 to 1965 and sand and gravel showed a four and one-half-fold increase. Also surface mined output of phosphate rock climbed sharply to satisfy farm demand for fertilizer.

Much of the technology and equipment for surface mining had been developed and perfected in such situations as the huge open pit copper mines of the Rocky Mountains or the iron ore mines of the Mesabi. The power shovels and hauling equipment inherited from these industries have grown with the years so that today there are shovels capable of digging 185 cubic yards at a single scoop, with larger ones planned. Machines currently under design have capacities of 200 yards. By 1965, about 3.2 million acres of land had been disturbed by surfacing mining, and about a third of this vast area has been adequately reclaimed.

Of the remaining 2.0 million acres, 800,000 had been mined for coal, and 800,000 for stone, phosphate, iron, gold, and other minerals. There is no exact information on how rapidly the total disturbed acreage is being extended, because this depends on the balance between rate of reclamation and volume of new surface mining activity. In general, as technology advances it becomes feasible to mine and process lower grade ores, so that more acreage is disturbed per unit of final product. The Department of Interior estimates that 153,000 acres of land were disturbed in 1964, 39 percent in mining sand and gravel, 30 percent for coal, 14 percent for stone, 6 percent each for phosphate and clay, and 5 percent for all others.

Mr. Karsch finds the RFF high projection for coal output best fits the experience of the 1960s. Using the high projection as the basis for his calculations, Mr. Karsch projects a cumulative total of 4.433 million acres disturbed by surface mining of coal through 2000. This makes no allowance for the amount of this land that will be reclaimed and devoted to useful purposes other than mining during the period. Under the impetus of legislation and with the aid of improvements in reclamation technology, a very large portion of the land disturbed by coal mining should be reclaimed.

Mr. Weisz has used RFF data and adapted their general methodology to create projections of the amount of stone, sand and gravel, and phosphate rock to be surface mined during the period through 2000. Since a continued substantial growth of construction and heavy application of phosphate fertilizer is expected, these projections imply enormous acreages surface mined for these purposes — as much as two and one-half times the amount similarly mined for coal. However, the net amount remaining in unreclaimed, disturbed condition for any length of time is likely to be no greater than for coal. This is because the land surface mined for construction materials is likely to be located fairly near urban areas where the demand for land for other uses is high. Likewise, land values are high in most of Florida which will be the site of most of the expansion in phosphate rock production. Accordingly, the reclamation of these lands may be expected to follow as the more or less inevitable consequence of operation of economic forces. Whether this happens with optimum efficiency will depend on the quality of the planning for the systematic restoration of such lands to productive uses.

One use suggested for abandoned mining properties of all sorts — surface and underground — is as a depository for the growing mountains of solid waste afflicting the cities of the United States. One community on the flat plains of Illinois created a mountain 118 feet high, covering thirty-nine acres at the base and three acres at the top. With the mountain of garbage covered and compacted by approved landfill methods, these prairie residents now have a proper slope for skiing and tobogganing.

For most cities, the problem of disposing of solid wastes has no such happy outcome. In the motion picture *Morgan,* the central character finds himself at one point in an active garbage dump, imminently threatened with inundation by trash. For many municipal officials this nightmare scene must have been too real for comfort.

In part, the increase in the amount of trash is nothing but a reflection of the growth in PCE (personal consumption expenditures); as the amount we spend as a nation on things to eat and wear and use, the more we discard as unnecessary, wornout or obsolete. However, the rate of increase in PCE has been about two percent annually and the medium forecast of RFF is for a continuance of this rate of increase. Most studies suggest that the annual rate of increase in the volume of all refuse subject to collection is and will be near this two percent figure. However, the same studies agree that the combustible rubbish, principally packing materials such as paper, plastics, cartons, boxes and barrels, will increase at a per capita rate of increase almost one-half again as high as the general trend of consumption.

The generation of trash in the form of empty containers is examined in Chapter 12 by N. Russell Wayne. His projections suggest a growth in packaging materials requiring disposal from 51.5 million tons in 1970 to more than double that amount, or 108.1 million tons, in 2000. Much — but by no means all — of these staggering totals consist of combustibles and would appear to be disposable by incineration. But before that is seized upon as an easy way out of the dilemma for large cities, three aspects must be noted:

1. An increasing portion of our larger cities — where the trash disposal problem is most acute — are also afflicted with serious air pollution, and many incinerators seriously exacerbate the problem, discharging large quantities of particulates to the atmosphere.

2. Glass bottles and plastics make up an increasing fraction of the rubbish destined for the incinerator and a portion that is inextricable for practical purposes. But the glass and plastics foul up the incinerators and interfere with their efficient operation.

3. Other noncombustible and potentially damaging constituents of the rubbish heap — such as large pieces of metal — may find their way into incinerators.

The oneway, nodeposit, no-return beer and soft drink bottles represent a segment of the flood of trash which is growing especially rapidly. From 1948 to 1967, annual domestic shipments of oneway bottles grew from 3.6 million to 65 million, while shipments of returnable bottles rose only from 11.9 million to 17.7 million. Output of cans for beer and soft drinks also skyrocketed during this period and these also sometimes interfered with efficient operation if they found their way into incinerators. But if tin cans and disposable bottles were a headache for incinerator operators, they were a nightmare for park and highway officials. Thousands of cans and bottles evaded the trash collection process and littered parks and highways where collection was enormously expensive.

The durable goods that are worn out or discarded for other reasons present special problems to municipal officials. Problems in the disposal of solid waste from durable goods is the subject of Chapter 8 by Kevin F. Frain. RFF projected an increase in the number of automobiles scrapped or abandoned annually from 5.0 million in 1960 to 19.5 million in 2000. Because the price of scrap has been depressed and disassembly costs are high, such outworn cars are less and less in demand by junk dealers. As any visitor to a large city may observe, more and more automobiles are simply abandoned. Mr. Frain collected new data from several leading cities on automobile abandonment; New York City, for example, estimated 30,000 cars left on its streets in 1968.

Somewhat comparable disposal problems characterize other products of our automated factories from television sets to washing machines. The ubiquity of oneway containers and throwaway durable goods has led many observers to recommend a disposal tax, assessed at the time of production and made available to states and local governments to defray the costs of the ultimate and inevitable disposal. In order to maximize the recycling of containers, such a tax on them might be made discriminatory in favor of the returnable variety.

The town dump was the destination of most of that trash which did find its way into regular collection channels. In practice, this might mean anything from the otherwise unregulated dumping of refuse at designated sites to the burying of trash at prescribed depths according to best practice in sanitary landfill. In some instances, this latter practice, properly conducted, has made it possible for cities to reclaim land otherwise valueless for public housing, recreation, or other social purposes. In the largest cities, the number of such opportunities for the beneficial use of garbage is rapidly diminishing; there is literally no place to throw it away. Compaction which reduces the space occupied by a given amount of refuse is one way of extending the capacity of the land available for disposal.

If the compacted garbage can also be coated with a protective seal to make it sanitary, the resulting cubes may be deposited in the sea for breakwaters, fishing reefs, or simple landfill. Similar use may be made of automobile bodies or other durable goods, with or without compaction. Rising urban land prices may be expected to restrict sanitary landfill and higher air pollution standards to inhibit incineration: compaction may be an increasingly attractive solution.

The mounting volume of solid waste like air and water pollution and the scars of surface mining are side effects primarily of rising *industrial* output. Time now to look at side effects associated with expanding *agricultural* output, made possible in large part by intensive use of artificial fertilizers and synthetic pesticides. None of the developments with which this volume is concerned has caused deeper alarm than the far-ranging environmental repercussions of the application of the post-war generation of chemical pesticides. Thomas Sassi examines pesticides in Chapter 14.

One of the features of the synthetic pesticides most attractive to the farmer is their persistence, that is their capacity to maintain their potency over long periods of time within the soil or when sprayed on crops. This reduces the required frequency of application to achieve whatever protective effect the pesticide may have. But this characteristic, so attractive from a profit standpoint, is profoundly troubling to observers who have found evidence of harmful side effects of synthetic organic pesticides such as DDT. Most forms of pollution tend to be temporary in some degree; a brisk wind will clear the most heavily polluted air, and the waters of a rapidly flowing river with abundant falls and rapids may have its purity restored despite heavy pollutant inputs. The more successfully persistent synthetic pesticides are, the longer their harmful effects will manifest themselves.

It has been found, moreover, that the combination of two insecticides or of an insecticide and certain pharmaceuticals may have harmful consequences vastly greater than would follow from one alone. This synergistic effect, as it is designated, has many more occasions to assert itself with persistent insecticides.

Finally, Mr. Sassi cites considerable evidence of a cumulative effect in building the concentrations of pesticides ingested by animals, including humans. Pesticides may be retained in the plant or fatty tissue of the animal and passed up the chain of life from plant to herbivore to predator in ever-increasing concentrations until potentially dangerous levels are reached.

These additive and multiplicative characteristics of the side effects of synthetic pesticides have so many alarming aspects that there have been increasingly frequent calls for a halt to their use. Even as Mr. Sassi was writing, three states — Arizona, Michigan and Wisconsin — adopted legislation banning the use of DDT. Senator Gaylord Nelson of the latter state, has introduced federal legislation to prohibit interstate sale or use of DDT.

At the present time, the future of synthetic organic pesticides is far from clear. The scientific findings of those who see grave dangers in the continued use of synthetic pesticides have been sharply disputed by leading authorities, and many others have asked that judgment be reserved. Such side effects are slow to manifest themselves with clarity. There is understandable reluctance to discard any tool capable of boosting farm output in a world where food is in short supply, many feel critically so.

On the basis of past trends in pesticide use per acre and RFF projections of acreage to be tilled in 1980 and 2000, Mr. Sassi estimated United States sales at 930 million pounds in 1980 and 996 million pounds in 2000. This compares with 763 million pounds actually sold in 1965. This is clearly a conservative estimate compared to the sixfold increase in their sales foreseen by 1985 by Senator Nelson of Wisconsin.

As an alternative to the massive expansion in the use of synthetic chemical pesticides, Mr. Sassi explores measures for the bioenvironmental control of destructive insects. Bioenvironmental controls involve too many varied techniques to be susceptible to summary treatment. Included are the careful search for natural enemies to control insects, manipulations of the environment such as changes in water levels to destroy larvae of mosquitos, the use of synthetic attractants which simulate natural ones, and genetic methods. Encouraging beginnings have been made which suggest that the material and application costs of these techniques will be much lower than the costs of chemical pesticide control.

Expanding agricultural output is also involved in Chapter 15 where Robert J. Butscher explores the phenomena grouped under the heading of eutrophication. It is significant that the work derives from the medical term eutrophic, defined by Webster as: "pertaining to, or being in a condition of eutrophy, or healthy nutrition." Just as Americans appear to be especially susceptible to heart disease believed to be associated with an overrich diet, so its waterways, and especially its lakes have been beset increasingly in recent years by an excessive growth of vegetable matter as a consequence of overenrichment with plant nutrients. A lake which receives the runoff from heavily fertilized farm lands may be subject to such eutrophication; thus it is not entirely coincidental that the nation has become aware of the problem of eutrophication during a period in which fertilizer output grew from eight million tons in 1940 to over thirty-five million in 1966. RFF projects a continuation of this trend in the future with dollar outlays on fertilizer and lime tripling between 1960 and 2000. Chemical fertilizers represent an especially important source of nitrogenous nutrients.

But artificial fertilizers are not the sole or even the most important source of plant nutrients reaching American waterways. Estimates of the amount of nutrients produced by various potential sources are available, but it is impossible to make even approximate judgments as to the amounts actually reaching the waterways. However, it is known that human wastes are rich in nitrogenous nutrients and in sewage the phosphatic constituents are heavily bolstered by detergents.

Lake Erie represents the most dramatic example of the cumulative effect of overfertilization combined with biological pollution. Lake Erie receives the runoff from an extensive farm area, plus treated and partially treated sewage effluent, plus much oxygen-demanding industrial waste. Heavy mats of algae floating on the surface mar large areas. When this dies and decays it places a further drain on the lake's overburdened defenses against biological pollution.

It is striking the degree to which eutrophication is an ailment of affluence and high industrial and agricultural productivity. Experiments have demonstrated that algae can be converted to feed for livestock or to a nitrogen-rich fertilizer, but no process of this sort has proven commercially viable in the United States. Similarly, poorer countries such as China, Indonesia, and Japan have for years grown substantial amounts of fish that feed on algae or on the lower forms that are so nourished. But again, affluence and high productivity of competitive food sources bars this solution for America. Moreover, this avenue — like the efforts at beneficent uses of thermal pollution — is attractive only if the water is biologically pure, and the harvesting of fish may be barred as well by heavy concentrations of dissolved synthetic pesticides. It is very difficult to remove plant nutrients in sewage treatment plants and only the most advanced effect any substantial reduction in the nutrient content of the effluent. Sale of fertilizer captured in this way might partially offset such costs but it has not proven commercially feasible for reasons already indicated.

The only reasonable expectation at the present time is that there will be an increasing discharge of nutrients that will threaten lakes in all parts of the country, and, perhaps later, rivers and estuaries with blighting eutrophican.

Conclusions

One thing is clear: We do not face problems of increasing pollution because of advances in technology; rather in one area after another the hope of overcoming pollution rests on technological advances and there are few areas where the amount of pollution per unit of production or consumption is not declining.

Why, then, do we appear more and more frequently to confront skies that are smokier, water that is dirtier, and landscapes more littered? Has there been increasingly flagrant disregard of the public interest by industry, local governments and ordinary citizens? There is no evidence of any widespread concern about the quality of the environment until very recent years either on the part of industry or private citizens. On the other hand, neither is there evidence that problems of pollution have arisen because of a sudden breakdown in public morality concerning our surrounding.

Rather, the conclusion is clear that pollution has become a matter of such commanding urgency because of the rise in the scale of the national output. The persistent boom in industrial production since the start of World War II, the unprecedented prosperity raising consumption levels for almost all sectors of the population — these are the villains responsible for the magnitude of the environmental side effects that are evident today.

Surely, the extent of air pollution in the United States becomes more understandable if we reflect that ten minutes consumption of fossil fuels in the United States today is equivalent to the cumulative total consumed by all mankind until the beginning of the sixteenth century — a period comprising tens of thousands of years of human life on earth. The next 350 years witnessed the first and second industrial revolutions. Use of fossil fuels increased over forty thousand times. Still, at the end of that time in 1960 in the United States, a year's consumption of fossil fuels was less than this nation uses in a single day today. RFF expects energy consumption to triple again between 1960 and 2000.

To some it may appear more pertinent to note that the number of new automobiles produced last year exceeded the nation's entire stock at the start of the 1920s. Looking ahead, we observe that the RFF projection of the new car purchases for 2000 is 28.8 million as compared to a total national stock of 28.2 million in 1947. It is evident that in automobile pollution control, we will — like Alice in Wonderland — have to run very fast to stay in the same place if the projections are anywhere near correct.

The RFF projections raise a fundamental question that has never received more than passing attention: Do our national goals really require an indefinite expansion of national output? So far in postwar United States, the furnace of national prosperity has been stoked in the first place by substantial military expenditures, and the voices questioning their necessity have been few and faint. Traumatized by the depression of the thirties, the sole concern has been that economic activity might slow down. There has scarcely been even abstract consideration given to the proposition that the quality of life might be maintained or even improved with a slower rate of increase in a better distributed national output.

If we do keep on expanding output at the present hectic pace, there seems likely to be a net increase in the impact of pollutional effects, even in the face of technological progress. This will be particularly true if the objectives of pollution control are regarded as subordinate to other national goals that are military. As a minimum, we must explore new routes to a stable economy. Possessed of a technical prowess capable of reaching the moon, we should be able to meet all reasonable productive responsibilities to our people and those of the world. And, in doing so, we need not be a bull in nature's china shop.

Appendixes

Appendix A

Appendix to Chapter 1

As a part of their original master's essays, candidates were required to make a comparison of the figure projected by RFF for a given series with the corresponding figure actually reported for some recent year (or years) by statistical agencies. In practice, this usually meant a comparison of the relevant reported figures for 1966 and 1967 with interpolated RFF projections for the same years. It was obviously necessary to make this comparison if the RFF projections were to be used as a basis for projections, however tentative, of future pollutional effects.

To reduce length and eliminate repetition, it appeared desirable to consolidate these comparisons to the extent possible, and the table accompanying this Appendix is the product of that effort. (No suitable RFF series were available for comparison with respect to the subject matters of Chapters 4, 11 and 14. The comparisons relevant to Chapters 6 and 12 have been retained within the text of the respective chapters. Comparison of the reported and projected output of coal was made a part of Chapter 10 (and this Appendix) rather than Chapter 7)

In general, the comparison suggests a reasonably close correspondence between the RFF "Medium" projection and the reported values. In part, this follows from the almost exact match between RFF population projections for 1966 and 1967 and the Census Bureau estimates for those years.

However, the RFF "Medium" projections did not fully reflect the impact of the sustained business boom on personal incomes. Thus, even the "High" RFF projections of personal consumption expenditures failed to top the figures reported for 1966 and 1967. One consequence of this immense flow of consumer funds was that the growth in the stock of passenger cars and in the extent of their use outstripped the RFF "High" projections for 1966.

Table A-1

Comparison of Reported Values and RFF Projections for Selected Series in 1966 and 1967

Item	Units	Source
Population	Millions	a
Personal Consumption Expenditures	Billion 1960 Dollars	e
Electric Power Generation	Billion kwh	b
Coal Production	Million Short Tons	c
Air: Revenue Passenger-Miles	Billions	d
Furniture and Furnishings	Billion 1960 Dollars	e
Household Appliances	Same	e
Passenger Cars	Same	e
Tires and Batteries	Same	e
Books, Toys and Sporting Equipment	Same	e
Total Passenger Car Stock	Million Vehicles	f
Passenger Car Miles	Billions	f
Fuel Consumed by Passenger Cars	Billion Gallons	f

Na - not available.

[a]Reported: U. S. Department of Commerce, Bureau of the Census, *Statistical Abstract of the United States - - 1968*, Table 2, p. 5. Projected: *Resources in America's Future*, op cit, Table A1-2, pp. 516-517. Straight line interpolation.

[b]Reported: Edison Electric Institute *Statistical Yearbook of the Electric Utility Industry for 1967* (New York, 1968) Number 35, Publication Number 68-26, p. 13, Table 7S. Projected: *Resources in America's Future*, op cit, Table A15-1, p. 837. Straight line interpolation.

[c]Reported: National Coal Association *Bituminous Coal Facts 1968* (Washington, D. C.: National Coal Association, 1968) p. 60. Total coal production, including about 2 percent anthracite. Projected: *Resources in America's Future*, op cit, Table A15-16, p. 854. Straight line interpolation.

Reported	1966 Projected		Reported	1967 Projected	
196.9	Med.	196.8	199.1	Med.	199.6
429	High	426	442	High	442
1,250	Med.	1,170	1,314	Med.	1,226
547	High	567	563	High	582
51.3	Med.	53.8	55.9	Med.	57.0
11.6	Med.	10.9	11.9	Med.	11.3
12.0	Med.	11.3	12.4	Med.	11.7
21.0	Med.	19.8	21.7	Med.	20.5
3.9	Med.	3.6	4.0	Med.	3.8
4.7	Med.	4.8	5.3	Med.	5.0
78.4	High	73.0	Na	High	75.7
745	High	715	Na	High	742
53.2	High	49.3	Na	High	51.2

(*continued*)

[d] Reported: U. S. Department of Transportation, Civil Aeronautics Board *Handbook of Airline Statistics* (Washington, D. C.: Government Printing Office, 1967, 1968). Projected: *Resources in America's Future*, op cit, Table A5-7, p. 648. Straight line interpolation.

[e] Reported: U. S. Department of Commerce, *Survey of Current Business* Vol. 48 No. 12, U. S. Government Printing Office, Dec. 1968, p. 36. Projected: *Resources in America's Future*, op cit, Table A1-27, p. 556. Straight line interpolation.

[f] Reported: U. S. Department of Transportation, Bureau of Public Roads, *Highway Statistics: 1966* (Washington, D. C.: U. S. Government Printing Office, 1967) p. 49. Projected: Based on data in *Resources in America's Future*, op cit, Table A5-15, p. 661 and Table A5-2, p. 641. RFF made the projections of "Total stock of vehicles" presented in Table A5-15 from projections of the population 20 years and over given in Table A5-2 divided by a projection of the ratio of population 20 years and over per vehicle. An identical methodology was employed in deriving the projections for 1966 and 1967 of "Total passenger car stock" shown here. Estimates of population 20 years and over for 1966 and 1967 were obtained by straight line interpolation between data for 1960 and 1970 in Table A5-2; interpolations were made in the "High" ratio corresponding to an annual average decrease of 1.7 percent. The projections of "Total passenger car stocks" for 1966 and 1967 (as given above) were obtained by dividing the appropriate population estimate for each year by the corresponding interpolated ratio. Estimates of "Passenger car miles" for each year were calculated using the RFF assumption of 9,880 miles per vehicle per year, and fuel consumption by dividing total passenger car miles by 14.5 miles per gallon.

Table A-1 (*continued*)

Item	Units	Source
Newsprint Production	Million Tons	g
Printing Paper Production	Same	g
Fine Paper Production	Same	g
Sanitary and Tissue Paper Production	Same	g
Industrial Paper Production	Same	g
All Other Paper Production	Same	g
Total of All Above Paper Production	Same	g
Iron and Steel Industrial Production Index	1957 = 100	h
Chemicals and Products Industrial Production Index	Same	h
Petroleum Products Industrial Production Index	Same	h
Farm Outlays on Fertilizers and Lime	Billion 1960 Dollars	i
Synthetic Detergent Production	Million Pounds	j

	1966			1967	
Reported		Projected	Reported		Projected
2.3	Low	2.6	2.3	Low	2.7
6.0	High	5.7	6.8	High	5.9
2.6	High	2.2	2.5	High	2.3
3.1	High	3.2	3.2	Med.	3.1
5.9	Med.	5.8	5.8	Low	5.7
22.6	Low	22.3	21.8	Low	22.9
42.6	Med.	42.8	42.4	Low	41.8
118.4	High	125.0	Na		Nc
200.8	High	193.1	Na		Nc
129.7	Med.	126.8	Na		Nc
1.90	Med.	1.78	2.05	Med.	1.84
4,298	Low	4,668	4,577	Low	4,816

Nc - not computed.

gReported: U. S. Department of Commerce *Pulp, Paper and Board: Quarterly Industrial Report July, 1969* Vol. XXIV, No. 2. Projected: *Resources in America's Future*, op cit, pp. 706-7. Straight line interpolation between values for 1965 and 1970; 1965 value represented by geometric mean of values for 1960 and 1970.

hReported: Federal Reserve System Board of Governors *Industrial Indexes, 1966* (Washington, D. C., 1967). Adjusted to reflect 1957 as base year. Projected: *Resources in America's Future*, op cit, Table A1-30, pp. 564-578. Straight line interpolation between values for 1965 and 1970; 1965 value represented by geometric mean of values for 1960 and 1970.

iReported: U. S. Department of Commerce, Bureau of the Census, *Statistical Abstract of the United States - - 1968*, Table 2, p. 5. Projected: *Resources in America's Future*, op cit, Table A1-30, pp. 578-579. Straight line interpolation.

jReported: Soap and Detergent Association *Sales Census Report*, March 20, 1969. Projected: *Resources in America's Future*, op cit, Table A17-11, p. 967. Straight line interpolation.

Appendix to Chapter 2

Pulping Processes

Unless otherwise indicated, the principal source of the discussion in this appendix was a publication of the U.S. Department of Commerce, Area Redevelopment Administration [29]. (Reference numbers designate items in the bibiliography of Chapter 2.)

Chemical Processes: Sulfite. In this process, woodchips under steam pressure are reduced to pulp by an acid. The chemicals used may be calcium, ammonium, sodium, or magnesium bisulfites plus sulfurous acid. The process frees the cellulose fibers from the wood by dissolving the lignin layer surrounding the fibers.

Unbleached sulfite pulp is generally used in paper in which color specks are not so important, e.g., to improve the strength of groundwood sheets for newsprint and catalog papers. Bleaching will yield a fine, high white, sulfite pulp used in bond, book, and other quality papers.

Kraft. The soda and sulfate (kraft) processes are alkaline pulping processes. In the soda process, the cooking liquor consists mainly of caustic soda, while the kraft process uses sodium sulfide along with sodium hydroxide. The use of sulfide produces a stronger pulp and results in faster cooking. Practically every soda mill today uses at least a small amount of sulfide and is in the process of converting to kraft pulping, so there is essentially no difference between the two processes.

Recovery of the cooking chemicals is an essential part of the kraft process, otherwise the cost of sewering would be prohibitive, and stream pollution would be so severe that operation on inland waters would be impossible. [29:3-5].

Unbleached kraft pulp is used for brown wrapping materials; bleached kraft pulp is used in printing papers, fine papers, sanitary and tissue papers, newsprint, and boxboards.

Semichemical Processes: Neutral Sulfite Semichemical (NSSC). This process falls between mechanical and chemical pulping, and involves two stages. First, the wood chips are partially softened under steam pressure with chemicals; then the fibers are separated into a papermaking pulp. Sodium sulfite is employed in most semichemical pulping.

During the early development of the NSSC process, it was hoped that the resulting pulp would be suited to the manufacture of a wide variety of products. It was subsequently discovered that the bleaching of NSSC pulp was a very expensive process. Today, NSSC pulp finds it chief use in the product of unbleached corrugating medium for shipping containers.

Chemimechanical Processes: Chemigroundwood. Here wood bolts undergo a mild chemical treatment with neutral sulfite liquor under steam pressure, followed by grinding. The chemical pretreatment softens the lignin and binding materials, allowing the grinding stone to remove whole fibers rather than fine particles.

This pulp is used in newsprint mixtures and is also suitable for the production of corrugating board.

Mason and Asplund. The first step of the Mason (exploded) process is the softening of wood chips by the action of saturated steam at elevated pressures. A sudden release of external pressure causes the chips to explode into fibers and fiber bundles, which are then refined mechanically.

The Asplund process subjects wood chips to high temperatures; the softening allows the whole, undamaged fibers to be rubbed apart mechanically.

Both of these processes are used to produce paperboards.

Cold Soda. In this process wood chips are impregnated with cold caustic soda and mechanically refined; this pulp is used as a partial substitute for groundwood pulp in newsprint and book paper.

Hot Sulfite Chemimechanical. Wood chips are subjected to a mild chemical treatment, cooked with a hot sodium sulfite solution and then mechanically fiberized into pulp. The pulp serves as a substitute for groundwood and may be mixed with a softwood kraft and sulfite pulp in the production of book papers.

Mechanical Processes Groundwood. The groundwood process forces the wood against a rapidly revolving grindstone.

This process utilizes practically all the wood in a log, both cellulose and lignin, with a resultant yield of 93 to 95 percent. The chemical processes, on the other hand, dissolve the lignin to varying degrees, so that their yield is about one-half that of groundwood [29:3-12].

Mechanical pulp is the least expensive and, therefore, is most desirable for use in non-permanent applications such as newsprint, magazines, and toweling.

Production Process Streams

A mill is generally classified as belonging the "older technology" when the processes employed are relatively inefficient, excessive quantities of wastewater are produced, no recovery of liquors is provided (except for sulfate mills), and little or no wastewater is reused. A representative subprocess series of the older technology which is in use today consists of:

1) wood preparation by mechanical debarking of logs without water reuse and without bark utilization

2) groundwood, sulfite, semichemical pulping or deinking without water reuse and without chemical or heat recovery or sulfate (kraft) with inefficient chemical recovery

3) screening without water reuse

4) pulp washing

5) bleaching without countercurrent water reuse

6) stock preparation by batch operation

7) paper machine operation with little or no fiber recovery and white water reuse

A mill is classified under "today's technology" when the processes employed are the most widely used among the industry, the wastewaters produced are within a typical range regarding both quantities and characteristics, moderate recovery of liquors is employed, and reuse of water is practiced [34]. The representative subprocess series of today's technology consist of:

1) wood preparation by mechanical debarking of logs with water reuse and bark utilization

2) groundwood or pretreated groundwood pulping from wood logs with water reuse; sulfate (kraft) pulping by batch process with water reuse and liquor recovery; sulfite pulping by use of calcium-base process with water reuse and heat recovery; neutral sulfite semichemical or kraft semichemical pulping by batch process with water reuse

3) screening with water reuse

4) pulp washing and thickening by vacuum filtration

5) bleaching with countercurrent water reuse among stages

6) stock preparation by continuous operations

7) paper machine operation with fiber recovery and white water reuse

A mill is classified in the "newer technology" group when the processes employed have been improved and are more efficient, a high degree of water reuse is employed, chemicals and heat are recovered with subsequent reduction of pollution loadings, and effluent wastewaters generated are low in quantity. The representative subprocesses series of the newer technology consist of:

1) wood preparation by long log debarking with water reuse and bark utilization

2) refining groundwood pulping from chips with water reuse; kraft pulping by continuous process with water reuse and liquor recovery; sulfite pulping by use of a soluble base (such as ammonium, sodium, or magnesium) with water reuse, heat and chemical recovery; semichemical pulping by kraft or neutral sulfite continuous process (often associated with sulfate pulping); or deinking by cooking and washing with extensive water reuse

3) screening with water reuse

4) pulp washing and thickening by multistage vacuum filters

5) bleaching with a high degree of water reuse within each washer and among stages

6) stock preparation by continuous operation

7) paper machine operation with segregation of white waters according to their quality, and with fiber recovery and extensive water reuse.

Appendix C

Adequacy of Water Resources for Waste Dilution

The RFF conclusions concerning the adequacy of the resource base (water for dilution purposes) for projected outputs of sewage cannot really be simply related to the needs of sanitary sewage dilution. RFF has made no national estimates for water resource needs because high transportation costs in relation to value, eliminate the possibility for a nationwide market for water [17:379]. Therefore, RFF has broken its study of water resource needs into three regional sections; the East, the West, and the Pacific Northwest. The East region is approximately divided from the semi-arid west region by a line running from the North Dakota-Wisconsin Border to the Texas-Louisiana Border. The Pacific Northwest contains the area of Washington, Idaho, the majority of Oregon, and parts of Montana and Wyoming.

Although RFF does isolate waste dilution flow projections from other component projections in computing total water resource needs for the period under study, they recognize a certain amount of interchangeability within these needs. For instance, according to their projections, the minimum flow that should be allowed in a river would normally be determined by the waste dilution need, but should processes be worked out for the treatment of pollutants, which would reduce that need, then other needs such as navigation, hydro-electric power or recreation might well govern the minimum flow.

Basically, RFF broke the water resource need requirements into three categories — withdrawal uses, on-site uses and waste dilution flow uses. Withdrawal uses are uses in which water is actually used up, such as by evaporation during a manufacturing process. Onsite uses would be those where water has such uses as maintenance of wetlands; as wildlife habitat; and land treatment measures for soil conservation [17:260]. Flow uses would be those such as for recreation, hyrdo-electric power generation and waste dilution. Since the flow could be used for many different needs, the one which would be the largest, in this case, waste dilution, would be the one quantified as the flow need. RFF does not, however, divide waste dilution flow into that flow needed for industrial wastes and sanitary waste dilution. Furthermore, a further possible dilution flow need, that of thermal pollution, is not covered to a significant degree. This failure to provide a breakdown complicates the already difficult problem of providing a quantified result.

Of the three regions into which RFF has broken up the continental United States, the East is by far the most humid and, therefore, has the highest average annual runoff. This, combined with the fact that the East is more highly populated than the other two regions, has caused its water supply problems to be more one of quality rather than quantity. The maximum dependable average daily flow is estimated to be 790.4 billion gallons per day (BgD). The estimated minimum flows with 1954 storage facilities would be: for 95 per cent of the time — 76 BgD and for 50 per cent of the time — 436.6 BgD [17:380]. The easiest way to increase these minimum flows is to increase the water storage

Table C-1

Waste Dilution Flow Projections, 1954-2000 (flow in billion gallons per day)

	Actual	Projected	
	1954	*1980*	*2000*
East	413.3	251.5	342.3
West except Pac. NW	101.9	51.9	76.2
Pacific Northwest	4.7	28.9	28.0

Source: *Resources in America's Future*, p. 381, Hans H. Landsberg, Leonard L. Fischman, and Joseph L. Fischer (Baltimore: The Johns Hopkins Press for Resources for the Future, Inc., 1963).

facilities in the form of reservoirs and such so that low flows may be supplemented from storage. Combined on-site and withdrawal uses in the East total only an estimated 59.6 BgD in 1980 and 85.4 BgD in 2000. Furthermore, RFF indicates these figures may well be conservative [17:381]. Flow uses, however, pose a very difficult problem. When the Flow uses shown in Table C-1 are added to the other uses, it is found that by the year 2000, required flow will be equal to that available only 50 per cent of the time. To assure at least a 95 per cent level of flow that would meet these needs would probably require that the 1954 available water storage area of 95 million acre-feet be more than quadrupled [17:382].

Waste dilution flow is:

Total streamflow needed to maintain dissolved oxygen at an average of 4 mg. per liter, for level of treatment that minimizes total cost of treatment and storage. 1954 waste dilutions estimated on basis of 70 per cent treatment for municipal and 50 per cent treatment for industrial wastes, both higher than actually prevailed [17:271].

Thus, there can be little doubt that in the East, by the year 2000, water resources will not be adequate to meet the needs unless something can be done to reduce waste dilution. The technological possibility of economically reducing the amount of flow required for waste dilution will be discussed later. Other methods of reducing this problem will also be discussed, although it must be remembered that the problem being considered is not precisely the RFF problem of whether water resources are adequate. The present study is concerned with that problem only indirectly, through its effect on the level of non-industrial pollution.

Even if the principal flow use, that of waste dilution, could be reduced, other flow uses such as navigation, hydro-electric power and recreation might require a high flow to maintain their optimum quantities. There are relatively good and economical alternates available for navigational and hydro-electrical use in the form of other means of transportation and alternate, relatively economical means of power production. RFF believes that supplies for the smaller need of recreation will be adequate through the year 2000. Even though these alternates are available, it must be remembered that their substitution will add to the economic cost or they would normally be the methods presently in use. Therefore, their cost of substitution must be included in the cost of reducing the waste dilution needs after certain limiting values are reached. This will be qualitatively true for all three regions.

Since their concern is primarily with fresh water, RFF has made no estimates which would affect the study of estuary pollution to be made. This is true for all three regions also.

In the Western Region, the water problem is a far more critical one. Although the region is larger than the East, the maximum, available, dependable flow is less than 20 per cent that of the East. This creates a severe quantity problem in the use of water supplies. The maximum available flow is estimated to be 154.1BgD. With 1954 storage facilities, the estimated minimum flows would be: for 95 per cent of the time — 6.8 BgD; for 50 per cent of the time — 69.3 BgD. Projected needs for storage and on-site uses are: for 1980 — 103.2 BgD and for 2000 — 139.2 BgD [17:380-381]. To complicate the problem further,

About 60 per cent of the total supply of the region occurs in the Western Gulf Basin and the Central Pacific Basin, leaving a relatively small amount for the remainder of the region [17:383].

In the Arizona area, the amount of water currently being used is about 2.5 million acre-feet per year in excess of long term sustainable supplies. (This is made possible by over drafts on ground water). It is, therefore, clear that by the year 2000, when dilution flow requirements are added to other uses, the regional demand will exceed the total available supply by more than 40 per cent. In specific areas within that region, the problem may even be far worse.

Waste treatment, thus, appears to be far more crucial in the West than in the East. The average amount of treatment required will probably be higher as will the sophistication required.

The third region, the Pacific Northwest, is similar to the East in that the supply is large in proportion to the prospective demand. The maximum available dependable flow is estimated to be 136.3 BgD. With the relatively small storage facilities available in 1954, the minimum available flows would be: for 95 per cent of the time — 9.7 BgD; and for 50 per cent of the time — 76.0 BgD. Projected withdrawal and on-site uses combined are: for 1980 — 14.4 BgD; and for 2000 — 21.3 BgD [17:380-381]. When the waste dilution flows from

Table IV-B1 are added, the Pacific Northwest appears to be considerably better off than even the East since by 2000, the total use of 49.3 BgD is projected.

Adding further to this favorable result is the fact that substantial future storage capacity is planned in conjunction with hydro-electric power requirements and flood control [15:421]. This should increase significantly the 50 per cent and 95 per cent flow levels.

In summation, then, the adequacy of the resource base for the safe disposal of non-industrial water pollutants varies for different regions of the country. Providing a certain pollution content standard is set, this means that for various localities, the degree of treatment required will vary.

Appendix D

Background: How the Atom is Used

Atomic Energy. The phenomenon of radioactivity gives rise to the high content of potential energy that may be converted to useful purposes. A pound of fissionable uranium 235 will provide the same energy as 1,400 tons of coal. A single gram of pure uranium-235 could (theoretically) release 23,000 kilowatt-hours of heat; sufficient, when converted to electricity, to provide a residence with full power for several years. (There are 453 grams per pound).

The more than 100 elements known to man may be converted to radioisotopes through irradiation from a high strength neutron beam. 900 known isotopes, similar to their "mother" element in atomic number, but with different atomic weight, are capable of particulate or radiant emission of unique characteristics and decay rate. Each radioisotope, whether synthesized or found naturally, must be explored to determine its radiological strength to establish type of control and safety in its handling and disposition.

The core of the atom, comprising protons and neutrons, maintains a stability sustained by a binding force that holds the particles together. The process of fission is simply an action that releases this binding force with an attendant release of energy emitted in the form of heat, particulate emissions, and high frequency radiation, known as gamma rays. Specifically, the fission process takes place when a neutron, traveling freely between molecules, is captured by an unstable element with a resulting fragmentation (and release of additional neutrons) of the nuclei into lighter elements the sum of whose atomic weights approximately equals that of the original element. Isotopes of the heavy elements of atomic numbers 84 to 92 (uranium) are said to be radioactive due to their instability. In this manner, isotopes of lighter elements such as hydrogen, helium, cesium, strontium and others are formed.

All isotopic elements, due to their inherent instability, are radioactive, and release radiation and energy while reverting to a stable form. This rate of decay to atomic stability is measured in terms of "half-life", or the time required to return to a 50 percent level of stability. The phenomenon of fission is peculiar to three heavy elements which release a stable form of energy while fragmenting under the impact of a neutron stream. These fissile substances are; thorium, uranium, and plutonium. Uranium-235, found in small quantities (0.71 percent) with natural uranium-238, is the only naturally occurring fissile element. Other fissionable materials are synthesized by neutron capture and consequent radioactive decay. These include plutonium-239, the end product of the irradiation of uranium-238 (transcending through uranium-239 to neptunium-239, to plutonium) and thorium-233 (resulting from the chain decay of thorium-232 to uranium-233 to thorium).

Fissile isotopes, under irradiation, fragment and release neutrons, sustaining the neutron stream essential to continuing fission. A single uranium-235 nuclei fissions at the rate of 31 billion impacts per second, producing one watt of power (One horsepower equals 746 watts). A rather large mass of fissile material is necessary to sustain fission due to the inefficiency of the neutron "shot gun effect". This, the critical mass, for sustained irradiation, may require 500 pounds of fission material, to obtain this much fissionable material may involve processing of many tons of natural uranium.

The Nuclear Reactor. The fission process is generally carried out in the reactor, a vessel containing the ingredients necessary to sustained fission. The components within the reactor are briefly summarized:

a. Fuel: when irradiated, liberates heat just as coal does when burned in a fossil-fuel plant.

b. A moderator serves to control the velocity of the neutron stream, and therefore, the energy of fission. Moderators may be water, heavy water, graphite, or a hydrocarbon.

c. A reflector to redirect scattered neutrons back into the fission process, increasing its efficiency.

d. Coolant to withdraw the heat of fission for utilization as a heat source. Many gases, water and liquid metals are used as coolants. The heat absorbed by the coolant is then applied to the flashing of water into steam for conventional steam-turbine operation.

e. Control rods, containing a neutron "poison" control the fission rate by their ability to absorb neutrons when it is inserted into the fuel matrix. Control of the neutron density also controls the rate of power production.

The present generation of nuclear reactors are thermal, or slow reactors functioning from a carefully moderated stream of neutrons. This effects a limited power density, or low burning rate of fuel. It is easily and safely controlled, also, permitting a wide choice of materials and configuration of design.

The "fast" reactor operates with fewer moderators with resulting high velocity of neutrons and impact force upon the fissile nuclei. The resulting "fast" chain reaction causes a conversion of fertile nuclei into fissionable fuels. This is a "breeding" of fuel such as the conversion of uranium-238 to plutonium, which is fissionable. Such breeder reactors are capable of manufacturing more fuel than contained in the startup fuel batch. Problems relating to highly enriched fuels, difficult control, coolant heat exchange and the high costs of construction, currently places the breeder in the research and development stage. Competitive operation is not anticipated by manufacturers until the 1980's.

The useful life of a fuel element within the reactor is limited by the accumulation of fission products that cling to the fuel, tending to smother the fission process. A second factor is structural degradation of the fuel element's cladding, due to intense heat and radiation. The fuel element is replaced long before the fuel is depleted. The high value of the remaining useful fuel materials, in fact, justifies reprocessing for extraction of the fission fuels. The separation and disposal of the highly radioactive wastes from the fuels, gives rise to the problems of long term storage, the focal topic of this paper.

Sources

a. C. B. Amphlett, *Treatment and Disposal of Radioactive Wastes* (New York: Pergamon Press, 1961).

b. Samual Glasstone and Alexander Seskonske, *Nuclear Reactor Engineering* (Princeton: D. Van Nostrand Co., 1963).

c. John F. Hogerton, *Nuclear Reactors* (USAEC, Oak Ridge: Division of Technical Information, 1967).

Nuclear Reactors: A Brief History

January 1939   Nuclear Fission process discovered and explained by Otto Hahn, F. Strassmann and Lisa Meisner.

December 1942   University of Chicago: Self sustained fission chain achieved and controlled by Enrico Fermi. Required 40 tons of natural uranium fuel, sandwiched between 385 tons of graphite piles serving as moderator and reflector. The fuel was metallic slugs of uranium. Designed for one megawatt output with forced air cooling, the unit is still operating and producing four megawatts.

November 1943   Oak Ridge: Experimental reactor built for production of plutonium. Graphite was used for the moderator and reflector. The "pile" generated two kilowatts of power.

September 1944   Hanford: Experimental reactor for plutonium production. Water coolant with graphite moderator. No electric output.

May 1944   Los Alamos, New Mexico: First water boiler research reactor. Enriched fuel of uranium salts. Water used as moderator and solvent.

June 1944   Argonne Labs, Chicago: Research reactor using heavy water as moderator. Enriched fuel with light water as coolant. Unit CP-3.

April 1945   Chalk River, Ontario, Canada: First zero energy experimental pile (zeep) using heavy water and natural uranium as fuel.

August 1947   Chalk River: Research reactor, "NRX". Heavy water moderator, natural uranium fuel and water coolant. High flux beam reactor.

March 1952   National Reactor Testing Station, Arco, Idaho: Materials testing reactor (MTR) with high flux beam for neutron research. Enriched fuel and water coolant and moderator. Generates 40 megawatts.

December 1950	Oak Ridge: "swimming pool" type bulk shielding research reactor. Fuel assemblies are suspended in 20 feet of water acting as coolant, moderator, reflector and shield. Generates one megawatt.
November 1946	Los Alamos: Fast breeder reactor using plutonium as fuel. Generates 25 kilowatts.
December 1951	Arco, Idaho: Experimental breeder reactor (ERB-1). A pseudo-breeder fast reactor using liquid sodium and potassium as coolant. Used uranium-238 to generate fissile plutonium-239.
March 1953	Arco, Idaho: Constructed prototype of submarine reactor.
August 1953	Arco, Idaho: Experimental boiling water reactor (BORAX).
January 1955	USS Nautilus: First operational submarine reactor.
December 1956	Argonne Laboratories: Experimental boiling water reactor (EBWR). Produced primary steam at 600 psi introduced directly into the steam turbine. Generated five kilowatts.
December 1957	Shippingport, Pennsylvania: First commercial central nuclear power plant. Pressurized with primary water at 2000 psi to produce secondary steam at 490 degrees and 600 psi. Generates 60 megawatts.

Sources

a. Samuel Glasstone and Alexander Seskonske, *Nuclear Reactor Engineering,* (Princeton: D. Van Nostrand, 1963) pp 22-28.

b. John F. Hogerton, *Nuclear Reactors,* (USAEC, Oak Ridge; Division of Technical Information, 1967) pp 16-30.

Table D-1a

**Nuclear Power: Growth and Projections—
a. Nuclear Power Generation for The
Period 1957 to 1976**

Parameter	*Statistic*			
1. Period	1957 to 1960	1961 to 1965	1966 to 1968	1969 to 1976
2. Description of period	R&D	Demonstrate and Experiment.	Operational On line	Competitive
3. Typical Reactor installed	Dresden 200 MW	Indian Point 255 MW	Oyster Creek 1 640 MW	Salem 993 MW
4. Available Power in megawatts at end of period	290 MW	925 MW	3,025 MW	44,000 MW
5. Cumulative Demand in megawatts	290 MW	1,215 MW	4,240 MW	48,000 MW
6. Annual production of nuclear energy at end of period. Billions of kilowatt-hours.	3.0	9.0	28.0	308.0
7. Projections by Resources For The Future (Landsberg) Billions of kilowatt-hours.	0.0	8.0	25.0	90.0

Sources: John Martone, *Nuclear Engineering Division, Long Island Lighting Company*; personal interview, October, 1968; John F. Hogerton, *Nuclear Reactors* (USAEC; Oak Ridge: Division of Technical Information, 1967), pp. 22-30; Hans H. Landsberg, et al, *Resources in America's Future* (Baltimore: Johns Hopkins Press, 1963), pp. 844-846.

Table D-1b

Nuclear Power Production for the Period 1970 to 2000

Projection	1970	1980	1990	2000
1. Resources For The Future				
a. Energy in billions of kilowatt-hours.	35	400	1,200	2,400
b. Power in megawatts	6,000	67,000	200,000	400,000
2. U. S. Bureau of Mines				
a. Energy in billions of kilowatt-hours.	180	700	2,200	5,000
b. Power in megawatts	35,000	130,000	400,000	900,000
3. H. R. Zeitlin, et al				
a. Energy in billions of kilowatt-hours	180	600	1,800	4,200
b. Power in megawatts	31,000	100,000	300,000	700,000
4. Colin A. Mawson				
a. Energy in billions of kilowatt-hours	120	600	1,680	4,500
b. Power in megawatts	20,000	100,000	280,000	750,000

Sources: *Resources in America's Future*, p. 843; W. E. Morrison, *IEEE-ASME Joint Power Conference* (San Francisco: U. S. Bureau of Mines, July 26, 1968); H. R. Zeitlin, et al, "Nuclear Power and The Generation of Waste," *Nucleonics*, Vol. 15 (January 1957), p. 58; Colin Ashley Mawson, *Management of Radioactive Wastes* (Princeton: Van Nostrand Co., 1965), Ch. 10, p. 246.

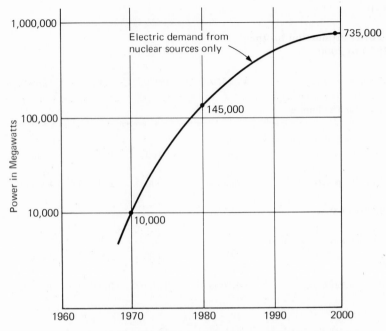

Note: Projection to 1973 is based on data extracted from utility load projections. Beyond 1973, the equation $f(t) = 33,000 + 12,500t + 500t^2$ was developed by the authors.

Figure D-1 Forecast of Nuclear Power Plant Capacity. Source: USAEC, Division of Operations Analysis and Forecasting, *Forecast of Growth of Nuclear Power,* December, 1967 (Washington, D.C.: Supt. of Documents, December, 1967), Report WASH-1084; TID-4500, p. 5.

Table D-2

Maximum Permissible Concentrations
of Radionuclides

A partial list of radioactive elements is offered below, with typical allowable concentrations in water and air, based on continuous non-occupational exposure of 168 hours per week:

Element	Atomic weight	Allowable Concentration In water In curies per mililiter	In air
1. Rubidium	86	7×10^{-4}	1×10^{-4}
2. Strontium	89	1×10^{-4}	1×10^{-8}
3. Strontium	90	1×10^{-6}	1×10^{-10}
4. Yttrium	91	3×10^{-4}	1×10^{-8}
5. Zirconium	95	1×10^{-3}	4×10^{-8}
6. Iodine	131	2×10^{-5}	3×10^{-9}
7. Xenen	135	—	1×10^{-6}
8. Cesium	137	2×10^{-4}	2×10^{-9}
9. Promethium	147	2×10^{-3}	2×10^{-8}
10. Uranium	238	2×10^{-5}	3×10^{-11}
11. Plutonium	239	5×10^{-5}	6×10^{-13}
12. Americum	241	4×10^{-5}	2×10^{-12}

Sources: Recommendations of The International Commission on Radiological Protection (ICRP), *Main Commission Report*, 9 September, 1959 (New York: Pergamon Press, 1959). National Bureau of Standards, Handbook No. 69, *Maximum Permissible Body Burdens and Concentrations of Radionuclides in Air and Water* (Washington, D. C.: National Bureau of Standards, 5 June, 1959).

Table D-3

**The Radioisotopes of the Decay Chain
of Uranium-238**

Isotope	Atomic Number	Atomic Weight	Half-life	Percent Found in natural uranium
1. Uranium	92	238	4.5×10^9 years	99.28
2. Thorium	90	234	24.1 days	1×10^{-9}
3. Protactinium	91	234	1.14 minutes	5×10^{-14}
4. Uranium	92	234	2.5×10 years	6×10^{-3}
5. Thorium	90	230	80 years	2×10^{-3}
6. Radium	88	226	1622 years	4×10^{-5}
7. Radon	86	222	3.8 days	2×10^{-10}
8. Polonium	84	218	3.1 minutes	1×10^{-13}
9. Lead	82	214	26.8 minutes	1×10^{-12}
10. Bismuth	83	214	19.7 minutes	8×10^{-13}
11. Polonium	84	214	1×10^{-4} seconds	1×10^{-15}
12. Lead	82	210	22 years	5×10^{-7}
13. Bismuth	83	210	5 days	3×10^{-10}
14. Polonium	84	210	138 days	8×10^{-9}
15. Lead	82	206	Infinity	Stable

Source: U. S. Congress: Subcommittee on
Air and Water Pollution, *Hearings On Indus-
trial Radioactive Waste Disposal*
(Washington, D. C.: Government Printing
Office, 1959), Vol. 1, Table 3, pp. 288-290.

Glossary to Chapter 6

Curie	Radioactivity measured in rate of disintegration of a specific radio-nuclide. Radium decays at the rate of 3.7×10^{10} disintegrations per second or *one curie.*
Roentgen	Quantity of radiation necessary to absorb 83.6 ergs per gram in air, or 93 ergs per gram in water or tissue.
Rad	Amount of radiation giving the energy adsorption of 100 ergs per gram of irradiated material.
Rem	Amount of radiation giving the same biological effect as one Roentgen of X-rays.
Half-life	Time interval during which the disintegration rate of a single radioactive species is halved.
MeV	Million of electron volts. The energy acquired by an electron when accelerated through a potential of one million volts. Equal to 1.6×10^6 ergs.
MeV Curies	Radioactive power equal to 0.06 watts (approximate). One million curies of strontium-90 (0.54 MeV Beta) develops heat at the rate of 32 kilowatts.
Burnup	Fraction of fissile atoms that have undergone fission. Expressed in number of megawatt-days of heat energy per metric ton of uranium. Sometimes termed, "exposure".
Breeding	Production of fissile material from fertile materials by neutron absorption. Uranium-233 generated from thorium-232, or plutonium-239 created from uranium-238 are examples.
Breeder reactor	A reactor which contains fertile material in its core, so arranged that it is converted to fissile material by neutron irradiation. The reactor produces more fuel than it consumes.
Dosimeter	An instrument which measures the dose of radiation over a given time.
Electroscope	An electrostatic instrument for measuring radioactivity intensity.

Scintillation Counter	A counter which detects ionizing radiation by the light emitted when passing through certain materials.
Alpha particle	A helium nucleus emitted in radioactive decay. Speed is of the order of 10^9 centimeters per second.
Beta particle	High velocity electrons (0.99 of the speed of light) emitted in radioactive decay.
Gamma radiation	Electromagnetic radiation of short wavelength, emitted in radioactive decay. Wavelengths are of order of 10^{-8} to 10^{-11} centimeters.
Fission	The process of atomic fragmentation caused by the neutron bombardment of the heavy elements thorium-232, uranium-233, uranium-235 and plutonium-239, with the attendant release of a stable, uniform emission of heat and radiant energy.
Fertile	Elements that are capable of conversion to fissionable materials by virtue of high speed neutron impaction. The conversion of uranium-238 to neptunium to plutonium-239 is such an example. This is the principle of breeding.
Natural fuel	The processed ores of uranium, containing 0.7 percent of uranium-235, as fissionable fuel.
Enriched fuel	The addition of fissionable fuels such as uranium-235 or plutonium-239 to natural fuel, resulting in a mixture containing more than 0.7 percent of fissionable materials. Typical enriched fuels may contain two to three percent of fissionable fuels.

Appendix E

Notes on Statistical Regression and
Correlation Analysis for
Population and Passenger Cars

Statistical Methods Employed. In obtaining the relationship between 1967 passenger cars and population, a linear regression analysis will be used. Data for major metropolitan areas will be plotted on a scatter diagram to determine the degree of the closeness of fit to a regression line. Any data which does not fit to the regression line on the scatter diagram will not be included in the regression analysis. If a straight line can be fit to the data, the linear regression equation ($Yc = a + bx$) can be applied in determining the relationship between passenger cars and population. In computing the values for the linear equation, passenger cars will be deemed the dependent variable (Y) and population will be considered the independent variable (X). The least squares method will be used in arriving at the values for the linear equation.

The degree of the closeness of the relationship between automobiles and population can then be determined using correlation analysis. The first product-moment formula will be applied to various sums and products of (X) and (Y) variables which will result in calculation of the correlation coefficient and the coefficient of determination. If the data appears to correlate, the linear regression equation will be used to predict future values of passenger cars (Y) given projected data for population (X). Public Health Service projections of future vehicle emission control levels (Table 8-19) will be applied to passenger car projections in arriving at projected emissions for various air pollutants.

Presentation of Data. Data on passenger car registrations and population for 1967 are presented in Table 8-20 for the twenty-five standard metropolitan statistical areas (S.M.S.A.'s) with largest automobile population. The U.S. Bureau of the Census was used as the source of population estimates for 1967, and the Standard Rate and Data Service was used for obtaining 1967 passenger car registrations. The data for the twenty-five S.M.S.A.'s represent 34 percent of all automobile registrations and 30 percent of total U.S. population. (Table 8-20).

Table 8-19 lists various automobile emission levels for various air pollutions. Data on this table represent rates of emissions for hydrocarbons, carbon monoxide, and nitrogen oxides. These emission factors indicate the average amount of air pollution, in pounds, caused by an automobile in a year. It will be the purpose of this analysis to project future air pollution based on these emission factors. From Table 8-19 it can be seen that developments in the field of pollution control may cause pollution levels to be greatly reduced in the future. In 1963, emission levels were not controlled and thus a total of 2,310 pounds of pollutants were emitted by an average car in a year. By 1968, however, the combination of federal legislation and technological developments by automobile manufacturers may reduce total air pollution to 1,020 pounds per year for automobiles. Unfortunately, the 1968 national standards for vehicle emissions apply to only new cars manufactured in that year. Vehicles produced prior to 1968 are controlled basically as in 1963. After 1980, it has been estimated that technological advances may result in reducing pollution to 140 pounds per car in a year.

In projecting 1980 emissions for metropolitan areas, 1975 commercially feasible emission control levels will be used. Projected emissions to the year 2000 will rely on expected ultimate pollution levels after 1980. Estimates will also be made of future emissions for 1980 and 2000 based on 1968 standards currently in effect. The latter projections are being developed because emission control levels in the future are uncertain and depend upon the willingness of government, industry and automobile users to share in the great cost of controlling air pollution.

Projections will also be made for 1967 emissions based on uncontrolled 1963 emission levels. These projections are being made in order to suggest the extent of the current automobile pollution problem, to indicate its growth if uncontrolled and for comparison with other projections assuming higher levels of control. Table 8-22 summarizes 1967 emission data.

Determination of the Closeness of Fit of Data to Regression Line. In determining the closeness of fit of the data on Table 8-20 to the regression equation, a scatter diagram has been used. The population data are plotted along the X axis since X is the independent variable. Passenger car figures are plotted along the Y axis because Y is the independent variable. When data for population (X) and passenger cars (Y) are plotted on a graph, it appears that all cities do cluster about a straight line drawn through the approximate center of the points on the graph, except Los Angeles-Long Beach. As such, this S.M.S.A. will be excluded from the linear regression analysis. All future projections will be based on 1967 passenger car density of 49 percent relative to population (Table 8-20).

Calculation of Regression Equation and Standard Deviation. The regression equation $(Yc = a + bx)$ is determined based on separate calculations for the (a) and (b) values in the equation. For formulas used, see S. P. Shao, *Statistics for Business and Economics* (Columbus, Ohio: Charles E. Merrill Books, Inc., 1967), p. 617. The linear regression equation is $Yc = 257.84 + .27x$. It is this equation which may be used to predict future passenger cars based upon a given population.

The standard deviation of regression has been calculated to be 246, which gives an indication of the scatter of the points from the regression line. The greater the dispersion of points from the regression line, the greater will be the standard deviation of regression. For formula used, see page 621 of reference above.

Calculation of the Coefficient of Determination and Correlation. The coefficient of determination has been calculated to be .94, based on a correlation coefficient of .97. There thus appears to be a high degree of correlation between population and passenger cars.

Conclusion to Statistical Analysis. The equation ($Yc = a + bx$) may be used to estimate passenger cars for 1980 and 2000, based on population projections by the Urban Land Institute [67:50-52]. By applying anticipated emission control factors to passenger car projections, projections can be made for air pollution for hydrocarbons, carbon monoxide, and nitrogen oxides.

Appendix F

*State License, Bonding and
Reclamation Requirements
for the Surface Mining of Coal*

Illinois:	License —	$50. for first acre plus $5.50 to $11.50 per additional acre
	Bonding —	$200. per acre with a $1,000. minimum.
	Reclamation —	Must be made suitable for productive use to include grading and planting of vegetation within 3 years of permit issuance. Acid material must be covered to support plant life.
Indiana:	License —	$50. plus $15. per acre.
	Bonding —	$300. per acre with a $2,000. minimum.
	Reclamation —	Plan must be submitted prior to mining. Acid material must be covered to support plant life. Grading and plant cover required.
Iowa:	License—	$50. with a renewal fee of $10. per year.
	Bonding —	Equal to established rehabilitation cost schedule.
	Reclamation—	Grading, and coverage of acid material required.
Kentucky:	License —	$50. per year plus $25. per acre.
	Bonding —	$100. to $500. per acre with $2000. minimum.
	Reclamation —	Grading and coverage of acid material required.
Maryland:	License —	$100. plus $10. renewal each year.
	Bonding —	$200. per acre with $1,600. minimum.
	Reclamation —	Grading, and coverage of final pit required.
Ohio:	License —	$75. per year plus $15. per acre.
	Bonding —	$300. per acre with $2,000 minimum.
	Reclamation —	Grading required within two years of completion of mining.
Oklahoma:	License —	$50. per year.
	Bonding —	$50. per acre or accessed value of land, whichever is less.
	Reclamation —	Grading, and coverage of acid material required.
Pennsylvania:	License —	$300. per acre.
	Bonding —	$500. to $1,000 per acre with $5,000. minimum.
	Reclamation —	Eliminate acid water. Grading, filling and vegetation required after one year.
Tennessee:	License —	$250. plus $25. per acre.
	Bonding —	$100. to $200. per acre.
	Reclamation —	Grading, coverage of exposed coal and provide favorable condition for vegetation.

Virginia:	License —	$150. plus submission of plan prior to mining.
	Bonding —	$75. per acre at time of issuance of license plus $50. per acre as mined.
	Reclamation —	Grading and vegetation required. Cover acid material and eliminate water impoundments.
West Virginia:	License —	$100. plus $50. annually and $30. per acre mined.
	Bonding —	$100. to $500. per acre with $3,000 minimum.
	Reclamation —	Grading, coverage of acid material and coal, treatment of run-off and planting of vegetation within one year required.

Source: *Restoring Surface-Mined Land,*
p. 12.

Appendix G

Appendix to Chapter 11

Table G-1

Land Disturbed by Strip and Surface
Mining in the United States, as of
January 1, 1965 by Mineral and Type
of Mining[1] (thousand acres)

	Strip mining			Quarry open pit				
Mineral	Contour	Area	Total	Into hillside	Below ground level	Total	Dredge, hydraulic, and other methods	Grand Total[2]
Coal[3]	665	637	1,302	—	—	—	—	1,302
Sand and gravel	38	258	296	82	371	453	74	823
Stone	6	8	14	100	127	227	—	241
Gold	—	8	8	1	3	4	191	203
Clay	10	26	36	22	44	66	7	109
Phosphate	28	49	77	13	93	106	—	183
Iron	7	31	38	30	96	126	—	164
All Other	11	12	23	59	81	140	—	163
Total	765	1,029	1,794	307	815	1,122	272	3,188

[1] Data by method of mining estimated on basis of information obtained by random sampling survey.

[2] Data compiled from reports submitted by the States on U. S. Department of the Interior form 6-1385X, from Soil Conservation Service, U. S. Department of Agriculture, and estimates prepared by the study group.

[3] Includes anthracite, bituminous, and lignite.

Source: U. S. Department of the Interior, Bureau of Mines, *Surface Mining and Our Environment* (Washington, D. C.: GPO, 1965), Table 2, p. 111.

Table G-2

Status of Land Disturbed by Strip and Surface Mining in the United States as of January 1, 1965, by State (thousand acres)

State	Land requiring reclamation[1]	Land not requiring reclamation[1]	Total land disturbed[2]
Alabama	83.0	50.9	133.9
Alaska	6.9	4.2	11.1
Arizona	4.7	27.7	32.4
Arkansas	16.6	5.8	22.4
California	107.9	66.1	174.0
Colorado	40.2	14.8	55.0
Connecticut	10.1	6.2	16.3
Delaware	3.5	2.2	5.7
Florida	143.5	45.3	188.8
Georgia	13.5	8.2	21.7
Hawaii	(3)	(3)	(3)
Idaho	30.7	10.3	41.0
Illinois	88.7	54.4	143.1
Indiana	27.6	97.7	125.3
Iowa	35.5	8.9	44.4
Kansas	50.0	9.5	59.5
Kentucky	79.2	48.5	127.7
Louisiana	17.2	13.6	30.8
Maine	21.6	13.2	34.8
Maryland	18.1	7.1	25.2
Massachusetts	25.0	15.3	40.3
Michigan	26.6	10.3	36.9
Minnesota	71.5	43.9	115.4
Mississippi	23.7	5.9	29.6
Missouri	43.7	15.4	59.1
Montana	19.6	7.3	26.9

(*continued*)

Table G-2 (*continued*)

State	Land requiring reclamation[1]	Land not requiring reclamation[1]	Total land disturbed[2]
Nebraska	16.8	12.1	28.9
Nevada	20.4	12.5	32.9
New Hampshire	5.1	3.2	8.3
New Jersey	21.0	12.8	33.8
New Mexico	2.0	4.5	6.5
New York	50.2	7.5	57.7
North Carolina	22.8	14.0	36.8
North Dakota	22.9	14.0	36.9
Ohio	171.6	105.1	276.7
Oklahoma	22.2	5.2	27.4
Oregon	5.8	3.6	9.4
Pennsylvania	229.5	140.7	370.2
Rhode Island	2.2	1.4	3.6
South Carolina	19.3	13.4	32.7
South Dakota	25.3	8.9	34.2
Tennessee	62.5	38.4	100.9
Texas	136.4	29.9	166.3
Utah	3.4	2.1	5.5
Vermont	4.2	2.5	6.7
Virginia	37.7	23.1	60.8
Washington	5.5	3.3	8.8
West Virginia	111.4	84.1	195.5
Wisconsin	27.4	8.2	35.6
Wyoming	6.4	4.0	10.4
Total	2,040.6	1,147.2	3,187.8

[1]Compiled from data supplied by Soil Conservation Service, U. S. Department of Agriculture.

[2]Data compiled from reports submitted by the States on U. S. Department of the Interior form 6-1385X, from Soil Conservation Service, U. S. Department of Agriculture, and estimates.

[3]Less than 100 acres.

Source: U. S. Department of the Interior, Bureau of Mines, *Surface Mining and Our Environment* (Washington, D. C.: GPO, 1965), Table 2, p. 111.

Table G-3

Solid Wastes by Type Generated by the Minerals and Fossil Fuels Industries in 1965 (1,000 short tons)

Industry	Mine Waste	Mill Tailings	Washing Plant Rejects
Copper	286,600	174,900	—
Iron and Steel	117,599	100,589	—
Phosphate Rock	72	—	54,823
Lead-Zinc	2,500	17,811	—
Alumina	—	—	—
Bituminous Coal	12,800	—	86,800
Anthracite Coal	1	—	2,000
Coal Ash	—	—	—
Other	NA[4]	NA	NA
Total	419,571	293,300	143,623

Industry	Slag	Processing Plant Wastes	Total
Copper	5,200	—	466,700
Iron and Steel	14,689	1,000	233,877
Phosphate Rock	4,030	9,383	68,308
Lead-Zinc	—	—	20,311
Alumina	—	5,350[2]	5,350
Bituminous Coal	—	—	99,600
Anthracite Coal	—	—	2,000
Coal Ash	—	24,500	24,500
Other	NA	NA	230,000[3]
Total	23,919	40,233	1,150,646

[1] Total not available but quantities negligible and are included in washing plant wastes.

[2] Of this total 1,700,000 tons are discharged directly into the Mississippi River annually by two alumina production plants in Louisiana. Annual accumulation thus is 3,650,000 tons.

[3] Represents wastes of remaining mineral mining and processing industries - 20 percent of the total wastes generated.

[4] NA - Not available.

Source: IIT Research Institute, *Proceedings of the Symposium: Mineral Waste Utilization* (Chicago, Ill., 1968), Table 1, p. 8.

Table G-4

Solid Wastes Generated by the Mineral
and Fossil Fuel Mining and Processing
Industries in 1965 and Accumulated
1942 to 1965 (1,000 short tons)

Industry	1965	Accumulated 1942 to 1965[1]
Copper	466,700	7,356,000
Iron and Steel	233,877	3,700,000
Phosphate Rock	68,308	850,000
Lead-Zinc	20,311	429,000
Alumina	5,350	36,000
Bituminous Coal	99,600	1,559,000
Anthracite Coal	2,000	910,000
Coal Ash	24,500	370,000
Other[2]	230,000	3,802,000
Total	1,150,646	19,012,000

[1] Most wastes deposited prior to 1942 believed no longer discernible.

[2] Wastes accumulated by remaining mineral mining and processing industries - 20 percent of total wastes discarded.

Source: IIT Research Institute, *Proceedings of the Symposium: Mineral Waste Utilization* (Chicago, Ill., 1968), Table 2, p. 9.

Appendix to Chapter 12

The following is a summary of the legislative developments which have taken place with respect to the problem of container waste.

Discriminatory Taxes And Outright Bans

Though the problem of solid waste produced by containers is beginning to receive recognition from a number of state and municipal governments, the theme of current efforts in the area is one of research and study as a prelude to later enactments as they may prove necessary. At present, there are no enacted laws dealing directly with this problem. Last year, thirty-five different bills were proposed banning disposable bottles and cans or placing a discriminatory tax upon them. None of these proposals were approved.

In February 1968, for example, State Senator Whitney North Seymour Jr. of New York introduced a bill in that state's legislature calling for imposition of a tax, in the form of a disposal fee, on distributors of food and beverages in nondisintegrating bottles and cans [1]. Though it was not passed, the bill is representative of laws which may be written on the books of many urban areas in the years ahead. The proposal was aimed at producers of the increasingly popular nonreturnable beverage containers. To the extent that their container production incurred waste disposal costs (assuming the container was not biodegradable), the producer would be proportionately taxed. The bill was designed to attack the problem from two angles. First, by holding out the threat of a tax, it would persuade producers to encourage their customers to return the containers for recycling and to avoid the waste problem. Or, if recycling proved to be impractical from an economic standpoint, the producers would be delegated the problem of waste disposal. Second, the producers would have been given the opportunity to pass the levy on to the consumer, thereby squarely placing the decision to return the container in the consumer's hands.

In 1953, Vermont passed an outright prohibition on the sale of beer and ale in one-way containers [25:104]. The bill was repealed in 1957 when it was determined that consumers were also throwing away returnable containers.

Other Enactments

Other legislation concerning solid waste tends to be quite general. Antilitter laws, in effect in virtually all urban areas, serve to route the waste products to a central collection point. Though perhaps desirable, there are as yet no enactments levying a tax in proportion to the pollution output of each individual, but this appears to be a distinct possibility for the future.

Laws relating to solid waste are primarily concerned with methods of getting rid of it. They run the gamut from approved forms of garbage collection to specifications for the construction of sanitary landfills and incinerators. The emphasis may well be misplaced. Present legislation avoids the prevention aspect and only serves to specify action to be taken after the problem has arisen. Ideally, the former should receive the emphasis.

Letter from Editor of *American City*

The following is the text of a letter from Mr. William S. Foster, editor of *American City* magazine:

Dear Mr. Wayne:

We, of course, are a magazine and not a governmental agency. Therefore, we have very little power to control the problem of solid waste, other than to talk about it and make recommendations. We have been cognizant of the fact that a contribution of waste products has been increasing as the standard of living rises, and we have endeavored to show how cities can cope with this problem by improved refuse collection and disposal facilities.

Industry, I am sorry to say, has been very slow in taking action. There have been a few faltering steps to indicate that the industry recognizes that a problem exists. However, all of their production and marketing is aimed at increasing the volume of solid waste, rather than decreasing it. I attach a copy of a talk I gave about a year ago relating to this problem. It attracted a fair amount of attention in the press. You might find it of interest since it deals with this aspect of urban society.

Sincerely yours,
(signed)
William S. Foster

Bibliography

Bibliography

Chapter 1
The Environment and Rising Output:
Methodology for a Study

1. Landsberg, Hans H., Fischman, Leonard L. and Fisher, Joseph L. *Resources in America's Future* (Published for Resources for the Future, Inc. by the Johns Hopkins Press, Baltimore, Md., 1963), 1,017 pages.

2. Sugden, Dr. Virginia M. and Wattel, Dr. Harold L., "A Group Approach to the Master's Essay," *Collegiate News and Views,* Vol. 23 No. 3 (March, 1970), pp. 11-14.

Chapter 2
The Social Costs of
Expanding Paper Production

1. Ackerman, E. A. and G.O.G. Lof. *Technology in American Water Development:* Baltimore: Johns Hopkins Press, 1959. 710 pages.

2. Americana Corporation. *Encyclopedia Americana.* New York, 1963.

3. Billings, R. M. "Testimony of R. M. Billings, Assistant to the Vice President of Research and Development, Kimberly-Clark Corporation, Neehan, Wisconsin, before the Subcommittee on Air and Water Pollution of the Senate Public Works Committee," June 25, 1963

4. _____ . and Q. A. Narum. "A River, A Mill, And A Need," a paper presented before the National Council for Stream Improvement, New York, February 22, 1966.

5. Britt, Kenneth W. (ed.) *Handbook of Pulp and Paper Technology.* New York: Reinhold, 1964.

6. Carr, Donald E. *Death of the Sweet Waters.* New York: W. W. Norton, 1966. 257 pages.

7. Casey, James P. *Pulp and Paper: Chemistry and Chemical Technology, Volume I: Pulping and Bleaching.* New York: Interscience Publishing, 1960.

8. Clark, John W. and Warren Veissman, Jr. *Water Supply and Pollution Control.* Scranton: International Textbook, 1965. 575 pages.

9. Gehm, H. W. "Pulp, Paper, and Paperboard," as cited in W. Rudolfs (ed.), *Industrial Wastes, Their Disposal and Treatment.* New York: Reinhold, 1953.

10. Glesinger, Egon. *The Coming Age of Wood.* New York: Simon and Schuster, 1949. 279 pages

11. Goldman, Marshall I. (ed.) *Controlling Pollution: The Economics of a Cleaner America.* Englewood Cliffs, New Jersey: Prentice Hall, 1967. 175 pages.

12. Graham, Frank, Jr. *Disaster By Default: Politics and Water Pollution.* New York: M. Evans, 1966. 256 pages.

13. Halacy, D. S. Jr. *The Water Crisis.* New York: E. P. Dutton, 1966.

14. Julson, J. O. "Environmental Protection: A Look At Its Costs And Its Future," a paper presented at the Annual Meeting of the Paperboard Group, American Paper Institute, New York, November 13, 1968.

15. Kneese, Allen V. *Water Pollution: Economic Aspects and Research Needs.* Washington, D.C.: Resources For The Future, 1962. 107 pages.

16. Kneese, Allen V. and S. Smith (ed.) *Water Research.* Baltimore: Johns Hopkins Press, 1966. 526 pages.

17. Landsberg, H. H., Fischman, L. L., and Fisher, J. L. *Resources in America's Future.* Baltimore: Johns Hopkins Press, 1963. 1017 pages.

18. Libby, C. Earl (ed.) *Pulp and Paper Science Technology, Volume II: Paper.* New York: McGraw-Hill, 1962.

19. Maine, Water Improvement Commission. "Androscoggin River Classification Report," 1966.

20. Mantel, Howard N. *Industrial Incentives for Water Pollution Abatement.* New York: Institute of Public Administration, 1965.

21. Moroney, M. J. *Facts From Figures.* Baltimore: Penguin Books, 1965. 472 pages.

22. New Hampshire Water Pollution Commission. "Staff Report on Portions of the Androscoggin River, Connecticut River, and Merrimack River Watersheds," July, 1966.

23. *New York Times.* "How Paper Serves America." October 17, 1965. p. 22.

24. Perry, John. *Our Polluted World: Can Man Survive?* New York: Franklin Watts, 1967. 213 pages.

25. *Pulp and Paper.* December 16, 1968.

26._____ . January, 1969.

27. Sutermeister, E. *The Story of Papermaking.* New York: R. R. Bowker, 1962. 209 pages.

28. Sanford, Robert (ed.) *Lockwood's Directory of the Paper and Allied Trades.* New York: Lockwood Publishing, 1968, 1962, 1957.

29. United States Department of Commerce, Area Redevelopment Administration. *Technical and Economic Feasibility of Establishing a Hardwood Pulp and Paper Mill in an Eight-County Area of Western Kentucky.* Washington, D.C., August 1964.

30._____ . Business and Defense Services Administration. *Pulp, Paper and Board: Quarterly Industrial Report.* Washington, D.C., July 1968.

31._____ . *Location of Manufacturing Plants by Industry, County and Employment Size: 1954, Part 4, Pulp, Paper, and Products.* Washington, D.C., 1959.

32._____ . *Pulp, Paper, and Board: Current Industrial Reports.* Washington, D.C., May 1968.

33. United States Department of the Interior, Federal Water Pollution Control Administration. *Cost of Clean Water: Volume 2, Detailed Analyses.* Washington, D.C., January 1968.

34._____ . *Cost of Clean Water: Volume 3, Industrial Waste Profiles, Paper Mills, Report Number 3.* Washington, D.C., November 1967.

35. Vermont Department of Water Resources. "Summary Report on Water Quality in the Lake Champlain — Ticonderoga Bay Area and Adjacent Vermont Waters. November 1968.

36. *Wastes Engineering.* April 1960.

37. Weyerhauser Company. "Progress in Air and Water Protection."

38. *Weyerhauser News.* "Pollution or Protection." April 1967.

39. Willrich, T. L. and Hines, N. W. (eds.) *Water Pollution and Abatement.* Ames, Iowa: Iowa State University Press, 1965. 194 pages.

40. Wisconsin Department of Natural Resources. "The Second Wave," biennial report of the Wisconsin Resource Development Board, August 1, 1966 to June 30, 1968.

41. Wisconsin, State of. "Report on an Investigation of the Pollution in the Upper Wisconsin River Drainage Made During 1963 and Early 1964," June 30, 1964.

Chapter 3
Water Pollution and Expanding Production
in the Steel, Chemical, and
Petroleum Industries

1. Besselievre, Edmund B. *Industrial Waste Treatment.* New York: McGraw-Hill Book Company, Inc., 1952.

2. Bird, David. "Pollution Data Called Lacking." *The New York Times,* February 19, 1969.

3. Bower, B. T.; Larson, G.; Michaels, A., and Phillips, W. *Waste Management: The Generation and Disposal of Solid, Liquid, and Gaseous Wastes in the New York Region.* New York: Regional Plan Association, 1967.

4. Carr, Donald E. *Death of the Sweet Waters.* New York: W. W. Norton & Co., Inc., 1966.

5. Connor, John T. "The Balanced Public Interest in Pollution: A Study in Corporate Responsibility." New York: By the Allied Chemical Corporation, 1967.

6. The Dow Chemical Company. *Waste Treatment and Pollution Control.* Midland, Michigan: The Dow Chemical Company, 1964.

7._____. *Instant Abatement.* Midland, Michigan: The Dow Chemical Company, 1967.

8._____. *Air, Water, and Industry.* Midland, Michigan: The Dow Chemical Company, 1967.

9. Kandle, Dr. Rosco P. and Shaw, Robert S. "Control of Water Pollution and Its Relation to Sportsmen." *Public Health News,* January 1961.

10. Drapkin, Michael K. and Ehrich, Thomas L. "The Dirty Ohio." *The Wall Street Journal,* March 17, 1969.

11. Eckenfelder, W. Wesley, Jr. *Industrial Water Pollution Control.* New York: McGraw-Hill Book Company, Inc., 1966.

12. Eckenfelder, W. Wesley, Jr. and McCabe, Brother Joseph, editors, *Advances in Biological Waste Treatment.* New York: Macmillan Company, 1963.

13. Edwards, Max. "Government and Industry – Partners in Pollution Control." Houston, Texas: National Pollution Control Exposition and Conference, 1968.

14. Hammond, R. J. *Benefit — Cost Analysis and Water Pollution Control.* Stanford, California: Food Research Institute, 1960.

15. Humble Oil & Refining Company. "Will We Have Enough Water?" Houston, Texas: Humble Oil and Refining Company.

16. Jones, Mellor A. "Mobil's Part in the Anti-Pollution Program." New York: Mobil Oil Corporation, 1969. (Mimeographed.)

17. Landsberg, Hans H.; Fischman, Leonard L.; and Fisher, Joseph L. *Resources in America's Future — Patterns of Requirements and Availabilities 1960-2000.* Maryland: Johns Hopkins Press, 1963.

18. Manufacturing Chemists Association. "Toward a Clean Environment — A 1967 Survey of Members of the Manufacturing Chemists Association." Washington, D.C.: Manufacturing Chemists Association, 1967.

19. *The New York Times.* "Maine Begins Pollution Plan to Protect Water Supplies," February 15, 1969.

20. Rivers, C. H. and Wright, W. W. "Treatment of Waste Waters — Shell Chemical's Houston Plant." Houston, Texas: National Pollution Control Exposition and Conference, 1968.

21. Shao, Stephen P. *Statistics for Business and Economics.* Columbus, Ohio: Charles E. Merrill Books, Inc., 1967.

22. Talbot, J. S. "Deep Well Disposal of Waste Water." Houston, Texas: National Pollution Control Exposition and Conference, 1968.

23. "The Chemical Industry." *World Book Encyclopedia.* 1965. Vol. III.

24. "The Killing of a Great Lake." *World Book Encyclopedia.* Yearbook 1968.

Government Publications:

25. Federal Reserve System Board of Governors. *Industrial Indexes.* 1966. Washington, D.C.: Government Printing Office, 1967.

26. U.S. Department of Commerce. *Location of Manufacturing Plants by Industry, County, and Employment Size: 1963, Part 5 — Chemicals and Allied Products, Petroleum and Coal Products, Rubber and Plastics Products, 1966.*

27._____. *Location of Manufacturing Plants by Industry, County, and Employment Size: 1963, Part 7 — Primary Metal Industries, Fabricated Metal Products, 1966.*

28. U.S. Department of the Interior. Federal Water Pollution Control Administration. *The Cost of Clean Water — Industrial Waste Profile No. 1: Blast Furnaces and Steel Mills.* Vol. III. Washington, D.C.: Government Printing Office, 1967.

29._____. *The Cost of Clean Water — Industrial Waste Profile No. 5: Petroleum Refining.* Vol. III. Washington, D.C.: Government Printing Office, 1967.

30._____. *The Cost of Clean Water — Industrial Waste Profile No. 10: Plastics Materials and Resins.* Vol. III. Washington, D.C.: Government Printing Office, 1967.

31._____. *A New Era for America's Waters.* Washington, D.C.: Government Printing Office, 1967.

32. U.S. Department of the Interior. *Proceedings, Progress Evaluation Meeting, In the Matter of Pollution of the Interstate Waters of the Grand Calumet River, Little Calumet River, Wolf Lake, Lake Michigan and Their Tributaries, Sept. 11, 1967.* Vol. I. Washington, D.C.: Government Printing Office, 1967.

33._____. *Proceedings, Conference on Pollution of Lake Erie and its Tributaries, Third Session, Buffalo, New York, March 22, 1967.* Vol. I-II. Washington, D.C.: Government Printing Office, 1967.

34._____. Federal Water Pollution Control Administration and the New York State Department of Health, Division of Pure Waters. *Lake Ontario and St. Lawrence River Basins: Water Pollution Problems and Improvement Needs.* Washington, D.C.: Government Printing Office, 1968.

35._____. . Federal Water Pollution Control Administration. *Proceedings: Conference in the Matter of Pollution of the Interstate Waters of the Hudson River and Its Tributaries — New York and New Jersey, 2nd Sess., September 20-21, 1967.* Washington, D.C.: Government Printing Office.

36._____. Federal Water Pollution Control Administration. *Proceedings: Conference — Pollution of Raritan Bay and Adjacent Interstate Waters, Third Sess., June 1967.* Washington, D.C.: Government Printing Office.

37._____. Federal Water Pollution Control Administration. *A Report to the Congress — Water Pollution Control 1969-1973: The Federal Costs.* Washington, D.C.: Government Printing Office, 1968.

38. U.S. Congress. House. *Federal Water Pollution Control Act Amendments — 1968. Hearings* before the Committee on Public Works, House of Representatives, on H.R. 15906, 90th Cong., 2nd Sess., 1968.

39. U.S. Congress. Joint Economic Committee. *Environmental Pollution,* by Robert U. Ayers and Allen V. Kneese. 1968, 90th Cong., 2nd Sess. *Federal Programs for the Development of Human Resources,* Vol. III.

40. California, State Water Resources Control Board. *Useful Waters for California.* California: Resources Agency, 1967.

41. California, Water Resources Control Board. *Final Report — San Francisco Bay-Delta Water Quality Control Program.* California: State Water Resources Control Board, 1969.

42. Illinois. *Water Quality Standards, Rules and Regulations, 1968.*

43. Rhode Island, Department of Health, Division of Water Pollution Control. *Report for the 12 Month Period July 1, 1967-June 30, 1968.* (Mimeographed.)

44._____. *Report for the 12 Month Period July 1, 1965 to June 30, 1966.* (Mimeographed.)

45. Rhode Island Water Pollution Advisory Board. "Annual Report: 1967-1968." (Mimeographed.)

Chapter 4
Population Growth and
Nonindustrial Water Pollution

1. Amratry, Aaron. "Waste Treatment for Ground Water Recharge." Advances in Water Pollution Research, Vol. 2. Washington, D.C.: The Water Pollution Control Federation, 1965. pp. 147-168.

2. Arizona Water Quality Council. *Water Quality Standards for Surface Waters in Arizona.* Phoenix, Arizona: Arizona State Department of Health, 1968. 54 pages.

3. Bohnke, B. "New Method of Calculation for Ascertaining the Oxygen Conditions in Waterways and the Influence on the Forces of Natural Purification." Advances in Water Pollution Research, Vol. I. Washington, D.C.: The Water Pollution Control Federation, 1967. pp. 157-180.

4. Clark, J. W. and Viessman, Warren Jr. *Water Supply and Pollution Control.* Scranton, Pennsylvania: International Textbook Company, 1965. 575 pages.

5. Cleary, Edward J. *The Orsanco Story.* Baltimore, Maryland: The Johns Hopkins Press, 1967. 335 pages.

6. Federal Water Pollution Control Administration. "Comprehensive Planning." *Clean Water Fact Sheet.* December 1967. 3 pages.

7. Federal Water Pollution Control Administration. *The Economic Impact of the Capital Outlays Required to Attain the Waste Water Quality Standards of the Federal Water Pollution Control Act.* Washington, D.C.: Government Printing Office, 1968.

8. Federal Water Pollution Control Administration. *Sewer and Sewage Treatment Plant Construction Cost Index.* Washington, D.C.: Government Printing Office, 1967.

9. Federal Water Pollution Control Administration. "Technical Programs" *Clean Water Fact Sheet.* November, 1967. 2 pages.

10. Federal Water Pollution Control Administration. "Water Quality Act of 1965." *Clean Water Fact Sheet.* March 1969. 3 pages.

11. Flynn, Michael J. and Thistlethwayte, D. K. B. "Sewage Pollution and Sea Bathing." Advances in Water Pollution Research, Vol. 3. Washington, D.C.: The Water Pollution Control Federation, 1965. pp. 1-25.

12. Grossman, Irving. "Experiences With Surface Water Quality Standards." *Journal of the Sanitary Division,* American Society of Civil Engineers, Vol. 94, February 1968. pp. 13-19.

13. Hardenbergh, W. A. and Rodie, Edward B. *Water Supply and Waste Disposal.* Scranton, Pennsylvania: International Textbook Company, 1960. 513 pages.

14. Heubeck, Andrew, Jr.; Coulter, James B.; McKee, Paul W.; O'Donnell, James J.; and Pritchard, Donald W. "Program for Water Pollution Control in Maryland." *Journal of the Sanitary Engineering Division,* American Society of Civil Engineers, Vol. 94. April 1968. pp. 283-294.

15. Klein, Louis. *River Pollution III. Control.* London: Butterworths, 1966. 484 pages.

16. Kneese, Allen V. "The Ruhr and the Delaware." *Journal of the Sanitary*

Engineering Division, American Society of Civil Engineers, Vol. 92. October 1966. pp. 83-92.

17. Landsberg, Hans H.; Fischman, Leonard L.; and Fischer, Joseph L. *Resources in America's Future: Patterns of Requirements and Availabilities 1960 – 2000.* Baltimore, Maryland: The Johns Hopkins Press for Resources for the Future, Inc., 1965. 1,017 pages.

18. McGauhey, P. H. and Klein, Stephen A. "Degradable Pollutants – A Study of the New Detergents." Advances in Water Pollution Research, Vol. I. Washington, D.C.: The Water Pollution Control Federation, 1967. pp. 353-373.

19. Merrill, John C.; Jopling, William F.; Bott, Roderick F.; Katko, Albert; and Pinter, Herbert E. *The Santee Recreation Project.* Cincinnati, Ohio: Federal Water Pollution Control Administration, 1967. 165 pages.

20. Missouri; Water Pollution Board. *Water Quality Standards: Missouri River Basin.* Jefferson City, Missouri: Missouri Water Pollution Board, 1968. 47 pages.

21. New York State Department of Health. *Introduction to the Pure Waters Program.* Albany, New York: New York State Department of Health, 1968. 5 pages.

22. *New York Times.* Nov. 14, 1968.

23. Ray, William C. and Walker, William R. "Low Flow Criteria for Stream Standards." *Journal of the Sanitary Division,* American Society of Civil Engineers, Vol. 94, June 1968. pp. 507-520.

24. Rosenberger, Richard L. and Walsh, Raymond. "Estuarine Water Quality Management." *Journal of the Sanitary Division,* American Society of Civil Engineers, Vol. 94, October, 1968. pp. 913-926.

25. Slanetz, L. W.; Bartley, Clara H.; and Metcalf, T. G. "Correlation of Coliform and Fecal Streptococcal Indices with the Presence of Salmonellae and Enteric Viruses in Sea Water and Shellfish." Advances in Water Pollution Research, Vol. 3. Washington, D.C.: The Water Pollution Control Federation, 1965. pp. 27-42.

26. Steel, Ernest W. *Water Supply and Sewage.* 4th ed. New York: McGraw Hill and Company, 1960. 655 pages.

27. Steinburg, Robert L.; Convery, John J.; and Swanson, Charles L. "New Approaches to Wastewater Treatment." *Journal of the Sanitary Division,* American Society of Civil Engineers, Vol. 94, December 1968. pp. 1121-1136.

28. U.S. Bureau of the Census. *Statistical Abstract of the United States: 1968.* Washington, D.C.: Government Printing Office, 1968. 1,034 pages.

29. U.S. Congress, House Committee on Government Operations. *Water Pollution Control and Abatement.* Hearings before a subcommittee of the Committee on Government Operations, House of Representatives, 88th Cong., 1st Sess., 1963.

30. Velz, Clarence J.; Calvert, James D.; Deininger, Rolf A.; Heilman, William L.; and Reynolds, John Z. "Pumped Storage for Water Resources Development." *Journal of the Sanitary Engineering Division,* American Society of Civil Engineers, Vol. 94. February 1968. pp. 159-170.

31. Letter dated May 2, 1969. From Hajinian, Charles H., Acting Director, Office of Water Quality Management. Missouri Basin Region, Federal Water Pollution Control Administration.

32. Letter dated April 14, 1969. From Hansen, George K., Sanitary Engineer, Basin Development Section, New York State Department of Public Health.

33. G. G. Cillie, *et al.* "The Reclamation of Sewage Effluents for Domestic Use," Advances in Water Pollution Research, Vol. 2 (Washington: The Water Pollution Control Federation, 1967), p. 18.

34. McGauhey, P.H. and Klein, Stephen A., "Degradable Pollutants — A Study of the New Detergents," Advances in Water Pollution Research, Vol. I (Washington, D.C.: The Water Pollution Control Federation, 1967), p. 353.

Chapter 5
Thermal Pollution

1. Briggs, Peter. *Water. The Vital Essence.* New York: Harper and Row, Publishers, 1967. 223 pages.

2. Carr, Donald E. *Death of the Sweet Waters.* New York: W. W. Norton and Company, Inc., 1966. 257 pages.

3 Clark, John W., and Viessman, Warren, Jr. *Water Supply and Pollution Control.* Scranton, Pa.: International Textbook Company, 1965. 575 pages.

4. Martin, Roscoe C. *Water For New York.* Syracuse: Syracuse University Press, 1960. 264 pages.

5. Perry, John. *Our Polluted World.* New York: Franklin Watts, Inc., 1967. 213 pages.

6. Taft, Clarence E. *Water and Algae.* Chicago, Illinois: Educational Publishers, Inc., 1965. 236 pages.

7. Wright, Jim. *The Coming Water Famine.* New York: Coward — McCann, Inc., 1966. 255 pages.

8. Arnold, D. E., et al. "Cornell Scientists See Thermal Pollution of Cayuga Lake by Planned Nuclear Power Plant" *The Conservationist*, (August-September, 1968), pp. 2-5, 36-37.

9. Edinger, John E.; Brady, Derek K.; and Graves, Willard L. "The Variation of Water Temperatures Due to Steam Electric Cooling Operations" *Journal: Water Pollution Control Federation*, XL (September 1968), pp. 1632-1639.

10. Hirsch, Allan; Agee, James L.; and Burd, Robert S., "Water Quality Standards: The Federal Perspective — Progress Toward Objectives," *Journal: Water Pollution Control Federation*, XL (September 1968), pp. 1601-1606.

11. Ignjatovic, Lazar R., "Effect of Photosynthesis on Oxygen Saturation" *Journal: Water Pollution Control Federation*, XL (May 1968), Part 2, pp. 151-161.

12. Jaske, Robert T., and Goebel, J. B., "Effects of Dam Construction on Temperatures of Columbia River" *Journal: American Water. Works Association*, LIX (August 1967), pp. 935-942.

13. Stephenson, J. Ben. "A Focus on Water Temperatures," *Industrial Water Engineering,* IV (April 1967), pp. 16-20.

14. Van Lopik, J. R.; Rambie, G. S.; and Pressman, A. E. "Pollution Surveillance by Noncontact Infrared Techniques" *Journal: Water Pollution Control Federation,* XL (March 1968), Part 1, pp. 425-438.

15. Wurtz, Charles B. "Misunderstandings about Heated Discharges" *Industrial Water Engineering,* IV (September 1967), pp. 28-30.

16. Stevens, William K. "An Infrared Device Is Mapping Water Temperatures," *New York Times,* September 11, 1968. p. 32.

17. Fenton, John H. "New Parley is Set for Boston on Lake Champlain Pollution," *New York Times,* November 17, 1968. p. 69.

18. Pecker, Scott, "Heat Pollution Roils Conservationists" *The Christian Science Monitor,* October 26, 1968. p. 3.

19. Lukens, John E. *Remote Sensing of Thermal Pollution.* HRB – Singer, Inc., A Subsidiary of the Singer Company, State College, Pennsylvania. A paper submitted for presentation at the American Water Resoùrces Conference in San Francisco, California on November 8-10, 1967.

20. Stingelin, Ronald W., and Fisher, Wilson, Jr. *Advancements in Airborne Infrared Imaging Techniques in Hydrological Studies.* Environmental Sciences Branch, HRB – Singer, Inc., A Subsidiary of the Singer Company. A paper submitted for presentation at the American Water Resources Conference in San Francisco, California on November 8-10, 1967.

21. Hoak, Richard D. *The Thermal Pollution Problem.* This source is from a paper presented at the Annual Meeting of the Pennsylvania Water Pollution Control Association in University Park, Pa. on August 10-12, 1960.

22. Mackenthum, Kenneth M., and Ingram, William Marcus. *Biological Associated Problems in Fresh Water Environments.* U.S. Department of the Interior, Federal Water Pollution Control Administration. Washington, D.C.: U.S. Government Printing Office, 1967. 287 pages.

23. Ingram, William Marcus; Mackenthum, Kenneth M.; and Bartsch, Alfred F., *Biological Field Investigative Data For Water Pollution Surveys.* Federal Water Pollution Control Administration. Washington, D.C.: U.S. Government Printing Office, 1966, 139 pages.

24. U.S. Congress. Senate. Committee on Public Works. *Hearings before Subcommittee on Air and Water Pollution: Thermal Pollution – 1968.* 90th Cong., 2nd sess., 1968.

25. U.S. Congress. Senate. Committee on Public Works. *Hearings before Subcommittee on Air and Water Pollution – 1967.* 90th Cong., 1st sess., 1967.

26. U.S. Department of Health, Education and Welfare. Public Health Service. *Report on the Pollution of Lake Erie and Its Tributaries, Part Three: New York and Pennsylvania Sources.* Washington, D.C.: U.S. Government Printing Office (July 1965).

27. U.S. Department of Health, Education, and Welfare. Public Health Service. *Report on Pollution of the Hudson River and Its Tributaries.* Washington, D.C.: U.S. Government Printing Office (September 1965).

28. U.S. Department of the Interior. Federal Water Pollution Control Administration. *Executive Order 11288, Section 4B and 4E, 1967.* Published as an appendix to the *Federal Water Pollution Control Act.* Washington, D.C.: U.S. Government Printing Office, 1967.

29. U.S. Department of the Interior. Federal Water Pollution Control Administration. *The Cost of Clean Water, Volume II, Detailed Analyses.* Washington, D.C.: U.S. Government Printing Office (January 10, 1968).

30. U.S. Department of the Interior. Federal Water Pollution Control Administration. *Pollution Caused Fish Kills in 1965,* Washington, D.C.: U.S. Government Printing Office, 1966.

31. Cronin, L. Eugene. *The Impact of Thermal Releases Along the East Coast on Shellfish.* A paper presented at the National Shellfisheries Association, Washington, D.C. on July 15, 1968. Maryland: Chesapeake Biological Laboratory, Natural Resources Institute, University of Maryland, 1968, Reference no. 68-66.

32. Gammon, M. G. "Planning the Use of Water for Cooling Purposes in Power Stations" *Water Research,* II (January 1968), pp. 131-136.

33. Winger, John G.; Emerson, John D.; and Gunning, Gerald, D. *Outlook for Energy in the United States.* Energy Division, The Chase Manhattan Bank, N.A., New York, 1968. 60 pages.

34. Resources for the Future, Inc. *Annual Report 1967.* Washington, D.C.: Resources for the Future, Inc., 1967. 134 pages.

35. Edison Electric Institute. *Statistical Yearbook of the Electric Utility Industry for 1967.* Report of the Statistical Committee of the Edison Electric Institute New York: Edison Electric Institute, 1968. Number 35. Publication Number 68-26. 70 pages.

36. Landsberg, Hans H.; Fischman, Leonard L.; and Fisher, Joseph L. *Resources in America's Future.* Maryland: The Johns Hopkins Press, 1963. 1,017 pages.

37. "Myths About Pollution" *Nation's Business,* LVI (September 1968), pp. 64-67.

38. U.S. Congress Senate. *Water Resources Activities in the United States.* Select Committee on National Water Resources. 86th Cong., 2nd sess., pursuant to S. Res 48, 1960, pp. 1-33.

39. Weiss, C. M., et al. "A Review of the Literature of 1967 on Waste Water and Water Pollution Control" *Journal of the Water Pollution Control Federation,* XL (June 1968), pp. 897-1,051.

40. U.S. Department of the Interior, Federal Water Pollution Control Administration. *Federal Water Pollution Control Act: Public Law 84-660 as amended by the Federal Water Pollution Control Act Amendments of 1961 — (PL 87-88), the Water Quality Act of 1965 — (PL 89-234), and the Clean Water Restoration Act of 1966 — (PL 89-753).* Washington, D.C.: U.S. Government Printing Office, 1967.

41. Long Island Lighting Company. *This Is Northport.* New York: Long Island Lighting Company, 1968.

42. *Air/Water Pollution Report,* VII (February 10, 1969), pp. 42-49.

43. Clark, John R. "Thermal Pollution and Aquatic Life," *Scientific American,* Vol. 220 (March 1969), pp. 19-28.

44. U.S. Department of the Interior, National Technical Advisory Committee on Water Quality Criteria, *Interim Report,* Washington, D.C.: U.S. Government Printing Office (June 1967).

Chapter 6
Nuclear Power Production and
Problems in the Disposal of
Atomic Wastes

Government and Special Commission Publications

1. Corliss, William R. USAEC, Division of Technical Information. *Direct Conversion of Energy.* Washington, D.C.: Government Printing Office, 1968. 75 pages.

2. Fox, Charles H. *Radioactive Wastes.* USAEC, Division of Technical Information, Washington, D.C.: Government Printing Office, 1965. 87 pages.

3. Hogerton, John F. *Atomic Fuel.* USAEC, Division of Technical Information. Washington, D.C.: Government Printing Office, 1963. 74 pages.

4. Hogerton, John F. *Nuclear Reactors.* USAEC, Division of Technical Information. Oak Ridge: Government Printing Office, 1967. 106 pages.

5. Howes, Merwin H. *Methods and Costs of Shaft Sinking; USAEC Project Gnome.* Bureau of Mines, Washington, D.C.: Government Printing Office, 1963. 64 pages.

6. International Commission on Radiological Protection, *Main Commission Report, 1959.* New York: Pergamon Press, 1959. 1,215 pages.

7. Langhaar, John W. *Safety Aspects of Spent Fuel Transports.* Third International Conference on Peaceful Uses of Atomic Energy. Vol. 1. Washington, D.C.: Government Printing Office, 1964.

8. Lyerly, Ray L. and Mitchell, Walter III. *Nuclear Power Plants.* USAEC, Division of Technical Information, Oak Ridge: Government Printing Office, 1966. 85 pages.

9. Nuclear Engineering and Science Congress. "Nuclear Physics and Waste Management", *Proceedings of meeting, Geneva,* 1958.

10. Pilkey, O. H. *The Storage of High Level Radioactive Wastes; Design and Operating Experience in the United States.* New York: United Nations Press, 1958, Paper 389. 176 pages.

11. Robinson, G. *The New Force of Atomic Energy.* USAEC, Division of Technical Information. Aiken: Government Printing Office, 1963. 55 pages.

12. Rodger, W. A. *Radiation Waste Disposal.* USAEC, Division of Technical Information. Washington, D.C.: Government Printing Office, 1960. 75 pages.

13. Taylor, H. A. and Cherubin, L. J. *Waste Management.* USAEC, Report TID-7517. Oak Ridge: Government Printing Office, 1956. pp. 406-457.

14. United Nations Scientific Committee, Seventh Session. *Report On Effects Of Atomic Radiation.* New York: United Nations Press, 1962.

15. U.S., Congress, Senate Committee on Government Operations. *Establishment Of A Select Committee on Government, Technology, and The Human Environment.* Testimony by Glenn T. Seaborg, Chairman of AEC, March 20, 1967. Washington, D.C.: Government Printing Office, 1967. 28 pages.

16. U.S., Congress, Sub-committee on Air and Water Pollution. Hearings on *Waste Management Research.* Senator Ed. S. Muskie, Chairman. Washington, D.C.: Government Printing Office, 1968. 224 pages.

17. U.S., Congress, Sub-committee on Air and Water Pollution. Hearings on *Industrial Radioactive Waste Disposal,* Vol. I. Washington, D.C.: Government Printing Office, 1959. pp. 2340-2372.

18. USAEC, *Civilian Nuclear Power: A Report to The President, 1962.* Washington, D.C.: Government Printing Office, 1962. 250 pages.

19. USAEC, *Civilian Power Reactor Program.* Report to U.S. Congress, Washington, D.C., 1960. Report TID-8517 part 2. Washington, D.C.: Government Printing Office, 1960. 650 pages.

20. USAEC, Division of Industrial Participation. *The Nuclear Industry, 1967.* Washington, D.C.: Government Printing Office, 1968. 223 pages.

21. USAEC, Division of Operations Analysis and Forecasting. *Forecasting of Growth of Nuclear Power.* Washington, D.C.: Government Printing Office, 1967. 166 pages.

22. USAEC, *Report on Nuclear Fission Production.* Washington, D.C.: Government Printing Office, 1957. Report WASH- 740. 368 pages.

Texts, Treatises and Topical Books

23. Amphlett, C. B. *Treatment and Disposal of Radioactive Wastes.* New York: Pergamon Press, 1961. 300 pages.

24. Burns, R. H. *The Treatment of Radioactive Liquid Effluents.* New York: John Wiley and Sons, 1960. 250 pages.

25. Collins, John C. *Radioactive Wastes, Their Treatment and Disposal.* New York: John Wiley, 1960. 450 pages.

26. Glasstone, Samuel and Seskonske, Alexander. *Nuclear Reactor Engineering* Princeton: D. Van Nostrand Co., 1963. 450 pages.

27. Gluekauf, E. Editor. *Atomic Energy Waste.* New York: International Publishers, 1961. 500 pages.

28. Grainger, L. *Uranium and Thorium.* London: Newnes Publishers, 1958. 430 pages.

29. Korff, D. A. *Electron and Nuclear Counters.* London: Van Nostrand, 1954. 475 pages.

30. Landsberg, Hans H.; Fischman Leonard L.; Fisher, Joseph L. *Resources In America's Future.* Baltimore: Johns Hopkins Press, 1963. 987 pages.

31. Lapp, R. E. and Andrews, H. L. *Nuclear Radiation Physics.* New York: Prentice Hall, 1954. 670 pages.

32. Mawson, Colin A. *Management of Radioactive Wastes.* Princeton: D. Van Nostrand Company, 1965. 460 pages.

33. Negaw, W. J. *Radioactive Wastes.* London: John Wiley, 1960. 325 pages.

34. Parsigian, V. Lawrence. *Industrial Management In The Atomic Age.* Reading: Addison-Wesley, 1965. 350 pages.

35. Saddington, K. *Chemical Processing of Reactor Fuels.* John F. Flagg, ed. New York: Academic Press, 1961. 610 pages.

Articles from Journals and Magazines

36. Anderson, Cleve R. "Why Recover The Used Nuclear Fuels?" *Electrical World,* Vol. 170, October 7, 1968. pp. 26-28.

37. Davison, W. C. "Need For Advanced Reactor is Moscow Meeting Refrain." *Electric World,* October 14, 1968. pp. 34-37.

38. Eiserer, L. A., ed. "General Electric Immersion Heater Reduces Liquid Radioactive Wastes at AEC Hanford Plant." *Air/Water Pollution Report.* January 6, 1969. p. 6.

39. Eiserer, L. A., ed. "AEC Begins Test Program for Disposal of Radioactive Wastes by Hydraulic Fracturing." *Air/Water Pollution Report.* February 10, 1969. p. 46.

40. Eiserer, L. A., ed. "Potential One Billion Dollar Savings Per Year Seen in Isotope Treatment of Sewage." *Air/Water Pollution Report.* November 18, 1968. p. 384.

41. Kenny, A. W. "Radioactive Discharge Into Sewers and Rivers." *Journal On Sewage Purification,* IV, 1957. pp. 383-395.

42. Schubert, Jack. "Radioactive Poisons." *Scientific American,* August 1955. pp. 35-44.

43. Weinberg, Alvin M. "Breeder Reactors." *Scientific American,* January 1960. pp. 82-94.

44. Young, J. F. "Nuclear Power Plans Of Many Nations Revealed." *Electrical World,* vol. 170, no. 26., Dec. 23, 1968. pp. 21-24.

45. Zeitlen, H. R. "Nuclear Power and The Future." *Nucleonics* XV, January 1957. pp. 58-71.

Unpublished Data Such as
Personal Correspondence and
Seminars Attended.

46. Carson, A. B. General Electric Nuclear Energy Division; Manager, Fuel Recovery Operation, Personal Correspondence on *Nuclear Fuel Reprocessing.* March 14, 1969.

47. Martone, John. Long Island Lighting Company. Manager, Nuclear Power

Engineering Division. Personal Interview on *Nuclear Power Projections*. November 2, 1968.

48. Tape, Dr. Gerald F., Former Commissioner, AEC, "Nuclear Power and Social and Technological Change." Session of Seminar at Columbia University Men's Faculty on, *Technology and Social Change*, May 9, 1969.

Organizational References and Reports

49. American Society of Mechanical Engineers. *Nuclear Reactor Plant Data.* New York: McGraw-Hill, 1958. Vol. I, pp. 72-77.

50. Atomfair International. *Proceedings of Joint Conference of The Atomic Industrial Forum and The American Nuclear Society.* Washington, D.C.: Atomic Industrial Forum Press, August 1968. 146 pages.

51. Benedict, Manson. *Breeder Reactors,* Conference of Atomic Industrial Forum, Washington, D.C., 16, August 1968.

52. Gower, Blair T.; Larson, Gordon P.; Michaels, Abraham; and Phillips, Walter M. *The Generation and Disposal of Wastes in The New York Region.* Report of The Second Regional Plan, New York City, March 1968, New York: Regional Plan Association Inc., March 1968. 150 pages.

53. Hogerton, John F.; Cline, James B.; Kupp, Robert W.; and Yulish, Charles B. *Background Information On Atomic Power Waste Handling.* Report of The Atomic Industrial Forum. New York: Atomic Industrial Forum Press, 1965. 90 pages.

54. Hogerton, John F. *Atomic Power Safety.* New York: Atomic Industrial Forum, 1968. 65 pages.

55. Morrison, W. E. *"Power Projections By The Bureau of Mines".* Report to *The IEEE-ASME Joint Power Committee.* San Francisco, Calif., July 1968.

56. National Bureau of Standards, Handbook 69. *Maximum Permissible Body Burdens and Concentrations of Radionuclides in Air and Water.* Washington, D.C.: Government Printing Office, 1959. 1,000 pages.

Chapter 7
Air Pollution and the
Projected Consumption of
Fossil Fuels for Purposes
Other than Internal Combustion Engines

1. Landsberg, Hans H., *Natural Resources for U.S. Growth,* Baltimore: The Johns Hopkins Press, 1964. 260 pages.

2. Landsberg, Hans H.; Fischman, Leonard L.; and Fisher, Joseph L. *Resources in America's Future,* Baltimore: The Johns Hopkins Press, 1962. 1,015 pages.

3. Bienstock, D., and Field, J. H., "Removal of Sulfur Oxides from Flue Gas

with Alkalized Alumina at Elevated Temperatures" *Journal of Engineering for Power,* (July 1964), 353-8.

4. Rohrman, F. A.; Ludwig, J. H.; and Steigerwald, B. J., "Residual Fuel Air Pollution." *The Oil and Gas Journal,* (June 27, 1966), 154.

5. Rohrman, F. A.; Ludwig, J. H.; and Steigerwald, B. J., "Low Sulfur Residual Supplies Fall Far Short of U.S. Needs." *The Oil and Gas Journal,* (August 15, 1966), 104-6.

6. Napier, D. H., and Stone, M. H., "Catalytic Oxidation of Sulfur Dioxide at Low Concentrations." *Journal of Applied Chemistry,* (Vol. 8, 1958), 781-6.

7. U.S. Department of the Interior, Bureau of Mines, *Sulfur Dioxide — Its Chemistry and Removal from Industrial Waste Gases.* Washington, D.C.: Government Printing Office, 1968.

8. U.S. Congress, House, Committee on Government Operations. *Federal Air Pollution R&D on Sulfur Oxides Pollution Abatement Hearings* before a subcommittee of the Committee on Government Operations, House of Representatives, 90th Congress, 1968.

9. U.S. Public Health Service. *Air Pollution A National Sample.* Washington, D.C.: Government Printing Office, 1966.

10. U.S. Public Health Service. *Compilation of Air Pollutant Emission Factors.* Washington, D.C.: Government Printing Office, 1968.

11. U.S. Department of Health, Education and Welfare. *The Air Quality Act of 1967.* Washington, D.C.: Government Printing Office, 1967.

12. U.S. Public Health Service. *A Digest of State Air Pollution Laws.* Washington, D.C.: Government Printing Office, 1967.

13. U.S. Public Health Service. *Atmospheric Emissions From Coal Combustion.* (Washington, D.C.: Government Printing Office, 1966) Public Health Service Publication No. 999-AP-24.

14. *New York Times,* October 24, 1968.

15. *New York Times,* February 4, 1969.

16. *New York Times,* March 16, 1969, Sec. 3, P. 14F.

17. *New York Times,* September 22, 1969.

18. The Monsanto Company, St. Louis, "The Catalytic — Oxidation System for Removing Sulfur Dioxide from Flue Gas, September 1968, 2-10.

19. *New York Times,* April 6, 1969.

Chapter 8
Air Pollution and the
Expanding Consumption of Fuels in
Internal Combustion Engines

Private Publications

1. Abrams, D. F. *Air Pollution Instrumentation.* Pittsburgh: Instrument Society of America, 1966. pp. 1-74.

2. American Association for the Advancement of Science. *Air Conservation.* Baltimore: American Association for the Advancement of Science, 1965. pp. 3-335.

3. Anderson, R. T., ed. *Waste Management.* New York: Regional Plan Association, 1968. pp. 1-107.

4. Battan, L. J. *The Unclean Sky.* Garden City, New York: Doubleday & Co., Inc., 1966. pp. 1-160.

5. Carr, D. E. *The Breath of Life: The Problem of Poisoned Air.* New York: W. W. Norton & Company, Inc., 1965. pp. 1-175.

6. Edelson, E. and Warshofsky, F. *Poisons in the Air.* New York: Pocket Books, 1966. pp. 1-160.

7. Goldman, M. I., ed. *Controlling Pollution.* Englewood Cliffs, New Jersey: Prentice-Hall, Inc., 1967. pp. 1-175.

8. Leighton, P. A. *Photochemistry of Air Pollution.* New York: Academic Press, 1961. pp. 1-300.

9. Marquis, R. W. *Environmental Improvement.* Washington: U.S. Department of Agriculture Graduate School, 1966. pp. 1-105.

10. *Physician's Guide to Air Pollution.* Chicago: American Medical Association, 1968. pp. 1-20.

11. Ridker, R. G. *Economic Costs of Air Pollution.* New York: Frederick A. Praeger, 1967. pp. 1-214.

12. Stern, A. C., ed. *Air Pollution.* Vol. 2: *Analysis, Monitoring, and Surveying.* New York: Academic Press, 1968. pp. 3-684.

13. Stern, A. C., ed. *Air Pollution.* Vol. 3: *Sources of Air Pollution and Their Control.* New York: Academic Press, 1968. pp. 3-866.

14. "Two Possible Alternatives to the Internal Combustion Engine." *1968 Annual Report-Resources for the Future, Inc.* Washington: Resources for the Future, Inc., 1968. pp. 14-22.

15. Wolozin, H., ed. *The Economics of Air Pollution.* New York: W. W. Norton & Company, Inc., 1966. pp. 1-308.

U.S. Government Publications

16. National Commission on Technology, Automation, and Economic Progress. "Technological Change as It Relates to Air Pollution." *Applying Technology to Unmet Needs.* Appendix Volume 5. Washington: National Commission on Technology, Automation, and Economic Progress, 1966. pp. 135-45.

17. U.S. Congress. House. Committee on Interstate and Foreign Commerce. *Report on the Air Quality Act of 1967.* H. Rept. To Accompany S. 780, 90th Cong., lst sess., 1967. pp. 1-97.

18. U.S. Congress. Senate. Committee on the District of Columbia. *Report on Controlling Air Pollution in the District of Columbia.* S. Rept. To Accompany S. 1941, 90th Cong., 1st sess., 1967. pp. 1-15.

19. U.S. Congress. Senate. Committee on Public Works. *Air Pollution-1967.* *Hearings* before a subcommittee on air and water pollution of the Committee on Public Works, Senate, 90th Cong., 1st sess., 1967. pp. 2231-2694.

20. U.S. Congress. Senate. Committee on Public Works. *Automobile Air Pollution-1967. Hearings* before a subcommittee on air and water pollution of the Committee on Public Works, Senate, 90th Cong., 1st sess., 1967. pp. 1-746.

21. U.S. Congress. Senate. Committee on Public Works. *Clean Air. Hearings* before a subcommittee on air and water pollution of the Committee on Public Works, Senate, 88th Cong., 2nd sess., 1964. pp. 1-1408.

22. U.S. Congress. Senate. Committee on Public Works. *Report on the Air Quality Act of 1967.* S. Rept. 403 To Accompany S. 780, 90th Cong., 1st sess., 1967. pp. 1-86.

23. U.S. Congress. Senate. "Environmental Pollution." *Federal Programs for the Development of Human Resources,* by R. U. Ayres, and A. V. Kneese. A Compendium of Papers Submitted to the subcommittee on economic progress, Vol. II. Washington: U.S. Government Printing Office, 1968. pp. 626-78.

24. U.S. Congress. Senate. *Fourth Report of the Secretary of Health, Education, and Welfare on Air Pollution.* S. Doc. 101, 89th Cong., 2nd sess., 1966. pp. 1-9.

25. U.S. Congress. Senate. *Fifth Report of the Secretary of Health, Education, and Welfare on Air Pollution.* S. Doc. 8, 90th Cong., 1st sess., 1967. pp. 1-11.

26. U.S. Congress. Senate. *Sixth Report of the Secretary of Health, Education, and Welfare on Air Pollution.* S. Doc. 47, 90th Cong., 1st sess., 1967. pp. 1-13.

27. U.S. Congress. Senate. "A Study of Pollution-Air." *A Staff Report to the Committee on Public Works.* 88th Cong., 2nd sess. pp. 1-62.

28. U.S. Congress, Senate. "Progress in the Prevention and Control of Air Pollution." *First Report of the Secretary of Health, Education, and Welfare.* S. Doc. 92, 90th Cong., 2nd sess., 1968. pp. 1-85.

29. U.S. Department of Commerce. *The Automobile and Air Pollution: A Program for Progress-Part I.* Washington: Government Printing Office, 1967. pp. 1-51.

30. U.S. Department of Commerce. *The Automobile and Air Pollution: A Program for Progress-Part II.* Washington: Government Printing Office, 1967. pp. 1-160.

31. U.S. Department of Health, Education, and Welfare. Consumer Protection and Environmental Health Service. *Thanksgiving 1966 Air Pollution Episode in the Eastern United States.* Durham, N.C.: U.S. Government Printing Office, 1968. pp. 1-45.

32. U.S. Department of Health, Education, and Welfare. Public Health Service. *Air Quality Data from the National Air Sampling Network and Contributing State and Local Networks-1964-1965.* Cincinnati: Government Printing Office, 1966. pp. 1-125.

33. U.S. Department of Health, Education, and Welfare. Public Health

Service. *Compilation of Air Pollutant Emission Factors.* Durham, N.C.: Government Printing Office, 1968. pp. 1-67.

34. U.S. Department of Health, Education, and Welfare. Public Health Service. *Digest of State Air Pollution Laws.* Washington: Government Printing Office, 1966. pp. 1-292.

35. U.S. Department of Health, Education, and Welfare. Public Health Service. *Interstate Air Pollution Study on the Effects of Air Pollution.* Cincinnati: Government Printing Office, 1966. pp. 1-62.

36. U.S. Department of Health, Education, and Welfare. Public Health Service. *Interstate Air Pollution Study on a Proposal for An Air Resource Management Program.* Cincinnati: Government Printing Office, 1967. pp. 1-132.

37. U.S. Department of Health, Education, and Welfare. Public Health Service. *Proceedings of the Third National Conference on Air Pollution.,* December 12-14, 1966. Washington: Government Printing Office, 1967. pp. 1-667.

38. U.S. Department of Health, Education, and Welfare. Public Health Service. *Report for Consultation on the Metropolitan Boston Intrastate Air Quality Control Region.* Washington: Government Printing Office, 1968. pp. 1-70.

39. U.S. Department of Health, Education, and Welfare, Public Health Service, *The Effects of Air Pollution* (Washington: Government Printing Office, 1967).

State and Local Government Publications

40. "Air Pollution in Michigan." Unpublished report by the Michigan State Department of Health, November 15, 1967. pp. 1-12.

41. The Governor's Committee on Air Resources. *Air Pollution in Minnesota.* Minneapolis: The Governor's Committee on Air Resources, 1966. pp. 1-52.

42. *Air Pollution in Nassau County, New York.* Albany, N.Y.: The Air Pollution Control Board of the State of New York, 1966. pp. 1-35.

43. *Air Pollution in Westchester County, New York.* Albany, N.Y.: The Air Pollution Control Board of the State of New York, 1965. pp. 1-79.

44. New Jersey State Department of Health. Division of Clean Air and Water. *Motor Vehicle Air Pollution Control Project.* Trenton, N.J.: New Jersey State Department of Health, 1968. pp. 1-6.

45. Wunderle, J. A. "Air Pollution Control in Ohio." *Ohio's Health,* January 1968. pp. 12-18.

Periodicals and Newspaper Articles

46. "Anti-Smog Gadgets on Your Car." *Changing Times,* April 1968. pp. 31-3.

47. Buchan, W. E., and Charlson, R. J. "Urban Haze: The Extent of Automotive Pollution." *Science,* January 12, 1968. pp. 192-4.

48. Flint, J. M. "Ford Says Radically New Antipollution Devices Must Be Built." *The New York Times.* November 19, 1968.

49. Heller, A. N. "The Role of the Scientist in Urban Ecology," *Transactions of the New York Academy of Sciences,* XXX, June 1968. pp. 1027-44.

50. Lessing, L. "The Revolt Against the Internal Combustion Engine." *Fortune Magazine,* July 1967, pp. 1-6. Article reprinted by U.S. Department of Health, Education, and Welfare. Public Health Service.

51. "The Polluted Air." *Time,* January 27, 1967, pp. 1-5. Article reprinted by U.S. Department of Health, Education, and Welfare. Public Health Service.

52. "The Polluted Air Around Us." *The Los Angeles Times.* April 16, 1967. pp. 1-3. Article reprinted by U.S. Department of Health, Education, and Welfare. Public Health Service.

53. Sitomer, C. J. "California Wars on Smog." *Christian Science Monitor.* Dec. 4, 1968.

Publications Relating to
Fields Other Than Air Pollution

54. Alexander, L. M. *The Northeastern United States.* Princeton, N.J.: D. Van Nostrand Company, Inc., 1967. pp. 1-122.

55. Eldredge, H., ed. *Taming Megalopis.* Vol. I. Garden City, N.Y.: Anchor Books, 1967. pp. 3-576.

56. Ezekiel, M., and Fox, K. *Methods of Correlation and Regression Analysis.* New York: John Wiley and Sons, Inc., 1959. pp. 1-548.

57. Owen, W. *Cities in the Motor Age.* New York: The Viking Press, 1959. pp. 3-176.

58. Owen, W. *The Metropolitan Transportation Problem.* Washington: The Brookings Institute, 1966. pp. 1-266.

59. Sell, G. *The Petroleum Industry.* London: Oxford University Press, 1963. pp. 1-276.

60. Shao, S. P. *Statistics for Business and Economics.* Columbus, Ohio: Charles E. Merrill Books, Inc., 1967. pp. 3-792.

61. *Automobile Facts and Figures-1967.* Detroit: Automobile Manufacturers Association, 1966. pp. 1-70.

62. *Automobile Facts and Figures-1968.* Detroit: Automobile Manufacturers Association, 1967. pp. 1-70.

63. Conway, H. M., ed. *The Weather Handbook.* Atlanta, Ga.: Conway Publications. 1963. pp. 3-255.

64. Felton, E. L. *California's Many Climates.* Palo Alto, Calif.: Pacific Books, 1965. pp. 1-169.

65. Lansberg, H. H.; Fischman, L. L.; and Fisher, J. L. *Resources in America's Future.* Baltimore: The Johns Hopkins Press, 1963. pp. 3-987.

66. *Petroleum Facts and Figures-1967.* New York: The American Petroleum Institute, 1967. pp. 6-344.

67. Pickard, J. P. *Dimensions of Metropolitanism.* Washington: Urban Land Institute, 1967. pp. 3-93.

68. Pickard, J. P. *The Metropolitanization of the United States.* Washington, Urban Land Institute, 1959. pp. 1-95.

69. *Spot Television Rates and Data.* Skokie, Ill.: Standard Rate and Data Service, January 15, 1968.

70. U.S. Department of Commerce. Bureau of the Census. *Americans at Mid-Decade,* Series P-23, No. 16. Washington: Government Printing Office, 1966. pp. 2-30.

71. U.S. Department of Commerce. Bureau of the Census. *Population Estimates,* Series P-25, No. 11. Washington: Government Printing Office, December 5, 1967. pp. 1-3.

72. U.S. Department of Transportation. Bureau of Public Roads. *Highway Statistics-1966.* Washington: Government Printing Office, 1967. pp. 1-186.

Chapter 9
The Crowded Skies and the
Projected Increase in Air Travel

1. U.S. Department of Transportation. Federal Aviation Agency. *FAA Air Traffic Activity: Calendar Year 1966.* Washington, D.C.: Government Printing Office 1966

2. U.S. Department of Transportation. Federal Aviation Agency. *FAA Air Traffic Activity: Calendar Year 1967.* Washington, D.C.: Government Printing Office 1967.

3. U.S. Department of Transportation. Federal Aviation Agency. *Handbook of Airline Statistics.* Washington, D.C. Government Printing Office 1967

4. Johnson, Harold, "Expansion Planned at 18 Major Airports" *American Aviation,* (September 2, 1968), p. 20

5. Judge, John F., "New Baggage System Studies" *American Aviation* XXXII, (August 5, 1968), p. 32

6. Robinson, William, "Miami Plans Airport In Swamp" *American Aviation* XXXII, (September 2, 1968), p. 47

7. Taylor, Hal, "NASA To Launch Quiet Engine Program" *American Aviation* XXXII, August 19, 1968), p. 32

8. Taylor, Hal, "Noise Reduction Could Cost Million" *American Aviation* XXXII, (August 5, 1968), p. 24

9. Twiss, Robert, "Robertson Successful In STOL Modifications" *American Aviation* XXXII, (June 10, 1968), p. 81

10. Van Osten, Richard, "Schiphol Airport Plans Ahead" *American Aviation* XXXII, (August 19, 1968), p. 52

11. "AirLine Plans Rescheduling To Ease Congestion." *American Aviation* XXXII, (September 2, 1968), p. 23

12. "Benguet 941 Test Set For EAL Shuttle." *American Aviation* XXXII, (June 24, 1968), p. 16

13. "Boyd Gives Policy On Airports, Airways." *American Aviation* XXXII, (June 24, 1968), p. 16

14. "Dow Attacks Runway Icing." *American Aviation* XXXII, (October 24, 1968), p. 74

15. "NASA To Test Low Cost Capital CAS." *American Aviation* XXXII, (August 5, 1968), p. 61

16. "NASA Plans Research Program to Expand V/STOL Technology." *American Aviation* XXXII, (June 24, 1968), p. 50

17. "Noise Bill Draws Opposing Views." *American Aviation* XXXII, (June 24, 1968), p. 21

18. "New Univac Computers OK'd For New York City Area." *American Aviation* XXXII, (June 10, 1968), p. 63

19. "Ryan Plans VTOL Business Jet in 1969" *American Aviation* XXXII, (September 2, 1968), p. 15

20. "Trends" *American Aviation* XXXII, (September 2, 1968), p. 31

21. "Warm Fog Dispersal Test 70% Successful." *American Aviation* XXXII, (June 10, 1968), p. 37.

22. "Twenty-five Dollar Minimum Airport Use Fees to be Implemented by PNYA." *American Aviation* XXXII, (July 22, 1968), p. 23

23. Roscoe, Stanley, "Airborne Displays For Flight and Navigation." *Human Factors*, X, (August 1968), p. 323

24. "Pilots Response in Combined Control Tasks." *Human Factors*, X, (October 1968), p. 282

25. Ruppenthal, Karl M., "No Money For Safe Landings." *Nation* CCVII, (August 26, 1968), p. 143

26. Eberhart, Jonathan, "Gemini Electronics Used For V/STOL." *Science News* VIIC, (August 17, 1968), p. 158

27. Eberhart, Jonathan, "Noise Survey by FAA." *Science News* VIIC, (July 20, 1968), p. 161

28. "Lights Signal Runway Runout." *Science News* VIIC, (April 13, 1968), p. 356

29. "STOL: A Takeoff Shortly." *Science News* VIIC, (September 7, 1968), p. 229

30. "STOL – Port Guidelines Issued." *Science News* VIIC, (October 19, 1968) p. 390

31. "The Organization Gap." *Science News* VIIC, (June 15, 1968), p. 570

32. "Can Air Travel Be Kept Safe." *U.S. News & World Report* LXU, (January 1, 1968), p. 55

33. "Coming Up: Another Crisis for U.S. Airports" *U.S. News & World Report* LXU, (October 3, 1968), pp. 96-7

34. "The Amazing Future for Air Travel." *U.S. News & World Report* LXU, (September 23, 1968), p. 92.

35. "U.S. Needs 800 New Airports in 5 Years: FAA." *Long Island Press* (Garden City, N.Y.) (November 12, 1968), p. 4.

36. Lowell, Vernon W., *Airline Safety is a Myth* Bartholomew House: New York 1967

37. U.S. Department of Transportation, Federal Aviation Agency, *FAA Air Traffic Activity: Fiscal Year 1968*, (Washington, D.C.: Government Printing Office, 1968) p. 36

38. "Chemical Fertilizer Bars Runway Ice." *New York Times*, (New York, New York), January 12, 1969, p. 93

39. F. D. Burnbaum, "FAA Tests New Localizer," *American Aviation*, XXXII, (August 5, 1968), p. 64

Chapter 10
The Social Costs of Surface Mined Coal

United States Government Publications

1. U.S. Bureau of Census. *Statistical Abstract of the United States, 1968.* 89th Edition, Washington, D.C.: Government Printing Office, 1968. 1,034 pages.

2. U.S. Congress. Senate. Committee on Interior and Insular Affairs. *Surface Mine Reclamation. Hearings* before the Committee on Interior and Insular Affairs, on S. 217, 3126 and 3132, 90th Cong., 1968. 375 pages.

3. U.S. Congress, Senate, Committee on Public Works. *Waste Management and Environmental Quality Management. Hearings* before a subcommittee of the Committee on Public Works, 90th Cong., 1968. 451 pages.

4. U.S. Department of Agriculture. *Restoring Surface-Mined Land.* Washington, D.C.: Government Printing Office, April 1968. 18 pages.

5. U.S. Department of Interior. *Coal Reserves of the United States – A Progress Report,* by Paul Averitt. Washington, D.C.: Government Printing Office, 1961. 116 pages.

6. U.S. Department of Interior. *Description of Physical Environment and of Strip-Mining Operations in Parts of Beaver Creek Basin Kentucky,* by John J. Musser. Washington, D.C.: Government Printing Office, 1963. 25 pages.

7. U.S. Department of Interior. *Office of Coal Research Annual Report, 1966.* Washington, D.C.: Government Printing Office, 1966. 60 pages.

8. U.S. Department of Interior. *Office of Coal Research Annual Report, 1967.* Washington, D.C.: Government Printing Office, 1967. 68 pages.

9. U.S. Department of Interior. *Office of Coal Research Annual Report, 1968.* Washington, D.C.: Government Printing Office, 1968. 56 pages.

10. U.S. Department of Interior. *Stripping-Coal Resources of the United States,* by Paul Averitt. Washington, D.C.: Government Printing Office, 1968. 20 pages.

11. U.S. Department of Interior. *Study of Strip and Surface Mining in Appalachia.* Washington, D.C.: Government Printing Office, 1966. 78 pages.

12. U.S. Department of Interior. *Surface Mining and Our Environment.* Washington, D.C.: Government Printing Office, 1967. 124 pages.

Other Publications

13. Brooks, David B. "Strip Mine Reclamation and Economic Analysis." *Natural Resources,* January 1966. pp. 13-44.

14. Dalrymple, Byron W. "They're Mining For Bass In Kansas." *True's Fishing Yearbook,* November 1965.

15. Emerson, John D; Gunning, Gerald D; and Winger, John G. *Outlook for Energy In the United States.* New York: The Chase Manhattan Bank, N.A., 1968. 60 pages.

16. Klimstra, W. D. and John L. Reseberry. "Recreational Activities on Illinois Strip-Mined Lands." *Journal of Soil and Water Conservation,* May-June 1964.

17. Lamm, Arnold E. "Surface Mine Reclamation — Why and How." *Mining Congress Journal,* March 1964.

18. Landsberg, Hans H; Fischman, Leonard L.; and Fisher, Joseph L. *Resources In America's Future.* Baltimore: The Johns Hopkins Press, 1963. 1,017 pages.

19. National Coal Association. *Bituminous Coal Facts 1968.* Washington, D.C.: National Coal Association, 1968. 107 pages.

20. Neter, John, and Wasserman, William. *Fundamental Statistics for Business and Economics.* Boston: Allyn and Bacon, Inc., 1961. 838 pages.

21. Sawyer, L. E. "The Strippers." *Landscape Architecture,* January 1966.

22. Stearn, Enoid W. "Surface Minings Conservation Program Pays Off." *Coal Mining and Processing,* April 1964.

23. Sullivan, G. D. "A New Science-Mined Land Reclamation." *Mining Engineering,* July 1965.

24. "Strip Mining Builds for Accelerated Growth." *Coal Age,* August 1966.

25. *The New York Times.* April 20, 1969.

26. Grant Davis and Walter H. Davidson, "Coal-Mine Spoil Banks Offer Good Potential For Timber and Wildlife Production," *Pennsylvania Forests,* Vol. LVIII, April 1968. pp. 20-22.

27. "Strip Mine Legislation Pro and Con," *Mined-Land Conservation State and Nation,* Vol. 4, No. 5 (Washington, D.C.: Mined Land Conservation Conference, 1968).

28. "Modern Techniques are Changing Reclamation Planting," *Mined-Land Conservation State and Nation,* Vol. 4, No. 4, (Washington, D.C.: Mined-Land Conservation Conference, 1968).

29. "Harvest 1968," *Mined-Land Conservation State and Nation,* Vol. 4, No. 8, (Washington, D.C.: Mined-Land Conservation Conference, 1968).

30. R. E. Melton and W. W. Ward, "Penn State Shifts Emphasis In Strip-Mine Vegetation Research," *Pennsylvania Forests,* Vol. LVIII, April 1968. pp. 11-14.

Chapter 11
The Environmental Efforts of
Surface Mining and
Mineral Waste Generation

Books

1. Landsberg, Hans H.; Fischman, Leonard L.; and Fisher, Joseph L. *Resources in America's Future.* Baltimore: The John Hopkins Press, 1963. 1,017 pages.
2. Pickard, J. P., *Dimensions of Metropolitanism,* (Washington: Urban Land Institute, 1967).

Periodicals

3. Bishop, Freeman. "Is Federal Control of Surface Mining Necessary?" *Mining Engineering,* August 1967, pp. 34-35.
4. Brooks, David B. "Strip Mine Reclamation and Economic Analysis." *Natural Resources Journal,* January 1966, pp. 13-44.
5. Brown, James H. "Fine Grind." *Mining Engineering,* June 1968, p. 36.
6. Herde, Roy S. "Open Pit Mining." *Mining Congress Journal,* February 1968, pp. 181-185.
7. Herod, Buren C. "NSA Anniversary Meeting Emphasizes Potential of Future." *Pit and Quarry,* December 1967, pp. 130-134.
8. Lam, Arnold E. "Surface Mine Reclamation – Why and How." *Mining Congress Journal,* March 1964, pp. 23-27.
9. May, Morton. "Mine Reclamation in the Western States." *Mining Congress Journal,* August 1967, pp. 101-105.
10. May, Robert F. "Strip-Mine Reclamation Research – Where are We?" *Mining Congress Journal,* April 1965, pp. 52-55.
11. Medvick, Charles. "Why Reforest Surface Mined Areas?" *Mining Congress Journal,* June 1965, pp. 86-89.
12. Murphy, Thomas D. "Land Use Regulation." *Mining Engineering,* June 1967, pp. 48-49.
13. Reilly, James D. "Planning Surface Mine Reclamation Before Mining." *Mining Congress Journal,* November 1965, pp. 93-96.
14. "Slag Fills Construction Needs." *Plant Engineering,* December 1966, pp. 123-125.
15. Stearn, Enid W. "States Draft Interstate Mining Compact." *Rock Products,* January 1966, p. 14.
16. Stephenson, R. L. The Future of Ironmaking and Its Effect on Blast-Furnace Slag." *Pit and Quarry,* March 1966, pp. 133-137.
17. Sullivan, G. Don. "A Blueprint of Federal Controls of Surface and Strip

Mining in the United States." *Mining Congress Journal,* August 1967, pp. 88-92.

18._____. "A New Science — Mined Land Reclamation." *Mining Engineering,* July 1965, pp. 142-144.

19._____. "Current Research Trends in Mined-Land Conservation and Utilization." *Mining Engineering,* March 1967, pp. 63-67.

20. "What Should be the Long-Range R&D Mission for the Mineral Industries." *Mining Engineering,* January 1968, pp. 54-66.

Proceedings

21. IIT Research Institute. *Proceedings of the Symposium: Mineral Waste Utilization.* Chicago, Ill., 1968. 154 pages.

22. The Council of State Governments. *Proceedings of a Conference on Surface Mining.* Roanoke, Virginia, 1964. 64 pages.

Public Documents

23. U.S. Congress. Senate. Committee on Interior and Insular Affairs. *Surface Mining Reclamation. Hearings* on S.3132, S.3126, and S.217, 90th Cong., 2nd sess., 1968. 375 pages.

24. U.S. Department of Agriculture. *Restoring Surface-Mined Land.* Washington, D.C.: GPO, 1968. 17 pages.

25. U.S. Department of Interior. *Study of Strip and Surface Mining in Appalachia.* Washington, D.C.: GPO, 1966. 78 pages.

26._____. *Surface Mining and our Environment.* A Special Report to the Nation. Washington, D.C.: GPO, 1967. 124 pages.

27. U.S. Department of Interior. Bureau of Mines. *Demonstration and Evaluation of Five Methods of Secondary Backfilling of Strip-Mine Areas.* Washington, D.C.: GPO, 1966. 17 pages.

28._____. *Mineral Facts and Problems.* Washington, D.C.: GPO, 1965. 643 pages.

29._____. *Revegetation Studies at Three Strip-Mine Sites in North-Central Pennsylvania.* Washington, D.C.: GPO, 1968. 8 pages.

30. U.S. Department of Commerce, Bureau of the Census, *Statistical Abstract of the United States,* (Washington, D.C.: Government Printing Office, 1968).

Chapter 12
Solid Waste Disposal Problems
Arising from the Projected Output
of Containers

Legislation

1. New York. *An Act to Amend the Tax Law In Relation to the Imposition of a Disposal Fee upon Distributors of Food and Beverages in Non-Disintegrating Bottles and Cans.* (1968)

Newspapers

2. *The New York Times,* January 1, 1967-April 15, 1969.
3. *Wall Street Journal.* Jan. 8, 1969.

Periodicals

4. "A Decomposable Bottle." *The American City,* October 1968. p. 6.
5. "Chicago Will Compact Its Refuse." *The American City,* June 1968. p. 58.
6. "In Defense Of Waste." *Time,* Nov. 18, 1966, pp. 56-57.
7. Manchester, Harland. "Refuse Is Reusable." *National Civic Review,* February 1968, pp. 81-87.
8. "New Precipitators For Old Incinerators." *The American City,* August 1967. p. 40.
9. Pearl, David R. "What The Future Holds For Incinerators." *The American City,* October 1968. pp. 121, 122, 124, 162.
10. "Planned Landfills Cut Costs And Complaints." *The American City,* December 1968. pp. 102-104.
11. Pollock, K. M. "Solid Wastes Division's Interim Report of Industry Based on Unsound Research." *Solid Wastes Management,* March 1969. pp. 6, 7, 49.
12. "Sanitary Landfill — its impact on water pollution." *The American City,* January 1968. p. 48.
13. Sebastian, Frank. "The Worldwide Rush To Incineration." *The American City,* December 1967. p. 40.
14. Seymour, Whitney N. Jr. "80,000,000 Bottles A Day." *The N.Y. State Conservationist,* February-March 1968. pp. 162-165.
15. "State Produces 71.5 Million Ton Mountain Of Refuse Every Year." *Solid Wastes Management,* April 1969. pp. 30, 31, 34, 50.
16. "The Garbage Apocalypse." *New York,* March 10, 1969. pp. 23-27.

Books

17. Landsberg, H. H.; Fischman, L. L.; and Fisher, J. L. *Resources in America's Future.* Baltimore: Johns Hopkins Press, 1963. pp. 1,017.

18. Stewart, George. *Not So Rich As You Think.* Boston: Houghton Mifflin Co., 1968. 248 pages.

Government Publications

19. U.S. Congress. Joint Economic Committee. *Federal Programs for the Development of Human Resources,* a compendium of papers submitted to the Subcommittee on Economic Progress of the Joint Economic Committee, Vol. 2, 90th Cong., 2nd sess., 1968.

20. U.S. Department of Commerce. Business and Defense Services Administration. *Containers and Packaging, Quarterly Industry Report, October, 1967.* Washington, D.C.: Government Printing Office, 1967.

21. U.S. Department of Commerce. Business and Defense Services Administration. *Containers and Packaging, Quarterly Industry Report, October, 1968.* Washington, D.C.: Government Printing Office, 1968.

22. U.S. Department of Commerce. Business and Defense Services Administration. *Survey of Current Business, March, 1969.* Washington, D.C.: Government Printing Office, 1969.

23. U.S. Department of Commerce. Business and Defense Services Administration. *U.S. Industrial Outlook, 1968.* Washington, D.C.: Government Printing Office, 1967.

Interview

24. Mullins, P. *Soft Drink Industry* magazine, interview held on April 15, 1969.

25. "The Waste-High Crisis." *Modern Packaging,* November 1968. pp. 102-104.

Reports — Published

26. Aerojet-General Corp. *California Waste Management Study,* report to the State of California, Department of Public Health, Report No. 3056, (Final), Azusa, Calif., August 1965.

27. Darnay, Arsen J. Jr. *The Role of Packaging in Solid Waste.* Kansas City Missouri: Midwest Research Institute, 1968.

28. Glass Container Manufacturers Institute. *Glass Containers 1967.* New York: Glass Container Manufacturers Institute, 1968.

29. Keep America Beautiful, Inc. *Informational Pamphlets on Littering.* New York: Keep America Beautiful, Inc., 1968.

30. National Forest Products Association. *Forest Products Industry Facts, 1966.* Washington, D.C.: National Forest Products Association, 1967.

31. Regional Plan Association. *Waste Management* . New York: Regional Plan Association, 1968.

Unpublished Materials

32. Foster, William S. "Municipal Engineering and the City of the Future." Speech given at the Tri-State Meeting of the American Public Works Association, Moline, Illinois, May 16, 1968.

33. The Aluminum Association. "Aluminum Packaging And The Solid Waste Disposal Problem," New York, 1968. (Mimeographed)

34. Weaver, L. "The U.S. Solid Wastes Burden, A Twentieth Century Challenge." Paper presented at the Solid Waste Conference, The Conservation Council of Ontario, Toronto, Canada, Nov. 11-12, 1968.

Miscellaneous

35. Huxley, Aldous. *Brave New World* (New York: Modern Library, 1946).

36. Packard, Vance. *The Waste Makers* (New York: David McKay Co., 1960). 340 pages.

37. *Soft Drink Industry Annual Manual 1968-1969* (New York: Magazines for Industry, Inc., 1968).

Chapter 13
Problems in the Disposal of
Solid Waste from Durable Goods

1. Biederman, Paul, ed. *Economic Almanac 1967-68.* National Industrial Conference Board, New York, Macmillan Co., 1967. 655 pages.

2. Committee on Refuse Disposal and the American Public Works Association, *Municipal Refuse Disposal,* Chicago, Public Administration Service 1961. 506 pages

3. Committee on Solid Wastes and American Public Works Association, *Refuse Collection Practice,* 3rd Edition Chicago, Public Administration Service, 1966. 525 pages.

4. Institute of Scrap, Iron and Steel, *Proceedings of the National Conference on Auto Salvage,* Washington, 1964. Various pagings.

5. Kneese, A.; Ayres, R. *Environmental Pollution,* Federal Programs for the Development of Human Resources Vol. 2; Joint Economic Committee Congress of the United States, U.S. Government Printing Office, 1968. pp. 626-684.

6. Public Health, Engineering Section, Proceedings of the Second Symposium in the Treatment of Waste Waters, *Waste Treatment* Newcastle University of Durham, 1960. 477 pages.

7. Stewart, George R. *Not So Rich As You Think,* Boston, Houghton Mifflin Company, 1968. 248 pages.

8. Stirrup, F. L., *Public Cleansing: Refuse Disposal,* London, Pergamon Press, 1965. 144 pages.

9. Ralph Stone and Company Inc., *Copper Control In Vehicular Scrap,* Washington, U.S. Department of Interior, 1968. 109 pages.

10. Regional Plan Association, *Waste Management,* New York: Regional Plan Association, 1968. 105 pages.

11. Street Sanitation Committee, American Public Works Association, *Street Cleaning Practice,* 2nd Edition, Chicago, Public Administration Service, 1959. 424 pages.

12. Thompson, Warren S. and Lewis, David T. *Population Problems,* 5th Edition, New York, McGraw Hill Inc., 1965. 593 pages.

13. U.S. Bureau of the Census, *County and City Data Book,* (A Statistical Abstract Supplement), Washington, U.S. Government Printing Office, 1967. 673 pages.

14. U.S. Department of Commerce, *Survey of Current Business,* Vol. 48, No. 12, U.S. Government Printing Office, Dec. 1968. 36 pages.

15. U.S. Department of Health Education and Welfare: *Summaries of Solid Wastes Research and Training Grants 1968.* Solid Waste Program, Cincinnati 1968. 43 pages.

16. U.S. Department of the Interior: *Automobile Disposal:* A National Problem, Washington, U.S. Government Printing Office, 1967. 569 pages.

17. Vaughan, Richard D., *The Solid Wastes Program of the U.S. Public Health Department,* presented at the Fourth Annual Refuse Equipment Show and Congress, Chicago, Illinois, June 7, 1968. 13 pages.

18. Vogely, William A. *Abandoned and Scrap Automobiles,* Proceedings, the Surgeon Generals Conference on Solid Waste Management for Metropolitan Washington, Washington, U.S. Department of Health, Education and Welfare. 194 pages.

19. Wolf, Karl W., *Solid Wastes Collection and Disposal Facilities,* State and Local Public Facility Needs and Financing, Vol. 1: Joint Economic Committee, Congress of the United States, Washington 1966. 693 pages.

20. "For Solid Wastes: Squeeze and Package," *Chemical Week,* April 6, 1968. p. 55.

21. "Garbage for Health and Power," *Business Week,* July 1, 1967. p. 62.

22. "Garbage Freighted to Dump in Desert in New S.F. Plan," U.S. *Municipal News,* Dec. 15, 1968. p. 95.

23. "Garbage: Rosy New Future As Raw Material," *Chemical Engineering* April 22, 1968. pp. 28-34.

24. Hannavy, A., "Can Engineering Cope with the Debris of Affluence," *Product Engineering,* Vol. 38, No. 21, Oct. 9, 1967. pp. 36-44.

25. Ludwig, Harvey F. and Block, Ralph J., "Report on the Solid Waste

Problem," *Proceedings of the American Society of Civil Engineers,* Vol. 84, No. SA2, April 1968. pp. 344-370.

26. Korbitz, W. E. "Looking to the Future with a Regional Refuse Disposal Plan," *Public Works,* Vol. 98, June 1967. pp. 120-1.

27. Mix, A. Sheldon, "Solid Wastes: Everyday Another 800 Million Pounds," Reprinted from *Today's Health,* American Medical Association, March 1966. pp. 1-3.

28. *Newsday,* Garden City, New York, Dec. 5, 1968.

29. *New York Times,* Oct. 17, 1968.

30. Nilsen, Joan, "Solid Wastes Challenge the Disposal Experts," *Chemical Engineering,* Vol. 73, No. 60, Dec. 19, 1966. pp. 60-64.

31. Quon, Jimmie; Tanaka, Massaru; and Charnes, Abraham, "Refuse Quantities and Frequency of Service," *Proceedings of the American Society of Civil Engineers,* Vol. 94, No. SA2, April 1968. pp. 403-422.

32. Reynolds, W. F., "Abandoned Strip Mines Studied for Solid Waste Disposal," *Public Works,* Vol. 98, May 1967. pp. 74-75.

33. "Rising Plastics Content of Wastes Will Pose Problems," *Chemical and Engineering News,* Vol. 46, No. 3, Jan. 8, 1968. p. 13.

34. Landsberg, Hans H.; Fischman, Leonard L.; and Fisher, Joseph L., *Resources in American Future,* Baltimore, Johns Hopkins Press, 1963. 1,017 pages.

35. *Newsday,* Garden City, New York, Dec. 18, 1968.

36. *Newsday,* Garden City, New York, May 26, 1969.

37. *New York Times,* Oct. 27, 1968.

38. *New York Times,* Feb. 11, 1969.

39. Vickers, Sir Geoffrey, *The Art of Judgment* (New York: Basic Books, Inc., 1965). p. 143.

Chapter 14
The Harmful Side Effects of Pesticide Use

U.S. Government Publications

1. U.S. Agricultural Stabilization and Conservation Service, *The Pesticide Review.* Washington, D.C.: U.S. Government Printing Office, 1967, 42 pages.

2. U.S. Department of Agriculture and Cooperators. *Progress Report on Pesticides and Related Activities.* Washington, D.C.: U.S. Government Printing Office, 1967. 256 pages.

3. U.S. Department of Agriculture, "Insects Friends of Man," *Yearbook of Agriculture,* by F. C. Bishopp, Washington, D.C.: U.S. Government Printing Office, 1952. pp. 1-7.

3a. U.S. Department of Agriculture, "Screw-worm vs. Screw-worm," *Agricultural Research* (Washington, D.C.: U.S. Government Printing Office, July, 1958). p. 58.

Eutrophication of Lake Washington." *Limnology and Oceanography*, I (1) (January 1956), pp. 47-53.

24. Ferguson, F. Alan. "A Nonmyopic Approach to the Problem of Excess Algal Growth." *Environmental Science and Technology*, II (3) (March 1968), pp. 188-193.

25. Golueke, C. G. and Oswald, W. J. "Harvesting and Processing Sewage-Grown Planktonic Algae." *Water Pollution Control Federation*, XXXVII (4) (April 1965), pp. 471-98.

26. Hasler, Arthur P. and Ingersoll, Bruce. "Dwindling Lakes." *Natural History*, LXXVII (9) (November 1968), pp. 8-19.

27. Oglesby, R. T. and Edmondson, W. T. "Control of Eutrophication." *Water Pollution Control Federation*, XXXVIII (9) (September 1966), pp. 1452-60.

28. Oswald, William J. and Golueke, C. G. "Eutrophication Trends in the United States — A Problem." *Water Pollution Control Federation*, XXXVIII (6) (June 1966), pp. 964-75.

29. Rawson, D. C. "Algal Indications of Trophic Lake Types." *Limnology and Oceanography*, I (1) (January 1956), pp. 18-25.

30. Reid, L. W. "Wastewater Pollution and General Eutrophication of a Hydroelectric Impoundment." *Water Pollution Control Federation*, XXXVIII (2) (February 1966), pp. 165-74.

31. Reimold, Robert J. and Daiber, Franklin C. "Eutrophication of Estuarine Areas by Rainwater." *Chesapeake Science*, VIII (2) (1967), pp. 132-33.

32. Woodbury, Richard. "Blighted Great Lakes." *Life*, August 23, 1968, pp. 36-47.

Other Sources

33. *Water in the News*, published by the Soap and Detergent Association, New York. October 1967 to March 1969.

34. "Scientists Study Polluted Water." *National Geographic School Bulletin*, XLVII (5) (October 7, 1968), 79 pages.

35. Tehle, Edward, Jr. "The Incidence of Various Algae in Open Recirculating Cooling Systems." *Dearborn Technical Digest*, I (1), published by Dearborn Chemical Company, Chicago. 4 pages.

36. Rohlich, Gerard A. "Eutrophication." Paper presented at the 41st Annual Convention of the Soap and Detergent Association, New York City, January 25, 1968. 11 pages.

39. Cornell University Water Resources Center. "Eutrophication of Water Resources of New York State — A Study of Phytoplankton and Nutrients in Lakes Cayuga and Seneca," Ithaca, New York, November 1966. (Mimeographed), 24 pages.

Chapter 16
Summary of Findings

1. *The New York Times,* September 4, 1969. p. 1.

2. Novick, Sheldon *The Careless Atom* (Boston, Houghton Mifflin Co., 1969), 222 pages.

3. *The New York Times,* September 23, 1969. p. 28.

4. Landsberg, Hans H. and Schurr, Sam H. *Energy in the United States* (New York, Random House, 1968), 241 pages.

Index

Index

About the Editor

Alfred J. Van Tassel is an Associate Professor of Business Research at the School of Business, Hofstra University, Hempstead, New York. He attended the University of California — Berkeley, the University of Pennsylvania, and earned a Ph.D. in Economics from Columbia University. In addition to serving with the United Nations as Executive Secretary of the Scientific Conference on Conservation and Utilization of Resources, Professor Van Tassel was Staff Studies Director, U.S. Senate Small Business Committee. He is the author of numerous articles on economics and conservation.

DATE DUE

~~DEC 14 1992~~		
RETURNED		

Demco, Inc. 38-293